THE NORTON
INTRODUCTION TO
POETRY

Second Edition

W · W · NORTON & COMPANY · NEW YORK · LONDON

J. Paul Hunter
The University of Rochester

THE NORTON
INTRODUCTION TO
POETRY

Second Edition

Library of Congress Cataloging in Publication Data
Main entry under title:
The Norton introduction to poetry.

    First ed. published in 1973 as: Poetry.
    Includes indexes.
    1. Poetry—Collections.   I. Hunter, J. Paul,
1934–   II. Title: Poetry.
PN6101.H85   1981   821′.008   81–11070
ISBN 0-393-95157-X   AACR2

W. W. Norton & Company, 500 Fifth Avenue, New York, N.Y. 10110
W. W. Norton & Company Ltd. 37 Great Russell Street, London, WC1B 3NU

2 3 4 5 6 7 8 9 0

Contents

CRAFT 81

3 SPEAKER 81

The Way a Poem Looks   192

9 STANZAS AND VERSE FORMS   201

10   POETIC "KINDS"   217

CONTEXTS 236

11 THE AUTHOR'S WORK 236

12 HISTORICAL CONTEXTS 288

13 LITERARY TRADITION 302

16 CULTURAL ASSUMPTIONS: IDEAS OF ORDER   369

Analogy and Correspondence   371

The World as Stage   382

Modern Metaphors   385

APPENDIX: POETRY IN PROCESS   **532**

FOREWORD TO THE SECOND EDITION

The Norton Introduction to Poetry is both a textbook and an anthology —a guide for students who are open to exploring the full variety of poetry and a resource for teachers who care about helping to inspire and direct that exploration.

In preparing this Second Edition, I have simplified the organization and provided clear guidance from one kind of problem to the next. In this edition are more direct helps for the student, and the teacher has the option of leaving students to consider some basic questions in preparation for class and thereby spending less classroom time on terminology and rudimentary matters of craft. As in the first edition, the emphasis here is on the poems themselves, not on talk about them. My own brief comments are designed to clarify terms and to ask questions of individual poems, increasingly prompting students to raise questions for themselves. I have tried only to suggest some directions, provide important terminology, and get out of the teacher's way.

The chapters move from basic issues in the study of poetry to more difficult and complex ones, beginning with simple questions in readily accessible poems and moving to more technical questions in more complex poems. The first two chapters are introductory, and illustrate the varieties of *subject matter, theme,* and *tone* that poetry offers. In Chapters 3–10, questions of *craft* are explored systematically, one by one. In the third section (Chapters 11–16), more complex issues of *context* are introduced—the context of an author's total work, temporal and historical backgrounds, and cultural assumptions. I have attempted to encourage students to begin with a close reading of the text and gradually move to a larger concern with how poetry is created and what human effects it brings about.

The edition contains nearly 540 poems, 158 of them new to this edition. In selecting these, I have tried to find poems that are both enjoyable to read for pure pleasure and teachable in the cleassroom. You will find not only the familiar but also the surprising, including the forgotten and the seldom anthologized, for one of the pleasures of reading— for teachers as well as students—is the joy of discovery. I have chosen to "overrepresent" 20th-century, especially recent 20th-century poems because most present-day students find these works more readily enjoyable and comprehensible than works from another age; but most of the poems traditionally taught in introductory poetry courses are also here, and teachers will find themselves among many old favorites. Sometimes these traditional poems sit side by side with new and innovative ones—not always comfortably but, I hope, always usefully—to suggest the many various things that poetry can do and be, and to show the continuity of the powerful verbal tradition even when radical changes take place. For any classroom direction or personal taste, there is plenty to choose from.

I have retained certain editorial procedures that proved their useful-
ness in the First Edition. The poems are annotated, as is customary in
Norton anthologies: beginning readers need help with references and
allusions, and the fact that the book supplies that help frees the
teacher for more important activities in the classroom. To offer the
texts in the form most immediately available to their particular audi-
ence, I have normalized spelling according to modern American usage
(but only in cases where the change does not alter semantic, phono-
logical, or metric qualities). In order to avoid giving the impression
that all literature was written at the same time, I have dated the selec-
tions: the date to the right is that of first book publication (when pre-
ceded by a *p* it refers to periodical publication); a date to the left,
when it occurs, is that of composition.

J.P.H.

ACKNOWLEDGMENTS

Anyone old enough to write a textbook is indebted to more people
than he or she can name—to teachers, students, colleagues, friends,
family, and to occasional conversations and bits of undirected reading
the particulars of which are long forgotten. I am grateful to the many
unspecifiable moments and thousands of human contacts that make life
worthwhile and that make the writing of a textbook on poetry possible.
But I am especially grateful to those who have made their mark on
this book in specific ways—by suggesting a poem or by talking me out
of another one, by turning a phrase in just the right way, or by helping
me see where I had something important to learn. To my colleagues at
the University of Rochester, to my former colleagues at Emory Univer-
sity, and to the many teachers and students who helped shape this
book, I am grateful beyond my ability to express it: Paula Backschei-
der, Jerome Beaty, Patricia Brocker, Martine Brownley, W. S. Dowden,
Alan Grob, Kathryn Hunter, Lisa Hunter, Elizabeth Lunz, Lore Metz-
ger, William Morgan, Lee Pederson, Richard Quaintance, Joseph N.
Riddell, Harry Rusche, Ronald Schuchard, Fred Stocking, Kristina
Straub, Dennis Todd, Richard Turner, Floyd C. Watkins, Arthur Wil-
liams, Sally Wolff, and Curt R. Zimansky. Special thanks are due to my
friends at W. W. Norton who coaxed, cajoled, and commanded this
book from me: John Benedict, George Brockway, Karen Fischer, John
W. N. Francis, Josepha Gutelius, Debbie Hunter, Fred McFarland,
Jack Neill, Diane O'Connor, Jennifer Sutherland, Roy Tedoff, and Barry
Wade. My friend, colleague, and coeditor Carl E. Bain died as this
book was being completed; in everything he was an inspiration, an
aide, and a joy, and to him it is dedicated.

J.P.H.

A PREFACE TO POETRY

ANONYMOUS

Western Wind

> Western wind, when wilt thou blow,
>   The small rain down can rain?
> Christ, if my love were in my arms
>   And I in my bed again!

ca. 1300   15th century

This poem is clearly not a story, although perhaps it could be part of one: the beginning, the middle, or the end. (Perhaps the hero is saying these words on the eve of a battle—the beginning; perhaps the heroine, banished for conduct unbecoming a heroine, is dying in the wilderness—the end). But we are not told what happened—how the lovers became separated, when, why, what happened meanwhile. What we have is only the expression of the emotion itself: in the last two short lines, nostalgia, outrage, lust, a sense of loss. The emotion is directly, concisely, profanely expressed, and the narrative questions are all left unanswered. Longer poems—and some short ones—sometimes set the stage as carefully as a story does and fill out the plot, characters, and so on; often, however, we are alone out there with somebody else's feelings.

Sound scary? Perhaps that's why people who enjoy stories and plays often find it hard to "relate" to poetry; for one thing, it is hard to "escape" into a poem—we haven't the chance that a story or play offers to live with the characters for a while and share another existence. Most poems move more quickly than stories—a moment and they are over. A poem uses fewer words, so poets pack more into each word.

The following poem looks very different from *Western Wind*, by once again somebody (the poet? someone he has overheard? someone he has imagined being?) who is feeling lonely.

e. e. cummings

l(a

l(a

le
af
fa

ll   5

s)
one
l

iness

1958

Poetry usually looks different on the page from prose, but this poem really looks odd. The poet has tried to show, by imitation and analogy, a leaf falling, as we read. Visually, even the word "loneliness" is fragmented by the falling of the solitary leaf, and the poet even uses a typewriter pun in the second-to-last line to repeat the emphasis on "one." Not many poems use visual effects so heavily, and here the story element is almost nonexistent. But once again we are alone confronting a particular expression of feeling.

Which of these two is a typical poem? Neither, really, although both are well within what we might expect of poems to be read in a course in literature. It's hard to say what a typical poem is. Poetry has many subjects, many themes, many tones, and it uses a great variety of devices and strategies to affect us in a great variety of ways. Here are some things that all poems are often said to do:
  —Rhyme.
  —Have a regular rhythm.
  —Describe something beautiful.
  —State a universal truth.
  —Elevate our thoughts.
  —Make us feel better.
  —Teach us something.
  —Give us a broader perspective on ourselves and our world.
  —Give us aesthetic pleasure.
Some poems do quite a few of these things, and most of them are decent enough things to do, but if we think of poems *having* to do these things we are in trouble. It's a bad list: forget it. Poems do share some common concerns: a sense of wordplay, a sharp consciousness of some particular feeling or emotion, tremendous concision of expression, whether the poem is long or short, the conscious use of sound effects, a constant concern with telling us what it is like to be in a

particular situation, or feel a particular way. But even these persistent habits of poetry might be dangerous to codify as musts. Poems go better if you scrap preconceived notions about *all* poetry and are prepared to respond instead to the varieties of possibility that individual poems provide. Every poem is, like every person, individual, different, unique—not just a representative of a group.

Still, knowing how to read one poem can help you with other poems, and you can accumulate some skills that will help with difficulties that are likely to recur. This book is arranged to make it easier to develop such skills and to transfer them from one poem to another. Basically, we move from simpler problems in the early chapters to more complex ones, and from fairly accessible poems to more difficult ones. Groups of poems are arranged at the end of each chapter so as to facilitate comparison. A lot of the ability to read poetry well develops from a sense of knowing what to expect, and the groupings are there to help you develop that sense.

The first two chapters suggest some of the appeals and uses of poems, and the groupings of poems at the end of these chapters are by subjects—love, death, family, and so on—so that the many themes and tones of poems can readily be seen and distinguished from one another. The eight chapters in the second section are devoted to problems of craft. The craft of the poet has a lot to do with the skills needed by a reader of poetry, and in this section you will find introductory discussions of standard problems—speaker, situation and setting, figurative language, structure, stanza forms, and so on. The chapters in the third section raise "contextual" questions about poetry. Obviously, poems don't exist in a vacuum; like any other art objects or cultural phenomena they are part of the time and place from which they spring, and the groupings in this section illustrate a poem's connection to some larger cultural and historical forces. An anthology at the end includes some poems for further reading, and "A Glossary of Poetic Terms" (pp. 543–560) provides a review of the central points discussed in the individual chapters, a more detailed consideration of some technical points (directions on how to do metrical scansion, for example), and a ready reference guide to terminology.

Usually a reader can experience a poem in a satisfactory way without a lot of special knowledge, but additional knowledge and developed skill can heighten the experience of almost any poem. Poems do not "hide" their meanings, and good poets usually communicate rather quickly in some basic way. Rereadings, reconsiderations, and the application of additional knowledge allow us to hear resonances built into the poem, qualities that make it enjoyable to experience again and again. The route to meaning is often clear on first reading a poem, but the full possibilities of experience may require more time, energy, and knowledge of the right questions to ask.

This poem, for example, is fairly accessible, but far more pointed and complex if one brings a little knowledge to it:

LOUIS MACNEICE

Aubade

Having bitten on life like a sharp apple
Or, playing it like a fish, been happy,

Having felt with fingers that the sky is blue,
What have we after that to look forward to?

Not the twilight of the gods but a precise dawn   5
Of sallow and grey bricks, and newsboys crying war.

1935

Here is an expression of how the best of human desires for beauty is often frustrated by reality: instead of an eternal skyblueness and divine twilight, we discover a dull, gray reality of buildings and news of human conflict. The expression of the contrast is sharp, and there seems to be a hint of a specific reference. We can pin the situation down a bit if we know that the poem was written by an English poet in the mid-1930s, when fears of Hitler and of an imminent world war were rampant and likely to depress even the most determined of optimists and lovers. (Poems in this book are always dated at the end so it is easy to find out approximately when the poem was written.) The poem hints at a more specific situation, too; the "we" in line 4 suggests that whoever is talking is speaking for two, and the images of pleasure in the early lines imply a close and pleasant relationship that might well represent a love affair. Actually, this short poem gives us quite a bit of information—but indirectly. The title of the poem is *Aubade*, and the title tells us something about the tale. An aubade is a kind of poem (defined, along with other poetic kinds in "A Glossary of Poetic Terms," §10, p. 556) which features a particular setting and situation: it is a dawn song, involving lovers who regret the coming of the dawn after a night of love. We still are not told much about the narrative situation—only enough to let us share the sense of frustration and loss of awakening to a very grim world that seems light-years removed from moments ago.

The more you know, the better a reader of poems you are likely to be; the more practice you have had in reading other poems, the more likely you are to be able to experience a poem new to you. But knowing facts is not by itself enough; willingness to discover something new is a crucial quality of mind for reading poems well, and being willing to let the poem itself dictate which questions to ask is important to locating the right facts and discovering the right way of putting them together. Most readers can find out what they need to know for most poems if they figure out what questions to ask.

Poetry reading has many hazards, and almost as many of them result from overeagerness as from apathy; many people who read poetry enthusiastically do not read it well, just as many poems that mean well do not mean much. The questions you ask of poetry should channel your enthusiasm and direct it toward meaningful experience, but they should not destroy it. Some people are rather protective about poetry, and think it shouldn't be analyzed lest it shrivel or collapse. But such an attitude toward the "poor little poem" is finally rather patronizing; good poems are hardy, and they won't disintegrate when confronted with difficult questions. The techniques of analysis mean to make you both tougher-minded (less subject to gimmicks and quackery) and more sensitive (to the nuances and depths of good poems), and they also aim to allow the poem to open itself to you.

No one can give you a method that will offer you total experience of all poems. But because many characteristics of an individual poem are characteristics that one poem shares with other poems, there are guidelines which can prompt you to ask the right questions. The chapters that follow will help you in detail with a variety of problems, but meanwhile here is a checklist of some things to remember:

1. *Identify the poem's situation.* What is said is often conditioned by where it is said and by whom. Identifying the speaker and his or her place in the situation puts what he or she says in perspective.

2. *Read the syntax literally.* What the words say literally in normal sentences is only a starting point, but it is the place to start. Not all poems use normal prose syntax, but most of them do, and you can save yourself embarrassment by paraphrasing accurately (that is, rephrasing what the poem literally says, in plain prose) and not simply free-associating from an isolated word or phrase.

3. *Articulate for yourself what the title, subject, and situation make you expect.* Poets often use false leads and try to surprise you by doing shocking things, but defining expectation lets you be conscious of where you are when you begin.

4. *Be willing to be surprised.* Things often happen in poems that turn them around. A poem may seem to suggest one thing at first, then persuade you to its opposite, or at least to a significant qualification or variation.

5. *Find out what is implied by the traditions behind the poem.* Verse forms, poetic kinds, and metrical patterns all have a frame of reference, traditions of the way they are usually used and for what. For example, the anapest is usually used for comic poems, and if a poet uses it "straight" he is aware of his "departure" and is probably making a point by doing it.

6. *Remember that poems exist in time, and times change.* Not only the meanings of words, but whole ways of looking at the universe and man's role vary in different ages. Consciousness of time works two ways: your knowledge of history provides a context for reading the poem, and the poem's *use* of a word or idea may modify your notion of a particular age.

7. *Bother the reference librarian.* Look up anything you don't understand: an unfamiliar word (or an ordinary word used in an unfamiliar way), a place, a person, a myth, an idea—anything the poem uses. When you can't find what you need or don't know where to look, ask for help.

8. *Take a poem on its own terms.* Adjust to the poem; don't make

the poem adjust to you. Be prepared to hear things you do not want to hear. Not all poems are about your ideas, nor will they always present emotions you want to feel. But be tolerant and listen to the poem's ideas, not only to your desire to revise them for yourself.

9. *Argue.* Discussion usually results in clarification and keeps you from being too dependent on personal biases and preoccupations which sometimes mislead even the best readers. Talking a poem over with someone else (especially someone very different) can expand the limits of a too narrow perspective.

10. *Assume there is a reason for everything.* Poets do make mistakes, but in poems that show some degree of verbal control it is usually safest to assume that the poet chose each word carefully; if the choice seems peculiar to us, it is usually *we* who are missing something. Craftsmanship obliges us to try to account for the specific choices and only settle for conclusions of ineptitude if no hypothetical explanation will make sense.

What *is* poetry? Let your definition be cumulative as you read the poems in this book. No dictionary definition will cover all that you find, and it is better to discover for yourself poetry's many ingredients, its many effects, its many ways of acting. What can it do for you? Wait and see. Begin to add up its effects after you have read carefully —after you have studied and reread—a hundred or so poems; that will be a beginning, and you will be able to add to that total as long as you continue to read new poems or reread old ones.

Subject, Theme, and Tone

1 EXPERIENCING POETRY

People seldom feel neutral about poetry. Those who love it sometimes give the impression that it is an adequate substitute for food, shelter, and love. It isn't. It won't feed you or do your work for you or help you defeat your enemies, and, however satisfying words can be, they are never an equivalent for life itself and its human experiences. Those who dislike poetry on principle sometimes claim, on the other hand, that poetry is only words and good for nothing. That's not true either. It is easy to become frustrated by words—in poetry or in life—but when words represent, express, and recreate genuine human feelings, as they often do in poetry, they can be crucially important. Poetry is, in fact, more than just words. It is an *experience* of words, and those who know how to read poetry can easily extend their experience of life, their sense of what other people are like, and especially their awareness of personal feelings.

Feelings. One reason why poetry can be so important is that it is so intimately concerned with feelings. Poetry is often full of ideas, too, and sometimes poems can be powerful experiences of the mind, but most poems are primarily about how people feel rather than how people think. Poems provide, in fact, a language for feeling, and one of poetry's most insistent virtues involves its attempt to express the inexpressible. How can anyone, for example, put into words what it means to be in love? or what it feels like to lose to death someone one cares about? Poetry tries, and it often captures exactly the shade of emotion that feels just right to the reader. No one poem can be said to express all the things that love or death feels like, or means, but one of the joys of experiencing poetry occurs when we read a poem and want to say, "Yes, that is just what it is like; I know exactly what that line means but I've never been able to express it so well." Poetry can be the mouthpiece of our feelings even when our minds are speechless with grief or joy.

Here are two poems that talk about the sincerity and depth of love between two people. Each is written as if it were spoken or read by one person to his or her lover, and each is definite and powerful about the intensity and quality of love; but the poems work in quite different ways—the first one asserting the strength and depth of love, the second implying intense feeling by reminiscing about events in the relationship between the two people.

ELIZABETH BARRETT BROWNING

How Do I Love Thee?

How do I love thee? Let me count the ways.
I love thee to the depth and breadth and height
My soul can reach, when feeling out of sight
For the ends of Being and ideal Grace.
I love thee to the level of every day's   5
Most quiet need, by sun and candlelight.
I love thee freely, as men strive for Right;
I love thee purely, as they turn from Praise;
I love thee with the passion put to use
In my old griefs, and with my childhood's faith.   10
I love thee with a love I seemed to lose
With my lost saints—I love thee with the breath,
Smiles, tears of all my life!—and, if God choose,
I shall but love thee better after death.

1850

JAROLD RAMSEY

The Tally Stick

Here from the start, from our first of days, look:
I have carved our lives in secret on this stick
of mountain mahogany the length of your arms
outstretched, the wood clear red, so hard and rare.
It is time to touch and handle what we know we share.   5

Near the butt, this intricate notch where the grains
converge and join: it is our wedding.
I can read it through with a thumb and tell you now
who danced, who made up the songs, who meant us joy.
These little arrowheads along the grain,   10
they are the births of our children. See,
they make a kind of design with these heavy crosses,
the deaths of our parents, the loss of friends.

Over it all as it goes, of course, I
have chiseled Events, History—random   15
hashmarks cut against the swirling grain.
See, here is the Year the World Went Wrong,
we thought, and here the days the Great Men fell.
The lengthening runes of our lives run through it all.

See, our tally stick is whittled nearly end to end;   20
delicate as scrimshaw, it would not bear you up.

Regrets have polished it, hand over hand.
Yet let us take it up, and as our fingers
like children leading on a trail cry back
our unforgotten wonders, sign after sign,
we will talk softly as of ordinary matters,
and in one another's blameless eyes go blind.

25

p. 1977

The first poem is direct, but fairly abstract. It lists several ways in which the poet feels love and connects them to some noble ideas of higher obligations—to justice (line 7), for example, and to spiritual aspiration (lines 2–4). It suggests a wide range of things that love can mean and notices a variety of emotions. It is an ardent statement of feeling and asserts a permanence that will extend even beyond death. It contains admirable thoughts and memorable phrases that many lovers would like to hear said to themselves. What it does not do is say very much about what the relationship between the two lovers is like on an everyday basis, what experiences they have had together, what distinguishes their relationship from that of other devoted or ideal lovers. Its appeal is to our general sense of what love is like and how intense feelings can be; it does not offer everyday details. Love may differ from person to person and even from moment to moment, and so can poems about love.

The Tally Stick is much more concrete. The whole poem concentrates on a single object that, like the poem above, "counts" or "tallies" the ways in which this couple love one another. The stick stands for their love and becomes a kind of physical reminder of it: its natural features—the notches and arrowheads and cross marks (lines 6, 10, and 12) along with the marks carved on it (lines 15–16, 20–21)—indicate events in the story of the relationship. (We could say that the stick *symbolizes* their love; later on, we will look at a number of terms like this that can be used to make it easier to talk about some aspects of poems, but for now it is enough to notice that the stick serves the lovers as a reminder of some specific details of their love.) It is a special kind of reminder to them because its language is "secret" (line 2), something they can share privately (except that we as readers of the poem are sort of looking over their shoulders, not intruding but sharing their secret). The poet interprets the particular features of the stick as standing for particular events—their wedding and the births of their children, for example—and carves marks into it as reminders of other events (lines 15ff.). The stick itself becomes a very personal object, and in the last stanza of the poem it is as if we watch the lovers touching the stick together and reminiscing over it, gradually dissolving into their emotions and each other as they recall the "unforgotten wonders" (line 25) of their lives together.

Both poems are powerful statements of feelings, each in its own way. Some readers will prefer one and some the other. Personal preference does not mean that objective standards for poetry cannot be found (some poems are better than others, and later we will look in detail at features which help us to evaluate poems), but we need have no preconceived standard that all poetry must be one thing or another or work in one particular way. Some good poems are quite abstract, others quite specific. Any poem that helps us to articulate and clarify human feelings and ideas has a legitimate claim on us as readers. We tend to like poems (or people) for what they do, what they are, and what they represent to us.

Both *How Do I Love Thee* and *The Tally Stick* are written as if they were addressed to the partner in the love relationship, and both talk directly about the intensity of the love. The next poem we will look at talks only indirectly about the quality and intensity of love. It is written as if it were a letter from a woman to her husband who has gone on a long journey on business, and it clearly expresses how much she misses him, but indirectly suggests how much she cares about him.

EZRA POUND

The River-Merchant's Wife: A Letter

(*after Rihaku*[1])

While my hair was still cut straight across my forehead
I played about the front gate, pulling flowers.
You came by on bamboo stilts, playing horse,
You walked about my seat, playing with blue plums.
And we went on living in the village of Chokan: 5
Two small people, without dislike or suspicion.

At fourteen I married My Lord you.
I never laughed, being bashful.
Lowering my head, I looked at the wall.
Called to, a thousand times, I never looked back.   10

At fifteen I stopped scowling,
I desired my dust to be mingled with yours
For ever and for ever and for ever.
Why should I climb the look out?

At sixteen you departed,   15
You went into far Ku-to-yen, by the river of swirling eddies,
And you have been gone five months.
The monkeys make sorrowful noise overhead.

You dragged your feet when you went out.
By the gate now, the moss is grown, the different mosses,   20

1. The Japanese name for Li Po, an 8th-century Chinese poet. Pound's poem is a loose paraphrase of Li Po's.

Too deep to clear them away!
The leaves fall early this autumn, in wind.
The paired butterflies are already yellow with August
Over the grass in the West garden;
They hurt me. I grow older.   25
If you are coming down through the narrows of the river Kiang,
Please let me know beforehand,
And I will come out to meet you
        As far as Cho-fu-Sa.

1915

The "letter" tells us only a few facts about the nameless merchant's wife: that she is about sixteen and a half years old, that she married at fourteen and fell in love with her husband a year later, that she is now very lonely. And about their relationship we know only that they were childhood playmates in a small Chinese village, that their marriage originally was not a matter of personal choice, and that the husband unwillingly went away on a long journey five months ago. But the words tell us a great deal about how the young wife feels, and the simplicity of her language suggests her sincere and deep longing. The daily noises she hears seem "sorrowful" (line 18), and she worries about the dangers of the far-away place where her husband is, thinking of it in terms of its perilous "river of swirling eddies" (line 16). She thinks of how moss has grown up over the unused gate, and more time seems to her to have passed than actually has (lines 22–25). She remembers nostalgically their innocent childhood, when they played together without deeper love or commitment (lines 1–6), and contrasts that with her later satisfaction in their love (lines 11–14) and with her present anxiety, loneliness, and desire. We do not need to know the details of the geography of the river Kiang or how far Cho-fu-Sa is to sense that her wish to see him is very strong, that her desire is powerful enough to make her venture beyond the ordinary geographical bounds of her existence so that their reunion will come sooner. The closest she comes to a direct statement about her love is her statement that she desired that her dust be mingled with his "For ever and for ever and for ever" (lines 12–13). But her single-minded vision of the world, her perception of even the beauty of nature as only a record of her husband's absence and the passage of time, and her plain, apparently uncalculated language about her rejection of other suitors and her shutting out of the rest of the world all show her to be committed, desirous, nearly desperate for his presence. In a different sense, she has also counted the ways that she loves her man.

Here is another poem that similarly expresses a woman's intense desire for her lover, but here the expression is much more openly physical and sexual.

DIANE WAKOSKI

Uneasy Rider[2]

Falling in love with a mustache
is like saying
you can fall in love with
the way a man polishes his shoes
      which,   5
      of course,
      is one of the things that turns on
      my tuned-up engine

    those trim buckled boots

    (I feel like an advertisement   10
      for men's fashions
      when I think of your ankles)

Yeats was hung up with a girl's beautiful face[3]

and I find myself

a bad moralist,   15

a failing aesthetician,

a sad poet,

wanting to touch your arms and feel the muscles
that make a man's body have so much substance,
that makes a woman   20
lean and yearn in that direction
that makes her melt/ she is a rainy day
in your presence
the pool of wax under a burning candle
the foam from a waterfall   25

You are more beautiful than any Harley-Davidson
She is the rain,
waits in it for you,
finds blood spotting her legs
from the long ride.   30

                                                 1971

2. From Wakoski's volume, *The Motor-cycle Betrayal Poems. Easy Rider* was one of the most popular motorcycle films of the late 1960s and early '70s.

3. See, for example, Yeats's "Among School Children," p. 345.

Physical details of the man's body and his clothing are plentiful here, and the woman is very direct about their effects—emotional and phys-ical—upon her as she talks about what "turns on" her "tuned-up en-gine" (lines 7–8), and how his muscles make her "lean and yearn" and her body "melt" (lines 18–22). So vivid and intense are the various pictures of melting ("a rainy day," "a pool of wax," and "foam from a waterfall") that the poem pulls its focus back a bit from the couple near the end and talks of them as "a man" and "a woman": the woman who is speaking the poem adopts the third-person "she" to distance herself (and us) from the fire and energy of passion.

Poems can, of course, be about the meaning of a relationship or about disappointment just as easily as about sex or emotional fulfill-ment, and poets are often very good at suggesting the contradictions and uncertainties that tend to affect most relationships. Like other people, poets often find love and its complications quaint or down-right funny, too, mainly because it involves human beings who, how-ever serious their intentions and concerns, are often inept, uncertain, and self-contradictory—in short, human. Showing us ourselves as oth-ers see us is one of the more useful tasks that poems perform, but the poems that result can be just as entertaining and pleasurable as they are educational. Here is a poem which imagines a very strange scene, a kind of fantasy of what happens when we *think* too much about the implications of sex or love, and it is likely to leave us laughing, whether or not we take it seriously as a statement of human anxiety and of the tendency to intellectualize too much.

TOM WAYMAN

Wayman in Love

At last Wayman gets the girl into bed.
He is locked in one of those embraces
so passionate his left arm is asleep
when suddenly he is bumped in the back.
"Excuse me," a voice mutters, thick with German.   5
Wayman and the girl sit up astounded
as a furry gentleman in boots and a frock coat
climbs in under the covers.

"My name is Doktor Marx," the intruder announces
settling his neck comfortably on the pillow.   10
"I'm here to consider for you the cost of a kiss."
He pulls out a notepad. "Let's see now,
we have the price of the mattress, this room must be rented,
your time off work, groceries for two,
medical fees in case of accidents . . ."   15

"Look," Wayman says,
"couldn't we do this later?"
The philosopher sighs, and continues: "You are affected too,
    Miss.
If you are not working, you are going to resent   20
your dependent position. This will influence
I assure you, your most intimate moments . . ."

"Doctor, please," Wayman says. "All we want
is to be left alone."
But another beard, more nattily dressed,   25
is also getting into the bed.
There is a shifting and heaving of bodies
as everyone wriggles out room for themselves.
"I want you to meet a friend from Vienna,"
Marx says. "This is Doktor Freud."   30

The newcomer straightens his glasses,
peers at Wayman and the girl.
"I can see," he begins,
"that you two have problems . . ."

                                                                   1973

Another traditional subject of poetry is death, and on this subject, too, poets often describe frequent, recurrent human emotions in a variety of ways. In the following poem, the emphasis is on the shock and dismay we feel in perceiving the stillness of death in contrast to the energy and vitality of life. Here the dead person is a child, and the poet struggles with a sense of disbelief that someone so much alive could now be motionless.

JOHN CROWE RANSOM

Bells for John Whiteside's Daughter

There was such speed in her little body,
And such lightness in her footfall,
It is no wonder her brown study [4]
Astonishes us all.

Her wars were bruited in our high window.   5
We looked among orchard trees and beyond
Where she took arms against her shadow,
Or harried unto the pond

---

4. Stillness, as if in meditation or deep thought.

The lazy geese, like a snow cloud
Dripping their snow on the green grass,   10
Tricking and stopping, sleepy and proud,
Who cried in goose, Alas,

For the tireless heart within the little
Lady with rod that made them rise
From their noon apple-dreams and scuttle   15
Goose-fashion under the skies!

But now go the bells, and we are ready,
In one house we are sternly stopped
To say we are vexed at her brown study,
Lying so primly propped.   20

1924

After an opening stanza that introduces the basic contrast between activity and stillness and between life and death, the center of the poem concentrates on one vivid scene in the dead girl's life, a moment when she played Mother Goose to her world and created a colorful, energetic, and noisy dramatic scene. The three middle stanzas are filled with a sense of energy and timelessness, and their main effect is to recall the child at the peak of her vitality and activity, an emphasis that heightens even more the stillness and quiet of the "brown study" of the first and last stanzas. The final picture of the girl "Lying so primly propped" seems grossly inappropriate for someone so restless and active and thoroughly alive. The poet finds hard to bear the restraint of being "sternly stopped" to pay memorial homage and tries to keep control by understating ("vexed," line 19) the deep feelings about how all has gone wrong. We do not know much about the girl except for her playful energy; we don't even know how she died. For the purposes of the poem, those facts are not relevant. What we do know is that her restless body is now at rest, and the stillness is eerie, incomprehensible, unbelievable. The important thing to this poem is the sense of inappropriateness and finality that death visits upon those who seem to be its least likely targets.

The following poem is more openly about a personal reaction to the death of a child. Here, a father struggles to understand and control his grief.

BEN JONSON

On My First Son

Farewell, thou child of my right hand,[5] and joy;
My sin was too much hope of thee, loved boy:

5. A literal translation of the son's name, Benjamin.

Seven years thou'wert lent to me, and I thee pay,
Exacted by thy fate, on the just[6] day.
O could I lose all father now! for why   5
Will man lament the state he should envý,
To have so soon 'scaped world's and flesh's rage,
And, if no other misery, yet age?
Rest in soft peace, and asked, say, "Here doth lie
Ben Jonson his[7] best piece of poetry."   10
For whose sake henceforth all his vows be such
As what he loves may never like too much.

                                                                      1616

The poem's attempts to rationalize the death are quite conventional, and although the father tries to be comforted by pious thoughts, his feelings keep showing through. The poem's beginning—with its formal "farewell" and the rather distant-sounding address to the dead boy ("child of my right hand")—cannot be sustained for long: both of the first two lines end with bursts of emotion. It is as if the father is trying to explain the death to himself and to keep his emotions under control, but cannot quite manage it. Even the punctuation suggests the way his feelings compete with conventional attempts to put the death into some sort of perspective that will soften the grief, and the comma near the end of each of the first two lines marks a pause that cannot quite hold back the overflowing emotion. But finally the only "idea" that the poem supports is that the father wishes he did not feel so intensely; in the fifth line he fairly blurts that he wishes he could lose his fatherly emotions, and in the final lines he resolves never again to "like" so much that he can be this deeply hurt. Philosophy and religion offer their useful counsels in this poem, but they prove far less powerful than feeling; and rather than drawing some kind of moral about what death means, the poem presents the actuality of feeling as inevitable and nearly all-consuming.

The poem that follows similarly tries to suppress the rawness of feelings about the death of a loved one, but here the survivor is haunted by memories of his wife when he sees a physical object—a vacuum cleaner—that was important in her life.

HOWARD NEMEROV

The Vacuum

The house is so quiet now
The vacuum cleaner sulks in the corner closet,

6. Exact; the son died on his seventh birthday, in 1603.

7. Ben Jonson s (a common Renaissance form of the possessive).

Its bag limp as a stopped lung, its mouth
Grinning into the floor, maybe at my
Slovenly life, my dog-dead youth.   5

I've lived this way long enough,
But when my old woman died her soul
Went into that vacuum cleaner, and I can't bear
To see the bag swell like a belly, eating the dust
And the woolen mice, and begin to howl   10

Because there is old filth everywhere
She used to crawl, in the corner and under the stair.
I know now how life is cheap as dirt,
And still the hungry, angry heart
Hangs on and howls, biting at air.   15

1955

The poem is about a vacuum in the husband's life, but the title re-
fers most obviously to the vacuum cleaner that, like the tally stick we
looked at earlier, seems to stand for many of the things that were once
important in their life together. The cleaner is a reminder of the dead
wife ("my old woman," line 7) because of her devotion to cleanliness,
but to the surviving husband buried in the filth of his life it seems as
if the machine has become almost human, a kind of ghost of her: it
"sulks" (line 2), it has lungs and a mouth (line 3), and it seems to
grin, making fun of what has become of him. He "can't bear" (line 8)
to see it in action because it then seems too much alive, too much a
reminder of her life. The poem records his paralysis, his inability to do
more than discover that life is "cheap as dirt" without her ordering
and cleansing presence for him. At the end it is *his* angry heart that
acts like the haunting machine, howling and biting at air as if he has
merged with her spirit and the physical object that memorializes her.
This poem, like *Bells for John Whiteside's Daughter,* puts a strong
emphasis on the stillness of death and the way it makes things seem
to stop; it captures in words the hurt, the anger, the inability to un-
derstand, the vacuum that remains when a loved one dies and leaves
a vacant space. But here we do not see the body or hear a direct
good-bye to the dead person; rather we encounter the feeling that
lingers and won't go away, recalled through memory by an especially
significant object, a mere thing but one that has been personalized to
the point of becoming nearly human in itself. (The event described
here is, by the way, fictional; the poet's wife did not in fact die. Like
a dramatist or writer of fiction, the poet may simply *imagine* an event
in order to analyze and articulate how such an event might feel in
certain circumstances.)

   The following poem, written three centuries earlier about an actual
death, expresses a sense of love and loss much more directly. Here, the
grieving widow addresses her beloved and expresses her desire to join
him in death. Her terms are openly sexual, uniting a concern with
love and death.

LADY CATHERINE DYER

Epitaph On the Monument of Sir William Dyer at Colmworth, 1641

My dearest dust, could not thy hasty day
Afford thy drowsy patience leave to stay
One hour longer: so that we might either
Sit up, or gone to bed together?
But since thy finished labor hath possessed   5
Thy weary limbs with early rest,
Enjoy it sweetly: and thy widow bride
Shall soon repose her by thy slumbering side.
Whose business, now, is only to prepare
My nightly dress, and call to prayer: 10
Mine eyes wax heavy and the day grows old,
The dew falls thick, my blood grows cold.
Draw, draw the closéd curtains: and make room:
My dear, my dearest dust; I come, I come.

1641

There is much more going on in the poems that we have glanced
at than we have taken time to consider, but even the quickest look at
these poems suggests something of the range of feelings that poems
can offer—the depth of feeling, the clarity, the experience that may be
articulately and precisely shared. Later we will look more carefully at
how these things happen.

A Gathering of Love Poems

ANONYMOUS

My Love in Her Attire

My love in her attire doth show her wit,[1]
It doth so well become her:
For every season she hath dressings fit,
For winter, spring, and summer.
No beauty she doth miss,   5
When all her robes are on;

---

1. Cleverness.

But Beauty's self she is,
When all her robes are gone.

1602

ROBERT HERRICK

Upon Julia's Clothes

Whenas in silks my Julia goes
Then, then, methinks, how sweetly flows
That liquefaction of her clothes.

Next, when I cast mine eyes, and see
That brave[2] vibration, each way free,   5
O, how that glittering taketh me!

1648

THEODORE ROETHKE

I Knew a Woman

I knew a woman, lovely in her bones,
When small birds sighed, she would sigh back at them;
Ah, when she moved, she moved more ways than one:
The shapes a bright container can contain!
Of her choice virtues only gods should speak,   5
Or English poets who grew up on Greek
(I'd have them sing in chorus, cheek to cheek).

How well her wishes went! She stroked my chin,
She taught me Turn, and Counter-turn, and Stand;[3]
She taught me Touch, that undulant white skin;   10
I nibbled meekly from her proffered hand;
She was the sickle; I, poor I, the rake,
Coming behind her for her pretty sake
(But what prodigious mowing we did make).

Love likes a gander, and adores a goose: 15
Her full lips pursed, the errant note to seize;
She played it quick, she played it light and loose;
My eyes, they dazzled at her flowing knees;
Her several parts could keep a pure repose,
Or one hip quiver with a mobile nose   20
(She moved in circles, and those circles moved).

2. Handsome, showy.   Pindaric ode.
3. Literary terms for the parts of a

Let seed be grass, and grass turn into hay:
I'm martyr to a motion not my own;
What's freedom for? To know eternity.
I swear she cast a shadow white as stone.   25
But who would count eternity in days?
These old bones live to learn her wanton ways:
(I measure time by how a body sways).

1958

CHRISTINA ROSSETTI

Echo

Come to me in the silence of the night;
    Come in the speaking silence of a dream;
Come with soft rounded cheeks and eyes as bright
    As sunlight on a stream;
        Come back in tears,   5
O memory, hope, love of finished years.

O dream how sweet, too sweet, too bitter sweet,
    Whose wakening should have been in Paradise,
Where souls brimful of love abide and meet;
    Where thirsting longing eyes   10
        Watch the slow door
That opening, letting in, lets out no more.

Yet come to me in dreams, that I may live
    My very life again though cold in death:
Come back to me in dreams, that I may give   15
    Pulse for pulse, breath for breath:
        Speak low, lean low,
As long ago, my love, how long ago.

1862

AUDRE LORDE

Recreation

Coming together
it is easier to work
after our bodies
meet
paper and pen   5

neither care nor profit
whether we write or not
but as your body moves
under my hands
charged and waiting   10
we cut the leash
you create me against your thighs
hilly with images
moving through our word countries
my body   15
writes into your flesh
the poem
you make of me.

Touching you I catch midnight
as moon fires set in my throat   20
I love you flesh into blossom
I made you
and take you made
into me.

                                            1978

JOHN WILMOT, EARL OF ROCHESTER

Love and Life

All my past life is mine no more;
    The flying hours are gone,
Like transitory dreams given o'er
Whose images are kept in store
    By memory alone.   5

Whatever is to come is not:
    How can it then be mine?
The present moment's all my lot,
And that, as fast as it is got,
    Phyllis, is wholly thine.   10

Then talk not of inconstancy,
    False hearts, and broken vows;
If I, by miracle, can be
This livelong minute true to thee,
    'Tis all that heaven allows.   15
                                            1677

EDNA ST. VINCENT MILLAY

What Lips My Lips Have Kissed

What lips my lips have kissed, and where, and why,
I have forgotten, and what arms have lain
Under my head till morning; but the rain
Is full of ghosts tonight, that tap and sigh
Upon the glass and listen for reply,   5
And in my heart there stirs a quiet pain
For unremembered lads that not again
Will turn to me at midnight with a cry.
Nor knows what birds have vanished one by one,   10
Thus in the winter stands the lonely tree,
Yet knows its boughs more silent than before:
I cannot say what loves have come and gone;
I only know that summer sang in me
A little while, that in me sings no more.

1923

WILLIAM SHAKESPEARE

Let Me Not to the Marriage of True Minds

Let me not to the marriage of true minds
Admit impediments.[4] Love is not love
Which alters when it alteration finds,
Or bends with the remover to remove:
Oh, no! it is an ever-fixéd mark,   5
That looks on tempests and is never shaken;
It is the star to every wandering bark,
Whose worth's unknown, although his height be taken.[5]
Love's not Time's fool, though rosy lips and cheeks
Within his bending sickle's compass come;   10
Love alters not with his brief hours and weeks,
But bears it out even to the edge of doom.[6]
If this be error and upon me proved,
I never writ, nor no man ever loved.

1609

4. The Marriage Service contained this
address to the observers: "If any of you
know cause or just impediments why these
persons should not be joined together . . . ."

5. I.e., measuring the altitude of stars
(for purposes of navigation) is not a meas-
urement of value.
6. End of the world.

WILLIAM CONGREVE

Song

Pious Selinda goes to prayers,
    If I but ask the favor;[7]
And yet the tender fool's in tears,
    When she believes I'll leave her.

Would I were free from this restraint,   5
    Or else had hopes to win her;
Would she could make of me a saint,
    Or I of her a sinner.

ca. 1690

ADRIENNE RICH

Two Songs

1.

Sex, as they harshly call it,
I fell into this morning
at ten o'clock, a drizzling hour
of traffic and wet newspapers.
I thought of him who yesterday   5
clearly didn't
turn me to a hot field
ready for plowing,
and longing for that young man
piercéd me to the roots   10
bathing every vein, etc.[8]
All day he appears to me
touchingly desirable,
a prize one could wreck one's peace for.
I'd call it love if love   15
didn't take so many years
but lust too is a jewel
a sweet flower and what
pure happiness to know
all our high-toned questions   20
breed in a lively animal.

2.

That "old last act"!
And yet sometimes

---

7. Sexual favor.
8. See the opening lines of the Prologue   to Chaucer's *Canterbury Tales*.

all seems post coitum triste[9]
and I a mere bystander.   25
Somebody else is going off,
getting shot to the moon.
Or, a moon-race!
my opposite number lands
Split seconds after   30
I make it—
we lie fainting together
at a crater-edge
heavy as mercury in our moonsuits
till he speaks—   35
in a different language
yet one I've picked up
through cultural exchanges . . .
we murmur the first moonwords:
Spasibo. Thanks. O.K.   40

                                                             1964

ANN DEAGON

Man and Wife Is One Flesh

I

Barely acceptable in grammar,
it is not mathematically sound.
An equation incapable of proof,
we assert it merely.

II

Because he was dying, they let me stay.   5
In the corridor speakers called over and over.
Something is happening in the corridor,
he said. (But nothing was.) They gave him
more morphine. Check the altitude,
he said, do we have enough? I told him,   10
Yes. The dog's collar is a quarter-
inch too small. I'll exchange it, I said.
(But we had no dog.) The monitor
faltered and beat on, faltered and beat.

On the third night he had not yet died.   15
I leaned back in the reclining chair.
It is hard to put in words: he lay
propped into living; I lay back
level with death. A great plane
sliced through the tissue of the world.   20
We lay against it, smears on a slide.

9. Sadness after sexual union.

Falling asleep I fell continually
into his body, feeling the tubes
dry my nostrils, feeling the slow
swell of fluid up my wrist,   25
my hair thinning to his fine golden
my eyes blurring blue, blue.

III

He lived, for the time. We all
live for the time only, the time
a great shearing between dead   30
flesh and the quick. No way
but by its sting to know
we live and live together.

1978

SIR JOHN SUCKLING

Out upon It! I Have Loved

Out upon it! I have loved
  Three whole days together;
And am like to love three more,
  If it prove fair weather.

Time shall moult away his wings   5
  Ere he shall discover
In the whole wide world again
  Such a constant lover.

But the spite on 'tis, no praise
  Is due at all to me: 10
Love with me had made no stays,
  Had it any been but she.

Had it any been but she
  And that very face,
There had been at least ere this   15
  A dozen dozen in her place.

1659

A Gathering of Poems about Death

A. E. HOUSMAN

To an Athlete Dying Young

The time you won your town the race
We chaired[1] you through the marketplace;
Man and boy stood cheering by,
And home we brought you shoulder-high.

Today, the road all runners come,   5
Shoulder-high we bring you home,
And set you at your threshold down,
Townsman of a stiller town.

Smart lad, to slip betimes away
From fields where glory does not stay,   10
And early though the laurel[2] grows
It withers quicker than the rose.

Eyes the shady night has shut
Cannot see the record cut,
And silence sounds no worse than cheers   15
After earth has stopped the ears:

Now you will not swell the rout
Of lads that wore their honors out,
Runners whom renown outran
And the name died before the man.   20

So set, before its echoes fade,
The fleet foot on the sill of shade,
And hold to the low lintel[3] up
The still-defended challenge-cup.

And round that early-laureled head   25
Will flock to gaze the strengthless dead,
And find unwithered on its curls
The garland[4] briefer than a girl's.

1896

WILLIAM WORDSWORTH

A Slumber Did My Spirit Seal

A slumber did my spirit seal;
I had no human fears:

---

1. Carried aloft in triumph.   3. Upper part of a door frame.
2. Wreath of honor.   4. Wreath of flowers.

She seemed a thing that could not feel
  The touch of earthly years.

No motion has she now, no force:
  She neither hears nor sees;
Rolled round in earth's diurnal[5] course,
  With rocks, and stones, and trees.

1800

MARK TWAIN

Ode to Stephen Dowling Bots, Dec'd[6]

And did young Stephen sicken,
  And did young Stephen die?
And did the sad hearts thicken,
  And did the mourners cry?

No; such was not the fate of   5
  Young Stephen Dowling Bots;
Though sad hearts round him thickened,
  'Twas not from sickness' shots.

No whooping-cough did rack his frame,
  Nor measles drear with spots;   10
Not these impaired the sacred name
  Of Stephen Dowling Bots.

Despised love struck not with woe
  That head of curly knots,
Nor stomach troubles laid him low,   15
  Young Stephen Dowling Bots.

O no. Then list with tearful eye,
  Whilst I his fate do tell.
His soul did from this cold world fly,
  By falling down a well.   20

They got him out and emptied him;
  Alas it was too late;
His spirit was gone for to sport aloft
  In the realms of the good and great.

1884

---

5. Daily.
6. The ode is supposedly written by Emmeline Grangerford, the 13-year-old daughter of one of the feuding families in *Huckleberry Finn*. Huck says, "She could write about anything you choose [sic] to give her to write about just so it was sadful. Every time a man died, or a woman died, or a child died, she would be on hand with her 'tribute' before he was cold."

DYLAN THOMAS

Do Not Go Gentle into That Good Night[7]

Do not go gentle into that good night,
Old age should burn and rave at close of day;
Rage, rage against the dying of the light.

Though wise men at their end know dark is right,
Because their words had forked no lightning they   5
Do not go gentle into that good night.

Good men, the last wave by, crying how bright
Their frail deeds might have danced in a green bay,
Rage, rage against the dying of the light.

Wild men who caught and sang the sun in flight,   10
And learn, too late, they grieved it on its way,
Do not go gentle into that good night.

Grave men, near death, who see with blinding sight
Blind eyes could blaze like meteors and be gay,
Rage, rage against the dying of the light.   15

And you, my father, there on the sad height,
Curse, bless, me now with your fierce tears, I pray.
Do not go gentle into that good night.
Rage, rage against the dying of the light.

1952

EMILY DICKINSON

Because I Could Not Stop for Death

Because I could not stop for Death—
He kindly stopped for me—
The Carriage held but just Ourselves—
And Immortality.

We slowly drove—He knew no haste   5
And I had put away
My labor and my leisure too,
For His Civility—

We passed the School, where Children strove
At Recess—in the Ring—   10
We passed the Fields of Gazing Grain—
We passed the Setting Sun—

7. Written during the final illness of the poet's father.

Or rather—He passed Us—
The Dews drew quivering and chill—
For only Gossamer,[8] my Gown—   15
My Tippet[9]—only Tulle[1]—

We paused before a House that seemed
A Swelling of the Ground—
The Roof was scarcely visible—
The Cornice—in the Ground—   20

Since then—'tis Centuries—and yet
Feels shorter than the Day
I first surmised the Horses' Heads
Were toward Eternity—

ca. 1863

JOHN DONNE

Death Be Not Proud

Death be not proud, though some have called thee
Mighty and dreadful, for thou art not so;
For those whom thou think'st thou dost overthrow
Die not, poor Death, nor yet canst thou kill me.
From rest and sleep, which but thy pictures[2] be,   5
Much pleasure; then from thee much more must flow,
And soonest[3] our best men with thee do go,
Rest of their bones, and soul's delivery.[4]
Thou art slave to Fate, Chance, kings, and desperate men,
And dost with Poison, War, and Sickness dwell;   10
And poppy or charms can make us sleep as well,
And better than thy stroke; why swell'st[5] thou then?
One short sleep past, we wake eternally
And death shall be no more; Death, thou shalt die.

1633

SYLVIA PLATH

Lady Lazarus[6]

I have done it again.
One year in every ten
I manage it——

A sort of walking miracle, my skin
Bright as a Nazi lampshade,   5
My right foot

8. A soft sheer fabric.
9. Scarf.
1. A fine net fabric.
2. Likenesses.
3. Most willingly.

4. Deliverance.
5. Puff with pride.
6. According to *John* 11, Jesus raised Lazarus, the brother of Mary and Martha, from the dead.

A paperweight,
My face a featureless, fine
Jew linen.

Peel off the napkin   10
O my enemy.
Do I terrify?——

The nose, the eye pits, the full set of teeth?
The sour breath
Will vanish in a day.   15

Soon, soon the flesh
The grave cave ate will be
At home on me

And I a smiling woman.
I am only thirty.   20
And like the cat I have nine times to die.

This is Number Three.
What a trash
To annihilate each decade.

What a million filaments.   25
The peanut-crunching crowd
Shoves in to see

Them unwrap me hand and foot——
The big strip tease.
Gentlemen, ladies   30

These are my hands
My knees.
I may be skin and bone,

Nevertheless, I am the same, identical woman.
The first time it happened I was ten.   35
It was an accident.

The second time I meant
To last it out and not come back at all.
I rocked shut

As a seashell.   40
They had to call and call
And pick the worms off me like sticky pearls.

Dying
Is an art, like everything else.
I do it exceptionally well.   45

I do it so it feels like hell.
I do it so it feels real.
I guess you could say I've a call.

It's easy enough to do it in a cell.
It's easy enough to do it and stay put.   50
It's the theatrical

Comeback in broad day
To the same place, the same face, the same brute
Amused shout:

"A miracle!"   55
That knocks me out.
There is a charge

For the eyeing of my scars, there is a charge
For the hearing of my heart——
It really goes.   60

And there is a charge, a very large charge
For a word or a touch
Or a bit of blood

Or a piece of my hair or my clothes.
So, so, Herr Doktor.   65
So, Herr Enemy.

I am your opus,
I am your valuable,
The pure gold baby

That melts to a shriek.   70
I turn and burn.
Do not think I underestimate your great concern.

Ash, ash—
You poke and stir.
Flesh, bone, there is nothing there——   75

A cake of soap,
A wedding ring,
A gold filling.

Herr God, Herr Lucifer
Beware   80
Beware.

Out of the ash
I rise with my red hair
And I eat men like air.

1965

THOMAS NASHE

A Litany in Time of Plague[7]

Adieu, farewell, earth's bliss;
This world uncertain is;
Fond[8] are life's lustful joys;
Death proves them all but toys;[9]
None from his darts can fly;   5
I am sick, I must die.
   Lord, have mercy on us!

Rich men, trust not in wealth,
Gold cannot buy you health;
Physic[1] himself must fade.   10
All things to end are made,
The plague full swift goes by;
I am sick, I must die.
   Lord, have mercy on us!

Beauty is but a flower   15
Which wrinkles will devour;
Brightness falls from the air;
Queens have died young and fair;
Dust hath closed Helen's[2] eye.
I am sick, I must die.   20
   Lord, have mercy on us!

Strength stoops unto the grave,
Worms feed on Hector[3] brave;
Swords may not fight with fate,
Earth still holds ope her gate.   25
"Come, come!" the bells[4] do cry.
I am sick, I must die.
   Lord, have mercy on us.

Wit with his wantonness
Tasteth death's bitterness;   30
Hell's executioner
Hath no ears for to hear
What vain art can reply.
I am sick, I must die.
   Lord, have mercy on us.   35

Haste, therefore, each degree,
To welcome destiny;
Heaven is our heritage,
Earth but a player's stage;

---

7. England was ravaged by bubonic plague in 1592.
8. Foolish.
9. Trifles.
1. Restorative powers, personified.

2. Helen of Troy, a traditional type of beauty.
3. The bravest Trojan, a traditional type of strength.
4. Church bells which toll for deaths.

Mount we unto the sky.   40
I am sick, I must die.
    Lord, have mercy on us.

1592

JONATHAN SWIFT

A Satirical Elegy

On the Death of a Late Famous General[5]

His Grace? impossible? what dead?
Of old age too, and in his bed?
And could that Mighty Warrior fall?
And so inglorious, after all!
Well, since he's gone, no matter how,   5
The last loud trump[6] must wake him now;
And, trust me, as the noise grows stronger,
He'd wish to sleep a little longer.

And could he be indeed so old
As by the newspapers we're told?[7]   10
Threescore, I think, is pretty high;
'Twas time in conscience he should die.
This world he cumbered long enough;
He burnt his candle to the snuff;
And that's the reason, some folks think,   15
He left behind *so great a stink*.

Behold his funeral appears,
Nor widow's sighs, nor orphan's tears,
Wont at such times each heart to pierce,
Attend the progress of his hearse.   20
But what of that, his friends may say,
He had those honors in his day;
True to his profit and his pride,
He made them weep before he died.

    Come hither, all ye empty things,   25
Ye bubbles[8] raised by breath of Kings,
Who float upon the tide of state,
Come hither, and behold your fate.
Let pride be taught by this rebuke,
How very mean a thing's a Duke;   30
From all his ill-got honors flung,
Turned to that dirt from whence he sprung.

1722

5. John Churchill, the first Duke of
Marlborough, whose brilliant military ex-
ploits had made him an English hero. His
later pettiness and civilian politics tar-
nished, in the eyes of some, his earlier
glory, but the poem exaggerates his loss
of reputation.

6. On Judgment Day, when the dead are
supposed to be awakened.
7. Marlborough died at age 72.
8. Insubstantial things. Marlborough was
made a Duke in 1689, two days before
William became king, in a deal made dur-
ing the succession crisis.

EXPECTATION AND SURPRISE

Poetry is full of surprises. Poems express anger or outrage just as effectively as love or sadness, and good poems can be written about going to a rock concert or having lunch or cutting the lawn, as well as about making love or gazing at a cloudless sky or smelling flowers. Even poems on "predictable" subjects can surprise us with unpredicted attitudes, unusual events, or a sudden twist. Knowing that a poem is about some particular subject—love, for example, or death—may give us a general idea of what to expect, but it never tells us altogether what we will find in a particular poem. Experiencing a poem fully means being open to the poem and its surprises, being willing to let the poem guide us to its own attitudes, feelings, and ideas. The following two poems—one about death and one about love —are rather different from those we looked at in Chapter 1.

MARGE PIERCY

Barbie Doll

This girlchild was born as usual
and presented dolls that did pee-pee
and miniature GE stoves and irons
and wee lipsticks the color of cherry candy.
Then in the magic of puberty, a classmate said: 5
You have a great big nose and fat legs.

She was healthy, tested intelligent,
possessed strong arms and back,
abundant sexual drive and manual dexterity.
She went to and fro apologizing.   10
Everyone saw a fat nose on thick legs.

She was advised to play coy,
exhorted to come on hearty,
exercise, diet, smile and wheedle.
Her good nature wore out   15
like a fan belt.
So she cut off her nose and her legs
and offered them up.

In the casket displayed on satin she lay
with the undertaker's cosmetics painted on,   20
a turned-up putty nose,
dressed in a pink and white nightie.
Doesn't she look pretty? everyone said.
Consummation at last.
To every woman a happy ending.   25

1973

34

W. D. SNODGRASS

Leaving the Motel

Outside, the last kids holler
Near the pool: they'll stay the night.
Pick up the towels; fold your collar
Out of sight.

Check: is the second bed   5
Unrumpled, as agreed?
Landlords have to think ahead
In case of need,

Too. Keep things straight: don't take
The matches, the wrong keyrings—   10
We've nowhere we could keep a keepsake—
Ashtrays, combs, things

That sooner or later others
Would accidentally find.
Check: take nothing of one another's   15
And leave behind

Your license number only,
Which they won't care to trace;
We've paid. Still, should such things get lonely,
Leave in their vase   20

An aspirin to preserve
Our lilacs, the wayside flowers
We've gathered and must leave to serve
A few more hours;

That's all. We can't tell when   25
We'll come back, can't press claims;
We would no doubt have other rooms then,
Or other names.

1968

The first poem has the strong note of sadness that characterizes many death poems, but its emphasis is not on the response to the girl's death but on the disappointments in her life. The only "scene" in the poem (lines 19–23) portrays the unnamed girl at rest in her casket, and as in *Bells for John Whiteside's Daughter*, her stillness contrasts with a restlessness in life, but the effect is very different. Here the still body in the casket contrasts not with vitality but with frustration and anxiety: her life since puberty (lines 5–6) had been full of apologies and attempts to change her physical appearance and emotional makeup. The rest she achieves in death is not, however, a triumph, despite what people say (line 23). Although the poem's last two words are "happy ending" this girl without a name has died in embarrassment and without fulfillment, and the final lines are **ironic**, meaning the opposite of what they say. The cheerful comments at the end lack force and truth because of what we already know; we understand them as ironic because they emphasize how unhappy the girl was and how false her cosmeticized corpse is to the sad truth of her life.

The poem's concern is to suggest the falsity and destructiveness of those standards of beauty which have led to the tragedy of the girl's life. In an important sense, the poem is not really *about* death at all in spite of the fact that the girl's death and her repaired corpse are central to it. As the title suggests, the poem dramatizes how standardized, commercialized notions of femininity and prettiness can be painful and destructive to those whose bodies do not precisely fit the conformist models, and the poem attacks vigorously those conventional standards and the widespread, unthinking acceptance of them.

Leaving the Motel similarly goes in quite a different direction from many poems on the subject of love. Instead of expressing assurance about how love lasts and endures, or about the sincerity and depth of affection, this poem dramatizes a brief sexual encounter. But it does not emphasize sexuality or eroticism in the meeting of the nameless lovers (we see them only as they prepare to leave), nor does it suggest why or how they have found each other, or what either of them is like as a person. Its emphasis is on how careful they must be not to get caught, how exact and calculating they must be in their planning, how finite and limited their encounter must be, how sealed off this encounter is from the rest of their lives. The poem stresses the tiny details the lovers must think of, the agreements they must observe, and the ritual checklist of their duties ("Check . . . Keep things straight . . . Check . . ." lines 5, 9, 15). Affection and sentiment have their small place in the poem (notice the care for the flowers, lines 19–24, and the thought of "pressing claims," line 26), but the emphasis is on temporariness, uncertainty, and limits. The poem is about an illicit, perhaps adulterous sexual encounter, but there is no sex in the poem, only a kind of archeological record of lust.

Labeling a poem as a "love poem" or a "death poem" is primarily a matter of convenience, a grouping based on the **subject matter** in a poem or the event or **topic** it chooses to engage. But as the poems we have been looking at suggest, poems that may be loosely called love poems or death poems may differ widely from one another, express totally different attitudes or ideas, and concentrate on very different aspects of the subject. The main advantages of grouping poems in this way for study is that a reader can become conscious of individual differences: a reading of two poems side by side may suggest how each is distinctive in what it has to say and how it says it.

What a poem has to say is often called its **theme**, the kind of statement it makes about its subject. We could say, for example, that the theme of *Leaving the Motel* is that illicit love is secretive, careful, transitory, and short on emotion and sentiment, or that secret sexual encounters tend to be brief, calculated, and characterized by restrained and insecure feelings. The theme of a poem usually may be expressed in several different ways, and poems often have more than one theme. *Barbie Doll* suggests that commercialized standards destroy human values; that rigid and idealized notions of normalty cripple people who are different; that false standards of appearance and behavior can destroy human beings and lead to personal tragedy; that people are easily and tragically led to accept evaluations thrust upon them by others; that American consumers tend to be conformists, easily influenced in their outlook by advertising and by commercial products; that children who do not conform to middle-class standards and notions don't have a chance. Each of these statements could be demonstrated to be said or implied in the poem and rather central to it. But none of these statements individually nor all of them together would be an adequate substitute for the poem itself. To state the theme in such a brief and abstract way—while it may be helpful in clarifiying what the poem does and does not say—never does justice to the experience of the poem, the way it works on us as readers. Poems affect us in all sorts of ways—emotional and psychological as well as rational—and often a poem's dramatization of a story, an event, or a moment bypasses our rational responses and affects us far more deeply than a clear and logical argument would.

Poems, then, may differ widely from one another even when they share a common subject. And the subjects of poetry also vary widely. It isn't true that there are certain "poetic" subjects and that there are others which aren't appropriate to poetry. Any human activity, any thought or feeling can be the subject of poetry. Poetry often deals with beauty and the softer, more attractive human emotions, but it can deal with ugliness and less attractive human conduct as well, for poetry seeks to mirror human beings and human events, showing us ourselves not only as we'd like to be but as we are. Good poetry gets written about all kinds of topics, in all kinds of forms. This poem, for example, celebrates a famous rock concert.

JONI MITCHELL

Woodstock[1]

I came upon a child of God
He was walking along the road
And I asked him, where are you going
And this he told me

---

1. Written after the rock festival there in 1969, celebrating not only the festival but what came to be called the "Woodstock Nation."

I'm going on down to Yasgur's farm   5
I'm going to join in a rock'n'roll band
I'm going to camp out on the land
And try an' get my soul free
    We are stardust
    We are golden   10
    And we've got to get ourselves
    Back to the garden

Then can I walk beside you
I have come here to lose the smog
And I feel to be a cog in something turning   15
Well maybe it is just the time of year
Or maybe it's the time of man
I don't know who I am
But life is for learning
    We are stardust   20
    We are golden
    And we've got to get ourselves
    Back to the garden

By the time we got to Woodstock
We were half a million strong   25
And everywhere there was song and celebration
And I dreamed I saw the bombers
Riding shotgun in the sky
And they were turning into butterflies
Above our nation   30
    We are stardust
    We are golden
    And we've got to get ourselves
    Back to the garden

1969

This particular poem is also a song. (The lyrics to some songs "work" as poems; others don't because they aren't sufficiently verbal or because their particular effects depend too much on the music that goes with the words.) The account it gives of Woodstock may now seem rather dated in its optimism about transforming, through love and togetherness, the machines of war (lines 27–30), but its ideals of simplicity and peace are stated powerfully. The recurrent idea of returning somehow to an original ideal of innocence (the Garden of Eden) suggests the high aspirations ("stardust") and urgency ("got to") of the sixties' sense of things gone wrong. The mental pictures portray rural simplicity, freedom, the power of united efforts, and the joys of music as an alternative to urban crowding and pollution (line 14), political conflict (lines 27–28), and confusion over personal identity (lines 18–19). The poem's theme—that human beings can, through love and working together, recreate a perfect age of innocence and peace—represents human aspirations at a very high level and does so persuasively and highmindedly, despite the particular details of time and place that anchor the poem to a particular moment in history and a specific experience.

Much less flattering to human nature is this poem about a prison inmate.

ETHERIDGE KNIGHT

Hard Rock Returns to Prison from the Hospital for the Criminal Insane

Hard Rock was "known not to take no shit
From nobody," and he had the scars to prove it:
Split purple lips, lumped ears, welts above
His yellow eyes, and one long scar that cut
Across his temple and plowed through a thick   5
Canopy of kinky hair.

The WORD was that Hard Rock wasn't a mean nigger
Anymore, that the doctors had bored a hole in his head,
Cut out part of his brain, and shot electricity
Through the rest. When they brought Hard Rock back,   10
Handcuffed and chained, he was turned loose,
Like a freshly gelded stallion, to try his new status.
And we all waited and watched, like indians at a corral,
To see if the WORD was true.

As we waited we wrapped ourselves in the cloak   15
Of his exploits: "Man, the last time, it took eight
Screws[2] to put him in the Hole." "Yeah, remember when he
Smacked the captain with his dinner tray?" "He set
The record for time in the Hole—67 straight days!"
"Ol Hard Rock! man, that's one crazy nigger."   20
And then the jewel of a myth that Hard Rock had once bit
A screw on the thumb and poisoned him with syphilitic spit.

The testing came, to see if Hard Rock was really tame.
A hillbilly called him a black son of a bitch
And didn't lose his teeth, a screw who knew Hard Rock 25
From before shook him down and barked in his face.
And Hard Rock did *nothing*. Just grinned and looked silly,
His eyes empty like knot holes in a fence.

---

2. Guards. "Hole": solitary confinement.

And even after we discovered that it took Hard Rock
Exactly 3 minutes to tell you his first name,   30
We told ourselves that he had just wised up,
Was being cool; but we could not fool ourselves for long,
And we turned away, our eyes on the ground. Crushed.
He had been our Destroyer, the doer of things
We dreamed of doing but could not bring ourselves to do,   35
The fears of years, like a biting whip,
Had cut grooves too deeply across our backs.

1968

The picture of Hard Rock as a kind of hero to other prison in-
mates is established early in the poem through a retelling of the
legends circulated about him; the straightforward chronology of the
poem sets up the mystery of how he will react after his "treatment"
in the hospital. The poem identifies with those who wait; they are
hopeful that Hard Rock's spirit has not been broken by surgery or shock
treatments, and the lines crawl almost to a stop with disappointment
in stanza four. The "nothing" (line 27) of Hard Rock's response to
teasing and taunting and the emptiness of his eyes ("like knot holes
in a fence," line 28) reduce the heroic hopes and illusions to despair.
The final stanza recounts the observers' attempts to reinterpret, to hang
onto hope that their symbol of heroism could stand up against the
best efforts to tame him, but the spirit has gone out of the hero-
worshipers too, and the poem records them as beaten, conformed,
deprived of their spirit as Hard Rock has been of his. The poem
records the despair of the hopeless and it protests against the exercise
of power that can curb even as rebellious a figure as Hard Rock.
   The following poem is equally full of anger and disappointment,
but it uses a kind of playfulness with words to make the seriousness of
the situation seem all the more relentless.

WILLIAM BLAKE

London

I wander through each chartered street,
Near where the chartered Thames does flow,
And mark in every face I meet
Marks of weakness, marks of woe.

In every cry of every man,   5
In every Infant's cry of fear,
In every voice, in every ban,
The mind-forged manacles I hear.

How the Chimney-sweeper's cry
Every black'ning Church appalls;   10
And the hapless Soldier's sigh
Runs in blood down Palace walls.

But most through midnight streets I hear
How the youthful Harlot's curse
Blasts the new-born Infant's tear,   15
And blights with plagues the Marriage hearse.

                                                          1794

The poem gives a strong sense of how London feels to this particular observer; it is cluttered, constricting, oppressive. The wordplay here articulates and connects the strong emotions he associates with London experiences. The repeated words—"every," for example, or "cry"—intensify the sense of total despair in the city and weld connections between things not necessarily related—the cries of street vendors, for example, the cries for help. The word "chartered" implies strong feelings too, and the word gives a particularly rigid sense of streets. Instead of seeming alive with people or bustling with movement, they are rigidly, coldly determined, controlled, cramped. And the same word is used for the river, as if it too were planned, programed, laid out by an oppressor. In fact, the course of the Thames had been altered (slightly) by the government before Blake's time, but most important is the word's emotional force, the sense it projects of constriction and artificiality: the person speaking experiences London as if human artifice had totally altered nature. According to the poem, people are victimized too, "marked" by their confrontations with urbanness and the power of institutions: the "soldier's sigh" that "runs in blood down Palace walls" vividly suggests, through a metaphor that visually dramatizes the speaker's feelings, both the powerlessness of the individual and the callousness of power. The "description" of the city has clearly become, by now, a subjective, highly emotional, and vivid expression of how the speaker feels about London and what it represents to him.

One more thing about *London:* at first it looks like an account of a personal experience, as if the speaker is describing and interpreting as he goes along: "I wander through each chartered street." But soon it is clear that he is describing many wanderings, putting together impressions from many walks, recreating a generalized or typical walk—which shows him "every" person in the streets, allows him to generalize about the churches being "appalled" (literally, made white) by the cry of the representative Chimney-sweeper, presents his conclusions about soldiers, prostitutes, and infants. What we are given is not a personal record of an event, but a re-presentation of it, as it seems in the mind in retrospect—not a story, not a narrative or chronological account of events, but a dramatization of self that compresses many experiences into one.

The **tone** of *London* is somber in spite of the poet's playfulness with words. Wordplay may be witty and funny if it calls attention to its own cleverness, but here it involves the discovery of unsuspected (but meaningful) connections between things. The term **tone** is used to describe the attitude the poem takes toward its subject and theme. If the theme of a poem is *what* the poem says, the tone involves *how* one says it. The "how" involves feelings, attitudes that are expressed by how one says the words. The tone of *London* is sad, despairing, and angry; reading *London* aloud, one would try to show in one's voice the strong feelings that the poem expresses, just as one would try to reproduce tenderness and caring in reading aloud *The Tally Stick* or *How Do I Love Thee*.

Subject, theme, and tone. Each of these categories gives us a way to begin considering poems and showing how one poem differs from another. Comparing poems on the same subject, or with a similar theme or tone, can lead to a clearer understanding of each individual poem and can refine our responses to the subtleties of individual differences. The title of a poem (*Leaving the Motel*, for example) or the way the poem first introduces its subject often can give us a sense of what to expect, but we need to be open to surprise too. No two poems are going to be exactly alike in their effect on us; the variety of possible poems multiplies when you think of all the possible themes and tones that can be explored within any single subject. Varieties of feeling often coincide with varieties of thinking, and readers open to the pleasures of the unexpected may find themselves learning, growing, becoming more sensitive to ideas and human issues as well as more articulate about feelings and thoughts they already have.

The following two poems might be said to be about animals, although both of them place their final emphasis on what human beings are like: the animal in each case is only the means to the end of exploring human nature. The poems share a common assumption that animals reflect human habits and conduct and may reveal much about ourselves, and in each case the woman central to the poem is revealed to be surprisingly unlike the way she thinks of herself. But the poems are very different from one another. As you read them, see if you can think of appropriate words to describe the main character and to indicate the right tone of voice to use in reading each poem.

MAXINE KUMIN

Woodchucks

Gassing the woodchucks didn't turn out right.
The knockout bomb from the Feed and Grain Exchange
was featured as merciful, quick at the bone
and the case we had against them was airtight,
both exits shoehorned shut with puddingstone,[3]
but they had a sub-sub-basement out of range.

3. A mixture of cement, pebbles, and gravel: a conglomerate.

Next morning they turned up again, no worse
for the cyanide than we for our cigarettes
and state-store Scotch, all of us up to scratch.
They brought down the marigolds as a matter of course   10
and then took over the vegetable patch
nipping the broccoli shoots, beheading the carrots.

The food from our mouths, I said, righteously thrilling
to the feel of the .22, the bullets' neat noses.
I, a lapsed pacifist fallen from grace   15
puffed with Darwinian pieties for killing,
now drew a bead on the littlest woodchuck's face.
He died down in the everbearing roses.

Ten minutes later I dropped the mother. She
flipflopped in the air and fell, her needle teeth   20
still hooked in a leaf of early Swiss chard.
Another baby next. O one-two-three
the murderer inside me rose up hard,
the hawkeye killer came on stage forthwith.

There's one chuck left. Old wily fellow, he keeps   25
me cocked and ready day after day after day.
All night I hunt his humped-up form. I dream
I sight along the barrel in my sleep.
If only they'd all consented to die unseen
gassed underground the quiet Nazi way.   30

1972

ADRIENNE RICH

Aunt Jennifer's Tigers

Aunt Jennifer's tigers prance across a screen,
Bright topaz denizens of a world of green.
They do not fear the men beneath the tree;
They pace in sleek chivalric certainty.

Aunt Jennifer's fingers fluttering through her wool   5
Find even the ivory needle hard to pull.
The massive weight of Uncle's wedding band
Sits heavily upon Aunt Jennifer's hand.

When Aunt is dead, her terrified hands will lie
Still ringed with ordeals she was mastered by.   10
The tigers in the panel that she made
Will go on prancing, proud and unafraid.

1951

How would your tone of voice change if you read *Woodchucks* aloud from beginning to end? What tone would you use to read the ending? How does the hunter feel about her increasing attraction to violence? Why does the poem begin by calling the gassing of the woodchucks "merciful" and end by describing it as "the quiet Nazi way"? What names does the hunter call herself? How does the name-calling affect your feelings about her? Exactly when does the hunter begin to *enjoy* the feel of the gun and the idea of killing? How does the poet make that clear?

Why are tigers a particularly appropriate contrast to the quiet and subdued manner of Aunt Jennifer? What words used to describe the tigers seem particularly significant? In what ways is the tiger an opposite of Aunt Jennifer? In what ways does it externalize her secrets? Why are Aunt Jennifer's hands described as "terrified"? What clues does the poem give about why Aunt Jennifer is so afraid? How does the poem make you feel about Aunt Jennifer? about her tigers? about her life? How would you describe the tone of the poem? How does the poet feel about Aunt Jennifer?

Twenty years after writing *Aunt Jennifer's Tigers*, Adrienne Rich said this about the poem:

> In writing this poem, composed and apparently cool as it is, I thought I was creating a portrait of an imaginary woman. But this woman suffers from the opposition of her imagination, worked out in tapestry, and her life style, "ringed with ordeals she was mastered by." It was important to me that Aunt Jennifer was a person as distinct from myself as possible—distanced by the formalism of the poem, by its objective, observant tone—even by putting the woman in a different generation. In those years formalism was part of the strategy—like asbestos gloves, it allowed me to handle materials I couldn't pick up bare-handed.[4]

Not often do we have such an explicit comment on a poem by its author, and we don't actually have to have it to understand and experience the force of the poem (although such a statement may clarify why the author chose particular modes of presentation and how the poem fits into the author's own patterns of thinking and growing). Most poems contain within them what we need to know in order to tap the human and artistic resources they offer us. Still, it is nice to have comments like this one, and later on (in Chapter 11) we will look at some of the advantages of knowing specific things about an author and other poems that he or she has written. (There, too, you will find a gathering of poems by Adrienne Rich.) In the chapters between now and then we will look at various technical aspects of poetry, considering how poems are put together and what sorts of things we need to know in order to read well, that is, how to experience sensitively and fully other poems you may want to read later. Not all poems are as accessible as those we've looked at so far, and even the

4. In *When We Dead Awaken: Writing as Re-Vision*, a talk given in December, 1971, at the Women's Forum of the Modern Language Association.

ones that are accessible usually yield themselves to us more readily and more completely if we approach them systematically by developing specific reading habits and skills—just as someone learning to play tennis systematically learns the rules, the techniques, the things to watch out for that are distinctive to the pleasures and hazards of that skill or craft. In the next eight chapters, we will consider the various aspects of language that come together in a poem, and we will methodically ask some questions that will help you to know how to approach a poem. It helps if you know what to expect, and the chapters that follow will help you to an understanding of the things that poets can do—and thus to what poems can do for you.

But knowing what to expect isn't everything, and I have one bit of advice to offer every prospective reader of poetry before going any further: Be open. Be open to new experience, be open to new feelings, be open to new ideas. No reader of poetry is perfect, and in learning what you learn in the next few chapters you will not become invincible and superior to all mistakes. It is important that you stay open to new information and new experiences—forever. Every poem in the world is a potential new experience, and no matter how sophisticated you become, you can still be surprised (and delighted) by new poems— and by rereading old ones. Good poems bear many, many rereadings, and often one discovers something new with every new reading. Learning about the standard devices and techniques of poetry can help you know what to expect, but it need not make you feel either overconfident or jaded; in fact, knowledge of poetry—like real knowledge of almost anything—will convince you that you do not know everything, or indeed as much as you want to know. No reader is a worse reader than a dogmatic or closed-minded one. This course will not teach you everything.

And it is especially important that you be open now. The information that follows will help give you a sense of what to expect, but will also count on your being open to surprises. Poetry is not Everything; there are many worthwhile things in the world besides poetry, but poetry considers most of these things and offers several perspectives on them. If you are open to poetry, you are open to much that the world can offer you. Be willing to let poems surprise you when you come to them; let them come on their own terms, let them be themselves. At the end of this chapter are four groups of poems on popular subjects of poetry. You can probably read most of them with interest and pleasure now. But you may want to come back to them later, too, when you have worked your way through some of the problems we will consider together in the chapters that follow, where you will become more familiar with what meeting a poem on its own terms can mean.

A Gathering of Poems about Animals

JOHN BUNYAN

Of the Boy and Butterfly

Behold, how eager this our little boy
Is for a butterfly, as if all joy,
All profits, honors, yea, and lasting pleasures,
Were wrapped up in her, or the richest treasures
Found in her would be bundled up together,   5
When all her all is lighter than a feather.

He halloos, runs, and cries out, "Here, boys, here!"
Nor doth he brambles or the nettles fear:
He stumbles at the molehills, up he gets,
And runs again, as one bereft of wits;   10
And all his labor and his large outcry
Is only for a silly butterfly.

Comparison

This little boy an emblem[1] is of those
Whose hearts are wholly at the world's dispose.
The butterfly doth represent to me   15
The world's best things at best but fading be.
All are but painted nothings and false joys,
Like this poor butterfly to these our boys.

His running through nettles, thorns, and briers,
To gratify his boyish fond desires,   20
His tumbling over molehills to attain
His end, namely, his butterfly to gain,
Doth plainly show what hazards some men run
To get what will be lost as soon as won.

1686

EMILY DICKINSON

A Narrow Fellow in the Grass

A narrow Fellow in the Grass
Occasionally rides—
You may have met Him—did you not
His notice sudden is—

1. Symbol.

The Grass divides as with a Comb—   5
A spotted shaft is seen—
And then it closes at your feet
And opens further on—

He likes a Boggy Acre
A Floor too cool for Corn—   10
Yet when a Boy, and Barefoot—
I more than once at Noon

Have passed, I thought, a Whip lash
Unbraiding in the Sun
When stooping to secure it   15
It wrinkled, and was gone—

Several of Nature's People
I know, and they know me—
I feel for them a transport
Of cordiality—   20

But never met this Fellow
Attended, or alone
Without a tighter breathing
And Zero at the Bone—

                                                     1866

KARL SHAPIRO

The Fly

O hideous little bat, the size of snot,
With polyhedral eye and shabby clothes,
To populate the stinking cat you walk
The promontory of the dead man's nose,
Climb with the fine leg of a Duncan-Phyfe[2]   5
  The smoking mountains of my food
    And in a comic mood
In mid-air take to bed a wife.

Riding and riding with your filth of hair
On gluey foot or wing, forever coy,   10
Hot from the compost and green sweet decay,
Sounding your buzzer like an urchin toy—
You dot all whiteness with diminutive stool,
  In the tight belly of the dead
    Burrow with hungry head   15
And inlay maggots like a jewel.

2. Furniture of the 19th-century American cabinetmaker Duncan Phyfe sometimes featured delicate, sharply angled legs.

At your approach the great horse stomps and paws
Bringing the hurricane of his heavy tail;
Shod in disease you dare to kiss my hand
Which sweeps against you like an angry flail;   20
Still you return, return, trusting your wing
 To draw you from the hunter's reach
  That learns to kill to teach
 Disorder to the tinier thing.

My peace is your disaster. For your death   25
Children like spiders cup their pretty hands
And wives resort to chemistry of war.
In fens of sticky paper and quicksands
You glue yourself to death. Where you are stuck
 You struggle hideously and beg,   30
  You amputate your leg
 Imbedded in the amber muck.

But I, a man, must swat you with my hate,
Slap you across the air and crush your flight,
Must mangle with my shoe and smear your blood,   35
Expose your little guts pasty and white,
Knock your head sidewise like a drunkard's hat,
 Pin your wings under like a crow's,
  Tear off your flimsy clothes
 And beat you as one beats a rat.   40

Then like Gargantua[3] I stride among
The corpses strewn like raisins in the dust,
The broken bodies of the narrow dead
That catch the throat with fingers of disgust.
I sweep. One gyrates like a top and falls   45
 And stunned, stone blind, and deaf
  Buzzes its frightful F
 And dies between three cannibals.

            1942

OGDEN NASH

The Turtle

The turtle lives 'twixt plated decks
Which practically conceal its sex.
I think it clever of the turtle
In such a fix to be so fertile.

            1940

3. Legendary medieval giant.

LEWIS CARROLL

How Doth the Little Crocodile

How doth the little crocodile
  Improve his shining tail,
And pour the waters of the Nile
  On every golden scale!

How cheerfully he seems to grin   5
  How neatly spreads his claws,
And welcomes little fishes in,
  With gently smiling jaws!

1865

SUSAN MITCHELL

From the Journals of the Frog Prince[4]

In March I dreamed of mud,
sheets of mud over the ballroom chairs and table,
rainbow slicks of mud under the throne.
In April I saw mud of clouds and mud of sun.
Now in May I find excuses to linger in the kitchen   5
for wafts of silt and ale,
cinnamon and river bottom,
tender scallion and sour underlog.

At night I cannot sleep.
I am listening for the dribble of mud   10
climbing the stairs to our bedroom
as if a child in a wet bathing suit ran
up them in the dark.

Last night I said, "Face it, you're bored.
How many times can you live over   15
with the same excitement
that moment when the princess leans
into the well, her face a petal
falling to the surface of the water
as you rise like a bubble to her lips,   20
the golden ball bursting from your mouth?"
Remember how she hurled you against the wall,
your body cracking open,
skin shriveling to the bone,

4. According to a popular fairy tale, a frog is transformed into a prince when a girl for whom he performs a favor kisses him and allows him to sleep in her bed.

the green pod of your heart splitting in two, 25
and her face imprinted with every moment
of your transformation?

I no longer tremble.

Night after night I lie beside her.
"Why is your forehead so cool and damp?" she asks. 30
Her breasts are soft and dry as flour.
The hand that brushes my head is feverish.
At her touch I long for wet leaves,
the slap of water against rocks.

"What are you thinking of?" she asks. 35
How can I tell her
I am thinking of the green skin
shoved like wet pants behind the Directoire desk?
Or tell her I am mortgaged to the hilt
of my sword, to the leek-green tip of my soul? 40
Someday I will drag her by her hair
to the river—and what? Drown her?
Show her the green flame of my self rising at her feet?
But there's no more violence in her
than in a fence or a gate. 45

"What are you thinking of?" she whispers.
I am staring into the garden.
I am watching the moon
wind its trail of golden slime around the oak,
over the stone basin of the fountain. 50
How can I tell her
I am thinking that transformations are not forever?

p. 1978

DELMORE SCHWARTZ

The Heavy Bear Who Goes with Me

"the withness of the body" [5]

The heavy bear who goes with me,
A manifold honey to smear his face,
Clumsy and lumbering here and there,
The central ton of every place,
The hungry beating brutish one 5
In love with candy, anger, and sleep,

5. Early editions attributed the epigraph to Alfred North Whitehead, the philosopher.

Crazy factotum, dishevelling all,
Climbs the building, kicks the football,
Boxes his brother in the hate-ridden city.

Breathing at my side, that heavy animal,   10
That heavy bear who sleeps with me,
Howls in his sleep for a world of sugar,
A sweetness intimate as the water's clasp,
Howls in his sleep because the tight-rope
Trembles and shows the darkness beneath.   15
—The strutting show-off is terrified,
Dressed in his dress-suit, bulging his pants,
Trembles to think that his quivering meat
Must finally wince to nothing at all.

That inescapable animal walks with me,   20
Has followed me since the black womb held,
Moves where I move, distorting my gesture,
A caricature, a swollen shadow,
A stupid clown of the spirit's motive,
Perplexes and affronts with his own darkness,   25
The secret life of belly and bone,
Opaque, too near, my private, yet unknown,
Stretches to embrace the very dear
With whom I would walk without him near,
Touches her grossly, although a word   30
Would bare my heart and make me clear,
Stumbles, flounders, and strives to be fed
Dragging me with him in his mouthing care,
Amid the hundred million of his kind,
The scrimmage of appetite everywhere.   35
                                                      1938

JOHN STONE

Explaining about the Dachshund

There's no badger in this sandbox.
There wasn't one here when I nailed it
four feet square and hauled
the sand ten miles.

There's not one in it now   5
despite this nosing
nosing around these tunnels
we dug by hand.

It's genes that have caught up with him,

an instinct for fur some ancestor   10
had to leave behind,
tremble-jawed but safe,
in other ground.

It's a grandfather's failure

makes him want to kill   15
something he hasn't seen
but can't forget

that comes back with him now to the house,
part of his cells, and sleeps beside him
in the red-eyed dark of my kitchen,   20

mixed in with the other smells.

1972

JOHN MASEFIELD

The Lemmings[6]

Once in a hundred years the Lemmings come
Westward, in search of food, over the snow,
Westward until the salt sea drowns them dumb,
Westward, till all are drowned, those Lemmings go.
Once, it is thought, there was a westward land   5
(Now drowned) where there was food for those starved things,
And memory of the place has burnt its brand
In the little brains of all the Lemming Kings.
Perhaps, long since, there was a land beyond
Westward from death, some city, some calm place,   10
Where one could taste God's quiet and be fond
With the little beauty of a human face;
But now the land is drowned. Yet still we press
Westward, in search, to death, to nothingness.

1920

6. Rodents noted for their periodic migrations caused by sharp population increases.

RICHARD WILBUR

The Pardon

My dog lay dead five days without a grave
In the thick of summer, hid in a clump of pine
And a jungle of grass and honeysuckle-vine.
I who had loved him while he kept alive

Went only close enough to where he was   5
To sniff the heavy honeysuckle-smell
Twined with another odor heavier still
And hear the flies' intolerable buzz.

Well, I was ten and very much afraid.
In my kind world the dead were out of range   10
And I could not forgive the sad or strange
In beast or man. My father took the spade

And buried him. Last night I saw the grass
Slowly divide (it was the same scene
But now it glowed a fierce and mortal green)   15
And saw the dog emerging. I confess

I felt afraid again, but still he came
In the carnal sun, clothed in a hymn of flies,
And death was breeding in his lively eyes.
I started in to cry and call his name,   20

Asking forgiveness of his tongueless head.
. . . I dreamt the past was never past redeeming:
But whether this was false or honest dreaming
I beg death's pardon now. And mourn the dead.

                                                     1950

W. S. MERWIN

Burning the Cat

In the spring, by the big shuck-pile
Between the bramble-choked brook where the copperheads
Curled in the first sun, and the mud road,
All at once it could no longer be ignored.
The season steamed with an odor for which
There has never been a name, but it shouted above all.
When I went near, the wood-lice were in its eyes
And a nest of beetles in the white fur of its armpit.

I built a fire there by the shuck-pile
But it did no more than pop the beetles   10
And singe the damp fur, raising a stench
Of burning hair that bit through the sweet day-smell.
Then thinking how time leches after indecency,
Since both grief is indecent and the lack of it,
I went away and fetched newspaper,   15
And wrapped it in dead events, days and days,
Soaked it in kerosene and put it in
With the garbage on a heaped nest of sticks:
It was harder to burn than the peels of oranges,
Bubbling and spitting, and the reek was like   20
Rank cooking that drifted with the smoke out
Through the budding woods and clouded the shining dogwood.
But I became stubborn: I would consume it
Though the pyre should take me a day to build
And the flames rise over the house. And hours I fed   25
That burning, till I was black and streaked with sweat;
And poked it out then, with charred meat still clustering
Thick around the bones. And buried it so
As I should have done in the first place, for
The earth is slow, but deep, and good for hiding;   30
I would have used it if I had understood
How nine lives can vanish in one flash of a dog's jaws,
A car or a copperhead, and yet how one small
Death, however reckoned, is hard to dispose of.

                                                                                    1955

A Gathering of Poems on Family and Ancestry

RICHARD HUGO

What Thou Lovest Well, Remains American

You remember the name was Jensen. She seemed old
always alone inside, face pasted gray to the window,
and mail never came. Two blocks down, the Grubskis
went insane. George played rotten trombone
Easter when they flew the flag. Wild roses   5
remind you the roads were gravel and vacant lots
the rule. Poverty was real, wallet and spirit,
and each day slow as church. You remember threadbare
church groups on the corner, howling their faith
at stars, and the violent Holy Rollers[1]   10

---

1. Slang for emotional evangelical Christians.

renting the barn for their annual violent sing
and the barn burned down when you came back from war.
Knowing the people you knew then are dead,
you try to believe these roads paved are improved,
the neighbors, moved in while you were away, good-looking,   15
their dogs well fed. You still have need
to remember lots empty and fern.
Lawns well trimmed remind you of the train
your wife took one day forever, some far empty town,
the odd name you never recall. The time: 6:23.   20
The day: October 9. The year remains a blur.
You blame this neighborhood for your failure.
In some vague way, the Grubskis degraded you
beyond repair. And you know you must play again
and again Mrs. Jensen pale at her window, must hear   25
the foul music over the good slide of traffic.
You loved them well and they remain, still with nothing
to do, no money and no will. Loved them, and the gray
that was their disease you carry for extra food
in case you're stranded in some odd empty town   30
and need hungry lovers for friends, and need feel
you are welcome in the secret club they have formed.

1975

JOHN STONE

Coming Home

About two thousand miles
into my life
the family bounced south
west   east
in an old Oldsmobile.   5

Two brothers tumbled
on the back seat
watching the world blur
upside down right side up
through windows   10
time fogged in
slowly from the corners.

Nights
cars came at us
wall-eyed   15
their lights sliding
over the ceiling
like night fighters

                    while in the front
              they talked parental   low   20
                    in a drone
                  we didn't hear .
              tossing through Arkansas
                toward Mississippi.

              When our eyes grew red   25
                  and blood bulged
            in our heads from laughing
                    we slept
                  he on the seat
                  and I bent over   30
              the humped transmission

              close to the only motor
                  in the world.

                                                              1972

DIANE WAKOSKI

The Photos

My sister in her well-tailored silk blouse hands me
the photo of my father
in naval uniform and white hat.
I say, "Oh, this is the one which Mama used to have on her
    dresser."

My sister controls her face and furtively looks at my mother,   5
a sad rag bag of a woman, lumpy and sagging everywhere,
like a mattress at the Salvation Army, though with no holes or
    tears,
and says, "No."

I look again,
and see that my father is wearing a wedding ring,   10
which he never did
when he lived with my mother. And that there is a legend on it,
"To my dearest wife,
          Love
          Chief"   15
And I realize the photo must have belonged to his second wife,
whom he left our mother to marry.

My mother says, with her face as still as the whole unpopulated
    part of the
state of North Dakota,

"May I see it too?"   20
She looks at it.

I look at my tailored sister
and my own blue-jeaned self. Have we wanted to hurt our
    mother,
sharing these pictures on this, one of the few days I ever visit or
spend with family? For her face is curiously haunted,   25
not now with her usual viperish bitterness,
but with something so deep it could not be spoken.

I turn away and say I must go on, as I have a dinner
    engagement with friends.
But I drive all the way to Pasadena from Whittier,
thinking of my mother's face; how I could never love her;   30
    how my father
could not love her either. Yet knowing I have inherited
the rag-bag body,
stony face with bulldog jaws.

I drive, thinking of that face.
Jeffers' California Medea[2] who inspired me to poetry.   35
I killed my children,
but there as I am changing lanes on the freeway, necessarily
    glancing in the
rearview mirror, I see the face,
not even a ghost, but always with me, like a photo in a   40
    beloved's wallet.

How I hate my destiny.

                                                                    1978

DOROTHY LIVESAY

Green Rain

I remember long veils of green rain
Feathered like the shawl of my grandmother—
Green from the half-green of the spring trees
Waving in the valley.

I remember the road   5
Like the one which leads to my grandmother's house,
A warm house, with green carpets,

2. Robinson Jeffers (1887–1962), American poet who migrated to California from the East, retold the Medea story in *Solstice*, 1935. According to Greek legend, Medea was a sorceress who killed her children.

Geraniums, a trilling canary
And shining horse-hair chairs;
And the silence, full of the rain's falling   10
Was like my grandmother's parlor
Alive with herself and her voice, rising and falling—
Rain and wind intermingled.

I remember on that day
I was thinking only of my love   15
And of my love's house.
But now I remember the day
As I remember my grandmother.
I remember the rain as the feathery fringe of her shawl.

p. 1929

ANN DEAGON

There Is No Balm in Birmingham

Among the agents used by counterfeiters
to age their stock are: glycerine,
whale oil, rose water. I know this art.
To make their tender legal, to pass current,
my petaled, my limpid aunts   5
distilled in the coiled copper of their afternoons
animal, vegetable, mineral
into a balmy essence that preserved
their beauty moist.
                        Leathered as I am,   10
Aunties, sisters, I smear my page
with crafty balsam, beauteous conceit,
hide to the last, last line the truth that's not
beauty but bone. bone. bone. bone.

1978

ETHERIDGE KNIGHT

The Idea of Ancestry

I

Taped to the wall of my cell[3] are 47 pictures: 47 black
faces: my father, mother, grandmothers (1 dead), grand

---

3. This poem is from Knight's volume, *Poems from Prison*; Knight began to write poetry while serving a sentence for armed robbery in the Ohio State Penitentiary.

fathers (both dead), brothers, sisters, uncles, aunts,
cousins (1st & 2nd), nieces, and nephews. They stare
across the space at my sprawling on my bunk. I know
their dark eyes, they know mine. I know their style,   5
they know mine. I am all of them, they are all of me;
they are farmers, I am a thief, I am me, they are thee.

I have at one time or another been in love with my mother,
1 grandmother, 2 sisters, 2 aunts (1 went to the asylum),   10
and 5 cousins. I am now in love with a 7 yr old niece
(she sends me letters written in large block print, and
her picture is the only one that smiles at me).

I have the same name as 1 grandfather, 3 cousins, 3 nephews,
and 1 uncle. The uncle disappeared when he was 15, just took 15
off and caught a freight (they say). He's discussed each year
when the family has a reunion, he causes uneasiness in
the clan, he is an empty space. My father's mother, who is 93
and who keeps the Family Bible with everybody's birth dates
(and death dates) in it, always mentions him. There is no   20
place in her Bible for "whereabouts unknown."

II

Each Fall the graves of my grandfathers call me, the brown
hills and red gullies of mississippi send out their electric
messages, galvanizing my genes. Last yr/like a salmon quitting
the cold ocean—leaping and bucking up his birthstream/I   25
hitchhiked my way from L.A. with 16 caps[4] in my pocket and a
monkey on my back, and I almost kicked it with the kinfolks.
I walked barefooted in my grandmother's backyard/I smelled
    the old
land and the woods/I sipped cornwhiskey from fruit jars with the
    men/
I flirted with the women/I had a ball till the caps ran out   30
and my habit came down. That night I looked at my grand-
    mother
and split/my guts were screaming for junk/but I was almost
contented/I had almost caught up with me.
    The next day in Memphis I cracked a croaker's crib[5]/for a fix.

This yr there is a gray stone wall damming my stream, and when
the falling leaves stir my genes, I pace my cell or flop on my
    bunk
and stare at 47 black faces across the space. I am all of them,
they are all of me, I am me, they are thee, and I have no sons
to float in the space between.

                                                          1968

---

4. Doses of heroin (?); "monkey on   5. Burglarized a doctor's house (or a
my back": drug habit.   drugstore).

A. M. KLEIN

Heirloom

My father bequeathed me no wide estates;
No keys and ledgers were my heritage;
Only some holy books with *yahrzeit*[6] dates
Writ mournfully upon a blank front page—

Books of the Baal Shem Tov,[7] and of his wonders;   5
Pamphlets upon the devil and his crew;
Prayers against road demons, witches, thunders;
And sundry other tomes for a good Jew.

Beautiful: though no pictures on them, save
The scorpion crawling on a printed track;   10
The Virgin floating on a scriptural wave,
Square letters twinkling in the Zodiac.

The snuff left on this page, now brown and old,
The tallow stains of midnight liturgy—
These are my coat of arms, and these unfold   15
My noble lineage, my proud ancestry!

And my tears, too, have stained this heirloomed ground,
When reading in these treatises some weird
Miracle, I turned a leaf and found
A white hair fallen from my father's beard.   20

                                                                    1940

SYLVIA PLATH

Daddy

You do not do, you do not do
Any more, black shoe
In which I have lived like a foot
For thirty years, poor and white,
Barely daring to breathe or Achoo.   5

Daddy, I have had to kill you.
You died before I had time——
Marble-heavy, a bag full of God,
Ghastly statue with one gray toe
Big as a Frisco seal   10

6. Anniversary of the death of a parent or near relative.
7. A title given to someone who pos- sesses the secret knowledge of Jewish holy men and who therefore could work miracles.

And a head in the freakish Atlantic
Where it pours bean green over blue
In the waters off beautiful Nauset.[8]
I used to pray to recover you.
Ach, du.[9]   15

In the German tongue, in the Polish town
Scraped flat by the roller
Of wars, wars, wars.
But the name of the town is common.
My Polack friend   20

Says there are a dozen or two.
So I never could tell where you
Put your foot, your root,
I never could talk to you.
The tongue stuck in my jaw.   25

It stuck in a barb wire snare.
Ich, ich, ich, ich,
I could hardly speak.
I thought every German was you.
And the language obscene   30

An engine, an engine
Chuffing me off like a Jew.
A Jew to Dachau, Auschwitz, Belsen.[1]
I began to talk like a Jew.
I think I may well be a Jew.   35

The snows of the Tyrol,[2] the clear beer of Vienna
Are not very pure or true.
With my gypsy-ancestress and my weird luck
And my Taroc[3] pack and my Taroc pack
I may be a bit of a Jew.   40

I have always been scared of *you*,
With your Luftwaffe,[4] your gobbledygoo.
And your neat moustache
And your Aryan eye, bright blue.
Panzer-man, panzer-man, O You—   45

Not God but a swastika
So black no sky could squeak through.
Every woman adores a Fascist,
The boot in the face, the brute
Brute heart of a brute like you.   50

8. An inlet on Cape Cod.
9. Literally, "Oh, you" in German.
Plath often portrays herself as Jewish and
her oppressors as German.
1. Sites of World War II German death
camps.
2. Alpine region in Austria and north-
ern Italy. The snow there is, legendarily,
as pure as the beer is clear in Vienna.
3. A variant of Tarot, playing cards
used mainly for fortune-telling, said to
have been introduced into Europe by gyp-
sies in the 15th century.
4. German air force.

You stand at the blackboard, daddy,
In the picture I have of you,
A cleft in your chin instead of your foot
But no less a devil for that, no not
Any less the black man who   55

Bit my pretty red heart in two.
I was ten when they buried you.
At twenty I tried to die
And get back, back, back to you.
I thought even the bones would do   60

But they pulled me out of the sack,
And they stuck me together with glue.
And then I knew what to do.
I made a model of you,
A man in black with a Meinkampf look   65

And a love of the rack and the screw.
And I said I do, I do.
So daddy, I'm finally through.
The black telephone's off at the root,
The voices just can't worm through.   70

If I've killed one man, I've killed two——
The vampire who said he was you
And drank my blood for a year,
Seven years, if you want to know.
Daddy, you can lie back now.   75

There's a stake in your fat black heart
And the villagers never like you.
They are dancing and stamping on you.
They always *knew* it was you.
Daddy, daddy, you bastard, I'm through.   80
                                                              1966

LUCILLE CLIFTON

Daddy

12/02–5/69

the days have kept on coming,
Daddy or not.   the cracks
in the sidewalk turn green
and the Indian women sell pussywillows
on the corner.   nothing remembers.   5
everything remembers.

in the days where Daddy was
there is a space.

my Daddy died as he lived,
a confident man.   10
"I'll go to Heaven," he said,
"Jesus knows me."
when his leg died, he cut it off.
"It's gone," he said, "it's gone
but I'm still here."   15

what will happen to the days
without you
my baby whispers to me.
the days have kept on coming
and Daddy's gone.   20
He knew.
He must have known and
I comfort my son with the hope
the life in the confident man.

                                                               1972

W. D. SNODGRASS

Here in the Scuffled Dust

Here in the scuffled dust
    is our ground of play.
I lift you on your swing and must
    shove you away,
see you return again,   5
    drive you off again, then

stand quiet till you come.
    You, though you climb
higher, farther from me, longer,
    will fall back to me stronger.   10
Bad penny, pendulum,
    you keep my constant time

to bob in blue July
    where fat goldfinches fly
over the glittering, fecund   15
    reach of our growing lands.
Once more now, this second,
    I hold you in my hands.

                                                               1959

A Gathering of Poems on Poetry

A. E. HOUSMAN

Terence, This Is Stupid Stuff

"Terence,[1] this is stupid stuff:
You eat your victuals fast enough;
There can't be much amiss, 'tis clear,
To see the rate you drink your beer.
But oh, good Lord, the verse you make,   5
It gives a chap the belly-ache.
The cow, the old cow, she is dead;
It sleeps well, the horned head:
We poor lads, 'tis our turn now
To hear such tunes as killed the cow.   10
Pretty friendship 'tis to rhyme
Your friends to death before their time
Moping melancholy mad:
Come, pipe a tune to dance to, lad."

     Why, if 'tis dancing you would be,   15
There's brisker pipes than poetry.
Say, for what were hop-yards meant,
Or why was Burton built on Trent?[2]
Oh many a peer of England brews
Livelier liquor than the Muse,   20
And malt does more than Milton can
To justify God's ways to man.[3]
Ale, man, ale's the stuff to drink
For fellows whom it hurts to think:
Look into the pewter pot   25
To see the world as the world's not.
And faith, 'tis pleasant till 'tis past:
The mischief is that 'twill not last.
Oh I have been to Ludlow fair[4]
And left my necktie God knows where,   30
And carried half-way home, or near,
Pints and quarts of Ludlow beer:
Then the world seemed none so bad,
And I myself a sterling lad;
And down in lovely muck I've lain,   35
Happy till I woke again.
Then I saw the morning sky:
Heigho, the tale was all a lie;

---

1. Housman originally titled the volume in which this poem appeared "The Poems of Terence Hearsay."
2. Burton was famous for its ales, originally brewed from special springs there.
3. Milton said his purpose in *Paradise Lost* was to "justify the ways of God to men."
4. Ludlow was a market town in Shropshire, and its town fair would be a social high point for a youth growing up in the county.

The world, it was the old world yet,
I was I, my things were wet,   40
And nothing now remained to do
But begin the game anew.

   Therefore, since the world has still
Much good, but much less good than ill,
And while the sun and moon endure   45
Luck's a chance, but trouble's sure,
I'd face it as a wise man would,
And train for ill and not for good.
'Tis true, the stuff I bring for sale
Is not so brisk a brew as ale: 50
Out of a stem that scored the hand
I wrung it in a weary land.
But take it: if the smack is sour,
The better for the embittered hour;
It should do good to heart and head   55
When your soul is in my soul's stead;
And I will friend you, if I may,
In the dark and cloudy day.

   There was a king reigned in the East:
There, when kings will sit to feast,   60
They get their fill before they think
With poisoned meat and poisoned drink.
He gathered all that springs to birth
From the many-venomed earth;
First a little, thence to more,   65
He sampled all her killing store;
And easy, smiling, seasoned sound,
Sate the king when healths went round.
They put arsenic in his meat
And stared aghast to watch him eat;   70
They poured strychnine in his cup
And shook to see him drink it up:
They shook, they stared as white's their shirt:
Them it was their poison hurt.
—I tell the tale that I heard told.   75
Mithridates,[5] he died old.

                          1896

MARIANNE MOORE

Poetry

I, too, dislike it: there are things that are important beyond all this
fiddle.

5. The king of Pontus, he was said to have developed a tolerance of poison by taking
gradually increasing quantities.

Reading it, however, with a perfect contempt for it, one discovers in
it after all, a place for the genuine.
    Hands that can grasp, eyes
       that can dilate, hair that can rise   5
          if it must, these things are important not because a

high-sounding interpretation can be put upon them but because they
      are
useful. When they become so derivative as to become unintelligible,
    the same thing may be said for all of us, that we
      do not admire what   10
        we cannot understand: the bat
          holding on upside down or in quest of something to

eat, elephants pushing, a wild horse taking a roll, a tireless wolf under
    a tree, the immovable critic twitching his skin like a horse that feels
      a flea, the base-
      ball fan, the statistician—   15
        nor is it valid
          to discriminate against "business documents and

school-books"[6]; all these phenomena are important. One must make a
      distinction
    however: when dragged into prominence by half poets, the result is
      not poetry,
    nor till the poets among us can be   20
      "literalists of
        the imagination"[7]—above
          insolence and triviality and can present

for inspection, "imaginary gardens with real toads in them," shall we
      have
    it. In the meantime, if you demand on the one hand,   25
      the raw material of poetry in
        all its rawness and
        that which is on the other hand
          genuine, you are interested in poetry.

                                  1921

6. *"Diary of Tolstoy*, p. 84: 'Where the boundary between prose and poetry lies, I shall never be able to understand. The question is raised in manuals of style, yet the answer to it lies beyond me. Poetry is verse: prose is not verse. Or else poetry is everything with the exception of business documents and school books.' " (Moore's note)

7. " 'Literalists of the imagination.' Yeats, *Ideas of Good and Evil* (A. H. Bullen, 1903), p. 182. 'The limitation of his view was from the very intensity of his vision; he was a too literal realist of imagination, as others are of nature; and because he believed that the figures seen by the mind's eye, when exalted by inspiration, were "eternal existences," symbols of divine essences, he hated every grace of style that might obscure their lineaments.' " (Moore's note)

NIKKI GIOVANNI

Poetry

poetry is motion graceful
as a fawn
gentle as a teardrop
strong like the eye
finding peace in a crowded room   5

we poets tend to think
our words are golden
though emotion speaks too
loudly to be defined
by silence   10

sometimes after midnight or just before
the dawn
we sit typewriter in hand
pulling loneliness around us
forgetting our lovers or children   15
who are sleeping
ignoring the weary wariness
of our own logic
to compose a poem
    no one understands it   20
it never says "love me" for poets are
beyond love
it never says "accept me" for poems seek not
acceptance but controversy
it only says "i am" and therefore   25
i concede that you are too

a poem is pure energy
horizontally contained
between the mind
of the poet and the ear of the reader   30
if it does not sing discard the ear
for poetry is song
if it does not delight discard
the heart for poetry is joy
if it does not inform then close   35
off the brain for it is dead
if it cannot heed the insistent message
that life is precious

which is all we poets
wrapped in our loneliness   40
are trying to say

1975

EMILY DICKINSON

I Dwell in Possibility

I dwell in Possibility—
A fairer House than Prose—
More numerous of Windows—
Superior—for Doors—

Of Chambers as the Cedars—   5
Impregnable of Eye—
And for an Everlasting Roof
The Gambrels[8] of the Sky—

Of Visitors—the fairest—
For Occupation—This—   10
The spreading wide my narrow Hands
To gather Paradise—

ca. 1862

ARCHIBALD MACLEISH

Ars Poetica[9]

A poem should be palpable and mute
As a globed fruit,

Dumb
As old medallions to the thumb,

Silent as the sleeve-worn stone   5
Of casement ledges where the moss has grown—

A poem should be wordless
As the flight of birds.

A poem should be motionless in time
As the moon climbs,   10

Leaving, as the moon releases
Twig by twig the night-entangled trees,

Leaving, as the moon behind the winter leaves,
Memory by memory the mind—

8. Roofs with double slopes.
9. "The Art of Poetry," title of a poetical

treatise by the Roman poet Horace (65–8
B.C.).

A poem should be motionless in time   15
As the moon climbs.

A poem should be equal to:
Not true.

For all the history of grief   20
An empty doorway and a maple leaf.

For love
The leaning grasses and two lights above the sea—

A poem should not mean
But be.

1926

ISHMAEL REED

beware : do not read this poem

tonite   ,   thriller was
abt an ol woman   , so vain she
surrounded herself w/
     many mirrors

it got so bad that finally she   5
locked herself indoors & her
whole life became the
     mirrors

one day the villagers broke
into her house   ,   but she was too   10
swift for them   .   she disappeared
     into a mirror

each tenant who bought the house
after that   ,   lost a loved one to
     the ol woman in the mirror   :   15
     first a little girl
     then a young woman
     then the young woman/s husband

the hunger of this poem is legendary
it has taken in many victims   20
back off from this poem
it has drawn in yr feet
back off from this poem
it has drawn in yr legs

back off from this poem   25
it is a greedy mirror
you are into this poem   from
       the waist down
nobody can hear you can they   ?
this poem has had you up to here   30
       belch
this poem aint got no manners
you cant call out frm this poem
relax now & go w/ this poem   35
move & roll on to this poem
do not resist this poem
this poem has yr eyes
this poem has his head
this poem has his arms
this poem has his fingers   40
this poem has his fingertips
this poem is the reader & the
reader this poem

statistic :   the us bureau of missing persons reports
                 that in 1968 over 100,000 people disappeared
                 leaving no solid clues
                         nor trace   only
          a space   in the lives of their friends

                                                    1970

WILLIAM SHAKESPEARE

Not Marble, Nor the Gilded Monuments

Not marble, nor the gilded monuments
Of princes, shall outlive this powerful rhyme;
But you shall shine more bright in these conténts
Than unswept stone, besmeared with sluttish time.
When wasteful war shall statues overturn,   5
And broils root out the work of masonry,
Nor Mars his[1] sword nor war's quick fire shall burn
The living record of your memory.
'Gainst death and all-oblivious enmity
Shall you pace forth; your praise shall still find room   10
Even in the eyes of all posterity
That wear this world out to the ending doom.[2]
So, till the judgment that yourself arise,
You live in this, and dwell in lovers' eyes.

                                                    1609

1. Mars's (a common Renaissance form   . . . nor.
of the possessive). "Nor . . . nor": neither   2. Judgment Day.

ARCHIBALD MACLEISH

"Not Marble Nor the Gilded Monuments"

for Adele

The praisers of women in their proud and beautiful poems,
Naming the grave mouth and the hair and the eyes,
Boasted those they loved should be forever remembered:
These were lies.

The words sound but the face in the Istrian sun is forgotten.   5
The poet speaks but to her dead ears no more.
The sleek throat is gone—and the breast that was troubled to listen:
Shadow from door.

Therefore I will not praise your knees nor your fine walking
Telling you men shall remember your name as long   10
As lips move or breath is spent or the iron of English
Rings from a tongue.

I shall say you were young, and your arms straight, and your mouth
        scarlet:
I shall say you will die and none will remember you:
Your arms change, and none remember the swish of your garments,   15
Nor the click of your shoe.

Not with my hand's strength, not with difficult labor
Springing the obstinate words to the bones of your breast
And the stubborn line to your young stride and the breath to your
        breathing
And the beat to your haste   20
Shall I prevail on the hearts of unborn men to remember.

(What is a dead girl but a shadowy ghost
Or a dead man's voice but a distant and vain affirmation
Like dream words most)

Therefore I will not speak of the undying glory of women.   25
I will say you were young and straight and your skin fair
And you stood in the door and the sun was a shadow of leaves on your
        shoulders
And a leaf on your hair—

I will not speak of the famous beauty of dead women:
I will say the shape of a leaf lay once on your hair.   30
Till the world ends and the eyes are out and the mouths broken
Look! It is there!

                                                        1930

ROBINSON JEFFERS

To the Stone-Cutters

Stone-cutters fighting time with marble, you foredefeated
Challengers of oblivion
Eat cynical earnings, knowing rock splits, records fall down,
The square-limbed Roman letters
Scale in the thaws, wear in the rain. The poet as well   5
Builds his monument mockingly;
For the man will be blotted out, the blithe earth die, the brave sun
Die blind and blacken to the heart:
Yet stones have stood for a thousand years, and pained thoughts found
The honey of peace in old poems.   10

                                                                        1924

DYLAN THOMAS

In My Craft or Sullen Art

In my craft or sullen art
Exercised in the still night
When only the moon rages
And the lovers lie abed
With all their griefs in their arms,   5
I labor by singing light
Not for ambition or bread
Or the strut and trade of charms
On the ivory stages
But for the common wages   10
Of their most secret heart.

Not for the proud man apart
From the raging moon I write
On these spindrift[3] pages
Nor for the towering dead   15
With their nightingales and psalms
But for the lovers, their arms
Round the griefs of the ages,
Who pay no praise or wages
Nor heed my craft or art.   20

                                                  1946

3. Literally, wind-driven sea spray.

X. J. KENNEDY

Ars Poetica

The goose that laid the golden egg
Died looking up its crotch
To find out how its sphincter worked.

Would you lay well? Don't watch.

1961

A Gathering of Poems of Satire and Protest

TOM WAYMAN

Picketing Supermarkets

Because all this food is grown in the store
do not take the leaflet.
Cabbages, broccoli and tomatoes
are raised at night in the aisles.   5
Milk is brewed in the rear storage areas.
Beef produced in vats in the basement.
Do not take the leaflet.
Peanut butter and soft drinks
are made fresh each morning by store employees.
Our oranges and grapes   10
are so fine and round
that when held up to the lights they cast no shadow.
Do not take the leaflet.

And should you take one
do not believe it.   15
This chain of stores has no connection
with anyone growing food someplace else.
How could we have an effect on local farmers?
Do not believe it.

The sound here is Muzak, for your enjoyment.   20
It is not the sound of children crying.
There *is* a lady offering samples
to mark Canada Cheese Month.
There is no dark-skinned man with black hair beside her
wanting to show you the inside of a coffin.   25
You would not have to look if there was.

And there are no Nicaraguan heroes
in any way connected with the bananas.

Pay no attention to these people.
The manager is a citizen.   30
All this food is grown in the store.

                                                                1973

DUDLEY RANDALL

Ballad of Birmingham

(On the bombing of a church in Birmingham, Alabama, 1963)

"Mother dear, may I go downtown
Instead of out to play,
And march the streets of Birmingham
In a Freedom March today?"

"No, baby, no, you may not go,   5
For the dogs are fierce and wild,
And clubs and hoses, guns and jails
Aren't good for a little child."

"But, mother, I won't be alone.
Other children will go with me,   10
And march the streets of Birmingham
To make our country free."

"No, baby, no, you may not go,
For I fear those guns will fire.
But you may go to church instead   15
And sing in the children's choir."

She has combed and brushed her night-dark hair,
And bathed rose petal sweet,
And drawn white gloves on her small brown hands,
And white shoes on her feet.   20

The mother smiled to know her child
Was in the sacred place,
But that smile was the last smile
To come upon her face.

For when she heard the explosion,   25
Her eyes grew wet and wild.
She raced through the streets of Birmingham
Calling for her child.

She clawed through bits of glass and brick,
Then lifted out a shoe.   30
"Oh, here's the shoe my baby wore,
But, baby, where are you?"

                                                          1969

DENISE LEVERTOV

What Were They Like?

1) Did the people of Viet Nam
   use lanterns of stone?
2) Did they hold ceremonies
   to reverence the opening of buds?
3) Were they inclined to rippling laughter?   5
4) Did they use bone and ivory,
   jade and silver, for ornament?
5) Had they an epic poem?
6) Did they distinguish between speech and singing?

1) Sir, their light hearts turned to stone.   10
   It is not remembered whether in gardens
   stone lanterns illumined pleasant ways.
2) Perhaps they gathered once to delight in blossom,
   but after the children were killed
   there were no more buds.   15
3) Sir, laughter is bitter to the burned mouth.
4) A dream ago, perhaps. Ornament is for joy.
   All the bones were charred.
5) It is not remembered. Remember,
   most were peasants; their life   20
   was in rice and bamboo.
   When peaceful clouds were reflected in the paddies
   and the water buffalo stepped surely along terraces,
   maybe fathers told their sons old tales.
   When bombs smashed the mirrors   25
   there was time only to scream.
6) There is an echo yet, it is said,
   of their speech which was like a song.
   It is reported their singing resembled
   the flight of moths in moonlight.   30
   Who can say? It is silent now.

                                                          1966

DELAWARE INDIAN SONG

Who Are They?[1]

A great land and a wide land was the east land,
A land without snakes, a rich land, a pleasant land.
Great Fighter was chief, toward the north.
At the Straight river, River-Loving was chief.
Becoming-Fat was chief at Sassafras land . . .   5

Affable was chief, and made peace with all,
All were friends, all were united under this great chief.
Great-Beaver was chief, remaining in Sassafras land.
White-Body was chief on the seashore.
Peace-Maker was chief, friendly to all.   10
He-Makes-Mistakes was chief, hurriedly coming . . .

Coming-as-a-Friend was chief; he went to the Great Lakes,
Visiting all his children, all his friends.
Cranberry-Eater was chief, friend of the Ottawas.
North-Walker was chief; he made festivals.   15
Slow-Gatherer was chief at the shore . . .

White-Crab was chief; a friend of the shore.
Watcher was chief; he looked toward the sea.
At this time, from north and south, the whites came.
They are peaceful; they have great things; who are they?   20

                                                    translated, 1885

ANONYMOUS

The Lady Fortune

The lady Fortune is bothe freend and fo.
Of poure she maketh riche, of riche poure also;
She turneth wo[2] al into wele,[3] and wele al into wo.
Ne truste no man to this wele, the wheel it turneth so.

ca. 1325

ANONYMOUS

The Silver Swan

The silver swan, who living had no note,
When death approached, unlocked her silent throat;

---

1. Translated by D. G. Brinton.   3. Weal: well-being, prosperity.
2. Woe.

Leaning her breast against the reedy shore,
Thus sung her first and last, and sung no more:
"Farewell, all joys; Oh death, come close mine eyes;   5
More geese than swans now live, more fools than wise."

1612

AUDRE LORDE

Outside

In the center of a harsh and spectrumed city
all things natural are strange.
I grew up in a genuine confusion
between grass and weeds and flowers
and what colored meant   5
except for clothes you couldn't bleach
and nobody called me nigger
until I was thirteen.
Nobody lynched my momma
but what she'd never been   10
had bleached her face of everything
but very private furies
and made the other children
call me yellow snot at school.

And how many times have I called myself back   15
through my bones confusion
black
like marrow meaning meat
and how many times have you cut me
and run in the streets   20
my own blood
who do you think me to be
that you are terrified of becoming
or what do you see in my face
you have not already discarded   25
in your own mirror
what face do you see in my eyes
that you will someday
come to
acknowledge your own?   30
Who shall I curse that I grew up
believing in my mother's face
or that I lived in fear of potent darkness
wearing my father's shape
they have both marked me   35
with their blind and terrible love
and I am lustful now for my own name.

Between the canyons of their mighty silences

mother bright and father brown
I seek my own shapes now   40
for they never spoke of me
except as theirs
and the pieces I stumble and fall over
I still record as proof
that I am beautiful   45
twice
blessed with the images
of who they were
and who I thought them once to be
of what I move   50
toward and through
and what I need
to leave behind me
most of all   55
I am blessed within my selves
who are come to make our shattered faces
whole.

                                                  1978

W. H. AUDEN

The Unknown Citizen

(To JS/07/M/378
This Marble Monument
Is Erected by the State)[4]

He was found by the Bureau of Statistics to be
One against whom there was no official complaint,
And all the reports on his conduct agree
That, in the modern sense of an old-fashioned word, he was a saint,
For in everything he did he served the Greater Community.   5
Except for the War till the day he retired
He worked in a factory and never got fired,
But satisfied his employers, Fudge Motors Inc.
Yet he wasn't a scab or odd in his views,
For his Union reports that he paid his dues,   10
(Our report on his Union shows it was sound)
And our Social Psychology workers found
That he was popular with his mates and liked a drink.
The Press are convinced that he bought a paper every day
And that his reactions to advertisements were normal in every way.   15
Policies taken out in his name prove that he was fully insured,
And his Health-card shows he was once in hospital but left it cured.
Both Producers Research and High-Grade Living declare
He was fully sensible to the advantages of the Installment Plan
And had everything necessary to the Modern Man,   20
A phonograph, a radio, a car and a frigidaire.
Our researchers into Public Opinion are content

4. The title and subtitle parallel the inscription on the Tomb of the Unknown Soldier.

That he held the proper opinions for the time of year;
When there was peace, he was for peace; when there was war, he
     went.
He was married and added five children to the population,   25
Which our Eugenist says was the right number for a parent of his
     generation,
And our teachers report that he never interfered with their education.
Was he free? Was he happy? The question is absurd:
Had anything been wrong, we should certainly have heard.

                                              1940

CLAUDE McKAY

America

Although she feeds me bread of bitterness,
And sinks into my throat her tiger's tooth,
Stealing my breath of life, I will confess
I love this cultured hell that tests my youth!
Her vigor flows like tides into my blood,   5
Giving me strength erect against her hate.
Her bigness sweeps my being like a flood.
Yet as a rebel fronts a king in state,
I stand within her walls with not a shred
Of terror, malice, not a word of jeer.   10
Darkly I gaze into the days ahead,
And see her might and granite wonders there,
Beneath the touch of Time's unerring hand,
Like priceless treasures sinking in the sand.

                                              1922

LANGSTON HUGHES

Harlem (A Dream Deferred)

What happens to a dream deferred?

    Does it dry up
    like a raisin in the sun?
    Or fester like a sore—
    And then run?   5
    Does it stink like rotten meat?
    Or crust and sugar over—
    like a syrupy sweet?

    Maybe it just sags
    like a heavy load.   10

    Or does it explode?

                                                1951

WILLIAM BLAKE

The Garden of Love

I went to the Garden of Love,
And saw what I never had seen:
A Chapel was built in the midst,
Where I used to play on the green.

And the gates of this Chapel were shut,   5
And "Thou shalt not" writ over the door;
So I turned to the Garden of Love,
That so many sweet flowers bore,

And I saw it was filled with graves,
And tomb-stones where flowers should be;   10
And Priests in black gowns were walking their rounds,
And binding with briars my joys and desires.

1794

KENNETH KOCH

You Were Wearing

You were wearing your Edgar Allan Poe printed cotton blouse.
In each divided up square of the blouse was a picture of Edgar Allan
    Poe.
Your hair was blonde and you were cute. You asked me, "Do most boys
    think that most girls are bad?"
I smelled the mould of your seaside resort hotel bedroom on your hair
    held in place by a John Greenleaf Whittier clip.
"No," I said, "it's girls who think that boys are bad." Then we read
    Snowbound together   5
And ran around in an attic, so that a little of the blue enamel was
    scraped off my George Washington, Father of His Country, shoes.

Mother was walking in the living room, her Strauss Waltzes comb in
    her hair.
We waited for a time and then joined her, only to be served tea in cups
    painted with pictures of Herman Melville
As well as with illustrations from his book *Moby Dick* and from his
    novella, *Benito Cereno*.
Father came in wearing his Dick Tracy necktie: "How about a drink,
    everyone?"   10
I said, "Let's go outside a while." Then we went onto the porch and sat
    on the Abraham Lincoln swing.
You sat on the eyes, mouth, and beard part, and I sat on the knees.
In the yard across the street we saw a snowman holding a garbage can
    lid smashed into a likeness of the mad English king, George the
    Third.

1962

Craft

3 SPEAKER

Poems are personal. The thoughts and feelings they express belong to a specific person, and however "universal" or general their sentiments seem to be, poems come to us as the expression of a human voice—an individual voice. That voice is often the voice of the poet. But not always. Poets sometimes create a "character" just as writers of fiction or drama do—people who speak for them only indirectly. A character may, in fact, be very different from the poet, just as a character in a play or story is different from the author, and that person, the **speaker** of the poem, may express ideas or feelings very different from the poet's own. In the following poem, *two* individual voices in fact speak, and it is clear that, rather than himself speaking directly to us, the poet has chosen to create two speakers, each of whom has a distinctive voice.

THOMAS HARDY

The Ruined Maid

"O 'Melia,[1] my dear, this does everything crown!
Who could have supposed I should meet you in Town?
And whence such fair garments, such prosperi-ty?"—
"O didn't you know I'd been ruined?" said she.

—"You left us in tatters, without shoes or socks,   5
Tired of digging potatoes, and spudding up docks;[2]
And now you've gay bracelets and bright feathers three!"—
"Yes: that's how we dress when we're ruined," said she.

—"At home in the barton[3] you said 'thee' and 'thou,'
And 'thik oon,' and 'theäs oon,' and 't'other'; but now   10
Your talking quite fits 'ee for high compa-ny!"—
"Some polish is gained with one's ruin," said she.

—"Your hands were like paws then, your face blue and bleak
But now I'm bewitched by your delicate cheek,
And your little gloves fit as on any la-dy!"—   15
"We never do work when we're ruined," said she.

1. Short for Amelia.   3. Farmyard.
2. Spading up weeds.

—"You used to call home-life a hag-ridden dream,
And you'd sigh, and you'd sock;[4] but at present you seem
To know not of megrims[5] or melancho-ly!"—
"True. One's pretty lively when ruined," said she.   20

—"I wish I had feathers, a fine sweeping gown,
And a delicate face, and could strut about Town!"—
"My dear—a raw country girl, such as you be,
Cannot quite expect that. You ain't ruined," said she.

1866

The first voice, that of the sister who has stayed home, is designated typographically (that is, by the way the poem is printed): there are dashes at the beginning and end of each of her speeches. The second sister regularly gets the last line in each stanza (and in the last stanza, two lines), so it is easy to tell who is talking at every point. Also, the two speakers are just as clearly distinguished by what they say, how they say it, and what sort of person each proves to be. The nameless stay-at-home shows little knowledge of the world, and everything surprises her: seeing her sister at all, but especially seeing her well clothed, cheerful, and polished; and as the poem develops she shows increasing envy of her more worldly sister. She is the "raw country girl" (line 23) that her sister says she is, and she still speaks the country dialect ("fits 'ee," line 11, for example) that she notices her sister has lost (lines 9–11). The "ruined" sister ('Melia), on the other hand, says little except to keep repeating the refrain about having been ruined, but even the slight variations she plays on that theme suggest her sophistication and amusement at her countrified sister, although she still uses a rural "ain't" at the end. We are not told the full story of their lives (was the ruined sister thrown out? did she run away from home?), but we know enough (that they've been separated for some time, that the stay-at-home did not know where her sister had gone) to allow the dialogue to articulate the contrast between them. The style of speech of each speaker then does the rest.

It is equally clear that there is a speaker (or, in this case, actually a singer) in stanzas two through nine of this poem:

X. J. KENNEDY

In a Prominent Bar in Secaucus One Day

*To the tune of "The Old Orange Flute" or
the tune of "Sweet Betsy from Pike"*

In a prominent bar in Secaucus[6] one day

4. Deliver angry blows.
5. Migraine headaches.
6. A small, smoggy town on the Hacken- sack River in New Jersey, a few miles west of Manhattan.

Rose a lady in skunk with a topheavy sway,
Raised a knobby red finger—all turned from their beer—
While with eyes bright as snowcrust she sang high and clear:

"Now who of you'd think from an eyeload of me 5
That I once was a lady as proud as could be?
Oh I'd never sit down by a tumbledown drunk
If it wasn't, my dears, for the high cost of junk.

"All the gents used to swear that the white of my calf
Beat the down of a swan by a length and a half. 10
In the kerchief of linen I caught to my nose
Ah, there never fell snot, but a little gold rose.

"I had seven gold teeth and a toothpick of gold,
My Virginia cheroot was a leaf of it rolled
And I'd light it each time with a thousand in cash— 15
Why the bums used to fight if I flicked them an ash.

"Once the toast of the Biltmore,[7] the belle of the Taft,
I would drink bottle beer at the Drake, never draft,
And dine at the Astor on Salisbury steak
With a clean tablecloth for each bite I did take. 20

"In a car like the Roxy[8] I'd roll to the track,
A steel-guitar trio, a bar in the back,
And the wheels made no noise, they turned over so fast,
Still it took you ten minutes to see me go past.

"When the horses bowed down to me that I might choose, 25
I bet on them all, for I hated to lose.
Now I'm saddled each night for my butter and eggs
And the broken threads race down the backs of my legs.

"Let you hold in mind, girls, that your beauty must pass
Like a lovely white clover that rusts with its grass. 30
Keep your bottoms off barstools and marry you young
Or be left—an old barrel with many a bung.

"For when time takes you out for a spin in his car
You'll be hard-pressed to stop him from going too far
And be left by the roadside, for all your good deeds, 35
Two toadstools for tits and a face full of weeds."

All the house raised a cheer, but the man at the bar
Made a phonecall and up pulled a red patrol car
And she blew us a kiss as they copped her away
From that prominent bar in Secaucus, N.J. 40

1961

---

7. Like the Taft, Drake, and Astor, a once fashionable New York hotel.
8. A luxurious old New York theater and movie house, the site of many "World Premieres" in the heyday of Hollywood.

Again, we learn about the character primarily through her own words, although we don't have to believe everything she tells us about her past. From her introduction in the first stanza we get some general notion of her appearance and condition, but it is she who tells us that she is a junkie (line 8), a prostitute (line 27), and that her face and figure are pretty well shot (lines 32, 36). That information could make her a sad case, and the poem might lament her state or allow her to lament it, but instead the poem presents her cheerfully. She is anxious to give advice and sound moralistic (line 31, for example), but she's also enormously cheerful about herself, and her spirit repeatedly bursts through her song. Her performance gives her a lot of pleasure as she exaggerates outrageously about her former luxury and prominence, and even her departure in a patrol car she chooses to treat as a grand exit, throwing a kiss to her audience. The comedy is bittersweet, perhaps, but she is allowed to present herself, through her own words and attitudes, as a likable character. The glorious fiction of her life, narrated with energy and polish in the manner of a practiced and accomplished liar, betrays some rather naive notions of good taste and luxurious living (lines 18–26). But this "lady in skunk" has a picturesque and engaging style, a refreshing sense of humor about herself, and (like the cheap fur she wears) her experiences in what she considers high life satisfy her sense of style and drama. The self-portrait accumulates, almost completely through how she talks about herself, and the poet develops our attitude toward her by allowing her to recount her story herself, in her own words—or rather in words chosen for her by the author.

It is, of course, equally possible to create a speaker who makes us dislike himself or herself, also because of what the poet makes him or her say, as the following poem does. Here the speaker, as the title implies, is a monk, but he shows himself to be most unmonklike: mean, self-righteous, and despicable.

ROBERT BROWNING

Soliloquy of the Spanish Cloister[9]

Gr-r-r—there go, my heart's abhorrence!
  Water your damned flower-pots, do!
If hate killed men, Brother Lawrence,
  God's blood, would not mine kill you!
What? your myrtle-bush wants trimming?   5
  Oh, that rose has prior claims—
Needs its leaden vase filled brimming?
  Hell dry you up with its flames!

9. Monastery.

At the meal we sit together:
 Salve tibi![1] I must hear   10
Wise talk of the kind of weather,
 Sort of season, time of year:
Not a plenteous cork-crop: scarcely
 Dare we hope oak-galls,[2] *I doubt:*
What's the Latin name for "parsley"? 15
 What's the Greek name for Swine's Snout?

Whew! We'll have our platter burnished,
 Laid with care on our own shelf!
With a fire-new spoon we're furnished,
 And a goblet for ourself,   20
Rinsed like something sacrificial
 Ere 'tis fit to touch our chaps[3]—
Marked with L. for our initial!
 (He-he! There his lily snaps!)

Saint, forsooth! While brown Dolores 25
 Squats outside the Convent bank
With Sanchicha, telling stories,
 Steeping tresses in the tank,
Blue-black, lustrous, thick like horsehairs,
 —Can't I see his dead eye glow,   30
Bright as 'twere a Barbary corsair's?[4]
 (That is, if he'd let it show!)

When he finishes refection,[5]
 Knife and fork he never lays
Cross-wise, to my recollection,   35
 As do I, in Jesu's praise.
I the Trinity illustrate,
 Drinking watered orange-pulp—
In three sips the Arian[6] frustrate;
 While he drains his at one gulp. 40

Oh, those melons? If he's able
 We're to have a feast! so nice!
One goes to the Abbot's table,
 All of us get each a slice.
How go on your flowers? None double? 45
 Not one fruit-sort can you spy?
Strange!—And I, too, at such trouble,
 Keep them close-nipped on the sly!

There's a great text in Galatians,[7]

1. Hail to thee. Italics usually indicate the words of Brother Lawrence.
2. Abnormal growth on oak trees, used for tanning.
3. Jaws.
4. African pirate's.
5. A meal.
6. A heretical sect which denied the Trinity.
7. "Cursed is every one that continueth not in all things which are written in the book of law to do them," *Galatians* 3:10. *Galatians* 5:15–23 provides a long list of possible offenses, but they do not add up to 29.

Once you trip on it, entails   50
    Twenty-nine distinct damnations,
        One sure, if another fails:
If I trip him just a-dying,
    Sure of heaven as sure can be,
Spin him round and send him flying   55
    Off to hell, a Manichee?[8]

Or, my scrofulous French novel
    On gray paper with blunt type!
Simply glance at it, you grovel
    Hand and foot in Belial's gripe:[9]   60
If I double down its pages
    At the woeful sixteenth print,
When he gathers his greengages,
    Ope a sieve and slip it in't?

Or, there's Satan!—one might venture   65
    Pledge one's soul to him, yet leave
Such a flaw in the indenture
    As he'd miss till, past retrieve,
Blasted lay that rose-acacia
    We're so proud of! *Hy, Zy, Hine* . . .[1]   70
'St, there's Vespers! *Plena gratiâ*
    Ave, Virgo.[2] Gr-r-r—you swine!

                                              1842

Not many poems begin with a growl, and in this one it turns out to be fair warning that we are about to get to know a real beast, even though he is in the clothing of a religious man. In line 1, he has already shown himself to hold a most uncharitable attitude toward his fellow monk, Brother Lawrence, and by line 4 he has uttered two profanities and admitted his intense feelings of hatred and vengefulness. His ranting and roaring is full of exclamation points (four in the first stanza), and he reveals his own personality and character when he imagines curses and unflattering nicknames for Brother Lawrence or plots malicious jokes on him. By the end, we have accumulated no knowledge of Brother Lawrence that makes him seem a fit target for such rage (except that he is pious, dutiful, and pleasant—perhaps enough to make this sort of speaker despise him), but we have discovered the speaker to be lecherous (stanza 4), full of false piety (stanza 5), malicious in trivial matters (stanza 6), ready to use his theological learning to sponsor damnation rather than salvation (stanza 7), a closet reader and viewer of pornography

8. A heretic. According to the Manichean heresy, the world was divided into the forces of good and evil, equally powerful.
9. In the clutches of Satan.

1. Possibly the beginning of an incantation or curse.
2. The opening words of the *Ave Maria*, here reversed: "Full of grace, Hail, Virgin."

within the monastery (stanza 8)—even willing to risk his own soul in order to torment Brother Lawrence (last stanza). The speaker is made to characterize himself; the details accrue and accumulate into a fairly full portrait, and here we do not have even an opening and closing "objective" description (as in *In a Prominent Bar*) or another speaker (as in *The Ruined Maid*) to give us perspective. Except for the moments when the speaker mimics or parodies Brother Lawrence (usually in italic type), we have only the speaker's own words and thoughts. But that is enough; the poet has controlled them so carefully that we clearly know what he thinks of the speaker he has created— that he is a mean-spirited, vengeful hypocrite, a thoroughly disreputable and unlikable character. The whole poem has been about him and his attitudes; the point of the poem has been to characterize the speaker and develop in us a dislike of him and what he stands for—total hypocrisy. In reading a poem like this aloud, we would want our voice to suggest all the unlikable features of a hypocrite. We would also need to suggest, through the tone of voice we used, the author's contemptuous mocking of the rage and hypocrisy, and we would want, like an actor, to create strong disapproval in the hearer. The poem's words (the ones the author has given to the speaker) clearly imply those attitudes, and we would want our voice to express them. Usually there is much more to a poem than the identification and characterization of the speaker, but in many cases it is necessary to identify the speaker and determine his or her character before we can appreciate what else goes on in the poem. And sometimes, as here, in looking for the speaker of the poem, we come near to the center of the poem itself.

The speaker in the following poem is, from the first, clearly much more likable, but we do not get a very full sense of her until the poem is well along. As you read, try to imitate the tone of voice you think this kind of person would use. Exactly when do you begin to feel that you know what she is like?

DOROTHY PARKER

A Certain Lady

Oh, I can smile for you, and tilt my head,
    And drink your rushing words with eager lips,
And paint my mouth for you a fragrant red,
    And trace your brows with tutored finger-tips.
When you rehearse your list of loves to me,   5
    Oh, I can laugh and marvel, rapturous-eyed.
And you laugh back, nor can you ever see
    The thousand little deaths my heart has died.
And you believe, so well I know my part,
    That I am gay as morning, light as snow,   10

And all the straining things within my heart
    You'll never know.

Oh, I can laugh and listen, when we meet,
    And you bring tales of fresh adventurings—
Of ladies delicately indiscreet,   15
    Of lingering hands, and gently whispered things.
And you are pleased with me, and strive anew
    To sing me sagas of your late delights.
Thus do you want me—marveling, gay, and true—
    Nor do you see my staring eyes of nights.   20
And when, in search of novelty, you stray,
    Oh, I can kiss you blithely as you go . . .
And what goes on, my love, while you're away,
    You'll never know.

                                      1937

To whom does the speaker seem to be talking? What sort of person is he? How do you feel about him? Which habits and attitudes of his do you like least? How soon can you tell that the speaker is not altogether happy about his conversation and conduct? In what tone of voice would you read the first 22 lines aloud? What attitude would you try to express toward the person spoken to? What tone would you use for the last two lines? How would you describe the speaker's personality? What aspects of her behavior are most crucial to the poem's effect?

It is easy to assume that the speaker in a poem is an extension of the poet. Is the speaker in this poem Dorothy Parker?—Maybe. A lot of Parker's poems present a similar world-weary posture and a kind of cynicism about romantic love (look, for example, at *Comment*, p. 231). But the poem is hardly an example of self-revelation, a giving away of personal secrets. If it were, it would be silly, not to say risky, to address her lover in a way that gives damaging facts about a pose she has been so careful to set up. We may be *tempted* to think of the speaker as Dorothy Parker, but it is best to resist the temptation and think of the character as an imagined person. Besides, the poem is called *A Certain Lady*, as if it were a speaking portrait of someone. Is the speaker based on any real person at all? Probably not; we are given no reason to think that the speaker is anyone in particular or that the poet has done anything but create a fictional character and situation. In any case, the poem's effect does not depend on our thinking that the speaker is someone specific and historical; it depends on our surprise at her honesty and openness in giving away a secret, something more likely in a fictional speaker than in real life. In poetry we can be overhearers of a conversation; in real life such a role could be dangerous to hearer as well as speaker—and seldom in real life do we get so quick and pointed a characterization as this poem develops in just a few well-organized and well-calculated lines.

In poems like *The Ruined Maid, In a Prominent Bar,* and *Soliloquy,* we are in no danger of mistaking the speaker for the poet, once we have recognized that poets may create speakers who participate in specific situations much as in fiction or drama. When there is a pointed discrepancy between the speaker and what we know of the poet—when the speaker is a woman, for example, and the poet is a man—we know we have a created speaker to contend with and that the point (or at least *one* point) in the poem is to observe the characterization carefully. In *A Certain Lady* we may be less sure, and in other poems the discrepancy between speaker and poet may be even more uncertain. What are we to make, for example, of the speaker in *Woodchucks* in the previous chapter (p. 42)? Is that speaker the real Maxine Kumin? At best (without knowing something quite specific about the author) we can only say "maybe" to that question. What we can be sure of is the sort of person the speaker is portrayed to be—someone (man? or woman?) surprised to discover feelings and attitudes that contradict values apparently held confidently. And that is exactly what we need to know for the poem to have its effect.

A similar kind of self-mocking of the speaker is present in the following poem, but here the mockery is put to less revelatory, more comic ends.

A. R. AMMONS

Needs

I want something suited to my special needs
I want chrome hubcaps, pin-on attachments
and year round use year after year
I want a workhorse with smooth uniform cut,
dozer blade and snow blade & deluxe steering 5
wheel
I want something to mow, throw snow, tow
and sow with
I want precision reel blades
I want a console styled dashboard 10
I want an easy spintype recoil starter
I want combination bevel and spur gears, 14
gauge stamped steel housing and
washable foam element air cleaner
I want a pivoting front axle and extrawide 15
turf tires
I want an inch of foam rubber inside a vinyl
covering
and especially if it's not too much, if I
can deserve it, even if I can't pay for it 20
I want to mow while riding.

1970

The poet here may be teasing himself about his desire for comfort and ease—and showing how readily advertisements and catalog descriptions manipulate us. But the speaker doesn't have to be the author for the teasing to work. In fact, the effect is to tease those attitudes no matter who holds them by teasing a speaker who illustrates the attitudes. It doesn't matter to the poem whether the speaker is the poet himself or some totally invented character. If the speaker is a version of the poet himself—perhaps a *side* of his personality that he is exploring—the portrait is still fictional in an important sense. The poem presents not a whole human being (*no* poem could do that) but only a version of him—a mood perhaps, an aspect, an attitude, a part of that person. Here, the poet presents someone with an obsession, in this case a small and not very damaging one, and allows him to spurt phrases as if he were reciting from an ad. Here the "portrait" is made more comic by a clear sense the poem projects that what we have is only a part of the person, an interest grown too intense, gone askew, gotten out of proportion, something that happens to most of us from time to time. The speaker may be a side of the poet, or maybe not. All we know about the speaker is that he has a one-track mind, that he is obsessed by his own luxurious comfort. He may not even be a "he": there is nothing in the poem that makes us certain that the speaker is male. It is customary to think of the speaker in a poem written by a man as "he" and in a poem written by a woman as "she" (as in Maxine Kumin's *Woodchucks*) unless the poem presents contrary evidence, but it is merely a convenience, a habit, nothing more.

Even when poets present themselves as if they were speaking directly to us in their own voices, their poems present only a partial portrait, something considerably less than the full personality of the poet. Even when there is not an obviously created character—someone with distinct characteristics which are different from those of the poet—strategies of characterization are used to present the person speaking in one way and not another. Even in a poem like the following one, it is still a good idea to talk of the speaker instead of the poet, although here it is probable that the poet is writing about a personal, actual experience.

WILLIAM WORDSWORTH

She Dwelt Among the Untrodden Ways

> She dwelt among the untrodden ways
>   Beside the springs of Dove,[3]
> A Maid whom there were none to praise
>   And very few to love:

3. A small stream in the Lake District in northern England, near where Wordsworth lived in Dove Cottage at Grasmere.

A violet by a mossy stone
   Half hidden from the eye!
—Fair as a star, when only one
   Is shining in the sky.

She lived unknown, and few could know
   When Lucy ceased to be;   10
But she is in her grave, and, oh,
   The difference to me!

                                         1800

It is hard to say whether this poem is more about Lucy or about how the speaker feels about her death. Her simple life, far removed from fame and known only to a few, is said nevertheless to have been beautiful. We know little else about her beyond her name and where she lived, in a beautiful but then isolated section of northern England. We don't know if she was young or old, only that the speaker thinks of her as "fair" and compares her to a "violet by a mossy stone." What we do know is that the speaker feels her loss deeply, so deeply that he is almost inarticulate with grief, lapsing into simple exclamation ("oh," line 11) and unable to articulate the "difference" that her death makes.

Did Lucy actually live? Was she a friend of the poet? We don't know; the poem doesn't tell us, and even biographers of Wordsworth are unsure. What we do know is that Wordsworth was able to represent grief over the death very powerfully. Whether the speaker is the historical Wordsworth or not, that speaker is a major focus of the poem, and it is his feelings which the poem isolates and expresses. We need to recognize some characteristics of the speaker and be sensitive to his feelings for the poem to work. We may be tempted to identify the speaker with the poet—it seems to be a natural tendency for most readers to make that assumption unless there is overwhelming evidence to the contrary in the poem—but it is still best to think of the voice we hear in the poem as that of the speaker. We don't need to give him a name, but we do need to understand his values as the poem expresses them and to recognize his deep feelings.

The poems we have looked at in this chapter—and the group that follows at the end of the chapter—all suggest the value of beginning the reading of any poem with a simple question: Who is speaking and what do we know about him or her? Putting together the evidence that the poem presents in answer to this question can often take us a long way into the poem. For some poems, this question won't help a great deal because the speaking voice is too indistinct or the character behind the poem too scantily presented, but in many cases asking this question will lead you toward the central experience the poem offers.

JOHN BETJEMAN

In Westminster Abbey[4]

Let me take this other glove off
    As the *vox humana*[5] swells,
And the beauteous fields of Eden
    Bask beneath the Abbey bells.
Here, where England's statesmen lie,   5
Listen to a lady's cry.

Gracious Lord, oh bomb the Germans.
    Spare their women for Thy Sake,
And if that is not too easy
    We will pardon Thy Mistake.   10
But, gracious Lord, whate'er shall be,
Don't let anyone bomb me.

Keep our Empire undismembered
    Guide our Forces by Thy Hand,
Gallant blacks from far Jamaica,   15
    Honduras and Togoland;
Protect them Lord in all their fights,
And, even more, protect the whites.

Think of what our Nation stands for,
    Books from Boots[6] and country lanes,   20
Free speech, free passes, class distinction,
    Democracy and proper drains.
Lord, put beneath Thy special care
One-eighty-nine Cadogan Square.[7]

Although dear Lord I am a sinner,   25
    I have done no major crime;
Now I'll come to Evening Service
    Whensoever I have the time.
So, Lord, reserve for me a crown,
And do not let my shares go down.   30

I will labor for Thy Kingdom,
    Help our lads to win the war,
Send white feathers to the cowards[8]
    Join the Women's Army Corps,[9]
Then wash the Steps around Thy Throne   35
In the Eternal Safety Zone.

---

4. The famous Gothic church in London in which English monarchs are crowned and famous Englishmen are buried (see lines 5, 39–40).
5. Organ tones which resemble the human voice.
6. A chain of London pharmacies.
7. Presumably where the speaker lives, in a fairly fashionable area.
8. White feathers were sometimes given, or sent, to men not in uniform, to suggest that they were cowards and should join the armed forces.
9. The speaker uses the old World War I name (Women's Army Auxiliary Corps) of the Auxiliary Territorial Service, an organization which performed domestic (and some foreign) defense duties.

Now I feel a little better,
    What a treat to hear Thy Word
Where the bones of leading statesmen,
    Have so often been interred.   40
And now, dear Lord, I cannot wait
Because I have a luncheon date.

                    1940

HENRY REED

Lessons of the War

Judging Distances

Not only how far away, but the way that you say it
Is very important. Perhaps you may never get
The knack of judging a distance, but at least you know
How to report on a landscape: the central sector,
The right of arc and that, which we had last Tuesday,   5
    And at least you know

That maps are of time, not place, so far as the army
Happens to be concerned—the reason being,
Is one which need not delay us. Again, you know
There are three kinds of tree, three only, the fir and the poplar,   10
And those which have bushy tops to; and lastly
    That things only seem to be things.

A barn is not called a barn, to put it more plainly,
Or a field in the distance, where sheep may be safely grazing.
You must never be over-sure. You must say, when reporting: 15
At five o'clock in the central sector is a dozen
Of what appear to be animals; whatever you do,
    Don't call the bleeders *sheep*.

I am sure that's quite clear; and suppose, for the sake of example,
The one at the end, asleep, endeavors to tell us   20
What he sees over there to the west, and how far away,
After first having come to attention. There to the west,
On the fields of summer the sun and the shadows bestow
    Vestments of purple and gold.

The still white dwellings are like a mirage in the heat,   25
And under the swaying elms a man and a woman
Lie gently together. Which is, perhaps, only to say
That there is a row of houses to the left of arc,
And that under some poplars a pair of what appear to be humans
    Appear to be loving.   30

Well that, for an answer, is what we might rightly call

Moderately satisfactory only, the reason being,
Is that two things have been omitted, and those are important.
The human beings, now: in what direction are they,
And how far away, would you say? And do not forget   35
    There may be dead ground in between.

There may be dead ground in between; and I may not have got
The knack of judging a distance; I will only venture
A guess that perhaps between me and the apparent lovers,
(Who, incidentally, appear by now to have finished,)   40
At seven o'clock from the houses, is roughly a distance
    Of about one year and a half.

                                                              1946

AUDRE LORDE

Hanging Fire

I am fourteen
and my skin has betrayed me
the boy I cannot live without
still sucks his thumb
in secret   5
how come my knees are
always so ashy
what if I die
before morning
and momma's in the bedroom   10
with the door closed.

I have to learn how to dance
in time for the next party
my room is too small for me
suppose I die before graduation   15
they will sing sad melodies
but finally
tell the truth about me
There is nothing I want to do
and too much   20
that has to be done
and momma's in the bedroom
with the door closed.

Nobody even stops to think
about my side of it   25
I should have been on Math Team
my marks were better than his
why do I have to be

the one
wearing braces   30
I have nothing to wear tomorrow
will I live long enough
to grow up
and momma's in the bedroom
with the door closed.   35

                                                1978

HOWARD NEMEROV

Boom!

Sees Boom in Religion, Too

Atlantic City, June 23, 1957 (AP).—President Eisenhower's pastor said
tonight that Americans are living in a period of "unprecedented religious
activity" caused partially by paid vacations, the eight-hour day and modern
conveniences.

"These fruits of material progress," said the Rev. Edward L. R. Elson
of the National Presbyterian Church, Washington, "have provided the
leisure, the energy, and the means for a level of human and spiritual
values never before reached."

Here at the Vespasian-Carlton,[1] it's just one
religious activity after another; the sky
is constantly being crossed by cruciform[2]
airplanes, in which nobody disbelieves
for a second and the tide, the tide   5
of spiritual progress and prosperity
miraculously keeps rising, to a level
never before attained. The churches are full,
the beaches are full, and the filling-stations
are full, God's great ocean is full   10
of paid vacationers praying an eight-hour day
to the human and spiritual values, the fruits,
the leisure, the energy, and the means, Lord,
the means for the level, the unprecedented level,
and the modern conveniences, which also are full. 15
Never before, O Lord, have the prayers and praises
from belfry and phonebooth, from ballpark and barbecue
the sacrifices, so endlessly ascended.

It was not thus when Job in Palestine
sat in the dust and cried, cried bitterly;[3]   20
when Damien kissed the lepers on their wounds

---

1. Vespasian was emperor of Rome 70–
79, shortly after the reign of Nero. In
French, *vespasienne* means public toilet.
2. Cross-shaped.
3. According to the *Book of Job*, he
was afflicted with the loss of prosperity,
children, and health as a test of his faith.
His name means, in Hebrew, "he cries";
see especially *Job* 2:7–13.

it was not thus;[4] it was not thus
when Francis worked a fourteen-hour day
strictly for the birds;[5] when Dante took
a week's vacation without pay and it rained   25
part of the time,[6] O Lord, it was not thus.

But now the gears mesh and the tires burn
and the ice chatters in the shaker and the priest
in the pulpit and Thy Name, O Lord,
is kept before the public, while the fruits   30
ripen and religion booms and the level rises
and every modern convenience runneth over,
that it may never be with us as it hath been
with Athens and Karnak and Nagasaki,[7]
nor Thy sun for one instant refrain from shining   35
on the rainbow Buick by the breezeway
or the Chris Craft with the uplift life raft;
that we may continue to be the just folks we are,
plain people with ordinary superliners and
disposable diaperliners, people of the stop'n'shop   40
'n'pray as you go, of hotel, motel, boatel,
the humble pilgrims of no deposit no return
and please adjust thy clothing, who will give to Thee,
if Thee will keep us going, our annual
Miss Universe, for Thy Name's Sake, Amen.   45

1960

GEORGE HERBERT

The Collar

I struck the board[8] and cried, "No more;
       I will abroad!
What? shall I ever sigh and pine?
My lines[9] and life are free, free as the road,
       Loose as the wind, as large as store.[1]   5
          Shall I be still in suit?[2]
    Have I no harvest but a thorn
    To let me blood, and not restore
What I have lost with cordial[3] fruit?

---

4. "Father Damien" (Joseph Damien de Veuster, 1840–1889), a Roman Catholic missionary from Belgium, was known for his work among lepers in Hawaii; he ultimately contracted leprosy himself and died there.

5. St. Francis of Assisi, 13th-century founder of the Franciscan order, was noted for his love of all living things, and one of the most famous stories about him tells of his preaching to the birds. "Strictly for the birds": a mid-20th-century expression for worthless or unfashionable activity.

6. Dante's journey through Hell, Purgatory, and Paradise (in *The Divine Comedy*) takes a week, beginning on Good Friday, 1300. It rains in the third chasm of Hell.

7. Athens, the cultural center of ancient civilization; Karnak, a village on the Nile, built on the site of ancient Thebes; Nagasaki, a large Japanese port city, virtually destroyed by a U.S. atomic bomb in 1945.

8. Table.

9. Lot.

1. A storehouse; i.e., in abundance.

2. In service to another.

3. Reviving, restorative.

Sure there was wine   10
Before my sighs did dry it; there was corn
    Before my tears did drown it.
Is the year only lost to me?
    Have I no bays[4] to crown it,
No flowers, no garlands gay? All blasted?   15
                All wasted?
Not so, my heart; but there is fruit,
                And thou hast hands.
Recover all thy sigh-blown age
On double pleasures: leave thy cold dispute   20
Of what is fit, and not. Forsake thy cage,
            Thy rope of sands,[5]
Which petty thoughts have made, and made to thee
    Good cable, to enforce and draw,
                And be thy law,   25
While thou didst wink[6] and wouldst not see.
            Away! take heed;
                I will abroad.
Call in thy death's-head[7] there; tie up thy fears.
            He that forbears   30
    To suit and serve his need,
            Deserves his load."
But as I raved and grew more fierce and wild
            At every word,
Methought I heard one calling, *Child!*   35
    And I replied, *My Lord.*

                                                        1633

JOHN DONNE

Song

Go, and catch a falling star,
    Get with child a mandrake root,[8]
Tell me, where all past years are,
    Or who cleft the devil's foot,
Teach me to hear mermaids singing   5
Or to keep off envy's stinging,
            And find
            What wind
Serves to advance an honest mind.

If thou beest born to strange sights,[9]   10
    Things invisible to see,

---

4. Wreaths of triumph.
5. Moral restrictions.
6. I.e., close your eyes to the weaknesses of such restrictions.
7. *Memento mori*, a skull intended to remind men of their mortality.
8. The forked mandrake root is said to be shaped like the lower half of a human torso.
9. I.e., if you have supernatural powers.

Ride ten thousand days and nights,
   Till age snow white hairs on thee;
Thou, when thou return'st, wilt tell me
All strange wonders that befell thee,   15
      And swear,
      No where
Lives a woman true, and fair.

If thou find'st one, let me know:
   Such a pilgrimage were sweet.   20
Yet do not, I would not go,
   Though at next door we might meet:
Though she were true when you met her,
And last till you write your letter,
      Yet she   25
      Will be
False, ere I come, to two, or three.

               1633

BEN JONSON

In the Person of Woman Kind

A Song Apologetic

Men if you love us, play no more
   The fools or tyrants with your friends,
To make us still sing o'er and o'er,
   Our own false praises, for your ends:
      We have both wits,[1] and fancies[2] too,   5
      And if we must, let's sing of you.

Nor do we doubt, but that we can,
   If we would search with care and pain,
Find some one good, in some one man;
   So going thorow[3] all your strain:[4]   10
      We shall, at last, of parcels[5] make
      One good enough for a song's sake.

And as a cunning painter takes
   In any curious piece you see
More pleasure while the thing he makes   15
   Then when 'tis made, why so will we.
      And having pleased our art, we'll try
      To make a new, and hang that by.

               1640

1. Intellects.
2. Imaginations.
3. Through.
4. Kind; i.e., all men.
5. Particles; i.e., make one good man from the good particles of all men.

SIR PHILIP SIDNEY

What, Have I Thus Betrayed My Liberty?

What, have I thus betrayed my liberty?
Can those black beams such burning marks[6] engrave
In my free side? or am I born a slave,
Whose neck becomes[7] such yoke of tyranny?
Or want[8] I sense to feel my misery?   5
Or sprite,[9] disdain of such disdain to have?
Who for long faith, though daily help I crave,
May get no alms but scorn of beggary.[1]
Virtue, awake! Beauty but beauty is.
I may, I must, I can, I will, I do   10
Leave following that which it is gain to miss.
Let her go! Soft, but here she comes! Go to,
Unkind, I love you not! O me, that eye
Doth make my heart give to my tongue the lie!

1582

---

6. Slaves had formerly been branded.
7. Befits.
8. Lack.

9. Spirit.
1. I.e., contempt for my beggarly condition.

4 SITUATION AND SETTING

Questions about speaker ("Who?" questions) in a poem almost always lead to questions of "Where?" "When?" and "Why?" Identifying the speaker usually is, in fact, part of a larger process of defining the entire imagined **situation** in a poem: What is happening? Where is it happening? Who is the speaker speaking to? Who else is present? Why is this event occurring? In order to understand the dialogue in *The Ruined Maid*, for example, we need to become aware that the sisters are meeting again after a period of absence and that they are meeting in a town large enough to seem substantially different in setting from the rural area in which they grew up together. And we infer (from the opening lines) that the meeting is accidental, and that no other family members are present for the conversation. The poem's whole "story" depends upon the fact of their situation: after leading separate lives for some time they have some catching up to do. We don't know what specific town is involved, or what year, season, or time of day because those details are not important to the poem's effect. But crucial to the poem are the where and when questions that define the situation and relationship of the two speakers, and the answer to the why question—that the meeting is by chance— is important too. In another poem we looked at in the previous chapter, *A Certain Lady*, the specific moment and place are not important, but we do need to notice that the "lady" is talking to (or having an imaginary conversation with) her man and that they are talking about a relationship of some duration.

Sometimes a *specific* time and place (**setting**) may be important. The "lady in skunk" sings her life story "in a prominent bar in Secaucus, N.J.," a smelly and unfashionable town, but on no particular occasion ("One Day"). In *Soliloquy of the Spanish Cloister*, the setting (a monastery) adds to the irony because of the gross inappropriateness of such sentiments and attitudes in such a supposedly holy place, and the setting of *In Westminster Abbey* similarly helps us to judge the speaker's ideas, attitudes, and self-conception.

The title of the following poem suggests that place may be important, and it is, although you may be surprised to discover exactly what exists at this address and what uses the speaker makes of it.

JAMES DICKEY

Cherrylog Road

Off Highway 106[1]
At Cherrylog Road I entered
The '34 Ford without wheels,

---

1. The poem is set in the mountains of North Georgia.

Smothered in kudzu,[2]
With a seat pulled out to run   5
Corn whiskey down from the hills,

And then from the other side
Crept into an Essex
With a rumble seat of red leather
And then out again, aboard   10
A blue Chevrolet, releasing
The rust from its other color,

Reared up on three building blocks.
None had the same body heat;
I changed with them inward, toward   15
The weedy heart of the junkyard,
For I knew that Doris Holbrook
Would escape from her father at noon

And would come from the farm
To seek parts owned by the sun   20
Among the abandoned chassis,
Sitting in each in turn
As I did, leaning forward
As in a wild stock-car race

In the parking lot of the dead.   25
Time after time, I climbed in
And out the other side, like
An envoy or movie star
Met at the station by crickets.
A radiator cap raised its head,   30

Become a real toad or a kingsnake
As I neared the hub of the yard,
Passing through many states,
Many lives, to reach
Some grandmother's long Pierce-Arrow   35
Sending platters of blindness forth

From its nickel hubcaps
And spilling its tender upholstery
On sleepy roaches,
The glass panel in between   40
Lady and colored driver
Not all the way broken out,

The back-seat phone
Still on its hook.
I got in as though to exclaim,   45

2. A rapidly growing vine, introduced from Japan to combat erosion but now
covering whole fields and groves of trees.

"Let us go to the orphan asylum,
John; I have some old toys
For children who say their prayers."

I popped with sweat as I thought
I heard Doris Holbrook scrape   50
Like a mouse in the southern-state sun
That was eating the paint in blisters
From a hundred car tops and hoods.
She was tapping like code,

Loosening the screws,   55
Carrying off headlights,
Sparkplugs, bumpers,
Cracked mirrors and gear-knobs,
Getting ready, already,
To go back with something to show   60

Other than her lips' new trembling
I would hold to me soon, soon,
Where I sat in the ripped back seat
Talking over the interphone,
Praying for Doris Holbrook   65
To come from her father's farm

And to get back there
With no trace of me on her face
To be seen by her red-haired father
Who would change, in the squalling barn,   70
Her back's pale skin with a strop,
Then lay for me

In a bootlegger's roasting car
With a string-triggered 12-gauge shotgun
To blast the breath from the air.   75
Not cut by the jagged windshields,
Through the acres of wrecks she came
With a wrench in her hand,

Through dust where the blacksnake dies
Of boredom, and the beetle knows   80
The compost has no more life.
Someone outside would have seen
The oldest car's door inexplicably
Close from within:

I held her and held her and held her,   85
Convoyed at terrific speed
By the stalled, dreaming traffic around us,
So the blacksnake, stiff
With inaction, curved back
Into life, and hunted the mouse   90

With deadly overexcitement,
The beetles reclaimed their field
As we clung, glued together,
With the hooks of the seat springs
Working through to catch us red-handed   95
Amidst the gray breathless batting

That burst from the seat at our backs.
We left by separate doors
Into the changed, other bodies
Of cars, she down Cherrylog Road   100
And I to my motorcycle
Parked like the soul of the junkyard

Restored, a bicycle fleshed
With power, and tore off
Up Highway 106, continually   105
Drunk on the wind in my mouth,
Wringing the handlebar for speed,
Wild to be wreckage forever.

                                                          1964

The *exact* location of the junkyard is not important (there is no Highway 106 near the real Cherrylog Road in North Georgia), but we do need to know that the setting is rural, that the time is summer and that the summer is hot, and that moonshine whiskey is native to the area. Following the story is no problem once we have sorted out these few facts, and we are prepared to meet the cast of characters: Doris Holbrook, her red-haired father, and the speaker. About each we learn just enough to appreciate the sense of vitality, adventure, and power that constitute the major effects of the poem.

The situation of love-making in another setting than the junkyard would not produce the same effects, and the exotic sense of a forbidden meeting in this unlikely place helps to recreate the speaker's sense of the episode. For him, it is memorable (notice all the tiny details he remembers), powerful (notice his reaction when he gets back on his motorcycle), dreamlike (notice the sense of time standing still, especially in lines 85–89), and important (notice how the speaker perceives his environment as changed by their love-making, lines 88–91 and 98–100). The wealth of details about setting also helps us to raise other, related questions. Why does the speaker fantasize about being shot by the father (lines 72–75)? Why, in a poem so full of details, do we find out so little about what Doris Holbrook looks like? What gives us the sense that this incident is a composite of episodes, an event that was repeated many times? What gives us the impression that the events occurred long ago? What makes the speaker feel so powerful at the end? What does he mean when he talks of himself as being "wild to be wreckage forever"? All of the poem's attention to the speaker's reactions, reflections, and memories is intricately tied up with the particulars of setting. Making love in a junkyard is crucial to the speaker's sense of both power and wreckage, and Doris is merely a matter of excitement, adventure, and pretty skin, appreciated because she makes the world seem different and because she is willing to take risks and to suffer for meeting him like this. The more we probe the poem with questions about situation, the more likely we are to catch the poem's full effect.

Cherrylog Road is a fairly easy poem to read, but its effect is more complex than its simple story line suggests. The next poem we will look at is, at first glance, much more difficult to follow. Part of the difficulty is that the poem is from an earlier age, and its language is a little different, and part is because the action in the poem is so closely connected to what is being said. But its opening lines— addressed to someone who is resisting the speaker's suggestions— disclose the situation, and gradually we can figure out the scene: a man is trying to convince a woman that they should make love. When a flea happens by, the speaker uses it for an unlikely example as part of his argument. And once we recognize the situation, we can readily follow (and be amused by) the speaker's witty and intricate argument.

JOHN DONNE

The Flea

Mark but this flea, and mark in this[3]
How little that which thou deny'st me is;
It sucked me first, and now sucks thee,
And in this flea our two bloods mingled be;
Thou know'st that this cannot be said   5
A sin, nor shame, nor loss of maidenhead,
    Yet this enjoys before it woo,
      And pampered[4] swells with one blood made of two,
    And this, alas, is more than we would do.[5]

Oh stay, three lives in one flea spare,   10
Where we almost, yea more than, married are.
This flea is you and I, and this
Our marriage bed, and marriage temple is;
Though parents grudge, and you, we're met
And cloistered in these living walls of jet.   15
    Though use[6] make you apt to kill me,
      Let not to that, self-murder added be,
    And sacrilege, three sins in killing three.

3. Medieval preachers and rhetoricians asked their hearers to "mark" (look at) an object which illustrated a moral or philosophical lesson they wished to emphasize.
4. Fed luxuriously.

5. According to contemporary medical theory, conception involved the literal mingling of the lovers' blood.
6. Habit.

Cruel and sudden, hast thou since
Purpled thy nail in blood of innocence? 20
Wherein could this flea guilty be,
Except in that drop which it sucked from thee?
Yet thou triumph'st, and say'st that thou
Find'st not thyself, nor me, the weaker now;
   'Tis true; then learn how false, fears be; 25
   Just so much honor, when thou yield'st to me,
   Will waste, as this flea's death took life from thee.

1633

The scene in *The Flea* develops almost as in a play. Action even occurs right along with the words. Between stanzas 1 and 2, the woman makes a move to kill the flea (as stanza 2 opens, the speaker is trying to stop her), and between stanzas 2 and 3 the woman has squished the flea with her fingernail. Once we try to make sense of what the speaker says, the action is just as clear from the words as if we had stage directions in the margin. All of the speaker's verbal cleverness and all of his specious arguments follow from the situation, and in this poem (as in *Soliloquy of the Spanish Cloister* or *In Westminster Abbey*) we watch as if we were observing a scene on the stage. The speaker is, in effect, giving a dramatic monologue for our benefit. (You may have noticed that in seduction poems, the seducer usually does all the talking and the seducer seldom gets a chance to speak; for some amusing inversions (reversals) of this pattern, and some witty variations on it, see the group of poems on pp. 312–316).

Neither time nor place is important to *The Flea*, except in the sense that the speaker and his friend have to be assumed to be in the same place and have the leisure for some playfulness. The situation could occur in any place where a man, a woman, and a flea could be together. Indoors, outdoors, morning, evening, city, country, it is all one; the situation could occur in cottage or palace, on a boat or in a bedroom. We do know, from the date of publication of the poem (1633), that the poet was writing about people of more than three centuries ago, but the conduct he describes might equally happen in later ages just as well. Only the habits of language (and perhaps the speaker's religious attitudes) date the poem; the situation could equally be set in any age or place.

Some poems, are, however, specifically **referential** about time or place; that is, they refer to a certain actual place and time. The following poem depends upon historical information (it also assumes that we know the terminology of children's games); if you don't know the history of atomic warfare, you may want to read the footnote before you read the poem.

ROBERT FROST

U. S. 1946 King's X[7]

Having invented a new Holocaust,
And been the first with it to win a war,
How they make haste to cry with fingers crossed,
King's X—no fairs to use it any more!

p. 1946

Our knowledge of the relevant historical facts does not necessarily mean that we will agree with the poet's criticism of U. S. policy at the end of World War II, but we certainly can't understand or appreciate the poem's equation of nuclear policy with a child's fear of consequence unless we do know the facts. Often it is hard to place ourselves fully enough in another time or place to imagine sympathetically what a particular historical moment would have been like, and even the best poetic efforts do not necessarily transport us there. But poets sometimes record a particular moment or event in order to commemorate it or comment upon it. A poem written about a specific occasion is usually called an **occasional poem,** and such a poem is **referential;** that is, it refers to a specific historical moment or event. For such poems we need, at the least, specific historical information— plus a willingness on our part as readers to be transported imaginatively to that particular time, sometimes (as in *U. S. 1946 King's X*) by mentioning explicitly a particular time, sometimes by recreating that moment in a dramatic situation. The poems about World War I on pp. 297–301 suggest something of the range of problems involved in reading consciously historical and referential poetry.

Time or place may, of course, be used much less specifically and still be important to a poem, and the most common uses of setting involve drawing upon common notions of a particular time or place. Setting a poem in a garden, for example, or writing about apples almost inevitably reminds us of the Garden of Eden because it is part of our common heritage of belief or knowledge. Even people who don't read at all or who lack Judaeo-Christian religious commitments are likely to know about Eden, and a poet writing in our culture can count on that. In Joni Mitchell's *Woodstock* (p. 37), for example (as we noticed in Chapter 2) the idea of the innocence in Woodstock is drawn into the poem by an allusion to Eden; the final refrain in each stanza of the poem insists that "we've got to get ourselves / Back to the garden." An **allusion** is a reference to something outside the poem that carries a history of meaning and strong emotional associations. For example, gardens may carry suggestions

7. Shortly after exploding the two atomic bombs that ended World War II, the United States proposed to share nuclear information with other countries in exchange for an agreement that the information would be used only for peaceful purposes. In children's games, time out is sometimes signaled by crossing fingers and saying "King's X."

of innocence and order, or temptation and the fall, or both, depending on how the poem handles the allusion. Well-known places from history or myth may be popularly associated with particular ideas or values or ways of life.

The place involved in a poem is its **spatial setting,** and the time is its **temporal setting.** The temporal setting may involve a specific date or an era, a season of the year or a time of day. We tend, for example, to think of spring as a time of discovery and growth, and poems set in spring are likely to draw upon that association; morning usually suggests discovery as well—beginnings, vitality, the world fresh and new—even to those of us who in reality take our waking slow. Temporal or spatial setting are often used to influence our expectation of theme and tone in a specific way, although the poet may then go on to surprise us by making something very different of our expectation. Setting is often an important factor in creating the mood in poems just as in stories, plays, or films. Often the details of setting have a lot to do with the way we ultimately respond to the poem's subject or theme, as in this poem:

SYLVIA PLATH

Point Shirley

From Water-Tower Hill to the brick prison
The shingle booms, bickering under
The sea's collapse.
Snowcakes break and welter. This year
The gritted wave leaps   5
The seawall and drops onto a bier
Of quahog chips,[8]
Leaving a salty mash of ice to whiten

In my grandmother's sand yard. She is dead,
Whose laundry snapped and froze here, who   10
Kept house against
What the sluttish, rutted sea could do.
Squall waves once danced
Ship timbers in through the cellar window;
A thresh-tailed, lanced   15
Shark littered in the geranium bed—

Such collusion of mulish elements
She wore her broom straws to the nub.
Twenty years out
Of her hand; the house still hugs in each drab   20

8. Chips from quahog clam shells, common on the New England coast.

Stucco socket
The purple egg-stones: from Great Head's knob
To the filled-in Gut
The sea in its cold gizzard ground those rounds.

Nobody wintering now behind   25
The planked-up windows where she set
Her wheat loaves
And apple cakes to cool. What is it
Survives, grieves
So, over this battered, obstinate spit   30
Of gravel? The waves'
Spewed relics clicker masses in the wind,

Gray waves the stub-necked eiders ride.
A labor of love, and that labor lost.
Steadily the sea   35
Eats at Point Shirley. She died blessed,
And I come by
Bones, bones only, pawed and tossed,
A dog-faced sea.
The sun sinks under Boston, bloody red.   40

I would get from these dry-papped stones
The milk your love instilled in them.
The black ducks dive.
And though your graciousness might stream,
And I contrive,   45
Grandmother, stones are nothing of home
To that spumiest dove.
Against both bar and tower the black sea runs.

                                                                 1960

One does not have to know the New England coast by personal experience to have it vividly recalled by Plath's poem. A reader who knows that coast or another like it may have an advantage in being able to respond more quickly to the poem's precision of description, but the poem does not depend on such knowledge from outside the poem. The precise location of Point Shirley, near Boston, is not especially important, but visualization of the setting is. Crucial to the poem's tone and mood is the sense of the sea as aggressor, a force powerful enough to change the contours of the coast and invade the privacy of yards and homes. The energy, relentlessness, and impersonality of the sea met their match, though a temporary one, in the speaker's grandmother who "Kept house against / What the sluttish, rutted sea could do" (lines 11–12). The grandmother *belonged* in this setting, and it seemed hers, but twenty years of her absence (since her death) now begin to show. Still, the marks of her obstinacy and love are there, although ultimately doomed by the sea's more enduring power.

Details—and how they are amassed—are important here rather than historic particulars of time and place. The grays and whites and drab colors of the sea and its leavings provide both a visual sense of the scene and the mood for the poem. The stubbornness which the speaker admired in the grandmother comes to seem a part of that tenacious grayness. Nothing happens rapidly here; things wear down. Even the "bloody red" (line 40) of the sun's setting—an ominous sign that adds a vivid fright to the dullness rather than brightening it— makes promises that seem slow and long-term. The toughness of the boarded-up house is a monument to the grandmother's loving care and becomes a way for the speaker to touch her human spirit, but the poem's final emphasis is on the relentless black sea which continues to run against the landmarks and fortresses that had been identified with the setting in the very first line.

Questions about situation and setting begin as simple questions of identification but often become more complex when we sort out all the implications. Often it takes only a moment to determine a poem's situation, but it may take much longer to discover all of the things that time and place imply, for their meanings may depend upon visual details, or upon actual historical occurrences, or upon habitual ways of thinking about certain times and places—or all three at once. As you read the following poem, notice how the setting—another shore—prepares us for the speaker's moods and ideas, and then watch how the movement of his mind is affected by what he sees.

MATTHEW ARNOLD

Dover Beach[9]

The sea is calm tonight.
The tide is full, the moon lies fair
Upon the straits; on the French coast the light
Gleams and is gone; the cliffs of England stand,
Glimmering and vast, out in the tranquil bay.   5
Come to the window, sweet is the night-air!
Only, from the long line of spray
Where the sea meets the moon-blanched land,
Listen! you hear the grating roar
Of pebbles which the waves draw back, and fling,   10
At their return, up the high strand,
Begin, and cease, and then again begin,
With tremulous cadence slow, and bring
The eternal note of sadness in.

9. At the narrowest point on the English Channel. The lights on the French coast (lines 3–4) would be about 20 miles away.

Sophocles long ago   15
Heard it on the Aegean, and it brought
Into his mind the turbid ebb and flow
Of human misery;[1] we
Find also in the sound a thought,
Hearing it by this distant northern sea.   20

The Sea of Faith
Was once, too, at the full, and round earth's shore
Lay like the folds of a bright girdle furled.
But now I only hear
Its melancholy, long, withdrawing roar,   25
Retreating, to the breath
Of the night-wind, down the vast edges drear
And naked shingles[2] of the world.

Ah, love, let us be true
To one another! for the world, which seems   30
To lie before us like a land of dreams,
So various, so beautiful, so new,
Hath really neither joy, nor love, nor light,
Nor certitude, nor peace, nor help for pain;
And we are here as on a darkling plain   35
Swept with confused alarms of struggle and flight,
Where ignorant armies clash by night.

ca. 1851

Exactly what is the dramatic situation in *Dover Beach*? How soon
are you aware that someone is being spoken to? How much are we
told about the person spoken to? How would you describe the speak-
er's mood? What does the speaker's mood have to do with time and
place? Do any details of present place and time help to account for
his tendency to talk repeatedly of the past and the future? How
important is it to the poem's total effect that the beach here involves
an international border? What particulars of the Dover Beach seem
especially important to the poem's themes? to its emotional effects?

Not all poems have an identifiable situation or setting, just as not
all poems have a speaker that is distinct from the author. Poems that
simply present a series of thoughts and feelings directly, in a con-
templative, meditative, or reflective way, may not set up any kind of
action, plot, or situation at all, preferring to speak directly without the
intermediary of a dramatic device. But most poems depend crucially
upon a sense of place, a sense of time, and an understanding of human
interaction in scenes that resemble the strategies of drama or film.
And questions about these matters will often lead you to define not
only the "facts" but also the feelings central to a poem's design upon us.

---

1. In *Antigone*, lines 583–91, the chorus
compares the fate of the house of Oedipus
to the waves of the sea.
2. Pebble-strewn beaches.

ROBERT BROWNING

My Last Duchess

Ferrara[3]

That's my last Duchess painted on the wall,
Looking as if she were alive. I call
That piece a wonder, now: Frà Pandolf's hands[4]
Worked busily a day, and there she stands.
Will't please you sit and look at her? I said   5
"Frà Pandolf" by design, for never read
Strangers like you that pictured countenance,
The depth and passion of its earnest glance,
But to myself they turned (since none puts by
The curtain I have drawn for you, but I)   10
And seemed as they would ask me, if they durst,
How such a glance came there; so, not the first
Are you to turn and ask thus. Sir, 'twas not
Her husband's presence only, called that spot
Of joy into the Duchess' cheek: perhaps   15
Frà Pandolf chanced to say "Her mantle laps
Over my lady's wrist too much," or "Paint
Must never hope to reproduce the faint
Half-flush that dies along her throat": such stuff
Was courtesy, she thought, and cause enough   20
For calling up that spot of joy. She had
A heart—how shall I say?—too soon made glad,
Too easily impressed; she liked whate'er
She looked on, and her looks went everywhere.
Sir, 'twas all one! My favor at her breast,   25
The dropping of the daylight in the West,
The bough of cherries some officious fool
Broke in the orchard for her, the white mule
She rode with round the terrace—all and each
Would draw from her alike the approving speech,   30
Or blush, at least. She thanked men,—good! but thanked
Somehow—I know not how—as if she ranked
My gift of a nine-hundred-years-old name
With anybody's gift. Who'd stoop to blame
This sort of trifling? Even had you skill   35
In speech—which I have not—to make your will
Quite clear to such an one, and say, "Just this
Or that in you disgusts me; here you miss,
Or there exceed the mark"—and if she let
Herself be lessoned so, nor plainly set   40
Her wits to yours, forsooth, and made excuse,

---

3. Alfonso II, Duke of Ferrara in Italy in the mid-16th century, is the presumed speaker of the poem, which is loosely based on historical events. The Duke's first wife —whom he had married when she was 14 —died under suspicious circumstances at 17, and he then negotiated through an agent (to whom the poem is spoken) for the hand of the niece of the Count of Tyrol in Austria.
4. Frà Pandolf is, like Claus (line 56), fictitious.

—E'en then would be some stooping; and I choose
Never to stoop. Oh sir, she smiled, no doubt,
Whene'er I passed her; but who passed without
Much the same smile? This grew; I gave commands;   45
Then all smiles stopped together. There she stands
As if alive. Will't please you rise? We'll meet
The company below, then. I repeat,
The Count your master's known munificence
Is ample warrant that no just pretense   50
Of mine for dowry will be disallowed;
Though his fair daughter's self, as I avowed
At starting, is my object. Nay, we'll go
Together down, sir. Notice Neptune, though,
Taming a sea-horse, thought a rarity,   55
Which Claus of Innsbruck cast in bronze for me!

1842

JOHN DONNE

A Valediction: Forbidding Mourning

As virtuous men pass mildly away,
    And whisper to their souls to go,
Whilst some of their sad friends do say,
    "The breath goes now," and some say, "No,"

So let us melt, and make no noise,   5
    No tear-floods, nor sigh-tempests move;
'Twere profanation of our joys
    To tell the laity our love.

Moving of the earth[5] brings harms and fears,
    Men reckon what it did and meant;   10
But trepidation of the spheres,[6]
    Though greater far, is innocent.

Dull sublunary[7] lovers' love
    (Whose soul is sense) cannot admit
Absence, because it doth remove   15
    Those things which elemented[8] it.

But we, by a love so much refined
    That our selves know not what it is,

---

5. Earthquakes.
6. The Renaissance hypothesis that the celestial spheres trembled and thus caused unexpected variations in their orbits. Such movements are "innocent" because earthlings do not observe or fret about them.
7. Below the moon; i.e., changeable.

According to the traditional cosmology which Donne invokes here, the moon was considered the dividing line between the immutable celestial world and the earthly mortal one.
8. Comprised.

Inter-assured of the mind,
　　Care less, eyes, lips, and hands to miss.   20

Our two souls therefore, which are one,
　　Though I must go, endure not yet
A breach, but an expansion,
　　Like gold to airy thinness beat.

If they be two, they are two so   25
　　As stiff twin compasses are two:
Thy soul, the fixed foot, makes no show
　　To move, but doth, if the other do;

And though it in the center sit,
　　Yet when the other far doth roam,   30
It leans, and hearkens after it,
　　And grows erect, as that comes home.

Such wilt thou be to me, who must,
　　Like the other foot, obliquely run;
Thy firmness makes my circle⁹ just,   35
　　And makes me end where I begun.

1611(?)

JAROLD RAMSEY

Lupine Dew¹

For Sophia

That summer, you were game for anything.
Someday, stepping out of the rectilinear shade
of a building, bearing your own share of Atlas's burden,²
the stone cocoon of the world,
may you remember how we left the others   5
swigging canteen water under a juniper
to close the gate at the head of Garrett Canyon.³
Hot, too hot for purposes—
we played we were deer, breaking from willow to willow
shade and dazzle and dappled shade again,   10
until we sprawled in a bower.
There you drank the gems of dew on a purple lupine,
leaves and flower, and I told you

9. A traditional symbol of perfection.
1. The lupine plant is a member of the genus *lupinus,* literally meaning wolflike; the plant was so named because of the ancient belief that it destroyed the soil. There are many other legends about the power of the plant.
2. In Greek mythology, Atlas was condemned to uphold the heavens on his shoulders.
3. In the state of Oregon.

"Those who drink the lupine dew at noon
turn into many things, child, in the sun."   15
"Well then," you said, "I'll be a butterfly."
And when in a moment a lusty Monarch
veered at us through the boughs
you cried, "So long, Dad, I'm off and away!"
And you were a butterfly, remember,   20
oh remember, all that day.

p. 1979

GALWAY KINNELL

To Christ our Lord

The legs of the elk punctured the snow's crust
And wolves floated lightfooted on the land
Hunting Christmas elk living and frozen;
Inside snow melted in a basin, and a woman basted
A bird spread over coals by its wings and head.   5

Snow had sealed the windows; candles lit
The Christmas meal. The Christmas grace chilled
The cooked bird, being long-winded and the room cold.
During the words a boy thought, it is fitting
To eat this creature killed on the wing?   10

He had killed it himself, climbing out
Alone on snowshoes in the Christmas dawn,
The fallen snow swirling and the snowfall gone,
Heard its throat scream as the rifle shouted,
Watched it drop, and fished from the snow the dead.   15

He had not wanted to shoot. The sound
Of wings beating into the hushed air
Had stirred his love, and his fingers
Froze in his gloves, and he wondered,
Famishing, could he fire? Then he fired.   20

Now the grace praised his wicked act. At its end
The bird on the plate
Stared at his stricken appetite.
There had been nothing to do but surrender,
To kill and to eat; he ate as he had killed, with wonder.   25

At night on snowshoes on the drifting field
He wondered again, for whom had love stirred?
The stars glittered on the snow and nothing answered.
Then the Swan spread her wings, cross of the cold north,
The pattern and mirror of the acts of earth.   30

1960

ANNE SEXTON

The Truth the Dead Know

for my mother, born March 1902, died March 1959
and my father, born February 1900, died June 1959

Gone, I say and walk from church,
refusing the stiff procession to the grave,
letting the dead ride alone in the hearse.
It is June. I am tired of being brave.

We drive to the Cape.[4] I cultivate   5
myself where the sun gutters from the sky,
where the sea swings in like an iron gate
and we touch. In another country people die.

My darling, the wind falls in like stones
from the whitehearted water and when we touch   10
we enter touch entirely. No one's alone.
Men kill for this, or for as much.

And what of the dead? They lie without shoes
in their stone boats. They are more like stone
than the sea would be if it stopped. They refuse   15
to be blessed, throat, eye and knucklebone.

1962

DONALD JUSTICE

Here in Katmandu[5]

We have climbed the mountain,
There's nothing more to do.
It is terrible to come down
To the valley
Where, amidst many flowers,   5
One thinks of snow,

As, formerly, amidst snow,
Climbing the mountain,
One thought of flowers,
Tremulous, ruddy with dew,   10
In the valley.
One caught their scent coming down.

It is difficult to adjust, once down,
To the absence of snow.

4. **Cape Cod, in Massachusetts.**   miles west of Mt. Everest.
5. The capital city of Nepal, about 100

Clear days, from the valley,   15
One looks up at the mountain.
What else is there to do?
Prayerwheels, flowers!

Let the flowers
Fade, the prayerwheels run down.   20
What have these to do
With us who have stood atop the snow
Atop the mountain,
Flags seen from the valley?

It might be possible to live in the valley,   25
To bury oneself among flowers,
If one could forget the mountain,
How, setting out before dawn,
Blinded with snow,
One knew what to do.   30

Meanwhile it is not easy here in Katmandu,
Especially when to the valley
That wind which means snow
Elsewhere, but here means flowers,
Comes down,   35
As soon it must, from the mountain.

1960

JONATHAN SWIFT

A Description of the Morning

Now hardly[6] here and there a hackney-coach[7]
Appearing, showed the ruddy morn's approach.
Now Betty[8] from her master's bed had flown,
And softly stole to discompose her own.
The slip shod 'prentice from his master's door   5
Had pared the dirt, and sprinkled round the floor.
Now Moll had whirled her mop with dext'rous airs,
Prepared to scrub the entry and the stairs.
The youth with broomy stumps began to trace[9]
The kennel-edge[1] where wheels had worn the place.   10
The small-coal man[2] was heard with cadence deep,
Till drowned in shriller notes of chimney-sweep:
Duns[3] at his lordship's gate began to meet;

6. Scarcely; i.e., they are just beginning to appear.
7. Hired coach.
8. A stock name for a servant girl. Moll (lines 7, 14) is a frequent lower-class nickname.
9. "To find old Nails." (Swift's note)
1. Edge of the gutter which ran down the middle of the street.
2. A seller of coal and charcoal.
3. Bill collectors.

And brick-dust Moll had screamed through half the street.[4]
The turnkey now his flock returning sees,   15
Duly let out a-nights to steal for fees;[5]
The watchful bailiffs[6] take their silent stands,
And schoolboys lag with satchels in their hands.

p. 1709

TURNER CASSITY

Grace at the Atlanta Fox[7]

Whenever, in that ceiling sky,
Familiar clouds once more go by,

And in the restrooms, far below,
One half the lamps of Islam glow;

When, overweight but overawed,   5
Undying Grace, eternal Maude,

Once more are en rapport—are one—
With Myrna Loy and Irene Dunne[8]

(Irene as essence, Maude; *Ur*-Myrna:
Now the new star Annapurna,   10

Nepalese and thick of tongue);
Or when, pure movie, pure, brave, young,

The Foreign Legion dare and do,
Each year is 1932;

Pre-Eleanor,[9] pre-war, pre-Fala;   15
Time as place: the Garden of Allah,

Near whose entrance, chill with Freon,
That time's great sign resists still neon,

To be through Moorish, Hoover nights
This fugue of incandescent lights;   20

---

4. Selling powdered brick which was used to clean knives.
5. Jailers collected fees from prisoners for their keep and often let them out at night so they could steal to pay expenses.
6. Looking for those on their "wanted" lists.
7. An ornate Atlanta moviehouse (built 1927) which featured an elaborate lighted ceiling with moving "clouds" and "stars" and Moorish decor throughout the building, extending even to the restrooms.
8. Early movie stars. *Annapurna* (line 10) was a 1953 movie version of the climbing of the Himalayan peak.
9. I.e., before Eleanor Roosevelt. "Fala" was the pet dog of the Roosevelt family in the White House.

As if to make some statement yet;
As if the tan brick minaret

Were point and counterpoint; not theme,
But theme to be, that when the dream

Maude dreams is ours, and we too nod,   25
States then "There is no God but God . . ."

1966

5   WORDS

Fiction and drama depend upon language just as poetry does, but in a poem almost everything comes down to words. In stories and plays, we are likely to keep our attention primarily on narrative and plot—what is happening in front of us or in the action as we imagine it in our minds—and although words are crucial to how we imagine the characters and how we respond to what happens to them, we are less likely to pause over any one word as we may need to in a poem. Besides, poems often are short and use only a few words, so a lot depends on every single one. Poetry sometimes feels like prose that is distilled: only the most essential words are there, just barely enough so that we communicate in the most basic way, using the most elemental signs of meaning and feeling—and each one chosen for exactly the right shade of meaning. But elemental does not necessarily mean simple, and these signs may be very rich in their meanings and complex in their effects.

Let's look first at two poems, each of which depends heavily upon a single key word.

RICHARD ARMOUR

Hiding Place

A speaker at a meeting of the New York State Frozen Food Locker Association declared that the best hiding place in event of an atomic explosion is a frozen-food locker, where "radiation will not penetrate."[1]   NEWS ITEM.

> Move over, ham
>   And quartered cow,
> My Geiger[2] says
>   The time is now.
>
> Yes, now I lay me   5
>   Down to sleep,
> And if I die,
>   At least I'll keep.

1954

YVOR WINTERS

At the San Francisco Airport

To my daughter, 1954

> This is the terminal: the light
> Gives perfect vision, false and hard;

1. Before home freezers became popular, many Americans rented lockers in specially equipped commercial buildings.

2. Geiger counter: used to detect radiation.

The metal glitters, deep and bright.
Great planes are waiting in the yard—
They are already in the night.   5

And you are here beside me, small,
Contained and fragile, and intent
On things that I but half recall—
Yet going whither you are bent.
I am the past, and that is all.   10

But you and I in part are one:
The frightened brain, the nervous will,
The knowledge of what must be done,
The passion to acquire the skill
To face that which you dare not shun.   15

The rain of matter upon sense
Destroys me momently. The score:
There comes what will come. The expense
Is what one thought, and something more—
One's being and intelligence.   20

This is the terminal, the break.
Beyond this point, on lines of air,
You take the way that you must take;
And I remain in light and stare—
In light, and nothing else, awake.   25

1954

In *Hiding Place*, almost all the poem's comedy depends on the final word, "keep." In the child's prayer which the poem echoes, to "pray the Lord my soul to keep" does not exactly involve cold storage, and so the poem depends upon an outrageous double meaning. The key word is chosen because it can mean more than one thing; in this case, the importance of the word involves its **ambiguity** (an ability to mean more than one thing) rather than its **precision** (exactness).

In the second poem, the several possible meanings of a single word are probed more soberly and thoughtfully. What does it *mean* to be in a place called a "terminal"? the poem asks. As the parting of father and daughter is explored, carefully, the place of parting and the means of transportation begin to take on meanings larger than their simple referential ones. The poem is full of contrasts—young and old, light and dark, past and present, security and adventure—as the parting of generations is pondered. The father ("I am the past," line 10) remains in the light, among known objects and experience familiar to his many years; the daughter is about to depart into the night, the unknown, the uncertain future. But they both share a sense of the necessity of the parting, of the need for the daughter to mature, gain knowledge, acquire experience. Is she going off to school? to college?

to her first job? The specifics are not given, but her plane ride clearly means a new departure and a clean break with childhood, dependency, the past.

So much depends upon the meanings of "terminal." It is the airport building, of course, but it also implies a boundary, an extremity, an end, something that is limited, a place where a connection is broken. The clear, crisp meanings of other words are important too. The words "break," "point," "lines," "way," and "remain" all express literally and sharply what the event means. The final stanza of the poem is full of words that state flatly and **denote** exactly, as if the speaker has recovered completely from the momentary confusion of stanza 4, when "being and intelligence" are lost in the emotion of the parting itself. The crisp articulation of the last stanza puts an almost total emphasis on the precise meaning of each word, its **denotation**, what it precisely denotes or refers to. The words "break," "point," "way," and "remain" are almost completely unemotional and colorless; they do not make value judgments or offer personal views, but rather define and describe. It is as if the speaker is trying to disengage himself from the emotion of the situation and just give the facts.

Words, however, are more than hard blocks of meaning on whose sense everyone agrees. They also have a more personal side, and they carry emotional force and shades of suggestion. The words we use indicate not only what we mean but how we feel about it, and we choose words that we hope will carry a persuasive emotional engagement with others, in conversation and daily usage as well as in poems. A person who holds office is, quite literally (and unemotionally), an "officeholder," a word that clearly denotes what he or she does. But if we want to convince someone that an officeholder is wise, trustworthy, and deserving of political support we may call that person a "political leader" or perhaps a "statesman"; whereas if we want to promote distrust or contempt of officeholders we might call them "politicians" or "bureaucrats" or "political hacks." These latter words have clear **connotations**—suggestions of emotional coloration that imply our attitude and invite a similar one on the part of our hearers. What words **connote** can be just as important to a poem as what they denote, although some poems depend primarily on denotation and some more on connotation.

At the San Francisco Airport seems to depend primarily on denotation; the speaker tries to *specify* the meanings and implications of the parting with his daughter, and his tendency to split categories neatly for the two of them at first contributes to the sense of clarity and certainty which the speaker wants to project. He is the past (line 10) and what remains (line 24); he has age and experience, his life is the known quantity, he stands in the light. She, on the other hand, is committed to the adventure of going into the night; she seems small, fragile, and her identity exists in the uncertain future. Yet the connotations of some words carry strong emotional force as well as clear definition: that the daughter seems "small" and "fragile" to the speaker suggests his fear for her, something quite different from her sense of adventure. The neat, clean categories keep breaking down, and the speaker's feelings keep showing through. In stanza 1, the speaker tells us that the light in the terminal gives "perfect vision" but he also notices, indirectly, its artificial quality: it is "false" and "hard," suggesting the limits of the rationalism he tries to maintain. That artificial light shines over most of the poem and honors the speaker's effort, but the whole poem represents his struggle, and in stanza 4 the signals of disturbance are very strong as, despite an insistence on a vocabulary of calculation, his rational facade collapses completely. If we have observed his verbal strategies carefully, we should not be surprised to find him at the end just *staring* in the artificial light, merely awake, although the poem has shown him to be unconsciously awake to much more than he will candidly admit.

At the San Francisco Airport is an unusually intricate and complicated poem, and it offers us, if we are willing to examine very precisely its carefully crafted fabric, an unusually rich insight into how complex a thing it is to be human and have human feelings and foibles when we think we must be rational machines. Connotations often work more simply. The following poem, for example, even though it describes the mixed feelings one person has about another, depends heavily on the common connotations of fairly common words.

WALTER DE LA MARE

Slim Cunning Hands

Slim cunning hands at rest, and cozening eyes—
Under this stone one loved too wildly lies;
How false she was, no granite could declare;
    Nor all earth's flowers, how fair.

1950

What the speaker in *Slim Cunning Hands* remembers about the dead woman—her hands, her eyes—tells part of the story; her physical presence was clearly important to him, and the poem's other nouns—stone, granite, flowers—all remind us of her death and its finality. All these words denote objects having to do with rituals that memorialize a departed life. Granite and stone connote finality as well, and flowers connote fragility and suggest the shortness of life (which is why they have become the symbolic language of funerals). The way the speaker talks about the woman expresses, in just a few words, how complexly he feels about his love for her. She was loved, he says, too "wildly"—by him perhaps, and by others. The excitement she offered is suggested by the word, and also the lack of control. The words "cunning" and "cozening" help us interpret both her wildness and falsity; they suggest her calculation, cleverness, and untrustworthiness as well as her skill, persuasiveness, and ability to place. And the word "fair," a simple yet very inclusive word, suggests how totally attractive the speaker finds her: her beauty is just as incapable of being expressed by flowers as her fickleness is of being expressed in something as permanent as stone. Simple words here tell us perhaps all we need to know of a long story.

Words like "fair" and "cozening" are clearly loaded: they have strong, clear connotations and tell us what to think, what evaluation to make. The connotations may also suggest or imply the basis for the evaluation. In the two poems that follow we can readily see why the specific words are chosen because, although both poems express a preference for the same sort of feminine appearance, the grounds of appeal are vastly different.

BEN JONSON

Still to Be Neat[3]

Still[4] to be neat, still to be dressed,
As you were going to a feast;
Still to be powdered, still perfumed;
Lady, it is to be presumed,
Though art's hid causes are not found,   5
All is not sweet, all is not sound.

Give me a look, give me a face
That makes simplicity a grace;
Robes loosely flowing, hair as free;
Such sweet neglect more taketh me   10
Than all th' adulteries of art.
They strike mine eyes, but not my heart.

                                                        1609

ROBERT HERRICK

Delight in Disorder

A sweet disorder in the dress
Kindles in clothes a wantonness.
A lawn[5] about the shoulders thrown
Into a fine distractiön;
An erring lace, which here and there   5
Enthralls the crimson stomacher,[6]
A cuff neglectful, and thereby
Ribbands[7] to flow confusedly;

3. A song from Jonson's play, *The Silent Woman.*
4. Continually.

5. Scarf of fine linen.
6. Ornamental covering for the breasts.
7. Ribbons.

A winning wave, deserving note,
In the tempestuous petticoat;   10
A careless shoestring, in whose tie
I see a wild civility;
Do more bewitch me than when art
Is too precise[8] in every part.

1648

The poem *Still to Be Neat* begins by describing a woman who looks too neat and orderly; she seems too perfect to be believed, the speaker says, and he has to assume that there is a reason for such overly fastidious grooming, that she is covering up something. He worries that something is wrong underneath—that not all is "sweet" and "sound." "Sweet" could mean several possible things, and its meaning becomes clearer when it is repeated in the next stanza in a more specific context. But "sound" begins to suggest the speaker's moral earnestness: it is a strong word, implying a suspicion that something is deeply wrong.

When "sweet" is repeated in line 10, it has taken on specific attributes from what the speaker has said about things he likes in a less calculated physical appearance. Now it appears to mean easy, attractive, unpremeditated. And when the speaker springs "adulteries" on us in the next line as a description of the woman's cosmeticizing, it is clear what he fears—that the appearance of the too neat, too made-up woman covers serious flaws, things which try to make her appear someone she is not. "Adulteries" suggests the addition of something foreign, something unlike her own nature, and it is a strong, disapproving word. The "soundness" he had worried about involves her integrity; his objection is certainly moral, probably sexual. He wants his women simple and chaste; he wants them to be just what they seem to be.

The speaker in *Delight in Disorder* wants his women easy and simple too, but for different reasons. He finds disorder "sweet" too (line 1), and seems almost to be answering the first speaker, providing a different rationale for artless appearance. His grounds of preference are clear early: his support of "wantonness" (line 2) is close to the opposite in its moral suppositions of the first speaker's disapproval of "adulteries." This speaker wants a careless look because he thinks it's sexy, and many of the words he chooses suggest sensuality and availability: "distraction" (line 4), "erring" (line 5), "tempestuous" (line 10), "wild" (line 12). The speakers in the two poems read informality of dress very differently and have very different expectations of the person who dresses in a particular way. We find out quite a lot about each speaker. Their common subject allows us to see clearly how different they both are, and how what one sees is in the eye

---

8. In the 16th and 17th centuries Puritans were often called Precisians because of their fastidiousness.

of the beholder, how values and assumptions are built into the words one chooses even for description. Jonson has created a speaker who wants an informally clad woman who has a natural grace and ease of manner because she is confident of herself, dependable, and chaste. Herrick has created a speaker who finds informality of dress fetching and sexy and indicative of sensuality and availability.

It would be hard to exaggerate how important words are to poems. Poets who know their craft pick each word with care, so that each word will express exactly what needs to be expressed and suggest every emotional shade that the poem is calculated to evoke in us. Often individual words qualify and amplify one another—suggestions clarify other suggestions, and meanings grow upon meanings—and thus the way the words are put together can be important too. Notice, for example, that in *Slim Cunning Hands* the final emphasis is on how *fair* the speaker's woman was; that is his last word, the thing he can't forget in spite of his distrust of her, and that is where the poem chooses to leave the emphasis, on that one word which, even though it doesn't justify everything else, qualifies all the disappointment and hurt.

That word does not stand all by itself, however, any more than any other word in a poem can be considered all alone. Every word exists within larger units of meaning—sentences, patterns of comparisons and contrasts, the whole poem—and where the word is and how it is used often are very important. The final word or words may be especially emphatic (as in *Slim Cunning Hands*), and words that are repeated take on a special intensity, as "terminal" does in *At the San Francisco Airport* or as "chartered" and "cry" do in *London,* a poem we looked at in Chapter 2. Certain words often stand out, because they are used in an unusual way (like "chartered" in *London* or "adulteries" in *Still To Be Neat*) or because they are given an artificial prominence, through unusual sentence structure, for example, or because the title calls special attention to them. In the following poem, notice how the title calls upon us to wonder, from the beginning, how playful and how patterned the boy's bedtime romp with his father is. As you read it, try to be conscious of the emotional effects created by the choice of words that seem to be key ones. Which words establish the bond between the two males?

THEODORE ROETHKE

My Papa's Waltz

The whiskey on your breath
Could make a small boy dizzy;
But I hung on like death:
Such waltzing was not easy.

We romped until the pans   5
Slid from the kitchen shelf;

My mother's countenance
Could not unfrown itself.

The hand that held my wrist
Was battered on one knuckle;   10
At every step you missed
My right ear scraped a buckle.

You beat time on my head
With a palm caked hard by dirt,
Then waltzed me off to bed   15
Still clinging to your shirt.

1948

Exactly what is the situation in *My Papa's Waltz?* What are the economic circumstances in the family? How can you tell? What indications are there of the family's social class? of the father's line of work? How would you characterize the speaker? How does the poem indicate his pleasure in the bedtime ritual? Which words suggest the boy's excitement? Which suggest his anxiety? How can you tell how the speaker feels about his father? What clues are there about what the mother is like? How can you tell that the experience is remembered at some years' distance? What clues are there in the word choice that an adult is remembering a childhood experience? In what sense is the poem a tribute to memories of the father? How would you describe the poem's tone?

The subtlety and force of word choice is sometimes very much affected by **word order,** the way the sentences are put together. Sometimes poems are driven to unusual word order because of the demands of rhyme and meter, but ordinarily poets use word order very much as prose writers do, to create a particular emphasis. When an unusual word order is used, you can be pretty sure that something worth noticing is going on. Notice, for example, the odd constructions in the second and third stanzas of *My Papa's Waltz.* In the third stanza, the way the speaker talks about the abrasion of buckle on ear is very unusual. He does not say that the buckle scraped his ear, but rather puts it the other way round—a big difference in the kind of effect created, for it avoids placing blame and refuses to specify any unpleasant effect. Had he said that the buckle scraped his ear—the normal way of putting it—we would have to worry about the fragile ear. The **syntax** (sentence structure) of the poem channels our feeling and helps to control what we think of the waltz.

The most curious part of the poem is the second stanza, for it is there that the silent mother appears, and the syntax there is peculiar in two places. In lines 5–6, the connection between the romping and the pans falling is stated oddly: "We romped *until* the pans / Slid from the kitchen shelf." The speaker does not say that they knocked down the pans or imply that there was awkwardness, but he does suggest energetic activity and duration. He implies intensity, almost design—as though the romping were not complete until the pans fell. And the sentence about the mother—odd but effective—makes her position clear. She is a silent bystander in this male ritual, and her frown seems molded on her face. It is not as if she is frightened or angry but as if she too is performing a ritual, holding a frown on her face as if it is part of her role in the ritual, as well as perhaps a facet of her stern character. The syntax implies that she *has to* maintain the frown, and the falling of the pans almost seems to be for her benefit. She disapproves, but she is still their audience.

Word order is not always as complicated or crucial as it is in *My Papa's Waltz*, but poets often manipulate the ordinary prose order of a sentence to make a specific point or create a specific emphasis or effect. In the passage below (pp. 130–133) from *Paradise Lost*, for example, notice how the syntax first sets a formal tone for the passage, then calls attention to the complexities of theology which it expresses, and (in lines 44ff.) imitates, by holding back key elements of the grammar, the fall that is being described. The poems that follow suggest some of the ways in which poets use words and word order to create for us the various experiences they want us to have of their words.

GERARD MANLEY HOPKINS

Pied Beauty[9]

Glory be to God for dappled things—
    For skies of couple-color as a brinded[1] cow;
        For rose-moles all in stipple[2] upon trout that swim;
Fresh-firecoal chestnut-falls;[3] finches' wings;
    Landscape plotted and pieced—fold, fallow, and plow;   5
        And all trades, their gear and tackle and trim.
All things counter, original, spare, strange;
    Whatever is fickle, freckled (who knows how?)
        With swift, slow; sweet, sour; adazzle, dim;
He fathers-forth whose beauty is past change: 10
        Praise him.

1877

EMILY DICKINSON

After Great Pain

After great pain, a formal feeling comes—
The Nerves sit ceremonious, like Tombs—

9. Particolored beauty: having patches or sections of more than one color.
1. Streaked or spotted.

2. Rose-colored dots or flecks.
3. Fallen chestnuts as red as burning coals.

The stiff Heart questions was it He, that bore,
And Yesterday, or Centuries before?

The Feet, mechanical, go round—   5
Of Ground, or Air, or Ought—
A Wooden way
Regardless grown,
A Quartz contentment, like a stone—

This is the Hour of Lead—   10
Remembered, if outlived,
As Freezing Persons recollect the Snow—
First—Chill—then Stupor—then the letting go—

ca. 1862

WILLIAM CARLOS WILLIAMS

The Red Wheelbarrow

so much depends
upon

a red wheel
barrow

glazed with rain   5
water

beside the white
chickens.

1923

[handwritten annotations:]
playful: last line teases William Butler Yeats (philos, not words)
photocopying is "reproduction": like children? like sex? how risqué! What is form? Isn't freeverse, no rhyme

ANN DEAGON

Certified Copy

I have xeroxed my navel
bare-bellied in the public library
borne on the hymeneal cries
of hysteric librarians, inserted a coin
prone on the glass slab steeled myself against   5
the green light's insolent stroke
and viewed emerging
instantaneously, parthenogenously from the slit
this reproduction of my reproduction
this evidence of my most human birth.   10

[handwritten annotations:]
diction >
vs. diction >
comb. tone?
use of jargon? >
diction ~ Keats q: "choice of words" w/ regard to concrete / abstract (high-falootedbooks→ordinary / exotic literal / figurative — any substitn. "that which" for "him w"

Archives forget, Bibles[4] prevaricate
aged witnesses from age grow witless—
only the skin remembers, swirling to clench
the archetypal wound: the center holds.[5]

1978

e. e. cummings

anyone lived in a pretty how town

anyone lived in a pretty how town
(with up so floating many bells down)
spring summer autumn winter
he sang his didn't he danced his did.

Women and men (both little and small)
cared for anyone not at all
they sowed their isn't they reaped their same
sun moon stars rain

children guessed (but only a few
and down they forgot as up they grew   10
autumn winter spring summer)
that noone loved him more by more

when by now and tree by leaf
she laughed his joy she cried his grief
bird by snow and stir by still   15
anyone's any was all to her

someones married their everyones
laughed their cryings and did their dance
(sleep wake hope and then) they
said their nevers they slept their dream   20

stairs rain sun moon
(and only the snow can begin to explain
how children are apt to forget to remember
with up so floating many bells down)

one day anyone died i guess   25
(and noone stooped to kiss his face)
busy folk buried them side by side
little by little and was by was

all by all and deep by deep
and more by more they dream their sleep   30

---

4. Genealogies in family Bibles.
5. See Yeats's *The Second Coming*, (p. 342), line 3.

noone and anyone earth by april
wish by spirit and if by yes.

Women and men (both dong and ding)
summer autumn winter spring
reaped their sowing and went their came   35
sun moon stars rain

1940

JOHN MILTON

from Paradise Lost[6]

I

Of man's first disobedience, and the fruit[7]
Of that forbidden tree whose mortal taste
Brought death into the world, and all our woe,
With loss of Eden, till one greater Man
Restore us, and regain the blissful seat,   5
Sing, Heav'nly Muse,[8] that, on the secret top
Of Oreb, or Sinai, didst inspire
That shepherd who first taught the chosen seed
In the beginning how the Heav'ns and Earth
Rose out of Chaos: or, if Sion hill   10
Delight thee more, and Siloa's brook that flowed
Fast[9] by the oracle of God, I thence
Invoke thy aid to my adventurous song,
That with no middle flight intends to soar
Above th' Aonian mount,[1] while it pursues   15
Things unattempted yet in prose or rhyme.
And chiefly thou, O Spirit,[2] that dost prefer
Before all temples th' upright heart and pure,
Instruct me, for thou know'st; thou from the first

6. The opening lines of Books I and II and a short passage from Book III. The first passage states the poem's subject, and the second describes Satan's beginning address to the council of fallen angels meeting to discuss strategy; in the third, God is looking down from Heaven at his new human creation and watching Satan approach the Earth.

7. The apple, but also the consequences.

8. Addressing one of the muses and asking for aid is a convention for the opening lines of an epic; Milton complicates the standard procedure here by describing sources and circumstances of Judeo-Christian revelation rather than specifically invoking one of the nine classical muses. Sinai is the spur of Mount Oreb, where Moses ("That shepherd," line 8, who was traditionally regarded as author of the first five books of the Bible) received the Law;

Sion hill and Siloa (lines 10–11), near Jerusalem, correspond to the traditional mountain (Helicon) and springs of classical tradition. Later, in Book VII, Milton calls upon Urania, the muse of astronomy, but he does not mention by name the muse of epic poetry, Calliope.

9. Close.

1. Mt. Helicon, home of the classical muses.

2. The divine voice that inspired the Hebrew prophets. *Genesis* 1:2 says that "the Spirit of God moved upon the face of the waters" as part of the process of the original creation; Milton follows tradition in making the inspirational and communicative function of God present in creation itself. The passage echoes and merges many Biblical references to divine creation and revelation.

Wast present, and, with mighty wings outspread, 20
Dovelike sat'st brooding on the vast abyss,
And mad'st it pregnant: what in me is dark
Illumine; what is low, raise and support;
That, to the height of this great argument,[3]
I may assert Eternal Providence, 25
And justify the ways of God to men.
    Say first (for Heav'n hides nothing from thy view,
Nor the deep tract of Hell), say first what cause
Moved our grand parents, in that happy state,
Favored of Heav'n so highly, to fall off 30
From their Creator, and transgress his will
For[4] one restraint, lords of the world besides?
Who first seduced them to that foul revolt?
Th' infernal serpent; he it was, whose guile,
Stirred up with envy and revenge, deceived 35
The mother of mankind, what time[5] his pride
Had cast him out from Heav'n, with all his host
Of rebel angels, by whose aid, aspiring
To set himself in glory above his peers,
He trusted to have equaled the Most High, 40
If he opposed; and with ambitious aim
Against the throne and monarchy of God,
Raised impious war in Heav'n and battle proud,
With vain attempt. Him the Almighty Power
Hurled headlong flaming from th' ethereal sky, 45
With hideous ruin and combustion down
To bottomless perdition, there to dwell
In adamantine chains and penal fire,
Who durst defy th' Omnipotent to arms.[6]

❖   ❖   ❖

II

High on a throne of royal state, which far
Outshone the wealth of Ormus and of Ind,[7]
Or where the gorgeous East with richest hand
Show'rs on her kings barbaric pearl and gold,
Satan exalted sat, by merit raised 5
To that bad eminence; and, from despair
Thus high uplifted beyond hope, aspires
Beyond thus high, insatiate to pursue
Vain war with Heav'n, and by success[8] untaught,
His proud imaginations thus displayed: 10
    "Powers and Dominions, Deities of Heav'n,
For since no deep within her gulf can hold

---

3. Subject.
4. Because of. "besides": in all other respects.
5. When.
6. After invoking the muse and giving a brief summary of the poem's subject, an epic regularly begins *in medias res* (in the midst of things).
7. Hormuz, an island in the Persian Gulf, famous for pearls, and India.
8. Outcome, either good or bad.

Immortal vigor, though oppressed and fall'n,
I give not Heav'n for lost. From this descent
Celestial virtues rising will appear   15
More glorious and more dread than from no fall,
And trust themselves to fear no second fate.
Me though just right and the fixed laws of Heav'n
Did first create your leader, next, free choice,
With what besides, in council or in fight,   20
Hath been achieved of merit, yet this loss,
Thus far at least recovered, hath much more
Established in a safe unenvied throne
Yielded with full consent. The happier state
In Heav'n, which follows dignity, might draw   25
Envy from each inferior; but who here
Will envy whom the highest place exposes
Foremost to stand against the Thunderer's aim
Your bulwark, and condemns to greatest share
Of endless pain? Where there is then no good   30
For which to strive, no strife can grow up there
From faction; for none sure will claim in hell
Precédence, none, whose portion is so small
Of present pain, that with ambitious mind
Will covet more. With this advantage then   35
To union, and firm faith, and firm accord,
More than can be in Heav'n, we now return
To claim our just inheritance of old,
Surer to prosper than prosperity
Could have assured us; and by what best way,   40
Whether of open war or covert guile,
We now debate; who can advise, may speak."

                          ❋   ❋   ❋

                            III

                          ❋   ❋   ❋

Now had th' Almighty Father from above,   56
From the pure empyrean where he sits
High throned above all height, bent down his eye,
His own works and their works at once to view:
About him all the sanctities of Heav'n[9]   60
Stood thick as stars, and from his sight received
Beatitude past utterance; on his right
The radiant image of his glory sat,
His only Son. On earth he first beheld
Our two first parents, yet the only two   65
Of mankind, in the happy garden placed,
Reaping immortal fruits of joy and love,
Uninterrupted joy, unrivaled love,
In blissful solitude. He then surveyed
Hell and the gulf between, and Satan there   70

---

9. The hierarchies of angels.

Coasting the wall of Heav'n on this side Night
In the dun air sublime,[1] and ready now
To stoop[2] with wearied wings and willing feet
On the bare outside of this world, that seemed
Firm land embosomed without firmament,   75
Uncertain which, in ocean or in air.

1667

ROBERT GRAVES

The Cool Web

Children are dumb to say how hot the day is,
How hot the scent is of the summer rose,
How dreadful the black wastes of evening sky,
How dreadful the tall soldiers drumming by.

But we have speech, to chill the angry day,   5
And speech, to dull the rose's cruel scent.
We spell away the overhanging night,
We spell away the soldiers and the fright.

There's a cool web of language winds us in,
Retreat from too much joy or too much fear: 10
We grow sea-green at last and coldly die
In brininess and volubility.

But if we let our tongues lose self-possession,
Throwing off language and its watery clasp
Before our death, instead of when death comes,   15
Facing the wide glare of the children's day,
Facing the rose, the dark sky and the drums,
We shall go mad no doubt and die that way.

1927

1. Aloft in the twilight atmosphere.   2. Swoop down, like a bird of prey.

2nd day: speaker is ageing → addressee? We assumed a woman, love
"love," sonnet trad: but is that necess. so?
— last 2 lines + "that which": self?
— or: friendship? (other sonnets in sequence)

6   FIGURATIVE LANGUAGE

Metaphor and Simile

"that which" and
"me")thou" need
some attention,
don't leap to assumption
→ 128-129

The language of poetry is almost always picturesque. Rather than depending primarily on abstract ideas and elaborate reasoning, poems depend mainly upon the creation of pictures in our minds, helping us to see things fresh and new, or to feel them suggestively through our other physical senses, such as hearing or the sense of touch. Poetry is most often vital in the sense that it helps us form, in our minds, visual impressions. We "see" a corpse at a funeral, a child chasing geese in the garden, or two lovers sitting together on the bank of a stream, so that our response begins from a vivid impression of exactly what is happening. Some people think that those arts and media which challenge the imagination of a reader or hearer—radio drama, for example, or poetry—allow us to respond more fully than arts (such as film or theater) that actually show things more fully to our physical senses. Certainly they leave more to our imagination, to our mind's eye.

But being visual does not just mean describing, telling us facts, indicating shapes, colors, and specific details. Often the vividness of the picture in our minds depends upon comparisons. What we are trying to imagine is pictured in terms of something else familiar to us, and we are asked to think of one thing as if it were something else. Many such comparisons, or **figures of speech,** in which something is pictured or imaged or figured forth in terms of something already familiar to us, are taken for granted in daily life. Things we can't see or which aren't familiar to us are pictured as things we can; for example, God is said to be like a father, Italy is said to be shaped like a boot. Poems use figurative language much of the time. A speaker may tell us that his ladylove is like a red rose, or that the way to imagine how it feels to be spiritually secure is to think of the way a shepherd takes care of his sheep. The pictorialness of our imagination may *clarify* things for us—scenes, states of mind, ideas— but at the same time it stimulates us to think of how those pictures make us *feel.* Pictures, even when they are mental pictures or imagined visions, may be both denotative and connotative, just as individual words are: they may clarify and make precise, and they may channel our feelings. In this chapter, we will look at some of the ways that poets create pictures in our minds—images that help us think clearly about what they are saying and feel clearly the emotions they want us to feel. Most poetry depends, at least in part, on the pictorial quality of words and upon the notion that something becomes clearer when we compare it with something else that is more familiar. In the poem that follows, the poet helps us to visualize the old age and approaching death of the speaker by making comparisons with familiar things—the coming of winter, the approach of sunset, and the dying embers of a fire.

① divisions? very clear, ordered

WILLIAM SHAKESPEARE

implausible or daring ext. met. = conceit — "this bed thy centre is, these walls thy sphere"

That Time of Year

extended
tenor = aging
veh = yellow leaves

That time of year thou mayst in me behold
When yellow leaves, or none, or few, do hang
Upon those boughs which shake against the cold, *pathetic fallacy*
Bare ruined choirs, where late the sweet birds sang. *define*
In me thou see'st the twilight of such day   5
As after sunset fadeth in the west;
Which by and by[1] black night doth take away, *night ≠ death*

personification

Death's second self,[2] that seals up all in rest.
In me thou see'st the glowing of such fire,
That on the ashes of his youth doth lie,   10
As the deathbed whereon it must expire,
Consumed with that which it was nourished by.
This thou perceiv'st, which makes thy love more strong, *difference? haste—*
To love that well which thou must leave ere long.

③ loss = what's autumn? night?

④ 3 images share loss, ending →

1609

universal

what possibilities?
Who's speaking? to self?? → accommodation?
(calmness above)

The first four lines of *That Time of Year* make the comparison to seasonal change; but notice that the poet does not have the speaker say directly that his physical condition and age make him resemble autumn. He draws the comparison without stating directly that it is a comparison: you can see, he says, my own state in the coming of winter in late autumn when the leaves are almost all off the trees. The speaker portrays himself *indirectly* by talking about the passing of the year. The poem uses **metaphor**; that is, one thing is pictured *as if* it were something else. *That Time of Year* goes on to another metaphor in lines 5–8 and still another in lines 9–12, and each of the metaphors contributes to our understanding of the speaker's sense of his old age and approaching death. Even more important, however, is the way the metaphors give us feelings, an emotional sense of the speaker's age and of his own attitude toward aging. Through the metaphors we come to understand, appreciate, and to some extent share the increasing sense of anxiety and urgency that the poem expresses. Our emotional sense of the poem is largely influenced by the way each metaphor is developed and by the way each metaphor leads, with its own kind of internal logic, to another.

The images of late autumn in the first four lines all suggest loneliness, loss, and nostalgia for earlier times. As in the rest of the poem, our eyes are imagined to be the main vehicle for noticing the speaker's age and condition; the phrase "thou mayst in me behold" (line 1) introduces what we are asked to see, and in both lines 5 and 9 we are similarly told "In me thou see'st. . . ." The picture of the trees shedding their leaves suggests that autumn is nearly over, and

1. Shortly.   2. Sleep.

we can imagine trees either with yellow leaves, or without leaves, or with just a trace of foliage remaining—the latter perhaps most feelingly suggesting the bleakness and loneliness that characterize the change of seasons, the ending of the life cycle. But other senses are invoked too. The boughs shaking against the cold represent an appeal to our tactile sense, and the next line appeals to our sense of hearing, although only as a reminder that the birds no longer sing. (Notice how exact the visual representation is of the bare, or nearly bare, limbs, even as the cold and the lack of birds are noted; birds lined up like a choir on risers would have made a striking visual image on the barren limbs one above the other, but now there is only the *reminder* of what used to be. The present is quiet, bleak, trembly, and lonely.)

The next four lines are slightly different in tone, and the color changes. From a black-and-white landscape with a few yellow leaves, we come upon a rich and almost warm reminder of a faded sunset. But a somber note does enter the poem in these lines through another figure of speech, **personification**, which involves treating an abstraction, such as death or justice or beauty, as if it were a person. The poem is talking about the coming of night and of sleep, and Sleep is personified and identified as the "second self" of Death (that is, as a kind of reflection of death). The main emphasis is on how night and sleep close in on our sense of twilight, and only secondarily does a reminder of death enter the poem. But it does enter.

The third metaphor—that of the dying embers of a fire—begins in line 9 and continues to color and warm the bleak cold that the poem began with, but it also sharpens the reminder of death. The three main metaphors in the poem work in a way to make our sense of old age and approaching death more friendly, but also more immediate: moving from barren trees, to fading twilight, to dying embers suggests a sensuous increase of color and warmth, but also an increasing urgency. The first metaphor involves a whole season, or at least a segment of one, a matter of days or possibly weeks; the second involves the passing of a single day, reducing the time scale to a matter of minutes, and the third draws our attention to that split second when a glowing ember fades into a simple ash. The final part of the fire metaphor introduces the most explicit sense of death so far, as the metaphor of embers shifts into a direct reminder of death. Embers which had been a metaphor of the speaker's aging body now themselves become, metaphorically, a deathbed; the vitality that nourishes youth is used up just as a log in a fire is. The urgency of the reminder of coming death has now peaked. It is friendlier but now seems immediate and inevitable, a natural part of the life process, and the final two lines then make an explicit plea to make good and intense use of the remaining moments of human relationship.

That Time of Year represents an unusually intricate use of images to organize a poem and focus its emotional impact. Not all poems are so skillfully made, and not all depend on such a full and varied use of metaphor. But most poems use metaphors for at least part of their effect, and often a poem is based on a single metaphor which is fully developed as the major way of making the poem's statement and impact, as in this poem about the role of a mother and wife.

LINDA PASTAN

Marks

My husband gives me an A
for last night's supper,
an incomplete for my ironing,
a B plus in bed.
My son says I am average,   5
an average mother, but if
I put my mind to it
I could improve.
My daughter believes
in Pass/Fail and tells me   10
I pass. Wait 'til they learn
I'm dropping out.

                                                          1978

The speaker in *Marks* is obviously not thrilled with the idea of continually being judged, and the metaphor of marks (or grades) as a way of talking about her performance of roles in the family suggests her irritation. The list of the roles implies the many things expected of her, and the three different systems of marking (letter grades, categories to be checked off on a chart, and pass/fail) detail the difficulties of multiple standards. The poem retains the language of schooldays all the way to the end ("learn," line 11; "dropping out," line 12), and the major effect of the poem depends on the irony of the speaker's agreeing to surrender to the metaphor the family has thrust upon her; if she is to be judged as if she were a student, she retains the right to drop out. Ironically, she joins the system (adopts the metaphor for herself) in order to defeat it.

The difficulty of conveying what some experiences are like and how we feel about them sometimes leads poets to startling comparisons and figures of speech that may at first seem far-fetched but which, in one way or another, do in fact suggest the quality of the experience or the feelings associated with it. Sometimes a series of metaphors is used, as if no one kind of visualization will serve, but several together may suggest the full complexity of the experience or cumulatively define the feeling precisely. Metaphors open up virtually endless possibilities of comparison, giving words a chance to be more than words, offering our mind's eye a challenge to keep up with the fertile and articulate imagination of writers who make it their business to see things that ordinary people miss, noticing the most surprising likenesses.

Sometimes, in poetry as in prose, comparisons are made explicitly, as in the following poem.

ROBERT BURNS

A Red, Red Rose

O, my luve's like a red, red rose
That's newly sprung in June.
O, my luve is like the melodie
That's sweetly played in tune.

As fair art thou, my bonnie lass,   5
So deep in luve am I;
And I will luve thee still, my dear,
Till a' the seas gang[3] dry.

Till a' the seas gang dry, my dear,
And the rocks melt wi' the sun;   10
And I will luve thee still, my dear,
While the sands o' life shall run.

And fare thee weel, my only luve,
And fare thee weel a while!
And I will come again, my luve,   15
Though it were ten thousand mile.

1796

The first four lines make two explicit comparisons: the speaker says that his love is "like a rose" and "like a melodie." Such *explicit* comparison is called a **simile,** and usually (as here) the comparison involves the words "like" or "as." Similes work much as do metaphors, except that they usually are used more passingly, more incidentally; they make a quick comparison and usually do not elaborate, whereas metaphors often extend over a long section of a poem (in which case they are called **extended metaphors**) or even over the whole poem as in Marks (in which case they are called **controlling metaphors**).

The two similes in *A Red, Red Rose* assume that we already have a favorable opinion of roses and of melodies. Here the poet does not develop the comparison or even remind us of attractive details about roses or tunes. He pays the quick compliment and moves on. Similes sometimes develop more elaborate comparisons than this and occasionally even control long sections of a poem (in which case they are

3. Go.

called **analogies**); but usually a simile is briefer and relies more fully on something we already know. The speaker in *My Papa's Waltz* says that he hung on "like death"; he doesn't have to explain or elaborate the comparison: we know the anxiety he refers to.

Like metaphors, similes may imply both meaning and feeling; they may both explain something and invoke feelings about it. All figurative language involves an attempt to clarify something *and* to help readers feel a certain way about it. Saying that one's love is like a rose implies a delicate and fragile beauty and invites our senses into play so that we can share sensuously a response to fragrant appeal and soft touch, just as the shivering boughs and dying embers in Shakespeare's poem explain separation and loss at the same time that they allow us to share the cold sense of loneliness and the warmth of old friendship. The poems that follow suggest some other varieties of figures of speech in poems. But you will also find metaphors and similes elsewhere, in fact nearly everywhere. Once you are alerted to look for them you will find figures in poem after poem; they are among the most common devices through which poets share their vision with us.

RANDALL JARRELL

The Death of the Ball Turret Gunner[4]

From my mother's sleep I fell into the State,
And I hunched in its belly till my wet fur froze.
Six miles from earth, loosed from its dream of life,
I woke to black flak and the nightmare fighters.
When I died they washed me out of the turret with a hose.   5

1945

JOHN DONNE

Batter My Heart

Batter my heart, three-personed God; for You
As yet but knock, breathe, shine, and seek to mend;
That I may rise and stand, o'erthrow me, and bend
Your force, to break, blow, burn, and make me new.
I, like an usurped town, to another due,   5

4. "A ball turret was a plexiglass sphere set into the belly of a B-17 or B-24 and inhabited by two .50 caliber machine-guns and one man, a short, small man. When this gunner tracked with his machine-guns a fighter attacking his bomber from below, he revolved with the turret; hunched upside-down in his little sphere, he looked like the foetus in the womb. The fighters which attacked him were armed with cannon firing explosive shells. The hose was a steam hose." (Jarrell's note)

[handwritten margin: ALLEGORY]
[handwritten margin: personif.]

Labor to admit You, but Oh, to no end!
Reason, Your viceroy[5] in me, me should defend,
But is captived, and proves weak or untrue.

[handwritten margin: a 3rd image for relat. of soul to God]

Yet dearly I love You, and would be loved fain.[6]
But am betrothed unto Your enemy: *[handwritten: = ?]*   10
Divorce me, untie, or break that knot again, *[handwritten: = what ? (tenor/vehicle)]*
Take me to You, imprison me, for I,

[handwritten margin: Couplet : — ambiguous wds → solve paradox]

Except You enthrall me, never shall be free,
Nor ever chaste, except You ravish me.

1633

[handwritten: Divine violence ; sexual image of soul's desire for God ! ?]

ANONYMOUS
(Traditionally attributed to King David)   *[handwritten: Sch Rose 149]*

The Twenty-Third Psalm

The Lord is my shepherd; I shall not want.

He maketh me to lie down in green pastures: he leadeth me beside
        the still waters.
He restoreth my soul: he leadeth me in the paths of righteousness
        for his name's sake.
Yea, though I walk through the valley of the shadow of death,
        I will fear no evil: for thou art with me;
        thy rod and thy staff they comfort me.
Thou preparest a table before me in the presence of mine enemies:
        thou anointest my head with oil; my cup runneth over.
Surely goodness and mercy shall follow me all the days of my life:
        and I will dwell in the house of the Lord for ever.

BOB DYLAN

Mister Tambourine Man

Chorus

Hey, Mister Tambourine Man, play a song for me,
I'm not sleepy and there ain't no place I'm going to.
Hey, Mister Tambourine Man, play a song for me,
In the jingle, jangle morning I'll come followin' you.

I

Though I know that evenin's empire has returned into sand   5
Vanished from my hand,
Left me blindly here to stand

5. One who rules as the representative   6. Gladly.
of a higher power.

But still no sleepin'.
My weariness amazes me,
I'm branded on my feet,   10
I have no one to meet,
And the ancient empty street's
Too dead for dreamin'.
Chorus

II

Take me on a trip upon your magic swirlin' ship,
My senses have been stripped,   15
My hands can't feel to grip,
My toes too numb to step,
Wait only for my boot heels to be wanderin'.
I'm ready to go anywhere,
I'm ready for to fade   20
Into my own parade.
Cast your dancin' spell my way,
I promise to go under it.
Chorus

III

Though you might hear laughin', spinnin', swingin' madly through the
        sun,
It's not aimed at anyone,   25
It's just escapin' on the run,
And but for the sky there are no fences facin'.
And if you hear vague traces
Of skippin' reels of rhyme
To your tambourine in time,   30
It's just a ragged clown behind,
I wouldn't pay it any mind,
It's just a shadow
You're seein' that he's chasin'.
Chorus

IV

Take me disappearin' through the smoke rings of my mind   35
Down the foggy ruins of time,
Far past the frozen leaves,
The haunted, frightened trees
Out to the windy beach
Far from the twisted reach of crazy sorrow.   40
Yes, to dance beneath the diamond sky
With one hand wavin' free,
Silhouetted by the sea,
Circled by the circus sands,
With memory and fate   45
Driven deep beneath the waves.
Let me forget about today until tomorrow.
Chorus

1964

PHILIP BOOTH

One Man's Wife

Not that he promised not to windowshop,
or refuse free samples; but he gave up
exploring warehouse bargains, and forgot
the trial offers he used to mail away for.

After, that is, she laid on the counter what   5
she'd long kept hidden under the penny-candy,
and demonstrated (one up-country Sunday)
the total inventory of one wife's general store.

                                                    1966

EDWARD TAYLOR

Housewifery

Make me, O Lord, Thy spinning-wheel complete.[7]
  Thy holy Word my distaff make for me;
Make mine affections Thy swift flyers neat;
  And make my soul Thy holy spool to be;
  My conversation make to be Thy reel,   5
  And reel the yarn thereon spun of Thy wheel.

Make me Thy loom then; knit therein this twine;
  And make Thy Holy Spirit, Lord, wind quills;
Then weave the web Thyself. The yarn is fine.
  Thine ordinances make my fulling mills.   10
  Then dye the same in heavenly colors choice,
  All pinked[8] with varnished[9] flowers of paradise.

Then clothe therewith mine understanding, will,
  Affections,[1] judgment, conscience, memory,
My words and actions, that their shine may fill   15
  My ways with glory and Thee glorify.
  Then mine apparel shall display before Ye
  That I am clothed in holy robes for glory.

ca. 1700

7. Stanzas 1 and 2 specify parts of the spinning wheel and loom: the distaff (line 2) holds the fibers, flyers (line 3) twist the fibers, the spool (line 4) receives the spun thread, and the reel (line 5) stores the thread; quills (line 8) are bobbins holding the thread in the shuttle of the loom, and in the fulling mills (line 10) the cloth is cleaned and thickened.
8. Decorated.
9. Shining.
1. Emotions.

Symbol

One can get into a good argument with a literary critic, a philosopher, or just about anybody else simply by mentioning the word symbol. A symbol is many things to many people, and often it means no more than that the person using the term is dealing with something he doesn't know how to describe or think about precisely. The term is difficult to be precise about, but it can be used quite sensibly. A symbol is, put simply, something which stands for something else. The everyday world is full of common examples; a flag, a logo, a trademark, or a skull and crossbones all suggest things beyond themselves, and everyone is likely to understand what their display is meant to signify, whether or not the viewer shares a commitment to what the object represents. In common usage a prison is a symbol of confinement, constriction, and loss of freedom, and in specialized traditional usage a cross may symbolize oppression, cruelty, suffering, death, resurrection, triumph, or the intersection of two separate things, traditions, or ideas (as in crossroads and crosscurrents, for example). The specific symbolic significance is controlled by the context; a reader may often decide by looking at contiguous details in the poem and by examining the poem's attitude toward a particular tradition or body of beliefs; a star means one kind of thing to a Jewish poet and something else to a Christian poet, still something else to a Nazi or to someone whose religion is surfing. In a very literal sense, words themselves are all symbols (they stand for an object, action, or quality, not just for letters or sounds), but symbols in poetry are said to be those words and groups of words which have a range of reference beyond their literal denotation.

Poems sometimes create a symbol out of a thing, action, or event which has no previously agreed upon symbolic significance. In the following poem, for example, a random gesture is given symbolic significance.

SHARON OLDS

Leningrad Cemetery, Winter of 1941[1]

That winter, the dead could not be buried.
The ground was frozen, the gravediggers weak from hunger,
the coffin wood used for fuel. So they were covered with
    something
and taken on a child's sled to the cemetery
in the sub-zero air. They lay on the soil,   5
some of them wrapped in dark cloth
bound with rope like the tree's ball of roots

when it waits to be planted; others wound in sheets,
their pale, gauze, tapered shapes
stiff as cocoons that will split down the center   10
when the new life inside is prepared;
but most lay like corpses, their coverings
coming undone, naked calves
hard as corded wood spilling
from under a cloak, a hand reaching out   15
with no sign of peace, wanting to come back
even to the bread made of glue and sawdust,
even to the icy winter, and the siege.

p. 1979

All of the corpses—frozen, neglected, beginning to be in disarray—vividly stamp upon our minds a sense of the horrors of war, and the detailed picture of the random, uncounted clutter of bodies is likely to stick in our minds long after we have finished reading the poem. Several of the details are striking, and the poem's language heightens our sense of them. The corpses wound in sheets, for example, are described in "their pale, gauze, tapered shapes," and they are compared to cocoons that one day will split and emit new life; and the limbs that dangle loose when the coverings come undone are said to be "hard as corded wood spilling." But clearly the most memorable sight is the hand dangling from one corpse that is coming unwrapped, for the poet invests that hand with special significance, giving its gesture *meaning*. The hand is described as "reaching out . . . wanting to come back": it is as if the dead can still gesture even if they cannot speak, and the gesture seems to signify the desire of the dead to come back at any price. They would be glad to be alive, even under the grim conditions that attend the living in Leningrad during this grim war. Suddenly the grimness which we—living—have been witnessing pales by comparison with what the dead have lost simply by being dead. The hand has been made to **symbolize** the desire of the dead to return, to be alive, to be still among us, anywhere. The hand reaches out in the poem as a gesture that means; the poet has made it a symbol of desire.

The whole array of dead bodies in the poem might be said to be symbolic as well. As a group, they stand for the human waste that the war has produced, and their dramatic visual presence on the scene provides the poem with a dramatic visualization of how war and its requirements have no time for decency, not even the decency of burial. The bodies are a symbol in the sense that they stand for what the poem as a whole asserts.

This next poem also arises out of a historical moment, but this time the event is a personal one which the poet gives a significance by the interpretation he puts upon it.

JAMES DICKEY

The Leap

The only thing I have of Jane MacNaughton
Is one instant of a dancing-class dance.
She was the fastest runner in the seventh grade,
My scrapbook says, even when boys were beginning
To be as big as the girls,   5
But I do not have her running in my mind,
Though Frances Lane is there, Agnes Fraser,
Fat Betty Lou Black in the boys-against-girls
Relays we ran at recess: she must have run

Like the other girls, with her skirts tucked up   10
So they would be like bloomers,
But I cannot tell; that part of her is gone.
What I do have is when she came,
With the hem of her skirt where it should be
For a young lady, into the annual dance   15
Of the dancing class we all hated, and with a light
Grave leap, jumped up and touched the end
Of one of the paper-ring decorations

To see if she could reach it. She could,
And reached me now as well, hanging in my mind   20
From a brown chain of brittle paper, thin
And muscular, wide-mouthed, eager to prove
Whatever it proves when you leap
In a new dress, a new womanhood, among the boys
Whom you easily left in the dust   25
Of the passionless playground. If I said I saw
In the paper where Jane MacNaughton Hill,

Mother of four, leapt to her death from a window
Of a downtown hotel, and that her body crushed-in
The top of a parked taxi, and that I held   30
Without trembling a picture of her lying cradled
In that papery steel as though lying in the grass,
One shoe idly off, arms folded across her breast,
I would not believe myself. I would say
The convenient thing, that it was a bad dream   35
Of maturity, to see that eternal process

Most obsessively wrong with the world
Come out of her light, earth-spurning feet
Grown heavy: would say that in the dusty heels
Of the playground some boy who did not depend   40
On speed of foot, caught and betrayed her.
Jane, stay where you are in my first mind:

It was odd in that school, at that dance.
I and the other slow-footed yokels sat in corners
Cutting rings out of drawing paper   45

Before you leapt in your new dress
And touched the end of something I began,
Above the couples struggling on the floor,
New men and women clutching at each other
And prancing foolishly as bears: hold on   50
To that ring I made for you, Jane—
My feet are nailed to the ground
By dust I swallowed thirty years ago—
While I examine my hands.

                                                    1967

Memory is crucial to *The Leap*. The fact that Jane MacNaughton's graceful leap in dancing class has stuck in the speaker's mind for all these years means that this leap was important to him, meant something to him, stood for something in his mind. For the speaker, the leap is an "instant" and the "only thing" he has of Jane. Its grace and ease are what he remembers, and he struggles at several points to articulate its meaning (lines 15–26, 44–50), but even without articulation or explanation it is there in his head as a visual memory, a symbol for him of something beyond himself, something he cannot do, something he wanted to be. What that leap had stood for, or symbolized, was boldness, confidence, accomplishment, maturity, the ability to go beyond her fellow students in dancing class—the transcending of childhood by someone beginning to be a woman. Her feet now seem "earth-spurning" (line 38) in that original leap, and they separate her from everyone else. Jane MacNaughton was beyond the speaker's abilities and any attempt he could make to articulate his hopes, but not beyond his dreams. And even before articulation, she symbolized that dream.

The leap to her death seems cruelly ironic in the context of her earlier leap. In memory she is suspended in air, as if there were no gravity, no coming back to earth, as if life could exist as dream. And so the photograph, recreated in precise detail, is a cruel dashing of the speaker's dream—a detailed record of the ending of a leap, a denial of the suspension in which his memory had held her. His dream is grounded; her mortality is insistent. But what the speaker wants to hang on to (line 42) is still that symbolic moment which, although now confronted in more mature implications, will never be altogether replaced or surrendered.

The leap is ultimately symbolic in the *poem*, too, not just in the speaker's mind. In the poem (and for us as readers) the symbolism of the leap is double: the first leap is aspiration, and the second is frustration of high hopes; the two are complementary, one unable to be imagined without the other. The poem is horrifying in some ways, a dramatic reminder that human beings don't ultimately transcend their mortality, their limits, no matter how heroic or unencumbered by gravity they may seem to an observer. But it is not altogether sad and despairing either, partly because it notices and affirms the validity of the original leap and partly because another symbol is created and elaborated in the poem. That symbol is the paper chain.

The chain connects Jane to the speaker both literally and figuratively. It is, in part, *his* paper chain which she had leaped to touch in dancing class (lines 18–19), and he thinks of her first leap as "touch[ing] the end of something I began" (line 47). He and the other "slow footed," earthbound "yokels" (line 44) were the makers of the chain, and thus they are connected to her original leap, just as a photograph glimpsed in a paper connects the speaker to her second leap. The paper in the chain is "brittle" (line 21), and its creators seem dull artisans compared to the artistic performer that Jane was. They are heavy and left in the dust (lines 25, 52–53), and she is "light" (line 16) and able to transcend them but even in transcendence touching their lives and what they are able to do. And so the paper chain becomes the poem's symbol of linkage, connecting lower accomplishment to higher possibility, the artisan to the artist, material substance to the act of imagination. And the speaker at the end examines the hands that made the chain because those hands certify his connection to her and the imaginative leap she had made for him. The chain thus symbolizes not only the lower capabilities of those who cannot leap like the budding Jane could, but (later) the connection with her leap as both transcendence and mortality. Like the leap itself, the chain has been elevated to special meaning, given symbolic significance, by the poet's treatment of it. A leap and a chain have no necessary significance in themselves to most of us—at least no significance that we have all agreed upon together.

But some objects and acts do have such significance. Over the years some things have acquired an agreed-upon significance, an accepted value in our minds. They already stand for something before the poet cites them; they are **traditional symbols.** Their uses in poetry have to do with the fact that poets can count on a recognition of their traditional suggestions and meanings outside the poem, and the poem does not have to propose or argue a particular symbolic value. Birds, for example, traditionally symbolize flight, freedom from confinement, detachment from earthbound limits, the ability to soar beyond rationality and transcend mortal limits. Traditionally, birds have also been linked with imagination, especially poetic imagination, and poets often identify with them as ideal singers of songs, as in Keats's *Ode to a Nightingale* (p. 254). One of the most traditional symbols is that of the rose. It may be a simple and fairly plentiful flower in its season, but it has been allowed to stand for particular qualities for so long that to name it raises predictable expectations. Its beauty, delicacy, fragility, shortness of life, and depth of color have made it a symbol of the transitoriness of beauty, and countless poets have counted on its accepted symbolism—sometimes to compliment a friend (as Burns does in *A Red, Red Rose*) or sometimes to make a point about the nature of symbolism. The following poem draws on, in a quite traditional way, the traditional meanings.

JOHN CLARE

Love's Emblem

Go, rose, my Chloe's[2] bosom grace:
  How happy should I prove,
Could I supply that envied place
  With never-fading love.

Accept, dear maid, now summer glows,   5
  This pure, unsullied gem,
Love's emblem in a full-blown rose,
  Just broken from the stem.

Accept it as a favorite flower
  For thy soft breast to wear;   10
'Twill blossom there its transient hour,
  A favorite of the fair.

Upon thy cheek its blossom glows,
  As from a mirror clear,
Making thyself a living rose,   15
  In blossom all the year.

It is a sweet and favorite flower
  To grace a maiden's brow,
Emblem of love without its power—
  A sweeter rose art thou.   20

The rose, like hues of insect wing,
  May perish in an hour;
'Tis but at best a fading thing,
  But thou'rt a living flower.

The roses steeped in morning dews   25
  Would every eye enthrall,
But woman, she alone subdues;
  Her beauty conquers all.

1873

The speaker in *Love's Emblem* sends the rose to Chloe to decorate her bosom (lines 1, 10) and reflect the blush of her cheek and brow (lines 13, 18), and he goes on to mention some of the standard meanings: the rose is pure (line 6), transitory (line 11), fragrant, beautiful, and always appreciated (line 17). The poet need not elaborate or argue these things; he can assume the reader's acquiescence. To

2. A standard "poetic" name for a woman in traditional love poetry.

say that the rose is an emblem of love is to say that it traditionally symbolizes love, and the speaker expects Chloe to accept his gift readily; she will understand it as a compliment, a pledge, and a bond. She will understand, too, that her admirer is being conventional and complimentary in going on to call her (and women in general) a rose (line 20), except that her qualities are said to be more lasting than those of a momentary flower.

Several of the poems at the end of this chapter explore the traditional meanings of the rose as symbol, sometimes playing with the meanings and modifying them, sometimes consciously trying to create new and untraditional meanings (as in *Roses and Revolutions*), sometimes calling attention to the deterioration of nature as well as to the tradition (*Southern Gothic*), or suggesting the primacy of symbol over physical artifact (*Poem*: "The rose fades").

Sometimes symbols—traditional or not—become so insistent in the world of a poem that the larger referential world is left almost totally behind. In such cases the symbol is everything, and the poem does not just *use* symbols but becomes a symbolic poem.

Here is an example of such a poem:

[handwritten: — read : not horticulture (flying invisible worms), not literal — contrast symbol + allegory → ok not to fully trap meaning here]

WILLIAM BLAKE

The Sick Rose[3]

O rose, thou art sick.
The invisible worm
That flies in the night
In the howling storm

Has found out thy bed
Of crimson joy,
And his dark secret love
Does thy life destroy.

1794

[handwritten: — sensual (sexual) see Hughes → — but why not for spiritual, "Donne? Lots of good/evil connotations as well as sensual —]

[handwritten: That Time B5]

The poem does not seem to be about a rose, but about what the rose represents—not in this case something altogether understandable through the traditional meanings of rose.

We know that the rose is usually associated with beauty and love, often with sex; and here several key terms have sexual connotations: "bed," "worm," and "crimson joy." The violation of the rose by the

3. In Renaissance emblem books, the scarab beetle, worm, and rose are closely associated: The beetle feeds on dung, and the smell of the rose is fatal to it.

worm is the poem's main concern; the violation seems to have involved secrecy, deceit, and "dark" motives, and the result is sickness rather than the joy of love. The poem is sad; it involves a sense of hurt and tragedy, nearly of despair. The poem cries out against the misuse of the rose, against its desecration, implying that instead of a healthy joy in sensuality and sexuality, in this case, there has been destruction and hurt because of misunderstanding and repression and lack of sensitivity.

do they?

But to say so much about this poem I have had to extrapolate from other poems by this poet, and have introduced information from outside the poem. Fully symbolic poems often require that, and thus they ask us to go beyond the normal procedures of reading which we have discussed here. As presented in this poem, the rose is not part of the normal world that we ordinarily see, and it is symbolic in a special sense. The poet does not simply take an object from that everyday world and give it special significance, making it a symbol in the same sense that the leap is a symbol, or the corpse's hand. Here the rose seems to belong to its own world, a world made entirely inside the poem. The rose is not referential. The whole poem is symbolic; it is not paraphrasable; it lives in its own world. But what is the rose here a symbol of? In general terms, we can say from what the poem tells us; but we may not be as confident as we can be in the more nearly everyday world of *The Leap* or *Leningrad Cemetery, Winter of 1941,* poems that contain actions we recognize from the world of probabilities in which we live. In *The Sick Rose,* it seems inappropriate to ask the standard questions: What rose? Where? Which worm? What are the particulars here? In the world of this poem worms can fly and may be invisible. We are altogether in a world of meanings.

Negotiation of meanings in symbolic poems can be very difficult indeed; the skill of reading symbolic poems is an advanced skill that depends on special knowledge of authors and of the traditions they work from, and these skills need to be developed carefully and cautiously under the tutelage of a skilled teacher. You will find in this book some examples of symbolic poems (*Sailing to Byzantium,* for example), but the symbols you will usually find in poems are referential, and these meanings are readily discoverable from the careful study of the poems themselves, as in poems like *The Leap* and *Love's Emblem.*

WILLIAM HABINGTON

To Roses in the Bosom of Castara

Ye blushing virgins happy are
In the chaste nunn'ry of her breasts,

For he'd profane so chaste a fair,[4]
Whoe'er should call them Cupid's nests.

Transplanted thus, how bright ye grow,   5
How rich a perfume do ye yield.
In some close garden, cowslips so
Are sweeter than i' th' open field.

In those white cloisters live secure
From the rude blasts of wanton breath,   10
Each hour more innocent and pure,
Till you shall wither into death.

Then that which living gave you room,
Your glorious sepulcher shall be;
There wants[5] no marble for a tomb,   15
Whose breast hath marble been to me.

                                                    1634

ROBERT FROST

The Rose Family[6]

The rose is a rose,
And was always a rose.
But the theory now goes
That the apple's a rose,
And the pear is, and so's
The plum, I suppose.
The dear only knows
What will next prove a rose.
You, of course, are a rose—
But were always a rose.   10

                                                    1928

DOROTHY PARKER

One Perfect Rose

A single flow'r he sent me, since we met.
    All tenderly his messenger he chose;
Deep-hearted, pure, with scented dew still wet—
    One perfect rose.

4. Beautiful woman.
5. Lacks.

6. A response to Gertrude Stein's famous line, "A rose is a rose is a rose."

I knew the language of the floweret;   5
  "My fragile leaves," it said, "his heart enclose."
Love long has taken for his amulet
    One perfect rose.

Why is it no one ever sent me yet
    One perfect limousine, do you suppose?   10
Ah no, it's always just my luck to get
    One perfect rose.

1937

DONALD JUSTICE

Southern Gothic

(*for W.E.B. & P.R.*)

Something of how the homing bee at dusk
Seems to inquire, perplexed, how there can be
No flowers here, not even withered stalks of flowers,
Conjures a garden where no garden is
And trellises too frail almost to bear   5
The memory of a rose, much less a rose.
Great oaks, more monumentally great oaks now
Than ever when the living rose was new,
Cast shade that is the more completely shade
Upon a house of broken windows merely   10
And empty nests up under broken eaves.
No damask any more prevents the moon,
But it unravels, peeling from a wall,
Red roses within roses within roses.

1960

DUDLEY RANDALL

Roses and Revolutions

Musing on roses and revolutions,
I saw night close down on the earth like a great dark wing,
and the lighted cities were like tapers in the night,
and I heard the lamentations of a million hearts
regretting life and crying for the grave,   5
and I saw the Negro lying in the swamp with his face blown off,
and in northern cities with his manhood maligned and felt the
   writhing
of his viscera like that of the hare hunted down or the bear at bay,

and I saw men working and taking no joy in their work
and embracing the hard-eyed whore with joyless excitement   10
and lying with wives and virgins in impotence.

And as I groped in darkness
and felt the pain of millions,
gradually, like day driving night across the continent,
I saw dawn upon them like the sun a vision   15
of a time when all men walk proudly through the earth
and the bombs and missiles lie at the bottom of the ocean
like the bones of dinosaurs buried under the shale of eras,
and men strive with each other not for power or the accumulation
   of paper
but in joy create for others the house, the poem, the game of   20
   athletic beauty.

Then washed in the brightness of this vision,
I saw how in its radiance would grow and be nourished and
   suddenly
burst into terrible and splendid bloom
the blood-red flower of revolution.

1968

WILLIAM CARLOS WILLIAMS

Poem

The rose fades
and is renewed again
by its seed, naturally
but where

save in the poem   5
shall it go
to suffer no diminution
of its splendor

1962

7 STRUCTURE

"Proper words in proper places": that is the way one great writer of English prose (Jonathan Swift) described good writing. Finding appropriate words is not the easiest of tasks for a poet, and in the last two chapters we have looked at some of the implications for readers of the choices a poet makes. But a poet's decision about where to put those words is also difficult, for individual words, metaphors, and symbols not only exist as part of a phrase or sentence or rhythmic pattern but also as part of the larger whole of the poem itself. How is the whole poem to be organized? What will come first and what last? How is some sort of structure to be created? How are words, sentences, images, ideas, feelings to be put together into something that holds together, seems complete, and will have a certain effect upon us as readers?

Looking at these questions from the point of view of the maker of the poem (What shall I plan? Where shall I begin?) can have the advantage of helping us as readers to notice the effect of structural decisions. In a sense, every single poem is different from every other, and therefore independent, individual decisions must be made about how to organize. But there are also patterns of organization that poems fall into, sometimes because of the subject matter, sometimes because of the effect intended, sometimes for other reasons. Often poets consciously decide on a particular organizational strategy, sometimes they may reach instinctively for one or happen into a structure that suits the needs of the moment, one onto which a creator can hang the words one by one.

When there is a story to be told, the organization of a poem may be fairly simple, as in this popular ballad:

ANONYMOUS

Frankie and Johnny

Frankie and Johnny were lovers,
    Lordy, how they could love,
Swore to be true to each other,
    True as the stars up above,
        He was her man, but he done her wrong.   5

Frankie went down to the corner,
    To buy her a bucket of beer,
Frankie says "Mister Bartender,
    Has my lovin' Johnny been here?
        He is my man, but he's doing me wrong."   10

"I don't want to cause you no trouble
    Don't want to tell you no lie,

I saw your Johnny half-an-hour ago
    Making love to Nelly Bly.
        He is your man, but he's doing you wrong."   15

Frankie went down to the hotel
    Looked over the transom so high,
There she saw her lovin Johnny
    Making love to Nelly Bly.
        He was her man; he was doing her wrong.   20

Frankie threw back her kimono,
    Pulled out her big forty-four;
Rooty-toot-toot: three times she shot
    Right through that hotel door,
        She shot her man, who was doing her wrong.   25

"Roll me over gently,
    Roll me over slow,
Roll me over on my right side,
    'Cause these bullets hurt me so,
        I was your man, but I done you wrong."   30

Bring all your rubber-tired hearses
    Bring all your rubber-tired hacks,
They're carrying poor Johnny to the burying ground
    And they ain't gonna bring him back,
        He was her man, but he done her wrong.   35

Frankie says to the sheriff,
    "What are they going to do?"
The sheriff he said to Frankie,
    "It's the 'lectric chair for you.
        He was your man, and he done you wrong."   40

"Put me in that dungeon,
    Put me in that cell,
Put me where the northeast wind
    Blows from the southeast corner of hell,
        I shot my man, 'cause he done me wrong."   45
                        (19th century)

When a strict narrative pattern organizes a poem, events follow upon one another in a generally chronological order, but even then a lot of artistic decisions need to be made just as in a short story or novel. Does one begin at the beginning, or begin in the middle at an exciting point, and then circle back and explain earlier events? How much detail should be given? How much description of setting is necessary and where should one stop or slow the narrative to insert it? How much explanation of motives is needed and when should it be provided? Should some details be held back for greater suspense? Should there be subplots or digressions? Is an interpretation or reflection desirable, at the end or at some earlier point?

Even in a poem with as straightforward a **narrative structure** as that of *Frankie and Johnny*, pure chronology is not the only consideration in finding places for the words. The first stanza of the poem provides an overview, some background, and even a hint of the catastrophe ("he done her wrong"). Stanzas 2 and 3 move the story along swiftly, but not by the most economical narrative means possible; instead, the poem adds some color and flavor by including the dialogue between Frankie and the bartender. Except for the repeated refrain (which keeps the whole story continuously in view), the next three stanzas are straightforward, and efficient, up through the shooting and Johnny's confession of infidelity. The final three stanzas also proceed chronologically—through the funeral, the conversation between Frankie and the sheriff, and Frankie's final reflections. The poem does not ever violate chronology, strictly speaking, but one can readily imagine quite a different emphasis from the very same facts told in much the same order. Chronology has guided the construction of the poem, but the final effects depend just as much upon the decision of which details to include, on the decision to include so much dialogue, on the decision to follow Frankie's progress through the events rather than Johnny's, and on the decision to include a summary refrain in each stanza.

Purely narrative poems can often be very long, much longer than can be included in a book like this, and often there are many features that are not, strictly speaking, closely connected to the narrative or linked to a strict chronology. Very often a poem moves on from a narrative of an event to some sort of commentary or reflection upon it, as in *Auto Wreck* (at the end of this chapter) or *When Lilacs Last in the Dooryard Bloomed* (p. 518). Reflection can be included along the way or may be implicit in the way the story is narrated, as in *Woodchucks* (p. 42) where our major attention is more on the narrator and her responses than on the events in the story as such.

Just as they sometimes take on a structure rather like that of a story, poems sometimes borrow the structures of plays. The following poem has a **dramatic structure**; it consists of a series of scenes, each of which is presented vividly and in detail:

HOWARD NEMEROV

The Goose Fish

On the long shore, lit by the moon
To show them properly alone,
Two lovers suddenly embraced
So that their shadows were as one.
The ordinary night was graced   5

For them by the swift tide of blood
That silently they took at flood,
And for a little time they prized
   Themselves emparadised.

Then, as if shaken by stage-fright   10
Beneath the hard moon's bony light,
They stood together on the sand
Embarrassed in each other's sight
But still conspiring hand in hand,
Until they saw, there underfoot,   15
As though the world had found them out,
The goose fish turning up, though dead,
   His hugely grinning head.

There in the china light he lay,
Most ancient and corrupt and gray   20
They hesitated at his smile,
Wondering what it seemed to say
To lovers who a little while
Before had thought to understand,
By violence upon the sand,   25
The only way that could be known
   To make a world their own.

It was a wide and moony grin
Together peaceful and obscene;
They knew not what he would express,   30
So finished a comedian
He might mean failure or success,
But took it for an emblem of
Their sudden, new and guilty love
To be observed by, when they kissed,   35
   That rigid optimist.

So he became their patriarch,
Dreadfully mild in the half-dark.
His throat that the sand seemed to choke,
His picket teeth, these left their mark   40
But never did explain the joke
That so amused him, lying there
While the moon went down to disappear
Along the still and tilted track
   That bears the zodiac.   45

                   1955

The first stanza sets the scene—a sandy shore in moonlight—and presents, in fact, the major action of the poem. The rest of the poem dramatizes the lovers' reactions: their initial embarrassment and feelings of guilt (stanza 2), their attempt to interpret the goose fish's smile (stanza 3), their decision to make him, whatever his meaning, the "emblem" of their love (stanza 4), and their acceptance of the fish's ambiguity and of their own relationship (stanza 5). The five stanzas do not exactly present five different scenes, but they do present separate dramatic moments, even if only a few minutes apart. Almost like a play of five very short acts, the poem traces the drama of the lovers' discovery of themselves, of their coming to terms with the meaning of their action. As in many plays, the central event (their love-making) is not the central focus of the drama, although the drama is based upon that event and could not take place without it. Here, that event is depicted only briefly but very vividly through figurative language: "they took at flood" the "swift tide of blood," and the immediate effect is to make them briefly feel "emparadised." But the poem concentrates on their later reactions, not on the act of love itself.

Their sudden discovery of the fish is a rude shock and injects a grotesque, almost macabre note into the poem. From a vision of paradise, the poem seems for a moment to turn toward a gothic horror story when the lovers discover that they have, after all, been seen—and by such a ghoulish spectator. The last three stanzas gradually recreate the intruder in their minds, as they are forced to admit that their act of love does not exist in isolation as they had at first hoped, and they begin to see it as part of a continuum, as part of their relationship to the larger world, even (at the end) putting it into the context of the rotating world and its seasons as the moon disappears into its zodiac. In retrospect, we can see that even at the moment of passion they were in touch with larger processes controlled by the presiding mood (the "swift tide of blood"), but neither the lovers nor we had understood their act as such then, and the poem is about their gradual recognition.

Stages of feeling and knowing rather than specific visual scenes are responsible for the poem's progress, and its dramatic structure depends upon internal perceptions and internal states of mind rather than dialogue and events. Visualization and images help to organize the poem too. Notice in particular how the two most striking visual features of the poem—the fish and the moon—are presented stanza by stanza. In stanza 1, the fish is not yet noticed, and the moon exists plain; it is only mentioned, not described, and its light serves as a stage spotlight to assure not center-stage attention, but rather total privacy: it is a kind of lookout for the lovers. The stage imagery, barely suggested by the light in stanza 1, is articulated in stanza 2, and there the moon is said to be "hard" and its light "bony"; its features have characteristics that seem more appropriate to the fish which has now become visible. In stanza 3, the moon's light has come to seem fragile ("china") as it is said to expose the fish directly; the role of the moon as lookout and protector seems abandoned, or at least endangered. No moon appears in stanza 4, but the fish's grin is described as "wide and moony," almost as if the two onlookers, one earthly and dead, the other heavenly and eternal, had become merged in the poem, as they nearly had been by the imagery in stanza 2. And by stanza 5, the fish has become a friend—by now he is a comedian, optimist, emblem, and a patriarch of their love—and his new position in collaboration with the lovers is presided over by the moon going about its eternal business. The moon has provided the stage light for the poem and the means by which not only the fish but the meaning of the lovers' act has been discovered. The moon has also helped to organize the poem, partly as a dramatic accessory, partly as imagery.

The following poem is also dramatic, but it seems to represent a composite of several similar experiences rather than a single event— a fairly common pattern in dramatic poems:

PHILIP LARKIN

Church Going

Once I am sure there's nothing going on
I step inside, letting the door thud shut.
Another church: matting, seats, and stone,
And little books; sprawlings of flowers, cut
For Sunday, brownish now; some brass and stuff   5
Up at the holy end; the small neat organ;
And a tense, musty, unignorable silence,
Brewed God knows how long. Hatless, I take off
My cycle-clips in awkward reverence,

Move forward, run my hand around the font.[1]   10
From where I stand, the roof looks almost new—
Cleaned, or restored? Someone would know: I don't.
Mounting the lectern, I peruse a few
Hectoring[2] large-scale verses, and pronounce
"Here endeth" much more loudly than I'd meant.   15
The echoes snigger briefly. Back at the door
I sign the book, donate an Irish sixpence,
Reflect the place was not worth stopping for.

Yet stop I did: in fact I often do,
And always end much at a loss like this,   20
Wondering what to look for; wondering, too,
When churches fall completely out of use
What we shall turn them into, if we shall keep
A few cathedrals chronically on show,
Their parchment, plate and pyx[3] in locked cases,   25
And let the rest rent-free to rain and sheep.
Shall we avoid them as unlucky places?

Or, after dark, will dubious women come
To make their children touch a particular stone;
Pick simples[4] for a cancer; or on some   30
Advised night see walking a dead one?

1. A bowl for baptismal water, mounted on a stone pedestal.
2. Intimidating.
3. A container for the Eucharist.
4. Medicinal herbs.

Power of some sort or other will go on
In games, in riddles, seemingly at random;
But superstition, like belief, must die,
And what remains when disbelief has gone?   35
Grass, weedy pavement, brambles, buttress, sky,

A shape less recognizable each week,
A purpose more obscure. I wonder who
Will be the last, the very last, to seek
This place for what it was; one of the crew   40
That tap and jot and know what rood-lofts[5] were?
Some ruin-bibber,[6] randy for antique,
Or Christmas-addict, counting on a whiff
Of gown-and-bands and organ-pipes and myrrh?
Or will he be my representative,   45

Bored, uninformed, knowing the ghostly silt
Dispersed, yet tending to this cross of ground
Through suburb scrub because it held unspilt
So long and equably what since is found
Only in separation—marriage, and birth,   50
And death, and thoughts of these—for whom was built
This special shell? For, though I've no idea
What this accoutered frowsty barn is worth,
It pleases me to stand in silence here;

A serious house on serious earth it is,   55
In whose blent air all our compulsions meet,
Are recognized, and robed as destinies.
And that much never can be obsolete,
Since someone will forever be surprising
A hunger in himself to be more serious,   60
And gravitating with it to this ground,
Which, he once heard, was proper to grow wise in,
If only that so many dead lie round.

1955

Ultimately, the poem's emphasis is upon what it means to visit churches, what sort of phenomenon church buildings represent, and what one is to make of the fact that "church going" (in the usual sense of the word) has declined so much. The poem uses a *different* sort of church-going (visitation by tourists) to consider larger philosophical questions about the relationship of religion to culture and history. The poem is, finally, a rather philosophical one about the directions of English culture, and through an enumeration of religious

5. Galleries atop the screens (on which crosses are mounted) which divide the naves or main bodies of churches from the choirs or chancels.
6. Literally, ruin-drinker: someone extremely attracted to antiquarian objects.

objects and rituals it reviews the history of how we got to our present historical circumstance. It tells a kind of story first, through one lengthy dramatized scene, in order to comment later on what the place and the experience may mean, and the larger conclusion derives from the particulars of what the speaker does and touches. The action is really over by the end of stanza 2, and that action, we are told, stands for many such visits to similar churches; after that, all is reflection and discussion, five stanzas' worth.

Church Going is a curious, funny poem in many ways. It goes to a lot of trouble to characterize its speaker, who seems a rather odd choice as a commentator on the state of religion. His informal attire (he takes off his cycle-clips at the end of stanza 1) and his not exactly worshipful behavior do not at first make us expect him to be a serious philosopher about what all this means. He is not disrespectful or sacrilegious, and before the end of stanza 1 he has tried to describe the "awkward reverence" he feels, but his overly somber imitation of part of the service stamps him as playful and as a tourist here, not someone who regularly drops in for prayer or meditation in the usual sense. And yet those early details do give him credentials, in a way; he clearly knows the names of religious objects and has some of the history of churches in his grasp. Clearly he does this sort of church-going often ("Yet stop I did; in fact I often do," line 19) because he wonders seriously what it all means—now—in comparison to what it meant to religious worshipers in times past. Ultimately, he takes the church itself seriously and its cultural meaning and function just as seriously (lines 55ff.), understanding its important place in the history of his culture. In this poem, the drama is, relatively speaking, brief, but it gives a context for the more digressive and rambling free-floating reflections that grow out of the dramatic experience.

Poems often have **discursive structures** too; that is, they are sometimes organized like a treatise, an argument, or an essay. "First," they say, "and second . . . and third. . . ." This sort of 1–2–3 structure takes a variety of forms depending on what one is enumerating or arguing. Here, for example, is a poem that is about three people who have died. The poem honors all three, but makes clear and sharp distinctions between them. As you read the poem, try to articulate just what sort of person each of the three is represented to be.

JAMES WRIGHT

Arrangements with Earth for Three Dead Friends

Sweet earth, he ran and changed his shoes to go
Outside with other children through the fields.
He panted up the hills and swung from trees
Wild as a beast but for the human laughter
That tumbled like a cider down his cheeks.   5
Sweet earth, the summer has been gone for weeks,
And weary fish already sleeping under water

Below the banks where early acorns freeze.
Receive his flesh and keep it cured of colds.
Button his coat and scarf his throat from snow.   10

And now, bright earth, this other is out of place
In what, awake, we speak about as tombs.
He sang in houses when the birds were still
And friends of his were huddled round till dawn
After the many nights to hear him sing.   15
Bright earth, his friends remember how he sang
Voices of night away when wind was one.
Lonely the neighborhood beneath your hill
Where he is waved away through silent rooms.
Listen for music, earth, and human ways.   20

Dark earth, there is another gone away,
But she was not inclined to beg of you
Relief from water falling or the storm.
She was aware of scavengers in holes
Of stone, she knew the loosened stones that fell   25
Indifferently as pebbles plunging down a well
And broke for the sake of nothing human souls.
Earth, hide your face from her where dark is warm.
She does not beg for anything, who knew
The change of tone, the human hope gone gray.   30

                                                                  1957

Why, in stanza 1, is the earth represented as a parent? What does
addressing the earth here as "sweet" seem to mean? How does the
address to earth as "bright" fit the dead person described in stanza 2?
In what different senses is the person described in stanza 3 "dark"?
Why is the earth asked to give attention secretly to this person? Ex-
actly what kind of person was she? How does the poem make you feel
about her? Is there any cumulative point in describing three such
different people in the same poem? What is accomplished by having
the poem's three stanzas addressed to various aspects of earth? Simi-
lar discursive structures help to organize poems such as Shelley's *Ode
to the West Wind* (p. 169), where the wind is shown driving a leaf
in Part I, a cloud in Part II, a wave in Part III, and then, after a
summary and statement of the speaker's ambitious hope in Part IV,
is asked to make the speaker a lyre in Part V; or Spenser's *Happy
Ye Leaves* (p. 168), in which the speaker addresses in the first four
lines the leaves of the book his love is holding, in the next four the
lines of the poem she is reading, and in the next four the rhymes in
that poem.

Different kinds of structures are sometimes combined for special
effects:

M. CARL HOLMAN

Three Brown Girls Singing

In the ribs of an ugly school building
Three rapt faces
Fuse one pure sound in a shaft of April light:
Three girls, choir robes over their arms, in a stairwell singing
Compose the irrelevancies of a halting typewriter,   5
Chalk dust and orange peel,
A French class drilling,
Into a shimmering column of flawed perfection;
Lasting as long
As their fresh, self-wondering voices climb to security;   10
Outlasting
The childbed death of one,
The alto's divorce,
The disease-raddled face of the third
Whose honey brown skin   15
Glows now in a nimbus[7] of dust motes,
But will be as estranged
As that faceless and voiceless typist
Who, unknown and unknowing, enters the limpid column,
Joins chalk, French verbs, the acrid perfume of oranges,   20
To mark the periphery
Of what shall be saved from calendars and decay.

                                                        p. 1963

The poem begins like a narrative and fades into a single dramatic scene. But the scene itself receives little attention. We are told of the "pure sound" created by the music, but instead of detailing the sound or providing metaphoric equivalents so that we almost hear it, or dramatizing its effect on someone, the poem enumerates all the things that it "composes," that is, brings together as one. The various sounds, sights, and smells from the school building—the typewriter, the peeling of an orange, writing on a chalkboard—seem harmonized by their music, and so do the lives of the three singers, whose brief and turbulent histories are also enumerated. The poem brings together different organizational patterns much as the music is said to "compose" (or harmonize) the disparate, miscellaneous, and fragmented sounds, smells, sights, and histories of those who create it and those within the range of its notes.

  Poems may borrow their organizational strategies from many places, imitating chronological, visual, or discursive shapes in reality or in other works of art. Sometimes poems strive to be almost purely descriptive of someone or something (using **descriptive structures**), in which case organizational decisions have to be made much as a

7. Halo.

painter or photographer would make them, deciding first how the whole scene should look, then putting the parts into proper place for the whole. But there are differences demanded by the poetic medium: a poem has to present the details sequentially, not all at once as an actual picture more or less can, so the poet must decide where the description starts (at the left? center? top?) and what sort of movement to use (linear across the scene? clockwise?). But if having words instead of paint or film has some disadvantages, it also has particular assets: figurative language can be a part of description, or an adjunct to it. A poet can insert a comparison at any point without necessarily disturbing the unity of what he or she describes—as long as the reader's main attention stays riveted on the tenor rather than the vehicle. A poem like Stevens's *Anecdote of the Jar* (p. 389) suggests some other complex things that a descriptive poem can do just *because* it has words to use to offer perspective on an object or scene.

Some poems use **imitative structures,** mirroring as exactly as possible the structure of something that already exists as an object and can be seen (another poem perhaps, as in Koch's *Variations on a Theme by William Carlos Williams,* p. 316) or a standard visual or vocal format, by asking and answering questions, as Levertov's *What Were They Like* (p. 75) does. Or a poem may use **reflective** (or **meditative**) **structures,** pondering a subject, theme, or event, and letting the mind play with it, skipping (sometimes illogically but still usefully) from one sound to another, or to related thoughts or objects as the mind receives them.

Patterns, forms, structures, models, paradigms—all these terms help to suggest ways that we organize experience every day on the basis of analogy, putting things into an order on the basis of some other order we already know about. And they help with organizing words, with putting together verbal structures into some kind of whole. But the whole process is hardly mechanical. We might try to draw diagrams and charts of the organizations of poems, but they wouldn't be very helpful, not nearly so accurate as a set of plans for a building or even a sketch of a painting might be. Words reflect and reverberate; they are always growing and expanding; they won't stay put in a single frame. Their shades of meaning, connotations, implications, and their participation in larger syntaxes and pictures mean that they modify structures even as they fill them out. No one has ever discovered how to talk precisely about the larger organizations of words, and yet we need some sense of how attempts are made to put words into orders that are, to some extent, controlled by larger principles. And so we use terms such as narrative and imitative structures as imprecise but suggestive indicators.

The paradigms (or models) for organizing poems are, finally, not all that different from those of prose. It may be easier to organize something short rather than something long, but the question of intensity becomes comparatively more important in shorter works. Basically, the problem of how to organize one's material is, for the writer, first of all a matter of deciding what kind of thing one wants to create, of having its purposes and effects clearly in mind, a matter we will look at from a different perspective in Chapter 10. That means that every poem will differ somewhat from every other, but it also means that patterns of purpose—narrative, dramatic, discursive, descriptive, imitative, or reflective—may help writers organize and formulate their ideas. A consciousness of purpose and effect can help the reader see *how* a poem proceeds toward its goal. Seeing how a poem is organized is, in turn, often a good way of seeing where it is going and what its real concerns and purposes may be. Often a poem's organization helps to make clear the particular effects that the poet wishes to generate. In a good poem, means and end are closely related, and a reader who is a good observer of one will be able to discover the other.

ANONYMOUS

Lord Randal

"O where hae ye been, Lord Randal, my son?
O where hae ye been, my handsome young man?"
"I hae been to the wild wood; mother, make my bed soon,
For I'm weary wi' hunting, and fain wald[8] lie down."

"Where gat ye your dinner, Lord Randal, my son?   5
Where gat ye your dinner, my handsome young man?"
"I dined wi' my true-love; mother, make my bed soon,
For I'm weary wi' hunting, and fain wald lie down."

"What gat ye to your dinner, Lord Randal, my son?
What gat ye to your dinner, my handsome young man?"   10
"I gat eels boiled in broo; mother, make my bed soon,
For I'm weary wi' hunting, and fain wald lie down."

"What became of your bloodhounds, Lord Randal, my son?
What became of your bloodhounds, my handsome young man?"
"O they swelled and they died; mother, make my bed soon, 15
For I'm weary wi' hunting, and fain wald lie down."

"O I fear ye are poisoned, Lord Randal, my son!
O I fear ye are poisoned, my handsome young man!"
"O yes! I am poisoned; mother, make my bed soon,
For I'm sick at the heart, and I fain wald lie down."   20
(date of composition uncertain)

8. Would like to.

KARL SHAPIRO

Auto Wreck

Its quick soft silver bell beating, beating,
And down the dark one ruby flare
Pulsing out red light like an artery,
The ambulance at top speed floating down
Past beacons and illuminated clocks   5
Wings in a heavy curve, dips down,
And brakes speed, entering the crowd.
The doors leap open, emptying light;
Stretchers are laid out, the mangled lifted
And stowed into the little hospital.   10
Then the bell, breaking the hush, tolls once,
And the ambulance with its terrible cargo
Rocking, slightly rocking, moves away,
As the doors, an afterthought, are closed.

We are deranged, walking among the cops   15
Who sweep glass and are large and composed.
One is still making notes under the light.
One with a bucket douches ponds of blood
Into the street and gutter.
One hangs lanterns on the wrecks that cling,   20
Empty husks of locusts, to iron poles.

Our throats were tight as tourniquets,
Our feet were bound with splints, but now,
Like convalescents intimate and gauche,
We speak through sickly smiles and warn   25
With the stubborn saw of common sense,
The grim joke and the banal resolution.
The traffic moves around with care,
But we remain, touching a wound
That opens to our richest horror.   30
Already old, the question Who shall die?
Becomes unspoken Who is innocent?

For death in war is done by hands;
Suicide has cause and stillbirth, logic;
And cancer, simple as a flower, blooms.   35
But this invites the occult mind,
Cancels our physics with a sneer,
And spatters all we knew of denouement
Across the expedient and wicked stones.

1942

LUCILLE CLIFTON

At Last We Killed the Roaches

at last we killed the roaches.
mama and me. she sprayed,
i swept the ceiling and they fell
dying onto our shoulders, in our hair
covering us with red. the tribe was broken,   5
the cooking pots were ours again
and we were glad, such cleanliness was grace
when i was twelve. only for a few nights,
and then not much, my dreams were blood
my hands were blades and it was murder murder   10
all over the place.

1974

ANONYMOUS

Sir Patrick Spens

The king sits in Dumferling toune,[9]
    Drinking the blude-reid[1] wine:
"O whar will I get guid sailor,
    To sail this ship of mine?"

Up and spake an eldern knicht,   5
    Sat at the king's richt knee:
"Sir Patrick Spens is the best sailor
    That sails upon the sea."

The king has written a braid[2] letter
    And signed it wi' his hand,   10
And sent it to Sir Patrick Spens,
    Was walking on the sand.

The first line that Sir Patrick read,
    A loud lauch[3] lauched he;
The next line that Sir Patrick read,   15
    The tear blinded his ee.[4]

"O wha is this has done this deed,
    This il deed done to me,
To send me out this time o' the year,
    To sail upon the sea?   20

9. Town.
1. Blood-red.
2. Broad: explicit.

3. Laugh.
4. Eye.

"Make haste, make haste, my merry men all,
    Our guid ship sails the morn."
"O say na sae,[5] my master dear,
    For I fear a deadly storm.

"Late, late yestre'en I saw the new moon   25
    Wi' the auld moon in her arm,
And I fear, I fear, my dear mastér,
    That we will come to harm."

O our Scots nobles were richt laith[6]
    To weet their cork-heeled shoon,[7]   30
But lang owre a'[8] the play were played
    Their hats they swam aboon.[9]

O lang, lang, may their ladies sit,
    Wi' their fans into their hand,
Or ere they see Sir Patrick Spens   35
    Come sailing to the land.

O lang, lang, may the ladies stand
    Wi' their gold kems[1] in their hair,
Waiting for their ain[2] dear lords,
    For they'll see them na mair.   40

Half o'er, half o'er to Aberdour
    It's fifty fadom deep,
And there lies guid Sir Patrick Spens
    Wi' the Scots lords at his feet.

(probably 13th century)

EDMUND SPENSER

Happy Ye Leaves

Happy ye leaves[3] whenas those lily hands,
Which hold my life in their dead-doing[4] might,
Shall handle you and hold in love's soft bands,
Like captives trembling at the victor's sight.
And happy lines on which, with starry light,   5
Those lamping eyes will deign sometimes to look,
And read the sorrows of my dying sprite,[5]

5. Not so.
6. Right loath: very reluctant.
7. To wet their cork-heeled shoes. Cork was expensive, and therefore such shoes were a mark of wealth and status.
8. Before all.
9. Their hats swam above them.

1. Combs.
2. Own.
3. Of the book of poems celebrating the woman these "lines" (line 5) go on to describe.
4. Death-dealing.
5. Spirit.

Written with tears in heart's close[6] bleeding book.
And happy rhymes bathed in the sacred brook
Of Helicon,[7] whence she derivéd is;   10
When ye behold that angel's blessed look,
My soul's long-lackéd food, my heaven's bliss.
Leaves, lines and rhymes, seek her to please alone,
Whom if ye please, I care for other none!

                                                                                1595

PERCY BYSSHE SHELLEY

Ode to the West Wind

I

O wild West Wind, thou breath of Autumn's being,
Thou, from whose unseen presence the leaves dead
Are driven, like ghosts from an enchanter fleeing,

Yellow, and black, and pale, and hectic red,
Pestilence-stricken multitudes: O thou,   5
Who chariotest to their dark wintry bed

The wingéd seeds, where they lie cold and low,
Each like a corpse within its grave, until
Thine azure sister of the Spring shall blow

Her clarion[8] o'er the dreaming earth, and fill   10
(Driving sweet buds like flocks to feed in air)
With living hues and odors plain and hill:

Wild Spirit, which art moving everywhere;
Destroyer and preserver; hear, oh, hear!

II

Thou on whose stream, mid the steep sky's commotion,   15
Loose clouds like earth's decaying leaves are shed,
Shook from the tangled boughs of Heaven and Ocean,

Angels[9] of rain and lightning: there are spread
On the blue surface of thine aëry surge,
Like the bright hair uplifted from the head   20

Of some fierce Maenad,[1] even from the dim verge
Of the horizon to the zenith's height,
The locks of the approaching storm. Thou dirge

6. Secretly.
7. A mountain sacred to the muses.
Classical writers described a fountain or
spring on the mountain as a source of
poetic inspiration; medieval writers often
called the spring itself Helicon.

8. Trumpet-call.
9. Messengers.
1. A frenzied female votary of Dionysus,
the Greek god of vegetation and fertility
who was supposed to die in the fall and
rise again each spring.

Of the dying year, to which this closing night
Will be the dome of a vast sepulcher,   25
Vaulted with all thy congregated might

Of vapors, from whose solid atmosphere
Black rain, and fire, and hail will burst: oh, hear!

III
Thou who didst waken from his summer dreams
The blue Mediterranean, where he lay,   30
Lulled by the coil of his crystálline streams,

Beside a pumice isle in Baiae's bay,[2]
And saw in sleep old palaces and towers
Quivering within the wave's intenser day,

All overgrown with azure moss and flowers   35
So sweet, the sense faints picturing them! Thou
For whose path the Atlantic's level powers

Cleave themselves into chasms, while far below
The sea-blooms and the oozy woods which wear
The sapless foliage of the ocean, know   40

Thy voice, and suddenly grow gray with fear,
And tremble and despoil themselves:[3] oh, hear!

IV
If I were a dead leaf thou mightest bear;
If I were a swift cloud to fly with thee;
A wave to pant beneath thy power, and share   45

The impulse of thy strength, only less free
Than thou, O uncontrollable! If even
I were as in my boyhood, and could be

The comrade by thy wanderings over Heaven,
As then, when to outstrip thy skyey speed   50
Scarce seemed a vision; I would ne'er have striven

As thus with thee in prayer in my sore need.
Oh, lift me as a wave, a leaf, a cloud!
I fall upon the thorns of life! I bleed!

A heavy weight of hours has chained and bowed   55
One too like thee: tameless, and swift, and proud.

V
Make me thy lyre,[4] even as the forest is:

2. Where Roman emperors had erected villas, west of Naples. "pumice": made of porous lava turned to stone.
3. "The vegetation at the bottom of the sea . . . sympathizes with that of the land in the change of seasons." (Shelley's note)
4. Aeolian lyre, a wind harp.

What if my leaves are falling like its own!
The tumult of thy mighty harmonies

Will take from both a deep, autumnal tone,   60
Sweet though in sadness. Be thou, Spirit fierce,
My spirit! Be thou me, impetuous one!

Drive my dead thoughts over the universe
Like withered leaves to quicken a new birth!
And, by the incantation of this verse,   65

Scatter, as from an unextinguished hearth
Ashes and sparks, my words among mankind!
Be through my lips to unawakened earth

The trumpet of a prophecy! O Wind,
If Winter comes, can Spring be far behind?   70

1820

ROBERT FROST

Stopping by Woods on a Snowy Evening

Whose woods these are I think I know.
His house is in the village, though;
He will not see me stopping here
To watch his woods fill up with snow.

My little horse must think it queer   5
To stop without a farmhouse near
Between the woods and frozen lake
The darkest evening of the year.

He gives his harness bells a shake
To ask if there is some mistake.   10
The only other sound's the sweep
Of easy wind and downy flake.

The woods are lovely, dark, and deep,
But I have promises to keep,
And miles to go before I sleep,   15
And miles to go before I sleep.

1923

GEORGE GORDON, LORD BYRON

The Destruction of Sennacherib[5]

The Assyrian came down like the wolf on the fold,
And his cohorts were gleaming in purple and gold;
And the sheen of their spears was like stars on the sea,
When the blue wave rolls nightly on deep Galilee.

Like the leaves of the forest when Summer is green,   5
That host with their banners at sunset were seen:
Like the leaves of the forest when Autumn hath blown,
That host on the morrow lay withered and strown.

For the Angel of Death spread his wings on the blast,
And breathed in the face of the foe as he passed;   10
And the eyes of the sleepers waxed deadly and chill,
And their hearts but once heaved, and for ever grew still!

And there lay the steed with his nostril all wide,
But through it there rolled not the breath of his pride;
And the foam of his gasping lay white on the turf,   15
And cold as the spray of the rock-beating surf.

And there lay the rider distorted and pale,
With the dew on his brow, and the rust on his mail:
And the tents were all silent, the banners alone,
The lances unlifted, the trumpet unblown.   20

And the widows of Ashur are loud in their wail,
And the idols are broke in the temple of Baal;[6]
And the might of the Gentile, unsmote by the sword,
Hath melted like snow in the glance of the Lord!

1815

EDWIN ARLINGTON ROBINSON

Miniver Cheevy

Miniver Cheevy, child of scorn,
  Grew lean while he assailed the seasons;
He wept that he was ever born,
  And he had reasons.

5. King of Assyria who besieged Jeru-
salem during Hezekiah's reign as king of
Judah. According to *II Kings* 18 and 19,
Hezekiah paid ransom but refused to give
up faith in his God, who promised that
Jerusalem would not be taken. Hezekiah's
loyalty was finally rewarded when "the
angel of the lord went out, and smote in
the camp of the Assyrians an hundred four
score and five thousand." (*II Kings* 19:35)
  6. God of the Assyrians.

Miniver loved the days of old [5]
  When swords were bright and steeds were prancing;
The vision of a warrior bold
  Would set him dancing.

Miniver sighed for what was not,
  And dreamed, and rested from his labors; [10]
He dreamed of Thebes and Camelot,
  And Priam's neighbors.[7]

Miniver mourned the ripe renown
  That made so many a name so fragrant;
He mourned Romance, now on the town, [15]
  And Art, a vagrant.

Miniver loved the Medici,[8]
  Albeit he had never seen one;
He would have sinned incessantly
  Could he have been one. [20]

Miniver cursed the commonplace
  And eyed a khaki suit with loathing;
He missed the mediæval grace
  Of iron clothing.

Miniver scorned the gold he sought, [25]
  But sore annoyed was he without it;
Miniver thought, and thought, and thought,
  And thought about it.

Miniver Cheevy, born too late,
  Scratched his head and kept on thinking; [30]
Miniver coughed, and called it fate,
  And kept on drinking.

1910

7. Thebes was a site in ancient Greek civilization and legend; Camelot, the legendary site of King Arthur's court; Priam, ancient king of Troy and father of Hector.

8. The Renaissance family of bankers and merchants who ruled Florence for two centuries. Great patrons of the arts and responsible for much significant architecture, sculpture, and painting, they were also known as one of the most ruthless ruling groups in history.

8 SOUND AND SIGHT

The Sounds of Poetry

A lot of what happens in a poem happens in your mind's eye, but some of it happens in your voice. Poems are full of sounds and silences as well as words and sentences that are meaningful. Besides choosing words for their meanings, poets sometimes choose words because they involve certain sounds, and use sound effects to create a mood or establish a tone, just as films do. Sometimes the sounds of words are crucial to what is happening in the text of the poem.

The following poem explores the sounds of a particular word, tries them on, and analyzes them in relation to the word itself.

HELEN CHASIN

The Word *Plum*

The word *plum* is delicious

pout and push, luxury of
self-love, and savoring murmur

full in the mouth and falling
like fruit   5

taut skin
pierced, bitten, provoked into
juice, and tart flesh

question
and reply, lip and tongue   10
of pleasure.

1968

The poem savors the sounds of the word as well as the taste and feel of the fruit itself. It is almost as if the poem is tasting the sounds and rolling them carefully on the tongue. The second and third lines even replicate the "p," "l," "uh," and "m" sounds of the word while at the same time imitating the squishy sounds of eating the fruit. Words like "delicious" and "luxury" sound juicy, and other words imitate sounds of satisfaction and pleasure—"murmur," for example. Even the process of eating is in part recreated aurally. The tight, clipped sounds of "taut skin / pierced" suggest the sharp breaking of the skin and solid flesh, and as the tartness is described, the words ("provoked," "question") force the mouth to pucker as it would if it were savoring a tart fruit. The poet is having fun here recreating the various sense appeals of a plum, teasing the sounds and meanings out of available words. The words must mean something appropriate and describe something accurately first of all, of course, but when they can also imitate the sounds and feel of the process, they can do double duty. Not all poems manipulate sound as consciously or as fully as *The Word Plum*, but many poems at least contain passages in which the sounds of life are reproduced by the human voice reading the poem. To get the full effect of this poem—and of many others—reading aloud is essential; that way, one can pay attention to the vocal rhythms and can articulate the sounds as the poem calls for them to be reproduced by the human voice.

Almost always a poem's effect will be helped by reading it aloud, using your voice to pronounce the words so that the poem becomes a spoken communication. Historically, poetry began as an oral phenomenon, and often poems that seem very difficult when looked at silently come alive when they are turned into sound. Early bards chanted their verses, and the music of poetry—its cadences and rhythms—developed from this kind of performance. Often in primitive poetry (and sometimes in later ages) poetry performances have been accompanied by some kind of musical instrument. The rhythms of any poem become clearer when you say or hear them.

Poetry is, almost always, a vocal art, dependent on the human voice to become its full self (for some exceptions look at the shaped verse at the end of this chapter). In a sense, it begins to exist as a real phenomenon when a reader reads and actualizes it. Poems don't really achieve their full meaning when they merely exist on a page; a poem on a page is more a set of stage directions for a poem than a poem itself. Sometimes, in fact, it is hard to experience the poem at all unless you hear it. A good poetry reading might easily convince you of the importance of a good voice sensitive to the poem's requirements, but you can also persuade yourself by reading poems aloud in the privacy of your own room. An audience is even better, however, because then there is someone to share the pleasure in the sounds themselves and consider what they imply.

MONA VAN DUYN

What the Motorcycle Said

Br-r-r-am-m-m, rackety-am-m, OM, *Am:*
All—r-r-room, r-r-ram, ala-bas-ter—
Am, the world's my oyster.

I hate plastic, wear it black and slick,

hate hardhats, wear one on my head,   5
that's what the motorcycle said.

Passed phonies in Fords, knocked down billboards, landed
on the other side of The Gap, and Whee,
bypassed history.

When I was born (The Past), baby knew best.   10
They shook when I bawled, took Freud's path,
threw away their wrath.

R-r-rackety-am-m, *Am*. War, rhyme,
soap, meat, marriage, the Phantom Jet
are shit, and like that.   15

Hate pompousness, punishment, patience, am into Love,
hate middle-class moneymakers, live on Dad,
that's what the motorcycle said.

Br-r-r-am-m-m. It's Nowsville, man. Passed Oldies, Uglies,
Straighties, Honkies. I'll never be   20
mean, tired or unsexy.

Passed cigarette suckers, souses, mother-fuckers,
losers, went back to Nature and found
how to get VD, stoned.

Passed a cow, too fast to hear her moo, "*I* rolled   25
our leaves of grass into one ball.
I am the grassy All."

Br-r-r-am-m-m, rackety-am-m, OM, *Am:*
All—gr-r-rin, oooohgah, gl-l-utton—
Am, the world's my smilebutton.   30

                                                                   1973

Saying this poem as if you were a motorcycle with the power of
speech (sort of) is part of the poem's fun, and the rich, loud sounds
of a motorcycle revving up concentrate and intensify the effect and
enrich the pleasure. It's a shame not to hear a poem like this aloud;
a lot of it is missed if you don't try to imitate the sounds or if you
don't try to pick up the motor's rhythms in the poem. A per-
formance here is clearly worth it: a human being as motorcycle,
motorcycle as human being.

And it's a good poem, too, that does something interesting, im-
portant, and maybe a bit subversive. The speaking motorcycle seems
to take on the values of some of its riders, the noisy and obtrusive
ones that readers are most likely to associate with motorcycles in
their minds. The riders made fun of here are themselves sort of mind-

less and mechanical; they are the sort who have cult feelings about their group, who travel in packs, and who live no life beyond their machines. The speaking motorcycle, like such riders, grooves on power and speed, lives for the moment, and has little respect for people, the past, for institutions, or for anything beyond its own small world. It is self-centered, modish, ignorant, and inarticulate; but proud, mighty proud, and feels important in its own sounds. That's what the motorcycle says.

The following poem uses sound effects efficiently, too.

KENNETH FEARING

Dirge

1-2-3 was the number he played but today the number came 3-2-1;
Bought his Carbide at 30, and it went to 29; had the favorite at Bowie
    but the track was slow—

O executive type, would you like to drive a floating-power, knee-action,
    silk-upholstered six? Wed a Hollywood star? Shoot the course in
    58? Draw to the ace, king, jack?
O fellow with a will who won't take no, watch out for three cigarettes
    on the same, single match; O democratic voter born in August
    under Mars, beware of liquidated rails—

Denouement to denouement, he took a personal pride in the certain,
    certain way he lived his own, private life,   5
But nevertheless, they shut off his gas; nevertheless, the bank foreclosed;
    nevertheless, the landlord called; nevertheless, the radio broke,

And twelve o'clock arrived just once too often,
Just the same he wore one gray tweed suit, bought one straw hat, drank
    one straight Scotch, walked one short step, took one long look,
    drew one deep breath,
Just one too many,

And wow he died as wow he lived,   10
Going whop to the office and blooie home to sleep and biff got married
    and bam had children and oof got fired,
Zowie did he live and zowie did he die,

With who the hell are you at the corner of his casket, and where the
    hell're we going on the right-hand silver knob, and who the hell
    cares walking second from the end with an American Beauty
    wreath from why the hell not,

Very much missed by the circulation staff of the New York Evening
    Post; deeply, deeply mourned by the B.M.T.[1]

1. A New York subway line.

Wham, Mr. Roosevelt; pow, Sears Roebuck; awk, big dipper; bop,   15
    summer rain;
Bong, Mr., bong, Mr., bong, Mr., bong.

                                                              1935

As the title implies, this poem is a kind of musical lament, in this
case for a certain sort of businessman who took a lot of chances and
saw his investments and life go down the drain in the depression of
the early thirties. Reading this poem aloud is a big help partly be-
cause it contains expressive words which echo the action, words like
"oof" and "blooie" (which primarily carry their meaning in their sounds,
for they have no literal or referential meaning). Reading aloud also
helps us notice that the poem employs rhythms much as a song would
and that it frequently shifts its pace and mood. Notice how carefully
the first two lines are balanced, and then how quickly the rhythm
shifts as the "executive type" begins to be addressed directly in line
3. (Line 2 is long and dribbles over in the narrow pages of a book
like this; a lot of the lines here are especially long, and the irregu-
larity of the line lengths is one aspect of the special sound effects
the poem creates.) In the direct address, the poem first picks up a
series of advertising features which it recites in rapid-fire order rather
like the advertising phrases in *Needs* in Chapter 3. In stanza 3 here,
the rhythm shifts again, but the poem gives us helpful clues about
how to read. Line 5 sounds like prose and is long, drawn out, and
rather dull (rather like its subject), but line 6 sets up a regular
(and monotonous) rhythm with its repeated "nevertheless" which
punctuates the rhythm like a drumbeat: "But nevertheless *tuh-tuh-
tuh-tuh-tuh*; nevertheless *tuh-tuh-tuh-tuh*; nevertheless *tuh-tuh-tuh-
tuh*; nevertheless *tuh-tuh-tuh-tuh-tuh*." In the next stanza, the repeti-
tive phrasing comes again, this time guided by the word "one" in
cooperation with other words of one syllable: "wore *one* gray tweed
suit, bought *one* straw hat, *tuh* one *tuh-tuh*; *tuh* one *tuh-tuh*; *tuh*
one *tuh-tuh*; *tuh* one *tuh-tuh*." And then a new rhythm and a new
technique in stanza 5 as the language of comic books is imitated
to describe in violent, exaggerated terms the routine of his life. You
have to say words like "whop" and "zowie" aloud and in the rhythm
of the whole sentence to get the full effect of how boring his life is,
no matter how he tries to jazz it up with exciting words. And so it
goes—repeated words, shifting rhythms, emphasis on routine and aver-
ageness—until the final bell ("Bong . . . bong . . . bong . . . bong")
tolls rhythmically for the dead man in the final clanging line.

Sometimes sounds in poems just provide special effects, rather like
a musical score behind a film, setting mood and getting us into an
appropriate frame of mind. But often sound and meaning go hand in
hand, and the poet finds words that in their sounds echo the action.
A word which captures or approximates the sound of what it de-
scribes, such as "splash" or "squish" or "murmur" is called an **onomat-
opoeic** word, and the device itself is called **onomatopoeia**. And simi-
lar things can be done poetically with pacing and rhythm, sounds and

pauses. The punctuation, the length of vowels, and the combination of consonant sounds help to control the way we read so that we imitate what is being described. The poems at the end of this discussion (pp. 186–192) suggest several ways that such imitations of pace and pause may occur: by echoing the lapping of waves on a shore, for example (*Like as the Waves*), or mimicking the sounds of a train on a variable terrain (*The Express*), or reproducing the rhythms of a musical style (*Dear John, Dear Coltrane*).

Here is a classic passage in which a skillful poet talks about the virtues of making the sound echo the sense—and shows at the same time how to do it:

ALEXANDER POPE

[Sound and Sense][2]

But most by numbers[3] judge a poet's song,	337
And smooth or rough, with them, is right or wrong;	
In the bright muse though thousand charms conspire,[4]	
Her voice is all these tuneful fools admire,	340
Who haunt Parnassus[5] but to please their ear,	
Not mend their minds; as some to church repair,	
Not for the doctrine, but the music there.	
These, equal syllables[6] alone require,	
Though oft the ear the open vowels tire,	345
While expletives[7] their feeble aid do join,	
And ten low words oft creep in one dull line,	
While they ring round the same unvaried chimes,	
With sure returns of still expected rhymes.	
Wheree'er you find "the cooling western breeze,"	350
In the next line, it "whispers through the trees";	
If crystal streams "with pleasing murmurs creep,"	
The reader's threatened (not in vain) with "sleep."	
Then, at the last and only couplet fraught	
With some unmeaning thing they call a thought,	355
A needless Alexandrine[8] ends the song,	
That, like a wounded snake, drags its slow length along.	
Leave such to tune their own dull rhymes, and know	
What's roundly smooth, or languishingly slow;	
And praise the easy vigor of a line,	360
Where Denham's strength and Waller's[9] sweetness join.	

2. From *An Essay on Criticism*, Pope's poem on the art of poetry and the problems of literary criticism. The passage excerpted here follows a discussion of several common weaknesses of critics: failure to regard an author's intention, for example, or overemphasis on clever metaphors and ornate style.
3. Meter, rhythm, sound.
4. Unite.
5. A mountain in Greece, traditionally associated with the muses and considered the seat of poetry and music.
6. Regular accents.
7. Filler words, such as "do."
8. A six-foot line, sometimes used in pentameter poems to vary the pace mechanically. Line 357 is an alexandrine.
9. Sir John Denham and Edmund Waller, 17th-century poets credited with perfecting the heroic couplet.

> True ease in writing comes from art, not chance,
> As those move easiest who have learned to dance.
> 'Tis not enough no harshness gives offense,
> The sound must seem an echo to the sense: 365
> Soft is the strain when Zephyr¹ gently blows,
> And the smooth stream in smoother numbers flows;
> But when loud surges lash the sounding shore,
> The hoarse, rough verse should like the torrent roar.
> When Ajax² strives, some rock's vast weight to throw,   370
> The line too labors, and the words move slow;
> Not so, when swift Camilla³ scours the plain,
> Flies o'er th' unbending corn, and skims along the main.
> Hear how Timotheus'⁴ varied lays surprise,
> And bid alternate passions fall and rise!   375
> While, at each change, the son of Libyan Jove⁵
> Now burns with glory, and then melts with love;
> Now his fierce eyes with sparkling fury glow,
> Now sighs steal out, and tears begin to flow:
> Persians and Greeks like turns of nature⁶ found,   380
> And the world's victor stood subdued by sound!
> The pow'r of music all our hearts allow,
> And what Timotheus was, is DRYDEN now.

> 1711

A lot of things go on here simultaneously. The poem uses a number of echoic or onomatopoeic words, and pleasant and unpleasant consonant sounds are used in some lines to underline a particular point or add some mood music. When the poet talks about a particular weakness in poetry, he illustrates it at the same time—by using open vowels (line 345), expletives (line 346), monosyllabic words (line 347), predictable rhymes (lines 350–353), or long, slow lines (line 357). And the good qualities of poetry he talks about and illustrates as well (line 360, for example). But the main effects of the passage come from an interaction of several strategies at once. The effects are fairly simple and easy to spot, but their causes involve a lot of poetic ingenuity. In line 340, for example, a careful cacophonous effect is achieved by the repetition of the o͞o vowel sound and the repetition of the L consonant sound together with the interruption (twice) of the rough F sound in the middle; no one wants to be caught admiring that music when the poet gets through with us, but the careful harmony of the preceding sounds has set us up beautifully. And in lines 347, 357, and 359, the pace of the lines is carefully con-

1. The west wind.
2. A Greek hero of the Trojan War, noted for his strength.
3. A woman warrior in *The Aeneid*.
4. The court-musician of Alexander the Great, celebrated in a famous poem by Dryden (see line 383) for the power of his music over Alexander's emotions.

5. In Greek tradition, the chief god of any people was often given the name Zeus (Jove), and the chief god of Libya (the Greek name for all of Africa) was called Zeus Ammon. Alexander visited his oracle and was proclaimed son of the god.
6. Similar alternations of emotion.

trolled by consonant sounds as well as by the use of long vowels.
Line 347 moves incredibly slowly and seems much longer than it is
because almost all the one-syllable words end in a consonant which
refuses to blend with the beginning of the next word, making the words
hard to say without distinct, awkward pauses between them. And in
lines 357 and 359, long vowels such as those in "wounded," "snake,"
"slow," "along," "roundly," and "smooth" help to slow down the pace,
and the same trick of juxtaposing awkward, unpronounceable con-
sonants is also employed. The commas also provide nearly a full stop
in the midst of each line to slow us down still more. Similarly, the harsh
lashing of the shore in lines 368–69 is partly accomplished by ono-
matopoeia, partly by a shift in the pattern of stress which creates
irregular waves in line 368, and partly by the dominance of rough
consonants in line 369. (In Pope's time, the English *r* was still trilled
gruffly so that it could be made to sound extremely rough and harsh.)
Almost every line in this passage could serve as a demonstration of
how to make sound echo sense.

As the passage from Pope and the poem *Dirge* suggest, sound is
most effectively manipulated in poetry when the rhythm of the voice
is carefully controlled so that not only are the proper sounds heard,
but they are heard at precisely the right moment. Pace and rhythm
are nearly as important to a good poem as they are to a good piece
of music. The human voice naturally develops certain rhythms in
speech; some syllables and some words receive more stress than others,
and a careful poet controls the flow of stresses to that, in many poems,
a certain basic rhythm develops almost like a quiet percussion instru-
ment in the background. The most common rhythm in English is the
regular alternation of unstressed and stressed syllables, as in the pas-
sage from Pope. There, most lines have five sets of unstressed/stressed
syllables, although plenty of lines have slight variations so that there is
little danger (if you read sensitively) of falling into too expected a
rhythm, a dull sing-song. The unstressed/stressed pattern (in that
order) is called **iambic** rhythm. Other fairly common rhythms are the
trochaic (a stressed syllable followed by an unstressed one), the
anapestic (two unstressed syllables followed by a stressed one), and
dactylic (a stressed syllable followed by two unstressed ones). Each
unit of measurement is called a **foot**. In "A Glossary of Poetic Terms,"
pp. 543–560, you will find definitions as well for some less frequently
used rhythms, a list of terms used to describe lengths of lines, and
some directions on how to **scan** (that is, analyze the rhythmic pat-
tern of) metered verse.

Here is a poem which names and illustrates many of the meters.
If you read it aloud and chart the unstressed (∪) and stressed (−)
syllables you should have a chart similar to that done by the poet
himself in the text.

SAMUEL TAYLOR COLERIDGE

Metrical Feet

Lesson for a Boy

Trōchĕe trĭps frŏm lŏng tŏ shŏrt;[7]
Frŏm long to long in solemn sort
Slōw Spōndēe stālks; strŏng fōōt! yet ill able
Ēvĕr tŏ cōme ŭp wĭth Dāctўl trĭsўllăblĕ.   5
Wĭth ă leāp ănd ă boūnd thĕ swĭft Ānăpĕsts thrōng;
Ĭāmbĭcs mārch frŏm shŏrt tŏ lōng—
One syllable long, with one short at each side,
Ămphĭbrăchўs hāstes wĭth ă stātelў stride—
Fĭrst ănd lāst bēĭng lōng, mĭddlĕ shŏrt, Ămphĭmācer
Strĭkes hĭs thūndĕrĭng hōōfs lĭke ă proūd hĭgh-brĕd Rācer.   10
If Derwent[8] be innocent, steady, and wise,
And delight in the things of earth, water, and skies;
Tender warmth at his heart, with these meters to show it,
With sound sense in his brains, may make Derwent a poet—
May crown him with fame, and must win him the love   15
Of his father on earth and his Father above.
          My dear, dear child!
Could you stand upon Skiddaw,[9] you would not from its whole ridge
See a man who so loves you as your fond s. t. COLERIDGE.
1806

The following poem exemplifies **dactylic** rhythm, and the limericks
that follow are written in **anapestic** meter.

JOHN HOLLANDER

Historical Reflections

      Higgledy-piggledy,
      Benjamin Harrison,
      Twenty-third President,
      Was, and, as such,

      Served between Clevelands,[1] and   5
      Save for this trivial
      Idiosyncrasy,
      Didn't do much.

                                                      1967

---

7. The long and short marks over syl-
lables are Coleridge's; the kinds of metrical
feet named and exemplified here are de-
fined in the glossary, p. 552.
8. Written originally for Coleridge's son
Hartley, the poem was later adapted for
his younger son, Derwent.
9. A mountain in the lake country of
northern England (where Coleridge lived
in his early years), near the town of Der-
went.
1. Grover Cleveland was 22nd and
24th president of the U.S. His two terms
were split by the four-year presidency of
Harrison.

ANONYMOUS

Limericks

There once was a spinster of Ealing,
Endowed with such delicate feeling,
    That she thought an armchair
    Should not have its legs bare—
So she kept her eyes trained on the ceiling.

* *

I sat next to the Duchess at tea.
It was just as I thought it would be:
    Her rumblings abdominal
    Were simply phenomenal
And everyone thought it was me.

* *

A charming young woman named Pat
Would invite one to do this and that.
    When speaking of this
    She meant more than a kiss
So imagine her meaning of that.

* *

A trendy young girl from St. Paul
Wore a newspaper dress to a ball,
    But the dress caught on fire
    And burned her entire
Front page, sporting section, and all.

* *

A swimmer whose clothing was strewed
By breezes that left her quite nude
    Saw a man come along,
    And unless I am wrong
You expected this line to be lewd.

* *

A staid schizophrenic named Struther,
When told of the death of his brother,
    Said: "Yes, I am sad;
    It makes me feel bad,
But then, I still have each other."

* *

There once was a pious young priest
Who lived almost wholly on yeast.
    He said, "It's so plain
    We must all rise again
That I'd like to get started at least."

* *

God's plan had a hopeful beginning,
But man spoiled his chances by sinning.
  We trust that the story
  Will end in God's glory,
But right now the other side's winning.

This poem is composed in the more common **trochaic** meter.

SIR JOHN SUCKLING

Song

Why so pale and wan, fond Lover?
 Prithee why so pale?
Will, when looking well can't move her,
 Looking ill prevail?
 Prithee why so pale?   5

Why so dull and mute, young Sinner?
 Prithee why so mute?
Will, when speaking well can't win her,
 Saying nothing do 't?
 Prithee why so mute?   10

Quit, quit, for shame, this will not move,
 This cannot take her;
If of her self she will not love,
 Nothing can make her,
 The Devil take her.   15

            1646

The basic meter in the following poem is the most common one in English, **iambic:**

JOHN DRYDEN

To the Memory of Mr. Oldham[2]

Farewell, too little, and too lately known,
Whom I began to think and call my own;

---

2. John Oldham (1653–83), who like Dryden (see lines 3–6) wrote satiric poetry.

For sure our souls were near allied, and thine
Cast in the same poetic mold with mine.
One common note on either lyre did strike, 5
And knaves and fools we both abhorred alike.
To the same goal did both our studies drive;
The last set out the soonest did arrive.
Thus Nisus fell upon the slippery place,
While his young friend performed and won the race.[3] 10
O early ripe! to thy abundant store
What could advancing age have added more?
It might (what nature never gives the young)
Have taught the numbers[4] of thy native tongue.
But satire needs not those, and wit will shine 15
Through the harsh cadence of a rugged line.[5]
A noble error, and but seldom made,
When poets are by too much force betrayed.
Thy generous fruits, though gathered ere their prime,
Still showed a quickness; and maturing time 20
But mellows what we write to the dull sweets of rhyme.
Once more, hail and farewell; farewell, thou young,
But ah too short, Marcellus[6] of our tongue;
Thy brows with ivy, and with laurels bound;
But fate and gloomy night encompass thee around. 25

1684

Once you have figured out the basic rhythm of a poem, you can often find some interesting things by looking carefully at the departures from the pattern. Departures from the basic iambic meter of *To the Memory of Mr. Oldham,* for example, suggest some of the imaginative things that poets can do within the apparently very restrictive requirements of traditional meter. Try marking the stressed and unstressed syllables in *To the Memory of Mr. Oldham* and then look carefully at each of the places which vary from the basic iambic pattern. Which of these variations call special attention to a particular sound or action being talked about in the poem? Which ones specifically mimic or echo the sense? Which variations seem to exist primarily for emphasis? Which ones seem primarily intended to mark structural breaks in the poem?

3. In Vergil's *Aeneid* (Book V), Nisus (who is leading the race) falls and then trips the second runner so that his friend Euryalus can win.
4. Rhythms.

5. In Dryden's time, R's were pronounced with a harsh, trilling sound.
6. The nephew of the Roman emperor Augustus; he died at 20, and Vergil celebrated him in *The Aeneid,* Book VI.

ALFRED, LORD TENNYSON

Break, Break, Break

Break, break, break,
  On thy cold gray stones, O Sea!
And I would that my tongue could utter
  The thoughts that arise in me.

O well for the fisherman's boy,   5
  That he shouts with his sister at play!
O well for the sailor lad,
  That he sings in his boat on the bay!
And the stately ships go on
  To their haven under the hill;   10
But O for the touch of a vanished hand,
  And the sound of a voice that is still!

Break, break, break,
  At the foot of thy crags, O Sea!
But the tender grace of a day that is dead   15
  Will never come back to me.

ca. 1834

DONALD JUSTICE

Counting the Mad

This one was put in a jacket,
This one was sent home,
This one was given bread and meat
But would eat none,
And this one cried No No No No   5
All day long.

This one looked at the window
As though it were a wall,
This one saw things that were not there,
This one things that were,   10
And this one cried No No No No
All day long.

This one thought himself a bird,
This one a dog,
And this one thought himself a man,   15
An ordinary man,
And cried and cried No No No No
All day long.

1960

THOMAS NASHE

Spring, the Sweet Spring

Spring, the sweet spring, is the year's pleasant king,
Then blooms each thing, then maids dance in a ring,
Cold doth not sting, the pretty birds do sing:
  Cuckoo, jug-jug, pu-we, to-witta-woo! [7]

The palm and may make country houses gay,   5
Lambs frisk and play, the shepherds pipe all day,
And we hear aye birds tune this merry lay:
  Cuckoo, jug-jug, pu-we, to-witta-woo!

The fields breathe sweet, the daisies kiss our feet,
Young lovers meet, old wives a-sunning sit,   10
In every street these tunes our ears do greet:
  Cuckoo, jug-jug, pu-we, to-witta-woo!
    Spring, the sweet spring!

1592

GERARD MANLEY HOPKINS

Spring and Fall:

To a Young Child

Márgarét áre you gríeving
Over Goldengrove unleaving?
Leáves, líke the things of man, you
With your fresh thoughts care for, can you?
Áh! ás the heart grows older   5
It will come to such sights colder
By and by, nor spare a sigh
Though worlds of wanwood[8] leafmeal lie;
And yet you wíll weep and know why.
Now no matter, child, the name: 10
Sórrow's spríngs áre the same.
Nor mouth had, no nor mind, expressed
What heart heard of, ghost[9] guessed:
It ís the blight man was born for,
It is Margaret you mourn for.   15

1880

---

7. The calls of the cuckoo, nightingale, lapwing, and owl, respectively.
8. Pale, gloomy woods. "leafmeal": broken up, leaf by leaf (analogous to "piecemeal").
9. Soul.

WILLIAM SHAKESPEARE

Like as the Waves

Like as the waves make towards the pebbled shore,
So do our minutes hasten to their end,
Each changing place with that which goes before,
In sequent[1] toil all forwards do contend. [2]
Nativity,[3] once in the main[4] of light,   5
Crawls to maturity, wherewith being crowned,
Crooked[5] eclipses 'gainst his glory fight,
And Time that gave doth now his gift confound.[6]
Time doth transfix[7] the flourish set on youth
And delves the parallels[8] in beauty's brow,   10
Feeds on the rarities of nature's truth,
And nothing stands but for his scythe to mow.
And yet to times in hope[9] my verse shall stand,
Praising thy worth, despite his cruel hand.

1609

STEPHEN SPENDER

The Express

After the first powerful, plain manifesto
The black statement of pistons, without more fuss
But gliding like a queen, she leaves the station.
Without bowing and with restrained unconcern
She passes the houses which humbly crowd outside,   5
The gasworks, and at last the heavy page
Of death, printed by gravestones in the cemetery.
Beyond the town, there lies the open country
Where, gathering speed, she acquires mystery,
The luminous self-possession of ships on ocean.   10
It is now she begins to sing—at first quite low
Then loud, and at last with a jazzy madness—
The song of her whistle screaming at curves,
Of deafening tunnels, brakes, innumerable bolts.
And always light, aerial, underneath,   15
Retreats the elate meter of her wheels.
Steaming through metal landscape on her lines,
She plunges new eras of white happiness,
Where speed throws up strange shapes, broad curves

1. Successive.
2. Struggle.
3. New-born life.
4. High seas.
5. Perverse.

6. Bring to nothing.
7. Pierce.
8. Lines, wrinkles.
9. In the future.

And parallels clean like trajectories from guns.   20
At last, further than Edinburgh or Rome,
Beyond the crest of the world, she reaches night
Where only a low stream-line brightness
Of phosphorus on the tossing hills is light.
Ah, like a comet through flame, she moves entranced,   25
Wrapt in her music no bird song, no, nor bough
Breaking with honey buds, shall ever equal.

                                                                1933

MICHAEL HARPER

Dear John, Dear Coltrane

                        a love supreme, a love supreme[1]
                        a love supreme, a love supreme

    Sex fingers toes
    in the marketplace
    near your father's church
    in Hamlet, North Carolina—[2]
    witness to this love   5
    in this calm fallow
    of these minds,
    there is no substitute for pain:
    genitals gone or going,
    seed burned out,   10
    you tuck the roots in the earth,
    turn back, and move
    by river through the swamps,
    singing: *a love supreme, a love supreme;*
    what does it all mean?   15
    Loss, so great each black
    woman expects your failure
    in mute change, the seed gone.
    You plod up into the electric city—
    your song now crystal and   20
    the blues. You pick up the horn
    with some will and blow
    into the freezing night:
    a love supreme, a love supreme—

    Dawn comes and you cook   25
    up the thick sin 'tween

1. Coltrane's record of "A Love Supreme," released in 1965, represents his moment of greatest public acclaim. The record was named Record of the Year and Coltrane was named jazz musician of the year in the *Downbeat* poll.

2. Coltrane's birthplace. His family shared a house with Coltrane's grandfather, who was the minister of St. Stephen's AME Zion Church there.

impotence and death, fuel
the tenor sax cannibal
heart, genitals and sweat
that makes you clean—   30
a love supreme, a love supreme—

Why you so black?
cause I am
why you so funky?
cause I am   35
why you so black?
cause I am
why you so sweet?
cause I am
why you so black?   40
cause I am
a love supreme, a love supreme:

So sick
you couldn't play *Naima,*[3]
so flat we ached   45
for song you'd concealed
with your own blood,
your diseased liver gave
out its purity,
the inflated heart   50
pumps out, the tenor kiss,
tenor love:
a love supreme, a love supreme—
a love supreme, a love supreme—

1970

BOB KAUFMAN

Blues Note

Ray Charles is the black wind of Kilimanjaro,[4]
Screaming up-and-down blues,
Moaning happy on all the elevators of my time.

Smiling into the camera, with an African symphony
Hidden in his throat, and (*I Got a Woman*)[5] wails, too.   5

He burst from Bessie's crushed black skull

3. Another standard Coltrane song, recorded in 1966 at the Village Vanguard.
4. The highest mountain in Africa, where the high winds are legendary.

5. One of Ray Charles's most famous hit recordings, the phrase "'way cross town" (line 14) is also from this song.

One cold night outside of Nashville,[6] shouting,
And grows bluer from memory, glowing bluer, still.

At certain times you can see the moon
Balanced on his head.   10

From his mouth he hurls chunks of raw soul.
} He separated the sea of polluted sounds
And led the blues into the Promised Land.[7]

Ray Charles is a dangerous man ('way cross town),
And I love him.   15

(for Ray Charles's birthday N.Y.C./1961)

LANGSTON HUGHES

Jazzonia

Oh, silver tree!
Oh, shining rivers of the soul!

In a Harlem cabaret
Six long-headed jazzers play.
A dancing girl whose eyes are bold   5
Lifts high a dress of silken gold.

Oh, singing tree!
Oh, shining rivers of the soul!

Were Eve's eyes
In the first garden   10
Just a bit too bold?
Was Cleopatra gorgeous
In a gown of gold?

Oh, shining tree!
Oh, silver rivers of the soul!   15

In a whirling cabaret
Six long-headed jazzers play.

1926

6. Bessie Smith (1898?–1937), American blues singer, died near Nashville when a segregated hospital refused to treat her after an accident.
7. According to *Exodus* 14, Moses caused the Red Sea waters to part so that the Israelites could cross and escape from the Egyptians who were pursuing them; he then led his people to the Promised Land, Canaan.

The Way a Poem Looks

The way a poem looks is not nearly so important as the way it sounds—usually. But there are exceptions. A few poems are written to be seen rather than heard or read aloud, and their appearance on the page is crucial to their effect. The poem *l(a*, for example (discussed in the Preface, p. 2), tries to visualize typographically what the poet asks you to see in your mind's eye. Occasionally, too, poems are composed in a specific shape so that the poem looks like a physical object. At the end of this chapter, several poems—some old, some new—illustrate some of the ways in which visual effects may be created. Even though poetry has traditionally been thought of as oral—words to be said, sung, or performed rather than looked at—the idea that poems can also be related to painting and the visual arts is also an old one. Theodoric in ancient Greece is credited with inventing **technopaegnia**—that is, constructing poems with visual appeal. Once, the shaping of words to resemble an object was thought to have mystical power, and especially in the Renaissance there was an active interest in **emblem poetry** (or **carmen figuratum**) such as that exemplified in *Easter Wings* (p. 195) or *The Pillar of Fame* (p. 195). But more recent attempts at **shaped verse** (the general term that may be applied to any poem that uses visual appeal dramatically) are usually playful exercises (such as Robert Hollander's *You Too? Me Too—Why Not? Soda Pop*, which is shaped like a Coke bottle), attempting to supplement (or replace) verbal meanings with devices from painting and sculpture.

Reading a poem like *Easter Wings* aloud wouldn't make much sense. Our eyes are everything for a poem like that. A more frequent poetic device is to ask us to use our eyes as a guide to sound. The following poem depends upon recognition of some standard typographical symbols and knowledge of their names. We have to say those names to read the poem:

FRANKLIN P. ADAMS

Composed in the Composing Room

At stated .ic times
I love to sit and — off rhymes
Till ,tose at last I fall
Exclaiming "I don't ∧ all."

Though I'm an ° objection
By running this in this here §
This ☞ of the Fleeting Hour,
This lofty -ician Tower—

5

A ¶er's hope dispels   10
All fear of deadly ‖.
You think these [ ] are a pipe?
Well, not on your †eotype.

                                                    1914

We create the right term here when we verbalize, putting the visual signs together with the words or letters printed in the poem, for example making the word "periodic" out of ".ic" or "high Phoenician" out of "-ician." This, too, involves an extreme instance and involves a game more than any serious emotional effect. More often poets give us—by the visual placement of sounds—a guide to reading, inviting us to regulate the pace of our reading, notice pauses or silences, pay attention both to the syntax of the poem and to the rhetoric of the voice, thus providing us a set of stage directions for reading.

e. e. cummings

portrait

Buffalo Bill's
defunct
            who used to
            ride a watersmooth-silver
                                    stallion   5
and break onetwothreefourfive pigeonsjustlikethat
                                            Jesus
he was a handsome man
                        and what i want to know is
how do you like your blueeyed boy   10
Mister Death

                                                    1923

The unusual spacing of words here, with some run together and others widely separated, provides a guide to reading, regulating both speed and sense, so that the poem can capture aloud some of the excitement and wonder of a boy's enthusiasm for a theatrical act as spectacular as that of Buffalo Bill. A good reader-aloud, with only this typographical guidance, can capture some of the wide-eyed boy's responses, remembered now in retrospect long after Buffalo Bill's act is out of business and the man himself is dead.

In prose, syntax and punctuation are the main guides to the voice of a reader, providing indicators of emphasis, pace, and speed, and in poetry they are also more conventional and more common guides than extreme forms of unusual typography as in *portrait*. Reading a poem sensitively is in some ways a lot like reading a piece of prose sensitively: one has to pay close attention to the way the sentences are put together and how they are punctuated. A good reader makes use of appropriate pauses as well as thundering emphasis; silence as well as sound is part of any poem, and reading punctuation is as important as knowing how to say the words.

Beyond punctuation, the placement and spacing of lines on the page may be helpful to a reader even when that placement is not as radical as in *portrait*. The fact that poetry looks different from prose is not an accident; decisions to make lines one length instead of another have as much to do with vocal breaks and phrasing as they have to do with functions of syntax or meaning. In a good poem, there are no accidents, not even in the way the poem meets the eye, for as readers our eyes are the most direct route to our voices; they are our scanner and director, our prompter and guide.

[handwritten margin note: form as appearance on page: emblem poetry; next to / course god]

GEORGE HERBERT

Easter Wings

[The following poem is printed sideways as a shaped "emblem" poem, the two stanzas forming wing shapes.]

Lord, who createdst man in wealth and store,¹
Though foolishly he lost the same,
Decaying more and more,
Till he became
Most poor:
With thee
O let me rise
As larks,² harmoniously,
And sing this day thy victories:
Then shall the fall further the flight in me.

My tender age in sorrow did begin;
And still with sicknesses and shame
Thou didst so punish sin,
That I became
Most thin.
With thee
Let me combine,
And feel this day thy victory;
For, if I imp³ my wing on thine,
Affliction shall advance the flight in me.

[handwritten annotations: ① diagram; meter is > form   ② wings as emblem of the idea? (lines = sin / redemption)   ③ 1st stanza is 2nd   image: graft the wing; paradox; contradic → resolution?]

1633

ROBERT HERRICK

The Pillar of Fame

Fame's pillar here, at last, we set,
Out-during *Marble, Brass,* or *Jet,*⁴
Charmed and enchanted so,
As to withstand the blow
Of   overthrow:
Nor shall the seas,
Or   OUTRAGES
Of storms o'erbear
What we up-rear,
Tho Kingdoms fall,
This   pillar   never   shall
Decline   or   waste   at   all;
But stand for ever by his own
Firm and well fixed foundation.

1648

1. In plenty.
2. Which herald the morning.
3. Engraft. In falconry, to engraft feathers in a damaged wing, so as to restore the powers of flight (OED).
4. Black lignite or black marble. "Out-during": out-lasting.

ANONYMOUS

Love Knot

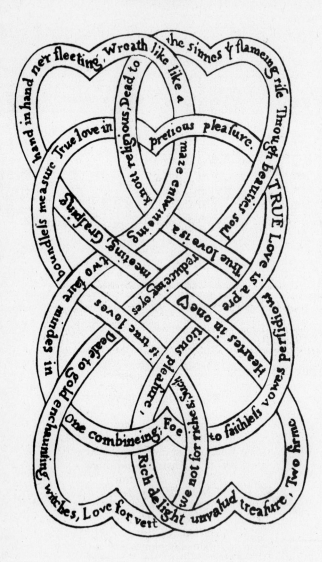

1640

EDWIN MORGAN

Message Clear

```
        am           i
                            if
    i am                 he
        he r       o
        h      ur    t                        5
        the re          and
        he     re      and
        he re
      a          n   d
        th   e   r          e                 10
    i am     r               ife
                 i n
             s       ion and
    i                d    i e
      am   e re    ct                         15
      am   e re    ction
                   o           f
        the                 life
                   o           f
      m          n                            20
            sur e
        the          d    i e
    i        s
             s  e t   and
    i am the  sur        d                     25
      a   t  res    t
                   o           life
    i am her                   e
    i a          ct
    i      r  u     n                          30
    i  m  e e     t
    i           t        i e
    i        s   t   and
    i am th       o     th
    i am   r        a                          35
    i am the  su    n
    i am the  s     on
    i am the  e   rect on     e if
    i am     re      n    t
    i am     s       a     fe                  40
    i am     s   e  n    t
    i    he e         d
    i    t e s    t
    i       re        a d
      a   th re        a d                     45
      a       s    t on       e
      a   t  re      a d
      a   th    r   on         e
    i       resurrect
                    a    life                  50
    i am         i n      life
    i am   resurrection
    i am the resurrection and
    i am
    i am the resurrection and the life[5]      55
```

EDWIN MORGAN

The Computer's First Christmas Card

```
       jollymerry
       hollyberry
       jollyberry
       merryholly
       happyjolly                    5
       jollyjelly
       jellybelly
       bellymerry
       hollyheppy
       jollyMolly                   10
       marryJerry
       merryHarry
       hoppyBarry
       heppyJarry
       boppyheppy                   15
       berryjorry
       jorryjolly
       moppyjelly
       Mollymerry
       Jerryjolly                   20
       bellyboppy
       jorryhoppy
       hollymoppy
       Barrymerry
       Jarryhappy                   25
       happyboppy
       boppyjolly
       jollymerry
       merrymerry
       merrymerry                   30
       merryChris
       ammerryasa
       Chrismerry
       aSMERRYCHR
       YSANTHEMUM                   35
```

1968

JOHN HOLLANDER

A State of Nature

```
                              Some broken
                           Iroquois adze
                          pounded southward
                          and resembled this
                          outline once But now
                          boundaries foul-lines
                          and even sea-coasts are
                          naturally involved with
                          mappers and followers of
                          borders So that we who grew
                       up here might think That steak is
              shaped too much like New York to be real And like
           the shattered flinty implement whose ghost lives
              inside our sense of what this rough chunk should
           by right of history recall the language spoken by
         its shapers now inhabits only streams and lakes and
       hills The natural names are only a chattering and mean
    only the land they label How shall we live in a forest of
                                  such murmurs with
                                  no ideas but in
                                  forms a state
                                  whose name
                                  passes
                                  for
                                  a city
                                  1969
```

ROBERT HOLLANDER

You Too? Me Too—Why Not?
Soda Pop

I am
look
ing at
the Co
caCola
bottle
which is
green wi
th ridges
just like

c   c   c
  o   o   o
l   l   l
u   u   u
  m   m   m
n   n   n
s   s   s

and on itself it says

COCA-COLA
reg.u.s.pat.off.

exactly like an art pop
statue of that kind of
bottle but not so green
that the juice inside
gives other than the co
lor it has when I pour
it out in a clear glass
glass on this table top
(It's making me thirsty
all this winking and
beading of Hippocrene
please let me pause
drinking the fluid in)
ah! it is enticing how
each color is the same
brown in green bottle
brown in uplifted glass
making each utensil on
the table laid a brown
fork in a brown shade
making me long to watch
them harvesting the crop
which makes the deep-aged
rich brown wine of America
that is to say which makes
soda   pop

p. 1968

9 STANZAS AND VERSE FORMS

Most poems of more than a few lines are divided into **stanzas,** groups of lines divided from other groups by white space on the page. Putting some space between the groupings of lines has the effect of sectioning off the poem, giving its physical appearance a series of divisions that often mark breaks in thought in the poem, or changes of scenery or imagery, or other shifts in the direction of the poem. In *The Flea* (p. 104), for example, the stanza divisions mark distinctive stages in the action; between the first and second stanzas, the speaker stops his companion from killing the flea, and between the second and third stanzas, the companion follows through on her intention and kills the flea. And in *The Goose Fish* (p. 156), the stanzas mark stages in the self-perception of the lovers; each of the stanzas is a more or less distinct scene, and the stanzas unfold almost like a series of slides. Not all stanzas are quite so neatly patterned, but any poem divided into stanzas calls attention on the page to the fact of the divisions and invites some sort of response to what appear to be gaps or silences that may be structural indicators.

Historically, stanzas have most often been organized internally by patterns of rhyme, and thus stanza divisions have been a visual indicator of patterns in sound. In most traditional stanza forms, the pattern of rhyme is repeated in stanza after stanza throughout the poem, and the voice and ear become familiar with the pattern so that, in a sense, we come to depend on it. We can thus "hear" variations, just as we do in music. In a poem of more than a few stanzas, the accumulation of pattern may even mean that our ear comes to expect repetition and finds a kind of comfort in its increasing familiarity. The rhyme thus becomes an organizational device in the poem, and ordinarily the metrical patterns stay constant from stanza to stanza. In Shelley's *Ode to the West Wind,* for example, the first and third lines in each stanza rhyme, and the middle line then rhymes with the first and third lines of the next stanza. (In indicating rhyme, a different letter of the alphabet is conventionally used to represent each sound; in the following example, if we begin with "being" as *a* and "dead" as *b*, then "fleeing" is also *a*, and "red" and "bed" are *b*.)

O wild West Wind, thou breath of Autumn's being,	a
Thou, from whose unseen presence the leaves dead	b
Are driven, like ghosts from an enchanter fleeing,	a
Yellow, and black, and pale, and hectic red,	b
Pestilence-stricken multitudes: O thou,	c
Who chariotest to their dark wintry bed	b
The wingéd seeds, where they lie cold and low,	c
Each like a corpse within its grave, until	d
Thine azure sister of the Spring shall blow	c

In this stanza form, known as **terza rima,** the stanzas are thus linked to each other by a common sound: one rhyme sound from each stanza is picked up in the next stanza, and so on to the end of the group of stanzas. This stanza form is the one used by Dante in *The Divine Comedy*; its use is not all that common in English because it is a rhyme-rich stanza form—that is, it requires many, many rhymes, and English is, relatively speaking, a rhyme-poor language (that is, not so rich in rhyme possibilities as are languages such as Italian or French). One reason for this is that English words derive from so many different language families that we have fewer similar word endings than languages that have remained more "pure," more dependent for vocabulary on roots and patterns in their own language system.

Shortly, we will look at some other stanza forms, but first a brief Defense of Rhyme, or at least an explanation of its uses. Contemporary poets seldom use it, finding it neither necessary nor appealing, but until the last half century or so rhyme was central to most poems. Historically, there are good reasons for rhyme. Why have most recent poets avoided rhyme as vigorously as older poets pursued it? There is no single easy answer, but one can suggest why poetry traditionally found rhyme attractive and notice that some of those needs no longer exist. Because poetry was originally an oral art (and its texts not always written down) various kinds of **memory devices** (sometimes called **mnemonic devices**) were built into poems to help reciters remember them. Rhyme was one such device, and most people still find it easier to memorize poetry that rhymes. The simple pleasure of hearing the repetition of familiar sounds may also help to account for the traditional popularity of rhyme, and perhaps plain habit (for both poets and hearers) had a lot to do with why rhyme flourished for so many centuries as a standard expectation. No doubt, too, rhyme helped to give poetry a special quality that distinguished it from prose, a significant advantage in ages that worried about decorum and propriety and that were anxious to preserve a strong sense of poetic tradition. Some ages have been very concerned that poetry should not in any way be mistaken for prose or made to serve prosaic functions, and the literary critics and theorists in those ages made extraordinary efforts to emphasize the distinctions between poetry, which was thought to be artistically superior, and prose, which was thought to be primarily utilitarian. A pride in elitism and a fear that an expanded reading public could ultimately mean a dilution of the possibilities of traditional art forms have been powerful cultural forces in Western civilization, and if such forces were not themselves responsible for creating rhyme in poetry, they did help to preserve a sense of its necessity.

But there are at least two other reasons for rhyme. One is complex and hard to state justly without long explanations. It involves traditional ideas of the symmetrical relationship of different aspects of the world and ideas about the function of poetry to reflect the universe as human learning understood it. Most poets in earlier centuries assumed that rhyme was proper to verse, perhaps even essential. They would have felt themselves eccentric to compose poems any other way. Some poets did experiment—very successfully—with **blank verse** (that is, verse which did not rhyme but which nevertheless had strict metrical requirements), but the cultural pressure was almost constantly for rhyme. Why? Custom or habit may account for part of the assumption that rhyme was necessary, but probably not all of it. Rather, the poets' sense that poetry was an imitation of larger relationships in the universe made it seem natural to use rhyme to recreate a sense of harmony, correspondence, symmetry, and order. The sounds of poetry were thus faint reminders of the harmonious cosmos, of the music of the spheres that animated the planets, the processes of nature, the interrelationship of all created things and beings. Probably poets never said to themselves, "I shall now tunefully emulate the harmony of God's carefully ordered universe," but the tendency to use rhyme and other repetitions or re-echoings of sound (such as **alliteration** or **assonance**, defined in "A Glossary of Poetic Terms" §8) nevertheless stems ultimately from basic assumptions about how the universe worked. In a modern world increasingly perceived as fragmented, rambling, and unrelated, there is of course a much lessened tendency to testify to a sense of harmony and symmetry. It would be too easy and too mechanical to think that rhyme in a poem specifically means that the poet has a firm sense of cosmic order, and that an unrhymed poem testifies to chaos, but cultural assumptions do affect the expectations of both poets and readers, and cultural tendencies create a kind of pressure upon the individual creator. In the third section, from Chapter 11 on, we will be looking at several similar effects upon individual poems of historical and cultural contexts.

One other reason for using rhyme is that it provides a kind of discipline for the poet, a way of harnessing poetic talents and keeping a rein on the imagination, so that the results are ordered, controlled, put into some kind of meaningful and recognizable form. Robert Frost used to be fond of saying that writing poems without rhyme was like playing tennis without a net. Writing good poetry does require a lot of discipline, and Frost speaks for many (perhaps most) traditional poets in suggesting that rhyme can be a major source of that discipline. But it is not the only possible source, and more recent poets have usually felt they would rather play by new rules or invent their own as they go along, and have therefore sought their sources of discipline elsewhere, preferring the more spare tones that unrhymed poetry provides. It is not that contemporary poets cannot think of rhyme words or that they do not care about the sounds of their poetry; rather, recent poets have consciously decided not to work with rhyme and to use instead other aural devices and other strategies for organizing stanzas, just as they have chosen to work with experimental and variable rhythms instead of writing primarily in the traditional English meters. Some few modern poets, though, have protested the abandonment of rhyme and have continued to write rhymed verse successfully in a more or less traditional way.

The amount and density of rhyme varies widely in stanza and verse forms, some requiring elaborate and intricate patterns of rhyme, others more casual or spare sound repetitions. The **Spenserian stanza,** for example, is even more rhyme rich than terza rima, using only three rhyme sounds in nine rhymed lines.

Her falt'ring hand upon the balustrade,	a
Old Angela was feeling for the stair,	b
When Madeline, St. Agnes' charméd maid,	a
Rose, like a missioned spirit, unaware:	b
With silver taper's light, and pious care,	b
She turned, and down the agéd gossip led	c
To a safe level matting. Now prepare,	b
Young Porphyro, for gazing on that bed;	c
She comes, she comes again, like ring dove frayed and fled.	c

On the other hand, the **ballad stanza** has only one rhyme in four lines; lines 1 and 3 in each stanza do not rhyme at all.

The king sits in Dumferling toune,	a
Drinking the blude-reid wine:	b
"O whar will I get guid sailor,	c
To sail this ship of mine?"	b

Most stanzas have a metrical pattern as well as a rhyme scheme. Terza rima, for example, involves five-beat lines (iambic pentameter), and most of the Spenserian stanza (the first 8 lines) is also in iambic pentameter, but the ninth line in each stanza has one extra foot (it is iambic hexameter). The ballad stanza, also iambic as are most English stanza and verse forms, alternates three-beat and four-beat lines; lines 1 and 3 are unrhymed iambic tetrameter, and lines 2 and 4 are rhymed iambic trimeter.

Several stanza forms are exemplified in this book, most of them based on rhyme schemes, but some (such as blank verse or syllabic verse) are based entirely on meter or other measures of sound, or on some more elaborate scheme such as the measured repetition of words, as in the **sestina,** or the repetition of whole lines, as in the **villanelle.** You can probably deduce the principles involved in each of the following stanza or verse forms by looking carefully at a poem which uses it; if you have trouble, look at the definitions in "A Glossary of Poetic Terms," §9.

[Sound and Sense]	heroic couplet	p. 179
To His Coy Mistress	tetrameter couplet	p. 310

What are stanza forms good for? What use is it to recognize them? Why do poets bother? Matters discussed in this chapter so far have suggested two reasons: 1. Breaks between stanzas provide convenient pauses for reader and writer, something roughly equivalent to paragraphs in prose. The eye thus picks up the places where some kind of pause or break occurs. 2. Poets sometimes use stanza forms, as they do rhyme itself, as a discipline: writing in a certain kind of stanza form imposes a shape on their act of imagination. To suggest some other uses, we will look in more detail at one particular verse form, the **sonnet**. A sonnet has only a single stanza and offers several related possibilities for its rhyme scheme, but it is always fourteen lines long and usually written in iambic pentameter. The sonnet has remained a popular verse form in English for more than four centuries, and even in an age that largely rejects rhyme it continues to attract a variety of poets, including (curiously) radical and even revolutionary poets who find its firm structure very useful. Its uses, although quite varied, can be illustrated fairly precisely.

As a verse form, the sonnet is contained, compact, demanding; whatever it does, it must do concisely and quickly. To be effective, it must take advantage of the possibilities inherent in its shortness and its relative rigidity. It is best suited to intensity of feeling and concentration of expression. Not too surprisingly, one subject it frequently discusses is confinement itself.

WILLIAM WORDSWORTH

Nuns Fret Not

Nuns fret not at their convent's narrow room;
And hermits are contented with their cells;
And students with their pensive citadels;
Maids at the wheel, the weaver at his loom,
Sit blithe and happy; bees that soar for bloom,   5
High as the highest Peak of Furness-fells,[1]
Will murmur by the hour in foxglove bells:[2]
In truth the prison, unto which we doom
Ourselves, no prison is: and hence for me,
In sundry moods, 'twas pastime to be bound   10

---

1. Mountains in England's Lake District, where Wordsworth lived.   2. Flowers from which digitalis (a heart medicine) began to be made in 1799.

Within the sonnet's scanty plot of ground;
Pleased if some souls (for such there needs must be)
Who have felt the weight of too much liberty,
Should find brief solace there, as I have found.

1807

Most sonnets are structured according to one of two principles of division. On one principle, the sonnet divides into three units of four lines each and a final unit of two lines. On the other, the fundamental break is between the first eight lines (called an octave) and the last six (called a sestet). The 4-4-4-2 sonnet is usually called the **English or Shakespearean sonnet,** and ordinarily its rhyme scheme reflects the structure: the scheme of *abab cdcd efef gg* is the classic one, but many variations from that pattern still reflect the basic 4-4-4-2 division. The 8-6 sonnet is usually called the **Italian or Petrarchan sonnet** (the Italian poet Petrarch was an early master of this structure), and its "typical" rhyme scheme is *abbaabba cdecde,* although it too produces many variations that still reflect the basic division into two parts.

The two kinds of sonnet structures are useful for two different sorts of argument. The 4-4-4-2 structure works very well for constructing a poem that wants to make a three-step argument (with a quick summary at the end), or for setting up brief, cumulative images. *That Time of Year* (p. 135), for example, uses the 4-4-4-2 structure to mark the progressive steps toward death and the parting of friends by using three distinct images, then summarizing. Shakespeare's *Let Me Not to the Marriage of True Minds* (p. 22) and Spenser's *Happy Ye Leaves* (p. 168) work very similarly, following the kind of organization that in Chapter 7 I called the 1-2-3 structure—and doing it compactly and economically.

Here, on the other hand is a poem which uses the 8-6 pattern:

HENRY CONSTABLE

My Lady's Presence Makes the Roses Red

My lady's presence makes the roses red
Because to see her lips they blush for shame.
The lily's leaves, for envy, pale became,
And her white hands in them this envy bred.
The marigold the leaves abroad doth spread   5
Because the sun's and her power is the same.
The violet of purple color came,
Dyed in the blood she made my heart to shed.
In brief, all flowers from her their virtue take;
From her sweet breath their sweet smells do proceed;   10

The living heat which her eyebeams doth make
Warmeth the ground and quickeneth the seed.
The rain wherewith she watereth the flowers
Falls from mine eyes, which she dissolves in showers.

1594

Here, the first eight lines argue that the lady's presence is respon-
sible for the color of all of nature's flowers, and the final six lines
summarize and extend that argument to smells and heat—and finally
to the rain that the lady draws from the speaker's eyes. That kind of
two-part structure, in which the octave states a proposition or gen-
eralization and the sestet provides a particularization or application of
it, has a variety of uses. The final lines may, for example, reverse
the first eight and achieve a paradox or irony in the poem, or the
poem may *nearly* balance two comparable arguments. Basically, the
8-6 structure lends itself to poems with two points to make, or to those
which wish to make one fairly brief point and illustrate it.

Sometimes the neat and precise structure I have described is al-
tered—either slightly, as in *Nuns Fret Not* above (where the 8-6
structure is more of an 8½-5½ structure) or more radically as par-
ticular needs or effects may demand. And the two basic structures
certainly do not define all the structural possibilities within a fourteen-
line poem, even if they do suggest the most traditional ways of taking
advantage of the sonnet's compact and well-kept container. Radical
departures like the *Joy Sonnet in a Random Universe* (p. 216), for
example, toy with the rigidity and use it lightheartedly to mock the
form.

The sonnets here by Sidney, Shakespeare, and Constable survive
from a golden age of sonnet writing in the late 16th century, an age
that set the pattern for expectations of form, subject matter, and tone.
The sonnet came to England from Italy via France, and imitations of
Petrarch's famous sonnet sequence to Laura became the rage. Thou-
sands upon thousands of sonnets were written in those years, often in
sequences of a hundred or more sonnets each; the sequences ex-
plored the many moods of love and usually had a light thread of nar-
rative that purported to recount a love affair between the poet and a
mistress who was almost always golden-haired, beautiful, disdainful,
and inaccessible. Her beauty was described in a series of exaggerated
comparisons: her eyes were like the sun (*When Nature Made Her
Chief Work, Stella's Eyes*), her teeth like pearls, her cheeks like
roses, her skin like ivory, and so on, but the adherence to these
conventions was always playful, and it became a game of wit to play
variations upon expectations (*My Lady's Presence Makes the Roses Red*
and *My Mistress' Eyes Are Nothing Like the Sun*). Almost always
teasing and witty (*What, Have I Thus Betrayed My Liberty*), these
poems were probably not as true to life as they pretended, but they
provided historically an expectation of what sonnets were to be.

Many modern sonnets continue to be about love or private life, and
many continue to use a personal, apparently open and sincere tone.

But poets often find the sonnet's compact form and rigid demands equally useful for many varieties of subject, theme, and tone. Besides love, sonnets often treat other subjects: politics, philosophy, discovery of a new world. And tones vary widely too, from the anger and remorse of *Th' Expense of Spirit* (p. 481) and righteous outrage of *On the Late Massacre in Piedmont* (p. 210) to the tender awe of *How Do I Love Thee* (p. 8). Many poets seem to take the kind of comfort Wordsworth describes in the careful limits of the form, finding in its two basic variations (the English sonnet such as *My Mistress' Eyes* and the Italian sonnet such as *On First Looking*) a sufficiency of convenient ways to organize their materials into coherent structures.

———

WILLIAM WORDSWORTH

Scorn Not the Sonnet

Scorn not the Sonnet; Critic, you have frowned,
Mindless of its just honors; with this key
Shakespeare unlocked his heart; the melody
Of this small lute gave ease to Petrarch's[3] wound;
A thousand times this pipe did Tasso sound;   5
With it Camoëns soothed an exile's grief;
The Sonnet glittered a gray myrtle leaf
Amid the cypress with which Dante crowned
His visionary brow: a glow-worm lamp,
It cheered mild Spenser, called from Faeryland   10
To struggle through dark ways; and when a damp
Fell round the path of Milton, in his hand
The Thing became a trumpet; whence he blew
Soul-animating strains—alas, too few!

1827

JOHN KEATS

On the Sonnet

If by dull rhymes our English must be chained,
And like Andromeda,[4] the sonnet sweet

3. Petrarch (1304–1374), Italian poet, was the model for English Renaissance sonneteers. The other poets named by Wordsworth—the Italians Tasso and Dante, the Portuguese Camoëns, and the English Shakespeare, Spenser, and Milton—also wrote sonnets extensively.

4. Who, according to Greek myth, was chained to a rock so that she would be devoured by a sea monster. She was rescued by Perseus, who married her. When she died she was placed among the stars.

Fettered, in spite of painéd loveliness,
Let us find, if we must be constrained,
Sandals more interwoven and complete   5
To fit the naked foot of Poesy:[5]
Let us inspect the lyre, and weigh the stress
Of every chord,[6] and see what may be gained
By ear industrious, and attention meet;
Misers of sound and syllable, no less   10
Than Midas[7] of his coinage, let us be
Jealous[8] of dead leaves in the bay-wreath crown;[9]
So, if we may not let the Muse be free,
She will be bound with garlands of her own.

1819

PERCY BYSSHE SHELLEY

Ozymandias[1]

I met a traveler from an antique land
Who said: Two vast and trunkless legs of stone
Stand in the desert. . . . Near them, on the sand,
Half sunk, a shattered visage lies, whose frown,
And wrinkled lip, and sneer of cold command,   5
Tell that its sculptor well those passions read
Which yet survive, stamped on these lifeless things,
The hand that mocked them, and the heart that fed:
And on the pedestal these words appear:
"My name is Ozymandias, King of Kings: 10
Look on my works, ye Mighty, and despair!"
Nothing beside remains. Round the decay
Of that colossal wreck, boundless and bare
The lone and level sands stretch far away.

1818

5. In a letter which contained this sonnet, Keats expressed impatience with the traditional Petrarchan and Shakespearean sonnet forms: "I have been endeavoring to discover a better sonnet stanza than we have."
6. Lyre-string.
7. The legendary king of Phrygia who asked, and got, the power to turn all he touched to gold.
8. Suspiciously watchful.
9. The bay tree was sacred to Apollo, god of poetry, and bay wreaths came to symbolize true poetic achievement. The withering of the bay tree is sometimes considered an omen of death.
1. The Greek name for Rameses II, 13th-century B.C. pharaoh of Egypt. According to a first century B.C. Greek historian, Diodorus Siculus, the largest statue in Egypt was inscribed: "I am Ozymandias, king of kings; if anyone wishes to know what I am and where I lie, let him surpass me in some of my exploits."

WILLIAM WORDSWORTH

London, 1802

Milton! thou should'st be living at this hour:
England hath need of thee: she is a fen[2]
Of stagnant waters: altar, sword, and pen,
Fireside, the heroic wealth of hall and bower,
Have forfeited their ancient English dower[3]   5
Of inward happiness. We are selfish men;
Oh! raise us up, return to us again;
And give us manners, virtue, freedom, power.
Thy soul was like a star, and dwelt apart:
Thou hadst a voice whose sound was like the sea: 10
Pure as the naked heavens, majestic, free,
So didst thou travel on life's common way,
In cheerful godliness; and yet thy heart
The lowliest duties on herself did lay.

1802

JOHN MILTON

On the Late Massacre in Piedmont[4]

Avenge, O Lord, thy slaughtered saints, whose bones
Lie scattered on the Alpine mountains cold;
Ev'n them who kept thy truth so pure of old,
When all our fathers worshiped stocks and stones,
Forget not: in thy book record their groans   5
Who were thy sheep, and in their ancient fold
Slain by the bloody Piedmontese, that rolled
Mother with infant down the rocks. Their moans
The vales redoubled to the hills, and they
To Heav'n. Their martyred blood and ashes sow   10
O'er all th' Italian fields, where still doth sway
The triple Tyrant:[5] that from these may grow
A hundredfold who, having learnt thy way,
Early may fly the Babylonian woe.[6]

1655

2. **Marsh.**
3. **Inheritance.**
4. On Easter Sunday, 1655, the Duke of Savoy's forces massacred 1700 members of the Waldensian sect in the Piedmont in northwestern Italy. The sect, founded in 1170, existed at first within the Roman Catholic Church, but its vigorous condemnation of church rites and policies (especially of the use of icons—see line 4) led to a total break. Until the year of the massacre the group had been allowed freedom ot worship.
5. The Pope's tiara has three crowns.
6. Protestants in Milton's day associated Catholicism with Babylonian decadence, called the church "the whore of Babylon," and read the prophecy of *Revelation* 17 and 18 as an allegory of its coming destruction.

GWENDOLYN BROOKS

First Fight. Then Fiddle.

First fight. Then fiddle. Ply the slipping string
With feathery sorcery; muzzle the note
With hurting love; the music that they wrote
Bewitch, bewilder. Qualify to sing
Threadwise. Devise no salt, no hempen thing   5
For the dear instrument to bear. Devote
The bow to silks and honey. Be remote
A while from malice and from murdering.
But first to arms, to armor. Carry hate
In front of you and harmony behind.   10
Be deaf to music and to beauty blind.
Win war. Rise bloody, maybe not too late
For having first to civilize a space
Wherein to play your violin with grace.

1949

JOHN KEATS

On First Looking into Chapman's Homer[7]

Much have I traveled in the realms of gold,
And many goodly states and kingdoms seen;
Round many western islands have I been
Which bards in fealty[8] to Apollo hold.
Oft of one wide expanse had I been told   5
That deep-browed Homer ruled as his demesne;[9]
Yet did I never breathe its pure serene[1]
Till I heard Chapman speak out loud and bold:
Then felt I like some watcher of the skies
When a new planet swims into his ken;[2]   10
Or like stout Cortez[3] when with eagle eyes
He stared at the Pacific—and all his men
Looked at each other with a wild surmise—
Silent, upon a peak in Darien.

1816

7. Chapman's were among the most famous Renaissance translations; his *Iliad* was completed in 1611, *The Odyssey* in 1616. Keats wrote the sonnet after being led to Chapman by his former teacher and reading *The Iliad* all night long.
8. Literally, the loyalty owed by a vassal to his feudal lord. Apollo was the Greek and Roman god of poetry and music.
9. Estate, feudal possession.
1. Atmosphere.
2. Range of vision.
3. Actually, Balboa; he first viewed the Pacific from Darien, in Panama.

GEORGE STARBUCK

On First Looking in on Blodgett's *Keats's* "*Chapman's Homer*" (*Sum.* ½C. M9–11)

Mellifluous as bees, these brittle men
droning of Honeyed Homer give me hives.
I scratch, yawn like a bear, my arm arrives
at yours—oh, Honey, and we're back again,
me the Balboa, you the Darien,   5
lording the loud Pacific sands, our lives
as hazarded as when a petrel dives
to yank the dull sea's coverlet, or when,
breaking from me across the sand that's rink
and record of our weekend boning up   10
on *The Romantic Agony*,[4] you sink
John Keats a good surf-fisher's cast out—plump
in the sun's wake—and the parched pages drink
that great whales' blanket party hump and hump.

1960

SIR PHILIP SIDNEY

When Nature Made Her Chief Work, Stella's Eyes[5]

When Nature made her chief work, Stella's eyes,[6]
In color black[7] why wrapped she beams so bright?
Would she in beamy black, like painter wise,
Frame daintiest luster mixed of shades and light?
Or did she else that sober hue devise,   5
In object best to knit and strength our sight,
Lest if no veil those brave gleams did disguise,
They sunlike should more dazzle than delight?
Or would she her miraculous power show,
That, whereas black seems Beauty's contrary,   10
She even in black doth make all beauties flow?
Both so and thus: she, minding[8] Love should be
Placed ever there, gave him this mourning weed
To honor all their deaths who for her bleed.

1582

---

4. The title, conveniently enough, of a scholarly book about several writers, including Keats.
5. From Sidney's sonnet sequence, *Astrophel and Stella*, usually credited with having started the vogue of sonnet sequences in Elizabethan England.
6. Following Petrarch's lead, Sidney and other English sonneteers developed a series of exaggerated conventions to describe the physical features of the women they celebrated. The excessive brightness of the eyes—almost always compared favorably with the sun's brightness—was an expected feature.
7. Black was frequently used in the Renaissance to mean absence of light, and ugly or foul (see line 10).
8. Remembering that.

WILLIAM SHAKESPEARE

My Mistress' Eyes Are Nothing like the Sun[9]

My mistress' eyes are nothing like the sun;
Coral is far more red than her lips' red;
If snow be white, why then her breasts are dun;[1]
If hairs be wires, black wires grow on her head.[2]
I have seen roses damasked[3] red and white,
But no such roses see I in her cheeks;
And in some perfumes is there more delight
Than in the breath that from my mistress reeks.
I love to hear her speak, yet well I know
That music hath a far more pleasing sound;
I grant I never saw a goddess go;[4]
My mistress, when she walks, treads on the ground.
And yet, by heaven, I think my love as rare
As any she belied with false compare.

1609

[handwritten margin notes:]
– conceits derived (TTR)
monstrous? (Brado / F. 3
NEG.; but idea is not to disparage beloved: how made 'neoPetrarchan' insofar as praise?
– endorsements e.g. on
– his assertion of truth + acceptance
– Ssp / Petr form? (engulfing the form)

HENRY CONSTABLE

Miracle of the World

Miracle of the world, I never will deny
That former poets praise the beauty of their days,
But all those beauties were but figures[5] of thy praise,
And all those poets did of thee but prophesy.
Thy coming to the world hath taught us to descry   5
What Petrarch's Laura[6] meant, for truth the lip bewrays.[7]
Lo, why th' Italians, yet which never saw thy rays,
To find out Petrarch's sense such forgéd glosses try:
The beauties, which he in a veil enclosed, beheld
But revelations were within his secret heart,[8]   10
By which in parables thy coming he foretold.
His songs were hymns of thee, which only now before
Thy image should be sung; for thou that goddess art
Which only we without idolatry adore.

1594

[handwritten margin notes:]
Milton: adapts. to various subjects

9. See Sidney's "When Nature Made Her Chief Work, Stella's Eyes," and notes.
1. Mouse-colored.
2. Women in traditional sonnets have hair of gold. Many poets who use the Petrarchan conventions also wrote poems which teased or deflated the conventions.
3. Variegated.
4. Walk.
5. Prefigurations, like people in the Old Testament who, according to Christian typology, prefigured Christ.
6. The woman celebrated in Petrarch's 14th-century sonnets. Constable's sequence of sonnets is addressed to "Diana."
7. Reveals.
8. I.e., once the beauties are actually seen (in Diana), Petrarch's mysterious descriptions turn out to be private revelations of the future.

LOUIS MACNEICE

Sunday Morning

Down the road someone is practicing scales,
The notes like little fishes vanish with a wink of tails,
Man's heart expands to tinker with his car
For this is Sunday morning, Fate's great bazaar;
Regard these means as ends, concentrate on this Now,   5
And you may grow to music or drive beyond Hindhead[9] anyhow,
Take corners on two wheels until you go so fast
That you can clutch a fringe or two of the windy past,
That you can abstract this day and make it to the week of time
A small eternity, a sonnet self-contained in rhyme.   10
But listen, up the road, something gulps, the church spire
Opens its eight bells out, skulls' mouths which will not tire
To tell how there is no music or movement which secures
Escape from the weekday time. Which deadens and endures.

1935

HELENE JOHNSON

Sonnet to a Negro in Harlem

You are disdainful and magnificent—
Your perfect body and your pompous gait,
Your dark eyes flashing solemnly with hate,
Small wonder that you are incompetent
To imitate those whom you so despise—   5
Your shoulders towering high above the throng,
Your head thrown back in rich, barbaric song,
Palm trees and mangoes stretched before your eyes.
Let others toil and sweat for labor's sake
And wring from grasping hands their meed[1] of gold.   10
Why urge ahead your supercilious feet?
Scorn will efface each footprint that you make.
I love your laughter arrogant and bold.
You are too splendid for this city street.

p. 1927

9. In Surrey; the direction of a typical   1. Reward.
Sunday outing from London.

CLAUDE MCKAY

The White House[2]

Your door is shut against my tightened face,
And I am sharp as steel with discontent;
But I possess the courage and the grace
To bear my anger proudly and unbent.
The pavement slabs burn loose beneath my feet,   5
And passion rends my vitals as I pass,
A chafing savage, down the decent street,
Where boldly shines your shuttered door of glass.
Oh, I must search for wisdom every hour,
Deep in my wrathful bosom sore and raw,   10
And find in it the superhuman power
To hold me to the letter of your law!
Oh, I must keep my heart inviolate
Against the poison of your deadly hate.

1937

e. e. cummings

a salesman

a salesman is an it that stinks Excuse

Me whether it's president of the you were say
or a jennelman name misder finger isn't
important whether it's millions of other punks
or just a handful absolutely doesn't   5
matter and whether it's in lonjewray

or shrouds is immaterial it stinks

a salesman is an it that stinks to please

but whether to please itself or someone else
makes no more difference than if it sells   10
hate condoms education snakeoil vac
uumcleaners terror strawberries democ
ra (caveat emptor[3]) cy superfluous hair

or Think We've Met subhuman rights Before

1944

2. For many years this poem was an-
thologized as "White Houses" because the
first anthologist to include the poem,
Alain Locke, had changed the title
against the author's wishes. In his auto-
biography, *A Long Way from Home*
(1937), McKay wrote: "My title . . . had
no reference to the official residence of
the President of the United States. . . .
The title 'White Houses' changed the
whole symbolic intent and meaning of the
poem, making it appear as if the burning
ambition of the black malcontent was to
enter white houses in general."
3. Literally, "let the buyer beware":
the principle that the seller is not responsi-
ble for a product unless he provides a
formal guarantee.

JOHN MILTON

When I Consider How My Light Is Spent

When I consider how my light is spent
Ere half my days,[4] in this dark world and wide,
And that one talent which is death to hide[5]
Lodged with me useless, though my soul more bent
To serve therewith my Maker, and present
My true account, lest He returning chide.
"Doth God exact day-labor, light denied?"
I fondly[6] ask. But Patience, to prevent
That murmur, soon replies, "God doth not need
Either man's work or his own gifts; who best   10
Bear His mild yoke, they serve Him best. His state
Is kingly. Thousands at His bidding speed
And post o'er land and ocean without rest;
They also serve who only stand and wait."

ca. 1652

[Handwritten marginal notes: "— Milton (PL next time) = long sent's"; "— blindness → allusion to talents: also pun? tr"; "(spiritual dangers)"; "paraphrase"; "figure? whose patience general → vise"; "Enjambment for shortest sentence"; "— repose, weight at center of sestet"; "paradox"; "— M. the prodigy, Sec. to Cromwell; failure of that (+ sight), dictated PL"]

HELEN CHASIN

Joy Sonnet in a Random Universe

Sometimes I'm happy: la la la la la la la
la la la la la la la la la la la la la la la la la la
la la la la. Tum tum ti tum. La la la la la la
la la la la la la la la la la la la la la la la la la.
Hey nonny nonny. La la la la la la la la la   5
la la la la la la la la la la la la. Vo do di o do.
Poo poo pi doo. La la la la la la la la la la la
la la la la la la la la la la la la la la la la la la
la la. Whack a doo. La la la la la la la. Sh-
boom, sh-boom. La la la la la la la la la la la   10
la la la la la la la la la la la la la la la la la la
la la. Dum di dum. La la la la la la la la la
la la la la la la la la la la. Tra la la. Tra la la
la la la la la la la la la la la la. Yeah yeah yeah.

1968

---

4. Milton was in his early forties when
he became totally blind.
5. In Jesus' parable of the talents, the
servant who buries his talent loses what
he has and is cast into "outer darkness";
see *Matthew* 25:14–30.
6. Foolishly.

10 POETIC "KINDS"

There are all sorts of poems. By now you have experienced poems on a variety of subjects and with a variation of tones, philosophical poems, political poems, witty poems, poems that tell stories, poems that recall events of long ago, poems of praise and of protest and attack, poems that concern abstractions and poems tied to a specific moment or occasion, poems that rhyme and poems that don't, short poems, long poems. And there are, of course, other sorts of poems which we haven't looked at. Some poems, for example, are thousands of lines long and differ rather substantially from the poems that can be included in a textbook like this. Poems may be classified in a variety of ways, by subject, topic, or theme; by their length, appearance, and formal features; by the way they are organized; by the level of language they use; by the poet's intention and what kinds of effects the poem tries to generate. Thinking about poems categorically can be useful in analytical ways because it enables us to put poems side by side for comparison and contrast, and in a sense almost any sort of sensible classification can help a reader experience a poem more precisely and fully. But, traditionally, there have been some more or less standard ways of classifying poems, ways that involve a combination of factors—subject matter, tone, style, intention, and effect. Knowledge of these classifications can help readers know what to expect. Poets, in fact, often consciously write a certain "kind" of poem and let us know what to expect, and when they do the poet and reader have entered into a kind of contract to think about a particular subject in a particular way. A poem that calls itself an "elegy," for example, gives us fair warning of what to expect: its label tells that it will be a serious poem memorializing the death of someone, and we may reasonably expect that its tone will be sad or angry about the death, and reflective about the meaning and direction of the dead person's life, and perhaps ruminative about the implications of the death itself.

Classification may be, of course, simply an intellectual exercise. Recognizing a poem that is an elegy, for example, or a satire, may be very much like the satisfaction involved in recognizing a scarlet tanager, a weeping willow tree, a Doric column, a French phrase, or a 1967 Ford Thunderbird. Just *knowing* what others don't know gives us a sense of importance, accomplishment, and power. But there are also *uses* for classification: we can experience a poem more fully if we understand early on exactly what kind of poem we are dealing with. A fuller response is possible because the poet has consciously chosen to play by certain defined rules, and the **conventions** he or she employs indicate that certain standard ways of saying things are being employed so as to achieve certain expected effects. The **tradition** that is involved in a particular poetic kind is thus employed by the poet and its effects are involved in us. For example, much of the humor and fun in the following poem is premised on the assumption that readers will know that they are reading a pastoral poem and will respond accordingly:

217

CHRISTOPHER MARLOWE

The Passionate Shepherd to His Love

Come live with me and be my love,
And we will all the pleasures prove[1]
That valleys, groves, hills, and fields,
Woods, or steepy mountain yields.

And we will sit upon the rocks,   5
Seeing the shepherds feed their flocks,
By shallow rivers to whose falls
Melodious birds sing madrigals.

And I will make thee beds of roses
And a thousand fragrant posies,   10
A cap of flowers, and a kirtle[2]
Embroidered all with leaves of myrtle;

A gown made of the finest wool
Which from our pretty lambs we pull;
Fair lined slippers for the cold,   15
With buckles of the purest gold;

A belt of straw and ivy buds,
With coral clasps and amber studs:
And if these pleasures may thee move,
Come live with me, and be my love.   20

The shepherd swains[3] shall dance and sing
For thy delight each May morning:
If these delights thy mind may move,
Then live with me and be my love.

1600

A naive reader might easily protest that a plea such as this one is unrealistic and fanciful and thus feel unsure of the poem's tone. What could such a reader think of a speaker who constructed his argument in such a dreamlike way? But the traditions behind the poem and the conventions of the poetic kind make its intention and effects quite clear. *The Passionate Shepherd* is a pastoral poem, a poetic kind that concerns itself with the simple life of country folk and describes that life in stylized, idealized terms. The people in a pastoral poem are usually (as here) shepherds, although they may be fishermen or other rustics who lead an outdoor life and are involved in tending basic human needs in a simplified society; the world of the poem is one

1. Try.
2. Gown.
3. Youths.

of simplicity, beauty, music, and love. The world always seems time-less in pastoral; people are eternally young, and the season is always spring, usually May. Nature seems endlessly green and the future entirely golden. Difficulty, frustration, disappointment, and obligation do not belong in this world at all; it is blissfully free of problems. Shepherds sing instead of tending sheep here, and they make love and play music instead of having to watch out for wolves in the night. If only the shepherd boy and shepherd girl can agree with each other to make love joyously and passionately, they will live happily ever after. The language of pastoral is informal and fairly simple, although always a bit more sophisticated than that of real shepherds with real problems and real sheep.

Unrealistic? Of course. No real shepherd gets to spend even a single whole day like that, and certainly the world of simple country folk has to cope with the ferocities of nature, human falsehood and knav-ery, disease, bad weather, old age, moments that are not all green and gold. And probably no poet ever thought that shepherds really live that way, but it is an attractive fantasy, and poets who write pastoral simply choose one formulaic way to isolate a series of ideal-ized moments. Fantasies can be personal and private, of course, but there is also a certain pleasure in shared public fantasies, and one central moment is that moment in a love relationship when two people are contemplating the joys of ecstatic love.

Pastoral poems are not written by shepherds. No doubt shepherds have fantasies too, but theirs probably involve ways of life far removed from sheepfolds and nights outdoors. Pastoral poems are usually written, as here, by city poets who are consciously indulging their "isn't it pretty to think so" thoughts. Pastoral poems involve an urban fantasy of rural bliss. It can be lovely to contemplate a world in which the birds sing only for our delight and other shepherds take care of the sheep, a world in which there is no work that does not turn into magic and in which the lambs bring themselves to us so that we can transform their wool instantly into a beautiful gown. It is also fun to "answer" such a vision. A group of poems on pp. 312–316 provide re-sponses to Marlowe's poem and thus offer a kind of critique of the pastoral vision. But in a sense none is necessary; the pastoral poet builds an awareness of artificiality into the whole idea of the poem. It is conceived in full consciousness that its fantasy avoids implication, and in filtering that implication carefully out of the poem, poets implicitly provide their own criticism of the fantasy world. Satire is, in a sense, the other side of the pastoral world—a city poet who fantasizes about being a shepherd usually knows all about dirt and grime and human failure and urban corruption—and satire and pas-toral are often seen as complementary poetic kinds.

Several other poetic kinds are exemplified in this book; and each has its own characteristics and conventions that have become estab-lished by tradition, repetition, and habit.

You will find definitions and brief descriptions of these poetic kinds in §10 of "A Glossary of Poetic Terms," p. 556. Each of these established kinds is worthy of detailed discussion and study, and your teacher may want to examine in depth how the conventions of several different kinds work. But rather than go through kind after kind with you, I have chosen to include quite a few poems that typify one particular kind, the epigram, so that you can examine one kind in some depth.

The poems at the end of this chapter are all epigrams, and together they add up almost to a definition of a poetic kind that has been in existence for centuries and that is still very popular. Some of these poems try definition directly (*What Is an Epigram?* or [*Epigrams*]); others, such as *Epitaph on Elizabeth, L. H.*, indirectly say what an epigram is for and how it works. Not all epigrams are so self-conscious, though, and they treat many subjects: politics (*Epigram: Of Treason*), love (*I'll Twine White Violets*), philosophies of life (*My Own Epitaph* and *Comment*), drinking (*Why I Drink*), social class (*For a Lady I Know*).

Like most poetic kinds, the epigram has a history that shaped its form and content. Originally, an **epigram** was an inscription upon some object such as a monument, triumphal arch, tombstone, or gate; hence it prized brevity and conciseness because they were absolutely necessary. But over a period of time, the term "epigram" came to mean a short poem that tried to attract attention in the same way that an inscription attracts the eyes of passersby.

As the poems here suggest, epigrams have been popular over a long period of time. The modern tradition of epigrams has two more or less separate ancient sources, one in Greece, one in Rome. In classical Greece, epigrams were composed over a period of 2,000 years; the earliest surviving ones date from the 8th century B.C. Apparently there were several anthologies of epigrams in early times, and fragments of these anthologies were later preserved, especially in large collections like the so-called *Greek Anthology*, which dates from the 10th century A.D. Largely short inscriptions, these epigrams also included some love poems (including many on homosexual love), comments on life and morality, riddles, etc. The father of the Roman tradition is generally agreed to be Martial (Marcus Valerius Martialis, A.D. 40–104 [?]), whose epigrams are witty and satirical. Modern epigrams have more frequently followed Martial's lead, but occasionally the distinctive influence of the older Greek tradition can be seen in the sadder poignancy of such poems as *Parting in Wartime*.

Knowing what to do with a poem often is aided by knowing what it is, or what it means to be. Many modern poems are not consciously conceived in terms of a traditional kind, and not all older poems are either, but a knowledge of kind can often provide one more way of deciding what to look for in a poem, helping one to find the right questions to ask.

———

SAMUEL TAYLOR COLERIDGE

What Is an Epigram?

What is an epigram? a dwarfish whole,
Its body brevity, and wit its soul.

p. 1802

ANONYMOUS translation of a Latin distich

[Epigrams]

Three things must epigrams, like bees, have all,
A sting, and honey, and a body small.

WILLIAM WALSH

An Epigram

An epigram should be—if right—
Short, simple, pointed, keen, and bright,
    A lively little thing!
Like wasp, with taper body—bound
By lines—not many, neat and round,
    All ending in a sting.

5

ca. 1690

WILLIAM BLAKE

Her Whole Life Is an Epigram

Her whole life is an epigram: smack, smooth & neatly penned,
  Platted quite neat to catch applause, with a sliding noose at the end.
ca. 1793–1811

BEN JONSON

Epitaph on Elizabeth, L. H.

Wouldst thou hear what man can say
In a little? Reader, stay.
Underneath this stone doth lie
As much beauty as could die;
Which in life did harbor give   5
To more virtue than doth live.
If at all she had a fault,
Leave it buried in this vault.
One name was Elizabeth;
Th' other, let it sleep with death: 10
Fitter, where it died, to tell,
Than that it lived at all. Farewell.

1616

MELEAGER (from the *Greek Anthology*)

I'll Twine White Violets[4]

I'll twine white violets and the myrtle green;
Narcissus will I twine and lilies sheen;
I'll twine sweet crocus and the hyacinth blue;
And last I twine the rose, love's token true:
That all may form a wreath of beauty, meet[5]
To deck my Heliodora's tresses sweet.

ca. 90 B.C.

MELEAGER (from the *Greek Anthology*)

That Morn Which Saw Me Made a Bride[6]

That morn which saw me made a bride,
The evening witnessed that I died.
Those holy lights, wherewith they guide
Unto the bed the bashful bride,
Served but as tapers for to burn,   5
And light my relics to their urn.
This epitaph which here you see,
Supplied the epithalamy.[7]

ca. 90 B.C.

---

4. Translated from the Greek by Goldwin Smith.
5. Appropriate.
6. Translated from the Greek by Robert Herrick.
7. Epithalamium: marriage song.

PALLADAS (from the *Greek Anthology*)

Naked I Came[8]

Naked I reached the world at birth;
Naked I pass beneath the earth:
Why toil I, then, in vain distress,
Seeing the end is nakedness?

ca. 400

PALLADAS (from the *Greek Anthology*)[9]

This Life a Theater[1]

This life a theater we well may call,
    Where every actor must perform with art;
Or laugh it through and make a farce of all,
    Or learn to bear with grace his tragic part.

ca. 400

MARTIAL

You've Told Me, Maro[2]

You've told me, Maro, whilst you live
You'd not a single penny give,
But that whene'er you chanced to die,
You'd leave a handsome legacy;
You must be mad beyond redress,   5
If my next wish you cannot guess.

ca. 100

MARTIAL

Tomorrow You Will Live[3]

Tomorrow you will live, you always cry;
In what fair country does this morrow lie,
That 'tis so mighty long ere it arrive?
Beyond the Indies does this morrow live?

8. Translated from the Greek by A. J. Butler.
9. A collection of epigrams compiled from earlier anthologies by a Byzantine scholar, Cephalus, in the 10th century.

1. Translated from the Greek by Robert Bland.
2. Translated from the Latin by F. Lewis.
3. Translated from the Latin by Abraham Cowley.

'Tis so far-fetched, this morrow, that I fear   5
'Twill be both very old and very dear.
"Tomorrow I will live," the fool does say;
Today itself's too late—the wise lived yesterday.

ca. 85–90

MARTIAL

Fair, Rich, and Young[4]

Fair, rich, and young? How rare is her perfection,
Were it not mingled with one foul infection?
I mean, so proud a heart, so cursed a tongue,
As makes her seem, nor fair, nor rich, nor young.

ca. 80–85

MARTIAL

He, unto Whom Thou Art So Partial[5]

He, unto whom thou art so partial,
Oh, reader! is the well-known Martial,
The Epigrammatist: while living,
Give him the fame thou wouldst be giving;
So shall he hear, and feel, and know it—   5
    Post-obits rarely reach a poet.

ca. 80–85

TOM BROWN

I Do Not Love Thee, Dr. Fell[6]

I do not love thee, Dr. Fell,
The reason why I cannot tell;
But this I know, and know full well,
I do not love thee, Dr. Fell.

ca. 1680

---

4. Translated from the Latin by Sir John Harington.
5. Translated from the Latin by George Gordon, Lord Byron.
6. A version of Martial's "Non Amo Te." According to tradition, Brown while a student at Oxford got into trouble and was taken to the dean, Dr. John Fell; Brown was expelled, but Dr. Fell decided to waive the expulsion if he could translate, extempore, a Martial epigram: this was the result.

JOHN GAY

My Own Epitaph

Life is a jest; and all things show it.
I thought so once; but now I know it.

1720

J. V. CUNNINGHAM

Here Lies My Wife

Here lies my wife. Eternal peace
Be to us both with her decease.

1959

WILLIAM BROWNE

On the Death of Marie, Countess of Pembroke

Underneath this sable hearse
Lies the subject of all verse:
Sidney's sister, Pembroke's mother;
Death, ere thou has slain another,
Fair, and learned, and good as she,   5
Time shall throw a dart at thee.
Marble piles let no man raise
To her name for after days;
Some kind woman borne as she,
Reading this, like Niobe[7]   10
Shall turn marble and become
Both her mourner and her tomb.

1621

SIR HENRY WOTTON

Upon the Death of Sir Albert Morton's Wife

He first deceased; she for a little tried
To live without him, liked it not, and died.

1651

7. In Greek fable, the mother of twelve children, all of whom died. She wept herself to death and was turned into a stone from which water ran.

RICHARD CRASHAW

An Epitaph upon a Young Married Couple, Dead and Buried Together

To these, whom death again did wed,
This grave's their second marriage-bed.
For though the hand of fate could force
'Twixt soul and body a divorce,
It could not sunder man and wife   5
'Cause they both livéd but one life.
Peace, good reader. Do not weep.
Peace, the lovers are asleep.
They, sweet turtles,[8] folded lie
In the last knot love could tie.   10
And though they lie as they were dead,
Their pillow stone, their sheets of lead,
(Pillow hard, and sheets not warm)
Love made the bed; they'll take no harm;
Let them sleep, let them sleep on.   15
Till this stormy night be gone,
Till th' eternal morrow dawn;
Then the curtains will be drawn
And they wake into a light,
Whose day shall never die in night.   20

1646

ALEXANDER POPE

Three Epitaphs on John Hewet and Sarah Drew

I

EPITAPH ON JOHN HEWET AND SARAH DREW
IN THE CHURCHYARD AT STANTON HARCOURT

NEAR THIS PLACE LIE THE BODIES OF
JOHN HEWET AND SARAH DREW,
AN INDUSTRIOUS YOUNG MAN AND
VIRTUOUS MAIDEN OF THIS PARISH;
CONTRACTED IN MARRIAGE
WHO BEING WITH MANY OTHERS AT HARVEST
WORK, WERE BOTH IN AN INSTANT KILLED
BY LIGHTNING ON THE LAST DAY OF JULY
1718

---

8. Turtledoves.

Think not by rigorous judgment seized,
  A pair so faithful could expire;
Victims so pure Heav'n saw well pleased
  And snatched them in celestial fire.

Live well and fear no sudden fate;   5
  When God calls virtue to the grave,
Alike 'tis justice, soon or late,
  Mercy alike to kill or save.

Virtue unmoved can hear the call,
And face the flash that melts the ball.   10

II

When Eastern lovers feed the fun'ral fire,
On the same pile the faithful fair expire;
Here pitying Heav'n that virtue mutual found,
And blasted both, that it might neither wound.
Hearts so sincere th' Almighty saw well pleased,   15
Sent his own lightning, and the victims seized.

III

Here lie two poor lovers, who had the mishap
Though very chaste people, to die of a clap.

1718

J. V. CUNNINGHAM

Epitaph for Someone or Other

Naked I came, naked I leave the scene,
And naked was my pastime in between.

1950

GEORGE GORDON, LORD BYRON

An Epitaph for Castlereagh[9]

Posterity will ne'er survey
  A nobler grave than this;
Here lie the bones of Castlereagh:
  Stop, traveler, . . .

1820

9. Robert Stewart Londonderry, known by the courtesy title of Viscount Castlereagh (1769–1822), was secretary of war 1805–09 and foreign secretary 1812–22; he was identified with the English government's repressive policies between 1815 and 1819 and often attacked by liberal Romantics.

X. J. KENNEDY

Epitaph for a Postal Clerk

Here lies wrapped up tight in sod
Henry Harkins c/o God.
On the day of Resurrection
May be opened for inspection.

1961

DAVID MC CORD

Epitaph on a Waiter

By and by
God caught his eye.

1935

WILLIAM STAFFORD

The Epitaph Ending in And

In the last storm, when hawks
blast upward and a dove is
driven into the grass, its broken wings
a delicate design, the air between
wracked thin where it stretched before,   5
a clear spring bent close too often
(that Earth should ever have such wings
burnt on in blind color!), this will be
good as an epitaph:

Doves did not know where to fly, and   10

1966

DOROTHY PARKER

Tombstones in the Starlight: The Very Rich Man

He'd have the best, and that was none too good;
No barrier could hold, before his terms.

He lies below, correct in cypress wood,
    And entertains the most exclusive worms.

                                                1937

DOROTHY PARKER

Tombstones in the Starlight: The Fisherwoman

The man she had was kind and clean
    And well enough for every day,
But, oh, dear friends, you should have seen
    The one that got away!

                                                1937

COUNTEE CULLEN

For a Lady I Know

She even thinks that up in heaven
    Her class lies late and snores,
While poor black cherubs rise at seven
    To do celestial chores.

                                                1925

J. V. CUNNINGHAM

All in Due Time

All in due time: love will emerge from hate,
And the due deference of truth from lies.
If not quite all things come to those who wait
They will not need them: in due time one dies.

                                                1950

THEODORE ROETHKE

Epigram: The Mistake

He left his pants upon a chair:
She was a widow, so she said:
But he was apprehended, bare,
By one who rose up from the dead.

                                          p. 1957

MATTHEW PRIOR

A True Maid

> No, no; for my virginity,
>   When I lose that, says Rose, I'll die:
> Behind the elms, last night, cried Dick,
>   Rose, were you not extremely sick?

1718

WILLIAM BLAKE

What Is It Men in Women Do Require?

> What is it men in women do require?
> The lineaments of Gratified Desire.
> What is it women do in men require?
> The lineaments of Gratified Desire.

ca. 1793–1811

GEORGE GRANVILLE, LORD LANSDOWNE

Cloe

> Bright as the day, and, like the morning, fair,
> Such Cloe is—and common as the air.

1732

RICHARD HARTER FOGLE

A Hawthorne Garland

Scarlet Letter

> Wrote the clergy: "Our Dear Madame Prynne:
> We keep mighty close watch upon sin:
>   And we think we had better
>   Proclaim by this Letter
> Our sense of how Active you've been."

1979

EZRA POUND

The Bathtub

As a bathtub lined with white porcelain,
When the hot water gives out or goes tepid,
So is the slow cooling of our chivalrous passion,
O my much praised but-not-altogether-satisfactory lady.

p. 1913

JOHN DONNE

Antiquary

If in his study Hammon hath such care
T'hang all old strange things, let his wife beware.

1633

ISAAC BICKERSTAFFE

An Expostulation

When late I attempted your pity to move,
What made you so deaf to my prayers?
Perhaps it was right to dissemble your love,
But—why did you kick me down stairs?

ca. 1765

DOROTHY PARKER

Comment

Oh, life is a glorious cycle of song,
A medley of extemporanea;
And love is a thing that can never go wrong;
And I am Marie of Rumania.

1926

HENRY ALDRICH

Why I Drink

If on my theme I rightly think,
There are five reasons why I drink—

Good wine, a friend, because I'm dry,
Or lest I should be by and by,
Or any other reason why.

ca. 1690

FRANCIS QUARLES

Be Sad, My Heart

Be sad, my heart, deep dangers wait thy mirth:
Thy soul's waylaid by sea, by hell, by earth:
Hell has her hounds; earth, snares; the sea, a shelf;
But, most of all, my heart, beware thyself.

1635

DAVID MC CORD

History of Education

The decent docent doesn't doze:
He teaches standing on his toes.
His student dassn't[1] doze—and does,
And that's what teaching is and was.

1945

J. V. CUNNINGHAM

History of Ideas

God is love. Then by inversion
Love is God, and sex conversion.

1947

SARAH CLEGHORN

Quatrain

The golf links lie so near the mill
That almost every day

---

1. Dares not.

The laboring children can look out
And see the men at play.

1936

JOHN WILMOT, EARL OF ROCHESTER

Impromptu on Charles II

God bless our good and gracious king,
   Whose promise none relies on,
Who never said a foolish thing,
   Nor ever did a wise one.

ca. 1670–80

WALTER SAVAGE LANDOR

The Georges

George the First was always reckoned
Vile, but viler George the Second;
And what mortal ever heard
Any good of George the Third?
When from earth the Fourth descended   5
(God be praised!) the Georges ended.

p. 1855

ANONYMOUS

Epigram on the Year 1390–1

The ax was sharpe, the stokke was harde,
In the xiiii yere of Kyng Richarde.

1391

PETER PINDAR

Epigram

Midas, they say, possessed the art of old
Of turning whatsoe'er he touched to gold;
This modern statesmen can reverse with ease—
Touch *them* with gold, *they'll turn to what you please.*

ca. 1780

HOWARD NEMEROV

Epigram: Political Reflexion

loquitur[2] the sparrow in the zoo.

No bars are set too close, no mesh too fine
To keep me from the eagle and the lion,
Whom keepers feed that I may freely dine.
This goes to show that if you have the wit
To be small, common, cute, and live on shit,   5
Though the cage fret kings, you may make free with it.

1958

SIR JOHN HARINGTON

Epigram: Of Treason

Treason doth never prosper, what's the reason?
For if it prosper, none dare call it treason.

1615

JOHN SHEFFIELD, DUKE OF BUCKINGHAM

Written over a Gate

Here lives a man, who, by relation,
Depends upon predestination;
For which the learnéd and the wise
His understanding much despise:
But I pronounce with loyal tongue   5
Him in the right, them in the wrong;
For how could such a wretch succeed,
But that, alas, it was decreed?

ca. 1680

FRANCES CORNFORD

Parting in Wartime

How long ago Hector[3] took off his plume,
Not wanting that his little son should cry,

---

2. I.e., the sparrow is the speaker.   3. The noblest chieftain in ancient Troy.

Then kissed his sad Andromache good-bye—
And now we three in Euston[4] waiting-room.

1948

WALTER SAVAGE LANDOR

Various the Roads of Life

Various the roads of life; in one
    All terminate, one lonely way.
We go; and "Is he gone?"
    Is all our best friends say.

1846

Contexts

11 THE AUTHOR'S WORK

Poems are not all written in the same style, as if they were produced by a corporation or put together in a committee. Just as every human individual is unique and has a distinct personality, every poet leaves a distinctive stamp on his or her work. Even though all poets share the same material (language) and usually have some common notions of their craft, they put the unique resources of their individual minds and consciousnesses into what they create. A poet may use the tradition extensively and share the crafts that others have developed without surrendering his or her own individuality, just as the integrity and uniqueness of an individual is not compromised by characteristics the individual may share with others—political affiliations, religious beliefs, tastes in clothes and music. Sometimes the uniqueness is hard to define—what exactly is it that defines the unique personality of an individual?—but it is always there, and the recognition of the distinctive quality is a large part of what we depend upon in our relationship with other people. And so with poets: most poets don't make a conscious effort to put an individual stamp on their work; they don't have to. The stamp is there, just in the way they choose subjects, words, configurations. Every individual's consciousness is unique, and that consciousness uniquely marks what it records, imagines, and decides to print.

Experienced readers can often identify a poem as the distinctive work of an individual poet even though they may never have seen the poem before. That may surprise you, but it is a lot like identifying a particular singer or group after hearing only a few phrases of a new song. Such an ability depends upon experience—a lot of reading of that author, or a lot of listening to music—but any reasonably sensitive reader can learn to do it with great accuracy. Developing such an ability, however, is not really an end in itself; rather, it is a by-product of learning to notice the particular, distinctive qualities in the workmanship of any poet. Once you've read several poems by a particular poet, you will usually begin to notice some features that the poems have in common, and gradually you may come to think of those features as characteristic. The poem that follows was written by Howard Nemerov, whose work you have read in some earlier chapters. Before you read it, you may want to look back at some of his poems printed earlier in this book and remind yourself of what those poems were like (*The Vacuum*, p. 16; *Boom!*, p. 95; *The Goose Fish*, p. 156; *Epigram: Political Reflexion*, p. 234). Another poem by Nemerov (*Life Cycle of the Common Man*, p. 463) appears in the anthology at the back.

HOWARD NEMEROV

A Way of Life

It's been going on a long time.
For instance, these two guys, not saying much, who slog
Through sun and sand, fleeing the scene of their crime,
Till one turns, without a word, and smacks
His buddy flat with the flat of an axe,   5
Which cuts down on the dialogue
Some, but is viewed rather as normal than sad
By me, as I wait for the next ad.

It seems to me it's been quite a while
Since the last vision of blonde loveliness   10
Vanished, her shampoo and shower and general style
Replaced by this lean young lunk-
head parading along with a gun in his back to confess
How yestereve, being drunk
And in a state of existential despair,   15
He beat up his grandma and pawned her invalid chair.

But here at last is a pale beauty
Smoking a filter beside a mountain stream,
Brief interlude, before the conflict of love and duty
Gets moving again, as sheriff and posse expound,   20
Between jail and saloon, the American Dream
Where Justice, after considerable horsing around,
Turns out to be Mercy; when the villain is knocked off,
A kindly uncle offers syrup for my cough.

And now these clean-cut athletic types   25
In global hats are having a nervous debate
As they stand between their individual rocket ships
Which have landed, appropriately, on some rocks
Somewhere in Space, in an atmosphere of hate
Where one tells the other to pull up his socks   30
And get going, he doesn't say where; they fade,
And an angel food cake flutters in the void.

I used to leave now and again;
No more. A lot of violence in American life
These days, mobsters and cops all over the scene.   35
But there's a lot of love, too, mixed with the strife,
And kitchen-kindness, like a bedtime story
With rich food and a more kissable depilatory.
Still, I keep my weapons handy, sitting here
Smoking and shaving and drinking the dry beer.

1967

What does this poem have in common with Nemerov's other poems? The concern with contemporary life, the tendency to concentrate on modern conveniences and luxuries, and the interest in isolating and defining aspects of the distinctively modern sensibility are all characteristic of Nemerov, and so is the tendency to create a short drama, with a speaker who is not altogether admirable. Several of Nemerov's other poems also share an attitude that seems deeply imbedded in this poem, a kind of anti-romanticism that emerges when someone tries to sound or feel *too* proud or cheerful and is shown, by events in the poem, to be part of a grimmer reality instead. The concentration upon one or more physical objects is also characteristic, and often (as in *The Vacuum*) the main object is a mechanical one that symbolizes modernity and our modern dependency on things rather than our concern with human relationships. Americanness is made emphatic here too, as if the poem were concerned to help us define our culture and its habits and values. The mood of loneliness is also characteristic, and so is the poem's witty conversational style. The verbal wit here, although not as prominent as the puns and double-entendres of *Boom!* and *Life Cycle,* is characteristically informal. Often it seems to derive from the language of commercials and street speech, and the undercutting of this language by the poet—having a paranoid and simple-minded speaker talk about a gangster in "a state of existential despair"—is similar to the strategy of *Boom!* or *The Vacuum.* The regular stanzas, rhymed but not in a traditional or regular way and with a number of near-rhymes, are also typical. Nemerov's thematic interests and ideas, his verbal style, and his cast of mind are all plainly visible in *A Way of Life.*

Noticing common features does not mean that every poem by a particular author will be predictable and contain all these features. Most poets like to experiment with new subjects, tones, forms, and various kinds of poetic strategies and devices. But the way of approach—the distinct stamp imposed by a unique consciousness—is likely to be visible anyway. The work of any writer will have certain *tendencies* that are identifiable, although not every single tendency will show up in any one poem.

Of what practical use is it to notice the distinctive voice and mind of a particular poet? One use (not the most important one for the casual reader, but one that nonetheless gives pleasure) is the pleasant surprise that occurs when you recognize something familiar. Reading a new poem by a poet with whom you are already familiar is a bit like meeting an old friend whose face or conversation reminds you of experiences you have had together. Poetic friendships can be treasures just as personal friendships are, even though they are necessarily more distant and somewhat more abstract. Just as novelty—meeting something or someone altogether new to you—is one kind of pleasure, so revisiting or recalling the familiar is another, its equal and opposite. Just *knowing* and *recognizing* often feel good—in and for themselves.

But there are other reasons, also, to look at the various works of a single writer. Just as you learn from watching other people—seeing how they react and respond to people and events, observing how they cope with their lives—you also learn from watching poets at work, seeing how they learn and develop, how they change their minds about things, how they discover the reach and limits of their minds and talents, how they find their distinctive voices and come to terms with their own identities. Watching someone at work over a period of years (as you can Adrienne Rich in the selection at the end of this chapter) is a little like watching an autobiography unfold, except that the individual poems continue to exist separately and for themselves as well as provide a record of a distinctive but gradually changing and evolving consciousness.

A third reason to study in some detail the work of a single individual is a very practical one: the more you know about the poet, the better a reader you are likely to be of any individual poem by that poet. It is not so much that the external facts of a writer's life find their way into whatever he or she writes—a poem or essay, as well as a letter or an autobiography—but that a reader gets used to habits and manners, of knowing what to expect. Coming to a new poem by a poet you already know is not completely an experience fresh and new. You adjust faster, know better what to look for, have some specific expectations (although they may be unconscious and unarticulated) of what the poem will be like. The more poems you read by any author, the better a reader you are likely to be of any one poem.

Before you read the following poem by John Donne, look at the poems by him that appear elsewhere in this book: *Death Be Not Proud* (p. 29), *Song* (p. 97), *The Flea* (p. 104), *A Valediction: Forbidding Mourning* (p. 112), *Batter My Heart* (p. 139), and *The Canonization* (p. 419). What features in these poems seem most striking and distinctive to you as you review them as a group?

JOHN DONNE

The Sun Rising

Busy old fool, unruly sun,
            Why dost thou thus,
Through windows, and through curtains, call on us?
Must to thy motions lovers' seasons run?
            Saucy pedantic wretch, go chide
            Late schoolboys, and sour prentices,[1]
Go tell court-huntsmen that the king will ride,
Call country ants[2] to harvest offices;
Love, all alike, no season knows, nor clime,
Nor hours, days, months, which are the rags of time.   10

---

1. Apprentices.   2. Farmworkers.

— Claim expands in 2nd stanza: from "we're outside rule of time" to — ?

- paraph. situation
→ we overpower sun (TR)

Thy beams, so reverend and strong
Why shouldst thou think?
I could eclipse and cloud them with a wink,
But that I would not lose her sight so long:
        If her eyes have not blinded thine,   15
        Look, and tomorrow late, tell me

- we are everything of value in world

Whether both the Indias[3] of spice and mine
Be where thou left'st them, or lie here with me.
Ask for those kings whom thou saw'st yesterday,
And thou shalt <u>hear</u>, all <u>here</u> in one bed lay. (homonym store)   20

HYPERBOLE:
comic? – line 1, 20...
but serious?
who is audience?

She is all states, and all princes I,
    Nothing else is.
Princes do but play us; compared to this,
All honor's mimic,[4] all wealth alchemy.[5]

final claim: they are world, rest is imitation

        Thou, sun, art half as happy as we,   25
        In that the world's contracted thus;
    Thine age asks[6] ease, and since thy duties be   so old sun can do
    To warm the world, that's done in warming us.   what? (Ptolomaic
Shine here to us, and thou art every where;   universe)
This bed thy center[7] is, these walls thy sphere.

                                                               1633

— universe of lovers —
(manaiacal if not for tone)

Was *The Sun Rising* somewhat easier to read than the first Donne poem you read this term? What kind of expectations did you have of the poem, knowing it was by the same author as other poems you had read? How conscious were you of those expectations? Did those expectations enable you to ask more intelligent questions of the poem as you read it? How conscious were you, as you read, of the subject matter of other Donne poems? of their themes? tone? style? form? sound effects? of other poetic devices? Did you consciously expect a speaker and a dramatic situation? How quickly did you decide what the situation was? How quickly did you identify the setting? Did you find that you had certain expectations of the speaker once you had sensed the poem's subject and situation? In retrospect, how similar to other Donne poems does this one seem? In what specific ways?

The skills involved here are progressive: they don't come all at once like a flash of lightning. Rather, they develop over time, as do most of the more sophisticated reading skills we will be considering in the final chapters of this book, and they develop in conjunction with skills you have already worked on in the previous chapters. Don't worry if you still have difficulty with a new Donne poem. You are in good company: Donne isn't easy. But the more you read, the better you will get. Reading ten or a dozen poems by a single author

3. The East and West Indies, commercial sources of spices and gold.
4. Hypocritical.
5. Imposture, like the "scientific" procedures for turning base metals into gold.
6. Requires.
7. Of orbit.

is better than reading three or four, not only because your generalizations and the expectations they create will be more reliable but also because you will feel increasingly comfortable. Spending some hours in the library reading several new poems by a poet you like and admire can be a very satisfying experience: work with any author long enough, and you will begin to feel positively at home. But even then, a good poet will still surprise you in every new poem, at least to some extent. Being reliable and distinctive is not the same as being totally predictable.

The two groups of poems that follow indicate both the distinctiveness of an individual poet's voice and the variety that often exists within that distinctiveness. The poems by John Keats suggest the pervasive sensuous and sensual quality of his work, his fascination with medieval times and gothic states of mind, his attraction both to nature and to highly ornate artifices, his distinctive patterns of phrasing and use of poetic devices, and the recurrent contrasts in his work between an external world of "objective" reality and internal states of "subjective" consciousness. Prose selections from a preface and from several of Keats's personal letters underscore some of his most persistent poetic and personal concerns. The poems are arranged chronologically, and a chronology of his life suggests the potential relevance of biographical information.

Adrienne Rich's distinctive poetic voice also emerges from the representative selection here, but the corpus of her work also illustrates change and development. Rich herself describes these changes in the prose selections and in notes appended to *Snapshots of a Daughter-in-Law, Orion,* and *Planetarium.* You may also want to look back at what Rich has said about *Aunt Jennifer's Tigers* (p. 43).

JOHN KEATS

On the Grasshopper and the Cricket

The poetry of earth is never dead:
When all the birds are faint with the hot sun,
And hide in cooling trees, a voice will run
From hedge to hedge about the new-mown mead;
That is the grasshopper's—he takes the lead   5
In summer luxury—he has never done
With his delights; for when tired out with fun
He rests at ease beneath some pleasant weed.
The poetry of earth is ceasing never:
On a lone winter evening, when the frost   10
Has wrought a silence, from the stove there shrills
The cricket's song, in warmth increasing ever,
And seems to one in drowsiness half lost,
The grasshopper's among some grassy hills.

December 30, 1816

On Seeing the Elgin Marbles[8]

My spirit is too weak—mortality
Weighs heavily on me like unwilling sleep,
And each imagined pinnacle and steep
Of godlike hardship tells me I must die
Like a sick eagle looking at the sky.   5
Yet 'tis a gentle luxury to weep
That I have not the cloudy winds to keep
Fresh for the opening of the morning's eye.
Such dim-conceived glories of the brain
Bring round the heart an indescribable feud;   10
So do these wonders a most dizzy pain,
That mingles Grecian grandeur with the rude
Wasting of old Time—with a billowy main—
A sun—a shadow of a magnitude.

1817

from Endymion (Book I.)[9]

A thing of beauty is a joy for ever:
Its loveliness increases; it will never
Pass into nothingness; but still will keep
A bower quiet for us, and a sleep
Full of sweet dreams, and health, and quiet breathing.   5
Therefore, on every morrow, are we wreathing
A flowery band to bind us to the earth,
Spite of despondence, of the inhuman dearth
Of noble natures, of the gloomy days,
Of all the unhealthy and o'er-darkened ways   10
Made for our searching: yes, in spite of all,
Some shape of beauty moves away the pall
From our dark spirits. Such the sun, the moon,
Trees old, and young sprouting a shady boon
For simple sheep; and such are daffodils   15
With the green world they live in; and clear rills
That for themselves a cooling covert make
'Gainst the hot season; the mid forest brake,[1]
Rich with a sprinkling of fair musk-rose blooms:
And such too is the grandeur of the dooms[2]   20
We have imagined for the mighty dead;
All lovely tales that we have heard or read:
An endless fountain of immortal drink,
Pouring unto us from the heaven's brink.

8. Figures and friezes from the Athenian Parthenon, purchased from the Turks by Lord Elgin and then sold to the British Museum, where Keats saw them.
9. Keats's long poem about the myth of a mortal (Endymion) loved by the goddess of the moon.
1. Thicket.
2. Judgments.

Nor do we merely feel these essences   25
For one short hour; no, even as the trees
That whisper round a temple become soon
Dear as the temple's self, so does the moon,
The passion poesy, glories infinite,
Haunt us till they become a cheering light   30
Unto our souls, and bound to us so fast,
That, whether there be shine, or gloom o'ercast,
They always must be with us, or we die.

1817

When I Have Fears

When I have fears that I may cease to be
Before my pen has gleaned my teeming brain,
Before high-piléd books, in charact'ry,
Hold like rich garners the full-ripened grain;
When I behold, upon the night's starred face,   5
Huge cloudy symbols of a high romance,
And think that I may never live to trace
Their shadows, with the magic hand of chance;
And when I feel, fair creature of an hour!
That I shall never look upon thee more,   10
Never have relish in the faery power
Of unreflecting love!—then on the shore
Of the wide world I stand alone, and think
Till Love and Fame to nothingness do sink.

1818

What the Thrush Said

O thou[3] whose face hath felt the Winter's wind,
Whose eye has seen the snow-clouds hung in mist,
And the black elm tops 'mong the freezing stars,
To thee the Spring will be a harvest-time.
O thou, whose only book has been the light   5
Of supreme darkness which thou feddest on
Night after night when Phœbus[4] was away,
To thee the spring shall be a triple morn.
O fret not after knowledge—I have none,
And yet my song comes native with the warmth.   10
O fret not after knowledge—I have none,
And yet the Evening listens. He who saddens
At thought of idleness cannot be idle,
And he's awake who thinks himself asleep.

1818

---

3. The thrush addresses the poet.   4. The sun.

The Eve of St. Agnes[5]

I

St. Agnes' Eve—Ah, bitter chill it was!
The owl, for all his feathers, was a-cold;
The hare limped trembling through the frozen grass,
And silent was the flock in woolly fold:
Numb were the Beadsman's[6] fingers, while he told   5
His rosary, and while his frosted breath,
Like pious incense from a censer old,
Seemed taking flight for heaven, without a death,
Past the sweet Virgin's picture, while his prayer he saith.

II

His prayer he saith, this patient, holy man;   10
Then takes his lamp, and riseth from his knees,
And back returneth, meager, barefoot, wan,
Along the chapel aisle by slow degrees:
The sculptured dead, on each side, seem to freeze,
Emprisoned in black, purgatorial rails: 15
Knights, ladies, praying in dumb orat'ries,[7]
He passeth by; and his weak spirit fails
To think[8] how they may ache in icy hoods and mails.

III

Northward he turneth through a little door,
And scarce three steps, ere Music's golden tongue   20
Flattered[9] to tears this aged man and poor;
But no—already had his deathbell rung:
The joys of all his life were said and sung:
His was harsh penance on St. Agnes' Eve:
Another way he went, and soon among   25
Rough ashes sat he for his soul's reprieve,
And all night kept awake, for sinners' sake to grieve.

IV

That ancient Beadsman heard the prelude soft;
And so it chanced, for many a door was wide,
From hurry to and fro. Soon, up aloft,   30
The silver, snarling trumpets 'gan to chide:
The level chambers, ready with their pride,[1]
Were glowing to receive a thousand guests:
The carvéd angels, ever eager-eyed,
Stared, where upon their heads the cornice rests,   35
With hair blown back, and wings put cross-wise on their breasts.

5. Martyred early in the fourth century at the age of 13, St. Agnes became the patron saint of virgins. According to popular belief, if a virgin performed the proper ritual on St. Agnes' Eve (January 20), she would dream of her future husband.
6. Someone paid to pray for the soul of another. "told": counted his beads.
7. Silent chapels inside the larger chapel.
8. When he thinks. "mails": suits of armor.
9. Coaxed, beguiled.
1. Splendor.

V

At length burst in the argent revelry, [2]
With plume, tiara, and all rich array,
Numerous as shadows haunting fairily
The brain, new stuffed, in youth, with triumphs gay   40
Of old romance. These let us wish away,
And turn, sole-thoughted, to one Lady there,
Whose heart had brooded, all that wintry day,
On love, and winged St. Agnes' saintly care,
As she had heard old dames full many times declare.   45

VI

They told her how, upon St. Agnes' Eve,
Young virgins might have visions of delight,
And soft adorings from their loves receive
Upon the honeyed middle of the night,
If ceremonies due they did aright;   50
As, supperless to bed they must retire,
And couch supine their beauties, lily white;
Nor look behind, nor sideways, but require
Of Heaven with upward eyes for all that they desire.

VII

Full of this whim was thoughtful Madeline: 55
The music, yearning like a God in pain,
She scarcely heard: her maiden eyes divine,
Fixed on the floor, saw many a sweeping train
Pass by—she heeded not at all: in vain
Came many a tiptoe, amorous cavalier,   60
And back retired; not cooled by high disdain,
But she saw not: her heart was otherwhere:
She sighed for Agnes' dreams, the sweetest of the year.

VIII

She danced along with vague, regardless eyes,
Anxious her lips, her breathing quick and short: 65
The hallowed hour was near at hand: she sighs
Amid the timbrels,[3] and the thronged resort
Of whisperers in anger, or in sport;
'Mid looks of love, defiance, hate, and scorn,
Hoodwinked with faery fancy; all amort,[4]   70
Save to St. Agnes and her lambs unshorn,[5]
And all the bliss to be before tomorrow morn.

IX

So, purposing each moment to retire,
She lingered still. Meantime, across the moors,
Had come young Porphyro, with heart on fire   75
For Madeline. Beside the portal doors,

---

2. Silver-clad revelers.
3. Small hand drums or tambourines.
4. Deadened: oblivious.
5. At the feast of St. Agnes the next day, lamb's wool was traditionally offered; later, nuns wove it into cloth (lines 115–17).

Buttressed[6] from moonlight, stands he, and implores
All saints to give him sight of Madeline,
But for one moment in the tedious hours,
That he might gaze and worship all unseen;   80
Perchance speak, kneel, touch, kiss—in sooth such things have been.

X

He ventures in: let no buzzed whisper tell:
All eyes be muffled, or a hundred swords
Will storm his heart, Love's fev'rous citadel:
For him, those chambers held barbarian hordes,   85
Hyena foemen, and hot-blooded lords,
Whose very dogs would execrations howl
Against his lineage:[7] not one breast affords
Him any mercy, in that mansion foul,
Save one old beldame,[8] weak in body and in soul.   90

XI

Ah, happy chance! the aged creature came,
Shuffling along with ivory-headed wand,[9]
To where he stood, hid from the torch's flame,
Behind a broad hall-pillar, far beyond
The sound of merriment and chorus bland:[1]   95
He startled her; but soon she knew his face,
And grasped his fingers in her palsied hand,
Saying, "Mercy, Porphyro! hie thee from this place;
They are all here tonight, the whole blood-thirsty race!

XII

Get hence! get hence! there's dwarfish Hildebrand;   100
He had a fever late, and in the fit
He curséd thee and thine, both house and land:
Then there's that old Lord Maurice, not a whit
More tame for his gray hairs—Alas me! flit!
Flit like a ghost away."—"Ah, Gossip[2] dear,   105
We're safe enough; here in this arm-chair sit,
And tell me how"—"Good Saints! not here, not here;
Follow me, child, or else these stones will be thy bier."

XIII

He followed through a lowly archéd way,
Brushing the cobwebs with his lofty plume,   110
And as she muttered "Well-a—well-a-day!"
He found him in a little moonlight room,
Pale, latticed, chill, and silent as a tomb.
"Now tell me where is Madeline," said he,
"O tell me, Angela, by the holy loom   115

6. Shaded by the wall supports.
7. Because of the feud between his
family and Madeline's.
8. Old, usually ugly, woman.

9. Walking stick, cane.
1. Soothing.
2. Old friend.

Which none but secret sisterhood may see,
When they St. Agnes' wool are weaving piously."

XIV

"St. Agnes! Ah! it is St. Agnes' Eve—
Yet men will murder upon holy days:
Thou must hold water in a witch's sieve,   120
And be liege-lord of all the Elves and Fays,
To venture so:[3] it fills me with amaze
To see thee, Porphyro!—St. Agnes' Eve!
God's help! my lady fair the conjuror plays [4]
This very night: good angels her deceive!   125
But let me laugh awhile, I've mickle [5] time to grieve."

XV

Feebly she laugheth in the languid moon,
While Porphyro upon her face doth look,
Like puzzled urchin on an aged crone
Who keepeth closed a wond'rous riddle-book,   130
As spectacled she sits in chimney nook.
But soon his eyes grew brilliant, when she told
His lady's purpose; and he scarce could brook [6]
Tears, at the thought of those enchantments cold
And Madeline asleep in lap of legends old.   135

XVI

Sudden a thought came like a full-blown rose,
Flushing his brow, and in his painéd heart
Made purple riot: then doth he propose
A stratagem, that makes the beldame start:
"A cruel man and impious thou art: 140
Sweet lady, let her pray, and sleep, and dream
Alone with her good angels, far apart
From wicked men like thee. Go, go!—I deem
Thou canst not surely be the same that thou didst seem."

XVII

"I will not harm her, by all saints I swear,"   145
Quoth Porphyro: "O may I ne'er find grace
When my weak voice shall whisper its last prayer,
If one of her soft ringlets I displace,
Or look with ruffian passion in her face:
Good Angela, believe me by these tears;   150
Or I will, even in a moment's space,
Awake, with horrid shout, my foemen's ears,
And beard[7] them, though they be more fanged than wolves and bears."

3. I.e., Porphyro would need to be a
magician to take such chances.
4. In trying to evoke the image of her
lover.

5. Plenty of.
6. Hold back.
7. Defy, affront.

XVIII

"Ah! why wilt thou affright a feeble soul?
A poor, weak, palsy-stricken, churchyard thing,   155
Whose passing-bell[8] may ere the midnight toll;
Whose prayers for thee, each morn and evening,
Were never missed."—Thus plaining,[9] doth she bring
A gentler speech from burning Porphyro;
So woeful, and of such deep sorrowing,   160
That Angela gives promise she will do
Whatever he shall wish, betide her weal or woe.[1]

XIX

Which was, to lead him, in close secrecy,
Even to Madeline's chamber, and there hide
Him in a closet, of such privacy   165
That he might see her beauty unespied,
And win perhaps that night a peerless bride,
While legioned fairies paced the coverlet,
And pale enchantment held her sleepy-eyed.
Never on such a night have lovers met,   170
Since Merlin paid his Demon all the monstrous debt.[2]

XX

"It shall be as thou wishest," said the Dame:
"All cates[3] and dainties shall be storéd there
Quickly on this feast-night: by the tambour frame[4]
Her own lute thou wilt see: no time to spare,   175
For I am slow and feeble, and scarce dare
On such a catering trust my dizzy head.
Wait here, my child, with patience; kneel in prayer
The while: Ah! thou must needs the lady wed,
Or may I never leave my grave among the dead."   180

XXI

So saying, she hobbled off with busy fear.
The lover's endless minutes slowly passed;
The dame returned, and whispered in his ear
To follow her; with agéd eyes aghast
From fright of dim espial. Safe at last,   185
Through many a dusky gallery, they gain
The maiden's chamber, silken, hushed, and chaste;
Where Porphyro took covert, pleased amain.[5]
His poor guide hurried back with agues in her brain.

XXII

Her falt'ring hand upon the balustrade,   190
Old Angela was feeling for the stair,

8. Bell that rings for death.
9. Complaining.
1. Whatever happens to her, good or bad.
2. Merlin was a powerful magician in the Arthurian legends; the incident referred to here has not been identified.
3. Delicacies.
4. Embroidery frame.
5. Greatly.

When Madeline, St. Agnes' charméd maid,
Rose, like a missioned spirit,[6] unaware:
With silver taper's light, and pious care,
She turned, and down the agéd gossip led   195
To a safe level matting. Now prepare,
Young Porphyro, for gazing on that bed;
She comes, she comes again, like ring dove frayed[7] and fled.

XXIII

Out went the taper as she hurried in;
Its little smoke, in pallid moonshine, died: 200
She closed the door, she panted, all akin
To spirits of the air, and visions wide:
No uttered syllable, or, woe betide!
But to her heart, her heart was voluble,
Paining with eloquence her balmy side;   205
As though a tongueless nightingale should swell
Her throat in vain, and die, heart-stifled, in her dell.

XXIV

A casement[8] high and triple-arched there was,
All garlanded with carven imag'ries
Of fruits, and flowers, and bunches of knot-grass,   210
And diamonded with panes of quaint device,
Innumerable of stains and splendid dyes,
As are the tiger moth's deep-damasked wings;
And in the midst, 'mong thousand heraldries,
And twilight saints, and dim emblazonings,   215
A shielded scutcheon blushed with blood of queens and kings.

XXV

Full on this casement shone the wintry moon,
And threw warm gules[9] on Madeline's fair breast,
As down she knelt for heaven's grace and boon;[1]
Rose-bloom fell on her hands, together pressed,   220
And on her silver cross soft amethyst,
And on her hair a glory,[2] like a saint:
She seemed a splendid angel, newly dressed,
Save wings, for heaven—Porphyro grew faint:
She knelt, so pure a thing, so free from mortal taint.   225

XXVI

Anon his heart revives: her vespers done,
Of all its wreathéd pearls her hair she frees;
Unclasps her warméd jewels one by one;
Loosens her fragrant bodice; by degrees
Her rich attire creeps rustling to her knees: 230

---

6. Angel on a mission.
7. Frightened.
8. Window, in which are stained-glass representations of many kinds, including a
royal coat of arms (line 216).
9. Heraldic red.
1. Gift, blessing.
2. Halo.

Half-hidden, like a mermaid in sea-weed,
Pensive awhile she dreams awake, and sees,
In fancy, fair St. Agnes in her bed,
But dares not look behind, or all the charm is fled.

XXVII

Soon, trembling in her soft and chilly nest,   235
In sort of wakeful swoon, perplexed she lay,
Until the poppied warmth of sleep oppressed
Her soothéd limbs, and soul fatigued away;
Flown, like a thought, until the morrow-day;
Blissfully havened both from joy and pain;   240
Clasped like a missal where swart Paynims[3] pray;
Blinded alike from sunshine and from rain,
As though a rose should shut, and be a bud again.

XXVIII

Stol'n to this paradise, and so entranced,
Porphyro gazed upon her empty dress,   245
And listened to her breathing, if it chanced
To wake into a slumberous tenderness;
Which when he heard, that minute did he bless,
And breathed himself: then from the closet crept,
Noiseless as fear in a wide wilderness,   250
And over the hushed carpet, silent, stepped,
And 'tween the curtains peeped, where, lo!—how fast she slept.

XXIX

Then by the bedside, where the faded moon
Made a dim, silver twilight, soft he set
A table, and, half anguished, threw thereon   255
A cloth of woven crimson, gold, and jet—
O for some drowsy Morphean amulet![4]
The boisterous, midnight, festive clarion,[5]
The kettledrum, and far-heard clarinet,
Affray his ears, though but in dying tone—   260
The hall door shuts again, and all the noise is gone.

XXX

And still she slept an azure-lidded sleep,
In blanchéd linen, smooth, and lavendered,
While he from forth the closet brought a heap
Of candied apple, quince, and plum, and gourd;   265
With jellies soother than the creamy curd,
And lucent syrups, tinct with cinnamon;
Manna[6] and dates, in argosy[7] transferred
From Fez; and spicéd dainties, every one,
From silken Samarcand to cedared Lebanon.   270

---

3. Pagans.
4. A charm of Morpheus, god of sleep.
5. Trumpet.
6. Sweet gum.

7. Merchant ships. Fez, Samarcand, and
Lebanon are in Morocco, central Asia, and
the Levant, respectively.

XXXI

These delicates he heaped with glowing hand
On golden dishes and in baskets bright
Of wreathéd silver: sumptuous they stand
In the retired quiet of the night,
Filling the chilly room with perfume light.   275
"And now, my love, my seraph[8] fair, awake!
Thou art my heaven, and I thine eremite:
Open thine eyes, for meek St. Agnes' sake,
Or I shall drowse beside thee, so my soul doth ache."

XXXII

Thus whispering, his warm, unnervéd arm   280
Sank in her pillow. Shaded was her dream
By the dusk curtains:—'twas a midnight charm
Impossible to melt as icéd stream:
The lustrous salvers in the moonlight gleam;
Broad golden fringe upon the carpet lies: 285
It seemed he never, never could redeem
From such a steadfast spell his lady's eyes;
So mused awhile, entoiled[9] in wooféd fantasies.

XXXIII

Awakening up, he took her hollow lute—
Tumultuous—and, in chords that tenderest be,   290
He played an ancient ditty, long since mute,
In Provence called, "La belle dame sans merci":[1]
Close to her ear touching the melody—
Wherewith disturbed, she uttered a soft moan.
He ceased—she panted quick—and suddenly   295
Her blue affrayéd eyes wide open shone:
Upon his knees he sank, pale as smooth-sculptured stone.

XXXIV

Her eyes were open, but she still beheld,
Now wide awake, the vision of her sleep:
There was a painful change, that nigh expelled   300
The blisses of her dream so pure and deep,
At which fair Madeline began to weep,
And moan forth witless words with many a sigh;
While still her gaze on Porphyro would keep;
Who knelt, with joinéd hands and piteous eye,   305
Fearing to move or speak, she looked so dreamingly.

XXXV

"Ah, Porphyro!" said she, "but even now
Thy voice was at sweet tremble in mine ear,
Made tunable with every sweetest vow;

---

8. The highest order of angel. "eremite":
devotee.
9. Entangled. "wooféd": woven.

1. "The beautiful lady without pity,"
the kind of love song played or sung in
medieval Provence.

And those sad eyes were spiritual and clear: 310
How changed thou art! how pallid, chill, and drear!
Give me that voice again, my Porphyro,
Those looks immortal, those complainings dear!
Oh leave me not in this eternal woe,
For if thou diest, my Love, I know not where to go."   315

XXXVI

Beyond a mortal man impassioned far
At these voluptuous accents, he arose,
Ethereal, flushed, and like a throbbing star
Seen mid the sapphire heaven's deep repose
Into her dream he melted, as the rose   320
Blendeth its odor with the violet—
Solution sweet: meantime the frost-wind blows
Like Love's alarum pattering the sharp sleet
Against the windowpanes; St. Agnes' moon hath set.

XXXVII

'Tis dark: quick pattereth the flaw-blown[2] sleet: 325
"This is no dream, my bride, my Madeline!"
'Tis dark: the icéd gusts still rave and beat:
"No dream, alas! alas! and woe is mine!
Porphyro will leave me here to fade and pine.
Cruel! what traitor could thee hither bring?   330
I curse not, for my heart is lost in thine,
Though thou forsakest a deceivéd thing—
A dove forlorn and lost with sick unprunéd wing."

XXXVIII

"My Madeline! sweet dreamer! lovely bride!
Say, may I be for aye[3] thy vassal blest?   335
Thy beauty's shield, heart-shaped and vermeil[4] dyed?
Ah, silver shrine, here will I take my rest
After so many hours of toil and quest,
A famished pilgrim—saved by miracle.
Though I have found, I will not rob thy nest   340
Saving of thy sweet self; if thou think'st well
To trust, fair Madeline, to no rude infidel.

XXXIX

"Hark! 'tis an elfin-storm from faery land,
Of haggard[5] seeming, but a boon indeed:
Arise—arise! the morning is at hand—   345
The bloated wassailers[6] will never heed—
Let us away, my love, with happy speed;
There are no ears to hear, or eyes to see—
Drowned all in Rhenish and the sleepy mead:[7]

2. Gust-blown.   6. Drunken revelers.
3. Forever.   7. Liquor made from honey. "Rhenish":
4. Vermilion: bright red.   rhine wine.
5. Wild.

Awake! arise! my love, and fearless be,   350
For o'er the southern moors I have a home for thee."

XL

She hurried at his words, beset with fears,
For there were sleeping dragons all around,
At glaring watch, perhaps, with ready spears—
Down the wide stairs a darkling way they found.   355
In all the house was heard no human sound.
A chain-drooped lamp was flickering by each door;
The arras,[8] rich with horseman, hawk, and hound,
Fluttered in the besieging wind's uproar;
And the long carpets rose along the gusty floor.   360

XLI

They glide, like phantoms, into the wide hall;
Like phantoms, to the iron porch, they glide;
Where lay the Porter, in uneasy sprawl,
With a huge empty flagon by his side:
The wakeful bloodhound rose, and shook his hide,   365
But his sagacious eye an inmate[9] owns:
By one, and one, the bolts full easy slide—
The chains lie silent on the footworn stones—
The key turns, and the door upon its hinges groans.

XLII

And they are gone: ay, ages long ago   370
These lovers fled away into the storm.
That night the Baron dreamt of many a woe,
And all his warrior-guests, with shade and form,
Of witch, and demon, and large coffin-worm,
Were long be-nightmared. Angela the old   375
Died palsy-twitched, with meager face deform;
The Beadsman, after thousand aves[1] told,
For aye unsought for slept among his ashes cold.

1819

To Sleep

O soft embalmer of the still midnight,
Shutting, with careful fingers and benign,
Our gloom-pleased eyes, embowered from the light,
Enshaded in forgetfulness divine;
O soothest[2] Sleep! if so it please thee, close,   5
In midst of this thine hymn, my willing eyes,

8. Tapestry.   1. Ave Maria's: Hail Mary's.
9. Member of the household. "owns":   2. Softest.
recognizes.

Or wait the amen, ere thy poppy[2] throws
Around my bed its lulling charities;
Then save me, or the passéd day will shine
Upon my pillow, breeding many woes;　　10
Save me from curious[4] conscience, that still lords
Its strength for darkness, burrowing like a mole;
Turn the key deftly in the oiléd wards,[5]
And seal the hushéd casket of my soul.

April, 1819

Ode to a Nightingale

I

My heart aches, and a drowsy numbness pains
　　My sense, as though of hemlock[6] I had drunk,
Or emptied some dull opiate to the drains
　　One minute past, and Lethe-wards[7] had sunk:
'Tis not through envy of thy happy lot,　　5
　　But being too happy in thine happiness,
　　　　That thou, light-wingéd Dryad[8] of the trees,
　　　　　　In some melodious plot
　　Of beechen green, and shadows numberless,
　　　　Singest of summer in full-throated ease.　　10

II

O, for a draught of vintage! that hath been
　　Cooled a long age in the deep-delvéd earth,
Tasting of Flora[9] and the country green,
　　Dance, and Provençal song,[1] and sunburnt mirth!
O for a beaker full of the warm South,　　15
　　Full of the true, the blushful Hippocrene,[2]
　　　　With beaded bubbles winking at the brim,
　　　　　　And purple-stainéd mouth;
　　That I might drink, and leave the world unseen,
　　　　And with thee fade away into the forest dim:　　20

III

Fade far away, dissolve, and quite forget
　　What thou among the leaves hast never known,
The weariness, the fever, and the fret
　　Here, where men sit and hear each other groan;
Where palsy shakes a few, sad, last gray hairs,　　25

3. Because opium derives from it, the poppy was associated with sleep.
4. Scrupulous. "lords": marshals.
5. Ridges in a lock that distinguish proper from improper keys.
6. A poisonous drug.
7. Toward the river of forgetfulness (Lethe) in Hades.

8. Wood nymph.
9. Roman goddess of flowers.
1. The medieval troubadors of Provence (in southern France) were famous for their love songs.
2. The fountain of the Muses on Mt. Helicon, whose waters bring poetic inspiration.

Where youth grows pale, and specter-thin, and dies;
    Where but to think is to be full of sorrow
        And leaden-eyed despairs,
    Where Beauty cannot keep her lustrous eyes,
        Or new Love pine at them beyond tomorrow.   30

IV

Away! away! for I will fly to thee,
    Not charioted by Bacchus and his pards,[3]
But on the viewless wings of Poesy,
    Though the dull brain perplexes and retards:
Already with thee! tender is the night,   35
    And haply the Queen-Moon is on her throne,
        Clustered around by all her starry Fays;[4]
        But here there is no light,
Save what from heaven is with the breezes blown
        Through verdurous glooms and winding mossy ways.   40

V

I cannot see what flowers are at my feet,
    Nor what soft incense hangs upon the boughs,
But, in embalméd[5] darkness, guess each sweet
    Wherewith the seasonable month endows
The grass, the thicket, and the fruit-tree wild;   45
    White hawthorn, and the pastoral eglantine;[6]
        Fast fading violets covered up in leaves;
        And mid-May's eldest child,
The coming musk-rose, full of dewy wine,
        The murmurous haunt of flies on summer eves.   50

VI

Darkling[7] I listen; and, for many a time
    I have been half in love with easeful Death,
Called him soft names in many a muséd rhyme,
    To take into the air my quiet breath;
Now more than ever seems it rich to die,   55
    To cease upon the midnight with no pain,
        While thou art pouring forth thy soul abroad
        In such an ecstasy!
Still wouldst thou sing, and I have ears in vain—
        To thy high requiem become a sod.   60

VII

Thou wast not born for death, immortal Bird!
    No hungry generations tread thee down;
The voice I hear this passing night was heard
    In ancient days by emperor and clown:

---

3. The Roman god of wine was sometimes portrayed in a chariot drawn by leopards. "viewless": invisible.
4. Fairies.
5. Fragrant, aromatic.
6. Sweetbriar or honeysuckle.
7. In the dark.

Perhaps the selfsame song that found a path   65
  Through the sad heart of Ruth,[8] when, sick for home,
    She stood in tears amid the alien corn;
      The same that ofttimes hath
  Charmed magic casements, opening on the foam
    Of perilous seas, in faery lands forlorn.   70

VIII

Forlorn! the very word is like a bell
  To toll me back from thee to my sole self!
Adieu! the fancy cannot cheat so well
  As she is famed to do, deceiving elf.
Adieu! adieu! thy plaintive anthem fades   75
  Past the near meadows, over the still stream,
    Up the hillside; and now 'tis buried deep
      In the next valley-glades:
  Was it a vision, or a waking dream?
    Fled is that music:—Do I wake or sleep?   80

May, 1819

Ode on a Grecian Urn

I

Thou still unravished bride of quietness,
  Thou foster-child of silence and slow time,
Sylvan[9] historian, who canst thus express
  A flowery tale more sweetly than our rhyme:
What leaf-fringed legend haunts about thy shape   5
  Of deities or mortals, or of both,
    In Tempe or the dales of Arcady?[1]
What men or gods are these? What maidens loath?
  What mad pursuit? What struggle to escape?
    What pipes and timbrels? What wild ecstasy?   10

II

Heard melodies are sweet, but those unheard
  Are sweeter; therefore, ye soft pipes, play on;
Not to the sensual[2] ear, but, more endeared,
  Pipe to the spirit ditties of no tone:
Fair youth, beneath the trees, thou canst not leave   15
  Thy song, nor ever can those trees be bare;
    Bold Lover, never, never canst thou kiss,
  Though winning near the goal—yet, do not grieve;

8. A virtuous Moabite widow who, according to the Old Testament *Book of Ruth*, found a husband while gleaning in the wheat fields of Judah.
9. Rustic. The urn depicts a woodland scene.
1. Arcadia. Tempe is a beautiful valley near Mt. Olympus in Greece, and the valley ("dales") of Arcadia a picturesque section of the Peloponnesus; both came to be associated with the pastoral ideal.
2. Of the senses, as distinguished from the "ear" of the spirit or imagination.

She cannot fade, though thou hast not thy bliss,
For ever wilt thou love, and she be fair!   20

III

Ah, happy, happy boughs! that cannot shed
  Your leaves, nor ever bid the Spring adieu;
And, happy melodist, unweariéd,
  For ever piping songs for ever new;
More happy love! more happy, happy love!   25
  For ever warm and still to be enjoyed,
    For ever panting, and for ever young;
All breathing human passion far above,
  That leaves a heart high-sorrowful and cloyed,
    A burning forehead, and a parching tongue.   30

IV

Who are these coming to the sacrifice?
  To what green altar, O mysterious priest,
Lead'st thou that heifer lowing at the skies,
  And all her silken flanks with garlands dressed?
What little town by river or sea shore,   35
  Or mountain-built with peaceful citadel,
    Is emptied of this folk, this pious morn?
And, little town, thy streets for evermore
  Will silent be; and not a soul to tell
    Why thou art desolate, can e'er return.   40

V

O Attic[3] shape! Fair attitude! with brede[4]
  Of marble men and maidens overwrought,
With forest branches and the trodden weed;
  Thou, silent form, dost tease us out of thought
As doth eternity: Cold Pastoral!   45
  When old age shall this generation waste,
    Thou shalt remain, in midst of other woe
Than ours, a friend to man, to whom thou say'st,
  Beauty is truth, truth beauty[5]—that is all
    Ye know on earth, and all ye need to know.   50

May, 1819

---

3. Attica was the district of ancient Greece surrounding Athens.
4. Woven pattern. "overwrought": ornamented all over.
5. In some texts of the poem "Beauty is truth, truth beauty" is in quotation marks and in some texts it is not, leading to critical disagreements about whether the last line and a half are also inscribed on the urn or spoken by the poet.

Ode on Melancholy

I

No, no, go not to Lethe,[6] neither twist
 Wolfsbane, tight-rooted, for its poisonous wine;[7]
Nor suffer thy pale forehead to be kissed
 By nightshade, ruby grape of Proserpine;
Make not your rosary of yew-berries,[8]   5
  Nor let the beetle, nor the death-moth be
   Your mournful Psyche,[9] nor the downy owl
A partner in your sorrow's mysteries;
  For shade to shade will come too drowsily,
   And drown the wakeful anguish of the soul. 10

II

But when the melancholy fit shall fall
 Sudden from heaven like a weeping cloud,
That fosters the droop-headed flowers all,
 And hides the green hill in an April shroud;
Then glut thy sorrow on a morning rose,   15
 Or on the rainbow of the salt sand-wave,
  Or on the wealth of globéd peonies;
Or if thy mistress some rich anger shows,
  Emprison her soft hand, and let her rave,
   And feed deep, deep upon her peerless eyes. 20

III

She[1] dwells with Beauty—Beauty that must die;
 And Joy, whose hand is ever at his lips
Bidding adieu; and aching Pleasure nigh,
 Turning to poison while the bee-mouth sips:
Ay, in the very temple of Delight   25
 Veiled Melancholy has her sov'reign shrine,
  Though seen of none save him whose strenuous tongue
Can burst Joy's grape against his palate fine;[2]
  His soul shall taste the sadness of her might,
   And be among her cloudy trophies hung.[3] 30

May, 1819

6. Like nightshade (line 4), wolfsbane is a poisonous plant. "Proserpine": Queen of Hades.
7. Which often grow in cemeteries and which are traditionally associated with death.
8. *Psyche* means both "soul" and "breath," and sometimes it was anciently represented by a moth leaving the mouth at death. Owls and beetles were also traditionally associated with darkness and death.
9. The river of forgetfulness in Hades.
1. The goddess Melancholy, whose chief place of worship ("shrine") is described in lines 25–26.
2. Sensitive, discriminating.
3. The ancient Greeks and Romans hung trophies in their gods' temples.

To Autumn

I

Season of mists and mellow fruitfulness,
  Close bosom-friend of the maturing sun;
Conspiring with him how to load and bless
  With fruit the vines that round the thatch-eves run;
To bend with apples the mossed cottage-trees,   5
  And fill all fruit with ripeness to the core;
    To swell the gourd, and plump the hazel shells
With a sweet kernel; to set budding more,
  And still more, later flowers for the bees,
    Until they think warm days will never cease,   10
      For Summer has o'er-brimmed their clammy cells.

II

Who hath not seen thee oft amid thy store?
  Sometimes whoever seeks abroad may find
Thee sitting careless on a granary floor,
  Thy hair soft-lifted by the winnowing wind;[4]   15
Or on a half-reaped furrow sound asleep,
  Drowsed with the fume of poppies, while thy hook[5]
    Spares the next swath and all its twinéd flowers:
And sometimes like a gleaner thou dost keep
  Steady thy laden head across a brook;   20
  Or by a cider-press, with patient look,
    Thou watchest the last oozings hours by hours.

III

Where are the songs of Spring? Ay, where are they?
  Think not of them, thou hast thy music too—
While barréd clouds bloom the soft-dying day,   25
  And touch the stubble-plains with rosy hue;
Then in a wailful choir the small gnats mourn
  Among the river sallows,[6] borne aloft
    Or sinking as the light wind lives or dies;
And full-grown lambs loud bleat from hilly bourn;[7]   30
  Hedge-crickets sing; and now with treble soft
  The red-breast whistles from a garden-croft;[8]
    And gathering swallows twitter in the skies.

September 19, 1819

from Letter to Benjamin Bailey, November 22, 1817[9]

  * * * I am certain of nothing but of the holiness of the Heart's affec-
tions and the truth of Imagination—What the imagination seizes as

---

4. Which sifts the grain from the chaff.
5. Scythe or sickle.
6. Willows.
7. Domain.

8. An enclosed garden near a house.
9. Keats's private letters, often carelessly written, are reprinted uncorrected.

Beauty must be truth—whether it existed before or not—for I have the same Idea of all our Passions as of Love they are all in their sublime, creative of essential Beauty ° ° ° The Imagination may be compared to Adam's dream[1]—he awoke and found it truth. I am the more zealous in this affair, because I have never yet been able to perceive how any thing can be known for truth by consequitive reasoning—and yet it must be—Can it be that even the greatest Philosopher ever ~~when~~ arrived at his goal without putting aside numerous objections—However it may be, O for a Life of Sensations rather than of Thoughts! It is "a Vision in the form of Youth" a Shadow of reality to come—and this consideration has further conv[i]nced me for it has come as auxiliary to another favorite Speculation of mine, that we shall enjoy ourselves here after by having what we called happiness on Earth repeated in a finer tone and so repeated—And yet such a fate can only befall those who delight in sensation rather than hunger as you do after Truth—Adam's dream will do here and seems to be a conviction that Imagination and its empyreal reflection is the same as human Life and its spiritual repetition. But as I was saying—the simple imaginative Mind may have its rewards in the repeti[ti]on of its own silent Working coming continually on the spirit with a fine suddenness—to compare great things with small—have you never by being surprised with an old Melody—in a delicious place—by a delicious voice, fe[l]t over again your very speculations and surmises at the time it first operated on your soul—do you not remember forming to yourself the singer's face more beautiful that [*for* than] it was possible and yet with the elevation of the Moment you did not think so—even then you were mounted on the Wings of Imagination so high—that the Prototype must be here after—that delicious face you will see—What a time! I am continually running away from the subject—sure this cannot be exactly the case with a complex Mind—one that is imaginative and at the same time careful of its fruits—who would exist partly on sensation partly on thought—to whom it is necessary that years should bring the philosophic Mind—such an one I consider your's and therefore it is necessary to your eternal Happiness that you not only ~~have~~ drink this old Wine of Heaven which I shall call the redigestion of our most ethereal Musings on Earth; but also increase in knowledge and know all things. ° ° °

from Letter to George and Thomas Keats,
December 21, 1817

° ° ° I spent Friday evening with Wells[2] & went the next morning to see *Death on the Pale horse*.[3] It is a wonderful picture, when West's age is considered; But there is nothing to be intense upon; no women one feels mad to kiss, no face swelling into reality. the excellence of

1. In *Paradise Lost*, VIII, 460–90.
2. Charles Wells (1800–1879), an author.
3. By Benjamin West (1738–1820), American painter and president of the Royal Academy; "Christ Rejected" (mentioned below) is also by West.

every Art is its intensity, capable of making all disagreeables evaporate, from their being in close relationship with Beauty & Truth—Examine King Lear & you will find this examplified throughout; but in this picture we have unpleasantness without any momentous depth of speculation excited, in which to bury its repulsiveness—The picture is larger than Christ rejected—I dined with Haydon the sunday after you left, & had a very pleasant day, I dined too (for I have been out too much lately) with Horace Smith & met his two Brothers with Hill & Kingston & one Du Bois,[4] they only served to convince me, how superior humour is to wit in respect to enjoyment—These men say things which make one start, without making one feel, they are all alike; their manners are alike; they all know fashionables; they have a mannerism in their very eating & drinking, in their mere handling a Decanter—They talked of Kean[5] & his low company—Would I were with that company instead of yours said I to myself! I know such like acquaintance will never do for me & yet I am going to Reynolds, on wednesday—Brown & Dilke walked with me & back from the Christmas pantomime. I had not a dispute but a disquisition with Dilke, on various subjects; several things dovetailed in my mind, & at once it struck me, what quality went to form a Man of Achievement especially in Literature & which Shakespeare posessed so enormously—I mean *Negative Capability*, that is when man is capable of being in uncertainties, Mysteries, doubts, without any irritable reaching after fact & reason—Coleridge, for instance, would let go by a fine isolated verisimilitude caught from the Penetralium of mystery, from being incapable of remaining content with half knowledge. This pursued through Volumes would perhaps take us no further than this, that with a great poet the sense of Beauty overcomes every other consideration, or rather obliterates all consideration.

Letter to John Hamilton Reynolds,
February 19, 1818

I have an idea that a Man might pass a very pleasant life in this manner—let him on any certain day read a certain Page of full Poesy or distilled Prose and let him wander with it, and muse upon it, and reflect from it, and bring home to it, and prophesy upon it, and dream upon it—untill it becomes stale—but when will it do so? Never—When Man has arrived at a certain ripeness in intellect any one grand and spiritual passage serves him as a starting post towards all "the two-and-thirty Pallaces"[6] How happy is such a "voyage of conception," what delicious diligent Indolence! A doze upon a Sofa does not hinder it, and a nap upon Clover engenders ethereal finger-pointings—the prattle of a child gives it wings, and the converse of middle age a strength to beat them—a strain of musick conducts to "an odd angle of

---

4. Thomas Hill (1760–1840), a book collector, and Edward duBois (1774–1850), a journalist.

5.]   nund Kean, a famous Shakespeare   actor.

6.   ices of delight" in Buddhism.

the Isle",[7] and when the leaves whisper it puts a "girdle round the earth",[8] Nor will this sparing touch of noble Books be any irreverance to their Writers—for perhaps the honors paid by Man to Man are trifles in comparison to the Benefit done by great Works to the "Spirit and pulse of good" by their mere passive existence. Memory should not be called knowledge—Many have original minds who do not think it— they are led away by Custom—Now it appears to me that almost any Man may like the Spider spin from his own inwards his own airy Citadel—the points of leaves and twigs on which the Spider begins her work are few and she fills the Air with a beautiful circuiting: man should be content with as few points to tip with the fine Webb of his Soul and weave a tapestry empyrean—full of Symbols for his spiritual eye, of softness for his spiritual touch, of space for his wandering of distinctness for his Luxury—But the Minds of Mortals are so different and bent on such diverse Journeys that it may at first appear impossible for any common taste and fellowship to exist ~~bettween~~ between two or three under these suppositions—It is however quite the contrary— Minds would leave each other in contrary directions, traverse each other in Numberless points, and all [*for at*] last greet each other at the Journeys end—An old Man and a child would talk together and the old Man be led on his Path, and the child left thinking—Man should not dispute or assert but whisper results to his neighbor, and thus by every germ of Spirit sucking the Sap from mould ethereal every human might become great, and Humanity instead of being a wide heath of Furse[9] and Briars with here and there a remote Oak or Pine, would become a grand democracy of Forest Trees. It has been an old Comparison for our urging on—the Bee hive—however it seems to me that we should rather be the flower than the Bee—for it is a false notion that more is gained by receiving than giving—no, the receiver and the giver are equal in their benefits—The f[l]ower I doubt not receives a fair guerdon from the Bee—its leaves blush deeper in the next spring—and who shall say between Man and Woman which is the most delighted? Now it is more noble to sit like Jove that [*for than*] to fly like Mercury—let us not therefore go hurrying about and collecting honey bee like, buzzing here and there impatiently from a knowledge of what is to be arrived at; but let us open our leaves like a flower and be passive and receptive—budding patiently under the eye of Apollo and taking hints from every noble insect that favors us with a visit—sap will be given us for Meat and dew for drink—I was led into these thoughts, my dear Reynolds, by the beauty of the morning operating on a sense of Idleness—I have not read any Books—the Morning said I was right —I had no Idea but of the Morning, and the Thrush said I was right— seeming to say—

> O thou whose face hath felt the Winter's wind,
> Whose eye has seen the snow-clouds hung in mist,
> And the black elm tops 'mong the freezing stars,
> To thee the spring will be a harvest-time.

---

7. *The Tempest*, Act I, sc. ii, 223. *Night's Dream*, Act II, sc. i, 175.
8. The phrase is from *Midsummer* 9. *The Tempest*, Act I, sc. i, 68–69.

O thou, whose only book has been the light
Of supreme darkness which thou feddest on
Night after night when Phœbus was away,
To thee the spring shall be a triple morn.
O fret not after knowledge—I have none,
And yet my song comes native with the warmth.
O fret not after knowledge—I have none,
And yet the Evening listens. He who saddens
At thought of idleness cannot be idle,
And he's awake who thinks himself asleep.

Now I am sensible all this is a mere sophistication, however it may neighbor to any truths, to excuse my own indolence—so I will not deceive myself that Man should be equal with jove—but think himself very well off as a sort of scullion-Mercury, or even a humble Bee—It is not [*for* no] matter whether I am right or wrong either one way or another, if there is sufficient to lift a little time from your Shoulders.

from Letter to John Taylor, February 27, 1818

* * * It is a sorry thing for me that any one should have to overcome Prejudices in reading my Verses—that affects me more than any hyper-criticism on any particular Passage. In *Endymion* I have most likely but moved into the Go-cart from the leading strings. In Poetry I have a few Axioms, and you will see how far I am from their Centre. 1st I think Poetry should surprise by a fine excess and not by Singularity—it should strike the Reader as a wording of his own highest thoughts, and appear almost a Remembrance—2nd Its touches of Beauty should never be half way therby making the reader breathless instead of content: the rise, the progress, the setting of imagery should like the Sun come natural natural too him—shine over him and set soberly although in magnificence leaving him in the Luxury of twilight—but it is easier to think what Poetry should be than to write it—and this leads me on to another axiom. That if Poetry comes not as naturally as the Leaves to a tree it had better not come at all. However it may be with me I cannot help looking into new countries with "O for a Muse of fire to ascend!"[1]—If Endymion serves me as a Pioneer perhaps I ought to be content. I have great reason to be content, for thank God I can read and perhaps understand Shakspeare to his depths, and I have I am sure many friends, who, if I fail, will attribute any change in my Life and Temper to Humbleness rather than to Pride—to a cowering under the Wings of great Poets rather than to a Bitterness that I am not appreciated. I am anxious to get Endymion printed that I may forget it and proceed. * * *

---

1. **Shakespeare,** *Henry V,* Prologue, 1.

from the Preface to *Endymion,* dated April 10, 1818

The imagination of a boy is healthy, and the mature imagination of a man is healthy; but there is a space of life between, in which the soul is in a ferment, the character undecided, the way of life uncertain, the ambition thick-sighted: thence proceeds mawkishness, and all the thousand bitters which those men I speak of must necessarily taste in going over the following pages.

I hope I have not in too late a day touched the beautiful mythology of Greece, and dulled its brightness: for I wish to try once more, before I bid it farewell.

from Letter to James Augustus Hessey, October 8, 1818

° ° ° Praise or blame has but a momentary effect on the man whose love of beauty in the abstract makes him a severe critic on his own Works. My own domestic criticism has given me pain without comparison beyond what Blackwood or the ~~Edinburgh~~ Quarterly[2] could possibly inflict. and also when I feel I am right, no external praise can give me such a glow as my own solitary reperception & ratification of what is fine. J. S.[3] is perfectly right in regard to the slip-shod Endymion. That it is so is no fault of mine.—No!—though it may sound a little paradoxical. It is as good as I had power to make it—by myself—Had I been nervous about its being a perfect piece, & with that view asked advice, & trembled over every page, it would not have been written; for it is not in my nature to fumble—I will write independantly.—I have written independently *without Judgment.*—I may write independently & *with judgment* hereafter.—The Genius of Poetry must work out its own salvation in a man: It cannot be matured by law & precept, but by sensation & watchfulness in itself—That which is creative must create itself—In Endymion, I leaped headlong into the Sea, and thereby have become better acquainted with the Soundings, the quicksands & the rocks, than if I had ~~stayed~~ stayed upon the green shore, and piped a silly pipe, and took tea & comfortable advice.—I was never afraid of failure; for I would sooner fail than not be among the greatest—But I am nigh getting into a rant. ° ° °

Chronology

1795   John Keats born October 31 at Finsbury, just north of London, the eldest child of Thomas and Frances Jennings Keats. Thomas Keats was head ostler at a livery stable.

1797–1803   Birth of three younger brothers and sisters: George in 1797, Thomas in 1799, Frances Mary (Fanny) in 1803.

2. *Endymion* was violently attacked by reviewers in *Blackwood's Edinburgh Magazine* and *The Quarterly Review.*

3. Whose letter to the *Morning Chronicle* defended Keats.

1803 With George, begins school in Enfield.

1804 Father killed by a fall from his horse, April 15. On June 27 his mother remarries, and the children go to live with their maternal grandparents at Enfield. The grandfather dies a year later, and the children move with their grandmother to Lower Edmonton.

1809 Begins a literary friendship with Charles Cowden Clarke, the son of the headmaster at the Enfield school, and develops a strong interest in reading.

1810 Mother dies of tuberculosis, after a long illness.

1811 Leaves school to become apprenticed to an apothecary-surgeon in Edmonton; completes a prose translation of the *Aeneid,* begun at school.

1814 Earliest known attempts at writing verse. In December his grandmother dies, and the family home is broken up.

1815 In October moves to next stage of his medical training at Guy's Hospital, south of the Thames in London.

1816 On May 5 his first published poem, *O Solitude,* appears in Leigh Hunt's *Examiner.* In October writes *On First Looking into Chapman's Homer,* published in December. Meets Hunt, Benjamin Haydon, John Hamilton Reynolds, and Shelley. By the spring of 1817, gives up the idea of medical practice.

1817 In March, moves with brothers to Hampstead, sees the Elgin Marbles with Haydon, and publishes his first collection of *Poems.* Composes *Endymion* between April and November. Reads Milton, Shakespeare, Coleridge and rereads Wordsworth during the year.

1818 *Endymion* published in April, unfavorably reviewed in September, defended by Reynolds in October. During the summer goes on walking tour of the lake country and Scotland, but returns to London in mid-August with a sore throat and severe chills. His brother Tom also seriously ill by late summer, dying on December 1. In September, Keats first meets Fanny Brawne (18 years old), with whom he arrives at an "understanding" by Christmas.

1819 Writes *The Eve of St. Agnes* in January, revises it in September. Fanny Brawne and her mother move into the other half of the double house in which Keats lives in April. During April and May writes *La Belle Dame sans Merci* and all the major odes except *To Autumn,* written in September. Rental arrangements force separation from Fanny Brawne during the summer (Keats on Isle of Wight from June to August), and in the fall he tries to break his dependence on her, but they become engaged by Christmas. Earlier in December suffers a recurrence of his sore throat.

1820 In February has a severe hemorrhage and in June an attack of blood-spitting. In July his doctor orders him to Italy for the winter; he sails in September and finally arrives in Rome on November 15. In July a volume of poems published, *Lamia, Isabella, The Eve of St. Agnes and Other Poems.* Fanny Brawne nurses him through the late summer.

1821 Dies at 11 P.M., February 23. Buried in the English Cemetery at Rome.

ADRIENNE RICH

A Clock in the Square

This handless clock stares blindly from its tower,
Refusing to acknowledge any hour.
But what can one clock do to stop the game
When others go on striking just the same?
Whatever mite of truth the gesture held,   5
Time may be silenced but will not be stilled,
Nor we absolved by any one's withdrawing
From all the restless ways we must be going
And all the rings in which we're spun and swirled,
Whether around a clockface or a world.   10

                                                                 1951

At a Bach Concert

Coming by evening through the wintry city
We said that art is out of love with life.
Here we approach a love that is not pity.

This antique discipline, tenderly severe,
Renews belief in love yet masters feeling,   5
Asking of us a grace in what we bear.

Form is the ultimate gift that love can offer—
The vital union of necessity
With all that we desire, all that we suffer.

A too-compassionate art is half an art.   10
Only such proud restraining purity
Restores the else-betrayed, too-human heart.

                                                                 1951

Storm Warnings

The glass has been falling all the afternoon,
And knowing better than the instrument
What winds are walking overhead, what zone
Of gray unrest is moving across the land,
I leave the book upon a pillowed chair   5
And walk from window to closed window, watching
Boughs strain against the sky

And think again, as often when the air
Moves inward toward a silent core of waiting,

How with a single purpose time has traveled 10
By secret currents of the undiscerned
Into this polar realm. Weather abroad
And weather in the heart alike come on
Regardless of prediction.

Between foreseeing and averting change 15
Lies all the mastery of elements
Which clocks and weatherglasses cannot alter.
Time in the hand is not control of time,
Nor shattered fragments of an instrument
A proof against the wind; the wind will rise, 20
We can only close the shutters.

I draw the curtains as the sky goes black
And set a match to candles sheathed in glass
Against the keyhole draught, the insistent whine
Of weather through the unsealed aperture. 25
This is our sole defense against the season;
These are the things that we have learned to do
Who live in troubled regions.

1951

Snapshots of a Daughter-in-Law

1

You, once a belle in Shreveport,
with henna-colored hair, skin like a peachbud,
still have your dresses copied from that time,
and play a Chopin prelude
called by Cortot: *"Delicious recollections* 5
float like perfume through the memory."

Your mind now, mouldering like wedding-cake,
heavy with useless experience, rich
with suspicion, rumor, fantasy,
crumbling to pieces under the knife-edge 10
of mere fact. In the prime of your life.

Nervy, glowering, your daughter
wipes the teaspoons, grows another way.

2

Banging the coffee-pot into the sink
she hears the angels chiding, and looks out 15
past the raked gardens to the sloppy sky.
Only a week since They said: *Have no patience.*

The next time it was: *Be insatiable.*

Then: *Save yourself; others you cannot save.*[4]
Sometimes she's let the tapstream scald her arm,   20
a match burn to her thumbnail,

or held her hand above the kettle's snout
right in the woolly steam. They are probably angels,
since nothing hurts her any more, except
each morning's grit blowing into her eyes.   25

3

A thinking woman sleeps with monsters.
The beak that grips her, she becomes. And Nature,
that sprung-lidded, still commodious
steamer-trunk of *tempora* and *mores*[5]
gets stuffed with it all: the mildewed orange-flowers,   30
the female pills, the terrible breasts
of Boadicea[6] beneath flat foxes' heads and orchids.

Two handsome women, gripped in argument,
each proud, acute, subtle, I hear scream
across the cut glass and majolica   35
like Furies[7] cornered from their prey:
The argument *ad feminam*,[8] all the old knives
that have rusted in my back, I drive in yours,
ma semblable, ma soeur![9]

4

Knowing themselves too well in one another: 40
their gifts no pure fruition, but a thorn,
the prick filed sharp against a hint of scorn . . .
Reading while waiting
for the iron to heat,
writing, *My Life had stood—a Loaded Gun—*[1]   45
in that Amherst pantry while the jellies boil and scum,
or, more often,
iron-eyed and beaked and purposed as a bird,
dusting everything on the whatnot every day of life.

5

Dulce ridens, dulce loquens,[2]   50
she shaves her legs until they gleam
like petrified mammoth-tusk.

---

4. According to *Matthew* 27:42, the chief priests, scribes, and elders mocked the crucified Jesus by saying, "He saved others; himself he cannot save."
5. Times and customs.
6. Queen of the ancient Britons. When her husband died, the Romans seized the territory he ruled and scourged Boadicea; she then led a heroic but ultimately unsuccessful revolt.
7. In Roman mythology, the three sisters were the avenging spirits of retributive justice.
8. Argument to the woman. The *argumentum ad hominem* (literally, argument to the man) is (in logic) an argument aimed at a person's individual prejudices or special interests.
9. "My mirror-image (or 'double'), my sister." Baudelaire, in the prefatory poem to *Les Fleurs du Mal*, addresses (and attacks) his "hypocrite reader" as "mon semblable, mon frère" (my double, my brother).
1. " 'My Life had stood—a Loaded Gun' [Poem No. 754], Emily Dickinson, *Complete Poems*, ed. T. H. Johnson, 1960, p. 369." (Rich's note)
2. "Sweet (or winsome) laughter, sweet chatter." The phrase (slightly modified here) concludes Horace's *Ode*, 1, 22, describing the appeal of a mistress.

6

When to her lute Corinna sings[3]
neither words nor music are her own;
only the long hair dipping   55
over her check, only the song
of silk against her knees
and these
adjusted in reflections of an eye.

Poised, trembling and unsatisfied, before   60
an unlocked door, that cage of cages,
tell us, you bird, you tragical machine—
is this *fertilisante douleur?*[4] Pinned down
by love, for you the only natural action,
are you edged more keen   65
to prise the secrets of the vault? has Nature shown
her household books to you, daughter-in-law,
that her sons never saw?

7

"To have in this uncertain world some stay
which cannot be undermined, is   70
of the utmost consequence."[5]
                              Thus wrote
a woman, partly brave and partly good,
who fought with what she partly understood.
Few men about her would or could do more,
hence she was labeled harpy, shrew and whore.   75

8

"You all die at fifteen," said Diderot,[6]
and turn part legend, part convention.
Still, eyes inaccurately dream
behind closed windows blankening with steam.
Deliciously, all that we might have been,   80
all that we were—fire, tears,
wit, taste, martyred ambition—
stirs like the memory of refused adultery
the drained and flagging bosom of our middle years.

9

Not that it is done well, but   85
that it is done at all?[7] Yes, think

---

3. The opening line of a famous Eliza-bethan lyric (by Thomas Campion) in which Corinna's music is said to control totally the poet's happiness or despair.
4. Enriching pain.
5. "'. . . is of the utmost consequence,' from Mary Wollstonecraft, *Thoughts on the Education of Daughters*, London, 1787." (Rich's note)
6. "'Vous mourez toutes à quinze ans,' from the *Lettres à Sophie Volland*, quoted by Simone de Beauvoir in *Le Deuxième Sexe*, vol. II, pp. 123–4." (Rich's note)

Editor of the *Encyclopédie* (the central document of the French Enlightenment), Diderot became disillusioned with the tra-ditional education of women and under-took an experimental education for his own daughter.
7. Samuel Johnson's comment on women preachers: "Sir, a woman's preaching is like a dog's walking on his hinder legs. It is not done well, but you are surprised to find it done at all." (Boswell's *Life of Johnson*, ed. Birbeck-Hill, I, 463)

of the odds! or shrug them off forever.
This luxury of the precocious child,
Time's precious chronic invalid,—
would we, darlings, resign it if we could?   90
Our blight has been our sinecure:
mere talent was enough for us—
glitter in fragments and rough drafts.

Sigh no more, ladies.
                    Time is male
and in his cups drinks to the fair.   95
Bemused by gallantry, we hear
our mediocrities over-praised,
indolence read as abnegation,
slattern thought styled intuition,
every lapse forgiven, our crime   100
only to cast too bold a shadow
or smash the mould straight off.

For that, solitary confinement,
tear gas, attrition shelling.
Few applicants for that honor.

                    10
                    Well,   105
she's long about her coming, who must be
more merciless to herself than history.[8]
Her mind full to the wind, I see her plunge
breasted and glancing through the currents,
taking the light upon her   110
at least as beautiful as any boy
or helicopter,
                    poised, still coming,
her fine blades making the air wince

but her cargo
no promise then: 115
delivered
palpable
ours.

1958–60

[*In* When We Dead Awaken, *Rich described her consciousness dur-
ing the time she was writing this poem:* "Over two years I wrote a
10-part poem called 'Snapshots of A Daughter-in-Law,' in a longer,
looser mode than I've ever trusted myself with before. It was an extra-

---

8. "Cf. *Le Deuxième Sexe,* vol. II, p.
574: '. . . elle arrive du fond des ages, de
Thèbes, de Minos, de Chichen Itza; et elle
est aussi le totem planté au coeur de la
brousse africaine; c'est un helicoptère et
c'est un oiseau; et voilà la plus grande mer-
veille: sous ses cheveux peints le bruisse-
ment des feuillages devient une pensée et
des paroles s'échappent de ses seins.' "
(Rich's note)

ordinary relief to write that poem. It strikes me now as too literary, too dependent on allusion; I hadn't found the courage yet to do without authorities, or even to use the pronoun 'I'—the woman in the poem is always 'she.' One section of it, #2, concerns a woman who thinks she is going mad; she is haunted by voices telling her to resist and rebel, voices which she can hear but not obey."]

Necessities of Life

Piece by piece I seem
to re-enter the world: I first began

a small, fixed dot, still see
that old myself, a dark-blue thumbtack

pushed into the scene,   5
a hard little head protruding

from the pointillist's[9] buzz and bloom.
After a time the dot

begins to ooze. Certain heats
melt it.
    Now I was hurriedly   10
blurring into ranges

of burnt red, burning green,
whole biographies swam up and
swallowed me like Jonah.

Jonah! I was Wittgenstein,[1]   15
Mary Wollstonecraft, the soul

of Louis Jouvet, dead
in a blown-up photograph.

Till, wolfed almost to shreds,
I learned to make myself   20

unappetizing. Scaly as a dry bulb
thrown into a cellar

I used myself, let nothing use me.
Like being on a private dole,

9. Post-impressionist painters (Seurat, for example) who fused small dots of paint with brush strokes.
1. Ludwig Wittgenstein (1889–1951), Austrian-born philosopher. His early thought heavily influenced logical positivism, and his later work expressed such strong skepticism about the reliability of language that he ultimately resigned his chair of philosophy lest his ideas be misunderstood or misinterpreted. Mary Wollstonecraft, an early feminist, wrote *Vindication of the Rights of Women* (1792). Louis Jouvet (1887–1951), innovative French actor and producer.

sometimes more like kneading bricks in Egypt.[2]   25
What life was there, was mine,

now and again to lay
one hand on a warm brick

and touch the sun's ghost
with economical joy,   30

now and again to name
over the bare necessities.

So much for those days. Soon
practice may make me middling-perfect, I'll

dare inhabit the world   35
trenchant in motion as an eel, solid

as a cabbage-head. I have invitations:
a curl of mist steams upward

from a field, visible as my breath,
houses along a road stand waiting   40

like old women knitting, breathless
to tell their tales.

1962

Orion

Far back when I went zig-zagging
through tamarack pastures
you were my genius, you
my cast-iron Viking, my helmed
lion-heart king in prison.   5
Years later now you're young

my fierce half-brother, staring
down from that simplified west
your breast open, your belt dragged down
by an oldfashioned thing, a sword   10
the last bravado you won't give over
though it weighs you down as you stride

and the stars in it are dim
and maybe have stopped burning.

2. According to *Exodus* 5, one of the most oppressive tasks imposed on the Is- raelites during their Egyptian bondage was the making of bricks.

But you burn, and I know it;   15
as I throw back my head to take you in
an old transfusion happens again:
divine astronomy is nothing to it.

Indoors I bruise and blunder,
break faith, leave ill enough   20
alone, a dead child born in the dark.
Night cracks up over the chimney,
pieces of time, frozen geodes
come showering down in the grate.

A man reaches behind my eyes   25
and finds them empty
a woman's head turns away
from my head in the mirror
children are dying my death
and eating crumbs of my life.   30

Pity is not your forte.
Calmly you ache up there
pinned aloft in your crow's nest,
my speechless pirate!
You take it all for granted   35
and when I look you back

it's with a starlike eye
shooting its cold and egotistical spear
where it can do least damage.
Breathe deep! No hurt, no pardon   40
out here in the cold with you
you with your back to the wall.

1965

[*In* When We Dead Awaken, *Rich described* Orion *as* "a poem of re-construction with a part of myself I had felt I was losing—the active principle, the energetic imagination, the 'half-brother' whom I projected, as I had for many years, into the constellation Orion. It's no accident that the words 'cold and egotistical' appear in this poem, and are applied to myself. The choice still seemed to be between 'love'—womanly, maternal love, altruistic love—a love defined and ruled by the weight of an entire culture—and egotism—a force directed by men into creation, achievement, ambition, often at the expense of others, but justifiably so. For weren't they men, and wasn't that their destiny as womanly love was ours? I know now that the alternatives are false ones—that the word 'love' is itself in need of re-vision."]

Planetarium

(Thinking of Caroline Herschel, 1750–1848,
astronomer, sister of William; and others)

A woman in the shape of a monster
a monster in the shape of a woman
the skies are full of them

a woman   "in the snow
among the Clocks and instruments   5
or measuring the ground with poles"

in her 98 years to discover
8 comets

she whom the moon ruled
like us   10
levitating into the night sky
riding the polished lenses

Galaxies of women, there
doing penance for impetuousness
ribs chilled   15
in those spaces   of the mind

An eye,
        "virile, precise and absolutely certain"
        from the mad webs of Uranisborg

                                encountering the NOVA

every impulse of light exploding   20
from the core
as life flies out of us

        Tycho[3] whispering at last
        "Let me not seem to have lived in vain"

What we see, we see   25
and seeing is changing

the light that shrivels a mountain
and leaves a man alive

Heartbeat of the pulsar
heart sweating through my body   30

3. Tycho Brahe (1546–1601), Danish astronomer whose cosmology tried to fuse the Ptolemaic and Copernican systems. He discovered and described (*"De Nova Stella,*" 1573) a new star in what had previously been considered a fixed star-system. Uraniborg (line 19) was Tycho's famous and elaborate palace-laboratory-observatory.

The radio impulse
pouring in from Taurus
        I am bombarded yet   I stand

I have been standing all my life in the
direct path of a battery of signals   35
the most accurately transmitted most
untranslatable language in the universe
I am a galactic cloud so deep   so invo-
luted that a light wave could take 15
years to travel through me   And has   40
taken   I am an instrument in the shape
of a woman trying to translate pulsations
into images   for the relief of the body
and the reconstruction of the mind.
1968

[*Rich described this poem, in* When We Dead Awaken, *as a* "companion poem to 'Orion,' " *above:* "at last the woman in the poem and the woman writing the poem become the same person. . . . It was written after a visit to a real planetarium, where I read an account of the work of Caroline Herschel, the astronomer, who worked with her brother William, but whose name remained obscure, as his did not."]

Trying to Talk with a Man

Perhaps my life is nothing but an image of this kind; perhaps I am doomed to retrace my steps under the illusion that I am exploring, doomed to try and learn what I should simply recognize, learning a mere fraction of what I have forgotten.
                    —ANDRE BRETON, *Nadja*[4]

Out in this desert we are testing bombs,

that's why we came here.

Sometimes I feel an underground river
forcing its way between deformed cliffs
an acute angle of understanding   5
moving itself like a locus of the sun
into this condemned scenery.

What we've had to give up to get here—
Whole LP collections, films we starred in
playing in the neighborhoods, bakery windows   10
full of dry, chocolate-filled Jewish cookies,
the language of love-letters, of suicide notes,
afternoons on the riverbank
pretending to be children

4. Breton (1896–1968), a French poet and critic, was one of the founders of both Dadaism and Surrealism. His novel *Nadja* was published in 1928.

Coming out to this desert   15
we meant to change the face of
driving among dull green succulents
walking at noon in the ghost-town
surrounded by a silence

that sounds like the silence of the place   20
except that it came with us
and is familiar
and everything we were saying until now
was an effort to blot it out
Coming out here we are up against it   25

Out here I feel more helpless
with you than without you.
You mention the danger
and list the equipment
we talk of people caring for each other   30
in emergencies—laceration, thirst—
but you look at me like an emergency

Your dry heat feels like power
your eyes are stars of a different magnitude
they reflect lights that spell out EXIT   35
when you get up and pace the floor

talking of the danger
as if it were not ourselves
as if we were testing anything else.

1971

Diving into the Wreck

First having read the book of myths,
and loaded the camera,
and checked the edge of the knife-blade,
I put on
the body-armor of black rubber   5
the absurd flippers
the grave and awkward mask.
I am having to do this
not like Cousteau with his
assiduous team   10
aboard the sun-flooded schooner
but here alone.

There is a ladder.
The ladder is always there

hanging innocently
close to the side of the schooner.
We know what it is for,
we who have used it.
Otherwise
it's a piece of maritime floss
some sundry equipment.

I go down.
Rung after rung and still
the oxygen immerses me
the blue light
the clear atoms
of our human air.
I go down.
My flippers cripple me,
I crawl like an insect down the ladder
and there is no one
to tell me when the ocean
will begin.

First the air is blue and then
it is bluer and then green and then
black I am blacking out and yet
my mask is powerful
it pumps my blood with power
the sea is another story
the sea is not a question of power
I have to learn alone
to turn my body without force
in the deep element.

And now: it is easy to forget
what I came for
among so many who have always
lived here
swaying their crenellated fans
between the reefs
and besides
you breathe differently down here.

I came to explore the wreck.
The words are purposes.
The words are maps.
I came to see the damage that was done
and the treasures that prevail.
I stroke the beam of my lamp
slowly along the flank
of something more permanent
than fish or weed

15

20

25

30

35

40

45

50

55

60

the thing I came for:
the wreck and not the story of the wreck
the thing itself and not the myth
the drowned face always staring
toward the sun   65
the evidence of damage
worn by salt and sway into this threadbare beauty
the ribs of the disaster
curving their assertion
among the tentative haunters.   70

This is the place.
And I am here, the mermaid whose dark hair
streams black, the merman in his armored body
We circle silently
about the wreck   75
we dive into the hold.
I am she: I am he

whose drowned face sleeps with open eyes
whose breasts still bear the stress
whose silver, copper, vermeil cargo lies   80
obscurely inside barrels
half-wedged and left to rot
we are the half-destroyed instruments
that once held to a course
the water-eaten log   85
the fouled compass

We are, I am, you are
by cowardice or courage
the one who find our way
back to this scene   90
carrying a knife, a camera
a book of myths
in which
our names do not appear.

1972

Origins and History of Consciousness

I

Night-life. Letters, journals, bourbon
sloshed in the glass. Poems crucified on the wall,
dissected, their bird-wings severed
like trophies. No one lives in this room
without living through some kind of crisis.   5

No one lives in this room
without confronting the whiteness of the wall
behind the poems, planks of books,
photographs of dead heroines.
Without contemplating last and late 10
the true nature of poetry. The drive
to connect. The dream of a common language.

Thinking of lovers, their blind faith, their
experienced crucifixions,
my envy is not simple. I have dreamed of going to bed 15
as walking into clear water ringed by a snowy wood
white as cold sheets, thinking, *I'll freeze in there.*
My bare feet are numbed already by the snow
but the water
is mild, I sink and float 20
like a warm amphibious animal
that has broken the net, has run
through fields of snow leaving no print;
this water washes off the scent—
You are clear now 25
of the hunter, the trapper
the wardens of the mind—

yet the warm animal dreams on
of another animal
swimming under the snow-flecked surface of the pool, 30
and wakes, and sleeps again.

No one sleeps in this room without
the dream of a common language.

II

It was simple to meet you, simple to take your eyes
into mine, saying: these are eyes I have known 35
from the first. . . . It was simple to touch you
against the hacked background, the grain of what we
had been, the choices, years. . . . It was even simple
to take each other's lives in our hands, as bodies.

What is not simple: to wake from drowning 40
from where the ocean beat inside us like an afterbirth
into this common, acute particularity
these two selves who walked half a lifetime untouching—
to wake to something deceptively simple: a glass
sweated with dew, a ring of the telephone, a scream 45
of someone beaten up far down in the street
causing each of us to listen to her own inward scream

knowing the mind of the mugger and the mugged

as any woman must who stands to survive this city,
this century, this life . . .   50

each of us having loved the flesh in its clenched or loosened
     beauty
better than trees or music (yet loving those too
as if they were flesh—and they are—but the flesh
of beings unfathomed as yet in our roughly literal life).

III

It's simple to wake from sleep with a stranger,   55
dress, go out, drink coffee,
enter a life again. It isn't simple
to wake from sleep into the neighborhood
of one neither strange nor familiar
whom we have chosen to trust. Trusting, untrusting,   60
we lowered ourselves into this, let ourselves
downward hand over hand as on a rope that quivered
over the unsearched. . . . We did this. Conceived
of each other, conceived each other in a darkness
which I remember as drenched in light.   65
                                        I want to call this, life.

But I can't call it life until we start to move
beyond this secret circle of fire
where our bodies are giant shadows flung on a wall
where the night becomes our inner darkness, and sleeps   70
like a dumb beast, head on her paws, in the corner.
1972–1974   1978

Coast to Coast

There are days when housework seems the only
outlet   old funnel I've poured caldrons through
old servitude   In grief and fury bending
to the accustomed tasks   the vacuum cleaner plowing
realms of dust   the mirror scoured   gray webs   5
behind framed photographs   brushed away
the gray-seamed sky enormous in the west
snow gathering in corners   of the north

Seeing through the prism
you who gave it me   10
                    You, bearing ceaselessly
yourself, the witness
Rainbow dissolves the Hudson   This chary, stinting
skin of late winter   ice   forming and breaking up

The unprotected seeing it through   15
with their ordinary valor
Rainbow composed of ordinary light
February-flat
gray-white of a cheap enameled pan
breaking into veridian, azure, violet   20
You write: *Three and a half weeks lost from writing.* . . .
I think of the word *protection*
who it is we try to protect   and why

Seeing through the prism   Your face, fog-hollowed   burning
cold of eucalyptus hung with butterflies   25
lavender of rockbloom
O and your anger uttered in silence word and stammer
shattering the fog   lances of sun
piercing the gray Pacific   unanswerable tide
carving itself in clefts and fissures of the rock   30
Beauty of your breasts   your hands
turning a stone a shell a weed a prism   in coastal light
traveler and witness
the passion of the speechless
driving your speech   35
protectless

If you can read and understand this poem
send something back: a burning strand of hair
a still-warm, still-liquid drop of blood
a shell   40
thickened from being battered year on year
send something back.
1979

from Talking with Adrienne Rich[5]

° ° ° I think of myself as using poetry as a chief means of self-exploration—one of several means, of which maybe another would be dreams, really thinking about, paying attention to dreams, but the poem, like the dream, does this through images and it is in the images of my poems that I feel I am finding out more about my own experience, my sense of things. But I don't think of myself as having a position or a self-description which I'm then going to present in the poem.

° ° °

When I started writing poetry I was tremendously conscious of, and very much in need of, a formal structure that could be obtained

5. A transcript of a conversation recorded March 9, 1971, and printed in The   *Ohio Review,* Fall, 1971.

from outside, into which I could pour whatever I had, whatever I thought I had to express. But I think that was a part of a whole thing that I see, now as a teacher, very much with young writers, of using language more as a kind of façade than as either self-revelation or as a probe into one's own consciousness. I think I would attribute a lot of the change in my poetry simply to the fact of growing older, undergoing certain kinds of experiences, realizing that formal metrics were not going to suffice me in dealing with those experiences, realizing that experience itself is much more fragmentary, much more sort of battering, much ruder than these structures would allow, and it had to find its own form.

*   *   *

I have a very strong sense about the existence of poetry in daily life and poetry being part of the world as it is, and that the attempt to reduce poetry to what is indited on a page just limits you terribly. . . . The poem is the poetry of things lodged in the innate shape of the experience. My saying "The moment of change is the only poem" is the kind of extreme statement you feel the need to make at certain times if only to force someone to say, "But I always thought a poem is something written on a piece of paper," you know, and to say: "But look, how did those words get on that piece of paper." There had to be a mind; there had to be an experience; the mind had to go through certain shocks, certain stresses, certain strains, and if you're going to carry the poem back to its real beginnings it's that moment of change. I feel that we are always writing.

*   *   *

When I was in my twenties * * * I was going through a very sort of female thing—of trying to distinguish between the ego that is capable of writing poems, and then this other kind of being that you're asked to be if you're a woman, who is, in a sense, denying that ego. I had great feelings of split about that for many years actually, and there are a lot of poems I couldn't write even, because I didn't want to confess to having that much aggression, that much ego, that much sense of myself. I had always thought of my first book as being a book of very well-tooled poems of a sort of very bright student, which I was at that time, but poems in which the unconscious things never got to the surface. But there's a poem in that book about a woman who sews a tapestry and the tapestry has figures of tigers on it. But the woman is represented as being completely—her hand is burdened by the weight of the wedding band, and she's meek, and she's fearful, and the only way in which she can express any other side of her nature is in embroidering these tigers. Well, I thought of that as almost a formal exercise, but when I go back and look at that poem I really think it's saying something about what I was going through. And now that's lessened a great deal for all sorts of reasons—that split.

from An Interview with Adrienne Rich[6]

I would have said ten or fifteen years ago that I would not even want to identify myself as a woman poet. That term *has* been used pejoratively; I just don't think it can be at this point. You know, for a woman the act of creation is prototypically to produce children, while the act of creating with language—I'm not saying that women writers haven't been accepted; certainly, more have been accepted than women lawyers or doctors. Still, a woman writer feels, she is going against the grain—or there has been this sense until very recently (if there isn't still). Okay, it's all right to be a young thing and write verse. But a friend of mine was telling me about meeting a noted poet at a cocktail party. She'd sent him a manuscript for a contest he was judging. She went up to him and asked him about it, and he looked at her and said, "Young girls *are* poems; they shouldn't write them." This attitude toward women poets manifests itself so strongly that you are made to feel you are becoming the thing you are not.

❖   ❖   ❖

If a man is writing, he's gone through all the nonsense and said "Okay, I am a poet and I'm still a man. They don't cancel each other out or, if they do, then I'll opt to be a poet." He's not writing for a hostile sex, a breed of critics who by virtue of their sex are going to look at his language and pass judgment on it. That does happen to a woman. I don't know why the woman poet has been slower than the woman novelist in taking risks though I'm very grateful that this is no longer so. I feel that I dare to think further than I would have dared to think ten years ago—and *that* certainly is going to affect my writing. And I now dare to entertain thoughts and speculations that then would have seemed unthinkable.

❖   ❖   ❖

Many of the male writers whom I very much admire—Galway Kinnell, James Wright, W. S. Merwin—are writing poetry of such great desolation. They come from different backgrounds, write in different ways, and yet all seem to write out of a sense of doom, as if we were fated to carry on these terribly flawed relationships. I think it's expressive of a feeling that "we, the masters, have created a world that's impossible to live in and that probably may not be livable in, in a very literal sense. What we thought, what we'd been given to think is our privilege, our right, and our sexual prerogative has led to this, to our doom." I guess a lot of women—if not a lot of women poets—are feeling that there has to be some other way, that human life is messed-up but that it doesn't have to be *this* desolate.

❖   ❖   ❖

Today, much poetry by women is charged with anger and uses voices of rage and anger that I don't think were ever used in poetry before. In poets like Sylvia Plath and Diane Wakoski, say, those voices are so convincing that it is impossible to describe them by using those

6. By David Kalstone, in *The Saturday Review*, April 22, 1972.

favorite adjectives of phallic criticism—shrill and hysterical. Well, Sylvia Plath is dead. I always maintained from the first time I read her last poems that her suicide was not necessary, that she could have gone on and written poems that would have given us even more insight into the states of anger and willfulness, even of self-destructiveness, that women experience. She didn't need literally to destroy herself in order to reflect and express those things. Diane Wakoski is a young woman. She's changing a lot and will continue to change. What I admire in her, besides her energy and dynamism and quite a beautiful gift for snatching the image that she wants out of the air, is her honesty. No woman has written before about her face and said she hated it, that it had served her ill, that she wished she could throw acid in it. That's very shocking. But I think all women, even the most beautiful women, at times have felt that in a kind of self-hatred. Because the *face* is supposed to be the *woman*.

* * *

A lot of poetry is becoming more oral. Certainly, it's true of women and black poets. Reading black poetry on the printed page gives no sense of the poem, if you're going to look at that poetry the way you look at poems by Richard Wilbur. Yet you can hear these poets read and realize it's the oldest kind of poetry.

* * *

I think the energy of language comes somewhat from the pressure and need and unbearableness of what's being done to you. It's not the same energy you find in the blues. The blues are a grief language, a lost language, and a cry of pain, usually in a woman's voice, which is interesting. For a long time you sing the blues, and then you begin to say, "I'm tired of singing the blues. I want something else." And that's what you're hearing now. There seems to be a connection between an oppressed condition and having access to certain kinds of energy, vitality, and subjectivity. For women as well as blacks. Though I don't feel there is a necessary cause-and-effect relationship; what seems to happen is that being on top, being in a powerful position leads to a divorce between one's unruly, chaotic, revolutionary sensitivity and one's reason, sense of order and of maintaining a hold. And, therefore, you have at the bottom of the pile, so to speak, a kind of churning energy that gets lost up there among the administrators.

* * *

I don't know how or whether poetry changes anything. But neither do I know how or whether bombing or even community organizing changes anything when we are pitted against a massive patriarchal system armed with supertechnology. I believe in subjectivity—that a lot of male Left leaders have turned into Omnipotent Administrators, because their "masculinity" forced them to deny their subjectivity. I believe in dreams and visions and "the madness of art." And at moments I can conceive of a women's movement that will show the way to humanizing technology and fusing dreams and skills and visions and reason to begin the healing of the human race. But I don't want women to take over the world and run it the way men have, or to take on—yet again!—the burden of carrying the subjectivity of the race. Women are a vanguard now, and I believe will increasingly become so, because we have—Western women, Third World women, all women—known and felt the pain of the human condition most consistently. But in the end it can't be women alone.

from When We Dead Awaken: Writing as Re-Vision

Most, if not all, human lives are full of fantasy—passive daydreaming which need not be acted on. But to write poetry or fiction, or even to think well, is not to fantasize or to put fantasies on paper. For a poem to coalesce, for a character or an action to take shape, there has to be an imaginative transformation of reality which is in no way passive. And a certain freedom of the mind is needed—freedom to press on, to enter the currents of your thought like a glider pilot, knowing that your motion can be sustained, that the buoyancy of your attention will not be suddenly snatched away. Moreover, if the imagination is to transcend and transform experience it has to question, to challenge, to conceive of alternatives, perhaps to the very life you are living at that moment. You have to be free to play around with the notion that day might be night, love might be hate, nothing can be too sacred for the imagination to turn into its opposite or to call experimentally by another name. For writing is re-naming.

Now, to be maternally with small children all day in the old way, to be with a man in the old way of marriage, requires a holding back, a putting aside of that imaginative activity, and seems to demand instead a kind of conservatism. I want to make it clear that I am *not* saying that in order to write well, or think well, it is necessary to become unavailable to others, or to become a devouring ego. This has been the myth of the masculine artist and thinker; and, I repeat, I do not accept it. But to be a female human being trying to fulfill traditional female functions in a traditional way *is* in direct conflict with the subversive function of the imagination. The word "traditional" is important here. There must be ways, and we will be finding out more and more about them, in which the energy of creation and the energy of relation can be united. But in those earlier years I always felt the conflict as a failure of love in myself. I had thought I was choosing a full life: the life available to most men, in which sexuality, work and parenthood could co-exist. But I felt, at 29, guilt toward the people closest to me, and guilty toward my own being.

I wanted, then, more than anything, the one thing of which there was never enough: time to think, time to write. The '50s and early '60s were years of rapid revelations: the sit-ins and marches in the South, the Bay of Pigs, the early antiwar movement, raised large questions—questions for which the masculine world of the academy around me seemed to have expert and fluent answers. But I needed desperately to think for myself—about pacifism and dissent and violence, about poetry and society, and about my own relationship to all these things. For about ten years I was reading in fierce snatches, scribbling in notebooks, writing poetry in fragments; I was looking desperately for clues, because if there were no clues then I thought I might be insane. I wrote in a notebook about this time:

> Paralyzed by the sense that there exists a mesh of relationships —e.g. between my anger at the children, my sensual life, pacifism, sex (I mean sex in its broadest significance, not merely sexual desire)—an interconnectedness which, if I could see it. make it valid, would give me back myself, make it possible to function lucidly and passionately. Yet I grope in and out among these dark webs.

I think I began at this point to feel that politics was not something "out there" but something "in here" and of the essence of my condition.

In the late '50s I was able to write, for the first time, directly about experiencing myself as a woman. The poem was jotted in fragments during children's naps, brief hours in a library, or at 3 A.M. after rising with a wakeful child. I despaired of doing any continuous work at this time. Yet I began to feel that my fragments and scraps had a common consciousness and a common theme, one which I would have been very unwilling to put on paper at an earlier time because I had been taught that poetry should be "universal," which meant, of course, nonfemale. Until then I had tried very much *not* to identify myself as a female poet.

Chronology

1929   Born in Baltimore, Maryland, May 16. Began writing poetry as a child under the encouragement and supervision of her father, Dr. Arnold Rich, from whose "very Victorian, pre-Raphaelite" library, Rich later recalled, she read Tennyson, Keats, Arnold, Blake, Rossetti, Swinburne, Carlyle, and Pater.

1951   A.B., Radcliffe College. Phi Beta Kappa. *A Change of World* chosen by W. H. Auden for the Young Poets Award and published.

1952–53   Guggenheim Fellowship; travel in Europe and England. Marriage to Alfred H. Conrad, an economist who taught at Harvard. Residence in Cambridge, Massachusetts, 1953–66.

1955   Birth of David Conrad. Publication of *The Diamond Cutters and Other Poems*, which won the Ridgely Torrence Memorial Award of the Poetry Society of America.

1957   Birth of Paul Conrad.

1959   Birth of Jacob Conrad.

1960   National Institute of Arts and Letters Award for poetry. Phi Beta Kappa poet at William and Mary College.

1961–62   Guggenheim Fellowship; residence with family in the Netherlands.

1962   Bollingen Foundation grant for translation of Dutch poetry.

1962–63   Amy Lowell Travelling Fellowship.

1963   *Snapshots of a Daughter-in-Law* published. Bess Hokin Prize of *Poetry* magazine.

1965 Phi Beta Kappa poet at Swarthmore College.
1966 *Necessities of Life* published, nominated for the National Book Award. Phi Beta Kappa poet at Harvard College. Move to New York City, where Alfred Conrad taught at City College of New York. Residence there from 1966 on. Increasingly active politically in protests against the Indochina war.
1966–68 Lecturer at Swarthmore College.
1967–69 Adjunct Professor of Writing in the Graduate School of the Arts, Columbia University.
1967 *Selected Poems* published in Britain. Litt.D., Wheaton College.
1968 Eunice Tietjens Memorial Prize of *Poetry* magazine. Began teaching in the SEEK and Open Admissions Programs at City College of New York.
1969 *Leaflets* published.
1970 Death of Alfred Conrad.
1971 *The Will to Change* published. Shelley Memorial Award of the Poetry Society of America. Increasingly identifies with the women's movement as a radical feminist.
1972–73 Fanny Hurst Visiting Professor of Creative Literature at Brandeis University.
1973 *Diving into the Wreck* published.
1973–74 Ingram Merrill Foundation research grant; began work on a book on the history and myths of motherhood.
1974 National Book Award for *Diving into the Wreck*. Rich rejected the award as an individual, but accepted it, in a statement written with Audre Lorde and Alice Walker. two other nominees, in the name of all women:

> "We . . . together accept this award in the name of all the women whose voices have gone and still go unheard in a patriarchal world, and in the name of those who, like us, have been tolerated as token women in this culture, often at great cost and in great pain. . . . We symbolically join here in refusing the terms of patriarchal competition and declaring that we will share this prize among us, to be used as best we can for women. . . . We dedicate this occasion to the struggle for self-determination of all women, of every color, identification or derived class . . . the women who will not understand yet; the silent women whose voices have been denied us, the articulate women who have given us strength to do our work."

Professor of English, City College of New York.
1975 *Poems: Selected and New* published.
1976 Professor of English at Douglass College. *Of Woman Born: Motherhood as Experience and Institution* published. *Twenty-one Love Poems* published.
1978 *The Dream of a Common Language: Poems 1974–1977* published.
1979 *On Lies, Secrets, and Silence: Selected Prose 1966–1978* published. Leaves Douglass College and New York City; moves to a small town in western Massachusetts with "the woman who shares my life."
1981 *A Wild Patience Has Taken Me This Far: Poems 1978–1981* published.

The more you know, the better a reader of poetry you are capable of being. Poems often draw upon a large fund of human knowledge, and sometimes they require a great deal from the reader. The earlier chapters in this book suggest some of the skills one needs to develop in order to cope with the demands they make. In these final chapters we will look at the knowledge poets often expect. Very little that you know will ultimately go to waste in your reading of poetry. The best potential reader of a poem is someone who has already developed reading skills to perfection, read everything, thought deeply about all sorts of things, and who is wise beyond belief—but that is the ideal reader we all strive to be, not the one any of us is, and no poet expects any reader to be all those things. Still, the point is to try. By knowing that these things are important to the reading of poetry, we won't discount too easily what we need, and so we will keep trying to do better, trying to bring more to the poem. The chapters that follow suggest some of the ways that poetry draws specifically upon the traditional fund of human knowledge, how it uses the history of literature, science, philosophy, religion—the "wisdom of the ages" that traditional humanistic education has long relied upon as the cornerstone of its existence. This chapter considers some of the historical particulars, matters that relate specifically to the moment in time when a particular poem was written, for every poem is, in the beginning, a timely act of creation.

Things that happen every day frequently find their way into poetry in an easy and yet often forceful manner. Making love in a junkyard, as in *Cherrylog Road,* is one kind of example; a reader doesn't need to know what particular junkyard was involved—or imaginatively involved—in order to understand the poem, but a reader does need to know what an auto junkyard was like in the middle of the 20th century, with more or less whole car bodies being scattered in various states of disarray over a large plot of ground. But what if, over the next generation or two, another way is developed to dispose of old cars? What if the metal is all melted down, or the junk is orbited into space? If something like that happens, readers then will need a footnote explaining what junkyards were like. The history of junkyards will not be lost—there will be pictures, films, records, and someone will write definitive books about the forms and functions of junkyards, probably even including the fact that lovers occasionally visited them—but the public memory of junkyards will soon disappear. No social customs, no things that are made, no institutions or sites last forever.

Readers may still be able to experience *Cherrylog Road* when that happens, but they will need some help, and they may think its particulars a little quaint, much as we regard literature that involves horses and buggies—or even making love in the back seat of a parked car—as quaint now. Institutions change, habits change, times change, particulars change, even when people's wants, needs, and foibles pretty much go on in the same way. Footnotes never provide a precise or adequate substitute for the ease and pleasure that come from already knowing, but they can help us understand and pave the way for feeling and experience. A kind of imaginative historical sympathy can be simulated and in fact created, for poems from earlier times that refer to specific contemporary details (and that have now become to us, in our own time, *historical* details) often describe human nature and human experiences very much as we still know and experience them. Today's poem may need tomorrow's footnote, but the poem need not be tomorrow's puzzle or only a curiosity or fossil.

The following poem, not many years old, already requires some explanation, not only because the factual details of its occasion may not be known to every reader, but also because the whole spirit of the poem may be difficult to appreciate unless one knows its circumstances.

RAYMOND R. PATTERSON

You Are the Brave

You are the brave who do not break
In the grip of the mob when the blow comes straight
To the shattered bone; when the sockets shriek;
When your arms lie twisted under your back.

Good men holding their courage slack   5
In their frightened pockets see how weak
The work that is done; and feel the weight
Of your blood on the ground for their spirits' sake;

And build their anger, stone on stone;
Each silently, but not alone.   10

1962

I can remember teaching this poem in class during the Viet Nam War and finding that a lot of students were hostile to it because they assumed it to be a poem in praise of patriotism and war. Sometimes the difficulty about factual information is that one doesn't know that one *needs* specific information. In a poem like *You Are the Brave*, it is fairly easy to assume (incorrectly, but understandably) that the conflict involved is a war and that the speaker addresses, and honors, a group of soldiers. Actually, there are clues in the poem that this conflict is, if as bitter as war, one in which mob violence (line 2) and enforced restraint (line 4) are involved. The date of the poem is a clue too—1962, when the American civil rights struggle was at its height. Once that "fact" is noticed, the whole historical context of the poem, if not its *immediate* occasion in terms of one specific civil rights march in one place on one day, becomes clear. In fact, since the poem doesn't mention a particular time and place, we may assume that the poem is not about the particulars of one specific incident, but instead gathers the kind of details that characterized many moments of the early sixties. The poem's details (generalized details about mob resentments and brutalities in a situation of passive resistance), its metaphors in the second and third stanzas, and its dignified tone of praise for "the brave" all make sense readily when the right information is available. The poem does not mention specific time and place because its concern is not confined to one event, but its location in time is important to finding what it refers to. Poems may be referential to one single event or moment (as in Berryman's *1 September 1939*, p. 399) or to some larger situation that may span weeks, months, or even years. The amount of particularity in the poem will tell you.

How do you know what you need to know? The easiest clue is your own puzzlement. When it seems that something is happening in a poem that you don't recognize—and yet the poem makes no apparent effort in itself to clarify it—you have a clue that readers at the time the poem was written must have recognized something which is not now such common knowledge. Once you know you don't know, it's only work to find out: most college libraries contain far more information than you will ever need, and the trick is to learn to search efficiently; that's why I have left a group of poems unannotated at the end of this chapter. An hour or two in the library will turn up most of the facts you will need for those poems, but of course your ability to find the information efficiently will depend upon how well you know the kinds of reference materials available to you. Practice helps. Knowledge accumulates. Most poems printed in textbooks like this one will be annotated for you with minimal facts, but often you may need additional information to interpret the poem's full meaning and resonance. An editor, trying to decide on the needs of a variety of readers, may not always have decided to write the footnote you yourself may need, so there may be digging to be done in the library for any poem you read, certainly for those you may come upon in magazines and books of poetry without footnotes. Few poets like to footnote their own work (they'd rather let you struggle a little to appreciate them), and besides, many things that now need footnotes didn't when they were first written, as in *You Are the Brave*.

To get at appropriate factual and historical information, it is important to learn to ask three kinds of questions. One kind is obvious: it is the "Do I understand the reference to . . . ?" kind of question. When events, places, or people unfamiliar to you come up, you will need to find out what or who they are. The second kind of question is more difficult: How do you know, in a poem like *You Are the Brave*, that you need to know more? When there are no specific references to look up, no people or events to identify, how do you know that there is a specific context? To get at this sort of question, you have to trust two people: the poet, and yourself. Learning to trust yourself, your own responses, is the more difficult—you can just decide to trust the poet. Usually, good poets know what they are doing.

If they do, they will not want to puzzle you more than necessary, so that you can safely assume that something which is not self-explanatory will merit close attention and possibly some digging in the library. (Poets do make mistakes and miscalculations about their readers, but it is safest to assume they know what they are doing and why they are doing it.) When a poem contains things that are not in themselves clear (such as "the grip of the mob" or the "arms . . . twisted under your back" in *You Are the Brave*) those things provide a strong clue that you need more information. And that is why you need to trust yourself: you need to be confident that when something doesn't click, when the information given you does not seem enough, that you trust your puzzlement and try to find the missing facts that will allow the poem to make sense. But how? Often the date of the poem is a help, as in *You Are the Brave*. Sometimes the title gives a clue or a point of departure. Sometimes you can discover, by reading about the author, some of the things he or she was interested in or concerned about. There is no single all-purpose way to discover what to look for, but that kind of research—looking for clues, adding up the evidence—can be interesting in itself and very rewarding when it is successful.

The third question is why? For every factual reference, one needs to ask why. Why does the poem refer to this particular person instead of some other? What function does the reference perform? Why, for example, does *In Memory of Radio* make such a big deal of its references to Lamont Cranston? What does that reference have to do with the whole poem? Why is Goody Knight mentioned in the poem? What particular aspect of Goodwin Knight's political career makes him useful to the poet in this poem?

Beyond the levels of simply understanding that a particular poem is about a particular event or place or movement is the matter of developing a full sense of historical context, a sense of the larger significance and resonance of the historical occurrence referred to. Often a poem expects you to bring some sense of that significance; equally often it wants to continue your education, telling you more, wanting you to understand and appreciate on a feeling level some further things about this occurrence. A second group of poems at the end of this chapter has as its point of reference World War I. These poems offer a variety of emphases and perspectives, and they isolate quite different facts about the war. What we need to bring to our reading varies from poem to poem. *Dulce et Decorum Est*, for example, needs our knowledge that poison gas was used in the war; the green tint through which the speaker sees the world in lines 13–14, comes from green-lensed glass in the goggles of the gas mask he has just put on. But some broader matters are important as well. Harder to specify but probably even more important is the climate of opinion that surrounded World War I. To idealists, it was "the war to end all wars," and many participants—as well as politicians and propagandists—felt holy about it, regarding the threat of Germany's expansionist policy as the potential destruction of Western civilization.

Here is some other background information you may find useful. The Allied Powers (France, Great Britain, and Russia, later joined by

Japan, Italy, and the United States) early in the war were very much weaker militarily than the combined force of the Central Powers (Germany, Austria-Hungary, and Turkey). Battles were fought on both Eastern and Western fronts; the Western battles in Flanders were especially brutal, and a long stalemate developed there in 1917, with huge casualties. On the sea, too, casualties ran high; the development of submarine warfare made transportation of ammunition and supplies very difficult, and German U-boats often attacked ships even from neutral nations. The United States joined the allied forces after one of the most celebrated incidents, the sinking of the *Lusitania*. Air power became militarily important for the first time, too; by 1915 fighter aircraft were equipped with machine guns, and there was some strategic bombing as early as the autumn of 1914.

Not everyone, however, was convinced of the dire danger to Western civilization and enthusiastic about the war effort. Great Britain entered the war reluctantly; after the British insisted that Germany respect the neutrality of Belgium, Germany ignored the British request and continued to occupy Belgium as part of its assault on France. The United States was even more reluctant to enter the war and stayed out until 1917. In both countries there were—although nearly forgotten now—strong peace movements; in Great Britain there were more than 16,000 conscientious objectors to the war, and their feelings were, for the most part, honored, despite incredible shortages of military manpower: by early 1918 Britain had raised the age of compulsory military service to 51. One of the poets represented here (Siegfried Sassoon) was a strong force in the peace movement; he had enlisted in the British military service early in the war and was twice wounded; later in the war, after winning the Military Cross and while still an officer in the army, Sassoon publicly affirmed his pacifism.

Because of its late entrance into the war, U. S. casualties were, relatively speaking, light; more Americans died in the flu epidemic of 1919 than had been killed in the war. But Britain was hit much harder. Fighting close to home soil for nearly five years—much of the time in savage combat in the Flanders mud, but also contributing forces and equipment to other fronts—Great Britain counted more than a million war dead. But even these figures do not begin to suggest the human loss. Nearly a whole generation of British youth was lost in the war, including many of its brightest and most promising potential leaders, and ultimately Britain suffered a loss of leadership in many fields, a loss that was not entirely felt until later years. Besides, Britain's international power and prestige were severely damaged; the British empire had rested on Britain's sea power and isolation, and at the war's end Britain faced a staggering war debt and a severe shrinkage of foreign markets, in addition to major shifts in the international power balance and shocking human losses.

No doubt you will read the poems more intelligently, and more feelingly, if you know quite a bit about World War I, and the same is true of poems about any historical occurrence or of poems that refer specifically or generally to things that happen or situations that exist in a temporal context. But it is also true that your sense of these events will grow as a result of reading sensitively and thoughtfully the poems themselves. Facts are no substitute for skills. Once you have read individually the poems in this section, try taking a breather, and then at one sitting read them all again. Reading poetry can be a form of gaining knowledge as well as an aesthetic experience. One doesn't go to poetry to seek information as such, but poems often give us more than we came for. The ways to wisdom are paved with facts, and although poetry is not primarily a data-conscious art, it often requires us to be aware, sometimes in detail, of its referents in the real world.

The Need for Factual Information

AMIRI BARAKA (LE ROI JONES)

In Memory of Radio

Who has ever stopped to think of the divinity of Lamont Cranston?
(Only Jack Kerouac, that I know of: & me.
The rest of you probably had on WCBS and Kate Smith,
Or something equally unattractive.)

What can I say?   5
It is better to have loved and lost
Than to put linoleum in your living rooms?

Am I a sage or something?
Mandrake's hypnotic gesture of the week?
(Remember, I do not have the healing powers of Oral Roberts . . .   10
I cannot, like F. J. Sheen, tell you how to get saved *& rich!*
I cannot even order you to gaschamber satori like Hitler or Goody Knight
& Love is an evil word.
Turn it backwards/see, what I mean?
An evol word. & besides   15
Who understands it?
I certainly wouldn't like to go out on that kind of limb.

Saturday mornings we listened to *Red Lantern* & his undersea folk.
At 11, *Let's Pretend*/& we did/& I, the poet, still do, Thank God!

What was it he used to say (after the transformation, when he was safe   20
& invisible & the unbelievers couldn't throw stones?) "Heh, heh, heh,
Who knows what evil lurks in the hearts of men? The Shadow knows."

O, yes he does
O, yes he does.
An evil word it is,   25
This Love.

1961

e. e. cummings

poem, or beauty hurts mr. vinal

take it from me kiddo
believe me
my country, 'tis of

you, land of the Cluett
Shirt Boston Garter and Spearmint   5
Girl With The Wrigley Eyes (of you
land of the Arrow Ide
and Earl &
Wilson
Collars) of you i   10
sing: land of Abraham Lincoln and Lydia E. Pinkham,
land above all of Just Add Hot Water And Serve—
from every B. V. D.

      let freedom ring

amen. i do however protest, anent the un   15
-spontaneous and otherwise scented merde which
greets one (Everywhere Why) as divine poesy per
that and this radically defunct periodical. i would
suggest that certain ideas gestures
rhymes, like Gillette Razor Blades   20
having been used and reused
to the mystical moment of dullness emphatically are
Not To Be Resharpened. (Case in point

if we are to believe these gently O sweetly
melancholy trillers amid the thrillers   25
these crepuscular violinists among my and your
skyscrapers—Helen & Cleopatra were Just Too Lovely,
The Snail's On The Thorn enter Morn and God's
In His andsoforth

do you get me?) according   30
to such supposedly indigenous
throstles Art is O World O Life
a formula: example, Turn Your Shirttails Into
Drawers and If It Isn't An Eastman It Isn't A
Kodak therefore my friends let   35
us now sing each and all fortissimo A-
mer
i

ca, I
love,
You. And there're a   40
hun-dred-mil-lion-oth-ers, like

all of you successfully if
delicately gelded(or spaded)
gentlemen(and ladies)—pretty   45

littleliverpill-
hearted-Nujolneeding-There's-A-Reason
americans(who tensetendoned and with
upward vacant eyes, painfully
perpetually crouched, quivering, upon the   50
sternly allotted sandpile
—how silently
emit a tiny violetflavoured nuisance:Odor?

ono.
comes out like a ribbon lies flat on the brush   55
                                                      1926

EUGENE MCCARTHY

Kilroy

Kilroy is gone,
the word is out,
absent without leave
from Vietnam.

Kilroy   5
who wrote his name
in every can
from Poland to Japan
and places in between
like Sheboygan and Racine   10
is gone
absent without leave
from Vietnam.

Kilroy
who kept the dice   15
and stole the ice
out of the BOQ
Kilroy
whose name was good
on every IOU   20
in World War II
and even in Korea
is gone
absent without leave
from Vietnam.   25

Kilroy
the unknown soldier
who was the first to land
the last to leave,
with his own hand   30
has taken his good name
from all the walls
and toilet stalls.
Kilroy
whose name around the world   35
was like the flag unfurled
has run it down
and left Saigon
and the Mekong
without a hero or a song   40
and gone
absent without leave
from Vietnam.

1968

JAMES A. EMANUEL

Emmett Till

I hear a whistling
Through the water.
Little Emmett
Won't be still.
He keeps floating   5
Round the darkness,
Edging through
The silent chill.
Tell me, please,
That bedtime story   10
Of the fairy
River Boy
Who swims forever,
Deep in treasures,
Necklaced in   15
A coral toy.

1968

World War I

WILFRED OWEN

Dulce Et Decorum Est[1]

Bent double, like old beggars under sacks,
Knock-kneed, coughing like hags, we cursed through sludge,
Till on the haunting flares we turned our backs
And towards our distant rest began to trudge.
Men marched asleep. Many had lost their boots   5
But limped on, blood-shod. All went lame; all blind;
Drunk with fatigue; deaf even to the hoots
Of disappointed shells that dropped behind.

Gas! Gas! Quick, boys!—An ecstasy of fumbling,
Fitting the clumsy helmets just in time;   10
But someone still was yelling out and stumbling
And floundering like a man in fire or lime.—
Dim, through the misty panes and thick green light
As under a green sea, I saw him drowning.

In all my dreams, before my helpless sight,   15
He plunges at me, guttering, choking, drowning.

If in some smothering dreams you too could pace
Behind the wagon that we flung him in,
And watch the white eyes writhing in his face,
His hanging face, like a devil's sick of sin;   20
If you could hear, at every jolt, the blood
Come gargling from the froth-corrupted lungs,
Obscene as cancer, bitter as the cud
Of vile, incurable sores on innocent tongues,—
My friend, you would not tell with such high zest   25
To children ardent for some desperate glory,
The old Lie: Dulce et decorum est
Pro patria mori.

1917

ISAAC ROSENBERG

Break of Day in the Trenches

The darkness crumbles away—
It is the same old druid[2] Time as ever.

---

1. Part of a phrase from Horace, quoted in full in the last lines: "It is sweet and proper to die for one's country."
2. Magician or priest.

Only a live thing leaps my hand—
A queer sardonic rat—
As I pull the parapet's poppy[3]   5
To stick behind my ear.
Droll rat, they would shoot you if they knew
Your cosmopolitan sympathies.
Now you have touched this English hand
You will do the same to a German—   10
Soon, no doubt, if it be your pleasure
To cross the sleeping green between.
It seems you inwardly grin as you pass
Strong eyes, fine limbs, haughty athletes
Less chanced than you for life,   15
Bonds to the whims of murder,
Sprawled in the bowels of the earth,
The torn fields of France.
What do you see in our eyes
At the shrieking iron and flame   20
Hurled through still heavens?
What quaver—what heart aghast?
Poppies whose roots are in man's veins
Drop, and are ever dropping;
But mine in my ear is safe,   25
Just a little white with the dust.

                                                    c. 1917

EZRA POUND

There Died a Myriad[4]

There died a myriad,
And of the best, among them,
For an old bitch gone in the teeth,
For a botched civilization,

Charm, smiling at the good mouth,   5
Quick eyes gone under earth's lid,

For two gross of broken statues,
For a few thousand battered books.

                                                    1920

3. Flower growing on the earthwork built to shield soldiers from enemy fire. The poppy became a standard symbol for the war dead because a large burial field in Flanders was covered with poppies.
4. Section V of "E. P. Ode pour L'Élection de Son Sépulcre."

EDGAR A. GUEST

The Things that Make a Soldier Great

The things that make a soldier great and send him out to die,
To face the flaming cannon's mouth, nor ever question why,
Are lilacs by a little porch, the row of tulips red,
The peonies and pansies, too, the old petunia bed,
The grass plot where his children play, the roses on the wall: 5
'Tis these that make a soldier great. He's fighting for them all.

'Tis not the pomp and pride of kings that make a soldier brave;
'Tis not allegiance to the flag that over him may wave;
For soldiers never fight so well on land or on the foam
As when behind the cause they see the little place called home.   10
Endanger but that humble street whereon his children run—
You make a soldier of the man who never bore a gun.

What is it through the battle smoke the valiant soldier sees?
The little garden far away, the budding apple trees,
The little patch of ground back there, the children at their play,   15
Perhaps a tiny mound behind the simple church of gray.
The golden thread of courage isn't linked to castle dome
But to the spot, where'er it be—the humble spot called home.

And now the lilacs bud again and all is lovely there,
And homesick soldiers far away know spring is in the air;   20
The tulips come to bloom again, the grass once more is green,
And every man can see the spot where all his joys have been.
He sees his children smile at him, he hears the bugle call,
And only death can stop him now—he's fighting for them all.

                                                        1918

SIEGFRIED SASSOON

Base Details

If I were fierce, and bald, and short of breath,
    I'd live with scarlet Majors at the Base,
And speed glum heroes up the line to death.
    You'd see me with my puffy petulant face,
Guzzling and gulping in the best hotel,   5
    Reading the Roll of Honor.[5] "Poor young chap,"
I'd say—"I used to know his father well;
    Yes, we've lost heavily in this last scrap."
And when the war is done and youth stone dead,
I'd toddle safely home and die—in bed.   10

                                                        1918

5. List of dead.

RUPERT BROOKE

The Soldier

If I should die, think only this of me:
   That there's some corner of a foreign field
That is forever England. There shall be
   In that rich earth a richer dust concealed;
A dust whom England bore, shaped, made aware,   5
   Gave, once, her flowers to love, her ways to roam,
A body of England's, breathing English air,
   Washed by the rivers, blest by suns of home.

And think, this heart, all evil shed away,
   A pulse in the eternal mind, no less   10
   Gives somewhere back the thoughts by England given;
Her sights and sounds; dreams happy as her day;
   And laughter, learnt of friends; and gentleness,
      In hearts at peace, under an English heaven.

                                                          1915

W. B. YEATS

On Being Asked for a War Poem

   I think it better that in times like these
   A poet's mouth be silent, for in truth
   We have no gift to set a statesman right;
   He has had enough of meddling who can please
   A young girl in the indolence of her youth,   5
   Or an old man upon a winter's night.

                                                    p. 1915

WILFRED OWEN

Disabled

He sat in a wheeled chair, waiting for dark,
And shivered in his ghastly suit of grey,
Legless, sewn short at elbow. Through the park
Voices of boys rang saddening like a hymn,
Voices of play and pleasure after day,   5
Till gathering sleep had mothered them from him.

About this time Town used to swing so gay
When glow-lamps budded in the light blue trees,

And girls glanced lovelier as the air grew dim,—
In the old times, before he threw away his knees.   10
Now he will never feel again how slim
Girls' waists are, or how warm their subtle hands;
All of them touch him like some queer disease.

There was an artist silly for his face,
For it was younger than his youth, last year.   15
Now, he is old; his back will never brace;
He's lost his color very far from here,
Poured it down shell-holes till the veins ran dry,
And half his lifetime lapsed in the hot race,
And leap of purple spurted from his thigh.   20

One time he liked a blood-smear down his leg,
After the matches,[6] carried shoulder-high
It was after football, when he'd drunk a peg,[7]
He thought he'd better join.—He wonders why.
Someone had said he'd look a god in kilts,   25
That's why; and may be, too, to please his Meg;
Aye, that was it, to please the giddy jilts
He asked to join. He didn't have to beg;
Smiling they wrote his lie; aged nineteen years.
Germans he scarcely thought of; all their guilt,   30
And Austria's, did not move him. And no fears
Of Fear came yet. He thought of jeweled hilts
For daggers in plaid socks; of smart salutes;
And care of arms; and leave; and pay arrears;
Esprit de corps; and hints for young recruits.   35
And soon, he was drafted out with drums and cheers.

Some cheered him home, but not as crowds cheer Goal.[8]
Only a solemn man who brought him fruits
Thanked him; and then inquired about his soul.
Now, he will spend a few sick years in Institutes,   40
And do what things the rules consider wise,
And take whatever pity they may dole.
Tonight he noticed how the women's eyes
Passed from him to the strong men that were whole.
How cold and late it is! Why don't they come   45
And put him into bed? Why don't they come?

1917

---

6. Soccer games. See A. E. Housman's
To an Athlete Dying Young, p. 26.

7. A drink, usually brandy and soda.
8. In soccer.

13   LITERARY TRADITION

The more poetry you read, the better a reader of poetry you are likely to be. This is not just because your skills will improve and develop, but also because you will come to know more about the poetic tradition and can thus understand more fully how poets draw upon each other. Poets are conscious of each other, and often they refer to each other's work or use it as a starting point for their own work in ways that may not be immediately obvious to an outsider. Sometimes a quiet (or even noisy) competitiveness is at the bottom of their concern with what other poems have done or can do; at other times, playfulness and a sense of humor about poetic possibilities take over, and the competitiveness dwindles to fun and poetic games. And often they want to tap the rich mine of artistic expression just to share in the bounty of our heritage. In any case, a poet's consciousness of what others have done leads to a sense of tradition that is often hard to articulate but nevertheless is very important to the effects of poetry —and this sense of tradition is something of a problem for a relatively new reader of poetry. How can I possibly read this poem intelligently, sometimes we are likely to ask in exasperation, until I've read all the other poems ever written? It's a real problem. Poets don't actually expect that all of their readers have Ph.D.s in literature, but sometimes it *seems* as if they do. For some poems—T. S. Eliot's *Love Song of J. Alfred Prufrock* (p. 424) is one example—it does help if one has read practically everything imaginable.

Why are poets so dependent on each other? What is the point of their continuous consciousness of what has already been done by others? Why do they repeatedly allude to and echo other poems? Why is a sense of tradition so important to them?

A sense of common task, a kind of communality of purpose, accounts for some traditional poetic practice, and the desire of individual poets to achieve a place in the English and American poetic tradition accounts for some more. Many poets show an anxiety to be counted among those who achieve, through their writing, a place in history, and a way of establishing that place is to define for oneself the relationship between one's own work and that of others whose place is already secure. There is, for many poets, a sense of a serious and abiding cultural tradition which they wish to share and pass on; but also important is a shared sense of playfulness, a kind of poetic gamesmanship. Making words dance on the page or in our heads provides in itself a satisfaction and delight for many writers; pride in craft that is rather like the pride of a painter or potter or tennis player. Often poets set themselves a particular task to see what they can do. One way of doing that is to introduce a standard traditional motif (a recurrent device, formula, or situation which deliberately connects a poem with common patterns of existing thought), and then to play variations on it much as a musician might do. Another way is to provide an alternative answer to a question that has repeatedly been asked and answered in a traditional way. Poetic playfulness by no means excludes serious intention—the poems in this chapter often make important statements about their subject, however humorous they may be in their method. Some teasing of the tradition and of other poets is pure fun, a kind of kidding among good friends; some is rather more harsh and represents an attempt to see the world very differently—to define and articulate a very different view.

The English poetic tradition is a rich and varied heritage, and individual poets draw upon it in countless ways. You have probably noticed, in the poems you have read so far, a number of allusions, glances at the tradition or at individual expressions of it, and the more poems you read the better equipped you will be to notice more. The more you read, the more you will yourself become a comfortable member of the audience poets write for. Poets do expect a lot—not always but often enough to make a new reader feel nervous and some-times inadequate. The other side of that discomfort comes when you begin to notice things that other readers don't. *After* you've read Yeats's *Second Coming* (p. 342), for example, you might want to reread Deagon's *Certified Copy* (p. 128): the comedy of the Deagon poem is funnier in the context of a knowledge of Yeats's serious worry and serious statement. The poetic tradition is a vast and various mine; poets find in it raw materials to make many fine things.

The three groups of poems in this chapter illustrate some of the ways that the tradition energizes individual poets and suggests some of the things poets like to do with their heritage. The first group con-sists of poems that share a common subject (love), theme (time is short), and urgency of tone (let's not wait; let's make love now). And most of them seem rather self-conscious—as if each poet is aware of a common tradition and is trying to do something a little bit different. However "sincere" these poems are as seduction poems (many of them do present a convincing sense of love and desire), their sense of play is equally important in its variation upon the standard *carpe diem* (seize the day: live for the moment) motif. The motif is an old one, dating back at least to classical Roman times; several of the poems (*Come, My Celia; Bridal Couch; To the Virgins, to Make Much of Time*) allude specifically to the following lines of a poem by Catullus, which is one of the fountains of the tradition:

> Let us live, my Lesbia, and love
> And not care about the gossip of old men.
> The sun that sets may rise again,
> But when our light has once set
> Our night will be unbroken.

The second group consists of poems that pick on (playfully) one poem which we looked at in Chapter 10, *The Passionate Shepherd to His Love* (p. 218). In effect, all these poems provide "answers" to that poem. It is as if "his love" were telling the shepherd what is the matter with his argument, and the poets are answering Marlowe, too. These poets know full well what Marlowe was doing in the fantasy of his original poem, and they clearly have a lot of fun telling him how people in various circumstances might feel about his fantasy. There is, repeatedly, a lot of joy in their "realistic" deflation of his magic, and not much hostility.

The third group similarly pokes fun at other famous poems, providing another version of what might have happened in each. Koch's *Variations on a Theme by William Carlos Williams* is the only **parody** in the group (that is, it pretends to write in the style of the original poem, but comically exaggerates that style). The other two **poems use** very different styles to alter, totally, the poetic intention of the original. *Ode on a Grecian Urn Summarized* teases Keats as well as the whole notion of poetic summaries; the effects of the summary are not very much like those of the Keats poem. *The Dover Bitch,* on the other hand, is as its subtitle suggests much more than just a different perspective on the situation portrayed in *Dover Beach*; it uses the tradition to criticize art *and* life.

The Carpe Diem *Motif*

ROBERT HERRICK

To the Virgins, to Make Much of Time

    Gather ye rosebuds while ye may,
        Old time is still a-flying;
    And this same flower that smiles today
        Tomorow will be dying.

    The glorious lamp of heaven, the sun,   5
        The higher he's a-getting,
    The sooner will his race be run,
        And nearer he's to setting.

    That age is best which is the first,
        When youth and blood are warmer;   10
    But being spent, the worse, and worst
        Times still succeed the former.

    Then be not coy, but use your time,
        And, while ye may, go marry;
    For, having lost but once your prime,   15
        You may forever tarry.

1648

EDMUND WALLER

Song

    Go, lovely rose!
Tell her that wastes her time and me
    That now she knows,
When I resemble[1] her to thee,
How sweet and fair she seems to be.   5

    Tell her that's young,
And shuns to have her graces spied,
    That hadst thou sprung
In deserts, where no men abide,
Thou must have uncommended died.   10

    Small is the worth
Of beauty from the light retired;
    Bid her come forth,
Suffer herself to be desired,
And not blush so to be admired.   15

    Then die! that she
The common fate of all things rare
    May read in thee;
How small a part of time they share
That are so wondrous sweet and fair!   20

           1645

RICHARD LOVELACE

To Amarantha, That She Would Dishevel Her Hair

    Amarantha sweet and fair,
Ah, braid no more that shining hair!
    As my curious hand or eye
Hovering round thee, let it fly.

    Let it fly as unconfined   5
As its calm ravisher, the wind,
    Who hath left his darling, th' East,
To wanton o'er that spicy nest.

    Every tress must be confessed
But neatly tangled at the best,   10
    Like a clue[2] of golden thread,
Most excellently raveléd.

1. Compare.   2. Ball.

Do not then wind up that light
In ribands, and o'ercloud in night;
   Like the sun in's early ray,
But shake your head and scatter day.   15

  See, 'tis broke! Within this grove,
The bower and the walks of love,
   Weary lie we down and rest
And fan each other's panting breast.   20

  Here we'll strip and cool our fire
In cream below, in milk-baths higher;
   And when all wells are drawn dry,
I'll drink a tear out of thine eye.

  Which our very joys shall leave,   25
That sorrows thus we can deceive;
   Or our very sorrows weep,
That joys so ripe so little keep.

1649

BEN JONSON

Come, My Celia[3]

Come, my Celia, let us prove,[4]
While we can, the sports of love;
Time will not be ours forever:
He at length our good will sever.
Spend not, then, his gifts in vain;   5
Suns that set may rise again,
But if once we lose this light,
'Tis with us perpetual night.
Why should we defer our joys?
Fame and rumor are but toys.   10
Cannot we delude the eyes
Of a few poor household spies?
Or his easier ears beguile,
Thus removéd by our wile?
'Tis no sin love's fruits to steal,   15
But the sweet thefts to reveal;
To be taken, to be seen,
These have crimes accounted been.

1606

---

3. A song from *Volpone*, sung by the play's villain and would-be seducer. Part of the poem paraphrases Catullus, V.

4. Try.

DONALD J. LLOYD

Bridal Couch

Follows this a narrower bed,
Wood at feet, wood at head;
Follows this a sounder sleep,
Somewhat longer and too deep.

All too meanly and too soon   5
Waxes once and wanes our moon;
All too swiftly for each one
Falls to dark our winter sun.

Let us here then wrestle death,
Intermingled limb and breath,   10
Conscious both that we beget
End of rest, endless fret,

And come at last to permanence,
Tired dancers from a dance,
Yawning, and content to fall   15
Into any bed at all.

                                                1956

JOHN FLETCHER

Love's Emblems

Now the lusty spring is seen;
    Golden yellow, gaudy blue,
    Daintily invite the view:
Everywhere on every green
Roses blushing as they blow   5
    And enticing men to pull,
Lilies whiter than the snow,
    Woodbines of sweet honey full:
        All love's emblems, and all cry,
        "Ladies, if not plucked, we die."   10

Yet the lusty spring hath stayed;
    Blushing red and purest white
    Daintily to love invite
Every woman, every maid:
Cherries kissing as they grow,   15
    And inviting men to taste,
Apples even ripe below,
    Winding gently to the waist:
        All love's emblems, and all cry,
        "Ladies, if not plucked, we die."   20

                                                1647

ROBERT HERRICK

Corinna's Going A-Maying

Get up, get up, for shame! the blooming morn
Upon her wings presents the god unshorn.[5]
   See how Aurora[6] throws her fair
   Fresh-quilted[7] colors through the air:
   Get up, sweet slug-a-bed, and see   5
   The dew bespangling herb and tree.
Each flower has wept, and bowéd toward the east,
Above an hour since; yet you not dressed,
   Nay, not so much as out of bed?
   When all the birds have matins[8] said,   10
   And sung their thankful hymns, 'tis sin,
   Nay, profanation to keep in,
Whenas a thousand virgins on this day
Spring, sooner than the lark, to fetch in May.[9]

Rise, and put on your foliage, and be seen   15
To come forth, like the springtime, fresh and green,
   And sweet as Flora.[1] Take no care
   For jewels for your gown, or hair;
   Fear not; the leaves will strew
   Gems in abundance upon you;   20
Besides, the childhood of the day has kept,
Against[2] you come, some orient[3] pearls unwept;
   Come, and receive them while the light
   Hangs on the dew-locks of the night,
   And Titan[4] on the eastern hill   25
   Retires himself, or else stands still,
Till you come forth. Wash, dress, be brief in praying:
Few beads[5] are best when once we go a-Maying.

Come, my Corinna, come; and, coming, mark
How each field turns[6] a street, each street a park   30
   Made green and trimmed with trees; see how
   Devotion gives each house a bough
   Or branch: each porch, each door, ere this,
   An ark, a tabernacle is,
Made up of whitethorn neatly interwove,   35
As if here were those cooler shades of love.
   Can such delights be in the street,
   And open fields, and we not see 't?
   Come, we'll abroad; and let's obey
   The proclamation made for May,   40

5. Apollo, the sun god, whose golden hair represents the sun's rays.
6. Goddess of the dawn.
7. Mingled.
8. Morning prayers.
9. The traditional celebration of May Day morning included the gathering of white hawthorn blossoms and boughs to decorate houses and streets.
1. Goddess of flowers.
2. Until.
3. Shining.
4. The sun.
5. Prayers.
6. Turns into.

And sin no more, as we have done, by staying.
But, my Corinna, come, let's go a-Maying.

There's not a budding boy or girl this day
But is got up, and gone to bring in May;
   A deal of youth, ere this, is come   45
   Back, and with whitethorn laden home.
   Some have dispatched their cakes and cream
   Before that we have left to dream;
And some have wept, and wooed, and plighted troth,
And chose their priest, ere we can cast off sloth.   50
   Many a green-gown[7] has been given,
   Many a kiss, both odd and even,
   Many a glance, too, has been sent
   From out the eye, love's firmament;
Many a jest told of the keys betraying   55
This night, and locks picked; yet we're not a-Maying.

Come, let us go while we are in our prime,
And take the harmless folly of the time.
   We shall grow old apace, and die
   Before we know our liberty.   60
   Our life is short, and our days run
   As fast away as does the sun;
And as a vapor, or a drop of rain,
Once lost, can ne'er be found again:
   So when or you or[8] I are made   65
   A fable, song, or fleeting shade,
   All love, all liking, all delight
   Lies drowned with us in endless night.
Then while time serves, and we are but decaying,
Come, my Corinna, come, let's go a-Maying.   70

1648

THOMAS MOORE

An Argument to Any Phillis or Cloë

     I've oft been told by learned friars,
       That wishing and the crime are one,
     And Heaven punishes desires
       As much as if the deed were done.

     If wishing damns us, you and I   5
       Are damned to all our heart's content;
     Come, then, at least we may enjoy
       Some pleasure for our punishment!

1801

7. Grass-stained gown.   8. Either . . . or.

ALFRED, LORD TENNYSON

Now Sleeps the Crimson Petal[9]

Now sleeps the crimson petal, now the white;
Nor waves the cypress in the palace walk;
Nor winks the gold fin in the porphyry font;[1]
The firefly wakens; waken thou with me.

Now droops the milk-white peacock like a ghost,   5
And like a ghost she glimmers on to me.

Now lies the Earth all Danaë[2] to the stars,
And all thy heart lies open unto me.

Now slides the silent meteor on, and leaves
A shining furrow, as thy thoughts in me.   10

Now folds the lily all her sweetness up,
And slips into the bosom of the lake;
So fold thyself, my dearest, thou, and slip
Into my bosom and be lost in me.

                                                    1847

ANDREW MARVELL

To His Coy Mistress

Had we but world enough, and time,
This coyness,[3] lady, were no crime.
We would sit down, and think which way
To walk, and pass our long love's day.
Thou by the Indian Ganges' side   5
Shouldst rubies[4] find: I by the tide
Of Humber[5] would complain. I would
Love you ten years before the Flood,
And you should if you please refuse
Till the conversion of the Jews.[6]   10
My vegetable love[7] should grow
Vaster than empires, and more slow;

9. A song from *The Princess,* in the form of a ghazal.
1. Stone fishbowl. "porphyry": a red stone containing fine white crystals.
2. A princess, confined in a tower, seduced by Zeus after he became a shower of gold in order to gain access to her.
3. Hesitancy, modesty (not necessarily suggesting calculation).
4. Talismans which are supposed to preserve virginity.
5. A small river which flows through Marvell's home town, Hull. "complain": write love complaints, conventional songs lamenting the cruelty of love.
6. Which, according to popular Christian belief, will occur just before the end of the world.
7. Which is capable only of passive growth, not of consciousness. The "Vegetable Soul" is lower than the other two divisions of the Soul, "Animal" and "Rational."

An hundred years should go to praise
Thine eyes, and on thy forehead gaze;
Two hundred to adore each breast,   15
But thirty thousand to the rest.
An age at least to every part,
And the last age should show your heart.
For, lady, you deserve this state;[8]
Nor would I love at lower rate.   20
   But at my back I always hear
Time's wingéd chariot hurrying near;
And yonder all before us lie
Deserts of vast eternity.
Thy beauty shall no more be found,   25
Nor, in thy marble vault, shall sound
My echoing song; then worms shall try
That long preserved virginity,
And your quaint honor turn to dust,
And into ashes all my lust: 30
The grave's a fine and private place,
But none, I think, do there embrace.
   Now therefore, while the youthful hue
Sits on thy skin like morning dew,[9]
And while thy willing soul transpires[1]   35
At every pore with instant fires,
Now let us sport us while we may,
And now, like am'rous birds of prey,
Rather at once our time devour
Than languish in his slow-chapped[2] pow'r.   40
Let us roll all our strength and all
Our sweetness up into one ball,
And tear our pleasures with rough strife
Thorough[3] the iron gates of life.
Thus, though we cannot make our sun   45
Stand still,[4] yet we will make him run.[5]

                                             1681

e. e. cummings

(ponder,darling,these busted statues

(ponder,darling,these busted statues
of yon motheaten forum be aware
notice what hath remained

---

8. Dignity.
9. The text reads "glew." "Lew" (warmth) has also been suggested as an emendation.
1. Breathes forth.
2. Slow-jawed. Chronos (Time), ruler of the world in early Greek myth, devoured all of his children except Zeus, who was hidden. Later, Zeus seized power (see line 46 and note).
3. Through.
4. To lengthen his night of love with Alcmene, Zeus made the sun stand still.
5. Each sex act was believed to shorten life by one day.

—the stone cringes
clinging to the stone,how obsolete   5

lips utter their extant smile . . . .
remark

a few deleted of texture
or meaning monuments and dolls

resist Them Greediest Paws of careful   10
time[6] all of which is extremely
unimportant)whereas Life

matters if or

when the your- and my-
idle vertical worthless   15
self unite in a peculiarly
momentary

partnership(to instigate
constructive
                    Horizontal   20
business . . . . even so,let us make haste
—consider well this ruined aqueduct

lady,
which used to lead something into somewhere)

                                                              1926

Replies to the Passionate Shepherd

SIR WALTER RALEGH

The Nymph's Reply to the Shepherd

If all the world and love were young,
And truth in every shepherd's tongue,
These pretty pleasures might me move
To live with thee and be thy love.

Time drives the flocks from field to fold,   5
When rivers rage, and rocks grow cold,
And Philomel[1] becometh dumb;
The rest complain of cares to come.

6. See "To His Coy Mistress," above,   1. The nightingale.
especially lines 39–40.

The flowers do fade, and wanton fields
To wayward winter reckoning yields: 10
A honey tongue, a heart of gall,
Is fancy's spring, but sorrow's fall.

Thy gowns, thy shoes, they beds of roses,
Thy cap, thy kirtle, and thy posies
Soon break, soon wither, soon forgotten;   15
In folly ripe, in reason rotten.

Thy belt of straw and ivy buds,
Thy coral clasps and amber studs,
All these in me no means can move
To come to thee and be thy love.   20

But could youth last, and love still breed,
Had joys no date,[2] nor age no need,
Then these delights my mind might move
To live with thee and be thy love.

1600

C. DAY LEWIS

Song

Come, live with me and be my love,
And we will all the pleasures prove
Of peace and plenty, bed and board,
That chance employment may afford.

I'll handle dainties on the docks   5
And thou shalt read of summer frocks:
At evening by the sour canals
We'll hope to hear some madrigals.

Care on thy maiden brow shall put
A wreath of wrinkles, and thy foot   10
Be shod with pain: not silken dress
But toil shall tire thy loveliness.

Hunger shall make thy modest zone
And cheat fond death of all but bone—
If these delights thy mind may move,   15
Then live with me and be my love.

1935

2. End.

JOHN DONNE

The Bait

Come live with me, and be my love,
And we will some new pleasures prove,
Of golden sands, and crystal brooks:
With silken lines, and silver hooks.

There will the river whispering run   5
Warmed by thy eyes, more than the sun.
And there th' enamored fish will stay,
Begging themselves they may betray.

When thou wilt swim in that live bath,
Each fish, which every channel hath,   10
Will amorously to thee swim,
Gladder to catch thee, than thou him.

If thou to be so seen be'st loath
By sun, or moon, thou dark'nest both,
And if myself have leave to see,   15
I need not their light, having thee.

Let others freeze with angling reeds,[3]
And cut their legs with shells and weeds,
Or treacherously poor fish beset
With strangling snare, or windowy net.   20

Let coarse bold hands, from slimy nest
The bedded fish in banks out-wrest;
Or curious traitors, sleave-silk[4] flies,
Bewitch poor fishes' wand'ring eyes.

For thee, thou need'st no such deceit,   25
For thou thyself art thine own bait;
That fish that is not catched thereby,
Alas, is wiser far than I.

1612

PETER DE VRIES

Bacchanal[5]

"Come live with me and be my love,"
He said, in substance. "There's no vine

---

3. Rods.
4. Untwisted silk.

5. A drunken or riotous celebration.

We will not pluck the clusters of,
   Or grape we will not turn to wine."

It's autumn of their second year.   5
   Now he, in seasonal pursuit,
With rich and modulated cheer,
   Brings home the festive purple fruit;

And she, by passion once demented
   —That woman out of Botticelli[6]—   10
She brews and bottles, unfermented,
   The stupid and abiding jelly.

                                                      1959

DELMORE SCHWARTZ

The Passionate Shepherd to His Love

Come live with me and be my wife,
We'll seek the peaks and pits of life
And run the gauntlet of the heart
On mountains or the depths of art.
         We'll do the most that thinking can   5
         Against emotion's Ghenghis Khan.
And we will play on Hallowe'en
Like all souls on the silver screen,
Or at a masked ball ask for fun
Dancing dressed as monk and nun.   10
         We'll ride a solemn music's boat
         When humors cough in breast and throat.
When snow comes like a sailing fleet
We'll skate a ballet in the street,
Though poor as saints or rocks, immense   15
Our chatter's rich irreverence.
         And sometimes speak of endless death
         To quicken ever conscious breath.
If one becomes too serious,
The other can bring down the house   20
With jokes which seem hilarious
About the self's pretentious Ows.
         I'll be your room-mate and your hoax,
         The scapeghost of your gentle jokes.
Like Molière's bourgeois gentleman,[7]   25
You may discover you have been

6. Italian painter (1445–1510) of the Florentine school, famous for his sensuous paintings of Venus and the Virgin Mary.

7. In Act II of *Le Bourgeois Gentilhomme*, M. Jourdain "discovers" that he has been speaking prose all his life.

Speaking blank verse all your life,
And hence you must become my wife.
    For you will know of metaphors,
    If I say aeroplanes are bores.   30
If these excursions seem to you
Interesting as a rendezvous,
    Rich as cake and revenue,
    Handsome as hope and as untrue,
    And full of travel's points of view,   35
    Vivid as red and fresh as dew,
Come live with me and try my life,
And be my night, my warmth, my wife.

                                                 1950

Another Version

KENNETH KOCH

Variations on a Theme by
William Carlos Williams[1]

1

I chopped down the house that you had been saving to live in next
    summer.
I am sorry, but it was morning, and I had nothing to do
and its wooden beams were so inviting.

2

We laughed at the hollyhocks together
and then I sprayed them with lye.   5
Forgive me. I simply do not know what I am doing.

3

I gave away the money that you had been saving to live on for the
    next ten years.
The man who asked for it was shabby
and the firm March wind on the porch was so juicy and cold.

4

Last evening we went dancing and I broke your leg.   10
Forgive me. I was clumsy, and
I wanted you here in the wards, where I am the doctor!

                                                 1962

1. See William Carlos Williams's *This
Is Just to Say*, p. 526. Williams was a   physician as well as poet (see line 12).

DESMOND SKIRROW

Ode on a Grecian Urn Summarized[2]

Gods chase
Round vase.
What say?
What play?
Don't know.
Nice, though.

p. 1960

ANTHONY HECHT

The Dover Bitch

A *Criticism of Life*

for Andrews Wanning

So there stood Matthew Arnold and this girl[3]
With the cliffs of England crumbling away behind them,
And he said to her, "Try to be true to me,
And I'll do the same for you, for things are bad
All over, etc., etc."   5
Well now, I knew this girl. It's true she had read
Sophocles in a fairly good translation
And caught that bitter allusion to the sea,[4]
But all the time he was talking she had in mind
The notion of what his whiskers would feel like   10
On the back of her neck. She told me later on
That after a while she got to looking out
At the lights across the channel, and really felt sad,
Thinking of all the wine and enormous beds
And blandishments in French and the perfumes.   15
And then she got really angry. To have been brought
All the way down from London, and then be addressed
As a sort of mournful cosmic last resort
Is really tough on a girl, and she was pretty.
Anyway, she watched him pace the room   20
And finger his watch-chain and seem to sweat a bit,
And then she said one or two unprintable things.
But you mustn't judge her by that. What I mean to say is,
She's really all right. I still see her once in a while
And she always treats me right. We have a drink   25

2. See Keats's *Ode on a Grecian Urn* (p. 256).
3. See Arnold's poem *Dover Beach*, p. 109.
4. In *Antigone*, lines 583–91. See *Dover Beach*, lines 9–18.

And I give her a good time, and perhaps it's a year
Before I see her again, but there she is,
Running to fat, but dependable as they come.
And sometimes I bring her a bottle of *Nuit d'Amour*.

1968

EDGAR A. GUEST

Home

It takes a heap o' livin' in a house t' make it home,
A heap o' sun an' shadder, an' ye sometimes have t' roam
Afore ye really 'preciate the things ye lef' behind,
An' hunger fer 'em somehow, with 'em allus on yer mind.
It don't make any differunce how rich ye get t' be,   5
How much yer chairs an' tables cost, how great yer luxury;
It ain't home t' ye, though it be the palace of a king,
Until somehow yer soul is sort o' wrapped round everything.

Home ain't a place that gold can buy or get up in a minute;
Afore it's home there's got t' be a heap o' livin' in it;   10
Within the walls there's got t' be some babies born, and then
Right there ye've got t' bring 'em up t' women good, an' men;
And gradjerly, as time goes on, ye find ye wouldn't part
With anything they ever used—they've grown into yer heart:
The old high chairs, the playthings, too, the little shoes they wore   15
Ye hoard; an' if ye could ye'd keep the thumbmarks on the door.

Ye've got t' weep t' make it home, ye've got t' sit an' sigh
An' watch beside a loved one's bed an' know that Death is nigh;
An' in the stillness o' the night t' see Death's angel come,
An' close the eyes o' her that smiled, an' leave her sweet   20
  voice dumb.
Fer these are scenes that grip the heart, an' when yer tears
  are dried,
Ye find the home is dearer than it was, an' sanctified;
An' tuggin' at ye always are the pleasant memories
O' her that was an' is no more—ye can't escape from these.

Ye've got t' sing an' dance fer years, ye've got t' romp an' play,   25
An' learn t' love the things ye have by usin' 'em each day;
Even the roses 'round the porch must blossom year by year
Afore they 'come a part o' ye, suggestin' someone dear
Who used t' love 'em long ago, an' trained ' em jes' t' run
The way they do, so's they would get the early mornin' sun;   30
Ye've got t' love each brick an' stone from cellar up t' dome:
It takes a heap o' livin' in a house t' make it home.

1916

LOUIS UNTERMEYER

Edgar A. Guest Considers the Good "Old Woman Who Lived in a Shoe" and the Good Old Truths Simultaneously

It takes a heap o' children to make a home that's true,
And home can be a palace grand, or just a plain, old shoe;
But if it has a mother dear, and a good old dad or two,
Why, that's the sort of good old home for good old me
    and you.

Of all the institutions this side the Vale o' Rest   5
Howe'er it be, it seems to me a good old mother's best;
And fathers are a blessing, too, they give the place a tone;
In fact each child should try and have some parents of
    its own.

The food can be quite simple; just a sop of milk and bread
Are plenty when the kiddies know it's time to go to bed.   10
And every little sleepy-head will dream about the day
When he can go to work because a Man's Work is his
    Play.

And, oh, how sweet his life will seem, with nought to
    make him cross;
And he will never watch the clock and always mind the boss.
And when he thinks (as may occur), this thought will
    please him best: 15
That ninety million think the same—including
    Eddie Guest.

1935

The Sister Arts

MICHAEL HAMBURGER

Lines on Brueghel's *Icarus*[1]

The plowman plows, the fisherman dreams of fish;
Aloft, the sailor through a world of ropes

1. "Landscape with the Fall of Icarus," by Pieter Brueghel the elder, located in the Brussels Museum. According to Greek myth, Daedalus and his son Icarus escaped from imprisonment by using homemade wings of wax; but Icarus flew too near the sun, the wax melted, and he fell into the sea and drowned. In the Brueghel painting the central figure is a peasant plowing, and several other figures are more immediately noticeable than Icarus who, disappearing into the sea, is easy to miss in the lower right-hand corner. Equally ignored by the figures is a dead body in the woods.

Guides tangled meditations, feverish
With memories of girls forsaken, hopes
Of brief reunions, new discoveries,   5
Past rum consumed, rum promised, rum potential.
Sheep crop the grass, lift up their heads and gaze
Into a sheepish present: the essential,
Illimitable juiciness of things,
Greens, yellows, browns are what they see.   10
Churlish and slow, the shepherd, hearing wings—
Perhaps an eagle's—gapes uncertainly.

Too late. The worst had happened: lost to man
The angel, Icarus, for ever failed,
Fallen with melted wings when, near the sun   15
He scorned the ordering planet, which prevailed
And, jeering, now slinks off, to rise once more.
But he—his damaged purpose drags him down—
Too far from his half-brothers on the shore,
Hardly conceivable, is left to drown.   20

                                                                  1952

WILLIAM CARLOS WILLIAMS

Landscape with the Fall of Icarus[2]

According to Brueghel
when Icarus fell
it was spring

a farmer was plowing
his field   5
the whole pageantry

of the year was
awake tingling
near

the edge of the sea   10
concerned
with itself

sweating in the sun
that melted
the wings' wax   15

---

2. See the notes to the poem above.

unsignificantly
off the coast
there was

a splash quite unnoticed
this was   20
Icarus drowning

                                                                            1962

X. J. KENNEDY

Nude Descending a Staircase[3]

Toe upon toe, a snowing flesh,
A gold of lemon, root and rind,
She sifts in sunlight down the stairs
With nothing on. Nor on her mind.

We spy beneath the banister   5
A constant thresh of thigh on thigh—
Her lips imprint the swinging air
That parts to let her parts go by.

One-woman waterfall, she wears
Her slow descent like a long cape   10
And pausing, on the final stair
Collects her motions into shape.

                                                                            1961

WILLIAM CARLOS WILLIAMS

The Dance

In Brueghel's great picture, The Kermess,[4]
the dancers go round, they go round and
around, the squeal and the blare and the
tweedle of bagpipes, a bugle and fiddles
tipping their bellies (round as the thick-   5
sided glasses whose wash they impound)
their hips and their bellies off balance
to turn them. Kicking and rolling about
the Fair Grounds, swinging their butts, those
shanks must be sound to bear up under such   10
rollicking measures, prance as they dance
in Brueghel's great picture, The Kermess.

                                                                            1944

3. A celebrated cubist-futurist painting   4. A drawing by Pieter Brueghel the elder.
by Marcel Duchamp (1913).

14   FRAMES OF REFERENCE: CONTEXTS OF MYTH

Whether or not we are a part of *all* that we have met, we take some of our identity from the cultures into which we were born and the traditions that lie behind them. Being so thoroughly culture-bound doesn't please everybody, and rebels often use a lot of energy kicking against the values and assumptions built into the people and institutions with whom they have grown up. But even in rebelling, we are stuck with the terms, values, and assumptions we rebel against. No matter how "individual" we succeed in being, we are still a part of something larger, something that has been here longer than we have and that has managed to clarify and articulate its values over generations and centuries.

Every culture develops stories to explain itself. These stories try to explain to us who we are and why we are the way we are. Taken together, they constitute what is often called a **myth**. Calling it a myth does not mean that it is false. In fact, it means nearly the opposite, for a culture takes its myths seriously as explanations of why things are the way they are, why the history of the culture has gone in a particular way. Myth, in the sense in which it is used here, involves the explanations that are more or less universally shared within a particular culture; it is a frame of reference that people within the culture understand and share. A sharing of this frame of reference does not mean that all people within a culture are carbon copies of each other or that popular stereotypes represent reality accurately, nor does it mean that every individual in the culture *knows* the perceived history and can articulate its events, ideas, and values. But it does mean that a shared history and a shared set of symbols lie behind any particular culture and that the culture is to some extent aware of its distinctiveness from other cultures.

A **culture,** in the sense in which it is used here, may be of many sizes and shapes. Often we think of a nation as a culture (and so speak of American culture, American history, the myth of America, the American dream, the American frame of reference), and it is equally useful to make smaller and larger divisions—as long as there is some commonality of history and some cohesiveness of purpose within the group. One can speak of Southern culture, for example, or of urban culture, or of the drug culture, or the rock music culture, or of a culture associated with a particular political belief, economic class, or social group. Most of us belong, willingly or not, to a number of such cultures at one time, and to some extent our identity and destiny are linked with the distinctive features of those cultures and with the ways the culture perceives its identity, values, and history. Some of these cultures we choose to join; some are thrust upon us by birth and circumstances. It is these larger and more persistent kinds of cultures that are illustrated in the frames of reference sampled in this chapter.

Poets, aware of their heritage, often like to probe its history and beliefs and plumb its depths, just as they like to articulate and play variations on the poetic tradition they feel a part of. For poetry written in the English language over the last 400 years or so, both the Judaeo-Christian frame of reference and the classical frame of reference (involving the civilizations of ancient Greece and Rome) have been quite important. Western culture, a broad culture that includes many nations and many sorts of religious and social groups, is largely defined within these two frames of reference—or it has been until quite recently. As religious belief has eroded over the past two or three centuries, and as classical civilization has been less emphasized and less studied, poets have felt increasingly less comfortable in assuming that their audiences share a knowledge of their systems, but they have often continued to use them to isolate and articulate human traits that have cultural continuity and importance. The poems in this chapter exemplify various kinds of attempts to define and investigate cultural contexts and what they continue to mean.

The question of shared values and a common heritage is prominent in all the poems in this chapter. Because communication necessarily involves some kind of common ground, poets in homogeneous cultures have had a relatively easier time of it than poets in very diverse cultures, and modern poets often lament the lack of a received tradition that they can count on. Still, they have to work with what is available, and the poems in the first two subgroups here draw upon two traditional sources of history and myth—the Judaeo-Christian and classical frames of reference. The third subgroup introduces elements from some non-Western frames of reference. The final subgroup represents one modern poet's individual solution to the problem of decaying certitudes in communication; W. B. Yeats's own mythology is highly individual and even eccentric but it amalgamates elements from traditional classical and Judaeo-Christian frames of reference as well as adding novelties of its own.

Judaeo-Christian History and Myth

JOHN MILTON

[Before the Fall][1]

She as a veil down to the slender waist   304
Her unadorned golden tresses wore
Disheveled, but in wanton[2] ringlets waved
As the vine curls her tendrils, which implied
Subjection,[3] but required with gentle sway,
And by her yielded, by him best received,

1. From *Paradise Lost,* Book IV. For the Biblical description of Eden, see *Genesis* 2:8–25.

2. Luxuriant.

3. The idea derives from *Genesis* 3:16 and *I Corinthians* 11:9–10.

Yielded with coy[4] submission, modest pride,   310
And sweet reluctant amorous delay.
Nor those mysterious parts were then concealed,
Then was not guilty shame, dishonest shame
Of nature's works, honor dishonorable,
Sin-bred, how have ye troubled all mankind   315
With shows instead, mere shows of seeming pure,
And banished from man's life his happiest life,
Simplicity and spotless innocence.
So passed they naked on, nor shunned the sight
Of God or angel, for they thought no ill.   320
So hand in hand they passed, the loveliest pair
That ever since in love's embraces met,
Adam the goodliest man of men since born
His sons, the fairest of her daughters Eve.
Under a tuft of shade that on a green   325
Stood whispering soft, by a fresh fountain side
They sat them down, and after no more toil
Of their sweet gardening labor than sufficed
To recommend cool zephyr, and made ease
More easy, wholesome thirst and appetite   330
More grateful, to their supper fruits they fell,
Nectarine[5] fruits which the compliant boughs
Yielded them, sidelong as they sat recline
On the soft downy bank damasked[6] with flowers:
The savory pulp they chew, and in the rind   335
Still as they thirsted scoop the brimming stream;
Nor gentle purpose,[7] nor endearing smiles
Wanted,[8] nor youthful dalliance as beseems
Fair couple, linked in happy nuptial league,
Alone as they. About them frisking played   340
All beasts of the earth, since wild, and of all chase[9]
In wood or wilderness, forest or den;
Sporting the lion ramped, and in his paw
Dandled the kid; bears, tigers, ounces,[1] pards,
Gamboled before them, the unwieldy elephant   345
To make them mirth used all his might, and wreathed
His lithe proboscis; close the serpent sly
Insinuating, wove with Gordian[2] twine
His braided train, and of his fatal guile
Gave proof unheeded; others on the grass   350
Couched, and now filled with pasture gazing sat,
Or bedward ruminating: for the sun
Declined was hasting now with prone career
To the Ocean Isles,[3] and in the ascending scale
Of heaven the stars that usher evening rose.   355

                                                        1667

4. Shy.
5. Sweet as nectar, the traditional drink
of the gods.
6. Variegated.
7. Conversation. "Nor . . . nor": neither
. . . nor (a common 17th-century con-
struction).

8. Were lacking.
9. Tracts of land.
1. Lynxes. "pards": leopards.
2. Like the Gordian knot, a legendary
intricate knot, finally cut by Alexander the
Great.
3. The Azores; i.e., westward.

JOHN HOLLANDER

Adam's Task

"And Adam gave names to all cattle, and to the fowl of the air, and to every beast of
the field . . ."—*Gen.* 2:20

      Thou, paw-paw-paw; thou, glurd; thou, spotted
         Glurd; thou, whitestap, lurching through
      The high-grown brush; thou, pliant-footed,
         Implex; thou, awagabu.

      Every burrower, each flier   5
         Came for the name he had to give:
      Gay, first work, ever to be prior,
         Not yet sunk to primitive.

      Thou, verdle; thou, McFleery's pomma;
         Thou; thou; thou—three types of grawl;   10
      Thou, flisket; thou, kabasch; thou, comma-
         Eared mashawk; thou, all; thou, all.

      Were, in a fire of becoming,
         Laboring to be burned away,
      Then work, half-measuring, half-humming,   15
         Would be as serious as play.

      Thou, pambler; thou, rivarn; thou, greater
         Wherret, and thou, lesser one;
      Thou, sproal; thou, zant; thou, lily-eater.
         Naming's over. Day is done.   20

                              1971

LINDA PASTAN

A Symposium: Apples

    Eve: Remember a season
         of apples, the orchard
         full of them, my apron
         full of them. One day
         we wandered from tree   5
         to tree, sharing a basket
         feeling the weight of apples
         increase between us.
         And how your muscles ripened
         with all that lifting.   10
         I felt them round and hard

under my teeth; white
and sweet the flesh
of men and apples.

Gabriel:[4] Nameless in Eden,   15
the apple itself
was innocent—an ordinary
lunchpail fruit.
Still it reddened
for the way it was used.   20
Afterward the apple
chose for itself
names untrusting
on the tongue: stayman,
gravenstein,   25
northern spy.

The Serpent: Ordinary, innocent
yes. But deep
in each center of whiteness
one dark star . . .   30

Adam: In the icebox
an apple
will keep
for weeks.
Then its skin   35
wrinkles up
like the skin of the old man
I have become,
from a single
bite.   40

1975

VASSAR MILLER

Adam's Footprint

Once as a child I loved to hop
On round plump bugs and make them stop
Before they crossed a certain crack.
My bantam brawn could turn them back,
My crooked step wrenched straight to kill   5
Live pods that then screwed tight and still.

Small sinner, stripping boughs of pears,
Shinnied past sweet and wholesome airs,

4. Traditionally, a messenger of God;   chief of the angelic guards in Paradise.
in *Paradise Lost*, Milton makes Gabriel the

How could a tree be so unclean?
Nobody knows but Augustine.[5]   10
He nuzzled pears for dam-sin's dugs[6]—
And I scrunched roly-poly bugs.

No wolf's imprint or tiger's trace
Does Christ hunt down to catch with grace
In nets of love the devious preys   15
Whose feet go softly all their days:
The foot of Adam leaves the mark
Of some child scrabbling in the dark.

                                         1956

CHRISTINA ROSSETTI

Eve

"While I sit at the door,
Sick to gaze within,
Mine eye weepeth sore
For sorrow and sin:
As a tree my sin stands   5
To darken all lands;
Death is the fruit it bore.

"How have Eden bowers grown
Without Adam to bend them!
How have Eden flowers blown,   10
Squandering their sweet breath,
Without me to tend them!
The Tree of Life was ours,
Tree twelvefold-fruited,[7]
Most lofty tree that flowers,   15
Most deeply rooted:
I chose the Tree of Death.[8]

"Hadst thou but said me nay,
    Adam, my brother,
I might have pined away—   20
    I, but none other:
God might have let thee stay
Safe in our garden,

5. In his *Confessions*, Book II, St. Augustine agonizes over his theft, from a nearby tree, of pears he did not really want and meditates on the human tendency to want what is forbidden.
6. I.e., as if they were the breasts of mother-sin (with, of course, more than one pun on "dam").
7. The tree of life is so described in *Revelation* 22:2, 14, but the account there is of the New Jerusalem, not of Eden.
8. The *Genesis* account distinguishes between the tree of life and the tree of the knowledge of good and evil; the latter is forbidden, and eating of it brings labor, sickness, and death into the world. See *Genesis* 2:9, 3:1–24.

By putting me away
Beyond all pardon.   25

"I, Eve, sad mother
Of all who must live,
I, not another,
Plucked bitterest fruit to give
My friend, husband, lover.   30
O wanton eyes run over!
Who but I should grieve?—
Cain hath slain his brother:[9]
Of all who must die mother,
Miserable Eve!"   35

Thus she sat weeping,
Thus Eve our mother,
Where one lay sleeping
Slain by his brother.
Greatest and least   40
Each piteous beast
To hear her voice
Forgot his joys
And set aside his feast.

The mouse paused in his walk   45
And dropped his wheaten stalk:
Grave cattle wagged their heads
In rumination;
The eagle gave a cry
From his cloud station: 50
Larks on thyme beds
Forbore to mount or sing;
Bees drooped upon the wing;
The raven perched on high
Forgot his ration;   55
The conies[1] in their rock,
A feeble nation,
Quaked sympathetical;
The mocking-bird left off to mock;
Huge camels knelt as if   60
In deprecation;
The kind hart's tears were falling;
Chattered the wistful stork;
Dove-voices with a dying fall
Cooed desolation   65
Answering grief by grief.

9. Abel (see *Genesis* 4:1–15).
1. A common term for rabbits, but here probably the small pachyderms mentioned in *Proverbs* 30:26.

Only the serpent in the dust,
Wriggling and crawling,
Grinned an evil grin, and thrust
His tongue out with its fork.   70

1865

ROB HOLLAND

Eve in Old Age

Over her shoulder, the window framed the stars.
The planets gathered—still, always for her,
Called out of the dark like thoughts. Venus a green
Firefly. The erratic pulse, Mars.
Inside the thoughts themselves gathered, the stir   5
Of a few leaves, the light fretful, serene.

The unicorn was not at her elbow now.
The pomegranate, split in the sudden cold,
Spilled its red chambers like a heart.[2]
She remembered it only so, and how   10
It was ever other she could not have told.
She was an old woman. This was God's part.

Her sons, once, had filled her like a snail,
Curled within her, beating like rain
Against a window. She remembered watching each   15
Drive into himself the hooked nail.
And the nameless daughters, who first had lain
With them. They watched the days pass without speech.

Adam, too, was silent. She could not forget
His calm weight beside her, as if nothing but light   20
Burned on the retina of God's eye.
There was a fine line where their bodies had met,
Crossed and yet never crossed. The white
Moon cut like a scythe across the sky.

She dreamed at last of the green skin of the snake,   25
In each scale the star, the tree, windless.
And her own face, scratched there like a mark.
The snow began to fall, flake by flake
Gathering the world around her. Transparent, endless,
The dark passed through her into the dark.

1977

2. In Christian iconography (most no-
tably in the Flemish tapestry "The Uni-
corn in Captivity" in the Cloisters in New
York), a unicorn and pomegranate tree
are associated with the *hortus conclusus*
(enclosed garden) tradition. The unicorn
is a traditional symbol of Christ.

RICHARD WILBUR

She

What was her beauty in our first estate
When Adam's will was whole,[3] and the least thing
Appeared the gift and creature of his king,
How should we guess? Resemblance had to wait

For separation, and in such a place   5
She so partook of water, light, and trees
As not to look like any one of these.
He woke and gazed into her naked face.

But then she changed, and coming down amid
The flocks of Abel and the fields of Cain,   10
Clothed in their wish, her Eden graces hid,
A shape of plenty with a mop of grain,

She broke upon the world, in time took on
The look of every labor and its fruits.
Columnar in a robe of pleated lawn   15
She cupped her patient hand for attributes,

Was radiant captive of the farthest tower
And shed her honor on the fields of war,
Walked in her garden at the evening hour,
Her shadow like a dark ogival[4] door,   20

Breasted the seas for all the westward ships
And, come to virgin country, changed again—
A moonlike being truest in eclipse,
And subject goddess of the dreams of men.

Tree, temple, valley, prow, gazelle, machine,   25
More named and nameless than the morning star,
Lovely in every shape, in all unseen,
We dare not wish to find you as you are,

Whose apparition, biding time until
Desire decay and bring the latter age,   30
Shall flourish in the ruins of our will
And deck[5] the broken stones like saxifrage.[6]

1961

3. Before the Fall.
4. In the form of a pointed (Gothic) arch.
5. Adorn.
6. A tufted plant with bright flowers, often rooted in the clefts of rocks.

NANCY SULLIVAN

The Death of the First Man

What was it?
How could they know what it was?
It had never happened before.
No one had ever gone out.
Whatever it was was happening.   5
Something was over.
Curled in a loose shape
the first dead man
drained out of himself
while the others shifted   10
the dead weight
(because it was dead);
they tried to make him get up.
They kicked and prodded.
Where had he gone?   15
Dead we now call that place
where he stayed in a heap
for maybe a week
until the stink told them
something was wrong.   20
Someone thought to bury him.
How could they know
from the animals that fell to their clubs
that they too could go down?
The first grave   25
mounded up over his weight.

What was it,
this going out?
That was what no one knew
even as it happened.   30
Even as it happens.

1975

ROBERT FROST

Never Again Would Birds' Song Be the Same

He would declare and could himself believe
That the birds there in all the garden round
From having heard the daylong voice of Eve
Had added to their own an oversound,
Her tone of meaning but without the words.   5
Admittedly an eloquence so soft

Could only have had an influence on birds
When call or laughter carried it aloft.
Be that as may be, she was in their song.
Moreover her voice upon their voices crossed   10
Had now persisted in the woods so long
That probably it never would be lost.
Never again would birds' song be the same.
And to do that to birds was why she came.

                                                    1942

Classical History and Myth

ALFRED, LORD TENNYSON

Ulysses[1]

It little profits that an idle king,
By this still hearth, among these barren crags,
Matched with an agéd wife,[2] I mete and dole
Unequal laws unto a savage race,
That hoard, and sleep, and feed, and know not me.   5
    I cannot rest from travel; I will drink
Life to the lees.[3] All times I have enjoyed
Greatly, have suffered greatly, both with those
That loved me, and alone; on shore, and when
Through scudding drifts the rainy Hyades[4]   10
Vexed the dim sea. I am become a name;
For always roaming with a hungry heart
Much have I seen and known—cities of men
And manners, climates, councils, governments,
Myself not least, but honored of them all—   15
And drunk delight of battle with my peers,
Far on the ringing plains of windy Troy.
I am a part of all that I have met;
Yet all experience is an arch wherethrough
Gleams that untraveled world, whose margin fades   20
For ever and for ever when I move.
How dull it is to pause, to make an end,
To rust unburnished, not to shine in use!
As though to breathe were life. Life piled on life
Were all too little, and of one to me   25

---

1. After the end of the Trojan War, Ulysses (or Odysseus), King of Ithaca and one of the Greek heroes of the war, returned to his island home (line 34). Homer's account of the situation is in the *Odyssey*, Book XI, but Dante's account of Ulysses in *The Inferno*, XXVI, is the more immediate background of the poem.
2. Penelope.
3. All the way down to the bottom of the cup.
4. A group of stars which were supposed to predict rain when they rose at the same time as the sun.

Little remains; but every hour is saved
From that eternal silence, something more,
A bringer of new things; and vile it were
For some three suns to store and hoard myself,
And this gray spirit yearning in desire   30
To follow knowledge like a sinking star,
Beyond the utmost bound of human thought.

    This is my son, mine own Telemachus,
To whom I leave the scepter and the isle—
Well-loved of me, discerning to fulfill   35
This labor by slow prudence to make mild
A rugged people, and through soft degrees
Subdue them to the useful and the good.
Most blameless is he, centered in the sphere
Of common duties, decent not to fail   40
In offices of tenderness, and pay
Meet adoration to my household gods,
When I am gone. He works his work, I mine.

    There lies the port; the vessel puffs her sail:
There gloom the dark, broad seas. My mariners,   45
Souls that have toiled, and wrought, and thought with me—
That ever with a frolic welcome took
The thunder and the sunshine, and opposed
Free hearts, free foreheads—you and I are old;
Old age hath yet his honor and his toil.   50
Death closes all; but something ere the end,
Some work of noble note, may yet be done,
Not unbecoming men that strove with Gods.
The lights begin to twinkle from the rocks;
The long day wanes; the slow moon climbs; the deep   55
Moans round with many voices. Come, my friends.
'Tis not too late to seek a newer world.
Push off, and sitting well in order smite
The sounding furrows; for my purpose holds
To sail beyond the sunset, and the baths   60
Of all the western stars, until I die.
It may be that the gulfs will wash us down;[5]
It may be we shall touch the Happy Isles,[6]
And see the great Achilles, whom we knew.
Though much is taken, much abides; and though   65
We are not now that strength which in old days
Moved earth and heaven, that which we are, we are:
One equal temper of heroic hearts,
Made weak by time and fate, but strong in will
To strive, to seek, to find, and not to yield.   70

1833

5. Beyond the Gulf of Gibraltar was supposed to be a chasm that led to Hades.
6. Elysium, the Islands of the Blessed, where heroes like Achilles (line 64) abide after death.

PETER VIERECK

Kilroy[7]

Also Ulysses once—that other war.[8]
      (Is it because we find his scrawl
      Today on every privy door
      That we forget his ancient role?)
Also was there—he did it for the wages—   5
When a Cathay-drunk Genoese set sail.[9]
Whenever "longen folk to goon on pilgrimages,"[1]
Kilroy is there;
        he tells The Miller's Tale.

At times he seems a paranoiac king   10
Who stamps his crest on walls and says "My Own!"
But in the end he fades like a lost tune,
Tossed here and there, whom all the breezes sing.
"Kilroy was here"; these words sound wanly gay,
      Haughty yet tired with long marching.   15
He is Orestes[2]—guilty of what crime?—
      For whom the Furies still are searching;
        When they arrive, they find their prey
(Leaving his name to mock them) went away.
Sometimes he does not flee from them in time: 20
"*Kilroy was*—"
            (*with his blood a dying man*
            Wrote half the phrase out in Bataan.[3])

Kilroy, beware. "HOME" is the final trap
That lurks for you in many a wily shape: 25
In pipe-and-slippers plus a Loyal Hound
      Or fooling around, just fooling around.
Kind to the old (their warm Penelope[4])
But fierce to boys,
           thus "home" becomes that sea,   30
Horribly disguised, where you were always drowned—
      (How could suburban Crete[5] condone

---

7. A fictitious character in World War II who symbolized American daring and ingenuity; the phrase "Kilroy was here" was carved and scribbled everywhere, all over the world.
8. The Trojan War, in which Ulysses became a hero and a mythic symbol of the bold voyager who thrived on action and adventure.
9. When Columbus set sail from Genoa, he intended to find a new trade route to China (Cathay).
1. An early line in the "General Prologue" to Chaucer's *Canterbury Tales*, explaining the rationale for the journey on which the *Tales* are built. "The Miller's Tale" (line 9) is the bawdiest of the tales, and one of the most spirited.
2. The son of Agamemnon and Clytemnestra in Greek myth. After his mother killed his father, he avenged the death by killing her, and the Furies (line 17) pursued him from country to country.
3. The site, in the Philippine Islands, of two major battle campaigns in World War II.
4. Wife of Ulysses.
5. According to Pindar, the Cretans were incredible liars.

The yarns you would have V-mailed[6] from the sun?)—
And folksy fishes sip Icarian tea.[7]

One stab of hopeless wings imprinted your   35
        Exultant Kilroy-signature
Upon sheer sky for all the world to stare:
        "I was there! I was there! I was there!"

God is like Kilroy. He, too, sees it all;
That's how He knows of every sparrow's fall;[8]   40
That's why we prayed each time the tightropes cracked
On which our loveliest clowns contrived their act.
The G. I. Faustus[9] who was
                        everywhere
Strolled home again. "What was it like outside?"   45
Asked Can't, with his good neighbors Ought and But
And pale Perhaps and grave-eyed Better Not;
For "Kilroy" means: the world is very wide.
        He was there, he was there, he was there!

And in the suburbs Can't sat down and cried.   50

                                              1948

WALLACE STEVENS

The World as Meditation

J'ai passé trop de temps à travailler mon violon, à voyager. Mais l'exercice essentiel du compositeur—la méditation—rien ne l'a jamais suspendu en moi . . . Je vis un rêve permanent, qui ne s'arrête ni nuit ni jour.

                                              GEORGES ENESCO[1]

Is it Ulysses that approaches from the east,[2]
The interminable adventurer? The trees are mended.
That winter is washed away. Someone is moving

On the horizon and lifting himself up above it.
A form of fire approaches the cretonnes of Penelope,   5
Whose mere savage presence awakens the world in which she dwells.

6. V-Mail was an overseas military mail system used in World War II. Letters were microfilmed, for compact transportation, and then re-enlarged before delivery.
7. Icarus, the son of Daedalus, flew with his father from Crete (line 32), but he strayed too near the sun, the wax which attached his wings melted, and he fell into the sea, which then became known as the Icarian Sea. "Icarian" once meant venturesome.
8. According to *Matthew* 10:29, even a sparrow "shall not fall on the ground" without God's knowledge of it.

9. The 16th-century astrologer and magician who became a symbol of man's desire to know everything regardless of the cost.
1. Rumanian violinist, conductor, and composer (1881–1955): "I have spent too much time working at my violin and traveling. But the essential exercise of the composer—meditation—nothing has ever kept me from that. I live a permanent dream which does not stop, night or day."
2. During Ulysses' absence to fight the Trojan War, Penelope remained at home for twenty years, besieged by suitors.

She has composed, so long, a self with which to welcome him,
Companion to his self for her, which she imagined,
Two in a deep-founded sheltering, friend and dear friend.

The trees had been mended, as an essential exercise   10
In an inhuman meditation, larger than her own.
No winds like dogs watched over her at night.

She wanted nothing he could not bring her by coming alone.
She wanted no fetchings. His arms would be her necklace
And her belt, the final fortune of their desire.   15

But was it Ulysses? Or was it only the warmth of the sun
On her pillow? The thought kept beating in her like her heart.
The two kept beating together. It was only day.

It was Ulysses and it was not. Yet they had met,
Friend and dear friend and a planet's encouragement.   20
The barbarous strength within her would never fail.

She would talk a little to herself as she combed her hair,
Repeating his name with its patient syllables,
Never forgetting him that kept coming constantly so near.

1954

EDMUND SPENSER

Penelope, for Her Ulysses' Sake

Penelope,[3] for her Ulysses' sake,
Devised a web her wooers to deceive;
In which the work that she all day did make,
The same at night she did again unreave:
Such subtle craft my damsel[4] doth conceive,   5
Th' importune suit of my desire to shun:
For all that I in many days do weave,
In one short hour I find by her undone.
So, when I think to end that I begun,
I must begin and never bring to end: 10
For with one look she spills[5] that long I spun;
And with one word my whole year's work doth rend.
Such labor like the spider's web I find,
Whose fruitless work is broken with least wind.

1595

3. Famous for her long-suffering faithfulness to her husband, Ulysses, during the Trojan War. She ingeniously devised a series of tricks to deceive the men who pursued her during Ulysses' 20-year absence. The "never-ending, still beginning" web was a shroud she was weaving for her father-in-law; she promised her suitors she would make a choice when she finished, but each night she unraveled what she had done during the day. See Homer's *Odyssey*, II, XIX, and XXIV.

4. Spenser's sonnet is part of a sequence recounting a courtship.

5. Destroys.

Non-Western History and Myth

LANGSTON HUGHES

The Negro Speaks of Rivers

I've known rivers:
I've known rivers ancient as the world and older than the flow of human
　　blood in human veins.

My soul has grown deep like the rivers.

I bathed in the Euphrates when dawns were young.
I built my hut near the Congo and it lulled me to sleep.　　　　　5
I looked upon the Nile and raised the pyramids above it.
I heard the singing of the Mississippi when Abe Lincoln went down
　　to New Orleans, and I've seen its muddy bosom turn all golden in
　　the sunset.

I've known rivers:
Ancient, dusky rivers.

My soul has grown deep like the rivers.　　　　　10
　　　　　　　　　　　　　　　　　　　　　　　1926

GABRIEL OKARA

Piano and Drums

When at break of day at a riverside
I hear jungle drums telegraphing
the mystic rhythm, urgent, raw
like bleeding flesh, speaking of
primal youth and the beginning,　　　　　5
I see the panther ready to pounce,
the leopard snarling about to leap
and the hunters crouch with spears poised;

And my blood ripples, turns torrent,
topples the years and at once I'm　　　　　10
in my mother's lap a suckling;
at once I'm walking simple
paths with no innovations,
rugged, fashioned with the naked
warmth of hurrying feet and groping hearts　　　　　15
in green leaves and wild flowers pulsing.

Then I hear a wailing piano
solo speaking of complex ways

in tear-furrowed concerto;
of far-away lands   20
and new horizons with
coaxing diminuendo, counterpoint,
crescendo. But lost in the labyrinth
of its complexities, it ends in the middle
of a phrase at a daggerpoint.   25

And I lost in the morning mist
of an age at a riverside keep
wandering in the mystic rhythm
of jungle drums and the concerto.

                                                   1963

MAYA ANGELOU

Africa

Thus she had lain
sugar cane sweet
deserts her hair
golden her feet
mountains her breasts   5
two Niles her tears
Thus she has lain
Black through the years.

Over the white seas
rime white and cold   10
brigands ungentled
icicle bold
took her young daughters
sold her strong sons
churched her with Jesus   15
bled her with guns.
Thus she has lain.

Now she is rising
remember her pain
remember the losses   20
her screams loud and vain
remember her riches
her history slain
now she is striding
although she had lain.   25

                                                   1975

BRUCE MCM. WRIGHT

The African Affair

Black is what the prisons are,
The stagnant vortex of the hours
Swept into totality,
Creeping in the perjured heart,
Bitter in the vulgar rhyme,   5
Bitter on the walls;

Black is where the devils dance
With time within
The creviced wall. Time pirouettes
A crippled orbit in a trance,   10
And crawls below, beneath the flesh
Where darkness flows;

Black is where the deserts burn,
The Niger and Sasandra flow,
From where the Middle Passage went   15
Within the Continent of Night
From Cameroons to Carisbrooke
And places conscience cannot go;

Black is where thatched temples burn
Incense to carved ebon-wood;   20
Where traders shaped my father's pain,
His person and his place,
Among dead statues in a frieze,
In the spectrum of his race.

1963

ISHMAEL REED

Sermonette

a poet was busted by a topless judge
his friends went to morristwn nj & put
black powder on his honah's doorstep
black powder into his honah's car
black powder on his honah's briefs   5
tiny dolls into his honah's mind

by nightfall his honah could a go go no mo
his dog went crazy & ran into a crocodile
his widow fell from a wall &

hanged herself   10
his daughter was run over by a black man
cming home for the wakes the two boys
skidded into mourning
all the next of kin's teeth fell out

gimmie dat ol time   15
                    religion
it's good enough
            for me!

                                                                  1972

Private History and Myth

WILLIAM BUTLER YEATS
Easter 1916[1]

I have met them at close of day
Coming with vivid faces
From counter or desk among gray
Eighteenth-century houses.
I have passed with a nod of the head   5
Or polite meaningless words,
Or have lingered awhile and said
Polite meaningless words,
And thought before I had done
Of a mocking tale or a gibe   10
To please a companion
Around the fire at the club,
Being certain that they and I
But lived where motley[2] is worn:
All changed, changed utterly: 15
A terrible beauty is born.

That woman's[3] days were spent
In ignorant good-will,
Her nights in argument
Until her voice grew shrill.   20
What voice more sweet than hers

---

fessional fool or jester, at court or in a play.
3. Countess Constance Georgina Markiewicz, a beautiful and well-born young woman from County Sligo who became a vigorous and bitter nationalist. At first condemned to death, she later had her sentence commuted to life imprisonment, and she gained amnesty in 1917.

When, young and beautiful,
She rode to harriers?[4]
This man[5] had kept a school
And rode our wingéd horse;[6]   25
This other[7] his helper and friend
Was coming into his force;
He might have won fame in the end,
So sensitive his nature seemed,
So daring and sweet his thought.   30
This other man[8] I had dreamed
A drunken, vainglorious lout.
He had done most bitter wrong
To some who are near my heart,
Yet I number him in the song;   35
He, too, has resigned his part
In the casual comedy;
He, too, has been changed in his turn,
Transformed utterly:
A terrible beauty is born.   40

Hearts with one purpose alone
Through summer and winter seem
Enchanted to a stone
To trouble the living stream.
The horse that comes from the road,   45
The rider, the birds that range
From cloud to tumbling cloud,
Minute by minute they change;
A shadow of cloud on the stream
Changes minute by minute;   50
A horse-hoof slides on the brim,
And a horse plashes within it;
The long-legged moor-hens dive,
And hens to moor-cocks call;
Minute by minute they live: 55
The stone's in the midst of all.

Too long a sacrifice
Can make a stone of the heart.
O when may it suffice?
That is Heaven's part, our part   60
To murmur name upon name,
As a mother names her child
When sleep at last has come

---

4. Hounds.
5. Patrick Pearse, who led the assault on the Dublin Post Office from which the proclamation of a republic was issued. A schoolmaster by profession, he had vigorously supported the restoration of the Gaelic language in Ireland and was an active political writer and poet.

6. Pegasus, the traditional symbol of poetic inspiration.
7. Thomas MacDonagh, also a writer and teacher.
8. Major John MacBride, who had married Yeats's beloved Maud Gonne in 1903 but separated from her two years later.

On limbs that had run wild.
What is it but nightfall?   65
No, no, not night but death;
Was it needless death after all?
For England may keep faith[9]
For all that is done and said.
We know their dream; enough
To know they dreamed and are dead;   70
And what if excess of love
Bewildered them till they died?
I write it out in a verse—
MacDonagh and MacBride   75
And Connolly[1] and Pearse
Now and in time to be,
Wherever green is worn,
Are changed, changed utterly:
A terrible beauty is born.   80

1916

The Second Coming[2]

Turning and turning in the widening gyre[3]
The falcon cannot hear the falconer;
Things fall apart; the center cannot hold;
Mere anarchy is loosed upon the world,
The blood-dimmed tide is loosed, and everywhere   5
The ceremony of innocence is drowned;
The best lack all conviction, while the worst
Are full of passionate intensity.

Surely some revelation is at hand;
Surely the Second Coming is at hand.   10
The Second Coming! Hardly are those words out
When a vast image out of *Spiritus Mundi*[4]
Troubles my sight: somewhere in sands of the desert
A shape with lion body and the head of a man,

9. Before the uprising the English had promised eventual home rule to Ireland.
1. James Connolly, the leader of the Easter uprising.
2. The Second Coming of Christ, according to *Matthew* 24:29–44, will come after a time of "tribulation." Disillusioned by Ireland's continued civil strife, Yeats saw his time as the end of another historical cycle. In *A Vision* (1937) Yeats describes his view of history as dependent on cycles of about 2000 years: the birth of Christ had ended the cycle of Greco-Roman civilization, and now the Christian cycle seemed near an end, to be followed by an antithetical cycle, ominous in its portents.
3. Literally, the widening spiral of a falcon's flight. "Gyre" is Yeats's term for a cycle of history, which he diagramed in terms of a series of interpenetrating cones.
4. Or *Anima Mundi*, the spirit or soul of the world, a consciousness in which the individual participates. Yeats considered this universal consciousness or memory a fund from which poets drew their images and symbols. In *Per Amica Silentia Lunae* he wrote: "Before the mind's eye, whether in sleep or waking, came images that one was to discover presently in some book one had never read, and after looking in vain for explanation . . . , I came to believe in a great memory passing on from generation to generation."

A gaze blank and pitiless as the sun,   15
Is moving its slow thighs, while all about it
Reel shadows of the indignant desert birds. [5]
The darkness drops again; but now I know
That twenty centuries of stony sleep
Were vexed to nightmare by a rocking cradle,   20
And what rough beast, its hour come round at last,
Slouches towards Bethlehem to be born?

p. 1920

Leda and the Swan[6]

A sudden blow: the great wings beating still
Above the staggering girl, her thighs caressed
By the dark webs, her nape caught in his bill,
He holds her helpless breast upon his breast.

How can those terrified vague fingers push   5
The feathered glory from her loosening thighs?
And how can body, laid in that white rush,
But feel the strange heart beating where it lies?

A shudder in the loins engenders there
The broken wall, the burning roof and tower   10
And Agamemnon dead.
                                        Being so caught up,
So mastered by the brute blood of the air,
Did she put on his knowledge with his power
Before the indifferent beak could let her drop?

1923

---

5. Yeats later writes of the "brazen winged beast . . . described in my poem *The Second Coming*" as "associated with laughing, ecstatic destruction." "Our civilization was about to reverse itself, or some new civilization about to be born from all that our age had rejected . . . ; because we had worshipped a single god it would worship many."

6. According to Greek myth, Zeus took the form of a swan to seduce Leda, who became the mother of Helen of Troy and also of Clytemnestra, Agamemnon's wife and murderer. Helen's abduction from her husband, Menelaus, brother of Agamemnon, began the Trojan War (line 10). Yeats described the visit of Zeus to Leda as an annunciation like that to Mary (see *Luke* 1:26–38): "I imagine the annunciation that founded Greece as made to Leda. . . ." (*A Vision*).

Sailing to Byzantium[7]

I

That[8] is no country for old men. The young
In one another's arms, birds in the trees
—Those dying generations—at their song,
The salmon-falls, the mackerel-crowded seas
Fish, flesh, or fowl, commend all summer long   5
Whatever is begotten, born, and dies.
Caught in that sensual music all neglect
Monuments of unaging intellect.

II

An aged man is but a paltry thing,
A tattered coat upon a stick, unless   10
Soul clap its hands and sing, and louder sing
For every tatter in its mortal dress,
Nor is there singing school but studying
Monuments of its own magnificence;
And therefore I have sailed the seas and come   15
To the holy city of Byzantium.

III

O sages standing in God's holy fire
As in the gold mosaic of a wall,
Come from the holy fire, perne in a gyre,[9]
And be the singing-masters of my soul.   20
Consume my heart away; sick with desire
And fastened to a dying animal
It knows not what it is; and gather me
Into the artifice of eternity.

---

7. The ancient name of Istanbul, the capital and holy city of Eastern Christendom from the late fourth century until 1453. It was famous for its stylized and formal mosaics, its symbolic, nonnaturalistic art, and its highly developed intellectual life. Yeats repeatedly uses it to symbolize a world of artifice and timelessness, free from the decay and death of the natural and sensual world. In *A Vision*, Yeats wrote: "I think if I could be given a month of Antiquity and leave to spend it where I chose, I would spend it in Byzantium a little before Justinian opened St. Sophia and closed the Academy of Plato [about 535 A.D.]. I think I could find in some little wineshop some philosophical worker in mosaic who could answer all my questions, the supernatural descending nearer to him than to Plotinus even, for the pride of his delicate skill would make what was an instrument of power to princes and clerics, a murderous madness in the mob, show as a lovely flexible presence like that of a perfect human body. I think that in early Byzantium, maybe never before or since in recorded history, religious, aesthetic and practical life were one, that architect and artificers . . . spoke to the multitude and the few alike. The painter, the mosaic worker, the worker in gold and silver, the illuminator of sacred books, were almost impersonal, almost perhaps without the consciousness of individual design, absorbed in their subject-matter and that the vision of the whole people. They could . . . weave all into a vast design, the work of many that seemed the work of one, that made building, picture, metal-work or rail and lamp, seem but a single image. . . ."

8. Ireland, as an instance of the natural, temporal world.

9. I.e., whirl in a coiling motion, so that his soul may merge with its motion as the timeless world invades the cycles of history and nature. The gyre in "The Second Coming" moves in the opposite direction, up and out centripetally, so that "things fall apart." "Perne" is Yeats's coinage (from the noun "pirn"): to spin around in the kind of spiral pattern that thread makes as it comes off a bobbin or spool.

IV

Once out of nature I shall never take   25
My bodily form from any natural thing,
But such a form as Grecian goldsmiths make
Of hammered gold and gold enameling
To keep a drowsy Emperor awake; [1]
Or set upon a golden bough [2] to sing   30
To lords and ladies of Byzantium
Of what is past, or passing, or to come.

1927

Among School Children

I

I walk through the long schoolroom questioning;
A kind old nun in a white hood replies;
The children learn to cipher and to sing,
To study reading-books and history,
To cut and sew, be neat in everything   5
In the best modern way—the children's eyes
In momentary wonder stare upon
A sixty-year-old smiling public man. [3]

II

I dream of a Ledaean body, [4] bent
Above a sinking fire, a tale that she   10
Told of a harsh reproof, or trivial event
That changed some childish day to tragedy—
Told, and it seemed that our two natures blent
Into a sphere from youthful sympathy,
Or else, to alter Plato's parable,   15
Into the yolk and white of the one shell. [5]

III

And thinking of that fit of grief or rage
I look upon one child or t'other there
And wonder if she stood so at that age—
For even daughters of the swan can share   20

1. "I have read somewhere that in the Emperor's palace at Byzantium was a tree made of gold and silver, and artificial birds that sang." (Yeats's note)
2. In Book VI of *The Aeneid*, the sybil tells Aeneas that he must pluck a golden bough from a nearby tree in order to descend to Hades. There is only one such branch there, and when it is plucked an identical one takes its place.
3. At 60 (in 1925) Yeats had been a senator of the Irish Free State.
4. Like that of Helen of Troy, daughter of Leda. The memory dream is of Maud Gonne (see also lines 29–30), with whom Yeats had long been hopelessly in love.
5. In Plato's *Symposium*, the origin of human love is explained by parable: Human beings were once spheres, but Zeus was fearful of their power and cut them in half; now each half longs to be reunited with its missing half. Helen and Pollux were hatched from one of two eggs born to Leda after her union with Zeus in the form of a swan; the other contained Castor and Clytemnestra. According to Yeats in *A Vision*, "from one of [Leda's] eggs came Love and from the other War."

Something of every paddler's heritage—
And had that color upon cheek or hair,
And thereupon my heart is driven wild:
She stands before me as a living child.

IV

Her present image floats into the mind—   25
Did Quattrocento finger[6] fashion it
Hollow of cheek as though it drank the wind
And took a mess of shadows for its meat?
And I though never of Ledaean kind
Had pretty plumage once—enough of that,   30
Better to smile on all that smile, and show
There is a comfortable kind of old scarecrow.

V

What youthful mother, a shape upon her lap
Honey of generation[7] had betrayed,
And that must sleep, shriek, struggle to escape   35
As recollection or the drug decide,
Would think her son, did she but see that shape
With sixty or more winters on its head,
A compensation for the pang of his birth,
Or the uncertainty of his setting forth?   40

VI

Plato thought nature but a spume that plays
Upon a ghostly paradigm of things;[8]
Solider Aristotle played the taws
Upon the bottom of a king of kings;[9]
World-famous golden-thighed Pythagoras[1]   45
Fingered upon a fiddle-stick or strings
What a star sang and careless Muses heard:
Old clothes upon old sticks to scare a bird.

VII

Both nuns and mothers worship images,
But those the candles light are not as those   50

6. Fifteenth-century artists, who fall within the 15th Phase of the Christian cycle. Yeats especially admired Botticelli, and in *A Vision* praises his "deliberate strangeness everywhere [which] gives one an emotion of mystery which is new to painting." Botticelli is grouped with those who make "intellect and emotion, *primary* curiosity and the *antithetical* dream . . . for the moment one."
7. "I have taken the 'honey of generation' from Porphyry's essay on 'The Cave of the Nymphs' [*Odyssey*, Book XIII], but find no warrant in Porphyry for considering it the 'drug' that destroys the 'recollection' of prenatal freedom. He blamed a cup of oblivion given in the zodiacal sign of Cancer." (Yeats's note) Porphyry, a third-century Greek scholar and neoplatonic

philosopher, says "honey of generation" means the "pleasure arising from copulation" which draws souls "downward" to generation.
8. Plato considered the world of nature an imperfect and illusory copy of the ideal world.
9. Aristotle, the teacher of Alexander the Great, disciplined him with a strap ("taw," line 43). His philosophy, insisting on the interdependence of form and matter, took the world of nature far more seriously than did Plato's.
1. Sixth-century B.C. Greek mathematician and philosopher, whose elaborate philosophical system included the doctrine of the harmony of the spheres. He was highly revered, and one legend describes his godlike golden thighs.

That animate a mother's reveries,
But keep a marble or a bronze repose.
And yet they too break hearts—O Presences
That passion, piety or affection knows,
And that all heavenly glory symbolize—   55
O self-born mockers of man's enterprise;

VIII

Labor is blossoming or dancing where
The body is not bruised to pleasure soul,
Nor beauty born out of its own despair,
Nor blear-eyed wisdom out of midnight oil.   60
O chestnut-tree, great-rooted blossomer,
Are you the leaf, the blossom or the bole?[2]
O body swayed to music, O brightening glance,
How can we know the dancer from the dance?

1927

Byzantium[3]

The unpurged images of day recede;
The Emperor's drunken soldiery are abed;
Night resonance recedes, night-walkers' song
After great cathedral gong;
A starlit or a moonlit dome[4] disdains   5
All that man is,
All mere complexities,
The fury and the mire of human veins.

Before me floats an image, man or shade,
Shade more than man, more image than a shade;   10
For Hades' bobbin bound in mummy-cloth
May unwind the winding path;[5]
A mouth that has no moisture and no breath
Breathless mouths may summon;
I hail the superhuman;   15
I call it death-in-life and life-in-death.

2. Trunk.
3. In his diary for April 30, 1930, Yeats sketched the following "Subject for a Poem": "Describe Byzantium as it is in the system towards the end of the first Christian millennium. A walking mummy. Flames at the street corners where the soul is purified, birds of hammered gold singing in the golden trees, in the harbor [dolphins], offering their backs to the wailing dead that they may carry them to paradise."
4. In *A Vision*, Yeats described the 28 phases of the moon in psychological terms related to his system. In Phase 1, only stars are visible ("starlit") and "body is completely absorbed in its supernatural environment." In its opposite, Phase 15, when the moon is full ("moonlit"), the mind is "completely absorbed in being."
5. A volume in which "Byzantium" appeared, *The Winding Stair and Other Poems*, contains many similar images; of this volume Yeats wrote: "In this book and elsewhere I have used towers, and one tower in particular, as symbols and have compared their winding stairs to the philosophical gyres, but it is hardly necessary to interpret what comes from the main track of thought and expression. Shelley uses towers constantly as symbols, and there are gyres in Swedenborg, and in Thomas Aquinas and certain classical authors."

Miracle, bird or golden handiwork,
More miracle than bird or handiwork,
Planted on the star-lit golden bough,
Can like the cocks of Hades crow,[6]   20
Or, by the moon embittered, scorn aloud
In glory of changeless metal
Common bird or petal
And all complexities of mire or blood.

At midnight on the Emperor's pavement flit   25
Flames that no fagot[7] feeds, nor steel has lit,
Nor storm disturbs, flames begotten of flame,
Where blood-begotten spirits come
And all complexities of fury leave,
Dying into a dance,   30
An agony of trance,
An agony of flame that cannot singe a sleeve.

Astraddle on the dolphin's mire and blood,[8]
Spirit after spirit! The smithies break the flood,
The golden smithies of the Emperor!   35
Marbles of the dancing floor
Break bitter furies of complexity,
Those images that yet
Fresh images beget,
That dolphin-torn, that gong-tormented sea.   40

                                                              1932

The Circus Animals' Desertion[9]

I

I sought a theme and sought for it in vain,
I sought it daily for six weeks or so.
Maybe at last, being but a broken man,
I must be satisfied with my heart, although
Winter and summer till old age began   5
My circus animals were all on show,
Those stilted boys, that burnished chariot,
Lion and woman and the Lord knows what.

II

What can I but enumerate old themes?
First that sea-rider Oisin[1] led by the nose   10

6. As the bird of dawn, the cock had from antiquity been a symbol of rebirth and resurrection.
7. Bundle of sticks.
8. In ancient art, dolphins symbolize the soul moving from one state to another, and sometimes they provide a vehicle for the dead. Palaemon, for example, in Greek tradition is often mounted on a dolphin.
9. The "animals" are early themes and images in Yeats's poetry, and he here reviews some of them.
1. The subject of an 1889 long poem. Oisin was a legendary figure, beguiled to faery land for 150 years, who returned to find his friends dead in his native Ireland.

Through three enchanted islands, allegorical dreams,
Vain gaiety, vain battle, vain repose,
Themes of the embittered heart, or so it seems,
That might adorn old songs or courtly shows;
But what cared I that set him on to ride,   15
I, starved for the bosom of his faery bride?

And then a counter-truth filled out its play,
The Countess Cathleen[2] was the name I gave it;
She, pity-crazed, had given her soul away,
But masterful Heaven had intervened to save it.   20
I thought my dear[3] must her own soul destroy,
So did fanaticism and hate enslave it,
And this brought forth a dream and soon enough
This dream itself had all my thought and love.

And when the Fool and Blind Man stole the bread   25
Cuchulain fought the ungovernable sea;[4]
Heart-mysteries there, and yet when all is said
It was the dream itself enchanted me:
Character isolated by a deed
To engross the present and dominate memory.   30
Players and painted stage took all my love,
And not those things that they were emblems of.

III

Those masterful images because complete
Grew in pure mind, but out of what began?
A mound of refuse or the sweepings of a street,   35
Old kettles, old bottles, and a broken can,
Old iron, old bones, old rags, that raving slut
Who keeps the till. Now that my ladder's gone,
I must lie down where all the ladders start,
In the foul rag-and-bone shop of the heart.   40

1939

---

2. An 1892 play, in which the countess
sells her soul to the devil to get food
for hungry people but nevertheless gains
Heaven.
3. Maud Gonne.
4. In a 1904 play, *On Baile's Strand*.

Tastes in poetry differ from age to age, and what individual poets choose to do in their poems depends to some extent on what their contemporaries are doing. Because the poetry of any age thus develops some common characteristics, it has become customary to think in terms of **periods** in literary history, segments of time in which the literature has a definable character. Literary historians and critics thus speak of the Elizabethan period, or the Romantic period, or the Modern period. What, exactly, characterizes these periods is often a matter of some debate—as is any generalization that is based upon a variety of somewhat contradictory particulars—but there is no denying that people who live and write more or less in the same temporal and spatial "world" do share some significant concerns, however strong their individuality may be. Partly, such similarities occur because people in a culture are conscious of each other: styles, fashions, and trends involve to some extent the way people think as well as the way they dress and the way they live from day to day. Anyone traveling from one country to another—or even from one section of homeland to another—quickly becomes conscious of how much customs differ in things great and small. People have always been creatures of habit and tradition, and although habits change and traditions are modified and reshaped, the people of any one time and place are a little different from those of any other.

Poets are especially conscious of the habits of their contemporary world—and of each other. Observation—close observation of how people act, what they think, how they feel—is the main business of poets, the subject and substance of their art, and however applicable their conclusions may be to other situations or to human nature generally, what they observe and what they say is based upon particulars that anchor them in a specific age. The things that poets write about—their topics, observations, and themes—tend to cluster, too, because those things which distinguish a particular age or culture seem to all sorts of observers worth commenting on so that a consciousness of distinctiveness develops. What makes us different? is a question thoughtful people in any age ask themselves, and poets (like other writers, artists, and commentators) often take it upon themselves to raise the question for the unthoughtful and phrase it for all of us.

Poets' consciousness of each other does not mean that they herd and prey. Few poets worth reading merely mimic what others say or the way they say it, and few are interested in establishing schools or cults of a particular political, philosophical, or social cast. Their awareness of each other does mean, however, two things: that they are tuned in to some of the best thinking that is going on in their age (when poets don't do it, they still record it), and that they notice how observations and thoughts are being formulated artistically. A literary period is thus characterized in part by *what* its writers find to write about and in part by *how* its writers write—by the prevalent styles practiced by its best artists.

The poems in this chapter are from what is usually called the *Elizabethan period*—so named because Elizabeth I was Queen of England at the time (1558–1603). Actually, most of the poems here come from the latter half of her reign when a substantial "flowering" of the arts took place, in part because she was a patron of poets and other artists (she even wrote poetry herself, p. 358), and in part because of much more complicated social and political factors, including England's rise to prominence as a world maritime power. I have tried to select poems that are, more or less, "typical" of the period, but any selection as short as this one obviously has its limitations. There is, for example, no room here to include a long poem such as Spenser's *Faerie Queene,* and one would need to include a variety of blank verse drama and some satirical verse to provide a full flavor of the period. Besides, no group of twenty-five poems is really fully representative, and any poem you read will offer at least a little something new.

What was the period like? I'm not going to tell you. You can decide for yourself. Rather than giving you a list of characteristics and having you check off examples in individual poems and passages, I want to invite you to do the characterizing yourself by reading, reflecting, summing up. Try reviewing the elements of poetic craft and seeing what patterns you notice as the poems accumulate in your mind. How are these poems different from other poems you have read? Keep this question repeatedly in mind.

Once you've constructed a description of the period, you may want to test it by reading other poems in this book written during the same years by the same authors: the index can help you to find them. You will find a gracious plenty of such poems, and some of them will challenge and extend your description—just as any particulars should at once test, confirm, and challenge any generalization.

———

ANONYMOUS

Crabbed Age and Youth

Crabbed age and youth cannot live together:
Youth is full of pleasance,[1] age is full of care;
Youth like summer morn, age like winter weather;
Youth like summer brave,[2] age like winter bare.
Youth is full of sport, age's breath is short;   5
    Youth is nimble, age is lame;
Youth is hot and bold, age is weak and cold;
    Youth is wild, and age is tame.
Age, I do abhor thee; youth, I do adore thee;
    Oh! my love, my love is young: 10
Age, I do defy thee: Oh! sweet shepherd, hie thee,
    For methinks thou stay'st too long.

p. 1599

1. Delight.   2. Showy, full of splendor.

ANONYMOUS

Though Amaryllis Dance in Green[3]

Though Amaryllis dance in green
  Like fairy queen;
  And sing full clear
Corinna can, with smiling cheer;
Yet since their eyes make heart so sore,   5
Heigh ho, heigh ho, 'chill[4] love no more.

My sheep are lost for want of food,
  And I so wood,[5]
  That all the day
I sit and watch a herdmaid gay,   10
Who laughs to see me sigh so sore,
Heigh ho, heigh ho, 'chill love no more.

Her loving looks, her beauty bright
  Is such delight,
  That all in vain   15
I love to like,[6] and lose my gain
For her that thanks me not therefor,
Heigh ho, heigh ho, 'chill love no more.

Ah wanton[7] eyes, my friendly foes,
  And cause of woes,   20
  Your sweet desire
Breeds flames of ice and freeze in fire.
Ye scorn to see me weep so sore,
Heigh ho, heigh ho, 'chill love no more.

Love ye who list,[8] I force him not,   25
  Sith, God it wot,[9]
  The more I wail,
The less my sighs and tears prevail.
What shall I do but say therefore,
Heigh ho, heigh ho, 'chill love no more.   30

1588

3. From a popular song book, *Psalms, Sonnets, and Songs of Sadness and Piety,* by William Byrd. Amaryllis (line 1) and Corinna (line 4) are typical women's names in Elizabethan lyrics.
4. I will (a rural dialect form: [i]ch [w]ill).
5. Frantic, wild, out of my mind.
6. Pretend. "gain": worldly possessions.
7. Playful, merciless.
8. Wish to.
9. Knows. "Sith": since.

NICHOLAS BRETON

Rare News

News from the heavens! All wars are at an end,
Twixt higher powers a happy peace concluded;
Fortune and Faith are sworn each other's friend,
And Love's desire shall never be deluded.

Time hath set down the compass of his course,   5
Nature her work and Excellence her art,
Care his content and Cruelty his curse,
Labor his desire and Honor his desert.

Words shall be deeds, and men shall be divine,
Women all saints or angels in degrees;   10
Clouds shall away, the sun shall ever shine,
Heavens shall have power to hinder none of these.
   These are the articles of the conclusion,
   Which, when they fall,[1] then look for a confusion.

1591

FULKE GREVILLE, LORD BROOKE

The World, That All Contains, Is Ever Moving

The world, that all contains, is ever moving,
The stars within their spheres for ever turned;
Nature (the queen of change) to change is loving,
And form to matter new is still adjourned.[2]

Fortune, our fancy-god,[3] to vary liketh;   5
Place is not bound to things within it placed;
The present time upon time passéd striketh;
With Phoebus'[4] wandering course the earth is graced.

The air still moves, and by its moving cleareth;
The fire up ascends, and planets[5] feedeth;   10
The water passeth on, and all lets weareth;[6]
The earth stands still, yet change of changes breedeth.

Her plants, which summer ripes, in winter fade;
Each creature in unconstant mother[7] lieth;

---

1. Occur.
2. Transferred.
3. Imaginary god.
4. The sun's.

5. Stars, which supposedly feed on fire,
the purest of the four elements.
6. Erodes all obstructions.
7. The earth.

Man made of earth, and for whom earth is made,   15
Still dying lives, and living ever dieth.
    Only like fate sweet Myra never varies,
     Yet in her eyes the doom of all change carries.

ca. 1585

THOMAS CAMPION

I Care Not for These Ladies

I care not for these ladies,
That must be wooed and prayed;
Give me kind Amaryllis,
The wanton country maid.
Nature art disdaineth;   5
Her beauty is her own.
    Her when we court and kiss,
    She cries, "Forsooth, let go!"
    But when we come where comfort is,
    She never will say no.   10

If I love Amaryllis,
She gives me fruit and flowers:
But if we love these ladies,
We must give golden showers.
Give them gold that sell love;   15
Give me the nut-brown lass
    Who, when we court and kiss,
    She cries, "Forsooth, let go!"
    But when we come where comfort is,
    She never will say no.   20

These ladies must have pillows
And beds by strangers wrought;
Give me a bower of willows,
Of moss and leaves unbought,
And fresh Amaryllis,   25
With milk and honey fed,
    Who, when we court and kiss,
    She cries, "Forsooth, let go!"
    But when we come where comfort is,
    She never will say no.   30

1601

THOMAS CAMPION

My Sweetest Lesbia[8]

My sweetest Lesbia, let us live and love,
And though the sager sort our deeds reprove,
Let us not weigh them. Heaven's great lamps do dive
Into their west, and straight again revive,
But soon as once set is our little light,   5
Then must we sleep one ever-during night.

If all would lead their lives in love like me,
Then bloody swords and armor should not be;
No drum nor trumpet peaceful sleeps should move,
Unless alarm came from the camp of love.   10
But fools do live, and waste their little light,
And seek with pain their ever-during night.

When timely death my life and fortune ends,
Let not my hearse be vexed with mourning friends,
But let all lovers, rich in triumph, come   15
And with sweet pastimes grace my happy tomb;
And Lesbia, close up thou my little light,
And crown with love my ever-during night.

1601

THOMAS CAMPION

There Is a Garden in Her Face

There is a garden in her face,
Where roses and white lilies grow,
A heavenly paradise is that place,
Wherein all pleasant fruits do flow.
There cherries grow, which none may buy   5
Till "Cherry ripe!"[9] themselves do cry.

Those cherries fairly do enclose
Of orient pearl a double row,
Which when her lovely laughter shows,
They look like rosebuds filled with snow.   10
Yet them nor peer nor prince can buy,
Till "Cherry ripe!" themselves do cry.

8. A version of Catullus, V, "Vivamus, mea Lesbia, atque amemus," one of the most frequently translated and imitated poems among English Renaissance poets.
9. A cry of London street vendors.

Her eyes like angels watch them still;
Her brows like bended bows do stand,
Threatening with piercing frowns to kill   15
All that attempt with eye or hand
Those sacred cherries to come nigh,
Till "Cherry ripe!" themselves do cry.

ca. 1617

SAMUEL DANIEL

Care-Charmer Sleep

Care-charmer Sleep, son of the sable Night,
Brother to Death, in silent darkness born:
Relieve my languish and restore the light;
With dark forgetting of my cares, return.
And let the day be time enough to mourn   5
The shipwreck of my ill-adventured youth;
Let waking eyes suffice to wail their scorn
Without the torment of the Night's untruth.
Cease, dreams, th' imagery of our day desires,
To model forth the passions of the morrow;   10
Never let rising sun approve you[1] liars,
To add more grief to aggravate my sorrow.
Still let me sleep, embracing clouds in vain,
And never wake to feel the day's disdain.

1592

MICHAEL DRAYTON

How Many Paltry, Foolish, Painted Things

How many paltry, foolish, painted things,
That now in coaches trouble every street,
Shall be forgotten, whom no poet sings,
Ere they be well wrapped in their winding sheet![2]
Where I to thee eternity shall give,   5
When nothing else remaineth of these days,
And queens hereafter shall be glad to live
Upon the alms of thy superfluous praise.
Virgins and matrons, reading these my rhymes,
Shall be so much delighted with thy story   10
That they shall grieve they lived not in these times,

1. Prove you to be.   2. Shroud.

To have seen thee, their sex's only glory.
So shalt thou fly above the vulgar throng,
Still to survive in my immortal song.

1619

SIR EDWARD DYER

My Mind to Me a Kingdom Is

My mind to me a kingdom is;
　　Such present joys therein I find
That it excels all other bliss
　　That earth affords or grows by kind.[3]
Though much I want[4] which most would have,   5
Yet still my mind forbids to crave.

No princely pomp, no wealthy store,
　　No force to win the victory,
No wily wit to salve a sore,
　　No shape to feed a loving eye;   10
To none of these I yield as thrall.
For why[5] my mind doth serve for all.

I see how plenty suffers oft,
　　And hasty climbers soon do fall;
I see that those which are aloft   15
　　Mishap doth threaten most of all:
They get with toil, they keep with fear.
Such cares my mind could never bear.

Content I live, this is my stay;
　　I seek no more than may suffice;   20
I press to bear no haughty sway;
　　Look, what I lack my mind supplies;
Lo, thus I triumph like a king,
Content with that my mind doth bring.

Some have too much, yet still do crave;   25
　　I little have, and seek no more.
They are but poor, though much they have,
　　And I am rich with little store.
They poor, I rich; they beg, I give;
They lack, I leave; they pine, I live.   30

I laugh not at another's loss;
　　I grudge not at another's gain;

3. Naturally.   5. Because.
4. Lack.

No worldly waves my mind can toss;
  My state at one doth still remain.
I fear no foe, I fawn no friend;   35
I loathe not life, nor dread my end.

Some weigh their pleasure by their lust,
  Their wisdom by their rage of will;
Their treasure is their only trust;
  A cloakéd craft their store of skill.   40
But all the pleasure that I find
Is to maintain a quiet mind.

My wealth is health and perfect ease;
  My conscience clear my choice defense;
I neither seek by bribes to please,   45
  Nor by deceit to breed offense.
Thus do I live; thus will I die.
Would all did so as well as I!

                                          1588

ELIZABETH

When I Was Fair and Young[6]

When I was fair and young, and favor graced me,
  Of many was I sought, their mistress for to be;
But I did scorn them all, and answered them therefore,
  "Go, go, go, seek some otherwhere,
    Importune me no more!"   5

How many weeping eyes I made to pine with woe,
  How many sighing hearts, I have no skill to show;
Yet I the prouder grew, and answered them therefore,
  "Go, go, go, seek some otherwhere,
    Importune me no more!"   10

Then spake fair Venus' son, that proud victorious boy,[7]
  And said: "Fine dame, since that you be so coy,
I will so pluck your plumes that you shall say no more,
  'Go, go, go, seek some otherwhere,
    Importune me no more!' "   15

When he had spake these words, such change grew in my breast
  That neither night nor day since that, I could take any rest.

6. The attribution of this poem to the
Queen is by no means certain; but she was
highly—and perhaps excessively—praised
by her subjects for her poetic talents.
7. Cupid.

Then lo! I did repent that I had said before,
  "Go, go, go, seek some otherwhere,
      Importune me no more!"   20
ca. 1585?

GILES FLETCHER

In Time the Strong

In time the strong and stately turrets fall,
In time the rose and silver lilies die,
In time the monarchs captive are and thrall,
In time the sea and rivers are made dry;
The hardest flint in time doth melt asunder;   5
Still-living fame in time doth fade away;
The mountains proud we see in time come under;
And earth, for age, we see in time decay.
The sun in time forgets for to retire
From out the east where he was wont to rise;   10
The basest thoughts we see in time aspire,
And greedy minds in time do wealth despise.
Thus all, sweet fair, in time must have an end,
Except thy beauty, virtues, and thy friend.

1593

BARTHOLOMEW GRIFFIN

Care-Charmer Sleep

Care-charmer Sleep, sweet ease in restless misery,
The captive's liberty, and his freedom's song,
Balm of the bruised heart, man's chief felicity,
Brother of quiet Death, when life is too, too long!
A comedy it is, and now an history—   5
What is not sleep unto the feeble mind!
It easeth him that toils and him that's sorry,
It makes the deaf to hear, to see the blind.
Ungentle Sleep, thou helpest all but me,
For when I sleep my soul is vexéd most.   10
It is Fidessa[8] that doth master thee;
If she approach, alas, thy power is lost.
But here she is. See, how he runs amain!
I fear at night he will not come again.

1596

8. The heroine of Griffin's sonnet sequence, of which this poem is a part.

CHRISTOPHER MARLOWE

[The Overreacher]⁹

In thee, thou valiant man of Persia,   166
I see the folly of thy emperor.
Art thou but captain of a thousand horse,
That, by characters graven in thy brows,
And by thy martial face and stout aspect,   170
Deserv'st to have the leading of an host?
Forsake thy king, and do but join with me,
And we will triumph over all the world.
I hold the Fates bound fast in iron chains,
And with my hand turn Fortune's wheel about;   175
And sooner shall the sun fall from his sphere
Than Tamburlaine be slain or overcome.
Draw forth thy sword, thou mighty man-at-arms,
Intending but to raze my charmèd skin,
And Jove himself will stretch his hand from heaven   180
To ward the blow, and shield me safe from harm.
See how he rains down heaps of gold in showers,
As if he meant to give my soldiers pay;
And, as a sure and grounded argument
That I shall be the monarch of the East,   185
He sends this Soldan's daughter rich and brave,
To be my queen and portly emperess.¹
If thou wilt stay with me, renownèd man,
And lead thy thousand horse with my conduct,
Besides thy share of this Egyptian prize,   190
Those thousand horse shall sweat with martial spoil
Of conquered kingdoms and of cities sacked.
Both we will walk upon the lofty cliffs;
And Christian merchants, that with Russian stems²
Plough up huge furrows in the Caspian Sea,   195
Shall vail³ to us as lords of all the lake.
Both we will reign as consuls of the earth,
And mighty kings shall be our senators.
Jove sometime maskèd in a shepherd's weed;
And by those steps that he hath scaled the heavens   200
May we become immortal like the gods.
Join with me now in this my mean⁴ estate
(I call it mean because, being yet obscure,
The nations far-removed admire me not)

9. From *Tamburlaine* (Part I), Marlowe's play about Tamburlaine's rise to
power from low beginnings as a shepherd
boy. Tamburlaine is usually considered the
epitome of the "overreacher," one whose
ambition is boundless and who will not rest
until he has extended himself too far. In
this speech from Act I, sc. ii, the hero
addresses a military leader of the enemy.

1. The beautiful daughter of the Soldan
of Egypt has, moments before, been led in
captive, bearing with her the considerable
wealth she carried when intercepted.
"brave": well-dressed; "portly": stately.
2. Prows of ships.
3. Lower their sails in salute. "lake":
ocean.
4. Low.

And when my name and honor shall be spread   205
As far as Boreas claps his brazen wings,
Or fair Boötes sends his cheerful light,
Then shalt thou be competitor with me,
And sit with Tamburlaine in all his majesty.

                                                ca. 1590

CHRISTOPHER MARLOWE

Was This the Face That Launched a Thousand Ships[5]

Was this the face that launched a thousand ships,
And burnt the topless towers of Ilium?[6]
Sweet Helen, make me immortal with a kiss!
Her lips suck forth my soul;[7] see where it flies.
Come, Helen, come, give me my soul again.   5
Here will I dwell, for heaven is in these lips,
And all is dross that is not Helena.
I will be Paris, and for love of thee
Instead of Troy shall Wittenberg[8] be sacked,
And I will combat with weak Menelaus,[9]   10
And wear thy colors on my pluméd crest.
Yea, I will wound Achilles in the heel,
And then return to Helen for a kiss.
O, thou art fairer than the evening's air,
Clad in the beauty of a thousand stars.   15
Brighter art thou than flaming Jupiter,
When he appeared to hapless Semele;[1]
More lovely than the monarch of the sky,
In wanton Arethusa's azured arms,[2]
And none but thou shalt be my paramour.   20

ca. 1588–92

5. From Marlowe's play, *Dr. Faustus*. The title character overwhelmingly desires power through knowledge and sells his soul to the devil to gain it. In the last act, he conjures up Helen from the dead and speaks these lines.
6. Another name for Troy.
7. In Greek, the word for soul and breath were the same (*psuche* or *psyche*), and according to some philosophers the soul was present in breath.
8. The setting for Marlowe's play.
9. Helen's husband. Paris, Helen's abductor, later fought with Menelaus in single combat during the Trojan War and was badly beaten (*Iliad*, III). He later killed

Achilles (line 12), however, when the gods directed his arrow so that it struck Achilles' only vulnerable part.
1. Jupiter (Zeus, Jove) was the father of Semele's child, Dionysus, but when she asked that he appear before her as the god of thunder, the lightning killed her.
2. In Greek mythology, Arethusa was a wood-nymph bathing in a river when Alpheus, the god of the stream, began to pursue her. Diana helped her escape underground, and she later re-emerged as a fountain, but even so Alpheus finally caught her and his waters were mingled with hers. See Ovid's *Metamorphoses*, Book V. "Wanton": merciless, luxuriant.

GEORGE PEELE

A Farewell to Arms[3]

His golden locks time hath to silver turned;
    Oh, time too swift, oh, swiftness never ceasing!
His youth 'gainst time and age hath ever spurned,[4]
    But spurned in vain; youth waneth by increasing.
Beauty, strength, youth, are flowers but fading seen;   5
Duty, faith, love, are roots, and ever green.

His helmet now shall make a hive for bees,
    And lover's sonnets turned to holy psalms,
A man-at-arms must now serve on his knees,
    And feed on prayers, which are age his[5] alms;   10
But though from court to cottage he depart,
His saint is sure of his unspotted heart.

And when he saddest sits in homely cell,
    He'll teach his swains this carol for a song:
Blest be the hearts that wish my sovereign well,   15
    Cursed be the souls that think her any wrong!
Goddess, allow this aged man his right,
To be your beadsman[6] now, that was your knight.

1590

SIR PHILIP SIDNEY

Come Sleep, O Sleep[7]

Come Sleep, O Sleep, the certain knot of peace,
The baiting-place[8] of wit, the balm of woe,
The poor man's wealth, the prisoner's release,
Th'indifferent[9] judge between the high and low;
With shield of proof[1] shield me from out the prease[2]   5
Of those fierce darts Despair at me doth throw;
O make in me those civil wars to cease:
I will good tribute pay, if thou do so.
Take thou of me smooth pillows, sweetest bed,
A chamber deaf to noise and blind to light,   10

3. From *Polyhymnia*, a verse description
of a 1590 jousting tournament on Queen
Elizabeth's birthday. Sir Henry Lee, who
had for years been the Queen's champion
in such contests, that year (at age 60)
retired in favor of a younger man.
4. Kicked.
5. Age's (a common Elizabethan pos-
sessive form).
6. One who prays for the soul of an-

other (OED).
7. A sonnet addressed to sleep was a
conventional part of the Elizabethan sonnet
sequences.
8. A refreshment stop for travelers and
horses.
9. Impartial.
1. Proven strength.
2. Press: throng.

A rosy garland and a weary head;
And if these things, as being thine by right,
Move not thy heavy grace, thou shalt in me,
Livelier[3] than elsewhere, Stella's image see.

1582

SIR PHILIP SIDNEY

Leave Me, O Love

Leave me, O Love, which reachest but to dust,
And thou, my mind, aspire to higher things;
Grow rich in that which never taketh rust:[4]
Whatever fades but fading pleasure brings.
   Draw in thy beams, and humble all thy might   5
To that sweet yoke where lasting freedoms be;
Which breaks the clouds and opens forth the light
That doth both shine and give us sight to see.
   O take fast hold; let that light be thy guide
In this small course which birth draws out to death,   10
And think how evil becometh him[5] to slide,
Who seeketh heav'n, and comes of heav'nly breath.
   Then farewell, world, thy uttermost I see;
Eternal Love, maintain thy life in me.

1581

EDMUND SPENSER

Prothalamion[6]

Calme was the day, and through the trembling ayre,
Sweete breathing Zephyrus[7] did softly play
A gentle spirit, that lightly did delay
Hot Titans[8] beames, which then did glyster fayre:
   When I whom sullein care,   5
Through discontent of my long fruitlesse stay
In Princes Court, and expectation vayne
Of idle hopes, which still doe fly away,

---

3. More lifelike.
4. According to *Matthew* 6:19–20, the difference between heavenly and earthly treasures is that in heaven "neither moth nor rust doth corrupt, and . . . thieves do not break through nor steal."
5. How badly it suits him. (In the 16th century evil was usually pronounced as one syllable, e'il.)

6. A marriage song celebrating the double marriage of Elizabeth and Katherine Somerset, daughters of the Earl of Worcester, to Henry Gilford and William Peter. Spenser's diction and spelling, deliberately archaic, are here left unmodernized.
7. The west wind.
8. The sun's.

Like empty shaddowes, did aflict my brayne,
Walkt forth to ease my payne   10
Along the shoare of silver streaming Themmes,
Whose rutty[9] Bancke, the which his River hemmes,
Was paynted all with variable flowers,
And all the meades[1] adornd with daintie gemmes,
Fit to decke maydens bowres,   15
And crowne their Paramours,
Against the Brydale day, which is not long:
    Sweete Themmes runne softly, till I end my Song.

There, in a Meadow, by the Rivers side,
A flocke of Nymphes I chauncéd to espy,   20
All lovely Daughters of the Flood[2] thereby,
With goodly greenish locks[3] all loose untyde,
As[4] each had bene a Bryde,
And each one had a little wicker basket,
Made of fine twigs entrayléd curiously,   25
In which they gathered flowers to fill their flasket:[5]
And with fine Fingers, cropt full feateously[6]
The tender stalkes on hye.
Of every sort, which in that Meadow grew,
They gathered some; the Violet pallid blew,   30
The little Dazie, that at evening closes,
The virgin Lillie, and the Primrose trew,
With store of vermeil[7] Roses,
To decke their Bridegromes posies,
Against the Brydale day, which was not long: 35
    Sweete Themmes runne softly, till I end my Song.

With that, I saw two Swannes[8] of goodly hewe,
Come softly swimming downe along the Lee,[9]
Two fairer Birds I yet never did see:
The snow which doth the top of Pindus[1] strew,   40
Did never whiter shew,
Nor Jove himselfe when he a Swan would be
For love of Leda, whiter did appeare:[2]
Yet Leda was they say as white as he,
Yet not so white as these, nor nothing neare;   45
So purely white they were,
That even the gentle streame, the which them bare,
Seem'd foule to them, and bad his billowes spare
To wet their silken feathers, least they might

9. Rooty.
1. Meadows.
2. River Thames.
3. Traditional for water nymphs and mermaids.
4. As if.
5. Shallow flower-basket.
6. Deftly.
7. Vermilion: bright red.

8. The ladies Somerset.
9. The River Lea, which flows into the Thames near Greenwich.
1. The Greek mountain range in which Parnassus, sacred to the Muses, is the highest peak.
2. Jove (Zeus) took the form of a swan to woo Leda, a mortal.

Soyle their fayre plumes with water not so fayre,   50
And marre their beauties bright,
That shone as heavens light,
Against their Brydale day, which was not long:
    Sweete Themmes runne softly, till I end my Song.

Eftsoones[3] the Nymphes, which now had Flowers their fill,   55
Ran all in haste, to see that silver brood,
As they came floating on the Christal Flood.
Whom when they sawe, they stood amazéd still,
Their wondring eyes to fill,
Them seem'd they never saw a sight so fayre,   60
Of Fowles so lovely, that they sure did deeme
Them heavenly borne, or to be that same payre
Which through the Skie draw Venus silver Teeme,[4]
For sure they did not seeme
To be begot of any earthly Seede,   65
But rather Angels or of Angels breede:
Yet were they bred of Somers-heat they say,
In sweetest Season, when each Flower and weede
The earth did fresh aray,
So fresh they seem'd as day,   70
Even as their Brydale day, which was not long:
    Sweete Themmes runne softly, till I end my Song.

Then forth they all out of their baskets drew,
Great store of Flowers, the honour of the field,
That to the sense did fragrant odours yeild,   75
All which upon those goodly Birds they threw,
And all the Waves did strew,
That like old Peneus[5] Waters they did seeme,
When downe along by pleasant Tempes shore
Scattred with Flowres, through Thessaly they streeme,   80
That they appeare through Lillies plenteous store,
Like a Brydes Chamber flore:
Two of those Nymphes, meane while, two Garlands bound,
Of freshest Flowres which in that Mead they found,
The which presenting all in trim Array,   85
Their snowie Foreheads therewithall they crownd,
Whil'st one did sing this Lay,
Prepar'd against that Day,
Against their Brydale day, which was not long:
    Sweete Themmes runne softly, till I end my Song.   90

Ye gentle Birdes, the worlds faire ornament,
And heavens glorie, whom this happie hower
Doth leade unto your lovers blisfull bower,

---

3. Very soon.
4. Venus, Roman goddess of love, was sometimes portrayed as riding on or drawn by white swans.

5. The chief river of Thessaly, which flows through the Vale of Tempe, near the legendary abode of the gods.

Joy may you have and gentle hearts content
Of your loves couplement: 95
And let faire Venus, that is Queene of love,
With her heart-quelling Sonne[6] upon you smile,
Whose smile they say, hath vertue to remove
All Loves dislike, and friendships faultie guile
For ever to assoile.[7]   100
Let endlesse Peace your steadfast hearts accord,
And blessed Plentie wait upon your bord,
And let your bed with pleasures chast abound,
That fruitfull issue may to you afford,
Which may your foes confound,   105
And make your joyes redound,
Upon your Brydale day, which is not long:
    Sweete Themmes run softly, till I end my Song.

So ended she; and all the rest around
To her redoubled that her undersong,[8]   110
Which said, their bridale daye should not be long.
And gentle Eccho from the neighbour ground,
Their accents did resound.
So forth those joyous Birdes did passe along,
Adowne the Lee, that to them murmurde low,   115
As he would speake, but that he lackt a tong,
Yet did by signes his glad affection show,
Making his streame run slow.
And all the foule which in his flood did dwell
Gan flock about these twaine, that did excell   120
The rest, so far, as Cynthia doth shend[9]
The lesser starres. So they enrangéd well,
Did on those two attend,
And their best service lend,
Against their wedding day, which was not long: 125
    Sweete Themmes run softly, till I end my Song.

At length they all to mery London came,
To mery London, my most kyndly Nurse,
That to me gave this Lifes first native sourse:
Though from another place I take my name,   130
An house of auncient fame.[1]
There when they came, whereas those bricky towres,[2]
The which on Themmes brode agéd backe doe ryde,
Where now the studious Lawyers have their bowers
There whylome wont the Templer Knights to byde,   135
Till they decayd through pride:

6. Cupid.
7. Absolve.
8. Re-echoed her refrain.
9. Surpass. "Cynthia," as a surname of Diana, was a name for the moon, and also one of the names often used by poets for

Queen Elizabeth.
    1. The Spencers of Althorpe, near Northampton, relatives of the author.
    2. The Temple, once the residence of the Knights Templar, later the residence of law students (line 134).

Next whereunto there standes a stately place,[3]
Where oft I gaynéd giftes and goodly grace
Of that great Lord, which therein wont to dwell,
Whose want too well now feeles my freendles case: 140
But Ah here fits not well
Olde woes but joyes to tell
Against the bridale daye, which is not long:
 Sweete Themmes runne softly, till I end my Song.

Yet therein now doth lodge a noble Peer,   145
Great Englands glory and the Worlds wide wonder,
Whose dreadfull name, late through all Spaine did thunder,
And Hercules two pillors[4] standing neere,
Did make to quake and feare:
Faire branch of Honor, flower of Chevalrie,   150
That fillest England with thy triumphes fame,
Joy have thou of thy noble victorie,
And endlesse happinesse of thine owne name
That promiseth the same:
That through thy prowesse and victorious armes, 155
Thy country may be freed from forraine harmes:
And great Elisaes[5] glorious name may ring
Through al the world, fil'd with thy wide Alarmes,
Which some brave muse may sing
To ages following,   160
Upon the Brydale day, which is not long:
 Sweete Themmes runne softly, till I end my Song.

From those high Towers, this noble Lord issuing,
Like Radiant Hesper[6] when his golden hayre
In th'Ocean billowes he hath Bathéd fayre,   165
Descended to the Rivers open vewing,
With a great traine ensuing.
Above the rest were goodly to bee seene
Two gentle Knights of lovely face and feature
Beseeming well the bower of anie Queene,   170
With gifts of wit and ornaments of nature,
Fit for so goodly stature:
That like the twins of Jove[7] they seem'd in sight,
Which decke the Bauldricke of the Heavens bright.
They two forth pacing to the Rivers side,   175
Received those two faire Brides, their Loves delight,
Which at th'appointed tyde,
Each one did make his Bryde,
Against their Brydale day, which is not long:
 Sweete Themmes runne softly, till I end my Song. 180

              1596

3. The house, until 1590, of Spenser's patron, the Earl of Leicester; but at the time of the poem, Essex House, occupied by the Earl of Essex (line 145), who sacked the city of Cadiz in August, 1596.
4. The straits of Gibraltar.
5. Elizabeth's.

6. Hesperus, the evening star.
7. Castor and Pollux, born of Jove to Leda (see lines 42–43), who as the constellation Gemini form part of the zodiac ("the Bauldricke of the Heavens," line 174).

EDMUND SPENSER

Was It a Dream

Was it a dream, or did I see it plain?
A goodly table of pure ivory,
All spread with junkets,[8] fit to entertain
The greatest prince with pompous[9] royalty:
'Mongst which, there in a silver dish did lie　　　　　5
Two golden apples of unvalued price;
Far passing those which Hercules[1] came by,
Or those which Atalanta[2] did entice.
Exceeding sweet, yet void of sinful vice;
That many sought, yet none could ever taste;　　　　10
Sweet fruit of pleasure, brought from Paradise
By Love himself, and in his garden placed.
　　Her breast that table was, so richly spread;
　　My thoughts the guests, which would thereon have fed.

1595

EDMUND SPENSER

Ye Tradeful Merchants

Ye tradeful merchants, that with weary toil
Do seek most precious things to make your gain;
And both the Indias[3] of their treasure spoil;
What needeth you to seek so far in vain?
For lo, my love doth in herself contain　　　　　5
All this world's riches that may far be found:
If sapphires, lo, her eyes be sapphires plain;
If rubies, lo, her lips be rubies sound;
If pearls, her teeth be pearls, both pure and round;
If ivory, her forehead ivory ween;[4]　　　　　10
If gold, her locks are finest gold on ground;
If silver, her fair hands are silver sheen;[5]
But that which fairest is, but few behold,
Her mind, adorned with virtues manifold.

1595

8. Sweetmeats.
9. Splendid.
1. Hercules' twelfth labor was to gain possession of the golden apples of the Hesperides.
2. In Greek myth, Atalanta agreed to marry anyone who could defeat her in a race; Milanion won by dropping, during the race, three golden apples which Atalanta paused to retrieve.
3. The East and West Indies, sources of spices and precious metals.
4. Seems to be ivory.
5. Shining silver.

16 CULTURAL ASSUMPTIONS: IDEAS OF ORDER

People of every age look at the world in their own way, but without always being conscious of why they do so. Many things in any culture seem to be done *just because*—just because, that is, people have done them that way before and it seems the "natural" way to do them. But those things that seem "natural" in one age or nation do not necessarily seem that way in another time and place. Some contemporaries of Columbus assumed, for example, that somewhere there was an edge to their flat earth; it seemed natural to them, and even after astronomers, mathematicians, and explorers had demonstrated that the earth was not flat, people still thought of "the four corners of the earth." In our culture today, with jet planes flying over our heads and circling the earth each day in all directions, it seems natural to us to assume that the earth is a globe, although people in another culture even today may not share our assumption. And despite our notion about a spinning earth orbiting the sun, we still speak of the sun as rising and setting. Habitual ways of thinking—based on assumptions that have lingered long—die slowly.

If there are distinctive features for every age (as the poems in Chapter 15 suggest), there are also cultural continuities, things that do not change or that only change slowly over a long period of time. Often there are continuities across national boundaries, and some traditions have such a wide geographical sweep and such a long history that they seem nearly universal—or at least central to the Western heritage that lies behind the cultures of the United States and Canada. In Chapter 14 we looked at poems based on the historical and mythological narratives and characters that Western culture has developed to explain some mysteries of existence; here we will read some poems related to a more subtle—and less conscious—form of cultural influence.

What is the world like? Is there some plan or purpose behind it? What are we doing here? Why are nations and cultures different from one another? Does some human bond hold us all together? How do we know what we know? How can we decide if some things are better—or truer—than others? These kinds of philosophical questions come up again and again, in one form or another, in all cultures: and religious and philosophical systems are built upon the answers that people give. Not many poems deal explicitly with questions like these, but poems that are primarily about other things are often influenced by such questions. Poems contain more than what poets consciously put into them. Beyond poets' conscious choices about the themes, words, and rhythms that they build into their poems—even beyond the events, preoccupations, and fashions of any literary period—are the ideas that sponsor a culture: assumptions about what the world is like and the place of human beings in it.

One of the most persistent assumptions in Western culture is that of a single ordered world, a cosmos, a *universe*—a sense that some central principle of order holds together all we see, all we know, all we are. The sense of order in Western culture has been, historically, very strong, and most poems in the past tended to reflect that sense in a confident, unquestioning way that mirrored the religious certainty and security of the ages in which they were written. More recently, even while poetry has reflected the growing insecurity and fragmentation of modernity, modern poets have continued to seek a sense of order that would help explain the larger world and justify a relationship between poetry and reality—even though the source for that order has seemed increasingly difficult for modern people to find. Virtually gone now are the old metaphors and formulas that earlier poetry had used to express that order—metaphors of organic growth and of parallel relationship between different orders of creation, images of the world as stage, or as dance, or as musical harmony. If, in former times, those formulas seemed "natural" ways of thinking about the order of the world—not metaphors really but literal expressions of cosmic organization and structure—now poets look for some new metaphor, some new way of expressing their sense of focus, connection, and relationship. Just as older poets usually assumed some version of cosmic order, modern poets usually assume that no objective and universal order exists, and in their descriptions of what they see they often isolate an object that focuses and holds—at least for a moment—some subjective vision that encompasses the world in a way that the modern mind can comprehend and relate to.

Some of the poems here argue an idea of order, but most more or less unconsciously assume the ideas of their age about order. The modern poems tend to be more argumentative than the older ones, perhaps because many of them are trying to assert some particular idea of order in an age which tends to be skeptical about universals. Thomas's *The Force That through the Green Fuse Drives the Flower*, for example, asserts a connection between man and nature (human seasons = natural seasons) and argues for it, whereas the Chaucer passage which is in many ways parallel to it simply assumes that human beings as part of the natural world are subject to its laws and processes. For Chaucer then, the organization of the passage is a rather simple when . . . when . . . then . . ., and the coming of spring leads as naturally to certain human activities (physical and spiritual) as it does to the rising of sap in plants and the singing of birds. Jonson's *To Penshurst* makes similar assumptions about the relation of human beings to their surroundings; the human order of the estate and buildings seems to grow out of the order of nature itself and thus to demonstrate that the family is in harmony with natural order. The two Shakespeare passages and the Addison poem assert standard Renaissance and Enlightenment ideas of order—that the stage as a miniature imitation of the world is a perfect metaphor for its temporal as well as spatial order, that social hierarchies mirror the carefully graduated orders of the larger universe, that the careful structure of the physical world demonstrates a divine plan with a Creator behind it. Most of the modern poems find a more subjective, less universal order to celebrate, and many of them assert and argue it rigorously through some particular object or event that comes to symbolize it. Thus, Gunn finds a kind of ordering principle in the fact of motion itself, Ammons and Stevens (*Anecdote of the Jar*) locate order in an object which organizes human sense perceptions around it, and Plath finds a relief from disorder when she allows her perceptions to center on the beauty of "a rook / Ordering its black feathers" (lines 27-28).

Analogy and Correspondence

GEOFFREY CHAUCER

Whan That Aprill with His Shoures Soote[1]

Whan that Aprill with his shoures soote[2]
The droghte[3] of March hath perced to the roote,
And bathed every veyne[4] in swich licour,
Of which vertu[5] engendred is the flour;
Whan Zephyrus[6] eek with his sweete breeth   5
Inspired hath in every holt and heeth[7]
The tendre croppes, and the yonge sonne[8]
Hath in the Ram his halfe cours yronne,
And smale foweles[9] maken melodye
That slepen[1] al the nyght with open yë—   10
So priketh hem[2] Nature in hir corages—
Thanne longen[3] folk to goon on pilgrimages,
And palmeres[4] for to seken straunge strondes
To ferne halwes, kowthe[5] in sondry londes;
And specially from every shires[6] ende   15
Of Engelond to Caunterbury they wende,[7]
The holy blisful martir for to seke
That hem hath holpen[8] whan that they were seeke.

ca. 1386

DYLAN THOMAS

The Force That through the Green Fuse
Drives the Flower

The force that through the green fuse drives the flower
Drives my green age; that blasts the roots of trees
Is my destroyer.
And I am dumb to tell the crooked rose
My youth is bent by the same wintry fever.   5

1. The opening lines of the "General Prologue" to *The Canterbury Tales*, a series of stories told by pilgrims going to Canterbury.
2. Sweet showers.
3. Drought. "perced": pierced.
4. Vein: vessel of sap. "swich licour": such liquid.
5. By the power ("vertu") of which. "flour": flower.
6. The west wind, traditionally the spring wind which renews life. "eek": also.
7. Woods and field.
8. Sun: "young" because it has run only halfway (line 8) through its course in Aries (the Ram), the first sign of the zodiac in the solar year. "croppes": shoots, sprouts.
9. Fowls: birds.
1. Sleep. "yë": eye.
2. Them. "hir corages": their hearts.
3. Long: desire. "goon": go.
4. Pilgrims who range widely to far-off shrines ("ferne halwes") on the foreign shores of the Holy Land ("straunge strondes").
5. Known.
6. Shire's: county's.
7. Go. At Canterbury was the shrine of St. Thomas à Becket ("the holy blisful martir"), murdered in Canterbury Cathedral in 1170.
8. Helped. "seeke": sick.

The force that drives the water through the rocks
Drives my red blood; that dries the mouthing streams
Turns mine to wax.
And I am dumb to mouth unto my veins
How at the mountain spring the same mouth sucks.   10

The hand that whirls the water in the pool
Stirs the quicksand; that ropes the blowing wind
Hauls my shroud sail.
And I am dumb to tell the hanging man
How of my clay is made the hangman's lime.   15

The lips of time leech to the fountain head;
Love drips and gathers, but the fallen blood
Shall calm her sores.
And I am dumb to tell a weather's wind
How time has ticked a heaven round the stars.   20

And I am dumb to tell the lover's tomb
How at my sheet goes the same crooked worm.

1934

HENRY HOWARD, EARL OF SURREY

The Soote Season

The soote[9] season, that bud and bloom forth brings,
With green hath clad the hill and eke[1] the vale;
The nightingale with feathers new she sings;
The turtle[2] to her make hath told her tale.
Summer is come, for every spray[3] now springs;   5
The hart hath hung his old head on the pale;
The buck in brake his winter coat he flings;
The fishes float with new repairéd scale;
The adder all her slough away she slings;
The swift swallow pursueth the flies small;   10
The busy bee her honey now she mings;[4]
Winter is worn, that was the flower's bale.[5]
   And thus I see among these pleasant things
   Each care decays, and yet my sorrow springs.

1557

9. Sweet.   3. Sprout, shoot.
1. Also.   4. Remembers.
2. Turtledove. "make": mate.   5. Enemy, instrument of death.

ARTHUR GUITERMAN

On the Vanity of Earthly Greatness

The tusks that clashed in mighty brawls
Of mastodons, are billiard balls.

The sword of Charlemagne the Just
Is ferric oxide known as rust.

The grizzly bear whose potent hug   5
Was feared by all, is now a rug.

Great Caesar's bust is on the shelf,
And I don't feel so well myself!

1930

BEN JONSON

To Penshurst [6]

Thou art not, Penshurst, built to envious show,
Of touch[7] or marble; nor canst boast a row
Of polished pillars, or a roof of gold;
Thou hast no lantern[8] whereof tales are told,
Or stair, or courts; but stand'st an ancient pile,   5
And, these grudged at,[9] art reverenced the while.
Thou joy'st in better marks, of soil, of air,
Of wood, of water; therein thou art fair.
Thou hast thy walks for health, as well as sport;
Thy mount, to which the dryads[1] do resort,   10
Where Pan and Bacchus[2] their high feasts have made,
Beneath the broad beech and the chestnut shade,
That taller tree, which of a nut was set
At his great birth[3] where all the Muses met.
There in the writhéd bark are cut the names   15
Of many a sylvan, taken with his flames;[4]
And thence the ruddy satyrs oft provoke
The lighter fauns to reach thy Lady's Oak.[5]

6. The country seat (in Kent) of the Sidney family, owned by Sir Robert, brother of the poet, Sir Philip. Jonson's celebration of the estate is one of the earliest "house" poems and a prominent example of topographical or didactic-descriptive poetry.
7. Touchstone: basanite, a smooth dark stone similar to black marble.
8. A glassed or open tower or dome atop the roof.
9. I.e., although these (more pretentious structures) are envied. "the while": anyway.

1. Wood nymphs.
2. Ancient gods of nature and wine, both associated with spectacular feasting and celebration.
3. Sir Philip Sidney's, on November 30, 1554; the tree stood for nearly 150 years.
4. Inspired by Sidney's love poetry. "sylvan": forest dweller, rustic.
5. Where, according to legend, a former lady of the house (Lady Leicester) began labor pains. "satyrs": half-men, half-goats who participated in the rites of Bacchus.

Thy copse too, named of Gamage,[6] thou hast there,
That never fails to serve thee seasoned deer   20
When thou wouldst feast, or exercise, thy friends.
The lower land, that to the river bends,
Thy sheep, thy bullocks, kine, and calves do feed;
The middle grounds thy mares and horses breed.
Each bank doth yield thee conies;[7] and the tops,   25
Fertile of wood, Ashore and Sidney's copse,[8]
To crown thy open table, doth provide
The purpled pheasant with the speckled side;
The painted partridge lies in every field,
And for thy mess is willing to be killed.   30
And if the high-swollen Medway[9] fail thy dish,
Thou hast thy ponds that pay thee tribute fish,
Fat agéd carps that run into thy net,
And pikes, now weary their own kind to eat,
As loath the second draught[1] or cast to stay,   35
Officiously[2] at first themselves betray;
Bright eels that emulate them, and leap on land
Before the fisher, or into his hand.
Then hath thy orchard fruit, thy garden flowers,
Fresh as the air, and new as are the hours.   40
The early cherry, with the later plum,
Fig, grape, and quince, each in his time doth come;
The blushing apricot and woolly peach
Hang on thy walls, that every child may reach.
And though thy walls be of the country stone,   45
They're reared with no man's ruin, no man's groan;
There's none that dwell about them wish them down,
But all come in, the farmer and the clown,[3]
And no one empty-handed, to salute
Thy lord and lady, though they have no suit.[4]   50
Some bring a capon, some a rural cake,
Some nuts, some apples; some that think they make
The better cheeses bring 'em, or else send
By their ripe daughters, whom they would commend
This way to husbands, and whose baskets bear   55
An emblem of themselves in plum or pear.
But what can this (more than express their love)
Add to thy free[5] provisions, far above
The need of such? whose liberal board doth flow
With all that hospitality doth know;   60
Where comes no guest but is allowed to eat,
Without his fear, and of thy lord's own meat;
Where the same beer and bread, and selfsame wine,
That is his lordship's shall be also mine.

6. The maiden name of the owner's wife. "copse": thicket.
7. Rabbits.
8. Two spinneys, or little woods.
9. A river bordering the estate.

1. Of a net. "stay": await.
2. Obligingly.

And I not fain[6] to sit (as some this day   65
At great men's tables), and yet dine away.[7]
Here no man tells[8] my cups; nor, standing by,
A waiter doth my gluttony envý,
But gives me what I call, and lets me eat;
He knows below he shall find plenty of meat.   70
Thy tables hoard not up for the next day;
Nor, when I take my lodging, need I pray
For fire, or lights, or livery;[9] all is there,
As if thou then wert mine, or I reigned here:
There's nothing I can wish, for which I stay.   75
That found King James when, hunting late this way
With his brave son, the prince,[1] they saw thy fires
Shine bright on every hearth, as the desires
Of thy Penates[2] had been set on flame
To entertain them; or the country came   80
With all their zeal to warm their welcome here.
What (great I will not say, but) sudden cheer
Didst thou then make 'em! and what praise was heaped
On thy good lady then! who therein reaped
The just reward of her high housewifery;[3]   85
To have her linen, plate, and all things nigh,
When she was far; and not a room but dressed
As if it had expected such a guest!
These, Penshurst, are thy praise, and yet not all.
Thy lady's noble, fruitful, chaste withal.   90
His children thy great lord may call his own,
A fortune in this age but rarely known.
They are, and have been, taught religion; thence
Their gentler spirits have sucked innocence.
Each morn and even they are taught to pray,   95
With the whole household, and may, every day,
Read in their virtuous parents' noble parts
The mysteries of manners, arms, and arts.
Now, Penshurst, they that will proportion[4] thee
With other edifices, when they see   100
Those proud, ambitious heaps, and nothing else,
May say, their lords have built, but thy lord dwells.

1616

---

3. Rustic, peasant.
4. Request for favors.
5. Generous.
6. Obliged.
7. Possibly, "elsewhere," because they do not get enough to eat; or "away" in the sense of far from the party of honor.

8. Counts.
9. Provisions (or, possibly, servants).
1. Prince Henry, who died in 1612.
2. Roman household gods who cared for the family's welfare.
3. Domestic economy.
4. Compare.

JOSEPH ADDISON

The Spacious Firmament on High[5]

The spacious firmament on high,
With all the blue ethereal sky,
And spangled heav'ns, a shining frame,
Their great Original proclaim:
Th' unwearied sun, from day to day,   5
Does his Creator's power display,
And publishes to ev'ry land
The work of an Almighty Hand.

Soon as the ev'ning shades prevail,
The moon takes up the wondrous tale,   10
And nightly to the list'ning earth
Repeats the story of her birth:
Whilst all the stars that round her burn,
And all the planets, in their turn,
Confirm the tidings as they roll,   15
And spread the truth from pole to pole.

What though, in solemn silence, all
Move round the dark terrestrial ball?
What though nor real voice nor sound
Amid their radiant orbs be found?   20
In reason's ear they all rejoice,
And utter forth a glorious voice,
Forever singing, as they shine,
"The Hand that made us is divine."

p. 1712

WILLIAM SHAKESPEARE

[Order and Degree][6]

The heavens themselves, the planets, and this center[7]   85
Observe degree, priority, and place,
Insisture,[8] course, proportion, season, form,
Office, and custom, in all line of order.
And therefore is the glorious planet Sol[9]
In noble eminence enthroned and sphered   90

5. In an essay accompanying this poem on its first publication in *The Spectator*, Addison cites *Psalm* 19 ("The heavens declare the glory of God; and the firmament showeth his handiwork") and writes: "The Supreme Being has made the best arguments for his own existence, in the formation of the heaven and the earth, and these are arguments which a man of sense cannot forbear attending to, who is out of the noise and hurry of human affairs."

6. A speech by Ulysses to other Greek leaders in *Troilus and Cressida*, Act I, sc. iii.

7. Earth.

8. Regularity.

9. The sun.

Amidst the other,[1] whose med'cinable eye
Corrects the influence[2] of evil planets,
And posts, like the commandment of a king,
Sans check to good and bad. But when the planets
In evil mixture to disorder wander,   95
What plagues, and what portents, what mutiny,
What raging of the sea, shaking of earth,
Commotion in the winds, frights, changes, horrors,
Divert and crack, rend and deracinate,
The unity and married calm of states   100
Quite from their fixure[3]? O, when degree is shaked,
Which is the ladder of all high designs,
The enterprise is sick. How could communities,
Degrees in schools, and brotherhoods in cities,
Peaceful commerce from dividable shores,   105
The primogenity[4] and due of birth,
Prerogative of age, crowns, scepters, laurels,
But by degree, stand in authentic place?
Take but degree away, untune that string,
And hark what discord follows. Each thing meets   110
In mere oppugnancy.[5] The bounded waters
Should lift their bosoms higher than the shores
And make a sop[6] of all this solid globe;
Strength should be lord of imbecility,[7]
And the rude son should strike his father dead;   115
Force should be right, or rather, right and wrong,
Between whose endless jar[8] justice resides,
Should lose their names, and so should justice too;
Then everything include itself in power,
Power into will, will into appetite,   120
And appetite, an universal wolf,
So doubly seconded with will and power,
Must make perforce an universal prey,
And last eat up himself. Great Agamemnon,[9]
This chaos, when degree is suffocate,   125
Follows the choking.
And this neglection of degree it is
That by a pace goes backward with a purpose
It hath to climb. The general's disdained
By him one step below, he by the next,   130
That next by him beneath; so every step,
Exampled by the first pace[1] that is sick
Of his superior, grows to an envious fever
Of pale and bloodless emulation.

                                                                ca. 1601

1. Others.
2. Astrological effect.
3. Fixed place, stability.
4. Rights of the first-born son.
5. Total war.
6. Sponge.
7. Weakness.
8. Conflict.
9. One of the leaders addressed by Ulysses.
1. Step of another rebel.

GEORGE BERKELEY

On the Prospect of Planting Arts and Learning
in America

The Muse, disgusted at an age and clime
  Barren of every glorious theme,
In distant lands now waits a better time,
  Producing subjects worthy fame:

In happy climes where from the genial sun   5
  And virgin earth such scenes ensue,
The force of art by nature seems outdone,
  And fancied beauties by the true:

In happy climes, the seat of innocence,
  Where nature guides and virtue rules,   10
Where men shall not impose, for truth and sense,
  The pedantry of courts and schools:

There shall be sung another golden age,
  The rise of empire and of arts,
The good and great inspiring epic rage,   15
  The wisest heads and noblest hearts.

Not such as Europe breeds in her decay;
  Such as she bred when fresh and young,
When heavenly flame did animate her clay,
  By future poets shall be sung.   20

Westward the course of empire takes its way;
  The first four acts already past,
A fifth shall close the drama with the day;
  Time's noblest offspring is the last.[2]

                                                           1752

GEORGE HERBERT

The Flower

How fresh, O Lord, how sweet and clean
Are thy returns! Ev'n as the flowers in spring,
  To which, besides their own demean,[3]
The late-past frosts tributes of pleasure bring.
          Grief melts away   5
          Like snow in May,
  As if there were no such cold thing.

2. The last stanza is the motto of the   3. Demesne: estate.
city of Berkeley, California.

Who would have thought my shriveled heart
Could have recovered greenness? It was gone
  Quite under ground, as flowers depart
To see their mother-root when they have blown;[4]
      Where they together
      All the hard weather,
Dead to the world, keep house unknown.

These are thy wonders, Lord of power,
Killing and quickning, bringing down to hell
  And up to heaven in an hour,
Making a chiming of a passing-bell.[5]
      We say amiss,
      This or that is:
Thy word is all, if we could spell.

O that I once past changing were,
Fast in thy Paradise, where no flower can wither!
  Many a spring I shoot up fair,
Off'ring[6] at heav'n, growing and groaning thither;
      Nor doth my flower
      Want a spring-shower,
My sins and I joining together.

But while I grow in a straight line,
Still upwards bent, as if heav'n were mine own,
  Thy anger comes, and I decline.
What frost to that? What pole is not the zone
      Where all things burn,
      When thou dost turn,
And the least frown of thine is shown?

And now in age I bud again,
After so many deaths I live and write;
  I once more smell the dew and rain,
And relish versing. O my only light,
      It cannot be
      That I am he
On whom thy tempests fell all night.

These are thy wonders, Lord of love,
To make us see we are but flowers that glide;
  Which when we once can find and prove,
Thou hast a garden for us where to bide.
      Who would be more,
      Swelling through store,[7]
Forfeit their Paradise by their pride.

1633

4. Bloomed.
5. Which tolls for death.

6. Aiming.
7. Possessions.

ANDREW MARVELL

On a Drop of Dew

See how the orient[8] dew,
  Shed from the bosom of the morn
    Into the blowing roses,
Yet careless of its mansion new
For[9] the clear region where 'twas born   5
    Round in itself incloses,
    And in its little globe's extent
Frames as it can its native element;
    How it the purple flow'r does slight,
    Scarce touching where it lies,   10
But gazing back upon the skies,
    Shines with a mournful light
        Like its own tear,
Because so long divided from the sphere.[1]
    Restless it rolls and unsecure,   15
        Trembling lest it grow impure,

Till the warm sun pity its pain,
And to the skies exhale it back again.
    So the soul, that drop, that ray
Of the clear fountain of eternal day,   20
Could it within the human flower be seen,
    Rememb'ring still its former height,
    Shuns the sweet leaves and blossoms green;
    And, recollecting its own light,
Does, in its pure and circling thoughts, express   25
The greater Heaven in an Heaven less.
    In how coy[2] a figure wound,
    Every way it turns away;
    So the world excluding round,
    Yet receiving in the day: 30
    Dark beneath, but bright above,
    Here disdaining, there in love.

How loose and easy hence to go,
How girt and ready to ascend;
Moving but on a point below,   35
It all about does upwards bend.
Such did the manna's sacred dew distill,
White and entire, though congealed and chill;[3]
Congealed on earth, but does, dissolving, run
Into the glories of th' almighty sun.   40

1681

8. Shining.
9. By reason of.
1. Of heaven.
2. Reserved, withdrawn, modest.
3. In the wilderness, the Israelites fed upon manna from heaven (distilled from the dew; see *Exodus* 16:10–21); manna became a traditional symbol for divine grace.

JOHN DONNE

I Am a Little World Made Cunningly

I am a little world made cunningly
Of elements, and an angelic sprite;
But black sin hath betrayed to endless night
My world's both parts, and Oh! both parts must die.
You which beyond that heaven which was most high   5
Have found new spheres, and of new lands can write,
Pour new seas in mine eyes, that so I might
Drown my world with my weeping earnestly,
Or wash it if it must be drowned no more.
But Oh, it must be burnt! Alas, the fire   10
Of lust and envy have burnt it heretofore,
And made it fouler. Let their flames retire,
And burn me, O Lord, with a fiery zeal
Of Thee and Thy house, which doth in eating heal.

1635

WILLIAM SHAKESPEARE

Poor Soul, the Center of My Sinful Earth

Poor soul, the center of my sinful earth,
Thrall to[4] these rebel pow'rs that thee array![5]
Why dost thou pine within and suffer dearth,
Painting thy outward walls so costly gay?
Why so large cost, having so short a lease,   5
Dost thou upon thy fading mansion spend?
Shall worms, inheritors of this excess,
Eat up thy charge? Is this thy body's end?
Then, soul, live thou upon thy servant's loss,
And let that pine to aggravate[6] thy store;   10
Buy terms divine in selling hours of dross:
Within be fed, without be rich no more.
So shalt thou feed on death, that feeds on men,
And death once dead, there's no more dying then.

1609

4. The original text is faulty here, and "Thrall to" is an emendation. Other possibilities include "Pressed by," "Rebuke," "Lord of," and "Starved by."
5. Deck out; or, possibly, afflict.
6. Increase.

The World as Stage

WILLIAM SHAKESPEARE

All the World's a Stage[1]

                    All the world's a stage,   139
And all the men and women merely players.
They have their exits and their entrances,
And one man in his time plays many parts,
His acts being seven ages. At first, the infant,
Mewling and puking in the nurse's arms.
Then the whining schoolboy, with his satchel   145
And shining morning face, creeping like snail
Unwillingly to school. And then the lover,
Sighing like furnace, with a woeful ballad[2]
Made to his mistress' eyebrow. Then a soldier,
Full of strange oaths and bearded like the pard,[3]   150
Jealous in honor,[4] sudden and quick in quarrel,
Seeking the bubble reputation
Even in the cannon's mouth. And then the justice,
In fair round belly with good capon lined,[5]
With eyes severe and beard of formal cut,   155
Full of wise saws[6] and modern instances;
And so he plays his part. The sixth age shifts
Into the lean and slippered pantaloon,[7]
With spectacles on nose and pouch on side;
His youthful hose, well saved, a world too wide   160
For his shrunk shank, and his big manly voice,
Turning again toward childish treble, pipes
And whistles in his sound. Last scene of all,
That ends this strange eventful history,
Is second childishness and mere oblivion,   165
Sans teeth, sans eyes, sans taste, sans everything.

                                              ca. 1599

EDMUND SPENSER

Of This World's Theater in Which We Stay

Of this world's theater in which we stay,
My love, like the spectator, idly sits;

1. A speech by Jaques in *As You Like It*, Act II, sc. vii. The metaphor of the world as stage (and the stage as a little world) dates from classical antiquity, and the motto of the newly opened Globe Theater (where *As You Like It* was played) was "Totus mundus agit histrionem": "All the world plays the actor."
2. Verse, song.
3. Leopard.
4. Zealous in pursuing fame; sensitive about his good name.
5. Well fed with presents (from those who seek his favorable judgment).
6. Sayings: maxims.
7. A ridiculous old man in Italian comedy.

Beholding me, that all the pageants[8] play,
Disguising diversly my troubled wits.
Sometimes I joy when glad occasion fits,   5
And mask in mirth like to a comedy:
Soon after, when my joy to sorrow flits,
I wail and make my woes a tragedy.
Yet she, beholding me with constant eye,
Delights not in my mirth, nor rues[9] my smart: 10
But when I laugh, she mocks; and when I cry
She laughs and hardens evermore her heart.
What then can move her? If nor mirth nor moan,
She is no woman, but a senseless stone.

                                                            1595

SIR WALTER RALEGH

What Is Our Life? A Play of Passion

What is our life? A play of passion;
Our mirth, the music of division;[1]
Our mothers' wombs the tiring-houses[2] be
Where we are dressed for this short comedy.
Heaven the judicious sharp spectator is,   5
That sits and marks still[3] who doth act amiss;
Our graves that hide us from the searching sun
Are like drawn curtains when the play is done.
Thus march we, playing, to our latest rest,
Only we die in earnest—that's no jest.   10

                                                            1612

FRANCIS QUARLES

My Soul, Sit Thou a Patient Looker-on[4]

My soul, sit thou a patient looker-on;
Judge not the play before the play is done.
Her plot has many changes: every day
Speaks a new scene. The last act crowns the play.

                                                            1635

---

8. Roles.
9. Pities.
1. A rapid melodic passage, or a varia-
tion on a musical theme.
2. Dressing rooms.

3. Observes constantly.
4. The concluding epigram to Quarles'
Emblem XV, depicting and then meditating
upon a scene presided over by Satan, who
has usurped God's throne.

JOHN DONNE

This Is My Play's Last Scene

This is my play's last scene, here heavens appoint
My pilgrimage's last mile; and my race,
Idly yet quickly run, hath this last pace,
My span's[5] last inch, my minute's last point;
And gluttonous death will instantly unjoint   5
My body and soul, and I shall sleep a space;
But my ever-waking part shall see that face
Whose fear[6] already shakes my every joint.
Then, as my soul to heaven, her first seat, takes flight,
And earth-born body in the earth shall dwell,   10
So, fall my sins, that all may have their right,
To where they're bred, and would press me, to hell.
Impute me righteous, thus purged of evil,
For thus I leave the world, the flesh, the devil.[7]

1633

ALGERNON   CHARLES   SWINBURNE

Stage Love

When the game began between them for a jest,
He played king and she played queen to match the best;
Laughter soft as tears, and tears that turned to laughter,
These were things she sought for years and sorrowed after.

Pleasure with dry lips, and pain that walks by night;   5
All the sting and all the stain of long delight;
These were things she knew not of, that knew not of her,
When she played at half a love with half a lover.

Time was chorus, gave them cues to laugh or cry;
They would kill, befool, amuse him, let him die;   10
Set him webs to weave today and break tomorrow,
Till he died for good in play, and rose in sorrow.

What the years mean; how time dies and is not slain;
How love grows and laughs and cries and wanes again;
These were things she came to know, and take their measure,   15
When the play was played out so for one man's pleasure.

1866

5. Literally, a "span" is the distance from the tip of the thumb to the tip of the little finger; traditionally, a representation of the shortness of human life.
6. The fear of whom.
7. The traditional Three Temptations.

Modern Metaphors

WALLACE STEVENS

The Idea of Order at Key West

She sang beyond the genius of the sea.
The water never formed to mind or voice,
Like a body wholly body, fluttering
Its empty sleeves; and yet its mimic motion
Made constant cry, caused constantly a cry,   5
That was not ours although we understood,
Inhuman, of the veritable ocean.

The sea was not a mask. No more was she.
The song and water were not medleyed sound
Even if what she sang was what she heard,   10
Since what she sang was uttered word by word.
It may be that in all her phrases stirred
The grinding water and the gasping wind;
But it was she and not the sea we heard.

For she was the maker of the song she sang.   15
The ever-hooded, tragic-gestured sea
Was merely a place by which she walked to sing.
Whose spirit is this? we said, because we knew
It was the spirit that we sought and knew
That we should ask this often as she sang.   20

If it was only the dark voice of the sea
That rose, or even colored by many waves;
If it was only the outer voice of sky
And cloud, of the sunken coral water-walled,
However clear, it would have been deep air,   25
The heaving speech of air, a summer sound
Repeated in a summer without end
And sound alone. But it was more than that,
More even than her voice, and ours, among
The meaningless plungings of water and the wind,   30
Theatrical distances, bronze shadows heaped
On high horizons, mountainous atmospheres
Of sky and sea.
                    It was her voice that made
The sky acutest at its vanishing.
She measured to the hour its solitude.   35
She was the single artificer of the world
In which she sang. And when she sang, the sea,
Whatever self it had, became the self
That was her song, for she was the maker. Then we,
As we beheld her striding there alone,   40

Knew that there never was a world for her
Except the one she sang and, singing, made.

Ramon Fernandez,[1] tell me, if you know,
Why, when the singing ended and we turned
Toward the town, tell why the glassy lights,   45
The lights in the fishing boats at anchor there,
As the night descended, tilting in the air,
Mastered the night and portioned out the sea,
Fixing emblazoned zones and fiery poles,
Arranging, deepening, enchanting night.   50

Oh! Blessed rage for order, pale Ramon,
The maker's rage to order words of the sea,
Words of the fragrant portals, dimly-starred,
And of ourselves and of our origins,
In ghostlier demarcations, keener sounds.   55

1935

WALLACE STEVENS

Of Modern Poetry

The poem of the mind in the act of finding
What will suffice. It has not always had
To find: the scene was set; it repeated what
Was in the script.
                    Then the theatre was changed   5
To something else. Its past was a souvenir.

It has to be living, to learn the speech of the place.
It has to face the men of the time and to meet
The women of the time. It has to think about war
And it has to find what will suffice. It has   10
To construct a new stage. It has to be on that stage
And, like an insatiable actor,   slowly   and
With meditation, speak words that in the ear,
In the delicatest ear of the mind,   repeat,
Exactly, that which it wants to hear, at the sound   15
Of which, an invisible audience listens,
Not to the play, but to itself, expressed
In an emotion as of two people, as of two

1, French classicist and critic, 1894–
1944, who emphasized the ordering role of
a writer's consciousness upon the materials
he used. Stevens denied that he had Fer-
nandez in mind, saying that he combined
a Spanish first name and surname at ran-
dom: "I knew of Ramon Fernandez, the
critic, and had read some of his criticisms,
but I did not have him in mind." (*Letters*
[New York: Knopf, 1960], p. 798) Later,
Stevens wrote to another correspondent
that he did not have the critic "consciously"
in mind. (*Letters*, p. 823)

Emotions becoming one. The actor is
A metaphysician in the dark, twanging   20
An instrument, twanging a wiry string that gives
Sounds passing through sudden rightnesses, wholly
Containing the mind, below which it cannot descend,
Beyond which it has no will to rise.
                              It must   25
Be the finding of a satisfaction, and may
Be of a man skating, a woman dancing, a woman
Combing. The poem of the act of the mind.

                                          p. 1940

SYLVIA PLATH

Black Rook in Rainy Weather

On the stiff twig up there
Hunches a wet black rook
Arranging and rearranging its feathers in the rain.
I do not expect miracle
Or an accident   5

To set the sight on fire
In my eye, nor seek
Any more in the desultory weather some design,
But let spotted leaves fall as they fall,
Without ceremony, or portent   10

Although, I admit, I desire,
Occasionally, some backtalk
From the mute sky, I can't honestly complain:
A certain minor light may still
Leap incandescent   15

Out of kitchen table or chair
As if a celestial burning took
Possession of the most obtuse objects now and then—
Thus hallowing an interval
Otherwise inconsequent   20

By bestowing largesse, honor,
One might say love. At any rate, I now walk
Wary (for it could happen
Even in this dull, ruinous landscape); skeptical,
Yet politic; ignorant   25

Of whatever angel may choose to flare
Suddenly at my elbow. I only know that a rook

Ordering its black feathers can so shine
As to seize my senses, haul
My eyelids up, and grant   30

A brief respite from fear
Of total neutrality. With luck,
Trekking stubborn through this season
Of fatigue, I shall
Patch together a content   35

Of sorts. Miracles occur,
If you care to call those spasmodic
Tricks of radiance miracles. The wait's begun again,
The long wait for the angel,
For that rare, random descent.[2]   40

1960

A. R. AMMONS

Cascadilla Falls

I went down by Cascadilla
Falls this
evening, the
stream below the falls,
and picked up a   5
handsized stone
kidney-shaped, testicular, and

thought all its motions into it,
the 800 mph earth spin,
the 190-million-mile yearly   10
displacement around the sun,
the overriding
grand
haul

of the galaxy with the 30,000   15
mph of where
the sun's going:
thought all the interweaving
motions
into myself: dropped   20

the stone to dead rest:
the stream from other motions

---

2. According to *Acts* 2, the Holy Ghost at Pentecost descended like a dove upon Christ's disciples.

broke
rushing over it:
shelterless,   25
I turned

to the sky and stood still:
oh
I do
not know where I am going   30
that I can live my life
by this single creek.

1970

WALLACE STEVENS

Anecdote of the Jar

I placed a jar in Tennessee,
And round it was, upon a hill.
It made the slovenly wilderness
Surround that hill.

The wilderness rose up to it,   5
And sprawled around, no longer wild.
The jar was round upon the ground
And tall and of a port in air.

It took dominion everywhere.
The jar was gray and bare.   10
It did not give of bird or bush,
Like nothing else in Tennessee.

1923

W. D. SNODGRASS

These Trees Stand . . .

These trees stand very tall under the heavens.
While *they* stand, if I walk, all stars traverse
This steep celestial gulf their branches chart.
Though lovers stand at sixes and at sevens
While civilizations come down with the curse,   5
Snodgrass is walking through the universe.

I can't make any world go around *your* house.
But note this moon. Recall how the night nurse

Goes ward-rounds, by the mild, reflective art
Of focusing her flashlight on her blouse.   10
Your name's safe conduct into love or verse;
Snodgrass is walking through the universe.

Your name's absurd, miraculous as sperm
And as decisive. If you can't coerce
One thing outside yourself, why you're the poet!   15
What irrefrangible atoms whirl, affirm
Their destiny and form Lucinda's skirts!
She can't make up your mind. Soon as you know it,
Your firmament grows touchable and firm.
If all this world runs battlefield or worse,   20
Come, let us wipe our glasses on our shirts:
Snodgrass is walking through the universe.

                                                                    1959

THOM GUNN

On the Move

"Man, you gotta Go."

The blue jay scuffling in the bushes follows
Some hidden purpose, and the gust of birds
That spurts across the field, the wheeling swallows,
Have nested in the trees and undergrowth.
Seeking their instinct, or their poise, or both,   5
One moves with an uncertain violence
Under the dust thrown by a baffled sense
Or the dull thunder of approximate words.

On motorcycles, up the road, they come:
Small, black, as flies hanging in heat, the Boys,   10
Until the distance throws them forth, their hum
Bulges to thunder held by calf and thigh.
In goggles, donned impersonality,
In gleaming jackets trophied with the dust,
They strap in doubt—by hiding it, robust—   15
And almost hear a meaning in their noise.

Exact conclusion of their hardiness
Has no shape yet, but from known whereabouts
They ride, direction where the tires press.
They scare a flight of birds across the field: 20
Much that is natural, to the will must yield.
Men manufacture both machine and soul,
And use what they imperfectly control
To dare a future from the taken routes.

It is a part solution, after all.   25
One is not necessarily discord
On earth; or damned because, half animal,
One lacks direct instinct, because one wakes
Afloat on movement that divides and breaks.
One joins the movement in a valueless world,   30
Choosing it, till, both hurler and the hurled,
One moves as well, always toward, toward.

A minute holds them, who have come to go:
The self-defined, astride the created will
They burst away; the towns they travel through   35
Are home for neither bird nor holiness,
For birds and saints complete their purposes.
At worst, one is in motion; and at best,
Reaching no absolute, in which to rest,
One is always nearer by not keeping still.   40

California, 1957

Poems for Further Reading

SAMUEL ALLEN

To Satch[1]

Sometimes I feel like I will *never* stop
Just go on forever
Till one fine mornin'
I'm gonna reach up and grab me a handfulla stars
Throw out my long lean leg   5
And whip three hot strikes burnin' down the heavens
And look over at God and say
How about that!

p. 1963

ANONYMOUS

Sumer Is Icumen In

Sumer is icumen in,
  Loudé sing cuccu!
Groweth sed[2] and bloweth med
  And springth the wodé[3] nu.
    Sing cuccu!   5

Ewé bleteth after lomb,
  Loweth after calvé cu;[4]
Bullock sterteth,[5] bucké verteth;
  Murie[6] sing cuccu!
    Cuccu, cuccu,   10
  Wel singes thu, cuccu,
  Ne swik[7] thu naver nu.

Sing cuccu nu! Sing cuccu!
Sing cuccu! Sing cuccu nu!

ca. 1225

---

1. Leroy ("Satchell") Paige, legendary pitcher in the Negro American League for many years. No one knows exactly how old he was when he finally was allowed to pitch in the Major Leagues after World War II, but he dates back to the era of Babe Ruth and Lou Gehrig (he pitched effectively against them in exhibition games); he is generally agreed to have been past 40, the oldest "rookie" in the history of Organized Baseball. He continued to pitch effectively for several years and made a one-game "comeback" in 1965, pitching 3 scoreless innings at about 60 years of age. His witty proverbs and formulas for staying young are nearly as legendary as his pitching.
2. Seed. "med": meadow.
3. Wood. "nu": now.
4. Cow.
5. Leaps. "verteth": farts.
6. Merrily.
7. Stop. "thu": thou; "naver": never.

MATTHEW ARNOLD

Lines Written in Kensington Gardens

In this lone, open glade I lie,
Screened by deep boughs on either hand;
And at its end, to stay the eye,
Those black-crowned, red-boled[8] pine-trees stand!

Birds here make song, each bird has his,   5
Across the girdling city's hum.
How green under the boughs it is!
How thick the tremulous sheep-cries come!

Sometimes a child will cross the glade
To take his nurse his broken toy;   10
Sometimes a thrush flit overhead
Deep in her unknown day's employ.

Here at my feet what wonders pass,
What endless, active life is here!
What blowing daisies, fragrant grass!   15
An air-stirred forest, fresh and clear.

Scarce fresher is the mountain-sod
Where the tired angler lies, stretched out,
And, eased of basket and of rod,
Counts his day's spoil, the spotted trout.   20

In the huge world, which roars hard by,
Be others happy if they can!
But in my helpless cradle I
Was breathed on by the rural Pan.[9]

I, on men's impious uproar hurled,   25
Think often, as I hear them rave,
That peace has left the upper world
And now keeps only in the grave.

Yet here is peace for ever new!
When I who watch them am away,   30
Still all things in this glade go through
The changes of their quiet day.

Then to their happy rest they pass!
The flowers upclose, the birds are fed,
The night comes down upon the grass,   35
The child sleeps warmly in his bed.

Calm soul of all things! make it mine
To feel, amid the city's jar,

---

8. Red-trunked.   9. God of shepherds and huntsmen.

That there abides a peace of thine,
Man did not make, and cannot mar.   40

The will to neither strive nor cry,
The power to feel with others give!
Calm, calm me more! nor let me die
Before I have begun to live.

1852

MARGARET ATWOOD

Five Poems for Dolls

I
Behind glass in Mexico
this clay doll draws
its lips back in a snarl;
despite its beautiful dusty shawl,
it wishes to be dangerous.   5

II
See how the dolls resent us,
with their bulging foreheads
and minimal chins, their flat bodies
never allowed to bulb and swell,
their faces of little thugs.   10

This is not a smile,
this glossy mouth, two stunted teeth;
the dolls gaze at us
with the filmed eyes of killers.

III
There have always been dolls   15
as long as there have been people.
In the trash heaps and abandoned temples
the dolls pile up;
the sea is filling with them.

What causes them?   20
Or are they gods, causeless,
something to talk to
when you have to talk
something to throw against the wall?

A doll is a witness   25
who cannot die,
with a doll you are never alone.

On the long journey under the earth,
in the boat with two prows,
there were always dolls.   30

IV

Or did we make them
because we needed to love someone
and could not love each other?

It was love, after all,
that rubbed the skins from their gray cheeks,   35
crippled their fingers,
snarled their hair, brown or dull gold.
Hate would merely have smashed them.

You change, but the doll
I made of you lives on,   40
a white body leaning
in a sunlit window, the features
wearing away with time,
frozen in the gaunt pose
of a single day,   45
holding in its plaster hand
your doll of me.

V

Or: all dolls come
from the land of the unborn,
the almost-born; each   50
doll is a future
dead at the roots,
a voice heard only
on breathless nights,
a desolate white memento.   55

Or: these are the lost children,
those who have died or thickened
to full growth and gone away.

The dolls are their souls or cast skins
which line the shelves of our bedrooms   60
and museums, disguised as outmoded toys,
images of our sorrow,
shedding around themselves
five inches of limbo.

1978

W. H. AUDEN

In Memory of W. B. Yeats

(*d. January, 1939*)

I

He disappeared in the dead of winter:
The brooks were frozen, the airports almost deserted,
And snow disfigured the public statues;
The mercury sank in the mouth of the dying day.
What instruments we have agree   5
The day of his death was a dark cold day.

Far from his illness
The wolves ran on through the evergreen forests,
The peasant river was untempted by the fashionable quays;
By mourning tongues   10
The death of the poet was kept from his poems.

But for him it was his last afternoon as himself,
An afternoon of nurses and rumors;
The provinces of his body revolted,
The squares of his mind were empty,   15
Silence invaded the suburbs,
The current of his feeling failed; he became his admirers.

Now he is scattered among a hundred cities
And wholly given over to unfamiliar affections,
To find his happiness in another kind of wood   20
And be punished under a foreign code of conscience.
The words of a dead man
Are modified in the guts of the living.

But in the importance and noise of tomorrow
When the brokers are roaring like beasts on the floor of the Bourse,[1]   25
And the poor have the sufferings to which they are fairly accustomed,
And each in the cell of himself is almost convinced of his freedom,
A few thousand will think of this day
As one thinks of a day when one did something slightly unusual.
What instruments we have agree   30
The day of his death was a dark cold day.

II

You were silly like us; your gift survived it all:
The parish of rich women, physical decay,
Yourself. Mad Ireland hurt you into poetry.
Now Ireland has her madness and her weather still,   35
For poetry makes nothing happen: it survives

1. The Paris stock exchange.

In the valley of its making where executives
Would never want to tamper, flows on south
From ranches of isolation and the busy griefs,
Raw towns that we believe and die in; it survives,   40
A way of happening, a mouth.

III

Earth, receive an honored guest:
William Yeats is laid to rest.
Let the Irish vessel lie
Emptied of its poetry.   45

In the nightmare of the dark
All the dogs of Europe bark,
And the living nations wait,
Each sequestered in its hate;

Intellectual disgrace   50
Stares from every human face,
And the seas of pity lie
Locked and frozen in each eye.

Follow, poet, follow right
To the bottom of the night,   55
With your unconstraining voice
Still persuade us to rejoice;

With the farming of a verse
Make a vineyard of the curse,
Sing of human unsuccess   60
In a rapture of distress;

In the deserts of the heart
Let the healing fountain start,
In the prison of his days
Teach the free man how to praise.   65

1939

W. H. AUDEN

Musée des Beaux Arts[2]

About suffering they were never wrong,
The Old Masters: how well they understood
Its human position; how it takes place
While someone else is eating or opening a window or just walking dully
    along;

2. The Museum of the Fine Arts, in Brussels.

How, when the aged are reverently, passionately waiting   5
For the miraculous birth, there always must be
Children who did not specially want it to happen, skating
On a pond at the edge of the wood:
They never forgot
That even the dreadful martyrdom must run its course   10
Anyhow in a corner, some untidy spot
Where the dogs go on with their doggy life and the torturer's horse
Scratches its innocent behind on a tree.

In Brueghel's *Icarus*,[3] for instance: how everything turns away
Quite leisurely from the disaster; the plowman may   15
Have heard the splash, the forsaken cry,
But for him it was not an important failure; the sun shone
As it had to on the white legs disappearing into the green
Water; and the expensive delicate ship that must have seen
Something amazing, a boy falling out of the sky,   20
Had somewhere to get to and sailed calmly on.
1938

AMIRI BARAKA (LEROI JONES)

Black Art

Poems are bullshit unless they are
teeth or trees or lemons piled
on a step. Or black ladies dying
of men leaving nickel hearts
beating them down. Fuck poems   5
and they are useful, they shoot
come at you, love what you are,
breathe like wrestlers, or shudder
strangely after pissing. We want live
words of the hip world live flesh &   10
coursing blood. Hearts Brains
Souls splintering fire. We want poems
like fists beating niggers out of Jocks
or dagger poems in the slimy bellies
of the owner-jews. Black poems to   15
smear on girdlemamma mulatto bitches
whose brains are red jelly stuck
between 'lizabeth taylor's toes. Stinking

---

3. "Landscape with the Fall of Icarus," by Pieter Brueghel the elder, located in the Brussels Museum. According to Greek myth, Daedalus and his son Icarus escaped from imprisonment by using homemade wings of wax; but Icarus flew too near the sun, the wax melted, and he fell into the sea and drowned. In the Brueghel painting the central figure is a peasant plowing, and several other figures are more immediately noticeable than Icarus who, disappearing into the sea, is easy to miss in the lower right-hand corner. Equally ignored by the figures is a dead body in the woods.

Whores! We want "poems that kill."
Assassin poems, Poems that shoot   20
guns. Poems that wrestle cops into alleys
and take their weapons leaving them dead
with tongues pulled out and sent to Ireland. Knockoff
poems for dope selling wops or slick halfwhite
politicians. Airplane poems. rrrrrrrrrrrrrrrrrrr   25
rrrrrrrrrr. . . . tuhtuhtuhtuhtuhtuhtuhtuhtuhtuh
. . . . rrrrrrrrrrrrrrr. . . Setting fire and death to
whities ass. Look at the Liberal
Spokesman for the jews clutch his throat
& puke himself into eternity. . . rrrrrrrrrr   30
There's a negroleader pinned to
a bar stool in Sardi's⁴ eyeballs melting
in hot flame. Another negroleader
on the steps of the white house one
kneeling between the sheriff's thighs   35
negotiating cooly for his people.
Aggh . . . stumbles across the room . . .
Put it on him, poem. Strip him naked
to the world! Another bad poem cracking
steel knuckles in a jewlady's mouth   40
Poem scream poison gas on beasts in green berets
Clean out the world for virtue and love,
Let there be no love poems written
until love can exist freely and
cleanly. Let Black People understand   45
that they are the lovers and the sons
of lovers and warriors and sons
of warriors Are poems & poets &
all the loveliness here in the world.

We want a black poem. And a   50
Black World.
Let the world be a Black Poem
And Let All Black People Speak This Poem
Silently

or LOUD   55
                                                                    1966

JOHN BERRYMAN

1 September 1939⁵

The first, scattering rain on the Polish cities.
That afternoon a man squat' on the shore

---

4. A fashionable New York bar and restau-   5. The first day of World War II.
rant.

Tearing a square of shining cellophane.
Some easily, some in evident torment tore,
Some for a time resisted, and then burst.   5
All this depended on fidelity . . .
One was blown out and borne off by the waters,
The man was tortured by the sound of rain.

Children were sent from London in the morning
But not the sound of children reached his ear.   10
He found a mangled feather by the lake,
Lost in the destructive sand this year
Like feathery independence, hope. His shadow
Lay on the sand before him, under the lake
As under the ruined library our learning.   15
The children play in the waves until they break.

The Bear crept under the Eagle's wing and lay
Snarling; the other animals showed fear,
Europe darkened its cities. The man wept,
Considering the light which had been there,   20
The feathered gull against the twilight flying.
As the little waves ate away the shore
The cellophane, dismembered, blew away.
The animals ran, the Eagle soared and dropt.

1939

EARLE BIRNEY

From the Hazel Bough

I met a lady
    on a lazy street
hazel eyes
    and little plush feet

her legs swam by   5
    like lovely trout
eyes were trees
    where boys leant out

hands in the dark and
    a river side   10
round breasts rising
    with the fingers' tide

she was plump as a finch
    and live as a salmon

gay as silk and
   proud as a Brahmin[6]   15

we winked when we met
   and laughed when we parted
never took time
   to be brokenhearted   20

but no man sees
   where the trout lie now
or what leans out
   from the hazel bough

1945–47

EARLE BIRNEY

Irapuato[7]

For reasons any
        brigadier
               could tell
this is a favorite nook for
               massacre   5

Toltex by Mixtex Mixtex by Aztex
Aztex by Spanishtex Spanishtex by
Mexitex by Mexitex by Mexitex by Texaco

So any farmer can see how the strawberries
are the biggest and reddest   10
   in the whole damn continent

but why
      when arranged under
             the market flies

do they look like small clotting hearts?   15

1962

---

6. A member of a socially elite class.
7. A city in central Mexico, northwest of Mexico City.

ELIZABETH BISHOP

Cootchie

Cootchie, Miss Lula's servant, lies in marl,
black into white she went
        below the surface of the coral-reef.
Her life was spent
        in caring for Miss Lula, who is deaf,   5
eating her dinner off the kitchen sink
while Lula ate hers off the kitchen table.
The skies were egg-white for the funeral
        and the faces sable.

Tonight the moonlight will alleviate   10
the melting of the pink wax roses
        planted in tin cans filled with sand
placed in a line to mark Miss Lula's losses;
        but who will shout and make her understand?
Searching the land and sea for someone else,   15
the lighthouse will discover Cootchie's grave
and dismiss all as trivial; the sea, desperate,
        will proffer wave after wave.

                                                         1946

WILLIAM BLAKE

Ah Sunflower

Ah Sunflower! weary of time,
Who countest the steps of the Sun,
Seeking after that sweet golden clime
Where the traveler's journey is done,

Where the Youth pined away with desire,   5
And the pale Virgin shrouded in snow,
Arise from their graves and aspire,
Where my Sunflower wishes to go.

                                                         1794

WILLIAM BLAKE

Song of Innocence[8]

Piping down the valleys wild,
Piping songs of pleasant glee,
On a cloud I saw a child,
And he laughing said to me:

"Pipe a song about a Lamb!"   5
So I piped with merry cheer.
"Piper, pipe that song again";
So I piped: he wept to hear.

"Drop thy pipe, thy happy pipe;
Sing thy songs of happy cheer!"   10
So I sung the same again,
While he wept with joy to hear.

"Piper, sit thee down and write
In a book that all may read."
So he vanished from my sight;   15
And I plucked a hollow reed,

And I made a rural pen,
And I stained the water clear,
And I wrote my happy songs
Every child may joy to hear.   20

                                        1789

WILLIAM BLAKE

The Lamb

Little Lamb, who made thee?
Dost thou know who made thee?
Gave thee life, and bid thee feed
By the stream and o'er the mead;
Gave thee clothing of delight,   5
Softest clothing woolly bright;
Gave thee such a tender voice,
Making all the vales rejoice?
Little Lamb, who made thee?
Dost thou know who made thee?   10

Little Lamb, I'll tell thee!
Little Lamb, I'll tell thee:

8. The introductory poem in Blake's volume, *Songs of Innocence*.

He is calléd by thy name,
For he calls himself a Lamb,
He is meek and he is mild;   15
He became a little child.
I a child and thou a lamb,
We are calléd by his name.
    Little Lamb, God bless thee!
    Little Lamb, God bless thee!   20

1789

WILLIAM BLAKE

The Tiger

Tiger, Tiger, burning bright
In the forests of the night,
What immortal hand or eye
Could frame thy fearful symmetry?

In what distant deeps or skies   5
Burnt the fire of thine eyes?
On what wings dare he aspire?
What the hand dare seize the fire?

And what shoulder and what art,
Could twist the sinews of thy heart?   10
And when thy heart began to beat,
What dread hand, and what dread feet?

What the hammer? What the chain?
In what furnace was thy brain?
What the anvil? What dread grasp   15
Dare its deadly terrors clasp?

When the stars threw down their spears
And watered heaven with their tears,
Did he smile his work to see?
Did he who made the Lamb make thee?   20

Tiger, Tiger, burning bright
In the forests of the night,
What immortal hand or eye
Dare frame thy fearful symmetry?

1794

LOUISE BOGAN

The Dragonfly

You are made of almost nothing
But of enough
To be great eyes
And diaphanous double vans;[9]
To be ceaseless movement,   5
Unending hunger
Grappling love.

Link between water and air,
Earth repels you.
Light touches you only to shift into iridescence   10
Upon your body and wings.

Twice-born, predator,
You split into the heat.
Swift beyond calculation or capture
You dart into the shadow   15
Which consumes you.

You rocket into the day.
But at last, when the wind flattens the grasses,
For you, the design and purpose stop.
And you fall   20
With the other husks of summer.

1968

JULIAN BOND

The Bishop of Atlanta: Ray Charles

The Bishop seduces the world with his voice
Sweat strangles mute eyes
As insinuations gush out through a hydrant of sorrow
Dreams, a world never seen
Molded on Africa's anvil, tempered down home   5
Documented in cries and wails
Screaming to be ignored, crooning to be heard
Throbbing from the gutter
On Saturday night
Silver offering only   10
The Right Reverend's back in town
Don't it make you feel all right?

p. 1963

9. Delicate and translucent double wings.

JULIAN BOND

Rotation

Like plump green floor plans
the pool tables squat
Among fawning mahogany Buddhas with felt heads.
Like clubwomen blessed with adultery
The balls dart to kiss   5
and tumble erring members into silent oblivion.
Right-angled over the verdant barbered turf
Sharks point long fingers at the multi-colored worlds
and play at percussion
Sounding cheap plastic clicks   10
in an 8-ball universe built for ivory.

p. 1964

GEORGE GORDON, LORD BYRON

She Walks in Beauty

She walks in beauty, like the night
   Of cloudless climes and starry skies;
And all that's best of dark and bright
   Meet in her aspect and her eyes:
Thus mellowed to that tender light   5
   Which heaven to gaudy day denies.

One shade the more, one ray the less,
   Had half impaired the nameless grace
Which waves in every raven tress,
   Or softly lightens o'er her face;   10
Where thoughts serenely sweet express
   How pure, how dear their dwelling place.

And on that cheek, and o'er that brow,
   So soft, so calm, yet eloquent,
The smiles that win, the tints that glow,   15
   But tell of days in goodness spent,
A mind at peace will all below,
   A heart whose love is innocent!

June 12, 1814

GEORGE GORDON, LORD BYRON

When a Man Hath No Freedom
to Fight for at Home

When a man hath no freedom to fight for at home,
  Let him combat for that of his neighbors;
Let him think of the glories of Greece and of Rome,
  And get knocked on his head for his labors.

To do good to mankind is the chivalrous plan,   5
  And is always as nobly requited;
Then battle for freedom wherever you can,
  And, if not shot or hanged, you'll get knighted.

November 5, 1820

LEWIS CARROLL

Jabberwocky[1]

'Twas brillig, and the slithy toves
  Did gyre and gimble in the wabe;
All mimsy were the borogoves,
  And the mome raths outgrabe.

"Beware the Jabberwock, my son!   5
  The jaws that bite, the claws that catch!
Beware the Jubjub bird, and shun
  The frumious Bandersnatch!"

He took his vorpal sword in hand:
  Long time the manxome foe he sought—   10
So rested he by the Tumtum tree,
  And stood awhile in thought.

And as in uffish thought he stood,
  The Jabberwock, with eyes of flame,
Came whiffling through the tulgey wood,   15
  And burbled as it came!

One, two! One, two! And through and through
  The vorpal blade went snicker-snack!

---

1. Of the "hard words" in this poem, Carroll wrote: "Humpty-Dumpty's theory, of two meanings packed into one word like a portmanteau, seems to me the right explanation for all. For instance, take the two words 'fuming' and 'furious.' Make up your mind that you will say both words, but leave it unsettled which you will say first. . . . If you have that rarest of gifts, a perfectly balanced mind, you will say 'frumious.'"

He left it dead, and with its head
  He went galumphing back.   20

"And hast thou slain the Jabberwock?
  Come to my arms, my beamish boy!
O frabjous day! Callooh! Callay!"
  He chortled in his joy.

'Twas brillig, and the slithy toves   25
  Did gyre and gimble in the wabe;
All mimsy were the borogoves,
  And the mome raths outgrabe.

            1871

TURNER CASSITY

Calvin in the Casino[2]

(He apostrophizes a roulette ball)

Sphere of pure chance, free agent of no cause,
Your progress is a motion without laws.

Let every casuist henceforth rejoice
To cite your amoralities of choice,

By whose autonomy one apprehends   5
The limits where predestination ends;

Where the Eternal Will divides its see[3]
In latitudes of probability,

And the divine election is obscured
Through being momently and long endured.   10

It is obscured and is rejustified,
That stands fulfilled in being here denied,

Lest its caprice should lead the mind to curse
A biased and encircling universe,

Or its vagaries urge us to reject   15
That one same Will which chooses the elect.

            1966

2. John Calvin (1509–1564), a French theologian best known for his doctrine of predestination.

3. Area of jurisdiction (usually used to describe the power of bishops).

ARTHUR HUGH CLOUGH

The Latest Decalogue

Thou shalt have one God only; who
Would be at the expense of two?
No graven images may be
Worshipped, except the currency.
Swear not at all; for, for thy curse   5
Thine enemy is none the worse.
At church on Sunday to attend
Will serve to keep the world thy friend.
Honor thy parents; that is, all
From whom advancement may befall.   10
Thou shalt not kill; but need'st not strive
Officiously to keep alive.
Do not adultery commit;
Advantage rarely comes of it.
Thou shalt not steal; an empty feat,   15
When it's so lucrative to cheat.
Bear not false witness; let the lie
Have time on its own wings to fly.
Thou shalt not covet; but tradition
Approves all forms of competition.   20

1862

LEONARD COHEN

Suzanne Takes You Down

Suzanne takes you down
to her place near the river,
you can hear the boats go by
you can stay the night beside her.
And you know that she's half crazy   5
but that's why you want to be there
and she feeds you tea and oranges
that come all the way from China.
Just when you mean to tell her
that you have no gifts to give her,   10
she gets you on her wave-length
and she lets the river answer
that you've always been her lover.
   And you want to travel with her,
   you want to travel blind   15
     and you know that she can trust you
     because you've touched her perfect body
     with your mind.

Jesus was a sailor
when he walked upon the water[4]   20
and he spent a long time watching
from a lonely wooden tower
and when he knew for certain
only drowning men could see him
he said All men will be sailors then   25
until the sea shall free them,
but he himself was broken
long before the sky would open,
forsaken, almost human,
he sank beneath your wisdom like a stone.   30
    And you want to travel with him,
    you want to travel blind
    and you think maybe you'll trust him
    because he touched your perfect body
    with his mind.   35

Suzanne takes your hand
and she leads you to the river,
she is wearing rags and feathers
from Salvation Army counters.
The sun pours down like honey   40
on our lady of the harbor
as she shows you where to look
among the garbage and the flowers,
there are heroes in the seaweed
there are children in the morning,   45
they are leaning out for love
they will lean that way forever
while Suzanne she holds the mirror.
    And you want to travel with her
    and you want to travel blind   50
    and you're sure that she can find you
    because she's touched her perfect body
    with her mind.

                              1968

SAMUEL TAYLOR COLERIDGE

Kubla Khan: or, a Vision in a Dream[5]

In Xanadu did Kubla Khan
    A stately pleasure-dome decree:

4. According to *Matthew* 14:22–26 and *Mark* 6:45–52, Jesus walked upon the water in order to join his disciples in a ship at sea.

5. Coleridge said he wrote this fragment immediately after waking from an opium dream and that after he was interrupted by a caller he was unable to finish the poem.

Where Alph, the sacred river, ran
Through caverns measureless to man
  Down to a sunless sea.   5
So twice five miles of fertile ground
With walls and towers were girdled round:
And here were gardens bright with sinuous rills
Where blossomed many an incense-bearing tree;
And here were forests ancient as the hills,   10
Enfolding sunny spots of greenery.
But oh! that deep romantic chasm which slanted
Down the green hill athwart a cedarn cover!6
A savage place! as holy and enchanted
As e'er beneath a waning moon was haunted   15
By woman wailing for her demon-lover!7
And from this chasm, with ceaseless turmoil seething,
As if this earth in fast thick pants were breathing,
A mighty fountain momently was forced,
Amid whose swift half-intermitted burst   20
Huge fragments vaulted like rebounding hail,
Or chaffy grain beneath the thresher's flail:
And 'mid these dancing rocks at once and ever
It flung up momently the sacred river.
Five miles meandering with a mazy motion   25
Through wood and dale the sacred river ran,
Then reached the caverns measureless to man,
And sank in tumult to a lifeless ocean:
And 'mid this tumult Kubla heard from far
Ancestral voices prophesying war!   30

      The shadow of the dome of pleasure
      Floated midway on the waves;
      Where was heard the mingled measure
      From the fountain and the caves.
It was a miracle of rare device,   35
A sunny pleasure-dome with caves of ice!
      A damsel with a dulcimer 8
      In a vision once I saw:
      It was an Abyssinian maid,
      And on her dulcimer she played,   40
      Singing of Mount Abora.
      Could I revive within me
      Her symphony and song,
      To such a deep delight 'twould win me,
That with music loud and long,   45
I would build that dome in air,
That sunny dome! those caves of ice!
And all who heard should see them there,

---

6. From side to side of a cover of cedar trees.

7. In a famous and often imitated German ballad, the lady Lenore is carried off on horseback by the specter of her lover and married to him at his grave.

8. A stringed instrument, prototype of the piano.

And all should cry, Beware! Beware!
His flashing eyes, his floating hair!   50
Weave a circle round him thrice,
And close your eyes with holy dread,
For he on honey-dew hath fed,
And drunk the milk of Paradise.

1798

SAMUEL TAYLOR COLERIDGE

This Lime-Tree Bower My Prison[9]

Well, they are gone, and here must I remain,
This lime-tree bower my prison! I have lost
Beauties and feelings, such as would have been
Most sweet to my remembrance even when age
Had dimmed mine eyes to blindness! They, meanwhile,   5
Friends, whom I never more may meet again,
On springy[1] heath, along the hilltop edge,
Wander in gladness, and wind down, perchance,
To that still roaring dell, of which I told;
The roaring dell, o'erwooded, narrow, deep,   10
And only speckled by the midday sun;
Where its slim trunk the ash from rock to rock
Flings arching like a bridge;—that branchless ash,
Unsunned and damp, whose few poor yellow leaves
Ne'er tremble in the gale, yet tremble still,   15
Fanned by the waterfall! and there my friends
Behold the dark green file of long lank weeds,[2]
That all at once (a most fantastic sight!)
Still nod and drip beneath the dripping edge
Of the blue clay-stone.

                         Now, my friends emerge   20
Beneath the wide wide Heaven—and view again
The many-steepled tract magnificent
Of hilly fields and meadows, and the sea,
With some fair bark, perhaps, whose sails light up
The slip of smooth clear blue betwixt two Isles   25
Of purple shadow! Yes! they wander on
In gladness all; but thou, methinks, most glad,
My gentle-hearted Charles![3] for thou hast pined
And hungered after Nature, many a year,
In the great City pent,[4] winning thy way   30

---

9. Coleridge wrote the poem during a visit to his cottage by some friends; an accident on the way of their arrival prevented him from accompanying them on walks, during one of which the poem is set.
1. "Elastic, I mean." (Coleridge's note)

2. Plants usually called adder's tongue or hart's tongue.
3. The poem is addressed to Charles Lamb, one of the visiting friends.
4. Lamb was a clerk at the India House, London.

With sad yet patient soul, through evil and pain
And strange calamity! Ah! slowly sink
Behind the western ridge, thou glorious Sun!
Shine in the slant beams of the sinking orb,
Ye purple heath-flowers! richlier burn, ye clouds!   35
Live in the yellow light, ye distant groves!
And kindle, thou blue Ocean! So my friend
Struck with deep joy may stand, as I have stood,
Silent with swimming sense; yea, gazing round
On the wide landscape, gaze till all doth seem   40
Less gross than bodily; and of such hues
As veil the Almighty Spirit, when yet he makes
Spirits perceive his presence.

                          A delight
Comes sudden on my heart, and I am glad
As I myself were there! Nor in this bower,   45
This little lime-tree bower, have I not marked
Much that has soothed me. Pale beneath the blaze
Hung the transparent foliage; and I watched
Some broad and sunny leaf, and loved to see
The shadow of the leaf and stem above   50
Dappling its sunshine! And that walnut-tree
Was richly tinged, and a deep radiance lay
Full on the ancient ivy, which usurps
Those fronting elms, and now, with blackest mass
Makes their dark branches gleam a lighter hue   55
Through the late twilight: and though now the bat
Wheels silent by, and not a swallow twitters,
Yet still the solitary humble-bee
Sings in the bean-flower! Henceforth I shall know
That Nature ne'er deserts the wise and pure;   60
No plot so narrow, be but Nature there,
No waste so vacant, but may well employ
Each faculty of sense, and keep the heart
Awake to Love and Beauty! and sometimes
'Tis well to be bereft of promised good,   65
That we may lift the soul, and contemplate
With lively joy the joys we cannot share.
My gentle-hearted Charles! when the last rook[5]
Beat its straight path along the dusky air
Homewards, I blessed it! deeming its black wing   70
(Now a dim speck, now vanishing in light)
Had crossed the mighty orb's dilated glory,
While thou stood'st gazing; or, when all was still,
Flew creeking o'er thy head, and had a charm
For thee, my gentle-hearted Charles, to whom   75
No sound is dissonant which tells of Life.

1797

---

5. Crow.

WILLIAM CONGREVE

Song

False though she be to me and love,
    I'll ne'er pursue revenge;
For still the charmer I approve,
    Though I deplore her change.

In hours of bliss we oft have met,   5
    They could not always last;
And though the present I regret,
    I'm grateful for the past.

                                            1710

e. e. cummings

chanson innocente

in Just-
spring   when the world is mud-
luscious the little
lame balloonman

whistles   far   and wee   5

and eddieandbill come
running from marbles and
piracies and it's
spring

when the world is puddle-wonderful   10

the queer
old balloonman whistles
far   and   wee
and bettyandisbel come dancing

from hop-scotch and jump-rope and   15

it's
spring
and
    the

      goat-footed   20

balloonMan   whistles
far
and
wee[6]

1923

e. e. cummings

the season 'tis, my lovely lambs

the season 'tis, my lovely lambs,

of Sumner Volstead Christ and Co.[7]
the epoch of Mann's righteousness
the age of dollars and no sense.

Which being quite beyond dispute   5

as prove from Troy (N. Y.) to Cairo
(Egypt) the luminous dithyrambs[8]
of large immaculate unmute
antibolshevistic gents
(each manufacturing word by word   10
his own unrivalled brand of pyro
-technic blurb anent[9] the (hic)
hero dead that gladly (sic)
in far lands perished of unheard
of maladies including flu)   15

my little darlings, let us now
passionately remember how—
braving the worst, of peril heedless,
each braver than the other, each
(a typewriter within his reach)   20
upon his fearless derrière
sturdily seated—Colonel Needless
To Name and General You know who
a string of pretty medals drew

6. Pan, whose Greek name means "everything," is traditionally represented with a syrinx (or the pipes of Pan). The upper half of his body is human, the lower half goat, and as the father of Silenus he is associated with the spring rites of Dionysus.

7. The Volstead Act (1919) gave the federal government power to enforce Prohibition. "Sumner": possibly Charles Sumner, a late 19th-century U. S. senator who was considered the leading representative of the Puritan spirit in American politics, but more probably William Sumner, a late 19th and early 20th-century laissez-faire theorist who opposed laws regulating monopolies. The Mann Act (1910) made taking a woman across a state line "for immoral purposes" a federal offense.

8. Vehement expressions on neon signs.

9. In reference to (a somewhat affected term common in early businessese). "Hic" (line 12), Latin for "here," and "sic" (line 13), Latin for "thus," sometimes appear in similar incongruent contexts, ostensibly as shortcuts to saying "here is an example" or "it is correct as it stands," but often to show off. There are, of course, also puns on both terms.

(while messrs jack james john and jim   25
in token of their country's love
received my dears the order of
The Artificial Arm and Limb)

—or, since bloodshed and kindred questions
inhibit unprepared digestions,   30
come: let us mildly contemplate
beginning with his wellfilled pants
earth's biggest grafter, nothing less;
the Honorable Mr. (guess)
who, breathing on the ear of fate,   35
landed a seat in the legislat-
ure whereas tommy so and so
(an erring child of circumstance
whom the bulls[1] nabbed at 33rd)

pulled six months for selling snow[2]   40

                                                     1926

EMILY DICKINSON

The Brain Is Wider Than the Sky

The Brain—is wider than the Sky—
For—put them side by side—
The one the other will contain
With ease—and You—beside—

The Brain is deeper than the sea—   5
For—hold them—Blue to Blue—
The one the other will absorb—
As Sponges—Buckets—do—

The Brain is just the weight of God—
For—Heft them—Pound for Pound—   10
And they will differ—if they do—
As Syllable from Sound—

ca. 1862

---

1. Police.
2. Cocaine, but also a reminder of the Season.

EMILY DICKINSON

My Life Closed Twice

My life closed twice before its close—
It yet remains to see
If Immortality unveil
A third event to me

So huge, so hopeless to conceive   5
As these that twice befell.
Parting is all we know of heaven,
And all we need of hell.

1896

EMILY DICKINSON

There Is No Frigate Like a Book

There is no Frigate like a Book
To take us Lands away
Nor any Coursers like a Page
Of prancing Poetry—
This Traverse may the poorest take   5
Without oppress of Toll—
How frugal is the Chariot
That bears the Human soul.

ca. 1873

EMILY DICKINSON

We Do Not Play on Graves

We do not play on Graves—
Because there isn't Room—
Besides—it isn't even—it slants
And People come—

And put a Flower on it—   5
And hang their faces so—
We're fearing that their Hearts will drop—
And crush our pretty play—

And so we move as far

As Enemies—away—   10
Just looking round to see how far
It is—Occasionally—

ca. 1862

EMILY DICKINSON

While We Were Fearing It, It Came

While we were fearing it, it came—
But came with less of fear
Because that fearing it so long
Had almost made it fair—

There is a Fitting—a Dismay—   5
A Fitting—a Despair—
Tis harder knowing it is Due
Than knowing it is Here.

The Trying on the Utmost
The Morning it is new   10
Is Terribler than wearing it
A whole existence through.

ca. 1873

EMILY DICKINSON

Wild Nights! Wild Nights!

Wild Nights—Wild Nights!
Were I with thee
Wild Nights should be
Our luxury!

Futile—the Winds—   5
To a Heart in port—
Done with the Compass—
Done with the Chart!

Rowing in Eden—
Ah, the Sea!   10
Might I but moor—Tonight—
In Thee!

ca. 1861

JOHN DONNE

The Canonization

For God's sake hold your tongue and let me love!
 Or chide my palsy or my gout,
My five gray hairs or ruined fortune flout;
With wealth your state, your mind with arts improve,
 Take you a course, get you a place,   5
 Observe his Honor or his Grace,
Or the king's real or his stampéd face [3]
 Contemplate; what you will, approve,
  So you will let me love.

Alas, alas, who's injured by my love?   10
 What merchant's ships have my sighs drowned?
Who says my tears have overflowed his ground?
When did my colds a forward spring remove?
 When did the heats which my veins fill
 Add one man to the plaguy bill? [4]   15
Soldiers find wars, and lawyers find out still
 Litigious men which quarrels move,
  Though she and I do love.

Call us what you will, we are made such by love.
 Call her one, me another fly,   20
We're tapers [5] too, and at our own cost die;
And we in us find th' eagle and the dove. [6]
 The phoenix riddle [7] hath more wit [8]
 By us; we two, being one, are it.
So to one neutral thing both sexes fit,   25
 We die and rise the same, and prove
  Mysterious by this love.

We can die by it, if not live by love;
 And if unfit for tombs and hearse
Our legend be, it will be fit for verse;
And if no piece of chronicle we prove, [9]   30
 We'll build in sonnets [1] pretty rooms
 (As well a well-wrought urn becomes [2]
The greatest ashes, as half-acre tombs),

3. On coins.
4. List of plague victims.
5. Which consume themselves. To "die" is Renaissance slang for consummating the sexual act, which was popularly believed to shorten life by one day. "fly": a traditional symbol of transitory life.
6. Traditional symbols of strength and purity.
7. According to tradition, only one phoenix existed at a time, dying in a funeral pyre of its own making and being reborn from its own ashes. The bird's existence was thus a riddle akin to a religious mystery (line 27), and a symbol sometimes fused with Christian representations of immortality.
8. Meaning.
9. I.e., if we don't turn out to be an authenticated piece of historical narrative.
1. Love poems. In Italian, *stanza* means rooms.
2. Befits.

And by these hymns all shall approve   35
    Us canonized for love.

And thus invoke us: "You whom reverent love
    Made one another's hermitage,
You to whom love was peace, that now is rage,
Who did the whole world's soul extract, and drove[3]   40
    Into the glasses of your eyes
    (So made such mirrors and such spies
That they did all to you epitomize)
    Countries, towns, courts; beg from above
        A pattern of your love!"   45

                                                      1633

JOHN DONNE

The Good-Morrow

I wonder, by my troth, what thou and I
    Did, till we loved? were we not weaned till then?
But sucked on country pleasures, childishly?
    Or snorted[5] we in the Seven Sleepers' den?[4]
'Twas so; but[6] this, all pleasures fancies be.   5
If ever any beauty[7] I did see,
Which I desired, and got,[8] 'twas but a dream of thee.

And now good-morrow to our waking souls,
    Which watch not one another out of fear;
For love, all love of other sights controls,   10
    And makes one little room an everywhere.
Let sea-discoverers to new worlds have gone,
Let maps to other,[9] worlds on worlds have shown,
Let us possess one world, each hath one, and is one.

My face in thine eye, thine in mine appears,[1]   15
    And true plain hearts do in the faces rest;
Where can we find two better hemispheres,
    Without sharp north, without declining west?
Whatever dies was not mixed equally,[2]
If our two loves be one, or, thou and I   20
Love so alike that none do slacken, none can die.

                                                      1633

3. Compressed.
4. Snored.
5. According to tradition, seven Chris-
tian youths escaped Roman persecution by
sleeping in a cave for 187 years.
6. Except for.
7. Beautiful woman.

8. Sexually possessed.
9. Other people.
1. I.e., each is reflected in the other's
eyes.
2. Perfectly mixed elements, according
to scholastic philosophy, were stable and
immortal.

JOHN DONNE

Hymn to God My God, in My Sickness

Since I am coming to that holy room
   Where, with Thy choir of saints forevermore,
I shall be made Thy Music, as I come
   I tune the instrument here at the door,
   And what I must do then, think here before.   5

Whilst my physicians by their love are grown
   Cosmographers, and I their map,[3] who lie
Flat on this bed, that by them may be shown
   That this is my South-west discovery[4]
   Per fretum febris,[5] by these straits to die,   10

I joy, that in these straits, I see my West;[6]
   For, though their current yield return to none,
What shall my West hurt me? As West and East
   In all flat maps (and I am one) are one,
   So death doth touch the resurrection.   15

Is the Pacific Sea my home? Or are
   The Eastern riches? Is *Jerusalem?*
Anyan,[7] and *Magellan*, and *Gibraltar*,
   All straits, and none but straits, are ways to them,
   Whether where *Japhet* dwelt, or *Cham*, or *Shem*.[8]   20

We think that *Paradise* and *Calvary*,
   Christ's Cross, and *Adam's* tree, stood in one place;
Look, Lord, and find both *Adams* met in me;
   As the first *Adam's* sweat surrounds my face,
   May the last *Adam's* blood my soul embrace.   25

So in His purple wrapped, receive me, Lord,
   By these His thorns give me His other crown;
And, as to others' souls I preached Thy word,
   Be this my text, my sermon to mine own,
   Therefore that He may raise, the Lord throws down.   30

1635

3. Because the various parts of the world and orders of being were thought to correspond closely and reflect one another, man was often called a "microcosm," or little world.
4. Magellan, in 1520, discovered the South American straits which are named for him; they are southwest of England.
5. Through the straits of fever.
6. West, because the sun sets there, often connotes death, and the East life or rebirth (line 13).
7. Bering.
8. Noah's sons who, after the Flood, settled Europe, Africa, and Asia, respectively.

JOHN DRYDEN

Why Should a Foolish Marriage Vow [9]

Why should a foolish marriage vow,
   Which long ago was made,
Oblige us to each other now
   When passion is decayed?
We loved, and we loved, as long as we could,   5
   Till our love was loved out in us both;
But our marriage is dead when the pleasure is fled:
   'Twas pleasure first made it an oath.

If I have pleasures for a friend,
   And farther love in store,   10
What wrong has he whose joys did end,
   And who could give no more?
'Tis a madness that he should be jealous of me,
   Or that I should bar him of another:
For all we can gain is to give ourselves pain,   15
   When neither can hinder the other.

                             1671

PAUL LAWRENCE DUNBAR

We Wear the Mask

We wear the mask that grins and lies,
It hides our cheeks and shades our eyes,—
This debt we pay to human guile;
With torn and bleeding hearts we smile,
And mouth with myriad subtleties.   5

Why should the world be over-wise,
In counting all our tears and sighs?
Nay, let them only see us, while
   We wear the mask.

We smile, but, O great Christ, our cries   10
To thee from tortured souls arise.
We sing, but oh the clay is vile
Beneath our feet, and long the mile;
But let the world dream otherwise,
   We wear the mask!   15

                             1896

9. A song from Dryden's play, *Marriage a la Mode.*

RICHARD EBERHART

The Fury of Aerial Bombardment

You would think the fury of aerial bombardment
Would rouse God to relent; the infinite spaces
Are still silent. He looks on shock-pried faces.
History, even, does not know what is meant.

You would feel that after so many centuries   5
God would give man to repent; yet he can kill
As Cain could, but with multitudinous will,
No farther advanced than in his ancient furies.

Was man made stupid to see his own stupidity?
Is God by definition indifferent, beyond us all?   10
Is the eternal truth man's fighting soul
Wherein the Beast ravens in its own avidity?

Of Van Wettering I speak, and Averill,
Names on a list, whose faces I do not recall
But they are gone to early death, who late in school   15
Distinguished the belt feed lever from the belt holding pawl. [1]

1947

T. S. ELIOT

Journey of the Magi[2]

"A cold coming we had of it,
Just the worst time of the year
For a journey, and such a long journey:
The ways deep and the weather sharp,
The very dead of winter."[3]   5
And the camels galled, sore-footed, refractory,
Lying down in the melting snow.
There were times we regretted
The summer palaces on slopes, the terraces,
And the silken girls bringing sherbet.   10
Then the camel men cursing and grumbling
And running away, and wanting their liquor and women,
And the night-fires going out, and the lack of shelters,
And the cities hostile and the towns unfriendly
And the villages dirty and charging high prices: 15
A hard time we had of it.

---

1. Machine-gun parts.
2. The wise men who followed the star of Bethlehem. See *Matthew* 2:1–12.

3. An adaptation of a passage from a 1622 sermon by Lancelot Andrewes.

At the end we preferred to travel all night,
Sleeping in snatches,
With the voices singing in our ears, saying
That this was all folly.   20

   Then at dawn we came down to a temperate valley,
Wet, below the snow line, smelling of vegetation;
With a running stream and a water-mill beating the darkness,
And three trees on the low sky,[4]
And an old white horse galloped away in the meadow.   25
Then we came to a tavern with vine-leaves over the lintel,
Six hands at an open door dicing for pieces of silver,
And feet kicking the empty wine-skins.
But there was no information, and so we continued
And arrived at evening, not a moment too soon   30
Finding the place; it was (you may say) satisfactory.

   All this was a long time ago, I remember,
And I would do it again, but set down
This set down
This: were we led all that way for   35
Birth or Death? There was a Birth, certainly,
We had evidence and no doubt. I had seen birth and death,
But had thought they were different; this Birth was
Hard and bitter agony for us, like Death, our death.
We returned to our places, these Kingdoms,[5]   40
But no longer at ease here, in the old dispensation,
With an alien people clutching their gods.
I should be glad of another death.

                          1927

T. S. ELIOT

The Love Song of J. Alfred Prufrock

S'io credesse che mia risposta fosse
A persona che mai tornasse al mondo,
Questa fiamma staria senza piu scosse.
Ma perciocche giammai di questo fondo
Non torno vivo alcun, s'i'odo il vero,
Senza tema d'infamia ti rispondo.[6]

Let us go then, you and I,
When the evening is spread out against the sky

---

4. Suggestive of the three crosses of the
Crucifixion (*Luke* 23:32–33). The Magi
see several objects which suggest later
events in Christ's life: pieces of silver (see
Matthew 26:14–16), the dicing (see
Matthew 27:35), the white horse (see
Revelation 6:2 and 19:11–16), and the
empty wine-skins (see *Matthew* 9:14–17,
possibly relevant also to lines 41–42).

5. The Bible only identifies the wise
men as "from the East," and subsequent
tradition has made them kings. In Persia,
Magi were members of an ancient priestly
caste.

6. Dante's *Inferno*, XXVII, 61–66. In
the Eighth Chasm, Dante and Vergil meet
Count Guido de Montefeltrano, one of the
False Counselors. The spirits there are in

Like a patient etherized upon a table;
Let us go, through certain half-deserted streets,
The muttering retreats   5
Of restless nights in one-night cheap hotels
And sawdust restaurants with oyster-shells:
Streets that follow like a tedious argument
Of insidious intent
To lead you to an overwhelming question . . .   10
Oh, do not ask, "What is it?"
Let us go and make our visit.

    In the room the women come and go
Talking of Michelangelo.

    The yellow fog that rubs its back upon the window-panes,   15
The yellow smoke that rubs its muzzle on the window-panes
Licked its tongue into the corners of the evening,
Lingered upon the pools that stand in drains,
Let fall upon its back the soot that falls from chimneys,
Slipped by the terrace, made a sudden leap,   20
And seeing that it was a soft October night,
Curled once about the house, and fell asleep.

    And indeed there will be time[7]
For the yellow smoke that slides along the street,
Rubbing its back upon the window-panes;   25
There will be time, there will be time
To prepare a face to meet the faces that you meet;
There will be time to murder and create,
And time for all the works and days[8] of hands
That lift and drop a question on your plate;   30
Time for you and time for me,
And time yet for a hundred indecisions,
And for a hundred visions and revisions,
Before the taking of a toast and tea.

    In the room the women come and go   35
Talking of Michelangelo.

    And indeed there will be time
To wonder, "Do I dare?" and, "Do I dare?"
Time to turn back and descend the stair,
With a bald spot in the middle of my hair—   40

---

the form of flames, and Guido speaks from the trembling tip of the flame, responding to Dante's request that he tell his life story: "If I thought that my answer were to someone who would ever go back to earth, this flame would be still, without any more movement. But because no one has ever gone back alive from this chasm (if what I hear is true) I answer you without fear of infamy."

7. See *Ecclesiastes* 3:1ff.: "To every-

thing there is a season, and a time to every purpose under the heaven: A time to be born, and a time to die; a time to plant, and a time to pluck up that which is planted; A time to kill, and a time to heal. . . ." Also see Marvell's "To His Coy Mistress": "Had we but world enough and time. . . ."

8. Hesiod's ancient Greek didactic poem *Works and Days* prescribed in practical detail how to conduct one's life.

(They will say: "How his hair is growing thin!")
My morning coat, my collar mounting firmly to the chin,
My necktie rich and modest, but asserted by a simple pin—
(They will say: "But how his arms and legs are thin!")
Do I dare   45
Disturb the universe?

In a minute there is time
For decisions and revisions which a minute will reverse.

    For I have known them all already, known them all:—
Have known the evenings, mornings, afternoons,   50
I have measured out my life with coffee spoons;
I know the voices dying with a dying fall
Beneath the music from a farther room.
    So how should I presume?

    And I have known the eyes already, known them all—   55
The eyes that fix you in a formulated phrase,
And when I am formulated, sprawling on a pin,
When I am pinned and wriggling on the wall,
Then how should I begin
To spit out all the butt-ends of my days and ways?   60
    And how should I presume?

    And I have known the arms already, known them all—
Arms that are braceleted and white and bare
(But in the lamplight, downed with light brown hair!)
Is it perfume from a dress   65
That makes me so digress?
Arms that lie along a table, or wrap about a shawl.
    And should I then presume?
    And how should I begin?

                . . . . .

Shall I say, I have gone at dusk through narrow streets   70
And watched the smoke that rises from the pipes
Of lonely men in shirt-sleeves, leaning out of windows? . . .

    I should have been a pair of ragged claws
Scuttling across the floors of silent seas.

                . . . . .

And the afternoon, the evening, sleeps so peacefully!   75
Smoothed by long fingers,
Asleep . . . tired . . . or it malingers,
Stretched on the floor, here beside you and me.
Should I, after tea and cakes and ices,
Have the strength to force the moment to its crisis?   80
But though I have wept and fasted, wept and prayed,
Though I have seen my head (grown slightly bald) brought in upon
    a platter,[9]

----

9. See *Matthew* 14:1–12 and *Mark*
6:17–29: John the Baptist was decapitated, upon Salome's request and at Herod's command, and his head delivered on a platter.

I am no prophet—and here's no great matter;
I have seen the moment of my greatness flicker,
And I have seen the eternal Footman hold my coat, and snicker,   85
And in short, I was afraid.

   And would it have been worth it, after all,
After the cups, the marmalade, the tea,
Among the porcelain, among some talk of you and me,
Would it have been worth while,   90
To have bitten off the matter with a smile,
To have squeezed the universe into a ball[1]
To roll it toward some overwhelming question,
To say: "I am Lazarus,[2] come from the dead,
Come back to tell you all, I shall tell you all"—   95
If one, settling a pillow by her head,
   Should say:"That is not what I meant at all.
   That is not it, at all."

   And would it have been worth it, after all,
Would it have been worth while,   100
After the sunsets and the dooryards and the sprinkled streets,
After the novels, after the teacups, after the skirts that trail along the
      floor—
And this, and so much more?—
It is impossible to say just what I mean!
But as if a magic lantern[3] threw the nerves in patterns on a screen: 105
Would it have been worth while
If one, settling a pillow or throwing off a shawl,
And turning toward the window, should say:
   "That is not it at all,
   That is not what I meant, at all."   110

                . . . . . .

No! I am not Prince Hamlet, nor was meant to be;
Am an attendant lord,[4] one that will do
To swell a progress,[5] start a scene or two,
Advise the prince; no doubt, an easy tool,
Deferential, glad to be of use,   115
Politic, cautious, and meticulous;
Full of high sentence, but a bit obtuse;
At times, indeed, almost ridiculous—
Almost, at times, the Fool.

   I grow old . . . I grow old . . .   120
I shall wear the bottoms of my trousers rolled.

---

1. See Marvell's "To His Coy Mistress," lines 41–42: "Let us roll all our strength and all / our sweetness up into one ball. . . ."
2. One Lazarus was raised from the dead by Jesus (see *John* 1:1 to 2:2), and another (in the parable of the rich man Dives) is discussed in terms of returning from the dead to warn the living (*Luke* 16:19–31).
3. A nonelectric projector used as early as the 17th century.
4. Like Polonius in *Hamlet*, who is full of maxims ("high sentence," line 117).
5. Procession of state.

Shall I part my hair behind? Do I dare to eat a peach?
I shall wear white flannel trousers, and walk upon the beach.
I have heard the mermaids singing, each to each.

I do not think that they will sing to me.   125

I have seen them riding seaward on the waves
Combing the white hair of the waves blown back
When the wind blows the water white and black.

We have lingered in the chambers of the sea
By sea-girls wreathed with seaweed red and brown   130
Till human voices wake us, and we drown.

1917

JULIA FIELDS

Madness One Monday Evening

Late that mad Monday evening
I made mermaids come from the sea
As the block sky sat
Upon the waves
And night came   5
Creeping up to me

(I tell you I made mermaids
Come from the sea)

The green waves lulled and rolled
As I sat by the locust tree   10
And the bright glare of the neon world
Sent gas-words bursting free—
Their spewed splendor fell on the billows
And gaudy it grew to me
As I sat up upon the shore   15
And made mermaids come from the sea.

1964

ROBERT FROST

Birches

When I see birches bend to left and right
Across the lines of straighter darker trees,

I like to think some boy's been swinging them.
But swinging doesn't bend them down to stay
As ice storms do. Often you must have seen them 5
Loaded with ice a sunny winter morning
After a rain. They click upon themselves
As the breeze rises, and turn many-colored
As the stir cracks and crazes their enamel.
Soon the sun's warmth makes them shed crystal shells 10
Shattering and avalanching on the snow crust—
Such heaps of broken glass to sweep away
You'd think the inner dome of heaven had fallen.
They are dragged to the withered bracken by the load,
And they seem not to break; though once they are bowed 15
So low for long, they never right themselves:
You may see their trunks arching in the woods
Years afterwards, trailing their leaves on the ground
Like girls on hands and knees that throw their hair
Before them over their heads to dry in the sun. 20
But I was going to say when Truth broke in
With all her matter of fact about the ice storm,
I should prefer to have some boy bend them
As he went out and in to fetch the cows—
Some boy too far from town to learn baseball, 25
Whose only play was what he found himself,
Summer or winter, and could play alone.
One by one he subdued his father's trees
By riding them down over and over again
Until he took the stiffness out of them, 30
And not one but hung limp, not one was left
For him to conquer. He learned all there was
To learn about not launching out too soon
And so not carrying the tree away
Clear to the ground. He always kept his poise 35
To the top branches, climbing carefully
With the same pains you use to fill a cup
Up to the brim, and even above the brim.
Then he flung outward, feet first, with a swish,
Kicking his way down through the air to the ground. 40
So was I once myself a swinger of birches.
And so I dream of going back to be.
It's when I'm weary of considerations,
And life is too much like a pathless wood
Where your face burns and tickles with the cobwebs 45
Broken across it, and one eye is weeping
From a twig's having lashed across it open.
I'd like to get away from earth awhile
And then come back to it and begin over.
May no fate willfully misunderstand me 50
And half grant what I wish and snatch me away
Not to return. Earth's the right place for love:
I don't know where it's likely to go better.
I'd like to go by climbing a birch tree,

And climb black branches up a snow-white trunk   55
Toward heaven, till the tree could bear no more,
But dipped its top and set me down again.
That would be good both going and coming back.
One could do worse than be a swinger of birches.

1916

ROBERT FROST

Departmental

An ant on the tablecloth
Ran into a dormant moth
Of many times his size.
He showed not the least surprise.
His business wasn't with such.   5
He gave it scarcely a touch,
And was off on his duty run.
Yet if he encountered one
Of the hive's enquiry squad
Whose work is to find out God   10
And the nature of time and space,
He would put him onto the case.
Ants are a curious race;
One crossing with hurried tread
The body of one of their dead   15
Isn't given a moment's arrest—
Seems not even impressed.
But he no doubt reports to any
With whom he crosses antennae,
And they no doubt report   20
To the higher-up at court.
Then word goes forth in Formic:[6]
"Death's come to Jerry McCormic,
Our selfless forager Jerry.
Will the special Janizary[7]   25
Whose office it is to bury
The dead of the commissary
Go bring him home to his people.
Lay him in state on a sepal.
Wrap him for shroud in a petal.   30
Embalm him with ichor of nettle.
This is the word of your Queen."
And presently on the scene
Appears a solemn mortician;

6, I.e., "ant language." Technically,
formic is an acid in a fluid emitted by
ants.
7. Military escort for travelers.

And taking formal position,   35
With feelers calmly atwiddle,
Seizes the dead by the middle,
And heaving him high in air,
Carries him out of there.
No one stands round to stare.   40
It is nobody else's affair.

It couldn't be called ungentle.
But how thoroughly departmental.

1936

ROBERT FROST

Design

I found a dimpled spider, fat and white,
On a white heal-all,[8] holding up a moth
Like a white piece of rigid satin cloth—
Assorted characters of death and blight
Mixed ready to begin the morning right,   5
Like the ingredients of a witches' broth—
A snow-drop spider, a flower like a froth,
And dead wings carried like a paper kite.

What had that flower to do with being white,
The wayside blue and innocent heal-all?   10
What brought the kindred spider to that height,
Then steered the white moth thither in the night?
What but design of darkness to appall?—
If design govern in a thing so small.

1936

ROBERT FROST

Provide, Provide

The witch that came (the withered hag)
To wash the steps with pail and rag,
Was once the beauty Abishag,[9]

---

8. A plant, also called the "all-heal" and "self-heal," with tightly clustered violet-blue flowers.

9. In *1 Kings* 1, a beautiful young woman named Abishag is brought to the aged King David.

The picture pride of Hollywood.
Too many fall from great and good   5
For you to doubt the likelihood.

Die early and avoid the fate.
Or if predestined to die late,
Make up your mind to die in state.[1]

Make the whole stock exchange your own!   10
If need be occupy a throne,
Where nobody can call *you* crone.

Some have relied on what they knew,
Others on being simply true.
What worked for them might work for you.   15

No memory of having starred
Atones for later disregard
Or keeps the end from being hard.

Better to go down dignified
With boughten friendship at your side   20
Than none at all. Provide, provide!

                                                    1936

ROBERT FROST

Range-Finding

The battle rent a cobweb diamond-strung
And cut a flower beside a groundbird's nest
Before it stained a single human breast.
The stricken flower bent double and so hung.
And still the bird revisited her young.   5
A butterfly its fall had dispossessed,
A moment sought in air his flower of rest,
Then lightly stooped to it and fluttering clung.
On the bare upland pasture there had spread
O'ernight 'twixt mullein[2] stalks a wheel of thread 10
And straining cables wet with silver dew.
A sudden passing bullet shook it dry.
The indwelling spider ran to greet the fly,
But finding nothing, sullenly withdrew.

                                                    1916

1. Ceremoniously, with official honor.   2. Weed.

ALLEN GINSBERG

Howl (Part I)[3]

(for Carl Solomon)

I saw the best minds of my generation destroyed by madness, starving
      hysterical naked,
dragging themselves through the negro streets at dawn looking for an
      angry fix,
angelheaded hipsters burning for the ancient heavenly connection to
      the starry dynamo in the machinery of night,
who poverty and tatters and hollow-eyed and high sat up smoking in
      the supernatural darkness of cold-water flats[4] floating across
      the tops of cities contemplating jazz,
who bared their brains to Heaven under the El[5] and saw Mohammedan
      angels staggering on tenement roofs illuminated,   5
who passed through universities with radiant cool eyes hallucinating
      Arkansas and Blake-light tragedy among the scholars of war,
who were expelled from the academies for crazy & publishing obscene
      odes on the windows of the skull,[6]
who cowered in unshaven rooms in underwear, burning their money
      in wastebaskets and listening to the Terror through the wall,
who got busted in their pubic beards returning through Laredo[7] with
      a belt of marijuana for New York,
who ate fire in paint hotels or drank turpentine in Paradise Alley,[8]
      death, or purgatoried their torsos night after night   10
with dreams, with drugs, with waking nightmares, alcohol and cock
      and endless balls,
incomparable blind streets of shuddering cloud and lightning in the
      mind leaping toward poles of Canada & Paterson,[9] illuminat-
      ing all the motionless world of Time between,
Peyote solidities of halls, backyard green tree cemetery dawns, wine
      drunkenness over the rooftops, storefront boroughs of teahead
      joyride neon blinking traffic light, sun and moon and tree
      vibrations in the roaring winter dusks of Brooklyn, ashcan
      rantings and kind king light of mind,
who chained themselves to subways for the endless ride from Battery
      to holy Bronx[1] on benzedrine until the noise of wheels and

---

3. Often regarded as the classic state-
ment of the Beat Generation, this poem
chronicles the counterculture experiences
and feelings of the author and many of his
friends in the 1950s. Various experiences
of different people are often conflated in
the telling, and the poem abounds in ref-
erences to drugs, mystical experiences, en-
counters with psychiatric clinics and men-
tal hospitals, and locales where the Beats
lived, especially in New York City. Gins-
berg met Carl Solomon, to whom the poem
is dedicated, at the Columbia Psychiatric
Institute in 1949; many of the experiences
alluded to are said to be Solomon's, al-
though the account he gave Ginsberg of
his life and adventures was part fiction.

4. Apartments without hot water.
5. Elevated railway.
6. Ginsberg was suspended from Co-
lumbia University in 1945 for tracing ob-
scenities in the grime on his dormitory
windows—in an effort to get the maid to
clean them.
7. A Texas border city.
8. A slum courtyard in the lower East
Side of New York—the setting for *The Sub-
terraneans*, a novel by another Beat writer,
Jack Kerouac (1922–69).
9. Paterson, N.J., where Ginsberg was
born.
1. Opposite ends of a north-south sub-
way line.

children brought them down shuddering mouth-wracked and
battered bleak of brain all drained of brilliance in the drear
light of Zoo,

who sank all night in submarine light of Bickford's [2] floated out and sat
through the stale beer afternoon in desolate Fugazzi's, [3]
listening to the crack of doom on the hydrogen jukebox,   15

who talked continuously seventy hours from park to pad to bar to
Bellevue [4] to museum to the Brooklyn Bridge,

a lost battalion of platonic conversationalists jumping down the stoops
off fire escapes off windowsills off Empire State out of the
moon,

yacketayakking screaming vomiting whispering facts and memories
and anecdotes and eyeball kicks and shocks of hospitals and
jails and wars,

whole intellects disgorged in total recall for seven days and nights with
brilliant eyes, meat for the Synagogue cast on the pavement,

who vanished into nowhere Zen New Jersey leaving a trail of ambiguous
picture postcards of Atlantic City Hall,   20

suffering Eastern sweats and Tangerian bone-grindings and migraines
of China under junk-withdrawal in Newark's bleak furnished
room,

who wandered around and around at midnight in the railroad yard
wondering where to go, and went, leaving no broken hearts,

who lit cigarettes in boxcars boxcars boxcars racketing through snow
toward lonesome farms in grandfather night,

who studied Plotinus Poe St. John of the Cross telepathy and bop
kaballa [5] because the cosmos instinctively vibrated at their
feet in Kansas,

who loned it through the streets of Idaho seeking visionary indian
angels who were visionary indian angels,   25

who thought they were only mad when Baltimore gleamed in super-
natural ecstasy,

who jumped in limousines with the Chinaman of Oklahoma on the
impulse of winter midnight streetlight smalltown rain,

who lounged hungry and lonesome through Houston seeking jazz or
sex or soup, and followed the brilliant Spaniard to converse
about America and Eternity, a hopeless task, and so took ship
to Africa,

who disappeared into the volcanoes of Mexico leaving behind nothing
but the shadow of dungarees and the lava and ash of poetry
scattered in fireplace Chicago,

who reappeared on the West Coast investigating the F.B.I. in beards
and shorts with big pacifist eyes sexy in their dark skin passing
out incomprehensible leaflets,   30

2. A chain of all-night cafeterias, where
Ginsberg worked while he was in college.
3. A bar near Greenwich Village in
New York.
4. New York's public hospital, the re-
ceiving center for mental patients.
5. Or cabala: an occult theosophy based
on mystical interpretations of Hebraic

Scriptures. Bop (or bebop) was a kind of
modern jazz popular just after World War
II. St. John of the Cross (1542–1591),
Spanish mystic and poet. Poe: Edgar Allan
Poe (1809–1849), American poet and au-
thor of Gothic and supernatural tales.
Plotinus: (205?–270?) Neo-Platonist phi-
losopher.

who burned cigarette holes in their arms protesting the narcotic
      tobacco haze of Capitalism,

who distributed Supercommunist pamphlets in Union Square[6] weeping
      and undressing while the sirens of Los Alamos wailed them
      down, and wailed down Wall, and the Staten Ferry also
      wailed,

who broke down crying in white gymnasiums naked and trembling
      before the machinery of other skeletons,

who bit detectives in the neck and shrieked with delight in policecars
      for committing no crime but their own wild cooking
      pederasty and intoxication,

who howled on their knees in the subway and were dragged off the
      roof waving genitals and manuscripts,   35

who let themselves be fucked in the ass by saintly motorcyclists, and
      screamed with joy,

who blew and were blown by those human seraphim, the sailors,
      caresses of Atlantic and Caribbean love,

who balled in the morning in the evenings in rosegardens and the grass
      of public parks and cemeteries scattering their semen freely
      to whomever come who may,

who hiccupped endlessly trying to giggle but wound up with a sob
      behind a partition in a Turkish Bath when the blonde &
      naked angel came to pierce them with a sword,

who lost their loveboys to the three old shrews of fate the one eyed
      shrew of the heterosexual dollar the one eyed shrew that
      winks out of the womb and the one eyed shrew that does
      nothing but sit on her ass and snip the intellectual golden
      threads of the craftsman's loom,   40

who copulated ecstatic and insatiate with a bottle of beer a sweetheart
      a package of cigarettes a candle and fell off the bed, and
      continued along the floor and down the hall and ended
      fainting on the wall with a vision of ultimate cunt and come
      eluding the last gyzym of consciousness,

who sweetened the snatches of a million girls trembling in the sunset,
      and were red eyed in the morning but prepared to sweeten
      the snatch of the sunrise, flashing buttocks under barns and
      naked in the lake,

who went out whoring through Colorado in myriad stolen night-cars,[7]
      N.C., secret hero of these poems, cocksman and Adonis of
      Denver—joy to the memory of his innumberable lays of girls
      in empty lots & diner backyards, moviehouses' rickety rows,
      on mountaintops in caves or with gaunt waitresses in familiar
      roadside lonely petticoat upliftings & especially secret gas-
      station solipsisms of johns, & hometown alleys too,

who faded out in vast sordid movies, were shifted in dreams, woke on
      a sudden Manhattan, and picked themselves up out of

---

6. Where radical speeches and demonstrations were centered in New York City in the 1930s. Los Alamos: where the atomic bomb was developed. Wall: Wall Street, New York's financial district.

7. Neal Cassady (1926–1968), Denver hipster whose picaresque adventures with Jack Kerouac are recorded in the latter's novel, *On the Road* (1957). Adonis: a beautiful youth, loved by Aphrodite in Greek mythology.

basements hungover with heartless Tokay and horrors of
  Third Avenue iron dreams & stumbled to unemployment
  offices,

who walked all night with their shoes full of blood on the snowbank
  docks waiting for a door in the East River to open to a room
  full of steamheat and opium,[8]   45

who created great suicidal dramas on the apartment cliff-banks of the
  Hudson under the wartime blue floodlight of the moon &
  their heads shall be crowned with laurel in oblivion,

who ate the lamb stew of the imagination or digested the crab at the
  muddy bottom of the rivers of Bowery,[9]

who wept at the romance of the streets with their pushcarts full of
  onions and bad music,

who sat in boxes breathing in the darkness under the bridge, and rose
  up to build harpsichords in their lofts,

who coughed on the sixth floor of Harlem crowned with flame under
  the tubercular sky surrounded by orange crates of theology,   50

who scribbled all night rocking and rolling over lofty incantations
  which in the yellow morning were stanzas of gibberish,

who cooked rotten animals lung heart feet tail borsht & tortillas dream-
  ing of the pure vegetable kingdom,

who plunged themselves under meat trucks looking for an egg,

who threw their watches off the roof to cast their ballot for Eternity
  outside of Time, & alarm clocks fell on their heads every day
  for the next decade,

who cut their wrists three times successively unsuccessfully, gave up
  and were forced to open antique stores where they thought
  they were growing old and cried,   55

who were burned alive in their innocent flannel suits on Madison
  Avenue[1] amid blasts of leaden verse & the tanked-up clatter
  of the iron regiments of fashion & the nitroglycerine shrieks
  of the fairies of advertising & the mustard gas of sinister
  intelligent editors, or were run down by the drunken taxicabs
  of Absolute Reality,

who jumped off the Brooklyn Bridge this actually happened and
  walked away unknown and forgotten into the ghostly daze of
  Chinatown soup alleyways & firetrucks, not even one free
  beer,

who sang out of their windows in despair fell out of the subway win-
  dow, jumped in the filthy Passaic,[2] leaped on negroes, cried
  all over the street, danced on broken wineglasses barefoot
  smashed phonograph records of nostalgic European 1930's
  German jazz finished the whiskey and threw up groaning
  into the bloody toilet, moans in their ears and the blast of
  colossal steamwhistles,

---

8. Herbert E. Huncke (1922–   ), a
drug addict, petty thief, and con artist,
arrived from jail into such a scene in Gins-
berg's apartment.
9. New York City's skid row.
1. The center of New York's advertising
industry, where William Burroughs (1914–
   ), author of *Junkie* (1953) and later
Naked Lunch (1962) had worked in the
1930s.
2. The river that runs through Pater-
son, N.J.

who barreled down the highways of the past journeying to each other's
    hotrod-Golgotha[3] jail-solitude watch or Birmingham jazz in-
    carnation,
who drove crosscountry seventytwo hours to find out if I had a vision
    or you had a vision or he had a vision to find out Eternity,   60
who journeyed to Denver, who died in Denver, who came back to
    Denver & waited in vain, who watched over Denver &
    brooded & loned in Denver and finally went away to find
    out the Time, & now Denver is lonesome for her heroes,
who fell on their knees in hopeless cathedrals praying for each other's
    salvation and light and breasts, until the soul illuminated its
    hair for a second,
who crashed through their minds in jail waiting for impossible crim-
    inals with golden heads and the charm of reality in their
    hearts who sang sweet blues to Alcatraz,[4]
who retired to Mexico to cultivate a habit,[5] or Rocky Mount to tender
    Buddha[6] or Tangiers to boys[7] or Southern Pacific to the
    black locomotive[8] or Harvard to Narcissus to Woodlawn[9] to
    the daisychain or grave,
who demanded sanity trials accusing the radio of hypnotism & were
    left with their insanity & their hands & a hung jury,   65
who threw potato salad at CCNY[1] lectures on Dadaism and subse-
    quently presented themselves on the granite steps of the
    madhouse with shaven heads and harlequin speech of suicide,
    demanding instantaneous lobotomy,
and who were given instead the concrete void of insulin metrasol
    electricity hydrotherapy psychotherapy occupational therapy
    pingpong & amnesia,
who in humorless protest overturned only one symbolic pingpong
    table, resting briefly in catatonia,
returning years later truly bald except for a wig of blood, and tears
    and fingers, to the visible madman doom of the wards of the
    madtowns of the East,
Pilgrim State's Rockland's and Greystone's[2] foetid halls, bickering
    with the echoes of the soul, rocking and rolling in the mid-
    night solitude-bench dolmen-realms of love, dream of life a
    nightmare, bodies turned to stone as heavy as the moon,   70
with mother finally******, and the last fantastic book flung out of the
    tenement window, and the last door closed at 4 AM and the
    last telephone slammed at the wall in reply and the last
    furnished room emptied down to the last piece of mental
    furniture, a yellow paper rose twisted on a wire hanger in

3. The hill where Christ was crucified; the name means "place of the skull."
4. An island in San Francisco Bay where a federal prison was located.
5. Burroughs.
6. Kerouac was then living in Rocky Mount, N.C.
7. Burroughs as well as Ginsberg had lived for a time in Tangier, Morocco.
8. Cassady had worked as a brakeman on the Southern Pacific Railroad.

9. A Bronx cemetery.
1. City College of New York. Dadaism: an early 20th century artistic and literary movement which rebelled against traditional forms and developed techniques based on intuition, irrationality, and chance.
2. Mental hospitals near New York. Ginsberg's mother was a patient at Greystone, and Carl Solomon at Pilgrim State and Rockland.

the closet, and even that imaginary, nothing but a hopeful
    little bit of hallucination—
ah, Carl, while you are not safe I am not safe, and now you're really
    in the total animal soup of time—
and who therefore ran through the icy streets obsessed with a sudden
    flash of the alchemy of the use of the ellipse the catalog the
    meter & the vibrating plane,
who dreamt and made incarnate gaps in Time & Space through images
    juxtaposed, and trapped the archangel of the soul between 2
    visual images and joined the elemental verbs and set the
    noun and dash of consciousness together jumping with sensa-
    tion of Pater Omnipotens Aeterna Deus[3]
to recreate the syntax and measure of poor human prose and stand
    before you speechless and intelligent and shaking with shame,
    rejected yet confessing out the soul to conform to the rhythm
    of thought in his naked and endless head,   75
the madman bum and angel beat in Time, unknown, yet putting down
    here what might be left to say in time come after death,
and rose reincarnate in the ghostly clothes of jazz in the goldhorn
    shadow of the band and blew the suffering of America's
    naked mind for love into an eli eli lamma lamma sabacthani[4]
    saxophone cry that shivered the cities down to the last radio
with the absolute heart of the poem of life butchered out of their own
    bodies good to eat a thousand years.

1955

THOMAS HARDY

Channel Firing[5]

That night your great guns, unawares,
Shook all our coffins as we lay,
And broke the chancel window squares,[6]
We thought it was the Judgment-day[7]

And sat upright. While drearisome   5
Arose the howl of wakened hounds:
The mouse let fall the altar-crumb,[8]
The worms drew back into the mounds,

3. Latin for "All-powerful Father, Eter-
nal God." Ginsberg apparently quotes the
phrase from one of Paul Cézanne's (1839–
1906) letters, in which it is used to cele-
brate the sensations derived from observ-
ing the natural world. Ginsberg later said
that *Howl* was, in part, an homage to
Cézanne and a verbal attempt to imitate
the method of his impressionist paintings.
4. According to *Matthew* 27:46 and
Mark 15:34, Christ's last words on the
cross: "My God, my God, why have you
forsaken me?"
5. Naval practice on the English Chan-
nel preceded the outbreak of World War I
in the summer of 1914.
6. The windows near the altar in a
church.
7. When, according to tradition, the
dead will be awakened.
8. Breadcrumbs from the sacrament.

The glebe cow[9] drooled. Till God called, "No;
It's gunnery practice out at sea   10
Just as before you went below;
The world is as it used to be:

"All nations striving strong to make
Red war yet redder. Mad as hatters
They do no more for Christés sake   15
Than you who are helpless in such matters.

"That this is not the judgment-hour
For some of them's a blessed thing,
For if it were they'd have to scour
Hell's floor for so much threatening . . .   20

"Ha, ha. It will be warmer when
I blow the trumpet (if indeed
I ever do; for you are men,
And rest eternal sorely need)."

So down we lay again. "I wonder,   25
Will the world ever saner be,"
Said one, "than when He sent us under
In our indifferent century!"

And many a skeleton shook his head.
"Instead of preaching forty year,"   30
My neighbor Parson Thirdly said,
"I wish I had stuck to pipes and beer."

Again the guns disturbed the hour,
Roaring their readiness to avenge.
As far inland as Stourton Tower,   35
And Camelot, and starlit Stonehenge.[1]

April, 1914

THOMAS HARDY

The Darkling Thrush

I leant upon a coppice gate
    When Frost was specter gray,

9. Parish cow pastured on the meadow next to the churchyard.
1. Stourton Tower, built in the 18th century to commemorate King Alfred's ninth-century victory over the Danes, in Stourhead Park, Wiltshire. Camelot is the legendary site of King Arthur's court, said to have been in Cornwall or Somerset. Stonehenge, a circular formation of upright stones dating from about 1800 B.C., is on Salisbury Plain, Wiltshire; it is thought to have been a ceremonial site for political and religious occasions or an early scientific experiment in astronomy.

And Winter's dregs made desolate
    The weakening eye of day.
The tangled bine-stems scored the sky   5
    Like strings of broken lyres,
And all mankind that haunted nigh
    Had sought their household fires.

The land's sharp features seemed to be
    The Century's corpse outleant,   10
His crypt the cloudy canopy,
    The wind his death-lament.
The ancient pulse of germ and birth
    Was shrunken hard and dry,
And every spirit upon earth   15
    Seemed fervorless as I.

At once a voice arose among
    The bleak twigs overhead
In a full-hearted evensong
    Of joy illimited;   20
An aged thrush, frail, gaunt, and small,
    In blast-beruffled plume,
Had chosen thus to fling his soul
    Upon the growing gloom.

So little cause for carolings   25
    Of such ecstatic sound
Was written on terrestrial things
    Afar or nigh around,
That I could think there trembled through
    His happy good-night air   30
Some blessed Hope, whereof he knew
    And I was unaware.

December 31, 1900

THOMAS HARDY

During Wind and Rain

They sing their dearest songs—
    He, she, all of them—yea,
Treble and tenor and bass,
    And one to play;
With the candles mooning each face. . . .   5
    Ah, no; the years O!
How the sick leaves reel down in throngs!

They clear the creeping moss—
    Elders and juniors—aye,

Making the pathway neat   10
    And the garden gay;
And they build a shady seat. . . .
    Ah, no; the years, the years;
See, the white stormbirds wing across!

They are blithely breakfasting all—   15
Men and maidens—yea,
Under the summer tree,
    With a glimpse of the bay,
While pet fowl come to the knee. . . .
    Ah, no; the years O!   20
And the rotten rose is ripped from the wall.

They change to a high new house,
He, she, all of them—aye,
Clocks and carpets, and chairs
    On the lawn all day,   25
And brightest things that are theirs. . . .
    Ah, no; the years, the years;
Down their carved names the rain drop ploughs.

1917

THOMAS HARDY

Hap[2]

If but some vengeful god would call to me
From up the sky, and laugh: "Thou suffering thing,
Know that thy sorrow is my ecstasy,
That thy love's loss is my hate's profiting!"

Then would I bear it, clench myself, and die,   5
Steeled by the sense of ire unmerited;
Half-eased in that a Powerfuller than I
Had willed and meted me the tears I shed.

But not so. How arrives it[3] joy lies slain,
And why unblooms the best hope ever sown?   10
—Crass Casualty[4] obstructs the sun and rain,
And dicing Time for gladness casts a moan. . . .
These purblind Doomsters[5] had as readily strown
Blisses about my pilgrimage as pain.

1866

2. Chance.   4. Chance.
3. How does it happen that.   5. Those who decide one's fate.

THOMAS HARDY

The Man He Killed

Had he and I but met
   By some old ancient inn,
We should have sat us down to wet
   Right many a nipperkin![6]

But ranged as infantry,   5
   And staring face to face,
I shot at him as he at me,
   And killed him in his place.

I shot him dead because—
   Because he was my foe,   10
Just so: my foe of course he was;
   That's clear enough; although

He thought he'd 'list,[7] perhaps,
   Off-hand like—just as I—
Was out of work—had sold his traps—[8]   15
   No other reason why.

Yes; quaint and curious war is!
   You shoot a fellow down
You'd treat if met where any bar is,
   Or help to half-a-crown.   20

1902

ANTHONY HECHT

"It Out-Herods Herod. Pray You, Avoid It."[9]

Tonight my children hunch
Toward their Western, and are glad
As, with a Sunday punch,
The Good casts out the Bad.

And in their fairy tales   5
The warty giant and witch

6. A measure or vessel for liquor, containing less than a half pint.
7. Enlist.
8. Personal belongings.
9. *Hamlet*, Act III, sc. ii. Hamlet's advice to the actors about to perform "The Mousetrap" includes a caution against overacting and excessive displays of passion. In medieval mystery plays, the character of Herod was portrayed as wild and bombastic, and the actor who played the part was sometimes allowed to improvise extravagant and spectacular behavior.

Get sealed in doorless jails
And the match-girl strikes it rich.

I've made myself a drink.
The giant and witch are set   10
To bust out of the clink
When my children have gone to bed.

All frequencies are loud
With signals of despair;
In flash and morse they crowd   15
The rondure of the air.

For the wicked have grown strong,
Their numbers mock at death,
Their cow brings forth its young,
Their bull engendereth.   20

Their very fund of strength,
Satan, bestrides the globe;
He stalks its breadth and length
And finds out even Job.[1]

Yet by quite other laws   25
My children make their case;
Half God, half Santa Claus,
But with my voice and face,

A hero comes to save
The poorman, beggarman, thief,   30
And make the world behave
And put an end to grief.

And that their sleep be sound
I say this childermas[2]
Who could not, at one time,   35
Have saved them from the gas.

1968

1. According to the *Book of Job* 1:7–12, Satan has been "going to and fro in the earth, and . . . walking up and down in it" before finding Job, a man of singular righteousness, to torment and tempt.

2. The festival of the Holy Innocents (Childermas) commemmorates Herod's slaughter of the children; see *Matthew* 2:16.

ANTHONY HECHT

A Lot of Night Music[3]

Even a Pyrrhonist[4]
Who knows only that he can never know
    (But adores a paradox)
Would admit it's getting dark. Pale as a wrist-
        Watch numeral glow,   5
Fireflies build a sky among the phlox,

        Imparting their faint light
Conservatively only to themselves.
        Earthmurk and flowerscent
Sweeten the homes of ants. Comes on the night   10
        When the mind rockets and delves
In blind hyperbolas of its own bent.

        Above, the moon at large,
Muse-goddess, slightly polluted by the runs
        Of American astronauts,   15
(Poor, poxed Diana, laid open to the charge
        Of social Actaeons)[5]
Mildly solicits our petty cash and thoughts.

        At once with their votive mites,
Out of the woods and woodwork poets come,   20
        Hauling their truths and booty,
Each one a Phosphor, writing by his own lights,
        And with a diesel hum
Of mosquitoes or priests, proffer their wordy duty.

        They speak in tongues, no doubt;   25
High glossolalia, runic gibberish.
        Some are like desert saints,
Wheat-germ ascetics, draped in pelt and clout.
        Some come in schools, like fish.
These make their litany of dark complaints;   30
        Those laugh and rejoice
At liberation from the bonds of gender,
        Race, morals and mind,
As well as meter, rhyme and the human voice.
        Still others strive to render   35
The cross-word world in perfectly declined

        Pronouns, starting with ME.
Yet there are honest voices to be heard:

---

3. Mozart wrote a lengthy four-part composition modestly called *Eine Kleine Nachtmusik* (a little night music).
4. Skeptic.

5. In Greek mythology, Actaeon (a huntsman) surprised Diana, goddess of the moon and of hunting, while she was bathing.

The crickets keep their vigil
Among the grass; in some invisible tree   40
Anonymously a bird
Whistles a fioritura, a light, vestigial

Reminder of a time,
An Aesopic Age when all the beasts were moral
And taught their ways to men;   45
Some herbal dream, some chlorophyll sublime
In which Apollo's laurel[6]
Blooms in a world made innocent again.

1977

GERARD MANLEY HOPKINS

The Windhover[7]

To Christ Our Lord

I caught this morning morning's minion,[8] king-
    dom of daylight's dauphin,[9] dapple-dawn-drawn Falcon, in his
        riding
    Of the rolling level underneath him steady air, and striding
High there, how he rung upon the rein of a wimpling[1] wing
In his ecstasy! then off, off forth on swing,   5
    As a skate's heel sweeps smooth on a bow-bend: the hurl and
        gliding
Rebuffed the big wind. My heart in hiding
Stirred for a bird,—the achieve of, the mastery of the thing!

Brute beauty and valor and act, oh, air, pride, plume, here
    Buckle![2] AND the fire that breaks from thee then, a billion   10
Times told lovelier, more dangerous, O my chevalier![3]

    No wonder of it: sheér plód makes plow down sillion[4]
Shine, and blue-bleak embers, ah my dear,
    Fall, gall themselves, and gash gold-vermilion.

1877

---

6. The symbol of excellence in poetry, and believed by the ancients to communicate the spirit of poetry and prophecy. Apollo was the Greek and Roman god of music and poetry as part of his function as sun-god and lifegiver.
7. A small hawk, the kestrel, which habitually hovers in the air, headed into the wind.
8. Favorite, beloved.

9. Heir to regal splendor.
1. Rippling.
2. Several meanings may apply: to join closely, to prepare for battle, to grapple with, to collapse.
3. Horseman, knight.
4. The narrow strip of land between furrows in an open field divided for separate cultivation.

A. E. HOUSMAN

1887[5]

From Clee[6] to heaven the beacon burns,[7]
  The shires[8] have seen it plain,
From north and south the sign returns
  And beacons burn again.

Look left, look right, the hills are bright,   5
  The dales are light between,
Because 'tis fifty years tonight
  That God has saved the Queen.

Now, when the flame they watch not towers
  About the soil they trod,   10
Lads, we'll remember friends of ours
  Who shared the work with God.

To skies that knit their heartstrings right,
  To fields that bred them brave,
The saviors come not home tonight: 15
  Themselves they could not save.[9]

It dawns in Asia, tombstones show
  And Shropshire[1] names are read;
And the Nile spills his overflow
  Beside the Severn's dead.[2]   20

We pledge in peace by farm and town
  The Queen they served in war,
And fire the beacons up and down
  The land they perished for.

"God save the Queen" we living sing,   25
  From height to height 'tis heard;
And with the rest your voices ring,
  Lads of the Fifty-third.[3]

Oh, God will save her, fear you not:
  Be you the men you've been,   30
Get you the sons your fathers got,
  And God will save the Queen.

1896

---

5. Queen Victoria's golden jubilee.
6. A small town in Shropshire.
7. Fires were lighted all over England in honor of the jubilee.
8. The provinces. ("The shires" was applied to other parts of England by the inhabitants of the London area.)
9. According to *Matthew* 25:42 and *Mark* 15:31, the scribes and elders or chief priests said of the crucified Jesus: "He saved others; himself he cannot save."
1. The volume containing this poem was entitled *A Shropshire Lad*.
2. The Severn is the chief river through Shropshire.
3. A Shropshire regiment.

A. E. HOUSMAN

Epitaph on an Army of Mercenaries

These, in the day when heaven was falling,
　The hour when earth's foundations fled,
Followed their mercenary calling
　And took their wages and are dead.

Their shoulders held the sky suspended;　　　　5
　They stood, and earth's foundations stay;
What God abandoned, these defended,
　And saved the sum of things for pay.

p. 1917

RICHARD HUGO

To Women

You start it all. You are lovely.
We look at you and we flow.
So a line begins, on the page, on air,
in the all of self. We have misused you,
invested you with primal sin. You bleed　　　　5
for our regret we are not more.
The dragon wins. We come home and sob
and you hold us and say we are brave
and in the future will do better.
So far, so good.　　　　10

Now some of you want out and I don't
blame you, not a tiny bit. You've caught on.
You have the right to veer off flaming
in a new direction, mud flat and diamond mine,
clavicord and dead drum. Whatever.　　　　15
Please know our need remains the same.
It's a new game every time, one on one.

In me today is less rage than ever, less hurt.
When I imagine some good woman young
I no longer imagine her cringing　　　　20
in cornstalks, cruel father four rows away
beating corn leaves aside with a club.
That is release you never expected
from a past you never knew you had.
My horse is not sure he can make it　　　　25
to the next star. You are free.

1980

BEN JONSON

The Hourglass

Do but consider this small dust,
  Here running in the glass,
    By atoms[4] moved;
Could you believe that this,
  The body ever was   5
    Of one that loved?
And in his mistress' flame, playing like a fly,[5]
  Turned to cinders by her eye?
    Yes; and in death, as life, unblest,
      To have't expressed,
  Even ashes of lovers find no rest.

1640

BEN JONSON

Inviting a Friend to Supper[6]

Tonight, grave sir, both my poor house and I
Do equally desire your company;
Not that we think us worthy such a guest,
But that your worth will dignify our feast,
With those that come, whose grace may make that seem   5
Something, which else could hope for no esteem.
It is the fair acceptance, sir, creates
The entertainment perfect, not the cates.[7]
Yet shall you have, to rectify[8] your palate,
An olive, capers, or some better salad   10
Ushering the mutton; with a short-legged hen,
If we can get her, full of eggs; and then,
Lemons, and wine for sauce: to these, a cony[9]
Is not to be despaired of for our money;
And though fowl now be scarce, yet there are clerks,   15
The sky not falling,[1] think we may have larks.
I'll tell you of more, and lie, so you will come:
Of partridge, pheasant, woodcock, of which some
May yet be there; and godwit if we can:
Gnat, rail, and ruff,[2] too. Howsoe'er,[3] my man[4]   20

---

4. Hypothetical bodies, thought to be incapable of further division and thus among the ultimate particles of matter (OED).
5. Any two-winged insect (including the moth and butterfly), a symbol of transitory life, especially in its self-destructive attraction to flame.
6. A 17th-century version of Horace, *Epistles* I, v.

7. Delicacies.
8. Restore to healthy condition.
9. Rabbit.
1. If the sky doesn't fall.
2. Fowl. "Gnat" was a nickname for the Lesser Tern.
3. In any case.
4. Servant.

Shall read a piece of Vergil, Tacitus,
Livy, or of some better book to us,
Of which we'll speak our minds, amidst our meat;
And I'll profess no verses to repeat:[5]
To this, if aught appear, which I not know of,   25
That will the pastry, not my paper, show of.
Digestive cheese, and fruit there sure will be;
But that which most doth take my muse and me,
Is a pure cup of rich Canary wine,
Which is the Mermaid's[6] now, but shall be mine: 30
Of which had Horace, or Anacreon tasted,
Their lives, as do their lines, till now had lasted.
Tobacco, nectar, or the Thespian[7] spring,
Are all but Luther's beer, to[8] this I sing.
Of this we will sup free, but moderately,   35
And we will have no Pooly or Parrot[9] by;
Nor shall our cups make any guilty men,
But at our parting, we will be as when
We innocently met. No simple word
That shall be uttered at our mirthful board   40
Shall make us sad next morning, or affright
The liberty that we'll enjoy tonight.

                                                        1616

X. J. KENNEDY

First Confession

Blood thudded in my ears. I scuffed,
    Steps stubborn, to the telltale booth
Beyond whose curtained portal coughed
    The robed repositor of truth.

The slat shot back. The universe   5
    Bowed down his cratered dome to hear
Enumerated my each curse,
    The sip snitched from my old man's beer,

My sloth pride envy lechery,
    The dime held back from Peter's Pence[1]   10
With which I'd bribed my girl to pee
    That I might spy her instruments.

5. I.e., I'll pretend I won't recite poems.
6. I.e., it now belongs to the Mermaid Tavern.
7. Associated with the Muses.
8. Inferior brew compared to.

9. Known government informers.
1. Hearth money: annual contributions by Roman Catholic households for the support of the Holy See (Rome).

Hovering scale-pans when I'd done
  Settled their balance slow as silt
While in the restless dark I burned   15
  Bright as a brimstone in my guilt

Until as one feeds birds he doled[2]
  Seven Our Fathers and a Hail
Which I to double-scrub my soul
  Intoned twice at the altar rail   20

Where Sunday in seraphic[3] light
  I knelt, as full of grace as most,
And stuck my tongue out at the priest:
  A fresh roost for the Holy Ghost.

1961

PHILIP LARKIN

Annus Mirabilis[4]

Sexual intercourse began
In nineteen sixty-three
(Which was rather late for me)
Between the end of the *Chatterley* ban[5]
And the Beatles' first LP.   5

Up till then there'd only been
A sort of bargaining,
A wrangle for a ring,
A shame that started at sixteen   10
And spread to everything.

Then all at once the quarrel sank:
Everyone felt the same,
And every life became
A brilliant breaking of the bank,   15
A quite unlosable game.

So life was never better than
In nineteen sixty three
(Though just too late for me)—
Between the end of the *Chatterley* ban   20
And the Beatles' first LP.

1974

2. Set penance at.
3. Angelic.
4. Latin for "the wonderful year."
5. D. H. Lawrence's novel *Lady Chat-* *terley's Lover* had been banned in the U.S. until court rulings of the early sixties.

D. H. LAWRENCE

Piano

Softly, in the dusk, a woman is singing to me;
Taking me back down the vista of years, till I see
A child sitting under the piano, in the boom of the tingling strings
And pressing the small, poised feet of a mother who smiles as she sings.

In spite of myself, the insidious mastery of song   5
Betrays me back, till the heart of me weeps to belong
To the old Sunday evenings at home, with winter outside
And hymns in the cozy parlor, the tinkling piano our guide.

So now it is vain for the singer to burst into clamor
With the great black piano appassionato. The glamour   10
Of childish days is upon me, my manhood is cast
Down in the flood of remembrance, I weep like a child for the past.

1918

RICHARD LOVELACE

To Lucasta, Going to the Wars

Tell me not, sweet, I am unkind
    That from the nunnery
Of thy chaste breast and quiet mind,
    To war and arms I fly.

True, a new mistress now I chase,   5
    The first foe in the field;
And with a stronger faith embrace
    A sword, a horse, a shield.

Yet this inconstancy is such
    As you too shall adore;   10
I could not love thee, dear, so much,
    Loved I not Honor more.

1649

ROBERT LOWELL

Skunk Hour

(For Elizabeth Bishop)

Nautilus Island's hermit
heiress still lives through winter in her Spartan cottage;
her sheep still graze above the sea.
Her son's a bishop. Her farmer
is first selectman[6] in our village,   5
she's in her dotage.

Thirsting for
the hierarchic privacy
of Queen Victoria's century,
she buys up all   10
the eyesores facing her shore,
and lets them fall.

The season's ill—
we've lost our summer millionaire,
who seemed to leap from an L. L. Bean[7]   15
catalogue. His nine-knot yawl
was auctioned off to lobstermen.
A red fox stain covers Blue Hill.

And now our fairy
decorator brightens his shop for fall,   20
his fishnet's filled with orange cork,
orange, his cobbler's bench and awl,
there is no money in his work,
he'd rather marry.

One dark night,   25
my Tudor Ford climbed the hill's skull,
I watched for love-cars. Lights turned down,
they lay together, hull to hull,
where the graveyard shelves on the town. . . .
My mind's not right.   30

A car radio bleats,
"Love, O careless Love. . . ."[8] I hear
my ill-spirit sob in each blood cell,
as if my hand were at its throat. . . .
I myself am hell;   35
nobody's here—

only skunks, that search
in the moonlight for a bite to eat.

6. An elected New England town official.   8. A popular song.
7. Famous old Maine sporting goods firm.

They march on their soles up Main Street:
white stripes, moonstruck eyes' red fire   40
under the chalk-dry and spar spire
of the Trinitarian Church.

I stand on top
of our back steps and breathe the rich air—
a mother skunk with her column of kittens swills the garbage pail.   45
She jabs her wedge head in a cup
of sour cream, drops her ostrich tail,
and will not scare.

1959

ELI MANDEL

Houdini[9]

I suspect he knew that trunks are metaphors,
could distinguish between the finest rhythms
unrolled on rope or singing in a chain
and knew the metrics of the deepest pools

I think of him listening to the words   5
spoken by manacles, cells, handcuffs,
chests, hampers, roll-top desks, vaults,
especially the deep words spoken by coffins

escape, escape: quaint Harry in his suit
his chains, his desk, attached to all attachments   10
how he'd sweat in that precise struggle
with those binding words, wrapped around him
like that mannered style, his formal suit

and spoken when? by whom? What think first said
"there's no way out"?; so that he'd free himself,   15
leap, squirm, no matter how, to chain himself again,
once more jump out of the deep alive
with all his chains singing around his feet
like the bound crowds who sigh, who sigh.

1967

9. Harry Houdini (1874–1926), Ameri-
can magician and escape-artist; he was
especially famous for spectacular "chal-
lenge" acts in which he allowed members
of his audience to tie him up, handcuff
him, and lock him in boxes, trunks,
coffins, etc., and for an act in which he
escaped from a Water Torture Cell while
submerged upside down.

ELI MANDEL

On the Death of Ho Chi Minh[1]

toward the end
he became frail as rice paper
his beard whispering thin ideograms

how unlike the great carved storm
that was Marx's face   5
                    how unlike
the darkness and fury
in Beethoven's head
                    scarcely
anything to be consumed   10

bombs destroy   destroy
you cannot touch his body now
or burn his poems

                                        1973

ANDREW MARVELL

The Garden

How vainly men themselves amaze[2]
To win the palm, the oak, or bays,[3]
And their incessant labors see
Crowned from some single herb, or tree,
Whose short and narrow-vergéd[4] shade   5
Does prudently their toils upbraid;
While all flowers and all trees do close[5]
To weave the garlands of repose!

Fair Quiet, have I found thee here,
And Innocence, thy sister dear?   10
Mistaken long, I sought you then
In busy companies of men.
Your sacred plants,[6] if here below,
Only among the plants will grow;
Society is all but rude[7]   15
To[8] this delicious solitude.

1. President of North Viet Nam and
highly regarded by many as a poet
(1890–1969).
2. Become frenzied.
3. Awards for athletic, civic, and literary
achievements.

4. Narrowly cropped.
5. Unite.
6. Cuttings.
7. Barbarous.
8. Compared to.

No white nor red was ever seen
So am'rous as this lovely green.
Fond lovers, cruel as their flame,
Cut in these trees their mistress' name: 20
Little, alas, they know, or heed
How far these beauties hers exceed!
Fair trees, wheresoe'er your barks I wound,
No name shall but your own be found.

When we have run our passion's heat,   25
Love hither makes his best retreat.
The gods, that mortal beauty chase,
Still in a tree did end their race:
Apollo hunted Daphne so,
Only that she might laurel grow;   30
And Pan did after Syrinx speed,
Not as a nymph, but for a reed.[9]

What wondrous life is this I lead!
Ripe apples drop about my head;
The luscious clusters of the vine   35
Upon my mouth do crush their wine;
The nectarine and curious[1] peach
Into my hands themselves do reach;
Stumbling on melons, as I pass,
Insnared with flowers, I fall on grass.   40

Meanwhile the mind, from pleasure less,
Withdraws into its happiness;[2]
The mind, that ocean where each kind
Does straight its own resemblance find;[3]
Yet it creates, transcending these,   45
Far other worlds and other seas,
Annihilating[4] all that's made
To a green thought in a green shade.

Here at the fountain's sliding foot,
Or at some fruit tree's mossy root,   50
Casting the body's vest[5] aside,
My soul into the boughs does glide:
There, like a bird, it sits and sings,
Then whets[6] and combs its silver wings,
And, till prepared for longer flight,   55
Waves in its plumes the various[7] light.

9. In Ovid's *Metamorphoses*, Daphne, pursued by Apollo, is turned into a laurel, and Syrinx, pursued by Pan, into a reed which Pan makes into a flute.
1. Exquisite.
2. I.e., the mind withdraws from lesser sense pleasure into contemplation.
3. All land creatures were supposed to have corresponding sea-creatures.
4. Reducing to nothing by comparison.
5. Vestment, clothing; the flesh is being considered as simply clothing for the soul.
6. Preens.
7. Many-colored.

Such was that happy garden-state,
While man there walked without a mate:
After a place so pure, and sweet,
What other help could yet be meet![8]   60
But 'twas beyond a mortal's share
To wander solitary there:
Two paradises 'twere in one
To live in paradise alone.

How well the skillful gardener drew   65
Of flowers and herbs this dial[9] new,
Where, from above, the milder sun
Does through a fragrant zodiac run;
And as it works, th' industrious bee
Computes its time as well as we!   70
How could such sweet and wholesome hours
Be reckoned but with herbs and flowers?

                                                          1681

JAMES MERRILL

Watching the Dance

1. BALANCHINE'S[1]

Poor savage, doubting that a river flows
But for the myriad eddies made
By unseen powers twirling on their toes,

Here in this darkness it would seem
You had already died, and were afraid.   5
Be still. Observe the powers. Infer the stream.

2. DISCOTHÈQUE.

Having survived entirely your own youth,
Last of your generation, purple gloom
Investing you, sit, Jonah,[2] beyond speech,

And let towards the brute volume VOOM whale mouth   10
VAM pounding viscera VAM VOOM
A teenage plankton luminously twitch.

                                                          1967

8. Appropriate.
9. A garden planted in the shape of a sundial, complete with zodiac.
1. George Balanchine, Russian-born (1894) ballet choreographer and teacher.

2. According to *Jonah* 4, Jonah sat in gloom near Nineveh after its residents repented and God decided to spare the city from destruction.

CZESLAW MILOSZ

A Poor Christian Looks at the Ghetto[3]

Bees build around red liver,
Ants build around black bone.
It has begun: the tearing, the trampling on silks,
It has begun: the breaking of glass, wood, copper, nickel, silver, foam
Of gypsum, iron sheets, violin strings, trumpets, leaves, balls, crystals.   5
Poof! Phosphorescent fire from yellow walls
Engulfs animal and human hair.

Bees build around the honeycomb of lungs,
Ants build around white bone.
Torn is paper, rubber, linen, leather, flax,   10
Fiber, fabrics, cellulose, snakeskin, wire.
The roof and the wall collapse in flame and heat seizes the foundations.
Now there is only the earth, sandy, trodden down,
With one leafless tree.

Slowly, boring a tunnel, a guardian mole makes his way,   15
With a small red lamp fastened to his forehead.
He touches burned bodies, counts them, pushes on,
He distinguishes human ashes by their luminous vapor,
The ashes of each man by a different part of the spectrum.
Bees build around a red trace.   20
Ants build around the place left by my body.

I am afraid, so afraid of the guardian mole.
He has swollen eyelids, like a Patriarch
Who has sat much in the light of candles
Reading the great book of the species.   25
What will I tell him, I, a Jew of the New Testament,
Waiting two thousand years for the second coming of Jesus?
My broken body will deliver me to his sight
And he will count me among the helpers of death:
The uncircumcised.   30

1943

---

3. Translated from the Polish by the author.

JOHN MILTON

Lycidas[4]

In this monody the author bewails a learned friend, unfortunately drowned in his passage from Chester on the Irish Seas, 1637.[5] And by occasion foretells the ruin of our corrupted clergy then in their height.

Yet once more, O ye laurels, and once more
Ye myrtles brown, with ivy never sere,[6]
I come to pluck your berries harsh and crude,[7]
And with forced fingers rude,
Shatter your leaves before the mellowing year.   5
Bitter constraint, and sad occasion dear,[8]
Compels me to disturb your season due:
For Lycidas is dead, dead ere his prime,
Young Lycidas, and hath not left his peer.
Who would not sing for Lycidas? He knew   10
Himself to sing, and build the lofty rhyme.
He must not float upon his wat'ry bier
Unwept, and welter[9] to the parching wind,
Without the meed[1] of some melodious tear.
    Begin then, sisters of the sacred well,[2]   15
That from beneath the seat of Jove doth spring,
Begin, and somewhat loudly sweep the string.
Hence with denial vain and coy excuse;
So may some gentle muse[3]
With lucky words favor my destined urn,   20
And as he passes turn,
And bid fair peace be to my sable shroud.
For we were nursed upon the self-same hill,
Fed the same flock, by fountain, shade, and rill.
    Together both, ere the high lawns[4] appeared   25
Under the opening eyelids of the morn,
We drove afield, and both together heard
What time the gray-fly winds[5] her sultry horn,
Batt'ning[6] our flocks with the fresh dews of night,
Oft till the star that rose, at ev'ning, bright,   30
Towards Heav'n's descent had sloped his westering wheel.
Meanwhile the rural ditties were not mute,
Tempered to the oaten flute;[7]
Rough satyrs danced, and fauns with clov'n heel,

4. The name of a shepherd in Vergil's *Eclogue* III. Milton's elegy works from the convention of treating the dead man as if he were a shepherd and also transforms other details to a pastoral setting and situation.

5. Edward King, a student with Milton at Cambridge, and at the time of his death a young clergyman. "monody": a song sung by a single voice.

6. Withered. The laurel, myrtle, and ivy were all materials used to construct traditional evergreen garlands signifying poetic accomplishment. "brown": dusky, dark.

7. Unripe.
8. Dire.
9. Tumble about.
1. Tribute.
2. The muses, who lived on Mt. Helicon. At the foot of the mountain were two fountains, or wells, where the muses danced around Jove's altar.
3. Poet.
4. Grasslands; pastures.
5. Blows; i.e., the insect hum of midday.
6. Fattening.
7. Shepherds' pipes.

From the glad sound would not be absent long,   35
And old Damaetas[8] loved to hear our song.

 But O the heavy change, now thou art gone,
Now thou art gone, and never must return!
Thee, shepherd, thee the woods and desert caves,
With wild thyme and the gadding[9] vine o'ergrown,   40
And all their echoes mourn.
The willows and the hazel copses[1] green
Shall now no more be seen,
Fanning their joyous leaves to thy soft lays.
As killing as the canker[2] to the rose,   45
Or taint-worm to the weanling herds that graze,
Or frost to flowers, that their gay wardrobe wear,
When first the white-thorn blows:[3]
Such, Lycidas, thy loss to shepherd's ear.

 Where were ye, nymphs,[4] when the remorseless deep   50
Closed o'er the head of your loved Lycidas?
For neither were ye playing on the steep,
Where your old Bards, the famous Druids, lie,
Nor on the shaggy top of Mona high,
Nor yet where Deva spreads her wizard stream:[5]   55
Ay me, I fondly[6] dream!
Had ye been there—for what could that have done?
What could the Muse[7] herself that Orpheus bore,
The Muse herself, for her enchanting[8] son
Whom universal nature did lament,   60
When by the rout that made the hideous roar,
His gory visage down the stream was sent,
Down the swift Hebrus to the Lesbian shore?

 Alas! What boots[9] it with uncessant care
To tend the homely slighted shepherd's trade,   65
And strictly meditate the thankless Muse?
Were it not better done, as others use,[1]
To sport with Amaryllis in the shade,
Or with the tangles of Neaera's hair?
Fame is the spur that the clear spirit doth raise   70
(That last infirmity of noble mind)
To scorn delights, and live laborious days;
But the fair guerdon[2] when we hope to find,

8. A traditional pastoral name, possibly referring here to a Cambridge tutor.
9. Wandering.
1. Thickets.
2. Cankerworm.
3. Blossoms.
4. Nature deities.
5. The River Dee, reputed to have prophetic powers. "Mona": the Isle of Anglesey. The steep (line 52) may be a burial ground, in northern Wales, for Druids, ancient priests and magicians; all three locations are near the place where King drowned.
6. Foolishly.
7. Calliope, the muse of epic poetry,

whose son Orpheus was torn limb from limb by frenzied orgiasts. His head, thrown into the Hebrus (lines 62–63), floated into the sea and finally to Lesbos, where it was buried.
8. Orpheus was reputed to be able to charm even inanimate things with his music; he once persuaded Pluto to release his dead wife, Eurydice, from the infernal regions.
9. Profits.
1. Customarily do. Amaryllis (line 68) and Neaera (line 69) are stock names of women celebrated in pastoral love poetry.
2. Reward.

And think to burst out into sudden blaze,
Comes the blind Fury[3] with th' abhorréd shears,   75
And slits the thin-spun life. "But not the praise,"
Phoebus[4] replied, and touched my trembling ears:
"Fame is no plant that grows on mortal soil,
Nor in the glistering foil[5]
Set off to th' world, nor in broad rumor lies,   80
But lives and spreads aloft by those pure eyes
And perfect witness of all-judging Jove;
As he pronounces lastly on each deed,
Of so much fame in Heav'n expect thy meed."

    O fountain Arethuse,[6] and thou honored flood,   85
Smooth-sliding Mincius, crowned with vocal reeds,
That strain I heard was of a higher mood.
But now my oat[7] proceeds,
And listens to the herald of the sea,[8]
That came in Neptune's plea.   90
He asked the waves and asked the felon-winds,
What hard mishap hath doomed this gentle swain,[9]
And questioned every gust of rugged wings
That blows from off each beakéd promontory.
They knew not of his story,   95
And sage Hippotades[1] their answer brings:
That not a blast was from his dungeon strayed;
The air was calm, and on the level brine,
Sleek Panopë[2] with all her sisters played.
It was that fatal and perfidious bark   100
Built in th' eclipse, and rigged with curses dark,
That sunk so low that sacred head of thine.

    Next Camus,[3] reverend sire, went footing slow,
His mantle hairy, and his bonnet sedge,
Inwrought with figures dim, and on the edge   105
Like to that sanguine flower inscribed with woe.[4]
"Ah! who hath reft," quoth he, "my dearest pledge?"
Last came, and last did go,
The pilot of the Galilean Lake;[5]
Two massy keys he bore of metals twain   110
(The golden opes, the iron shuts amain).

3. Atropos, the Fate who cuts the threads of human life after they are spun and measured by her two sisters.
4. Apollo, god of poetic inspiration. In Roman tradition, touching the ears of one's hearers meant asking them to remember what they heard.
5. Flashy setting, used to make inferior gems glitter.
6. A Sicilian fountain, associated with the pastoral poetry of Theocritus. The River Mincius (line 86) is associated with Vergil's pastorals.
7. Oaten pipe: pastoral song.
8. Triton, who maintains the innocence of Neptune, the Roman god of the sea, in the death of Lycidas.
9. Youth, shepherd, poet.

1. Aeolus, god of the winds and son of Hippotas.
2. According to Vergil, the greatest of the Nereids (sea nymphs).
3. God of the River Cam, which flows through Cambridge.
4. The hyacinth, which was supposed to bear marks that meant "alas" because the flower was created by Phoebus from the blood of a youth he had killed accidentally.
5. St. Peter, a fisherman before he became a disciple. According to *Matthew* 16:19, Christ promised him "the keys of the kingdom of heaven"; he was traditionally regarded as the first head of the church, hence the bishop's miter in line 112.

He shook his mitered locks, and stern bespake:
"How well could I have spared for thee, young swain,
Enow[6] of such as for their bellies' sake
Creep and intrude, and climb into the fold![7]   115
Of other care they little reck'ning make,
Than how to scramble at the shearers' feast,
And shove away the worthy bidden guest.
Blind mouths! that scarce themselves know how to hold
A sheep-hook,[8] or have learned aught else the least   120
That to the faithful herdman's art belongs!
What recks it[9] them? What need they? They are sped,[1]
And when they list,[2] their lean and flashy songs
Grate on their scrannel[3] pipes of wretched straw.
The hungry sheep look up and are not fed,   125
But swoln with wind, and the rank mist they draw,
Rot inwardly, and foul contagion spread,
Besides what the grim wolf with privy paw[4]
Daily devours apace, and nothing said;
But that two-handed engine[5] at the door   130
Stands ready to smite once, and smite no more."
    Return, Alpheus,[6] the dread voice is past,
That shrunk thy streams; return, Sicilian Muse,
And call the vales, and bid them hither cast
Their bells and flowrets of a thousand hues.   135
Ye valleys low, where the mild whispers use,[7]
Of shades and wanton winds and gushing brooks,
On whose fresh lap the swart star[8] sparely looks,
Throw hither all your quaint enameled eyes,
That on the green turf suck the honeyed showers,   140
And purple all the ground with vernal flowers.
Bring the rathe[9] primrose that forsaken dies,
The tufted crow-toe, and pale jessamine,
The white pink, and the pansy freaked[1] with jet,
The glowing violet,   145
The musk-rose, and the well-attired woodbine,
With cowslips wan that hang the pensive head,
And every flower that sad embroidery wears.
Bid amaranthus[2] all his beauty shed,
And daffodillies fill their cups with tears,   150
To strew the laureate hearse[3] where Lycid lies.

6. The old plural of "enough."
7. According to *John* 10:1, "He that entereth not by the door into the sheepfold, but climbeth up some other way . . . is a thief and a robber."
8. A bishop's staff was shaped like a sheephook to suggest his role as "pastor" (shepherd) of the flock of saints.
9. Does it matter to.
1. Have attained their purpose—but also, destroyed.
2. Desire.
3. Feeble.
4. The Roman Catholic Church.
5. Not identified. Guesses include the two-handed sword of the archangel Michael, the two houses of Parliament, and St. Peter's keys.
6. A river god who, according to Ovid, fell in love with Arethusa. She fled in the form of an underground stream and became a fountain in Sicily, but Alpheus dived under the sea and at last his waters mingled with hers. See above, line 85. "Sicilian Muse": the muse of Theocritus.
7. Frequent.
8. Sirius, the Dog Star, which supposedly withers plants in late summer.
9. Early.
1. Flecked.
2. A legendary flower that cannot fade.
3. Bier.

For so to interpose a little ease,
Let our frail thoughts dally with false surmise.
Ay me! Whilst thee the shores and sounding seas
Wash far away, where'er thy bones are hurled,   155
Whether beyond the stormy Hebrides,[4]
Where thou perhaps under the whelming tide
Visit'st the bottom of the monstrous world;[5]
Or whether thou to our moist vows denied,
Sleep'st by the fable of Bellerus old,[6]   160
Where the great vision of the guarded mount
Looks toward Namancos and Bayona's hold;
Look homeward, Angel, now, and melt with ruth.[7]
And, O ye dolphins,[8] waft the hapless youth.
  Weep no more, woeful shepherds, weep no more,   165
For Lycidas your sorrow is not dead,
Sunk though he be beneath the wat'ry floor,
So sinks the day-star[9] in the ocean bed,
And yet anon repairs his drooping head,
And tricks[1] his beams, and with new-spangled ore   170
Flames in the forehead of the morning sky:
So Lycidas sunk low, but mounted high,
Through the dear might of him that walked the waves,[2]
Where, other groves and other streams along,
With nectar pure his oozy locks he laves,   175
And hears the unexpressive nuptial song,[3]
In the blest kingdoms meek of joy and love.
There entertain him all the saints above,
In solemn troops and sweet societies
That sing, and singing in their glory move,   180
And wipe the tears forever from his eyes.
Now, Lycidas, the shepherds weep no more;
Henceforth thou art the genius[4] of the shore,
In thy large recompense, and shalt be good
To all that wander in that perilous flood.   185
  Thus sang the uncouth swain[5] to th' oaks and rills,
While the still morn went out with sandals gray;
He touched the tender stops of various quills,[6]
With eager thought warbling his Doric[7] lay.
And now the sun had stretched out all the hills,   190
And now was dropped into the western bay.
At last he rose, and twitched his mantle blue:
Tomorrow to fresh woods, and pastures new.

                                                                 1637

4. Islands off Scotland, the northern edge of the sea where King drowned.
5. World where monsters live.
6. A legendary giant, supposedly buried at Land's End in Cornwall. At the tip of Land's End is St. Michael's Mount (line 161), from which the archangel is pictured looking south across the Atlantic toward Spanish (Catholic) strongholds ("Namancos and Bayona," line 162).
7. Pity.
8. According to Roman legend, dolphins brought the body of a drowned youth, Melicertes, to land, where a temple was erected to him as the protector of sailors.
9. The sun.
1. Dresses.
2. Christ. See *Matthew* 14:25–26.
3. Sung at the "marriage of the Lamb," according to *Revelation* 19. "unexpressive": inexpressible.
4. Protecting deity.
5. Unlettered shepherd: i.e., Milton.
6. Reeds in the shepherd's pipes.
7. The Greek dialect of Theocritus, Bion, and Moschus, the first writers of pastoral.

HOWARD NEMEROV

Life Cycle of Common Man

Roughly figured, this man of moderate habits,
This average consumer of the middle class,
Consumed in the course of his average life span
Just under half a million cigarettes,
Four thousand fifths of gin and about   5
A quarter as much vermouth; he drank
Maybe a hundred thousand cups of coffee,
And counting his parents' share it cost
Something like half a million dollars
To put him through life. How many beasts   10
Died to provide him with meat, belt and shoes
Cannot be certainly said.
                  But anyhow,
It is in this way that a man travels through time,
Leaving behind him a lengthening trail   15
Of empty bottles and bones, of broken shoes,
Frayed collars and worn out or outgrown
Diapers and dinnerjackets, silk ties and slickers.

Given the energy and security thus achieved,
He did . . . ? What? The usual things, of course,   20
The eating, dreaming, drinking and begetting,
And he worked for the money which was to pay
For the eating, et cetera, which were necessary
If he were to go on working for the money, et cetera,
But chiefly he talked. As the bottles and bones   25
Accumulated behind him, the words proceeded
Steadily from the front of his face as he
Advanced into the silence and made it verbal.
Who can tally the tale of his words? A lifetime
Would barely suffice for their repetition;   30
If you merely printed all his commas the result
Would be a very large volume, and the number of times
He said "thank you" or "very little sugar, please,"
Would stagger the imagination. There were also
Witticisms, platitudes, and statements beginning   35
"It seems to me" or "As I always say."

Consider the courage in all that, and behold the man
Walking into deep silence, with the ectoplastic
Cartoon's balloon of speech proceeding
Steadily out of the front of his face, the words   40
Borne along on the breath which is his spirit
Telling the numberless tale of his untold Word[8]
Which makes the world his apple, and forces him to eat.

                                      1960

---

8. *Logos,* the principle of creation and order.

HOWARD NEMEROV

Pockets

Are generally over or around
Erogenous zones, they seem to dive
In the direction of those

Dark places, and indeed
It is their nature to be dark   5
Themselves, keeping a kind

Of thieves' kitchen for the things
Sequestered from the world
For long or little while,

The keys, the handkerchiefs,   10
The sad and vagrant little coins
That are really only passing through.

For all they locate close to lust,
No pocket ever sees another;
There is in fact a certain sadness   15

To pockets, going their lonesome ways
And snuffling up their sifting storms
Of dust, tobacco bits and lint.

A pocket with a hole in it
Drops out; from shame, is that, or pride?   20
What is a pocket but a hole?

                                                          1975

HOWARD NEMEROV

The Town Dump

"The art of our necessities is strange,
That can make vile things precious."[9]

A mile out in the marshes, under a sky
Which seems to be always going away
In a hurry, on that Venetian land threaded
With hidden canals, you will find the city
Which seconds ours (so cemeteries, too,   5
Reflect a town from hillsides out of town),
Where Being most Becomingly[1] ends up

9. *King Lear*, Act III, sc. ii, lines 70–71.
1. "Being" and "Becoming" have been, since Heraclitus, the standard antinomies in Western philosophy, standing for (respectively) the eternal and that which changes.

Becoming some more. From cardboard tenements,
Windowed with cellophane, or simply tenting
In paper bags, the angry mackerel eyes   10
Glare at you out of stove-in, sunken heads
Far from the sea; the lobster, also, lifts
An empty claw in his most minatory
Of gestures; oyster, crab, and mussel shells
Lie here in heaps, savage as money hurled   15
Away at the gate of hell. If you want results,
These are results.
           Objects of value or virtue,
However, are also to be picked up here,
Though rarely, lying with bones and rotten meat,
Eggshells and mouldy bread, banana peels   20
No one will skid on, apple cores that caused
Neither the fall of man nor a theory
Of gravitation.[2] People do throw out
The family pearls by accident, sometimes,
Not often; I've known dealers in antiques   25
To prowl this place by night, with flashlights, on
The off-chance of somebody's having left
Derelict chairs which will turn out to be
By Hepplewhite,[3] a perfect set of six
Going to show, I guess, that in any sty   30
Someone's heaven may open and shower down
Riches responsive to the right dream; though
It is a small chance, certainly, that sends
The ghostly dealer, heavy with fly-netting
Over his head, across these hills in darkness,   35
Stumbling in cut-glass goblets, lacquered cups,
And other products of his dreamy midden[4]
Penciled with light and guarded by the flies.

For there are flies, of course. A dynamo
Composed, by thousands, of our ancient black   40
Retainers, hums here day and night, steady
As someone telling[5] beads, the hum becoming
A high whine at any disturbance; then,
Settled again, they shine under the sun
Like oil-drops, or are invisible as night,   45
By night.
           All this continually smoulders,
Crackles, and smokes with mostly invisible fires
Which, working deep, rarely flash out and flare,

---

2. According to legend, Sir Isaac New-
ton's discovery of the principle of gravi-
tation followed his being hit on the head
by a falling apple.
3. A late 18th-century cabinet maker
and furniture designer, famed for his sim-
plification of neoclassic lines. No pieces
known to have been actually made by
Hepplewhite survive.
4. Refuse heap. (The term is usually
used to describe those primitive refuse
heaps which have been untouched for
centuries and in which archeologists dig
for shards and artifacts of older cultures.)
5. Counting.

And never finish. Nothing finishes;
The flies, feeling the heat, keep on the move.   50

Among the flies, the purefying fires,
The hunters by night, acquainted with the art
Of our necessities, and the new deposits
That each day wastes with treasure, you may say
There should be ratios. You may sum up   55
The results if you want results. But I will add
That wild birds, drawn to the carrion and flies,
Assemble in some numbers here, their wings
Shining with light, their flight enviably free,
Their music marvelous, though sad, and strange.   60

                                                                  1958

MARGE PIERCY

Beauty I Would Suffer for

Last week a doctor told me
anemic after an operation
to eat: ordered to indulgence,
given a papal dispensation to run
amok in Zabar's.[6]   5
Yet I know that in
two weeks, a month I
will have in my nostrils
not the savor of rendering goosefat,
not the burnt sugar of caramel topping   10
the Saint-Honoré cake, not the pumpernickel
bearing up the sweet butter, the sturgeon
but again the scorched wire,
burnt rubber smell
of willpower, living   15
with the brakes on.

I want to pass into the boudoirs
of Rubens' women.[7] I want to dance
graceful in my tonnage like Poussin nymphs.
Those melon bellies, those vast ripening thighs,   20
those featherbeds of forearms, those buttocks
placid and gross as hippopotami:
how I would bend myself
to that standard of beauty, how faithfully

6. A fashionable New York delicatessen.
7. The women in the paintings of the
Flemish painter Peter Paul Rubens
(1577–1640) are of ample magnitude.

The French painter Nicolas Poussin
(1595–1665) features women of precision
and grace.

I would consume waffles and sausage for breakfast   25
with croissants on the side, how dutifully
I would eat for supper the blackbean soup
with madeira, followed by the fish course,
the meat course, and the Bavarian cream.
Even at intervals during the day I would   30
suffer an occasional eclair
for the sake of appearance.

1978

EDGAR ALLAN POE

To Helen[8]

Helen, thy beauty is to me
　　Like those Nicéan[9] barks of yore,
That gently, o'er a perfumed sea,
　　The weary, way-worn wanderer bore
　　To his own native shore.   5

On desperate seas long wont to roam,
　　Thy hyacinth hair, thy classic face,
Thy Naiad airs[1] have brought me home
　　To the glory that was Greece
And the grandeur that was Rome.   10

Lo! in yon brilliant window-niche
　　How statue-like I see thee stand,
　　The agate lamp within thy hand!
Ah, Psyche,[2] from the regions which
　　Are Holy Land![3]   15

1831

---

8. Helen of Troy, the traditional type of beauty. Hers was "the face that launched a thousand ships," and her elopement caused the siege and destruction of Troy described in Homer's *Iliad* and the first books of Vergil's *Aeneid*. After the war she returned to her husband.
9. The reference is uncertain: possibly, the island of Nysa (which Milton's *Paradise Lost* calls the "Nyseian Isle," IV, 275) in the river Triton in North Africa, where Bacchus was safely protected from Rhea; or pertaining to the ancient city of Nicaea, a Byzantine seaport.

1. Graceful manners of a water nymph.
2. A beautiful maiden who, according to Apuleius's *Golden Ass*, was beloved by Cupid but deprived of him when she lit a lamp, disobeying his order that she never seek to know who he was. The word *psyche* in Greek means "soul."
3. In an 1836 review essay, Poe facetiously quotes a medieval monk who said that "Helen represents the Human Soul—Troy is Hell."

ALEXANDER POPE

[The Hunt]⁴

Ye vig'rous swains!⁵ while youth ferments your blood,   93
And purer spirits swell the sprightly flood,
Now range the hills, the gameful woods beset,
Wind the shrill horn, or spread the waving net.
When milder autumn summer's heat succeeds,
And in the new-shorn field the partridge feeds,
Before his lord the ready spaniel bounds,
Panting with hope, he tries the furrowed grounds;   100
But when the tainted gales the game betray,
Couched close he lies, and meditates the prey;
Secure they trust th' unfaithful field, beset,
'Till hov'ring o'er 'em sweeps the swelling net.
Thus (if small things we may with great compare)⁶   105
When Albion⁷ sends her eager sons to war,
Some thoughtless town, with ease and plenty blest,
Near, and more near, the closing lines invest;
Sudden they seize th' amazed, defenseless prize,
And high in air Britannia's standard flies.   110
    See! from the brake the whirring pheasant springs,
And mounts exulting on triumphant wings:
Short is his joy; he feels the fiery wound,
Flutters in blood, and panting beats the ground.
Ah! what avail his glossy, varying dyes,   115
His purple crest, and scarlet-circled eyes,
The vivid green his shining plumes unfold,
His painted wings, and breast that flames with gold?
    Nor yet, when moist Arcturus⁸ clouds the sky,
The woods and fields their pleasing toils deny.   120
To plains with well-breathed beagles we repair,
And trace the mazes of the circling hare.
(Beasts, urged by us, their fellow-beasts pursue,
And learn of man each other to undo.)
With slaught'ring guns th' unwearied fowler roves,   125
When frosts have whitened all the naked groves;
Where doves in flocks the leafless trees o'ershade,
And lonely woodcocks haunt the wat'ry glade.
He lifts the tube, and levels with his eye;
Strait a short thunder breaks the frozen sky.   130
Oft, as in airy rings they skim the heath,
The clam'rous lapwings feel the leaden death:
Oft, as the mounting larks their notes prepare,
They fall, and leave their little lives in air.

                                                                        1713

4. From *Windsor Forest*, Pope's didactic descriptive poem about the Peace of Utrecht and the uses of nature.
5. Youths.
6. In *Paradise Lost*, II, 921–22, Milton must "compare great things with small" to suggest the noise Satan hears as he is about to journey toward Hell.
7. England.
8. A large star thought to bring rain when it rises in September.

EZRA POUND

Commission[9]

Go, my songs, to the lonely and the unsatisfied,
Go also to the nerve-racked, go to the enslaved-by-convention,
Bear to them my contempt for their oppressors.
Go as a great wave of cool water,
Bear my contempt of oppressors.   5

Speak against unconscious oppression,
Speak against the tyranny of the unimaginative,
Speak against bonds.
Go to the bourgeoise who is dying of her ennuis,
Go to the women in suburbs.   10
Go to the hideously wedded,
Go to them whose failure is concealed,
Go to the unluckily mated,
Go to the bought wife,
Go to the woman entailed.[1]   15

Go to those who have delicate lust,
Go to those whose delicate desires are thwarted,
Go like a blight upon the dullness of the world;
Go with your edge against this,
Strengthen the subtle cords,   20
Bring confidence upon the algae and the tentacles of the soul.

Go in a friendly manner,
Go with an open speech.
Be eager to find new evils and new good,
Be against all forms of oppression.   25
Go to those who are thickened with middle age,
To those who have lost their interest.

Go to the adolescent who are smothered in family—
Oh how hideous it is
To see three generations of one house gathered together!   30
It is like an old tree with shoots,
And with some branches rotted and falling.

Go out and defy opinion,
Go against this vegetable bondage of the blood.
Be against all sorts of mortmain.[2]   35

p. 1913

9. Poems or books of poems are sometimes sent into the world with an "envoi" or commission ("Go, little book . . .").
1. Involuntarily committed. Property limited to a specific line of heirs is said to be entailed; the term is not usually applied to people.
2. Impersonal ownership.

EZRA POUND

The Garden

En robe de parade.—Samain[3]

Like a skein of loose silk blown against a wall
She walks by the railing of a path in Kensington Gardens,[4]
And she is dying piece-meal
        of a sort of emotional anæmia.

And round about there is a rabble   5
Of the filthy, sturdy, unkillable infants of the very poor.
They shall inherit the earth.

In her is the end of breeding.
Her boredom is exquisite and excessive.
She would like some one to speak to her,   10
And is almost afraid that I
        will commit that indiscretion.

                                                          1916

EZRA POUND

In a Station of the Metro[5]

The apparition of these faces in the crowd;
Petals on a wet, black bough.

                                                       p. 1913

EZRA POUND

A Virginal

No, no! Go from me. I have left her lately.
I will not spoil my sheath with lesser brightness,
For my surrounding air hath a new lightness;
Slight are her arms, yet they have bound me straitly
And left me cloaked as with a gauze of æther;   5
As with sweet leaves; as with a subtle clearness.

3. Albert Samain, late 19th-century French poet. The phrase is from the first line of the prefatory poem in his first book of poems, *Au Jardin de l'Infante:* "Mon âme est une infante en robe de parade" ("My soul is an Infanta in ceremonial dress"). An "Infanta" is a daughter of the Spanish royal family which, long inbred, had for many years been afflicted with a real blood disease, hemophilia.

4. A fashionable park near the center of London.

5. The Paris subway.

Oh, I have picked up magic in her nearness
To sheathe me half in half the things that sheathe her.
No, no! Go from me, I have still the flavor,
Soft as spring wind that's come from birchen bowers.   10
Green come the shoots, aye April in the branches,
As winter's wound with her sleight hand she staunches,
Hath of the trees a likeness of the savor:
As white their bark, so white this lady's hours.

1912

JOHN PRESS

Womanizers

Adulterers and customers of whores
And cunning takers of virginities
Caper from bed to bed, but not because
The flesh is pricked to infidelities.

The body is content with homely fare;   5
It is the avid, curious mind that craves
New pungent sauce and strips the larder bare,
The palate and not hunger that enslaves.

1959

MATTHEW PRIOR

To a Child of Quality Five Years Old,
the Author Supposed Forty[6]

Lords, knights, and squires, the numerous band
    That wear the fair Miss Mary's fetters,
Were summoned, by her high command,
    To show their passions by their letters.

My pen amongst the rest I took,   5
    Lest those bright eyes that cannot read
Should dart their kindling fires, and look
    The power they have to be obeyed.

6. Addressed to Lady Mary Villiers, daughter of Edward Villiers, the first Earl of Jersey. Prior was actually about 30 or 35 when the poem was written. "Quality" (see line 9) connotes aristocratic social degree.

Nor quality nor[7] reputation
    Forbid me yet my flame to tell;   10
Dear five years old befriends my passion,
    And I may write till she can spell.

For while she makes her silk-worms beds
    With all the tender things I swear,
Whilst all the house my passion reads,   15
    In papers round her baby's[8] hair,

She may receive and own[9] my flame,
    For though the strictest prudes should know it,
She'll pass for a most virtuous dame,
    And I for an unhappy poet.   20

Then too, alas! when she shall tear
    The lines some younger rival sends,
She'll give me leave to write, I fear,
    And we shall still continue friends.

For, as our different ages move,   25
    'Tis so ordained, would fate but mend it!
That I shall be past making love
    When she begins to comprehend it.

ca. 1700

JAROLD RAMSEY

Ontogeny

"Then there are the stories and after a while I think something
Else must connect them besides just this me"
    —W.S. Merwin, "The Child"

"Mommy, take me home, I'm a changed boy!"
they say I promised
after Grandpa kept me for a week
drilling on my lisping *l*'s and *r*'s
until I had them safely tongued-in-cheek   5
and had ceased to be the insufferable,
the unspeakable "Jewwy Wamsey."
Now, presumably, I was me? Wrong—
though storied, I was indecipherable.

In all this folklore of my growing, I miss   10
knowing the primitive little boy, the Urknabe.[1]

---

7. Neither . . . nor (a common 18th-
century construction).
8. Doll's.

9. Acknowledge.
1. Literally, the forerunner of a male
child.

Some days I feel like a tattered biplane, viz.
the Cal Rodgers Special, "Vin Fiz,"
first aeroplane from coast to coast in 1912,
which finished up its flight with only four   15
original parts, three wing-ribs and a strut.
Poor rickety bionic windhover—
a crash a day, tut tut, that's me all over.

How can there be a plot worth scanning
when the hero metamorphosizes every inning?   20
Still, once more into the book of changes
I leap, for love's ultimate ploy,
crying, "Darling, take me, I'm a changed boy!"

1978

JOHN CROWE RANSOM

The Equilibrists

Full of her long white arms and milky skin
He had a thousand times remembered sin.
Alone in the press of people traveled he,
Minding her jacinth,[2] and myrrh,[3] and ivory.

Mouth he remembered: the quaint orifice   5
From which came heat that flamed upon the kiss,
Till cold words came down spiral from the head.
Grey doves from the officious tower illsped.

Body: it was a white field ready for love,
On her body's field, with the gaunt tower above,   10
The lilies grew, beseeching him to take,
If he would pluck and wear them, bruise and break.

Eyes talking: Never mind the cruel words,
Embrace my flowers, but not embrace the swords.
But what they said, the doves came straightway flying   15
And unsaid: Honor, Honor, they came crying.

Importunate her doves. Too pure, too wise,
Clambering on his shoulder, saying, Arise,
Leave me now, and never let us meet,
Eternal distance now command thy feet.   20

2. An ancient blue gem.   3. An ingredient in perfume and incense.

Predicament indeed, which thus discovers
Honor among thieves, Honor between lovers.
O such a little word is Honor, they feel!
But the grey word is between them cold as steel.

At length I saw these lovers fully were come   25
Into their torture of equilibrium;
Dreadfully had forsworn each other, and yet
They were bound each to each, and they did not forget.

And rigid as two painful stars, and twirled
About the clustered night their prison world,   30
They burned with fierce love always to come near,
But Honor beat them back and kept them clear.

Ah, the strict lovers, they are ruined now!
I cried in anger. But with puddled brow
Devising for those gibbeted[4] and brave   35
Came I descanting: Man, what would you have?

For spin your period out, and draw your breath,
A kinder saeculum[5] begins with Death.
Would you ascend to Heaven and bodiless dwell?
Or take your bodies honorless to Hell?   40

In Heaven you have heard no marriage is,
No white flesh tinder to your lecheries,
Your male and female tissue sweetly shaped
Sublimed away, and furious blood escaped.

Great lovers lie in Hell, the stubborn ones   45
Infatuate of the flesh upon the bones;
Stuprate,[6] they rend each other when they kiss,
The pieces kiss again, no end to this.

But still I watched them spinning, orbited nice.
Their flames were not more radiant than their ice.   50
I dug in the quiet earth and wrought the tomb
And made these lines to memorize their doom:

EPITAPH

Equilibrists lie here; stranger, tread light;
Close, but untouching in each other's sight;
Mouldered the lips and ashy the tall skull.   55
Let them lie perilous and beautiful.

1927

---

4. Hanged and publicly displayed.   6. Having violent sexual intercourse.
5. Generation; era.

DAVID RAY

A Piece of Shrapnel

The Rock That Doesn't Break, she calls
it that, picks it up in a field of clover,
brushes off the mud, asks me what it is
but who am I to explain war to a five-
year-old, who myself see something which   5
even to touch is dangerous, it is so sharp
and unshiny. I can feel it wanting
to hurt, to whizz through the air, land
in a tangle, be sold and resold. I can feel
how restless it is, not having found after   10
all this search a grave, where it can rest
and not be picked up, once more estranged,
searching again through hands and delicate
faces. It is like a small, tired heart
begging not to be stolen still again from   15
this grave, which is in a field of clover.

1974

EDWIN ARLINGTON ROBINSON

Mr. Flood's Party

Old Eben Flood, climbing alone one night
Over the hill between the town below
And the forsaken upland hermitage
That held as much as he should ever know
On earth again of home, paused warily.   5
The road was his and not a native near;
And Eben, having leisure, said aloud,
For no man else in Tilbury Town to hear:

"Well, Mr. Flood, we have the harvest moon
Again, and we may not have many more;   10
The bird is on the wing, the poet says,[7]
And you and I have said it here before.
Drink to the bird." He raised up to the light
The jug that he had gone so far to fill,
And answered huskily: "Well, Mr. Flood,   15
Since you propose it, I believe I will."

---

7. Edward Fitzgerald, in "The Rubáiyat of Omar Khayyám," so describes the "Bird of Time."

Alone, as if enduring to the end
A valiant armor of scarred hopes outworn,
He stood there in the middle of the road
Like Roland's ghost winding a silent horn.[8]   20
Below him, in the town among the trees,
Where friends of other days had honored him,
A phantom salutation of the dead
Rang thinly till old Eben's eyes were dim.

Then, as a mother lays her sleeping child   25
Down tenderly, fearing it may awake,
He set the jug down slowly at his feet
With trembling care, knowing that most things break;
And only when assured that on firm earth
It stood, as the uncertain lives of men   30
Assuredly did not, he paced away,
And with his hand extended paused again:

"Well, Mr. Flood, we have not met like this
In a long time; and many a change has come
To both of us, I fear, since last it was   35
We had a drop together. Welcome home!"
Convivially returning with himself,
Again he raised the jug up to the light;
And with an acquiescent quaver said:
"Well, Mr. Flood, if you insist, I might.   40

"Only a very little, Mr. Flood—
For auld lang syne. No more, sir; that will do."
So, for the time, apparently it did,
And Eben evidently thought so too;
For soon amid the silver loneliness   45
Of night he lifted up his voice and sang,
Secure, with only two moons listening,
Until the whole harmonious landscape rang—

"For auld lang syne." The weary throat gave out,
The last word wavered, and the song was done.   50
He raised again the jug regretfully
And shook his head, and was again alone.
There was not much that was ahead of him,
And there was nothing in the town below—
Where strangers would have shut the many doors   55
That many friends had opened long ago.

                                                          1921

---

8. In French legend Roland's powerful ivory horn was used to warn his allies of impending attack.

EDWIN ARLINGTON ROBINSON

Richard Cory

Whenever Richard Cory went down town,
We people on the pavement looked at him:
He was a gentleman from sole to crown,
Clean favored, and imperially slim.

And he was always quietly arrayed,   5
And he was always human when he talked;
But still he fluttered pulses when he said,
"Good-morning," and he glittered when he walked.

And he was rich—yes, richer than a king—
And admirably schooled in every grace: 10
In fine, we thought that he was everything
To make us wish that we were in his place.

So on we worked, and waited for the light,
And went without the meat, and cursed the bread;
And Richard Cory, one calm summer night,   15
Went home and put a bullet through his head.

1897

EDWIN ARLINGTON ROBINSON

Uncle Ananias[9]

His words were magic and his heart was true,
　　And everywhere he wandered he was blessed.
Out of all ancient men my childhood knew
　　I choose him and I mark him for the best.
Of all authoritative liars, too,   5
　　I crown him loveliest.

How fondly I remember the delight
　　That always glorified him in the spring;
The joyous courage and the benedight[1]
　　Profusion of his faith in everything!   10
He was a good old man, and it was right
　　That he should have his fling.

And often, underneath the apple-trees,
　　When we surprised him in the summer time,

9. The Biblical character Ananias was famous because he lied to God. See *Acts* 5:1–10.　　1. Blessed.

With what superb magnificence and ease   15
   He sinned enough to make the day sublime!
And if he liked us there about his knees,
   Truly it was no crime.

All summer long we loved him for the same
   Perennial inspiration of his lies;   20
And when the russet wealth of autumn came,
   There flew but fairer visions to our eyes—
Multiple, tropical, winged with a feathery flame,
   Like birds of paradise.

So to the sheltered end of many a year   25
   He charmed the seasons out with pageantry
Wearing upon his forehead, with no fear,
   The laurel of approved iniquity.
And every child who knew him, far or near,
   Did love him faithfully.   30

1910

THEODORE ROETHKE

The Dream

1

I met her as a blossom on a stem
Before she ever breathed, and in that dream
The mind remembers from a deeper sleep:
Eye learned from eye, cold lip from sensual lip.
My dream divided on a point of fire;   5
Light hardened on the water where we were;
A bird sang low; the moonlight sifted in;
The water rippled, and she rippled on.

2

She came toward me in the flowing air,
A shape of change, encircled by its fire.   10
I watched her there, between me and the moon;
The bushes and the stones danced on and on;
I touched her shadow when the light delayed;
I turned my face away, and yet she stayed.
A bird sang from the center of a tree;   15
She loved the wind because the wind loved me.

3

Love is not love until love's vulnerable.
She slowed to sigh, in that long interval.
A small bird flew in circles where we stood;
The deer came down, out of the dappled wood.   20

All who remember, doubt. Who calls that strange?
I tossed a stone, and listened to its plunge.
She knew the grammar of least motion, she
Lent me one virtue, and I live thereby.

4

She held her body steady in the wind;   25
Our shadows met, and slowly swung around;
She turned the field into a glittering sea;
I played in flame and water like a boy
And I swayed out beyond the white seafoam;
Like a wet log, I sang within a flame.   30
In that last while, eternity's confine,
I came to love, I came into my own.

1958

THEODORE ROETHKE

She

I think the dead are tender. Shall we kiss?—
My lady laughs, delighting in what is.
If she but sighs, a bird puts out its tongue.
She makes space lonely with a lovely song.
She lilts a low soft language, and I hear   5
Down long sea-chambers of the inner ear.

We sing together; we sing mouth to mouth.
The garden is a river flowing south.
She cries out loud the soul's own secret joy;
She dances, and the ground bears her away.   10
She knows the speech of light, and makes it plain
A lively thing can come to life again.

I feel her presence in the common day,
In that slow dark that widens every eye.
She moves as water moves, and comes to me,   15
Stayed by what was, and pulled by what would be.

1956

THEODORE ROETHKE

The Waking

I wake to sleep, and take my waking slow.
I feel my fate in what I cannot fear.

I learn by going where I have to go.

We think by feeling. What is there to know?
I hear my being dance from ear to ear.   5
I wake to sleep, and take my waking slow.

Of those so close beside me, which are you?
God bless the Ground! I shall walk softly there,
And learn by going where I have to go.

Light takes the Tree; but who can tell us how?   10
The lowly worm climbs up a winding stair;
I wake to sleep, and take my waking slow.

Great Nature has another thing to do
To you and me; so take the lively air,
And, lovely, learn by going where to go.   15

This shaking keeps me steady. I should know.
What falls away is always. And is near.
I wake to sleep, and take my waking slow.
I learn by going where I have to go.

1953

JOHN SCOTT

I Hate That Drum's Discordant Sound

I hate that drum's discordant sound,
Parading round, and round, and round:
To thoughtless youth it pleasure yields,
And lures from cities and from fields,
To sell their liberty for charms   5
Of tawdry lace, and glittering arms;
And when Ambition's voice commands,
To march, and fight, and fall, in foreign lands.

I hate that drum's discordant sound,
Parading round, and round, and round: 10
To me it talks of ravaged plains,
And burning towns, and ruined swains,[2]
And mangled limbs, and dying groans,
The widows' tears, and orphans' moans;
And all that Misery's hand bestows,   15
To fill the catalogue of human woes.

1782

2. Youths.

ANNE SEXTON

The Kiss

My mouth blooms like a cut.
I've been wronged all year, tedious
nights, nothing but rough elbows in them
and delicate boxes of Kleenex calling *crybaby
crybaby, you fool!*   5

Before today my body was useless.
Now it's tearing at its square corners.
It's tearing old Mary's garments off, knot by knot
and see—Now it's shot full of these electric bolts.
Zing! A resurrection!   10

Once it was a boat, quite wooden
and with no business, no salt water under it
and in need of some paint. It was no more
than a group of boards. But you hoisted her, rigged her.
She's been elected.   15

My nerves are turned on. I hear them like
musical instruments. Where there was silence
the drums, the strings are incurably playing. You did this.
Pure genius at work. Darling, the composer has stepped
into fire.   20

1969

WILLIAM SHAKESPEARE

Th' Expense of Spirit

Th' expense[3] of spirit in a waste[4] of shame
Is lust in action; and, till action, lust
Is perjured, murderous, bloody, full of blame,
Savage, extreme, rude, cruel, not to trust;
Enjoyed no sooner but despiséd straight: 5
Past reason hunted; and no sooner had,
Past reason hated, as a swallowed bait,
On purpose laid to make the taker mad:
Mad in pursuit, and in possession so;
Had, having, and in quest to have, extreme;   10
A bliss in proof;[5] and proved, a very woe;
Before, a joy proposed; behind, a dream.

3. Expending.   5. In the act.
4. Using up; also, desert.

All this the world well knows; yet none knows well
To shun the heaven that leads men to this hell.

                                                        1609

WILLIAM SHAKESPEARE

Hark, Hark! the Lark[6]

Hark, hark! the lark at heaven's gate sings,
    And Phoebus[7] 'gins arise,
His steeds to water at those springs
    On chaliced[8] flowers that lies;
And winking Mary-buds[9] begin   5
    To ope their golden eyes:
With every thing that pretty is,
    My lady sweet, arise!
    Arise, arise!

ca. 1610

WILLIAM SHAKESPEARE

Shall I Compare Thee to a Summer's Day?

Shall I compare thee to a summer's day?
Thou art more lovely and more temperate:
Rough winds do shake the darling buds of May,
And summer's lease hath all too short a date:
Sometimes too hot the eye of heaven shines,   5
And often is his gold complexion dimmed;
And every fair from fair sometimes declines,
By chance or nature's changing course untrimmed;[1]
But thy eternal summer shall not fade,
Nor lose possession of that fair thou ow'st;[2]   10
Nor shall Death brag thou wander'st in his shade,
When in eternal lines to time thou grow'st:
So long as men can breathe, or eyes can see,
So long lives this, and this gives life to thee.

                                                        1609

6. From *Cymbeline*, Act II, sc. iii.   9. Buds of marigolds.
7. Apollo, the sun god.   1. Disordered.
8. Cup-shaped.   2. Ownest.

WILLIAM SHAKESPEARE

Two Loves I Have

Two loves I have of comfort and despair,
Which like two spirits do suggest[3] me still:
The better angel is a man right fair,
The worser spirit a woman, color'd ill.[4]
To win me soon to hell, my female evil   5
Tempteth my better angel from my side,
And would corrupt my saint to be a devil,
Wooing his purity with her foul pride.
And whether that my angel be turn'd fiend
Suspect I may, but not directly tell   10
But being both from me,[5] both to each friend,
I guess one angel in another's hell:
    Yet this shall I ne'er know, but live in doubt,
    Till my bad angel fire[6] my good one out.

1609

WILLIAM SHAKESPEARE

Spring[7]

When daisies pied and violets blue
    And ladysmocks all silver-white
And cuckoobuds of yellow hue
    Do paint the meadows with delight,
The cuckoo then, on every tree,   5
Mocks married men;[8] for thus sings he,
                Cuckoo;
Cuckoo, cuckoo: Oh word of fear,
Unpleasing to a married ear!

When shepherds pipe on oaten straws,   10
    And merry larks are plowmen's clocks,
When turtles tread,[9] and rooks, and daws,
    And maidens bleach their summer smocks,
The cuckoo then, on every tree,
Mocks married men; for thus sings he,   15
                Cuckoo;
Cuckoo, cuckoo: Oh word of fear,
Unpleasing to a married ear!

ca. 1595

3. Tempt. "Still": constantly.
4. Badly.
5. Away from me. "both to each friend": friends to each other.
6. Drive out with fire ("fire" is Elizabethan slang for venereal disease).

7. Like "Winter" (below), a song from *Love's Labors Lost*, Act V, sc. ii.
8. By the resemblance of its call to the word "cuckold."
9. Copulate. "turtles": turtledoves.

WILLIAM SHAKESPEARE

Winter

When icicles hang by the wall
    And Dick the shepherd blows[1] his nail,
And Tom bears logs into the hall,
    And milk comes frozen home in pail.
When blood is nipped and ways be foul,   5
Then nightly sings the staring owl,
            Tu-who;
Tu-whit, tu-who: a merry note,
While greasy Joan doth keel[2] the pot.

When all aloud the wind doth blow,   10
    And coughing drowns the parson's saw,[3]
And birds sit brooding in the snow,
    And Marian's nose looks red and raw,
When roasted crabs[4] hiss in the bowl,
Then nightly sings the staring owl,   15
            Tu-who;
Tu-whit, tu-who: a merry note
While greasy Joan doth keel the pot.

ca. 1595

PERCY BYSSHE SHELLEY

England in 1819

An old, mad, blind, despised, and dying king[5]—
Princes, the dregs of their dull race, who flow
Through public scorn—mud from a muddy spring;
Rulers who neither see, nor feel, nor know,
But leechlike to their fainting country cling,   5
Till they drop, blind in blood, without a blow;
A people starved and stabbed in the untilled field—
An army, which liberticide and prey
Makes as a two-edged sword to all who wield;
Golden and sanguine[6] laws which tempt and slay;   10
Religion Christless, Godless—a book sealed;
A Senate—Time's worst statute[7] unrepealed—
Are graves, from which a glorious Phantom[8] may
Burst, to illumine our tempestuous day.

1819

1. Breathes on for warmth. "nail": fingernail; i.e., hands.
2. Cool: stir to keep it from boiling over.
3. Maxim, proverb.
4. Crabapples.
5. George III, senile for many years, had ruled England since 1760. He died the year after the poem was written.
6. Motivated by greed, resulting in bloodshed.
7. A law discriminating against Catholics.
8. Revolution.

PERCY BYSSHE SHELLEY

Mont Blanc[9]

Lines Written in the Vale of Chamouni

I

The everlasting universe of things
Flows through the mind, and rolls its rapid waves,
Now dark—now glittering—now reflecting gloom—
Now lending splendor, where from secret springs
The source of human thought its tribute brings   5
Of waters—with a sound but half its own,
Such as a feeble brook will oft assume
In the wild woods, among the mountains lone,
Where waterfalls around it leap forever,
Where woods and winds contend, and a vast river   10
Over its rocks ceaselessly bursts and raves.

II

Thus thou, Ravine of Arve—dark, deep Ravine—
Thou many-colored, many-voicéd vale,
Over whose pines, and crags, and caverns sail
Fast cloud-shadows and sunbeams: awful scene,   15
Where Power in likeness of the Arve comes down
From the ice-gulfs that gird his secret throne,
Bursting through these dark mountains like the flame
Of lightning through the tempest; thou dost lie,
Thy giant brood of pines around thee clinging,   20
Children of elder time, in whose devotion
The chainless winds still come and ever came
To drink their odors, and their mighty swinging
To hear—an old and solemn harmony;
Thine earthly rainbows stretched across the sweep   25
Of the ethereal waterfall, whose veil
Robes some unsculptured image; the strange sleep
Which when the voices of the desert fail
Wraps all in its own deep eternity;
Thy caverns echoing to the Arve's commotion,   30
A loud, lone sound no other sound can tame;
Thou art pervaded with that ceaseless motion,
Thou art the path of that unresting sound—
Dizzy Ravine! and when I gaze on thee
I seem as in a trance sublime and strange   35
To muse on my own separate fantasy,
My own, my human mind, which passively
Now renders and receives fast influencings,
Holding an unremitting interchange

9. The highest peak in Europe, inaccessible at the summit. Its snows melt into the River Arve and the Chamonix valley in France, near the borders of Switzerland and Italy.

With the clear universe of things around;   40
One legion of wild thoughts, whose wandering wings
Now float above thy darkness, and now rest
Where that or thou art no unbidden guest,
In the still cave of the witch Poesy,
Seeking among the shadows that pass by   45
Ghosts of all things that are, some shade of thee,
Some phantom, some faint image; till the breast
From which they fled recalls them, thou art there!

III

Some say that gleams of a remoter world
Visit the soul in sleep, that death is slumber,   50
And that its shapes the busy thoughts outnumber
Of those who wake and live. I look on high;
Has some unknown omnipotence unfurled
The veil of life and death? or do I lie
In dream, and does the mightier world of sleep   55
Spread far around and inaccessibly
Its circles? For the very spirit fails,
Driven like a homeless cloud from steep to steep
That vanishes among the viewless[1] gales!
Far, far above, piercing the infinite sky,   60
Mont Blanc appears—still, snowy, and serene—
Its subject mountains their unearthly forms
Pile around it, ice and rock; broad vales between
Of frozen floods, unfathomable deeps,
Blue as the overhanging heaven, that spread   65
And wind among the accumulated steeps;
A desert peopled by the storms alone,
Save when the eagle brings some hunter's bone,
And the wolf tracks her there—how hideously
Its shapes are heaped around! rude, bare, and high,   70
Ghastly, and scarred, and riven. Is this the scene
Where the old Earthquake-demon taught her young
Ruin? Were these their toys? or did a sea
Of fire envelop once this silent snow?[2]
None can reply—all seems eternal now.   75
The wilderness has a mysterious tongue
Which teaches awful doubt, or faith, so mild,
So solemn, so serene, that man may be,
But for such faith, with nature reconciled;
Thou hast a voice, great Mountain, to repeal   80
Large codes of fraud and woe; not understood
By all, but which the wise, and great, and good
Interpret, or make felt, or deeply feel.

1. Invisible.
2. According to scientific theories of the time, the earth was originally round and smooth, and mountains resulted from floods, earthquakes, or fires bursting from the earth's center.

IV

The fields, the lakes, the forests, and the streams,
Ocean, and all the living things that dwell   85
Within the daedal³ earth; lightning, and rain,
Earthquake, and fiery flood, and hurricane,
The torpor of the year when feeble dreams
Visit the hidden buds, or dreamless sleep
Holds every future leaf and flower; the bound   90
With which from that detested trance they leap;
The works and ways of man, their death and birth,
And that of him and all that his may be;
All things that move and breathe with toil and sound
Are born and die; revolve, subside, and swell.   95
Power dwells apart in its tranquillity,
Remote, serene, and inaccessible:
And *this*, the naked countenance of earth,
On which I gaze, even these primeval mountains
Teach the adverting mind. The glaciers creep   100
Like snakes that watch their prey, from their far fountains,
Slow rolling on; there, many a precipice,
Frost and the Sun in scorn of mortal power
Have piled: dome, pyramid, and pinnacle,
A city of death, distinct with many a tower   105
And wall impregnable of beaming ice.
Yet not a city, but a flood of ruin
Is there, that from the boundaries of the sky
Rolls its perpetual stream; vast pines are strewing
Its destined path, or in the mangled soil   110
Branchless and shattered stand; the rocks, drawn down
From yon remotest waste, have overthrown
The limits of the dead and living world,
Never to be reclaimed. The dwelling place
Of insects, beasts, and birds, becomes its spoil   115
Their food and their retreat for ever gone,
So much of life and joy is lost. The race
Of man flies far in dread; his work and dwelling
Vanish, like smoke before the tempest's stream,
And their place is not known. Below, vast caves   120
Shine in the rushing torrents' restless gleam,
Which from those secret chasms in tumult welling
Meet in the vale, and one majestic River,
The breath and blood of distant lands, forever
Rolls its loud waters to the ocean waves,   125
Breathes its swift vapors to the circling air.

V

Mont Blanc yet gleams on high—the power is there,
The still and solemn power of many sights,
And many sounds, and much of life and death.

3. Varied.

In the calm darkness of the moonless nights,   130
In the lone glare of day, the snows descend
Upon that Mountain; none beholds them there,
Nor when the flakes burn in the sinking sun,
Or the star-beams dart through them—Winds contend
Silently there, and heap the snow with breath   135
Rapid and strong, but silently! Its home
The voiceless lightning in these solitudes
Keeps innocently, and like vapor broods
Over the snow. The secret Strength of things
Which governs thought, and to the infinite dome   140
Of Heaven is as a law, inhabits thee!
And what were thou, and earth, and stars, and sea,
If to the human mind's imaginings
Silence and solitude were vacancy?

                                                1817

LOUIS SIMPSON

The Green Shepherd

Here sit a shepherd and a shepherdess,
He playing on his melancholy flute;
The sea wind ruffles up her simple dress
And shows the delicacy of her foot.

And there you see Constantinople's wall   5
With arrows and Greek fire, molten lead;
Down from a turret seven virgins fall,
Hands folded, each one praying on her head.

The shepherd yawns and puts his flute away.
It's time, she murmurs, we were going back.   10
He offers certain reasons she should stay—
But neither sees the dragon on their track.

A dragon like a car in a garage
Is in the wood, his long tail sticking out.
Here rides St. George[4] swinging his sword and targe,[5]   15
And sticks the grinning dragon in the snout.

Puffing a smoke ring, like the cigarette
Over Times Square,[6] Sir Dragon snorts his last.
St. George takes off his armor in a sweat.
The Middle Ages have been safely passed.   20

4. The patron saint of England and legendary slayer of the dragon.
5. Shield.

6. A cigarette billboard which emitted steam to simulate smoke.

What is the sail that crosses the still bay,
Unnoticed by the shepherds? It could be
A caravel that's sailing to Cathay,[7]
Westward from Palos[8] on the unknown sea.

But the green shepherd travels in her eye   25
And whispers nothings in his lady's ear,
And sings a little song, that roses die,
Carpe diem,[9] which she seems pleased to hear.

The vessel they ignored still sails away
So bravely on the water, Westward Ho!   30
And murdering, in a religious way,
Brings Jesus to the Gulf of Mexico.

Now Portugal is fading, and the state
Of Castile rising purple on Peru;
Now England, now America grows great—   35
With which these lovers have nothing to do.

What do they care if time, uncompassed, drift
To China, and the crew is a baboon?
But let him whisper always, and her lift
The oceans in her eyelids to the moon.   40

The dragon rises crackling in the air,
And who is god but Dagon?[1] Wings careen,
Rejoicing, on the Russian hemisphere.
Meanwhile, the shepherd dotes upon her skin.

Old Aristotle, having seen this pass,   45
From where he studied in the giant's cave,
Went in and shut his book and locked the brass
And lay down with a shudder in his grave.

The groaning pole had gone more than a mile;
These shepherds did not feel it where they loved,   50
For time was sympathetic all the while
And on the magic mountain nothing moved.

1959

---

7. China.
8. Columbus sailed from the Spanish port of Palos on his first voyage; Cortez returned there after his conquest of Mexico.

9. "Live for the day": a traditional theme in love poetry.
1. The god of the Philistines, half man, half fish. See *Judges* 16.

W. D. SNODGRASS

The Campus on the Hill

Up the reputable walks of old established trees
They stalk, children of the *nouveaux riches;* chimes
Of the tall Clock Tower drench their heads in blessing:
"I don't wanna play at your house;
I don't like you any more."   5
My house stands opposite, on the other hill,
Among meadows, with the orchard fences down and falling;
Deer come almost to the door.
You cannot see it, even in this clearest morning.
White birds hang in the air between   10
Over the garbage landfill and those homes thereto adjacent,
Hovering slowly, turning, settling down
Like the flakes sifting imperceptibly onto the little town
In a waterball of glass.
And yet, this morning, beyond this quiet scene,   15
The floating birds, the backyards of the poor,
Beyond the shopping plaza, the dead canal, the hillside lying tilted in
        the air,
Tomorrow has broken out today:
Riot in Algeria, in Cyprus, in Alabama;
Aged in wrong, the empires are declining,   20
And China gathers, soundlessly, like evidence.
What shall I say to the young on such a morning?—
Mind is the one salvation?—also grammar?—
No; my little ones lean not toward revolt. They
Are the Whites, the vaguely furiously driven, who resist   25
Their souls with such passivity
As would make Quakers swear. All day, dear Lord, all day
They wear their godhead lightly.
They look out from their hill and say,
To themselves, "We have nowhere to go but down;   30
The great destination is to stay."
Surely the nations will be reasonable;
They look at the world—don't they?—the world's way?
The clock just now has nothing more to say.

1959

STEPHEN SPENDER

An Elementary School Classroom in a Slum

Far far from gusty waves these children's faces.
Like rootless weeds, the hair torn round their pallor.
The tall girl with her weighed-down head. The paper-

seeming boy, with rat's eyes. The stunted, unlucky heir
Of twisted bones, reciting a father's gnarled disease,   5
His lesson from his desk. At back of the dim class
One unnoted, sweet and young. His eyes live in a dream
Of squirrel's game, in tree room, other than this.
On sour cream walls, donations. Shakespeare's head,
Cloudless at dawn, civilized dome riding all cities.   10
Belled, flowery, Tyrolese valley.² Open-handed map
Awarding the world its world. And yet, for these
Children, these windows, not this world, are world,
Where all their future's painted with a fog,
A narrow street sealed in with a lead sky,   15
Far far from rivers, capes, and stars of words.

Surely, Shakespeare is wicked, the map a bad example
With ships and sun and love tempting them to steal—
For lives that slyly turn in their cramped holes
From fog to endless night? On their slag heap, these children   20
Wear skins peeped through by bones and spectacles of steel
With mended glass, like bottle bits on stones.
All of their time and space are foggy slum.
So blot their maps with slums as big as doom.

Unless, governor, teacher, inspector, visitor,   25
This map becomes their window and these windows
That shut upon their lives like catacombs,
Break O break open till they break the town
And show the children to green fields, and make their world
Run azure on gold sands, and let their tongues   30
Run naked into books, the white and green leaves open
History theirs whose language is the sun.

1939

STEPHEN SPENDER

Judas Iscariot³

The eyes of twenty centuries
Pursue me along corridors to where
I am painted at their ends on many walls.
    Ever-revolving future recognize
This red hair and red beard, where I am seated   5
Within the dark cave of the feast of light.

2. A rich and beautiful section of Austria with many scenes like those in typical paintings of hamlets and picturesque countrysides.
3. According to New Testament accounts, Judas, one of the twelve disciples, betrayed Jesus to his enemies for 30 pieces of silver. The betrayal occurred shortly after the Last Supper; Judas indicated to his confederates who Jesus was by kissing him.

Out of my heart-shaped shadow I stretch my hand
Across the white table into the dish
But not to dip the bread. It is as though
The cloth on each side of one dove-bright face   10
Spread dazzling wings on which the apostles ride
Uplifting them into the vision
Where their eyes watch themselves enthroned.
　　My russet hand across the dish
Plucks enviously against one feather   15
　　—But still the rushing wings spurn me below!

　　Saint Sebastian[4] of wickedness
I stand: all eyes legitimate arrows piercing through
The darkness of my wickedness. They recognize
My halo hammered from thirty silver pieces   20
And the hemp rope around my neck
Soft as that Spirit's hanging arms
When on my cheek he answered with the kiss
Which cuts for ever—
　　　　　　　　　　My strange stigmata,   25
All love and hate, all fire and ice!

　　But who betrayed whom? O you,
Whose light gaze forms the azure corridor
Through which those other pouring eyes
Arrow into me—answer! Who   30
Betrayed whom? Who read
In his mind's light from the first day
That the kingdom of heaven on earth must always
Reiterate the garden of Eden,
And each day's revolution be betrayed   35
Within man's heart, each day?
　　　　　　　　　　　　Who wrapped
The whispering serpent round the tree
And hung between the leaves the glittering purse
And trapped the fangs with God-appointed poison?   40
Who knew
I must betray the truth, and made the lie
Betray its truth in me?

　　Those hypocrite eyes which aimed at you
Now aim at me. And yet, beyond their world   45
Each turning on his pole of truth, your pole
Invisible light, and mine
Becoming what man is. We stare
Across two thousand years, and heaven, and hell,
Into each other's gaze.   50

1949

4. Early Christian martyr who was a
favorite subject of Renaissance painters.
According to legend, St. Sebastian was
sentenced to be shot with arrows, but his
many wounds were miraculously healed.

WALLACE STEVENS

Disillusionment of Ten O'clock

The houses are haunted
By white night-gowns
None are green,
Or purple with green rings,
Or green with yellow rings,   5
Or yellow with blue rings.
None of them are strange,
With socks of lace
And beaded ceintures.[5]
People are not going   10
To dream of baboons and periwinkles.[6]
Only, here and there, an old sailor,
Drunk and asleep in his boots,
Catches tigers
In red weather.   15

1923

WALLACE STEVENS

The Emperor of Ice-Cream

Call the roller of big cigars,
The muscular one, and bid him whip
In kitchen cups concupiscent curds.[7]
Let the wenches dawdle in such dress
As they are used to wear, and let the boys   5
Bring flowers in last month's newspapers.
Let be be finale of seem.[8]
The only emperor is the emperor of ice-cream.

Take from the dresser of deal,
Lacking the three glass knobs, that sheet   10
On which she embroidered fantails[9] once
And spread it so as to cover her face.
If her horny feet protrude, they come

---

5. Cinctures: belts, girdles.
6. Sea snails.
7. "The words 'concupiscent curds' have no genealogy; they are merely expressive: at least, I hope they are expressive. They express the concupiscence of life, but, by contrast with the things in relation in the poem, they express or accentuate life's destitution, and it is this that gives them something more than a cheap lustre" Wallace Stevens, *Letters* (New York: Knopf, 1960), p. 500.
8. ". . . the true sense of Let be be the finale of seem is let being become the conclusion or denouement of appearing to be: in short, ice cream is an absolute good. The poem is obviously not about ice cream, but about being as distinguished from seeming to be." *Letters*, p. 341.
9. Fantail pigeons.

> To show how cold she is, and dumb.
> Let the lamp affix its beam.   15
> The only emperor is the emperor of ice-cream.

                                                                        1923

WALLACE STEVENS

Martial Cadenza

I

Only this evening I saw again low in the sky
The evening star, at the beginning of winter, the star
That in spring will crown every western horizon,
Again . . . as if it came back, as if life came back,
Not in a later son, a different daughter, another place,   5
But as if evening found us young, still young,
Still walking in a present of our own.

II

It was like sudden time in a world without time,
This world, this place, the street in which I was,
Without time: as that which is not has no time,   10
Is not, or is of what there was, is full
Of the silence before the armies, armies without
Either trumpets or drums, the commanders mute, the arms
On the ground, fixed fast in a profound defeat.

III

What had this star to do with the world it lit,   15
With the blank skies over England, over France
And above the German camps? It looked apart.
Yet it is this that shall maintain—Itself
Is time, apart from any past, apart
From any future, the ever-living and being,   20
The ever-breathing and moving, the constant fire,

IV

The present close, the present realized,
Not the symbol but that for which the symbol stands,
The vivid thing in the air that never changes,
Though the air change. Only this evening I saw it again,   25
At the beginning of winter, and I walked and talked
Again, and lived and was again, and breathed again
And moved again and flashed again, time flashed again.

                                                                        1942

WALLACE STEVENS

Sunday Morning

I

Complacencies of the peignoir, and late
Coffee and oranges in a sunny chair,
And the green freedom of a cockatoo
Upon a rug mingle to dissipate
The holy hush of ancient sacrifice.   5
She dreams a little, and she feels the dark
Encroachment of that old catastrophe,[1]
As a calm darkens among water-lights.
The pungent oranges and bright, green wings
Seem things in some procession of the dead,   10
Winding across wide water, without sound.
The day is like wide water, without sound,
Stilled for the passing of her dreaming feet
Over the seas, to silent Palestine,
Dominion of the blood and sepulchre.   15

II

Why should she give her bounty to the dead?
What is divinity if it can come
Only in silent shadows and in dreams?
Shall she not find in comforts of the sun,
In pungent fruit and bright, green wings, or else   20
In any balm or beauty of the earth,
Things to be cherished like the thought of heaven?
Divinity must live within herself:
Passions of rain, or moods in falling snow;
Grievings in loneliness, or unsubdued   25
Elations when the forest blooms; gusty
Emotions on wet roads on autumn nights;
All pleasures and all pains, remembering
The bough of summer and the winter branch.
These are the measures destined for her soul.   30

III

Jove[2] in the clouds had his inhuman birth.
No mother suckled him, no sweet land gave
Large-mannered motions to his mythy mind
He moved among us, as a muttering king,
Magnificent, would move among his hinds,[3]   35
Until our blood, commingling, virginal,
With heaven, brought such requital to desire
The very hinds discerned it, in a star.[4]
Shall our blood fail? Or shall it come to be
The blood of paradise? And shall the earth   40

---

1. The Crucifixion.   3. Lowliest rural subjects.
2. Jupiter, the chief Roman god.   4. The star of Bethlehem.

Seem all of paradise that we shall know?
The sky will be much friendlier then than now,
A part of labor and a part of pain,
And next in glory to enduring love,
Not this dividing and indifferent blue.   45

IV

She says, "I am content when wakened birds,
Before they fly, test the reality
Of misty fields, by their sweet questionings;
But when the birds are gone, and their warm fields
Return no more, where, then, is paradise?"   50
There is not any haunt of prophecy,
Nor any old chimera of the grave,
Neither the golden underground, nor isle
Melodious, where spirits gat[5] them home,
Nor visionary south, nor cloudy palm   55
Remote on heaven's hill, that has endured
As April's green endures, or will endure
Like her remembrance of awakened birds,
Or her desire for June and evening, tipped
By the consummation of the swallow's wings.   60

V

She says, "But in contentment I still feel
The need of some imperishable bliss."
Death is the mother of beauty; hence from her,
Alone, shall come fulfillment to our dreams
And our desires. Although she strews the leaves   65
Of sure obliteration on our paths,
The path sick sorrow took, the many paths
Where triumph rang its brassy phrase, or love
Whispered a little out of tenderness,
She makes the willow shiver in the sun   70
For maidens who were wont to sit and gaze
Upon the grass, relinquished to their feet.
She causes boys to pile new plums and pears
On disregarded plate.[6] The maidens taste
And stray impassioned in the littering leaves.   75

VI

Is there no change of death in paradise?
Does ripe fruit never fall? Or do the boughs
Hang always heavy in that perfect sky,
Unchanging, yet so like our perishing earth,
With rivers like our own that seek for seas   80

5. Got.
6. "Plate is used in the sense of so-called family plate. Disregarded refers to the disuse into which things fall that have been possessed for a long time. I mean, therefore, that death releases and renews. What the old have come to disregard, the young inherit and make use of" (*Letters of Wallace Stevens* [1966], pp. 183–184).

They never find, the same receding shores
That never touch with inarticulate pang?
Why set the pear upon those river-banks
Or spice the shores with odors of the plum?
Alas, that they should wear our colors there,   85
The silken weavings of our afternoons,
And pick the strings of our insipid lutes!
Death is the mother of beauty, mystical,
Within whose burning bosom we devise
Our earthly mothers waiting, sleeplessly.   90

VII
Supple and turbulent, a ring of men
Shall chant in orgy[7] on a summer morn
Their boisterous devotion to the sun,
Not as a god, but as a god might be,
Naked among them, like a savage source.   95
Their chant shall be a chant of paradise,
Out of their blood, returning to the sky;
And in their chant shall enter, voice by voice,
The windy lake wherein their lord delights,
The trees, like serafin,[8] and echoing hills,   100
That choir among themselves long afterward.
They shall know well the heavenly fellowship
Of men that perish and of summer morn.
And whence they came and whither they shall go
The dew upon their feet shall manifest.   105

VIII
She hears, upon that water without sound,
A voice that cries, "The tomb in Palestine
Is not the porch of spirits lingering.
It is the grave of Jesus, where he lay."
We live in an old chaos of the sun,   110
Or old dependency of day and night,
Or island solitude, unsponsored, free,
Of that wide water, inescapable.
Deer walk upon our mountains, and the quail
Whistle about us their spontaneous cries;   115
Sweet berries ripen in the wilderness;
And, in the isolation of the sky,
At evening, casual flocks of pigeons make
Ambiguous undulations as they sink,
Downward to darkness, on extended wings.   120

1915

---

7. Ceremonial revelry.   orders of angels.
8. Seraphim, the highest of the nine

NANCY SULLIVAN

Burial in the Sand

The sand is a gritty flesh
mounding her aching mounds.
He piles her tight
    up to her throat.
On her head a flare of cloth hat,   5
in her mouth the glare of gold teeth.
Pat, pat. The drooling sand dribbles
  over
her arthritis quiet under its warm compress.
He is Henry Moore[9] building his old woman. 10
  Then
from this burial in the sand his beach Venus[1]
rises out of the maw of Zeus,
    her jewelry toothy, her crown canvas.
He rises and she rises,   15
    breaking the mold
the way it never happens out of
real statues, risky and rare,
although the same deep force
buried deep in the stone   20
is poised for the pounce.

              1975

JONATHAN SWIFT

A Beautiful Young Nymph Going to Bed

Corinna, pride of Drury-Lane,[2]
For whom no shepherd sighs in vain;
Never did Covent Garden[3] boast
So bright a battered, strolling toast;[4]
No drunken rake to pick her up,   5
No cellar where on tick[5] to sup;
Returning at the midnight hour;
Four stories climbing to her bow'r;
Then, seated on a three-legged chair,
Takes off her artificial hair: 10
Now, picking out a crystal eye,

---

9. English sculptor, b. 1898.
1. Roman goddess of love, usually said
to have sprung from the foam of the sea
or (alternatively) to have been the daugh-
ter of Dione and Jupiter (Greek name
Zeus), the supreme deity.

2. The London theatre district, inhabited
by many prostitutes.
3. A rival area.
4. A celebrated lady, one who is toasted.
5. Credit.

She wipes it clean, and lays it by.
Her eyebrows from a mouse's hide,
Stuck on with art on either side,
Pulls off with care, and first displays 'em,   15
Then in a play-book smoothly lays 'em.
Now dextrously her plumpers⁶ draws,
That serve to fill her hollow jaws.
Untwists a wire; and from her gums
A set of teeth completely comes.   20
Pulls out the rags contrived to prop
Her flabby dugs and down they drop.
Proceeding on, the lovely goddess
Unlaces next her steel-ribbed bodice;
Which by the operator's skill,   25
Press down the lumps, the hollows fill,
Up goes her hand, and off she slips
The bolsters that supply her hips.
With gentlest touch, she next explores
Her shankers,⁷ issues, running sores,   30
Effects of many a sad disaster;
And then to each applies a plaster.
But must, before she goes to bed,
Rub off the daubs of white and red;
And smooth the furrows in her front,   35
With greasy paper stuck upon't.
She takes a bolus⁸ e'er she sleeps;
And then between two blankets creeps.
With pains of love tormented lies;
Or if she chance to close her eyes,   40
Of Bridewell and the Compter⁹ dreams,
And feels the lash, and faintly screams;
Or, by a faithless bully drawn,
At some hedge-tavern lies in pawn;
Or to Jamaica seems transported,   45
Alone, and by no planter courted;¹
Or, near Fleet-Ditch's oozy brinks,²
Surrounded with a hundred stinks,
Belated, seems on watch to lie,
And snap some cully³ passing by;   50
Or, struck with fear, her fancy runs
On watchmen, constables and duns,
From whom she meets with frequent rubs;
But, never from religious clubs;
Whose favor she is sure to find,   55
Because she pays them all in kind.

6. Small balls or discs held in the mouth to fill out hollow cheeks.
7. Cankers.
8. Large pill.
9. Prisons; Bridewell held mostly vagrants and prostitutes.
1. Felons were sometimes transported to America rather than being hanged; they were then indentured for a number of years unless someone bought their freedom.
2. Most of London's sewage went to Fleet Ditch before being dumped into the Thames.
3. Dupe.

Corinna wakes. A dreadful sight!
Behold the ruins of the night!
A wicked rat her plaster stole,
Half eat, and dragged it to his hole.   60
The crystal eye, alas, was missed;
And Puss had on her plumpers pissed.
A pigeon picked her issue-peas;[4]
And Shock her tresses filled with fleas.
 The nymph though in this mangled plight,   65
Must ev'ry morn her limbs unite.
But how shall I describe her arts
To recollect the scattered parts?
Or show the anguish, toil, and pain,
Of gath'ring up herself again?   70
The bashful muse will never bear
In such a scene to interfere.
Corinna in the morning dizened,
Who sees, will spew; who smells, be poisoned.

1734

JONATHAN SWIFT

On Stella's Birthday, 1719

Stella this day is thirty-four,[5]
(We shan't dispute a year or more)
However Stella, be not troubled,
Although thy size and years are doubled,
Since first I saw thee at sixteen   5
The brightest virgin on the green,
So little is thy form declined
Made up so largely in thy mind.
Oh, would it please the gods to split
Thy beauty, size, and years, and wit,   10
No age could furnish out a pair
Of nymphs so graceful, wise and fair
With half the luster of your eyes,
With half your wit, your years and size:
And then before it grew too late,   15
How should I beg of gentle Fate,
(That either nymph might have her swain,[6])
To split my worship too in twain.

1719

---

4. Peas or other small round objects
placed in incisions to drain sores by coun-
ter-irritation.
5. Stella is Swift's pet name for Hester

Johnson, a close friend for many years. She
was actually 38.
 6. Servant, admirer, lover.

ALFRED, LORD TENNYSON

The Charge of the Light Brigade[7]

I

Half a league, half a league,
Half a league onward,
All in the valley of Death
    Rode the six hundred.[8]
"Forward the Light Brigade!   5
Charge for the guns!" he said.
Into the valley of Death
    Rode the six hundred.

II

"Forward, the Light Brigade!"
Was there a man dismayed?   10
Not though the soldier knew
    Someone had blundered.
Theirs not to make reply,
Theirs not to reason why,
Theirs but to do and die.   15
Into the valley of Death
    Rode the six hundred.

III

Cannon to right of them,
Cannon to left of them,
Cannon in front of them   20
    Volleyed and thundered;
Stormed at with shot and shell,
Boldly they rode and well,
Into the jaws of Death,
Into the mouth of hell   25
    Rode the six hundred.

IV

Flashed all their sabres bare,
Flashed as they turned in air
Sabring the gunners there,
Charging an army, while   30
    All the world wondered.
Plunged in the battery-smoke
Right through the line they broke;
Cossack and Russian

---

7. The Crimean charge took place on October 25, 1854; nearly half the officers and men were wounded or killed, and immediate reports suggested even heavier casualties. Legend says Tennyson took the rhythm of the poem from an item in the London *Times* which contained the phrase "Someone had blundered" (but the phrase doesn't actually occur in the item).

8. Pronounced "hunderd" in Tennyson's native Lincolnshire.

Reeled from the sabre-stroke   35
  Shattered and sundered.
Then they rode back, but not,
  Not the six hundred.

V

Cannon to right of them,
Cannon to left of them,   40
Cannon behind them
  Volleyed and thundered;
Stormed at with shot and shell,
While horse and hero fell.
They that had fought so well   45
Came through the jaws of Death,
Back from the mouth of hell,
All that was left of them,
  Left of six hundred.

VI

When can their glory fade?   50
O the wild charge they made!
  All the world wondered.
Honor the charge they made!
Honor the Light Brigade,
  Noble six hundred!   55

                                          p. 1854

ALFRED, LORD TENNYSON

Flower in the Crannied Wall

Flower in the crannied wall,
I pluck you out of the crannies,
I hold you here, root and all, in my hand.
Little flower—but if I could understand
What you are, root and all, and all in all,   5
I should know what God and man is.

                                          1869

ALFRED, LORD TENNYSON

Morte d'Arthur[9]

So all day long the noise of battle rolled
Among the mountains by the winter sea,
Until King Arthur's table, man by man,
Had fallen in Lyonnesse[1] about their lord,
King Arthur; then, because his wound was deep,   5
The bold Sir Bedivere uplifted him,
Sir Bedivere, the last of all his knights,
And bore him to a chapel nigh the field,
A broken chancel with a broken cross,
That stood on a dark strait of barren land.   10
On one side lay the ocean, and on one
Lay a great water, and the moon was full.
    Then spake King Arthur to Sir Bedivere:
"The sequel[2] of today unsolders all
The goodliest fellowship of famous knights   15
Whereof this world holds record. Such a sleep
They sleep—the men I loved. I think that we
Shall never more, at any future time,
Delight our souls with talk of knightly deeds,
Walking about the gardens and the halls   20
Of Camelot, as in the days that were.
I perish by this people which I made—
Though Merlin sware that I should come again
To rule once more—but let what will be be,
I am so deeply smitten through the helm   25
That without help I cannot last till morn.
Thou therefore take my brand[3] Excalibur,
Which was my pride; for thou rememberest how
In those old days, one summer noon, an arm
Rose up from out the bosom of the lake,   30
Clothed in white samite,[4] mystic, wonderful,
Holding the sword—and how I rowed across
And took it, and have worn it, like a king;
And, wheresoever I am sung or told
In aftertime, this also shall be known.   35
But now delay not; take Excalibur,
And fling him far into the middle mere;[5]
Watch what thou seest, and lightly[6] bring me word."
    To him replied the bold Sir Bedivere:
"It is not meet, Sir King, to leave thee thus,   40
Aidless, alone, and smitten through the helm.

9. Tennyson once intended to write an epic poem on the Arthurian legend, but this narrative of Arthur's death is all that he completed. He later published it in two forms: separately with a brief dramatic framework which introduces a narrator to tell the story, and then, in expanded form, as a part of *Idylls of the King.*

1. According to legend, an island country off the coast of Cornwall.
2. Result.
3. Sword.
4. A heavy silk fabric, often interwoven with silver or gold.
5. Middle of the lake.
6. Quickly.

A little thing may harm a wounded man.
Yet I thy hest will all perform at full,
Watch what I see, and lightly bring thee word."
    So saying, from the ruined shrine he stepped   45
And in the moon athwart the place of tombs,
Where lay the mighty bones of ancient men,
Old knights, and over them the sea-wind sang
Shrill, chill, with flakes of foam. He, stepping down
By zigzag paths and juts of pointed rock,   50
Came on the shining levels of the lake.
    There drew he forth the brand Excalibur,
And o'er him, drawing it, the winter moon,
Brightening the skirts of a long cloud, ran forth
And sparkled keen with frost against the hilt;   55
For all the haft twinkled with diamond sparks,
Myriads of topaz-lights, and jacinth-work
Of subtlest jewelry. He gazed so long
That both his eyes were dazzled, as he stood,
This way and that dividing the swift mind,   60
In act to throw; but at the last it seemed
Better to leave Excalibur concealed
There in the many-knotted water-flags,
That whistled stiff and dry about the marge.[7]
So strode he back slow to the wounded king.   65
    Then spake King Arthur to Sir Bedivere:
"Hast thou performed my mission which I gave?
What is it thou hast seen, or what hast heard?"
    And answer made the bold Sir Bedivere:
"I heard the ripple washing in the reeds,   70
And the wild water lapping on the crag."
    To whom replied King Arthur, faint and pale:
"Thou hast betrayed thy nature and thy name,
Not rendering true answer, as beseemed
Thy fealty,[8] nor like a noble knight;   75
For surer sign had followed, either hand,
Or voice, or else a motion of the mere.
This is a shameful thing for men to lie.
Yet now, I charge thee, quickly go again
As thou art lief[9] and dear, and do the thing   80
I bade thee, watch, and lightly bring me word."
    Then went Sir Bedivere the second time
Across the ridge, and paced beside the mere,
Counting the dewy pebbles, fixed in thought;
But when he saw the wonder of the hilt,   85
How curiously[1] and strangely chased,[2] he smote
His palms together, and he cried aloud:
    "And if indeed I cast the brand away,
Surely a precious thing, one worthy note,

7. Margin: edge.   1. Artfully.
8. Obligation of loyalty.   2. Engraved or embossed.
9. Beloved.

Should thus be lost forever from the earth,   90
Which might have pleased the eyes of many men.
What good should follow this, if this were done?
What harm, undone? deep harm to disobey,
Seeing obedience is the bond of rule.
Were it well to obey then, if a king demand   95
An act unprofitable, against himself?
The king is sick, and knows not what he does.
What record, or what relic of my lord
Should be to aftertime, but empty breath
And rumors of a doubt? but were this kept,   100
Stored in some treasure-house of mighty kings,
Someone might show it at a joust of arms,
Saying, 'King Arthur's sword, Excalibur,
Wrought by the lonely maiden of the lake.
Nine years she wrought it, sitting in the deeps   105
Upon the hidden bases of the hills.'
So might some old man speak in the aftertime
To all the people, winning reverence;
But now much honor and much fame were lost."
     So spake he, clouded with his own conceit,[3]   110
And hid Excalibur the second time,
And so strode back slow to the wounded king.
     Then spoke King Arthur, breathing heavily:
"What is it thou hast seen, or what hast heard?"
     And answer made the bold Sir Bedivere: 115
"I heard the water lapping on the crag,
And the long ripple washing in the reeds."
     To whom replied King Arthur, much in wrath:
"Ah, miserable and unkind, untrue,
Unknightly, traitor-hearted! Woe is me!   120
Authority forgets a dying king,
Laid widowed of the power in his eye
That bowed the will. I see thee what thou art,
For thou, the latest-left of all my knights,
In whom should meet[4] the offices of all,   125
Thou wouldst betray me for the precious hilt;
Either from lust of gold, or like a girl
Valuing the giddy pleasure of the eyes.
Yet, for a man may fail in duty twice,
And the third time may prosper, get thee hence;   130
But, if thou spare to fling Excalibur,
I will arise and slay thee with my hands."
     Then quickly rose Sir Bedivere, and ran,
And, leaping down the ridges lightly, plunged
Among the bulrush-beds, and clutched the sword,   135
And strongly wheeled and threw it. The great brand
Made lightnings in the splendor of the moon,

3. Fanciful notion.   4. Unite.

And flashing round and round, and whirled in an arch,
Shot like a streamer of the northern morn,[5]
Seen where the moving isles[6] of winter shock   140
By night, with noises of the northern sea.
So flashed and fell the brand Excalibur;
But ere he dipped the surface, rose an arm
Clothed in white samite, mystic, wonderful,
And caught him by the hilt, and brandished him   145
Three times, and drew him under in the mere.
And lightly went the other to the king.
    Then spoke King Arthur, drawing thicker breath:
"Now see I by thine eyes that this is done.
Speak out; what is it thou hast heard, or seen?"   150
    And answer made the bold Sir Bedivere:
"Sir King, I closed mine eyelids, lest the gems
Should blind my purpose, for I never saw,
Nor shall see, here or elsewhere, till I die,
Not though I live three lives of mortal men,   155
So great a miracle as yonder hilt.
Then with both hands I flung him, wheeling him;
But when I looked again, behold an arm,
Clothed in white samite, mystic, wonderful,
That caught him by the hilt, and brandished him   160
Three times, and drew him under in the mere."
    And answer made King Arthur, breathing hard:
"My end draws nigh; 'tis time that I were gone.
Make broad thy shoulders to receive my weight,
And bear me to the margin; yet I fear   165
My wound hath taken cold, and I shall die."
    So saying, from the pavement he half rose,
Slowly, with pain, reclining on his arm,
And looking wistfully with wide blue eyes
As in a picture. Him Sir Bedivere   170
Remorsefully regarded through his tears,
And would have spoken, but he found not words,
Then took with care, and kneeling on one knee,
O'er both his shoulders drew the languid hands,
And rising bore him through the place of tombs.   175
    But, as he walked, King Arthur panted hard,
Like one that feels a nightmare on his bed
When all the house is mute. So sighed the king,
Muttering and murmuring at his ear, "Quick, quick!
I fear it is too late, and I shall die."   180
But the other swiftly strode from ridge to ridge,
Clothed with his breath, and looking, as he walked,
Larger than human on the frozen hills.
He heard the deep behind him, and a cry
Before. His own thought drove him like a goad.   185

---

5. The Northern Lights.   6. Icebergs.

Dry clashed his harness in the icy caves
And barren chasms, and all to left and right
The bare black cliff clanged round him, as he based
His feet on juts of slippery crag that rang
Sharp-smitten with the dint of arméd heels—   190
And on a sudden, lo! the level lake,
And the long glories of the winter moon.
    Then saw they how there hove a dusky barge,
Dark as a funeral scarf from stem to stern,
Beneath them; and descending they were ware   195
That all the decks were dense with stately forms
Black-stoled, black-hooded, like a dream—by these
Three queens with crowns of gold—and from them rose
A cry that shivered to the tingling stars,
And, as it were one voice, an agony   200
Of lamentation, like a wind that shrills
All night in a waste land, where no one comes,
Or hath come, since the making of the world.
    Then murmured Arthur, "Place me in the barge,"
And to the barge they came. There those three queens   205
Put forth their hands, and took the king, and wept.
But she that rose the tallest of them all
And fairest laid his head upon her lap,
And loosed the shattered casque,[7] and chafed his hands,
And called him by his name, complaining loud,   210
And dropping bitter tears against his brow
Striped with dark blood; for all his face was white
And colorless, and like the withered moon
Smote by the fresh beam of the springing east;
And all his greaves and cuisses[8] dashed with drops   215
Of onset,[9] and the light and lustrous curls—
That made his forehead like a rising sun
High from the dais-throne—were parched with dust;
Or, clotted into points and hanging loose,
Mixed with the knightly growth that fringed his lips.   220
So like a shattered column lay the king;
Not like that Arthur who, with lance in rest,
From spur to plume a star of tournament,
Shot through the lists at Camelot, and charged
Before the eyes of ladies and of kings.   225
    Then loudly cried the bold Sir Bedivere:
"Ah! my Lord Arthur, whither shall I go?
Where shall I hide my forehead and my eyes?
For now I see the true old times are dead,
When every morning brought a noble chance,   230
And every chance brought out a noble knight.
Such times have been not since the light that led
The holy Elders with the gift of myrrh.[1]

---

7. Helmet.
8. Armor to protect the shins and thighs.
9. Blood from the battle.

1. The star that guided the Magi to Bethlehem.

But now the whole ROUND TABLE is dissolved
Which was an image of the mighty world;   235
And I, the last, go forth companionless,
And the days darken round me, and the years,
Among new men, strange faces, other minds."
   And slowly answered Arthur from the barge:
"The old order changeth, yielding place to new,   240
And God fulfills himself in many ways,
Lest one good custom should corrupt the world.
Comfort thyself: what comfort is in me?
I have lived my life, and that which I have done
May He within Himself make pure! but thou,   245
If thou shouldst never see my face again,
Pray for my soul. More things are wrought by prayer
Than this world dreams of. Wherefore, let thy voice
Rise like a fountain for me night and day.
For what are men better than sheep or goats   250
That nourish a blind life within the brain,
If, knowing God, they lift not hands of prayer
Both for themselves and those who call them friend?
For so the whole round earth is every way
Bound by gold chains about the feet of God.   255
But now farewell. I am going a long way
With these thou seest—if indeed I go—
For all my mind is clouded with a doubt—
To the island-valley of Avilion;[2]
Where falls not hail, or rain, or any snow,   260
Nor ever wind blows loudly, but it lies
Deep-meadowed, happy, fair with orchard lawns
And bowery hollows crowned with summer sea,
Where I will heal me of my grievous wound."
   So said he, and the barge with oar and sail   265
Moved from the brink, like some full-breasted swan
That, fluting a wild carol ere her death,
Ruffles her pure cold plume, and takes the flood
With swarthy webs. Long stood Sir Bedivere
Revolving many memories, till the hull   270
Looked one black dot against the verge of dawn,
And on the mere the wailing died away.

1833–34

---

2. Avalon, where, according to Celtic mythology, heroes dwell after death.

ALFRED, LORD TENNYSON

Tears, Idle Tears[3]

Tears, idle tears, I know not what they mean,
Tears from the depth of some divine despair
Rise in the heart, and gather to the eyes,
In looking on the happy autumn-fields,
And thinking of the days that are no more.   5

Fresh as the first beam glittering on a sail,
That brings our friends up from the underworld,
Sad as the last which reddens over one
That sinks with all we love below the verge;
So sad, so fresh, the days that are no more.   10

Ah, sad and strange as in dark summer dawns
The earliest pipe of half-awakened birds
To dying ears, when unto dying eyes
The casement slowly grows a glimmering square;
So sad, so strange, the days that are no more.   15

Dear as remembered kisses after death,
And sweet as those by hopeless fancy feigned
On lips that are for others; deep as love,
Deep as first love, and wild with all regret;
O Death in Life, the days that are no more!   20

1847

DYLAN THOMAS

Fern Hill

Now as I was young and easy under the apple boughs
About the lilting house and happy as the grass was green,
   The night above the dingle starry,
    Time let me hail and climb
   Golden in the heydays of his eyes,   5
And honored among wagons I was prince of the apple towns
And once below a time I lordly had the trees and leaves
    Trail with daisies and barley
   Down the rivers of the windfall light.

And as I was green and carefree, famous among the barns   10
About the happy yard and singing as the farm was home,

---

3. A song from *The Princess*, a long narrative poem about what the mid-nineteenth century called the "new woman."

In the sun that is young once only,
  Time let me play and be
  Golden in the mercy of his means,
And green and golden I was huntsman and herdsman, the calves   15
Sang to my horn, the foxes on the hills barked clear and cold,
   And the sabbath rang slowly
  In the pebbles of the holy streams.

All the sun long it was running, it was lovely, the hay
Fields high as the house, the tunes from the chimneys, it was air   20
  And playing, lovely and watery
   And fire green as grass.
  And nightly under the simple stars
As I rode to sleep the owls were bearing the farm away,
All the moon long I heard, blessed among stables, the nightjars[4]   25
  Flying with the ricks,[5] and the horses
   Flashing into the dark.

And then to awake, and the farm, like a wanderer white
With the dew, come back, the cock on his shoulder: it was all
  Shining, it was Adam and maiden,   30
   The sky gathered again
  And the sun grew round that very day.
So it must have been after the birth of the simple light
In the first, spinning place, the spellbound horses walking warm
  Out of the whinnying green stable   35
   On to the fields of praise.

And honored among foxes and pheasants by the gay house
Under the new made clouds and happy as the heart was long,
  In the sun born over and over,
   I ran my heedless ways,   40
  My wishes raced through the house-high hay
And nothing I cared, at my sky-blue trades, that time allows
In all his tuneful turning so few and such morning songs
  Before the children green and golden
   Follow him out of grace,   45

Nothing I cared, in the lamb white days, that time would take me
Up to the swallow-thronged loft by the shadow of my hand,
  In the moon that is always rising,
   Nor that riding to sleep
  I should hear him fly with the high fields   50
And wake to the farm forever fled from the childless land.
Oh as I was young and easy in the mercy of his means,
  Time held me green and dying
  Though I sang in my chains like the sea.

             1946

---

4. Birds.   5. Haystacks.

JEAN TOOMER

Song of the Son[6]

Pour O pour that parting soul in song,
O pour it in the sawdust glow of night,
Into the velvet pine-smoke air tonight,
And let the valley carry it along.
And let the valley carry it along.   5

O land and soil, red soil and sweet-gum tree,
So scant of grass, so profligate of pines,
Now just before an epoch's sun declines
Thy son, in time, I have returned to thee,
Thy son, I have in time returned to thee.   10

In time, for though the sun is setting on
A song-lit race of slaves, it has not set;
Though late, O soil, it is not too late yet
To catch thy plaintive soul, leaving, soon gone,
Leaving, to catch thy plaintive soul soon gone.   15

O Negro slaves, dark purple ripened plums,
Squeezed, and bursting in the pine-wood air,
Passing, before they strip the old tree bare
One plum was saved for me, one seed becomes

An everlasting song, a singing tree,   20
Caroling softly souls of slavery,
What they were, and what they are to me,
Caroling softly souls of slavery.

                                                               1923

HENRY VAUGHAN

The Retreat

Happy those early days! when I
Shined in my angel infancy.
Before I understood this place
Appointed for my second race,
Or taught my soul to fancy aught   5
But a white, celestial thought;
When yet I had not walked above
A mile or two from my first love,
And looking back, at that short space,

---

6. From the novel *Cane*.

Could see a glimpse of His bright face;   10
When on some gilded cloud or flower
My gazing soul would dwell an hour,
And in those weaker glories spy
Some shadows of eternity;
Before I taught my tongue to wound   15
My conscience with a sinful sound,
Or had the black art to dispense
A several[7] sin to every sense,
But felt through all this fleshly dress
Bright shoots of everlastingness.   20
   O, how I long to travel back,
And tread again that ancient track!
That I might once more reach that plain
Where first I left my glorious train,
From whence th' enlightened spirit sees   25
That shady city of palm trees.
But, ah! my soul with too much stay
Is drunk, and staggers in the way.
Some men a forward motion love;
But I by backward steps would move,   30
And when this dust falls to the urn,
In that state I came, return.

1650

DIANE WAKOSKI

Belly Dancer

Can these movements which move themselves
be the substance of my attraction?
Where does this thin green silk come from that covers
   my body?
Surely any woman wearing such fabrics
would move her body just to feel them touching every
   part of her.   5

Yet most of the women frown, or look away, or
   laugh stiffly.
They are afraid of these materials and these movements
in some way.
The psychologists would say they are afraid of
   themselves, somehow.
Perhaps awakening too much desire—   10
that their men could never satisfy?

7. Separate.

So they keep themselves laced and buttoned and
   made up
in hopes that the framework will keep them stiff
   enough not to feel
the whole register.
In hopes that they will not have to experience that
   unquenchable desire for rhythm and contact.   15

If a snake glided across this floor
most of them would faint or shrink away.
Yet that movement could be their own.
That smooth movement frightens them—
awakening ancestors and relatives to the tips of the
   arms and toes.   20

So my bare feet
and my thin green silks
my bells and finger cymbals
offend them—frighten their old-young bodies.
While the men simper and leer—   25
glad for the vicarious experience and exercise.
They do not realize how I scorn them:
or how I dance for their frightened,
unawakened, sweet
women.   30

            1966

DIANE WAKOSKI

A Poet Recognizing the Echo of the Voice

I. Isolation of Beautiful Women

> "How were you able to get ten of the world's
> most beautiful women to marry you?"
> "I just asked them. You know, men all over
> the world dream about Lana Turner, desire
> her want to be with her. But very very
> few ever ask her to marry them."
>
>   paraphrase of an interview with Artie Shaw

We are burning
in our heads
at night,
bonfires of our own bodies.
Persia reduces our heads   5
to star sapphires and lapis lazuli.[8]
Silver threads itself
into the lines of our throats
and glitters every time we speak.

8. Blue gems.

Old alchemical riddles[9]   10
are solved in the dreams of men
who marry other women and think of us.
Anyone who sees us
will hold our small hands,
like mirrors in which they see themselves,   15
and try to initial our arms
with desperation.
Everyone wants to come close to
the cinnamon of our ears.
Every man wants to explore our bodies   20
and fill up our minds.
Riding their motorcycles along collapsing grey highways,
they sequester their ambivalent hunting clothes
between our legs,
reminding themselves of their value   25
by quoting mining stock prices, and ours.
But men do not marry us,
do not ask us to share their lives,
do not survive the bonfires
hot enough to melt steel.   30
To alchemize rubies.

We live the loneliness
that men run after,
and we,
the precious rocks of the earth   35
are made harder,
more fiery
more beautiful,
more complex,
by all the pressing,   40
the burying,
the plundering;

even your desertions,
your betrayals,
your failure to understand and love us,   45
your unwillingness to face the world
as staunchly as we do;
these things
which ravage us,
cannot destroy our lives,   50
though they often take our bodies.
We are the earth.
We wake up
finding ourselves
glinting in the dark   55
after thousands of years
of pressing.

9. Problems. Alchemy was devoted to   metals to gold (line 31).
finding an elixir which would turn baser

II. Movement to Establish My Identity

I know what wages beauty gives,
How hard a life her servant lives . . .
"To A Young Beauty," W. B. YEATS

A woman wakes up
finds herself
glinting in the dark;   60
the earth holds her
as a precious rock
in a mine

her breath is a jumble
of sediments,   65
of mixed strata,
of the valuable,
beautiful,
of bulk.

All men are miners;   70
willing to work hard
and cover themselves with pit dirt;
to dig out;
to weigh;
to possess.   75

Mine is a place.
Mine is a designation.
A man says, "it is mine,"
but he hacks,
chops apart the mine   80
to discover,
to plunder,
what's in it/ Plunder,
that is the word.
Plunder.   85

A woman wakes up
finds herself
scarred
but still glinting
in the dark.   90

III. Beauty

only God, my dear,
Could love you for yourself alone
And not your yellow hair.
"For Anne Gregory," W. B. YEATS

and if I cut off my long hair,
if I stopped speaking,
if I stopped dreaming for other people about parts of the car,
stopped handing them tall creamy flowered silks

and loosing the magnificent hawks to fly in their direction,   95
stopped exciting them with the possibilities
of a thousand crystals under the fingernail
to look at while writing a letter,
if I stopped crying for the salvation of the tea ceremony,
stopped rushing in excitedly with a spikey bird-of-paradise,[1]   100
and never let them see how accurate my pistol shooting is,
who would I be?

Where is the real me
I want them all to love?

We are all the textures we wear.   105

We frighten men with our steel;
we fascinate them with our silk;
we seduce them with our cinnamon;
we rule them with our sensuous voices;
we confuse them with our submissions.   110
Is there anywhere
a man
who
will not punish us
for our beauty?   115

He is the one
we all search for,
chanting names for exotic oceans of the moon.

He is the one
we all anticipate,   120
pretending these small pedestrians
jaywalking into our lives
are he.
He is the one
we all anticipate;   125
beauty looks for its match,
confuses the issue
with a mystery that does not exist:
the rock
that cannot burn.   130

We are burning
in our heads at night
the incense of our histories, finding
you have used our skulls
for ashtrays.   135

1970

1. A bright, spectacular plant.

ALEXANDER WHITAKER

Leaving the Dance

The dinosaurus courteously
Went to join prehistory.
He mildly told our hosts that he
Had quite enjoyed their company,
And going out, as some might do,   5
He may have bent a shrub or two,
But nothing more—with elegance
He tipped his hat and left the dance.

I rather think such form is best;
Without disturbing any guest   10
He simply left, and all the rest
Continued dancing undistressed.
(Though some, I've noticed, quite deplore
The way we scar the ballroom floor
Or swing upon the chandelier—   15
They quietly sneak out the rear.)

The violinists in the wings,
Who all night long have strummed such things
As made us move like gorgeous kings,
Now scrape their bows on loosened strings.   20
Our hosts yawn in the smoke-filled air,
And the drummer has removed his snare.
It's time to go—with elegance
Let's get our things and leave the dance.

p. 1971

WALT WHITMAN

A Noiseless Patient Spider

A noiseless patient spider,
I marked where on a little promontory it stood isolated,
Marked how to explore the vacant vast surrounding,
It launched forth filament, filament, filament, out of itself,
Ever unreeling them, ever tirelessly speeding them.   5

And you O my soul where you stand,
Surrounded, detached, in measureless oceans of space,
Ceaselessly musing, venturing, throwing, seeking the spheres
          to connect them,
Till the bridge you will need be formed, till the ductile anchor hold,
Till the gossamer thread you fling catch somewhere, O my soul.   10

1881

WALT WHITMAN

When Lilacs Last in the Dooryard Bloomed[2]

1

When lilacs last in the dooryard bloomed,
And the great star early drooped in the western sky in the night,
I mourned, and yet shall mourn with ever-returning spring.

Ever-returning spring, trinity sure to me you bring,
Lilac blooming perennial and drooping star in the west,   5
And thought of him I love.

2

O powerful western fallen star!
O shades of night—O moody, tearful night!
O great star disappeared—O the black murk that hides the star!
O cruel hands that hold me powerless—O helpless soul of me!   10
O harsh surrounding cloud that will not free my soul.

3

In the dooryard fronting an old farm-house near the white-washed
      palings,
Stands the lilac-bush tall-growing with heart-shaped leaves of rich
      green,
With many a pointed blossom rising delicate, with the perfume strong
      I love,
With every leaf a miracle—and from this bush in the dooryard,   15
With delicate-colored blossoms and heart-shaped leaves of rich green,
A sprig with its flower I break.

4

In the swamp in secluded recesses,
A shy and hidden bird is warbling a song.

Solitary the thrush,   20
The hermit withdrawn to himself, avoiding the settlements,
Sings by himself a song.

Song of the bleeding throat,
Death's outlet song of life (for well dear brother I know,
If thou wast not granted to sing thou would'st surely die).   25

5

Over the breast of the spring, the land, amid cities,
Amid lanes and through old woods, where lately the violets peeped
      from the ground, spotting the gray debris,
Amid the grass in the fields each side of the lanes, passing the endless
      grass,
Passing the yellow-speared wheat, every grain from its shroud in the
      dark-brown fields uprisen,

2. The "occasion" of the poem is the assassination of Abraham Lincoln.

Passing the apple-tree blows of white and pink in the orchards,   30
Carrying a corpse to where it shall rest in the grave,
Night and day journeys a coffin.

6

Coffin that passes through lanes and streets,[3]
Through day and night with the great cloud darkening the land,
With the pomp of the inlooped flags with the cities draped in black,   35
With the show of the States themselves as of crepe-veiled women
 standing,
With processions long and winding and the flambeaus of the night,
With the countless torches lit, with the silent sea of faces and the un-
 bared heads,
With the waiting depot, the arriving coffin, and the somber faces,
With dirges through the night, with the thousand voices rising strong
 and solemn,   40
With all the mournful voices of the dirges poured around the coffin,
The dim-lit churches and the shuddering organs—where amid these
 you journey,
With the tolling tolling bells' perpetual clang,
Here, coffin that slowly passes,
I give you my sprig of lilac.   45

7

(Nor for you, for one alone,
Blossoms and branches green to coffins all I bring,
For fresh as the morning, thus would I chant a song for you O sane
 and sacred death.

All over bouquets of roses,
O death, I cover you over with roses and early lilies,   50
But mostly and now the lilac that blooms the first,
Copious I break, I break the sprigs from the bushes,
With loaded arms I come, pouring for you,
For you and the coffins all of you O death.)

8

O western orb sailing the heaven,   55
Now I know what you must have meant as a month since I walked,
As I walked in silence the transparent shadowy night,
As I saw you had something to tell as you bent to me night after night,
As you drooped from the sky low down as if to my side (while the
 other stars all looked on),
As we wandered together the solemn night (for something I know
 not what kept me from sleep),   60
As the night advanced, and I saw on the rim of the west how full you
 were of woe,
As I stood on the rising ground in the breeze in the cool transparent
 night,

---

3. The funeral cortege stopped at many towns between Washington and Springfield,
Illinois, where Lincoln was buried.

As I watched where you passed and was lost in the netherward black
    of the night,
As my soul in its trouble dissatisfied sank, as where you sad orb,
Concluded, dropped in the night, and was gone.   65

9

Sing on there in the swamp,
O singer bashful and tender, I hear your notes, I hear your call,
I hear, I come presently, I understand you,
But a moment I linger, for the lustrous star has detained me,
The star my departing comrade holds and detains me.   70

10

O how shall I warble myself for the dead one there I loved?
And how shall I deck my song for the large sweet soul that has gone?
And what shall my perfume be for the grave of him I love?
Sea-winds blown from east and west,
Blown from the Eastern sea and blown from the Western sea, till there
    on the prairies meeting,   75
These and with these and the breath of my chant,
I'll perfume the grave of him I love.

11

O what shall I hang on the chamber walls?
And what shall the pictures be that I hang on the walls,
To adorn the burial-house of him I love?   80

Pictures of growing spring and farms and homes,
With the Fourth-month eve at sundown, and the gray smoke lucid and
    bright,
With floods of the yellow gold of the gorgeous, indolent, sinking sun,
    burning, expanding the air,
With the fresh sweet herbage under foot, and the pale green leaves of
    the trees prolific,
In the distance the flowing glaze, the breast of the river, with a wind-
    dapple here and there,   85
With ranging hills on the banks, with many a line against the sky, and
    shadows,
And the city at hand with dwellings so dense, and stacks of chimneys,
And all the scenes of life and the workshops, and the workmen home-
    ward returning.

12

Lo, body and soul—this land,
My own Manhattan with spires, and the sparkling and hurrying tides,
    and the ships,   90
The varied and ample land, the South and the North in the light,
    Ohio's shores and flashing Missouri,
And ever the far-spreading prairies covered with grass and corn.

Lo, the most excellent sun so calm and haughty,
The violet and purple morn with just-felt breezes,
The gentle soft-born measureless light,   95

The miracle spreading bathing all, the fulfilled noon,
The coming eve delicious, the welcome night and the stars,
Over my cities shining all, enveloping man and land.

13

Sing on, sing on you gray-brown bird,
Sing from the swamps, the recesses, pour your chant from the bushes, 100
Limitless out of the dusk, out of the cedars and pines.

Sing on dearest brother, warble your reedy song,
Loud human song, with voice of uttermost woe.
O liquid and free and tender!
O wild and loose to my soul—O wondrous singer!   105
You only I hear—yet the star holds me (but will soon depart),
Yet the lilac with mastering odor holds me.

14

Now while I sat in the day and looked forth,
In the close of the day with its light and the fields of spring, and the
    farmers preparing their crops,
In the large unconscious scenery of my land with its lakes and forests, 110
In the heavenly aerial beauty (after the perturbed winds and the
    storms),
Under the arching heavens of the afternoon swift passing, and the
    voices of children and women.
The many-moving sea-tides, and I saw the ships how they sailed,
And the summer approaching with richness, and the fields all busy
    with labor,
And the infinite separate houses, how they all went on, each with its
    meals and minutia of daily usages,   115
And the streets how their throbbings throbbed, and the cities pent—lo,
    then and there,
Falling upon them all and among them all, enveloping me with the rest,
Appeared the cloud, appeared the long black trail,
And I knew death, its thought, and the sacred knowledge of death.

Then with the knowledge of death as walking one side of me,   120
And the thought of death close-walking the other side of me,
And I in the middle as with companions, and as holding the hands of
    companions,
I fled forth to the hiding receiving night that talks not,
Down to the shores of the water, the path by the swamp in the dim-
    ness,
To the solemn shadowy cedars and ghostly pines so still.   125

And the singer so shy to the rest received me,
The gray-brown bird I know received us comrades three,
And he sang the carol of death, and a verse for him I love.

From deep secluded recesses,
From the fragrant cedars and the ghostly pines so still,   130
Came the carol of the bird.

And the charm of the carol rapt me,
As I held as if by their hands my comrades in the night,
And the voice of my spirit tallied the song of the bird.

Come lovely and soothing death,   135
Undulate round the world, serenely arriving, arriving,
In the day, in the night, to all, to each,
Sooner or later delicate death.

Praised be the fathomless universe,
For life and joy, and for objects and knowledge curious,   140
And for love, sweet love—but praise! praise! praise!
For the sure-enwinding arms of cool-enfolding death.

Dark mother always gliding near with soft feet,
Have none chanted for thee a chant of fullest welcome?
Then I chant it for thee, I glorify thee above all,   145
I bring thee a song that when thou must indeed come, come unfalter-
     ingly.

Approach strong deliveress,
When it is so, when thou hast taken them I joyously sing the dead,
Lost in the loving floating ocean of thee,
Laved in the flood of thy bliss O death.   150

From me to thee glad serenades,
Dances for thee I propose saluting thee, adornments and feastings for
     thee,
And the sights of the open landscape and the high-spread sky are
     fitting,
And life and the fields, and the huge and thoughtful night.

The night in silence under many a star,   155
The ocean shore and the husky whispering wave whose voice I know,
And the soul turning to thee O vast and well-veiled death,
And the body gratefully nestling close to thee.

Over the tree-tops I float thee a song,
Over the rising and sinking waves, over the myriad fields and the
     prairies wide,   160
Over the dense-packed cities all and the teeming wharves and ways,
I float this carol with joy, with joy to thee O death.

15

To the tally of my soul,
Loud and strong kept up the gray-brown bird,
With pure deliberate notes spreading filling the night.   165

Loud in the pines and cedars dim,
Clear in the freshness moist and the swamp-perfume,
And I with my comrades there in the night.

While my sight that was bound in my eyes unclosed,
As to long panoramas of visions. 170

And I saw askant[4] the armies,
I saw as in noiseless dreams hundreds of battle-flags,
Borne through the smoke of the battles and pierced with missiles I saw
  them,
And carried hither and yon through the smoke, and torn and bloody,
And at last but a few shreds left on the staffs (and all in silence), 175
And the staffs all splintered and broken.

I saw battle-corpses, myriads of them,
And the white skeletons of young men, I saw them,
I saw the debris and debris of all the slain soldiers of the war,
But I saw they were not as was thought, 180
They themselves were fully at rest, they suffered not,
The living remained and suffered, the mother suffered,
And the wife and the child and the musing comrade suffered,
And the armies that remained suffered.

16

Passing the visions, passing the night, 185
Passing, unloosing the hold of my comrades' hands,
Passing the song of the hermit bird and the tallying song of my soul,
Victorious song, death's outlet song, yet varying ever-altering song,
As low and wailing, yet clear the notes, rising and falling, flooding the
  night,
Sadly sinking and fainting, as warning and warning, and yet again
  bursting with joy, 190
Covering the earth and filling the spread of the heaven,
As that powerful psalm in the night I heard from recesses,
Passing, I leave thee lilac with heart-shaped leaves,
I leave thee there in the door-yard, blooming, returning with spring.

I cease from my song for thee, 195
 From my gaze on thee in the west, fronting the west, communing with
  thee,
O comrade lustrous with silver face in the night.

Yet each to keep and all, retrievements out of the night,
The song, the wondrous chant of the gray-brown bird,
And the tallying chant, the echo aroused in my soul, 200
With the lustrous and drooping star with the countenance full of woe,
With the holders holding my hand nearing the call of the bird,
Comrades mine and I in the midst, and their memory ever to keep, for
  the dead I loved so well,
For the sweetest, wisest soul of all my days and lands—and this for his
  dear sake,
Lilac and star and bird twined with the chant of my soul, 205
There in the fragrant pines and the cedars dusk and dim.
1865–66

4. Askance: sideways.

RICHARD WILBUR

The Beautiful Changes

One wading a Fall meadow finds on all sides
The Queen Anne's Lace[5] lying like lilies
On water; it glides
So from the walker, it turns
Dry grass to a lake, as the slightest shade of you   5
Valleys my mind in fabulous blue Lucernes.[6]

The beautiful changes as a forest is changed
By a chameleon's tuning his skin to it;
As a mantis, arranged
On a green leaf, grows   10
Into it, makes the leaf leafier, and proves
Any greenness is deeper than anyone knows.

Your hands hold roses always in a way that says
They are not only yours; the beautiful changes
In such kind ways,   15
Wishing ever to sunder
Things and things' selves for a second finding, to lose
For a moment all that it touches back to wonder.

1947

RICHARD WILBUR

Love Calls Us to the Things of This World[7]

The eyes open to a cry of pulleys,[8]
And spirited from sleep, the astounded soul
Hangs for a moment bodiless and simple
As false dawn.
                    Outside the open window   5
The morning air is all awash with angels.

Some are in bed-sheets, some are in blouses,
Some are in smocks: but truly there they are.
Now they are rising together in calm swells
Of halcyon[9] feeling, filling whatever they wear   10
With the deep joy of their impersonal breathing;

5. A delicate-looking plant, with finely divided leaves and flat clusters of small white flowers, sometimes called "wild carrot."
6. Alfalfa, a plant resembling clover, with small purple flowers. Lake Lucerne is famed for deep blue color and its picturesque Swiss setting amid limestone mountains.
7. A phrase from St. Augustine's *Commentary on the Psalms.*
8. Laundry pulleys, designed so that clothes can be hung on the line inside and then sent outdoors to dry.
9. Serene.

Now they are flying in place,[1] conveying
The terrible speed of their omnipresence, moving
And staying like white water; and now of a sudden
They swoon down into so rapt a quiet   15
That nobody seems to be there.
                              The soul shrinks

      From all that it is about to remember,
From the punctual rape of every blessèd day,
And cries,   20
            "Oh, let there be nothing on earth but laundry,
Nothing but rosy hands in the rising steam
And clear dances done in the sight of heaven."

      Yet, as the sun acknowledges
With a warm look the world's hunks and colors,   25
The soul descends once more in bitter love
To accept the waking body, saying now
In a changed voice as the man yawns and rises,

      "Bring them down from their ruddy gallows;
Let there be clean linen for the backs of thieves;   30
Let lovers go fresh and sweet to be undone,
And the heaviest nuns walk in a pure floating
Of dark habits,
                keeping their difficult balance."

                                              1956

RICHARD WILBUR

Museum Piece

      The good gray guardians of art
      Patrol the halls on spongy shoes,
      Impartially protective, though
      Perhaps suspicious of Toulouse.[2]

      Here dozes one against the wall,   5
      Disposed upon a funeral chair.
      A Degas[3] dancer pirouettes
      Upon the parting of his hair.

      See how she spins! The grace is there,
      But strain as well is plain to see.   10

1. Like planes in a formation.
2. Toulouse-Lautrec, 19th-century French painter famous for his posters, drawings, and paintings of singers, dancers, and actresses.
3. Degas, a 19th-century French impressionist, usually considered the master of the human figure in movement.

Degas loved the two together:
Beauty joined to energy.

Edgar Degas purchased once
A fine El Greco,[4] which he kept
Against the wall beside his bed   15
To hang his pants on while he slept.

1950

WILLIAM CARLOS WILLIAMS

This Is Just to Say

I have eaten
the plums
that were in
the icebox

and which   5
you were probably
saving
for breakfast

Forgive me
they were delicious   10
so sweet
and so cold

1934

WILLIAM WORDSWORTH

It Is a Beauteous Evening

It is a beauteous evening, calm and free,
The holy time is quiet as a Nun
Breathless with adoration; the broad sun
Is sinking down in its tranquillity;
The gentleness of heaven broods o'er the Sea: 5
Listen! the mighty Being is awake,
And doth with his eternal motion make
A sound like thunder—everlastingly.
Dear Child! dear Girl![5] that walkest with me here,

4. El Greco, a 16th-century Spanish painter, known for the mannered disproportion of his figures.

5. Wordsworth's 10-year-old daughter, Caroline.

If thou appear untouched by solemn thought,   10
Thy nature is not herefore less divine:
Thou lies in Abraham's bosom[6] all the year,
And worship'st at the Temple's inner shrine,
God being with thee when we know it not.

1807

WILLIAM WORDSWORTH

Lines Composed a Few Miles above Tintern Abbey on Revisiting the Banks of the Wye During a Tour, July 13, 1798[7]

Five years have passed; five summers, with the length
Of five long winters! and again I hear
These waters, rolling from their mountain-springs
With a soft inland murmur. Once again
Do I behold these steep and lofty cliffs,   5
That on a wild secluded scene impress
Thoughts of more deep seclusion; and connect
The landscape with the quiet of the sky.
The day is come when I again repose
Here, under this dark sycamore, and view   10
These plots of cottage-ground, these orchard tufts,
Which at this season, with their unripe fruits,
Are clad in one green hue, and lose themselves
'Mid groves and copses.[8] Once again I see
These hedge-rows, hardly hedge-rows, little lines   15
Of sportive wood run wild: these pastoral farms,
Green to the very door; and wreaths of smoke
Sent up, in silence, from among the trees!
With some uncertain notice, as might seem
Of vagrant dwellers in the houseless woods,   20
Or of some hermit's cave, where by his fire
The hermit sits alone.
                            These beauteous forms,
Through a long absence, have not been to me
As is a landscape to a blind man's eye;
But oft, in lonely rooms, and 'mid the din   25
Of towns and cities, I have owed to them,
In hours of weariness, sensations sweet,
Felt in the blood, and felt along the heart;
And passing even into my purer mind,
With tranquil restoration—feelings too   30

6. After death, a resting place for Heaven-bound souls (see *Luke* 16:22).
7. Wordsworth had first visited the Wye valley and the ruins of the medieval abbey there in 1793, while on a solitary walking tour. He was 23 then, 28 when he wrote this poem.
8. Thickets.

Of unremembered pleasure: such, perhaps,
As have no slight or trivial influence
On that best portion of a good man's life,
His little, nameless, unremembered acts
Of kindness and of love. Nor less, I trust,   35
To them I may have owed another gift,
Of aspect more sublime; that blesséd mood,
In which the burthen[9] of the mystery,
In which the heavy and the weary weight
Of all this unintelligible world,   40
Is lightened—that serene and blesséd mood,
In which the affections gently lead us on—
Until, the breath of this corporeal frame
And even the motion of our human blood
Almost suspended, we are laid asleep   45
In body, and become a living soul;
While with an eye made quiet by the power
Of harmony, and the deep power of joy,
We see into the life of things.
                                If this
Be but a vain belief, yet, oh! how oft—   50
In darkness and amid the many shapes
Of joyless daylight; when the fretful stir
Unprofitable, and the fever of the world,
Have hung upon the beatings of my heart—
How oft, in spirit, have I turned to thee,   55
O sylvan Wye! thou wanderer through the woods,
How often has my spirit turned to thee!

    And now, with gleams of half-extinguished thought,
With many recognitions dim and faint,
And somewhat of a sad perplexity,   60
The picture of the mind revives again;
While here I stand, not only with the sense
Of present pleasure, but with pleasing thoughts
That in this moment there is life and food
For future years. And so I dare to hope,   65
Though changed, no doubt, from what I was when first
I came among these hills; when like a roe
I bounded o'er the mountains, by the sides
Of the deep rivers, and the lonely streams,
Wherever nature led: more like a man   70
Flying from something that he dreads than one
Who sought the thing he loved. For nature then
(The coarser[1] pleasures of my boyish days,
And their glad animal movements all gone by)
To me was all in all—I cannot paint   75
What then I was. The sounding cataract
Haunted me like a passion; the tall rock,

9. Burden.   1. Physical.

The mountain, and the deep and gloomy wood,
Their colors and their forms, were then to me
An appetite; a feeling and a love,   80
That had no need of a remoter charm,
By thought supplied, nor any interest
Unborrowed from the eye. That time is past,
And all its aching joys are now no more,
And all its dizzy raptures. Not for this   85
Faint I,[2] nor mourn nor murmur; other gifts
Have followed; for such loss, I would believe,
Abundant recompense. For I have learned
To look on nature, not as in the hour
Of thoughtless youth; but hearing oftentimes   90
The still, sad music of humanity,
Nor harsh nor grating, though of ample power
To chasten and subdue. And I have felt
A presence that disturbs me with the joy
Of elevated thoughts; a sense sublime   95
Of something far more deeply interfused,
Whose dwelling is the light of setting suns,
And the round ocean and the living air,
And the blue sky, and in the mind of man:
A motion and a spirit, that impels   100
All thinking things, all objects of all thought,
And rolls through all things. Therefore am I still
A lover of the meadows and the woods
And mountains; and of all that we behold
From this green earth; of all the mighty world   105
Of eye, and ear—both what they half create,
And what perceive; well pleased to recognize
In nature and the language of the sense
The anchor of my purest thoughts, the nurse,
The guide, the guardian of my heart, and soul   110
Of all my moral being.
                         Nor perchance,
If I were not thus taught, should I the more
Suffer my genial spirits[3] to decay:
For thou art with me here upon the banks
Of this fair river; thou my dearest Friend,[4]   115
My dear, dear Friend; and in thy voice I catch
The language of my former heart, and read
My former pleasures in the shooting lights
Of thy wild eyes. Oh! yet a little while
May I behold in thee what I was once,   120
My dear, dear Sister! and this prayer I make,
Knowing that Nature never did betray
The heart that loved her; 'tis her privilege,
Through all the years of this our life, to lead
From joy to joy: for she can so inform   125

2. Am I discouraged.
3. Natural disposition; i.e., the spirits   that are part of his individual genius.
                                                      4. His sister Dorothy.

The mind that is within us, so impress
With quietness and beauty, and so feed
With lofty thoughts, that neither evil tongues,
Rash judgments, nor the sneers of selfish men,
Nor greetings where no kindness is, nor all   130
The dreary intercourse of daily life,
Shall e'er prevail against us, or disturb
Our cheerful faith that all which we behold
Is full of blessings. Therefore let the moon
Shine on thee in thy solitary walk;   135
And let the misty mountain-winds be free
To blow against thee: and, in after years,
When these wild ecstasies shall be matured
Into a sober pleasure; when thy mind
Shall be a mansion for all lovely forms,   140
Thy memory be as a dwelling-place
For all sweet sounds and harmonies; oh! then,
If solitude, or fear, or pain, or grief,
Should be thy portion, with what healing thoughts
Of tender joy wilt thou remember me,   145
And these my exhortations! Nor, perchance—
If I should be where I no more can hear
Thy voice, nor catch from thy wild eyes these gleams
Of past existence—wilt thou then forget
That on the banks of this delightful stream   150
We stood together; and that I, so long
A worshiper of Nature, hither came
Unwearied in that service; rather say
With warmer love—oh! with far deeper zeal
Of holier love. Nor wilt thou then forget,   155
That after many wanderings, many years
Of absence, these steep woods and lofty cliffs,
And this green pastoral landscape, were to me
More dear, both for themselves and for thy sake!

                                                    1798

*[handwritten: Speaker: preocc w/ THEM but reveals self —
Puzzle: who are "they" of 1–7? (guess): how tell?]*

SIR THOMAS WYATT

They Flee from Me

They flee from me, that sometime did me seek,
With naked foot stalking in my chamber.
I have seen them, gentle, tame, and meek,
That now are wild, and do not remember
That sometime they put themselves in danger   5
To take bread at my hand; and now they range,
Busily seeking with a continual change.

*[handwritten: women imagined
as animals
(a surprise of
2nd stanza)]*

Thankéd be Fortune it hath been otherwise, — *one case of general*
Twenty times better; but once in special,
In thin array, after a pleasant guise,   10
When her loose gown from her shoulders did fall,
And she me caught in her arms long and small.[5]
And therewith all sweetly did me kiss
And softly said, "Dear heart, how like you this?" : *contrast 1st 2nd*
                                                    general / exception
read ↓
It was no dream, I lay broad waking.   *Why the denial?* 15
But all is turned, thorough[6] my gentleness,   — *dreamy*
Into a strange fashion of forsaking;   — *transition*
And I have leave to go, of her goodness,
And she also to use newfangleness.[7]   *what has happened?*
But since that I so kindely[8] am servéd,   *Who left whom?* 20
I fain[9] would know what she hath deservéd.   *whose fault?*
                                                    1557

tone? return to animal/natural idea?
What kind of relat. to women?

— ("character" more
than persona?)

— dram. irony if we see
him at fault, while he
excuses self

<hr>

5. Slender.   8. In a way natural to women.
6. Through.   9. Eagerly.
7. Fondness for novelty.

APPENDIX: POETRY IN PROCESS

Poems do not write themselves. Even if the idea for a poem comes in a flash (as it sometimes does), poets often struggle to get the final effect just right. For some poems that means draft after draft, and sometimes poets complete more than one version of a poem or later revise the poem and alter it in some crucial way. Often a study of the manuscript or of the several drafts suggests the various kinds of decisions a poet may make as a poem moves toward its final form. In this appendix you will find examples of several poems in the process of growth in the poet's mind.

The first example involves early drafts of the first stanza of Richard Wilbur's *Love Calls Us to the Things of This World,* which appears on p. 524. Wilbur is one of the most careful craftsmen writing today, and in the early drafts of the first stanza we can see him moving toward the brilliant and surprising effects he achieves in the final version. Someone is just awaking, and through a window sees laundry on a clothesline blowing in the breeze. But he is not quite awake and not quite sure what he sees: his body and soul, the poet says playfully in lines 26 and 27, are not yet quite reunited, and he seems for a moment still suspended in a world of spirit and dream, and the blowing clothes look like disembodied angels. Ultimately, the poem captures that sense of suspension between worlds, the uncertainty of where one is and what is happening in that first half-conscious moment when normal physical laws don't seem to apply. It is a delicate moment to catch, and in the six successive drafts printed below we can see the poet moving toward the precise effect of the final version.

In the first three drafts the speaker seems to speak about himself—not quite right because that device makes him too conscious, and part of the basic effect of the poem involves a lack of consciousness and control. By the fourth draft "My eyes came open" has become "The eyes open," and the effect of being a little lost and unsure of identity is on its way to being created. Another major change in the early drafts is that the sound of the laundry pulley changes from "squeak" to "shriek" to "cry": the first two words capture the shrill sound of a moving pulley faithfully, but "cry" makes it seem personal and human, and now it is as if the pulleys were in fact calling the speaker from sleep. The image changes too: in the first draft the world of sleep is a brothel, but those connotations are eliminated in later drafts, and instead by the sixth draft the "spirit" has become "soul" and is bodiless. Every new draft changes the conception just a little, and in the drafts printed here we can see effects gradually getting clearer in the poet's mind and falling into place. Notice how rhyme appears in draft and then disappears again, notice how the poet tries out and rejects words that don't have quite the right connotation: "wallow" (draft c), "frothing" (draft d), "rout" (draft f). In a detailed set of drafts like this one, we can see the poet weighing different visual and verbal possibilities, choosing every single word with care.

The other poems and passages similarly give us a chance to compare the effects of more than one version of a poem or passage. In several cases, a poem is "finished" in more than one version, and the poets

invite us to choose among the competing versions instead of them-
selves choosing. In each selection a few crucial words create significant
differences in the text.

1. Early drafts of the first stanza of *Love Calls Us to the Things of
This World*, reprinted by permission of the author:

(a) My eyes came open to the squeak of pulleys
     My spirit, shocked from the brothel of itself

(b) My eyes came open to the shriek of pulleys,
     And the soul, spirited from its proper wallow,
     Hung in the air as bodiless and hollow

(c) My eyes came open to the pulleys' cry.
     The soul, spirited from its proper wallow,
     Hung in the air as bodiless and hollow
     As light that frothed upon the wall opposing;
     But what most caught my eyes at their unclosing
     Was two gray ropes that yanked across the sky.
     One after one into the window frame
        . . . the hosts of laundry came

(d)   The eyes open to a cry of pulleys,
     And the soul, so suddenly spirited from sleep,
     As morning sunlight frothing on the floor,
        While just outside the window
     The air is solid with a dance of angels.

(e)   The eyes open to a cry of pulleys,
     And spirited from sleep, the astounded soul
     Hangs for a moment bodiless and simple
     As dawn light in the moment of its breaking:
        Outside the open window
     The air is crowded with a

(f)   The eyes open to a cry of pulleys,
     And spirited from sleep, the astounded soul
     Hangs for a moment bodiless and simple
     As false dawn.
        Outside the open window,
     Their air is leaping with a rout of angels.
        Some are in bedsheets, some are in dresses,
           it does not seem to matter

2. Here are two versions of Keats's *Bright Star*.

Original Version

> Bright star! would I were stedfast as thou art!
> Not in lone splendor hung amid the night;
> Not watching, with eternal lids apart,
> Like Nature's devout sleepless Eremite,
> The morning waters at their priestlike task   5
> Of pure ablution round earth's human shores;
> Or, gazing on the new soft fallen mask
> Of snow upon the mountains and the moors:—
> No;—yet still stedfast, still unchangeable.
> Cheek-pillow'd on my Love's white ripening breast,   10
> To touch, for ever, its warm sink and swell,
> Awake, for ever, in a sweet unrest;
> To hear, to feel her tender taken breath,
> Half-passionless, and so swoon on to death.

Revised Version

> Bright star! would I were steadfast as thou art—
>   Not in lone splendor hung aloft the night
> And watching, with eternal lids apart,
>   Like nature's patient, sleepless Ermite,
> The moving waters at their priestlike task   5
>   Of pure ablution round earth's human shores,
> Or gazing on the new soft fallen mask
>   Of snow upon the mountains and the moors—
> No—yet still steadfast, still unchangeable,
>   Pillowed upon my fair love's ripening breast,   10
> To feel for ever its soft fall and swell, ·
>   Awake for ever in a sweet unrest,
> Still, still to hear her tender-taken breath,
> And so live ever—or else swoon to death.

3 Keats's *Eve of St. Agnes* appears on pp. 244–253. Here are some
manuscript variants.

In manuscript, Keats had placed this stanza after stanza 6:

'Twas said her future lord would there appear
Offering as sacrifice—all in the dream—
Delicious food even to her lips brought near;
Viands and wine and fruit and sugar'd cream,
To touch her palate with the fine extreme
Of relish: then soft music heard; and then
More pleasure followed in a dizzy stream
Palpable almost: then to wake again
Warm in the virgin morn, no weeping Magdalen.

Here is a manuscript variant on lines 314–22:

So while she speaks his arms encroaching slow
Have zon'd her, heart to heart—loud the dark winds blow.

For on the midnight came a tempest fell
More sooth for that his quick rejoinder flows
Into her burning ear:—and still the spell
Unbroken guards her in serene repose.
With her wild dream he mingled as a rose
Marryeth its odor to a violet.
Still, still she dreams—louder the frost wind blows. . .

A manuscript version of the last four lines of the poem (375–78)
reads this way:

Were long be-nightmared. Angela went off
Twitch'd with the palsy; and with face deform
The beadsman stiffen'd, 'twixt a sigh and laugh
Ta'en sudden from his beads by one weak little cough.

4. Here are two published versions of Keats's *La Belle Dame sans Merci: A Ballad.*

Original Version

O what can ail thee, knight-at-arms,
    Alone and palely loitering?
The sedge has withered from the lake,
    And no birds sing.

O what can ail thee, knight-at-arms,   5
    So haggard and so woe-begone?
The squirrel's granary is full,
    And the harvest's done.

I see a lily on thy brow,
    With anguish moist and fever dew,   10
And on thy cheeks a fading rose
    Fast withereth too.

I met a lady in the meads[1]
    Full beautiful—a faery's child,
Her hair was long her foot was light,   15
    And her eyes were wild.

I made a garland for her head,
    And bracelets too, and fragrant zone,[2]
She looked at me as she did love,
    And made sweet moan.   20

I set her on my pacing steed,
    And nothing else saw all day long,
For sidelong would she bend, and sing
    A faery's song.

She found me roots of relish sweet   25
    And honey wild, and manna dew,
And sure in language strange she said,
    "I love thee true."

She took me to her elfin grot,
    And there she wept, and sighed full sore,   30
And there I shut her wild wild eyes
    With kisses four.

And there she lullèd me asleep,
    And there I dreamed—Ah! woe betide!
The latest[3] dream I ever dreamed   35
    On the cold hill side.

1. Meadows.   3. Last.
2. Girdle.

Revised Version

Ah, what can ail thee, wretched wight,
    Alone and palely loitering;
The sedge is withered from the lake,
    And no birds sing.

Ah, what can ail thee, wretched wight,   5
    So haggard and so woe-begone?
The squirrel's granary is full,
    And the harvest's done.

I see a lily on thy brow,
    With anguish moist and fever dew;   10
And on thy cheek a fading rose
    Fast withereth too.

I met a lady in the meads
    Full beautiful, a fairy's child;
Her hair was long, her foot was light,   15
    And her eyes were wild.

I set her on my pacing steed,
    And nothing else saw all day long;
For sideways would she lean, and sing
    A fairy's song.   20

I made a garland for her head,
    And bracelets too, and fragrant zone:
She looked at me as she did love,
    And made sweet moan.

She found me roots of relish sweet,   25
    And honey wild, and manna dew;
And sure in language strange she said,
    "I love thee true."

She took me to her elfin grot,
    And there she gazed and sighéd deep,   30
And there I shut her wild sad eyes—
    So kissed to sleep.

And there we slumbered on the moss,
    And there I dreamed, ah woe betide,
The latest dream I ever dreamed   35
    On the cold hill side.

I saw pale kings and princes too,
    Pale warriors, death-pale were they all;
They cried—"La Belle Dame sans Merci
    Hath thee in thrall!"   40

I saw their starved lips in the gloam,
    With horrid warning gapéd wide,
And I awoke and found me here,
    On the cold hill's side.

And this is why I sojourn here,   45
    Alone and palely loitering,
Though the sedge has withered from the lake,
    And no birds sing.

---

5. Here are three versions of Alexander Pope's *Ode on Solitude*.

The 1709 Manuscript Version

    Happy the man, who free from care,
    The business and the noise of towns,
    Contented breathes his native air,
        In his own grounds.

    Whose herds with milk, whose fields with bread,   5
    Whose flocks supply him with attire,
    Whose trees in summer yield him shade,
        In winter fire.

    Blest! who can unconcern'dly find
    His years slide silently away,   10
    In health of body, peace of mind,
        Quiet by day,

    Repose at night; study and ease
    Together mix'd; sweet recreation,
    And innocence, which most does please,   15
        With meditation.

    Thus let me live, unseen, unknown;
    Thus unlamented let me die;
    Steal from the world, and not a stone
        Tell where I lie.   20

The First Printed Version, 1717

    How happy he, who free from care,
    The rage of courts, and noise of towns;
    Contented breathes his native air,
        In his own grounds.
    Whose herds with milk, whose fields with bread,   5
    Whose flocks supply him with attire,

I saw pale kings,and princes too,
   Pale warriors, death-pale were they all;
Who cried—"La belle Dame sans merci
   Hath thee in thrall!"   40

I saw their starved lips in the gloom
   With horrid warning gapéd wide,
And I awoke, and found me here
   On the cold hill side.

And this is why I sojourn here   45
   Alone and palely loitering,
Though the sedge is withered from the lake,
   And no birds sing.

   Whose trees in summer yield him shade,
       In winter fire.
Blest! who can unconcern'dly find
Hours, days, and years slide swift away,   10
In health of body, peace of mind,
       Quiet by day,
Sound sleep by night; study and ease
Together mix'd; sweet recreation,
And innocence, which most does please,   15
       With meditation.
Thus let me live, unheard, unknown;
Thus unlamented let me die;
Steal from the world, and not a stone
       Tell where I lie.   20

The Final Version, 1736

   Happy the man, whose wish and care
   A few paternal acres bound,
   Content to breathe his native air,
       In his own ground.
Whose herds with milk, whose fields with bread,   5
Whose flocks supply him with attire,
Whose trees in summer yield him shade,
       In winter fire.
Blest! who can unconcern'dly find
Hours, days, and years slide soft away,
In health of body, peace of mind,   10
       Quiet by day,
Sound sleep by night; study and ease
Together mix'd; sweet recreation,
And innocence, which most does please,
       With meditation.   15
Thus let me live, unseen, unknown;
Thus unlamented let me die;
Steal from the world, and not a stone
       Tell where I lie.   20

6. This famous folk ballad was sung and recited in many variations; here are two written versions. Neither version can be dated precisely.

"O where ha' you been, Lord Randal, my son?
And where ha' you been, my handsome young man?"
"I ha' been at the greenwood; mother, mak my bed soon,
For I'm wearied wi' huntin', and fain wad[4] lie down."

"And wha met ye there, Lord Randal, my son?   5
And wha met you there, my handsome young man?"
"O I met wi' my true-love; mother, mak my bed soon,
For I'm wearied wi' huntin', and fain wad lie down."

"And what did she give you, Lord Randal, my son?
And what did she give you, my handsome young man?"   10
"Eels fried in a pan; mother, mak my bed soon,
For I'm wearied wi' huntin', and fain wad lie down."

"And wha gat your leavin's, Lord Randal, my son?
And wha gat your leavin's, my handsome young man?"
"My hawks and my hounds; mother, mak my bed soon,   15
For I'm wearied wi' huntin', and fain wad lie down."

"And what becam of them, Lord Randal, my son?
And what becam of them, my handsome young man?"
"They stretched their legs out and died; mother, mak my bed soon,
For I'm wearied wi' huntin', and fain wad lie down."   20

"O I fear you are poisoned, Lord Randal, my son!
I fear you are poisoned, my handsome young man!"
"O yes, I am poisoned; mother, mak my bed soon,
For I'm sick at the heart, and I fain wad lie down."

"What d' ye leave to your mother, Lord Randal, my son?   25
What d' ye leave to your mother, my handsome young man?"
"Four and twenty milk kye;[5] mother, mak my bed soon,
For I'm sick at the heart, and I fain wad lie down."

"What d'ye leave to your sister, Lord Randal, my son?
What d'ye leave to your sister, my handsome young man?"   30
"My gold and my silver; mother, mak my bed soon,
For I'm sick at the heart, and I fain wad lie down."

"What d' ye leave to your brother, Lord Randal, my son?
What d'ye leave to your brother, my handsome young man?"
"My houses and my lands; mother, mak my bed soon,   35
For I'm sick at the heart, and I fain wad lie down."

"What d' ye leave to your true-love, Lord Randal, my son?
What d' ye leave to your true-love, my handsome young man?"
"I leave her hell and fire; mother, mak my bed soon,
For I'm sick at the heart, and I fain wad lie down."   40

4. Would like to.   5. Cows.

The Shorter Version

"O where hae ye been, Lord Randal, my son?
O where hae ye been, my handsome young man?"
"I hae been to the wild wood; mother, make my bed soon,
For I'm weary wi' hunting, and fain wald lie down."

"Where gat ye your dinner, Lord Randal, my son?   5
Where gat ye your dinner, my handsome young man?"
"I dined wi' my true-love; mother, make my bed soon,
For I'm weary wi' hunting, and fain wald lie down."

"What gat ye to your dinner, Lord Randal, my son?
What gat ye to your dinner, my handsome young man?"   10
"I gat eels boiled in broo; mother, make my bed soon,
For I'm weary wi' hunting, and fain wald lie down."

"What became of your bloodhounds, Lord Randal, my son?
What became of your bloodhounds, my handsome young man?"
"O they swelled and they died; mother, make my bed soon, 15
For I'm weary wi' hunting, and fain wald lie down."

"O I fear ye are poisoned, Lord Randal, my son!
O I fear ye are poisoned, my handsome young man!"
"O yes! I am poisoned; mother, make my bed soon,
For I'm sick at the heart, and I fain wald lie down."   20

7. *Poetry*, by Marianne Moore, appears on p. 65 in the version that was originally published in 1921. Here are two later versions.

The 1924 Version

> I too, dislike it:
> there are things that are important beyond all this fiddle.
> The bat, upside down; the elephant pushing,
> the tireless wolf under a tree,
> the base-ball fan, the statistician—   5
> "business documents and schoolbooks"—
> these phenomena are pleasing,
> but when they have been fashioned
> into that which is unknowable,
> we are not entertained.   10
> It may be said of all of us
> that we do not admire what we cannot understand;
> enigmas are not poetry.

The version Moore chose to print in her *Complete Poems* in 1967:

I, too, dislike it.
      Reading it, however, with a perfect contempt for it, one discovers in it after all, a place for the genuine.

8. Two versions of Emily Dickinson's *Safe in Their Alabaster Chambers*

The 1859 Version

> Safe in their Alabaster Chambers—
> Untouched by Morning
> And untouched by Noon—
> Sleep the meek members of the Resurrection—
> Rafter of satin,   5
> And Roof of stone.
>
> Light laughs the breeze
> In her Castle above them—
> Babbles the Bee in a stolid Ear,
> Pipe the Sweet Birds in ignorant cadence—   10
> Ah, what sagacity perished here!

The 1861 Version

> Safe in their Alabaster Chambers—
> Untouched by Morning—
> And untouched by Noon—
> Lie the meek members of the Resurrection—
> Rafter of Satin—and Roof of Stone!   5
>
> Grand go the Years—in the Crescent—above them—
> Worlds scoop their Arcs—
> And Firmaments—row—
> Diadems—drop—and Doges—surrender—
> Soundless as dots—on a Disc of Snow—   10

A GLOSSARY OF POETIC TERMS

1. SUBJECT, THEME, AND MEANING

Most readers would agree with Archibald MacLeish that "a poem should not mean but be," but discovering what a poem "is" often involves identifying what it contains. Poets often used to provide an **argument** for their poems, a prose summary of what "happens"; now they seldom provide such a convenience, but to begin interpretation and experience of a poem readers often find it useful to **paraphrase,** put into prose exactly what the poem says, line by line, in words that are different but as nearly equivalent as possible.

The **subject,** or **topic,** of a poem is its general or specific area of concern, usually something categorical such as death (or the death of a particular person), war (or a specific war, or specific battle), love, or the simple life. Most poems make **statements** about a subject and define the degree and kind of their interest in it; a poem about war, for example, may ultimately be more concerned to say something about the nature of man or about honor or about peace than about war itself. Subjects offer a great variety of **themes: that death** is a release from pain, or a gateway to immortality, that war is senseless, or brutal, or a necessary evil, or a heroic quest for justice. A poem's theme is the statement it makes about its subject; summarizing a paraphrase in one or two sentences often yields the theme.

An **explication,** or **exegesis,** explains how all of the elements in an individual poem or passage work; in explication, a critic analyzes the various component parts in order to interpret the poem's statement. Explication takes a step beyond paraphrase in attempting to discover a poem's meaning. The terms **message** and **moral,** once used to summarize the poem's meaning, are now usually considered misleading because they tend to oversimplify and confuse statement with meaning. Similarly objectionable to many is the term **hidden meaning,** which implies that a poem is a puzzle or that the author is deliberately obscuring his or her point. **Meaning** is the poem's combination of themes and statements about a subject or series of subjects *and* the emotions that it artfully evokes toward them by means of poetic devices and strategies. But meaning—however well defined and articulated—is never the precise equivalent of the poem itself.

2. ATTITUDE, TONE, AND AUDIENCE

It is not only what is said that determines a poem's meaning and effect but how it is said and to whom. The term **tone** represents an attempt to be precise about the author's attitude toward what his or her poem literally says. Descriptions of tone try to characterize the way the words of the poem are (or should be) spoken when one sensitively reads the poem aloud. Tone literally tries to describe the vocal sounds which a poem seems to demand, and one may speak of the tone of an individual word or phrase, of a longer passsage, or of a whole poem. Words such as "ironic," "comic," "playful," "sincere," and "straightforward" may sometimes accurately describe tone, as may more particular adjectives such as "angry," "boastful," "taunting," "apologetic," "plaintive," or "bemused."

It is often useful, too, to know about the imagined **audience** of a poem, for much of what poets do involves an attempt to move and influence their hearers. Because poems are meant to be read and experienced by someone besides the poet, they are more than simple records of an event, or idea, or state of mind. Poets fictionalize or imagine circumstances and reflections, and they usually try to communicate by evoking in the reader a particular attitude or emotion.

The means by which poems generate an effect are usually called **poetic** (or **artistic**) **devices** or **strategies**. Almost everything in a poem is in some sense (but not a bad sense) a device: the choice of one word rather than another one, the use of metaphor, of certain sounds and rhythms, of allusions, conventions, forms—all contribute to a total effect. The **rhetoric** of a poem is the sum of the persuasive devices used to affect readers, with or without their consent.

Many of the most important **rhetorical devices** (or **rhetorical figures**) date from classical antiquity, and some of these are so common in ordinary life that we scarcely recognize them as devices, even in a poem. **Comparison** and **contrast** may clarify the identity and properties of a person, place, or thing, but persuasive values may also be built in, depending on what is being compared with what. Acceptance by **association** is as common as guilt by association; naming admired names may lull a reader into easy submission or be part of a complex web of interrelationships in which an author places his or her values among things certain to be admired, or expected to be admired among readers of a certain kind. An **allusion** is a reference to something outside the poem (in history, perhaps, or in another poem) which has built-in emotional associations. **Example** is simply the giving of a specific instance to back up a generalization, and many whole poems are built upon the principle, directly or indirectly.

Several classic figures of speech, though not restricted to poetry, are often found in poems. **Hyperbole** (or extravagant **exaggeration**) may be serious or comic or both at the same time, pushing something so far toward absurdity that its ordinary manifestation may seem normal and acceptable. **Meiosis** (or **understatement**) consciously underrates something or portrays it as lesser than it is usually thought to be; its psychology is to bring the reader instinctively to the defense of the thing being undervalued. It is closely related to **irony** (§3), especially in one of its forms, **litotes**, which affirms something by denying its opposite, as in colloquial expressions such as "He's no Einstein." **Periphrasis** (or **circumlocution**) is deliberate avoidance of the obvious, writing which circles its subject and refuses to take the simplest route toward clear meaning. **Synecdoche** is using a part of something to signify the whole (as in "hired hands" for "workmen"), and **metonymy** is naming something associated with what is being talked about rather than the thing itself, as in the use of "crown" for "king." **Hyperbaton** is the rearrangement of sentence elements for special effects; Milton, in *Paradise Lost*, for example, often uses extreme instances of the figure, as in the sentence beginning in line 44 of Book I (p. 131). **Prolepsis** is the **foreshadowing** of a future event as if it were already influencing the present, as in Eliot's *Journey of the Magi* (p. 423) when the wise men on their way to Bethlehem see objects suggestive of the Crucifixion.

These terms merely describe and categorize standard ways in which words may affect pyschological processes. Many kinds of attempts to persuade—sermons, political speeches, TV commercials, informal conversations—use some version of such devices, although often in more simple and less subtle ways than good poetry. Identifying the devices is only a way of discovering what a poem advocates, how it tries to develop emotional energy, and whether its methods are effective. Being able to identify the devices is useful but only as a means to a more important end.

Poems which openly and directly advocate a particular ideology, argue for a specific cause, or try to teach us something are called **didactic** poems. Critics sometimes distinguish between didactic poems and **mimetic** (or **imaginative**) poems, which are more concerned to present than to persuade. But the distinction is one of degree, for most poems mean at the very least to make their attitudes, their vision, their presentation of reality plausible and attractive. The term **propaganda** is almost always used pejoratively, to suggest that a writer's main aim is to arouse readers toward immediate action in a specific situation; poems so specifically and narrowly directed are usually assumed to be ephemeral, although good "occasional poems" (§11) and "satires" (§10) often transcend their occasions.

Paradox : copy from dict.

3. SPEAKER

It has become traditional to distinguish between the person who wrote the poem and the person who speaks in a poem, for an author often deliberately chooses to speak through a **character** quite different from his or her real self. Poets thus sometimes create a fictional person as a **speaker**, just as playwrights create a character who is then obliged to say things in a way appropriate to the character as created. In many poems the speaker is very like the author, or very like what the author wishes to think he or she is like. Between the speaker who is a fully distinct character and the author speaking honestly and directly are many degrees of detachment.

The term **persona** is often used synonymously with speaker, especially in satire, where the author usually speaks in a voice very like his own except that he often pretends to be more innocent, more earnest, and more pure than he knows himself to be. Such a **pose** (or **posture**, or **mask**) is not really dishonest any more than the creation of a character in a play or story is dishonest; it is part of the author's strategy of making a point effectively and persuasively.

When the author's attitude is different from that of the speaker the poem is said to be ironic, although the term **irony** also means several other things. Irony is not only saying one thing and meaning its opposite; it is also any manner of being oblique rather than straightforward and often involves exaggeration or understatement. A whole poem may be said to be ironic (or to have **structural irony**) when its total effect is to reverse the attitude presented by the speaker, but poems which are not wholly ironic may use ironic words and phrases (**verbal irony**) to generate a more complex statement or attitude.

When irony is stark, simple, snide, exactly inverted—that is, when what is said is exactly the opposite of what is meant—it is called **sarcasm.** The term "irony," qualified in various ways, may indicate almost any kind of discrepancy between what is apparent in a literary work and what someone else knows to be so. **Dramatic irony** (which may be used in a poem as well as in a play) occurs when the speaker is unaware of something about himself or his situation but the reader is not.

4.   SITUATION AND SETTING

A poem's relationship to time and space is sometimes very simple and sometimes very complicated. Some poems have a **setting** specified as clearly as do stories and plays, and in many cases the effect of a poem may depend heavily upon our recognizing the setting. In *Channel Firing* (p. 438), for example, the setting has to be a graveyard in England just before Britain's entry into World War I for the poem to make any sense. But the poem does not immediately tell us where and when the action is taking place; in *Channel Firing* the facts accumulate: first a dead body awakens and sits up, wondering what the noise is about. A little later we find out that gunnery practice in the English channel is the cause of the commotion, and finally we are given information (about the echoes moving inland) that indicates which side of the channel we are concerned with.

Poems which celebrate a certain occasion (see **occasional poem,** §11) often depend upon a reader's knowledge of the event and its cultural context. Poems about specific events or circumstances may be said to be **referential** in their use of setting, and they generally require us to recognize not only historical facts but the cultural interpretation placed upon the facts at the time. If a poem requires a particular location, there is usually information in the poem that leads to such specificity. When no such information exists in the poem, it is safe to assume that you don't need it to understand the poem's use of setting. Even a general setting may, however, recall other settings in literature, art, history, or myth. Such **allusive settings** (for a definition of **allusion,** see §2) are very common; garden settings, for example, almost inevitably call up memories of the Garden of Eden and its features and events—innocence, perfection, temptation, or the fall. Closely related to allusive settings are **symbolic settings,** which depend upon the psychological association of a particular quality with a particular place.

Temporal settings (that is, settings in time) may be symbolic or allusive or both at the same time. *Sunday Morning* (p. 495) depends upon both the traditional sense of sabbath and the modern custom of using Sunday mornings for luxurious leisure. Temporal settings may also be historically specific, or depend instead upon time of day or season of the year. The temporal setting often helps to set a particular mood in the poem or anchors the poem in a particular psychological reality.

The **situation** may need to be identified even in poems that do not have a specific setting. In *The Flea* (p. 104), for example, a male speaker is delivering a monologue to a woman, but we don't know

subject plus occasion?

where or when; the significant thing is that the man is arguing for making love, and the woman is reluctant. In some poems, too, the situation is a remembered one from the distance of later years; such a device is called **retrospection.** *Cherrylog Road* (p. 100), for example, although detailed in its presentation of setting and situation, makes it clear that the speaker is recalling events from many years before.

5. LANGUAGE AND POETRY

Words are the bricks and mortar of poetry, and whatever design the poet has in mind has to be carried out through the words available in the language. Word choice (**diction**) in poems is usually calculated carefully; often words are chosen because of their **precision** or their **ambiguity,** the multiple possibilities of suggestivity which can complicate reader responses. Where words are placed is important, too; like prose, poetry usually follows the normal **syntax** (word order) of the language in which it is written, but sometimes words are moved around for special effects in sound, emphasis, or meaning.

Most nouns, verbs, adjectives, and adverbs not only **denote** a thing, action, or attribute, but also **connote** feelings and associations suggested by it. A horse is literally a four-legged, whinnying, rideable, workable animal, but the word "horse" connotes to most people strength, vitality, vigor. To be even more emphatic about its vigor and strength and to imply wildness as well, one might call it a steed or stallion. Not all words have clear, universally accepted connotations built into them, and writers often use the more elaborate devices of metaphor and symbolism (§6) to build a specific set of associations and values into the words and combinations of words that they use.

Imagery is used by different critics to mean three related but distinct things: 1. the mental pictures suggested by the verbal descriptions in a poem; 2. the visual descriptions in the poem itself; or 3. the figurative language (including metaphors, similes, and analogies) in the poem. In all three uses, imagery is technically a visual term, though other sense impressions are sometimes included under its large umbrella; imagery which mingles different sense impressions (sound or touch, for exmple, with sight) is said to be **synesthetic imagery.**

The first definition of imagery is the least precise one, for it tries to describe the effect of the poem on the reader; because each reader's response is likely to be a little different from every other reader's, critics usually find it safer and more precise to articulate the poem's efforts to create the effect; the second and third definitions of imagery are attempts to describe these efforts, the *means* of bringing about a certain effect. The third definition is the most common one, and it has the advantage of greater précision in describing different indirect ways that a poem may use to translate words into less abstract sense experience. Critics who use the term "imagery" in this third way may refer to nonfigurative description simply as description and to the presumed effect on the reader of both description and imagery as **visual impressions** or **sense impressions.** Imagery is the collective term for a group of individual **images.** One may speak of an **image cluster** (a group of similar images concentrated in a short passage), of a **controlling image** (when a single image seems to dominate a passage or even a whole poem, making other images subservient to it), or of an **image pattern** (when one or more images recur in a passage or poem). Sometimes it is convenient to speak of **kinds of imagery** ("animal imagery" or "architectural imagery") as well as to define individual images in greater detail. When imagery is defined in the third way, it is **figurative language**, which is defined in §6.

6. FIGURATIVE LANGUAGE

Figurative language (that is, language that uses figures of speech) includes the use of simile, metaphor, analogy, and personification. A **simile** is a direct, explicit comparison of one thing to another and usually uses "like" or "as" in drawing the connection. A simile may **extend** throughout a poem and be elaborated (it is then called an **analogy**) or be used to make a brief comparison in only one specified sense.

A **metaphor** pretends that one thing is something else, thus making an implicit comparison between the things. Even more than similes, metaphors are often **extended** because, in describing a thing in terms of something else, a metaphor often implies a detailed and complex resemblance between the two, one which may not be obvious at first glance. When a metaphor compares things which seem radically unlike, but which can be developed into a striking parallel, it is called a **conceit**; the "metaphysical poets" of the 17th century specialized in finding surprising likenesses in things usually considered unlike, and their poems often elaborate a single **metaphysical conceit**. The terms **tenor** and **vehicle** are often used to distinguish the primary object of attention from the thing being used to clarify that object. In Shakespeare's *That Time of Year* (p. 135) the primary object of attention (**tenor**) is the aging speaker, and late autumn is the **vehicle** which in the first few lines clarifies his aging. Metaphors are often said to be **extended metaphors** or **controlling metaphors** (in the same sense I have described above for images) when they dominate or organize a passage or poem.

A **mixed metaphor** is one in which terms from one metaphor are incorporated into another one, usually by mistake. A **dead metaphor** is one that has passed into such common usage as to have obscured its origins: we speak of a "leg" of a chair or the "heart" of the problem without remembering that the terms are metaphors implying a comparison to living bodies. When language, metaphorical or not, becomes unnecessarily specialized and self-consciously unavailable to an outsider, it is **jargon**. When such language is used mindlessly, it is called **cant**. When it is slangy and lives the short life of fashion among a select in-group, it is called **argot**. A **cliché** is any expression or idea which, through repeated use, has become commonplace, tiresome, and trite.

Personification (or **prosopopeia**) is the strategy of giving human qualities to abstract concepts or inanimate things: Beauty, Honor, Cruelty, Death, flowers, and various aspects of the natural landscape have been personified in various ages, but the strategy has been largely out of favor except for specialized and comic uses in the 20th century. Closely related is the strategy of ascribing to nature emotions which reflect human happenings (the **pathetic fallacy**), as in *The Darkling Thrush* (p. 439).

A **symbol** is something which stands for something else. In a very literal sense, words themselves are all symbols (they stand for an object, action, or quality, not just for letters or sounds), but symbols in poetry are said to be those words and groups of words which have a range of reference beyond their literal denotation. When a poem pervasively uses symbols as a major strategy and when the poem is more committed to the things which the symbols represent than to everyday reality, it is called a **symbolic poem** and is said to use **symbolism**. Poems, like everyday conversation, may use symbols occasionally and casually without being called symbolic.

In **allegory**, the action of the poem consistently and systematically describes another order of things beyond the obvious one. Spenser's *The Faerie Queene* is allegorical on several levels at the same time; the narrative action makes literal sense as a story, but the characters and actions also stand for political happenings, religious events, and moral values. *The Faerie Queene* is thus said to be a political, religious, and moral allegory.

Poets sometimes develop a highly specialized and personal set of **private symbols**—words, objects, and phrases which take on specific meanings as a result of repeated use by the poet in poem after poem. At the opposite extreme from private symbols are those which are universally shared within a defined culture. The framework of such shared symbols is called a **myth**, and the myth may include characters, events, and recurrent patterns of experience which the culture recognizes as, on some deep level, true. Poets sometimes too use particulars of a myth no longer literally or generally accepted; the wide recognition of standard myths allows writers to employ examples either in or out of their full mythic context. In recent years, critics have been heavily influenced by **myth criticism**, which usually signifies an attempt to discover **archetypes**, patterns of experience and action which are similar in different nations and cultures. In this sense, myth is not restricted to a single system, but rather attempts to transcend the particulars of time and place and locate fundamental recurrent patterns in human nature and human history.

7. FORM AND STRUCTURE

The **form** of a poem has to do with its appearance, just as does the form of a building, and one can describe that form in many different ways, just as a description of the form of a building depends upon the angle of vision (from the ground or from the air), the distance of the viewer, and to what other buildings the building is being compared. The simplest sense of poetic form involves the literal appearance on the page, the poem's shape seen physically, conceived literally. On the page most traditional poems look regular—that is, they are either divided into regular "stanzas" (§9) or they flow continually down the page in lines of more or less equal length. Modern poems tend to be less regular and thus to look more scattered and fragmented on the page, reflecting a general modern attitude that poetic meaning accumulates in a less regular and less programmed way. Occasionally the words are even shaped like a particular object, as in Renaissance **emblem poetry** (or **carmen figuratum** or **shaped verse**) or recent **concrete poetry.**

More enduring, more significant, and more complex senses of form involve less easily seeable ways of classifying external characteristics. Poetry is itself a sort of **formal** classification as distinguished from drama or fiction, and one can also distinguish between kinds of poetry (elegy, for example, or epigram) on the basis of subject matter, tone; conventions, etc. (see §10). Stanza varieties and rhythmic patterns (see §9 and §8) are also formal matters, for each involves external patterns which may be described relative to other poems.

As in a building, **structure** supports form and makes it possible. The order and arrangement of all of a poem's constituent parts—words, images, figures of speech, ideas, everything—involve structure, and the ways of discussing the relationship between parts vary from matters of word arrangement (grammar, syntax) to the development and presentation of ideas. Structure enables the form; the planning and craft of poetry are all, finally, structural matters.

The distinction I have made between form and structure corresponds to distinctions that some critics make between **external** and **internal form** (or external and internal structure). Another frequent distinction is that between **organic** structure or form and **architechtonic** structure or form (those who make this distinction do not necessarily use the terms "form" and "structure" as they have been explained above). Things organic are said to take their shape from natural forces, like living organisms, and things architechtonic to have shape artificially imposed upon them from without; a strong bias is usually implied toward the former, for the distinction implies the livingness, wholeness, and uniqueness of an individual poem.

Some works are shaped by other works which they **imitate** or **parody**; *The Dover Bitch* (p. 317), for example, is a response to *Dover Beach* (p. 109). An **imitation** which makes fun of another work is a **burlesque** or **parody** of it, exaggerating its distinctive features and holding them up to ridicule; it is a parody if its attitude is one of gentle teasing, a burlesque if it is harsh and vicious: Imitation may also be a kind of flattery, honoring the methods, values, and meanings of another work and expropriating them into the new one. Many great poems have their basis in imitation and a good imitation is never a simple copy; it often derives major effects from its similarities to and differences from the original.

Questions of form and structure are related to questions about the integrity and autonomy of individual poems. For many years, critics were reluctant to deal with **parts** of a poem, insisting that as self-existent **wholes** poems deserved to be dealt with **holistically**, as creations having their own laws. More recently, criticism has dealt more directly with parts of poems, admitting that they too have organizational principles and facing squarely the difficulty that knowing whether a poem is whole or not is, even for the author, very nearly a mystical matter. Besides, an individual poem is often part of a larger **sequence** or **cycle**—that is, a group of poems which have significant features in common: they may be about a similar subject, tell a story progressively, or be calculated to produce a particular effect. Almost all poets themselves arrange the poems in their individual volumes, and it is often useful and revealing to read individual poems in the context of these volumes.

8. PROSODY

Prosody is the study of sound and rhythm in poetry. It is not a very exact science, but properly used it can be an aid to reading and *hearing* poems more fully.

The **rhythm** of a passage—in prose or poetry—is the pattern of sound pulsations in the voice as one reads it. Almost all spoken language has some kind of rhythm, however irregular, and simply listening to a human voice reciting, reading, or talking informally reveals recurrent systems of **stress** or **accent**. Stress is a relative matter (and this fact is a major difficulty for prosodic analysis), but in listening to the human voice we can always hear that some words and syllables are **stressed** (accented), and that others are, relatively, **unstressed** (unaccented). When the stress recurs at quite regular intervals—that is, when the rhythm has a pattern—the result is **meter**. The systematic analysis of patterns of stress, syllable by syllable, sound unit by sound unit, is called **scansion**; a reader who can **scan** a poem will discern the poem's basic rhythmic pattern (meter) and may then notice variations in the pattern or departures from it.

In the sentence,

Throw the ball to me

stresses "naturally" fall on "throw," "ball," and "me," but another context of meaning might considerably alter the stress pattern:

I said, throw the ball to me, not over my head.

Stress here would likely fall on "to," and there might be some other "unusual" stresses, provided by the demands of meaning in particular instances or by particular speakers. When a sentence or phrase appears in a certain rhythmic context (in, for example, a poem written in a certain meter), the sound context also affects it, tending to bend it (or "wrench" it) toward the basic pattern in the surrounding passage. There are, then, three factors which determine stress: (1.) the "natural" stress or stresses of each word; (2.) meaning and emphasis in a sentence or phrase; and (3.) the patterns of stress in the surrounding context.

Meter is measured in feet; a **foot** normally consists of a stressed syllable and one or more unstressed syllables. In the following line, in which stressed syllables have marked "–" and unstressed syllables "∪," the division into five feet is indicated by a **virgule**, or **slash mark** (/):

∪ – ∪ – ∪ – ∪ – ∪ –
A lit/tle lear/ning is/a dang/'rous thing

Each of its feet is an *iambic* foot—that is, it has an unstressed syllable followed by a stressed one. Iambic meter is the most common one in English poetry, but three other meters are of some importance:

Trochaic (a stressed syllable followed by an unstressed one):

Tell me/ not in/ mourn ful/ num bers

Anapestic (two unstressed syllables followed by a stressed one):

'Twas the night/ be fore Christ/ mas and all/ through the house

Dactylic (a stressed syllable followed by two unstressed ones):

Hig gle dy/ pig gle dy/ Al fred Lord/ Ten ny son.

Most English poems use one of these meters as their basic meter, but not with absolute regularity. An iambic poem will often contain trochaic feet (for emphasis, perhaps, or just for change), and some variation is almost a requirement if a poem is not to lull the ear into total dull deafness. Besides the standard meters, there are special feet used for variations.

Here is a table of the basic metrical feet and the most frequent variations:

ADJECTIVE FORM OF THE NAME	NOUN FORM	PATTERN
iambic	iamb (or iambus)	˘ –
trochaic	trochee	– ˘
anapestic	anapest	˘ ˘ –
dactylic	dactyl	– ˘ ˘
spondaic	spondee	– –
pyrrhic	pyrrhic	˘ ˘
amphibrachic	amphibrach (or amphibrachys or rocking foot)	˘ – ˘
amphimacric	amphimacer (or amphimac or cretic)	– ˘ –

Coleridge's *Metrical Feet* (p. 182) exemplifies most of them.

The most common line length in English poetry is pentameter, five feet. Here is a table of all the common line lengths:

monometer	one foot
dimeter	two feet
trimeter	three feet
tetrameter	four feet
pentameter	five feet
hexameter	six feet
heptameter	seven feet
octameter	eight feet

Iambic and anapestic meters are sometimes called **rising rhythms** (or **rising meters**) because their basic movement is from unstressed to stressed syllables; and trochaic and dactylic meters are called **falling rhythms** (or **falling meters**). When a foot lacks a syllable it is called **catalectic**; the first foot of anapestic lines is often catalectic, and the final foot of most trochaic lines is catalectic because lines that end with an unstressed syllable are usually thought to "sound funny"; such lines usually occur only in comic poetry. Lines that rhyme by using an unstressed final syllable are said to have **feminine rhyme**. Certain meters are also said to incline toward comic effects; anapestic rhythm tends to produce comic effects, although it can be used to produce more serious tones. Iambic tetrameter also seems more liable than most meters to comic effects, though it also has been used for great varieties of tone. The number and length of pauses in a line affect the speed with which the line is read and, indirectly, the tone in any meter, for a slow-paced line seems less emphatic in its rhythm than a rapid-paced one. Almost all lines contain one or more natural pauses, some very short and some fairly long; any significant pause within a line is called a **caesura**, and in scansion it is indicated by a double virgule (//).

The distinction between stressed and unstressed is not a very precise one, for many degrees of stress are possible, and even an untrained ear can usually hear great variety of stress in the reading of a single line from a single poem. Division into feet is sometimes arbitrary, for there is often more than one way to count the number of feet, even assuming that the stresses are all accurately marked. Students often get bogged down in the technicalities of such matters and lose sight of the point of metrical analysis—which is to *hear* poems more accurately and notice those surprising places when the poem departs from its basic pattern.

Not all English poetry uses meter in the traditional senses I have described. Much modern poetry is in **free verse**, which avoids regularized meter and has no significant recurrent stress rhythms, although it may use other repetitive patterns—of words, phrases, structures—as Whitman often does. (**Free verse** should not be confused with **blank verse**, which is unrhymed but is by definition written in iambic pentameter.) Many modern poems that may appear unpatterned are, however, very tightly controlled metrically; the absence of rhyme does not mean the absence of metrical pattern, and many untraditional-looking modern poems use traditional meter in traditional ways. Many poems, old as well as new, experiment with meter too, trying odd combinations within the definitions I have given or using different principles altogether. The **sprung rhythm** used by Gerard Manley Hopkins avoids the usual distinctions about kinds of feet and only counts the numbers of stressed syllables; each foot begins with a stressed syllable, but any number of unstressed syllables may follow before the next foot begins, so that traditional scansion would make the pattern seem unpatterned. **Quantitative verse**, imitating the metrical principles used by Latin and Greek poets, has been attempted in almost every age, but seldom with success. Unlike stress meters of any kind, quantitative verse determines pattern by the duration of sounds and sets up various meters in combinations of long and short syllables. Some modern experimenters have fused quantitative and stress patterns, and still others have tried patterns based on the number of sounds (see the discussion of syllabic verse in §9), on the kind of sounds used rather than either duration or stress, or on attempts at precise distinctions in the *amount* of stress in stressed syllables.

Until recently **rhyme** has been nearly as important as meter to most poetry. Rhyme is based on the duplication of the vowel sound and all sounds after the vowel in the relevant words. Most rhyme is **end-rhyme** (that is, the near-duplication of sounds takes place at the ends of the lines), but other patterns are possible. **Internal rhyme** involves rhyming sounds within the same line; in **beginning rhyme**, the first word or syllable rhymes in two or more lines. Not-quite rhyme is often used to vary strict rhyme schemes; the most common form is **slant rhyme** (or **half rhyme**) in which the relevant words have similar but not exactly rhyming sounds because either the vowel or consonant varies slightly (as in backs/box, bent/want, or web/step). **Visual** (or **eye**) **rhyme** uses words with identical endings but different pronunciations (bread/bead), and **rime riche** uses words that sound exactly the same but have different spellings and meanings (knight/night; lead/led; him/hymn). In poetry of earlier ages, one needs to watch, too, for **historical rhyme**—rhyme that was perfect when the poem was written but, because of historical changes in pronunciation, is no longer so; tea/day and join/divine were once good rhymes in the easiest and simplest sense.

Sound effects not involving rhyme continue to be important to poetry, and many of them are (like rhyme and meter) based on the ordering principle of repetition. **Alliteration** is the repetition of sounds in nearby words; usually alliteration involves the initial consonant sounds of words (and sometimes internal consonants in stressed syllables). **Assonance** is a repetition of vowel sounds in a line or series of lines; assonance often affects pace (by unbalancing short and long vowel patterns) and the way words included in the pattern tend to seem underscored. **Consonance** involves a repeated sequence of consonants but with varied vowels (as in stop/step, rope/reap, or hip/hop).

Onomatopoeia is the attempt to imitate or echo sounds being described. Some words are in themselves **onomatopoeic** (buzz, fizz, murmur), and others suggest action or qualities related to their literal meaning (slippery, lull). Passages may use rhythms and vocal sounds for onomatopoeic purposes; the famous "Sound and Sense" passage by Pope (p. 179) exemplifies many of the possibilities of sound to produce imitative, hormonious, or cacophonous effects.

9. STANZA AND VERSE FORMS

Most poems of more than a few lines are divided into **stanzas,** groups of lines with a specific cogency of their own and usually set off from one another by a space. Traditionally, stanzas are linked by a common **rhyme scheme** (pattern of rhyme words) or by a common pattern of rhythms; modern poems which are divided into stanzas often, however, lack such patterns. Stanza lengths vary considerably, and so do the patterns and complexity of rhyme. Poets often invent distinctive patterns of their own—sometimes for novelty, sometimes to generate a particular effect—but over the years some stanza patterns have proved quite durable.

The **ballad stanza** is one of the oldest; it consists of four lines, the second and fourth of which are iambic trimeter and rhyme with each other. The first and third lines, in iambic tetrameter, do not rhyme. **Terza rima** is the three-line stanza in which Dante wrote *The Divine Comedy;* each iambic pentameter stanza (*aba*) interlocks with the next (*bcb, cdc, ded,* etc.). Among longer stanza forms are **ottava rima,** an Italian form adapted to English as eight lines of iambic pentameter rhyming *abababcc,* and the **Spenserian stanza,** the nine-line form Spenser invented for his *Faerie Queene*—eight lines of iambic pentameter and a ninth line of iambic hexameter, called an **alexandrine,** rhymed *ababbcbcc.* Stanzas with no official names are simply designated by the number of lines; a three-line stanza is called a **tristich, triplet,** or **tercet** (the latter is also a term for part of the sonnet—see the discussion below); a four-line stanza is a **quatrain;** a five-line stanza is a **quintain** or **quintet;** a six-line stanza is a **sextain** or **sixain.**

Many modern poems, rather than using traditional stanzas, are divided spatially according to breaks in syntax, meaning, or tone, and the individual characteristics of a particular poem may dictate such breaks. Some modern experiments have also produced patterns as demanding in their own way as rhyme-based stanzas. **Syllabic verse,** for example, requires that the number of syllables in each line of the first stanza be duplicated in each subsequent stanza; stanzas (and lines within them) may thus be of any length, but the poet commits himself or herself to a pattern in the first stanza and thereafter sticks to it.

The **couplet** is a rather special case among stanza forms. It consists of two lines (of any specifiable length or rhythm) which rhyme with one another, and seldom is one couplet divided by space from another one. Larger divisions within couplet verse are usually indicated (as in blank verse) by indentation, and the units are called **verse paragraphs,** which may or may not be separated by space. The **heroic couplet,** rhyming lines of iambic pentameter, has been the most popular and durable of couplet forms; it dominated English poetry during much of the 17th and 18th centuries and has been used successfully by many earlier and later poets. When the syntax of one couplet carries over into the next couplet, the couplets are said to be **open** or **enjambed; enjambment** is the continuation of syntax beyond the borders of a single couplet. **Closed** (or **end-stopped**) **couplets** are—as far as the technicalities of syntax are concerned—complete in themselves. Couplets written in iambic tetrameter tend to be used for comic effect because of the emphatic regularity of the rhythms and the abrupt underscoring of the rhyme.

Several **fixed poetic forms** (which contain a certain number of stanzas organized in a determined way) have been popular, from time to time, with English poets. Most of them were introduced by French troubadours in Provence, some of them as early as the 12th century. The **villanelle,** for example, contains five three-line stanzas and a final four-line stanza; only two rhyme sounds are permitted in the entire poem, and the first and third lines of the first stanza are repeated, alternately, as the third line of subsequent stanzas until the last. In the last stanza, the repeating lines become the final two lines of the poem. The **sestina** contains six six-line stanzas and a final three-line stanza, all unrhymed; but the final word in each line of the first stanza then becomes the final word in other stanzas (but in a different specified pattern); the final stanza uses these words again in a specified way, one in each half line. Some poets have even written **double** and **triple sestinas**, in which the demands increase geometrically. Repetition (probably originally for mnemonic purposes) is a major feature in fixed poetic forms.

10. GENRES AND KINDS

Here the term **genre** is used to indicate the traditional classroom distinction between fiction, poetry, and drama. Other less inclusive terms may then be used for subdividing genres and for different ways of classifying literary works according to characteristics they have in common.

A **mode** is, literally, a way of doing something; as a literary term it may most usefully be employed to indicate basic literary patterns of organizing experience. The **narrative mode** tells a story and organizes experience along a time continuum. The **dramatic mode** presents a change, usually an abrupt one, and organizes experience emotionally according to the rise and fall of someone's fortunes. The **lyric mode** reflects upon an experience or an idea and organizes experience irrespective of time and space, although it may describe a particular time or specific place. These traditional modes represent basic ways of viewing experience and have been around for a very long time. They obviously influenced the development of genres, which represent a somewhat artificial stiffening or rigidification of the narrative, dramatic, and lyric modes.

One may also think of modes in terms of the conclusions they draw about experience or the dominant emotions they arouse in their presentations of experience. **Tragedy**, or the **tragic mode**, describes someone's downfall, usually in stately language. **Comedy**, or the **comic mode**, describes in more common language someone's triumph or the successful emergence of some order which encompasses and mutes all disorderly forces. **Romance**, or the **romantic mode**, describes the ideal, or what ought to be, often in terms of nostalgia or fantasy or longing. **Satire**, or the **satiric mode**, attacks the way things are and usually distributes the blame. In *The Anatomy of Criticism*, Northrop Frye argues that these modes correspond to the **myths** of the four seasons (comedy—spring; romance—summer; tragedy—autumn; satire—winter) and thus considers them universal ways of organizing experience.

Poetry considered as a genre may also be subdivided into **kinds** (or **types**, or **subgenres**). The **epic**, or **heroic poetry**, has been traditionally regarded as the highest in a hierarchy of kinds because it describes the great deeds of mighty heroes and heroines, usually in founding a nation or developing a distinctive culture, and uses elevated language and a grand, high style. **Pastoral poetry** describes the simple life of country folk, usually shepherds who live a timeless, painless (and sheepless) life in a world that is full of beauty, music, and love, and that remains forever green. The pastoral poem is also sometimes called an **eclogue**, a **bucolic**, or an **idyll**. The **elegy** was, in classical times, a poem on any subject written in "elegiac" meter, but since the

Renaissance the term has usually indicated a formal lament for the death of a particular person; a **dirge,** or **threnody,** is similar but less formal and is supposed to be sung. A dirge or elegy supposed to be sung by one person is called a **monody.** An **epigram** was originally any poem carved in stone (on tombstones, buildings, gates, etc.), but in modern usage it denotes a very short, usually witty verse with a quick turn at the end; it is often, but not always, comic. The **epitaph** is a variety of epigram in which the poem is to be carved on someone's tombstone, but many epitaphs are comic, written about people not yet dead, and of course not really intended for engraving. A **lyric** is a short poem in which a speaker expresses intense personal emotion rather than describing a narrative or dramatic situation; sometimes the term is used even more broadly for *any* short poem. Originally the term "lyric" designated poems meant to be sung to the accompaniment of the lyre, and the names of several other kinds also specify their original connection with music. Many **songs** (whose words are usually called lyrics) are poems which have been set to music. A **ballad** is a narrative poem which is, or originally was, meant to be sung. Characterized by much repetition and often by a repeated **refrain** (recurrent phrase or series of phrases), ballads were originally a folk creation, transmitted orally from person to person and age to age. Once **folk ballads** began to be written down (in the 18th century), **literary ballads** in imitation of folk ballads began to be created by individual authors. A **hymn** is a song of praise, usually in praise of God but sometimes of abstract qualities. A **chanson** (which in French simply means "song") was originally a song written in **couplets** (§9), but the term now describes any simple song. An ⌐**aubade**⌐ is a morning song in which the coming of dawn is either celebrated or denounced as a nuisance. An **aube** is a more rigidly defined morning poem; the speaker of an aube is the woman in a love triangle, and she expresses regret that dawn is coming so that she and her lover must part. In a **complaint** a lover bemoans his sad condition as a result of neglect by his mistress. In a **palinode,** an author recants his previous attitude toward something, often apologizing for his earlier poetry, which he now claims to have been trivial. The **confessional poem** is a relatively new (or at least only recently defined) kind in which the speaker describes his confused chaotic state, which becomes a metaphor for the state of the world around him. A **meditation** is a contemplation of some physical object as a way of reflecting upon some larger truth, often (but not necessarily) a spiritual one.

Many of the kinds (confessional, complaint, aube, and many others) are traditionally **monologues** (one clearly distinguishable speaker does all the speaking). Monologues are sometimes called **interior monologues** (as in fiction) if the speaker seems to be thinking thoughts rather than speaking to someone. A monologue set in a specific situation and spoken to someone is called **dramatic monologue;** if the character is alone and speaking only to him- or herself, it is called **soliloquy. Light verse** encompasses many poems in many kinds; it is not necessarily trivial, but its speaker takes or affects a whimsical, twitting attitude toward his or her subject. Light verse that deals with the manners and mores of polite society is called **vers de société.** And some terms which properly describe a kind also properly describe some other sort of grouping. If **satire,** for example, is in one sense a mode, it is also a kind, for there is **formal verse satire** that attacks a specific vice in the manner of a verse essay. And the term "satire" also describes an attitude toward experience and a tone; as the opposite of **panegyric** (poetry praising something) satire attacks something, usually by analyzing, specifying, and naming names. **Satire** that is mild, civilized, and gentle is called **Horatian satire** (named after the Roman poet Horace); vicious, violent, loud satire is **Juvenalian satire** (named after Juvenal), or **invective;** a satire that attacks a specific person is a **lampoon.**

11. WIDER CONTEXTS

In a sense, every poem creates a world all its own, but every poem also reflects aspects of a larger world from which it derives. Often it is important—and sometimes it is crucial—for a reader to recognize **context,** the circumstances that surrounded the making of the poem. The most obvious and compelling contexts are in poems that refer explicitly to some historical event or situation. A poem written about a specific event or occasion is called an **occasional** poem; the occasion may be a well known public one or a private one. All matters of time and circumstance that might affect either the conception or execution are part of the poem's **historical** or **cultural context.** It is not always easy to determine exactly which factors are relevant to a poem and which are not; deciding just what information is necessary and how to use it once acquired is one of the most delicate tasks in good interpretation.

Literary historians often designate **periods** in which cultural and aesthetic assumptions are more or less shared, speaking, for example, of the Elizabethan period (literally, 1558–1603, the reign of Queen Elizabeth in England) or the Romantic period (approximately 1790–1830) to describe certain common tendencies in a given historical era. The ideas and assumptions built into poems often reflect trends of thinking in a particular historical period. Poets sometimes consciously evoke their sense of shared ideas by using a **motif** (plural, **motifs** or **motives**): a recurrent device, formula or situation which deliberately connects a poem with common patterns of existing thought. One common motif is that of **carpe diem.** The phrase literally means "seize the day," and *carpe diem* poems invariably remind us of the shortness of life and beauty and the necessity to take advantage of the present. Such recurring situations as temptations in the garden, flights into the country, and journeys into experience are also motifs.

Poets often consciously evoke, too, a particular frame of reference or system of belief as a way of anchoring their own vision in a common pattern of experience that is understandable to an audience. In English poetry, the Judaeo-Christian and classical frames of reference are the most common, and the events and symbols of Biblical and classical history and myth are often prominent. Poets have, however, increasingly worried, especially since the 18th century, about the deterioration of a common heritage that was once based in Judaeo-Christian or classical terms, and the use of other, non-Western myths has become increasingly popular. Some poets have also developed private symbolic systems, sometimes extended into full-blown myths as in the poetry of Yeats. Most authors do not, of course, develop a complex private system of their own, but all authors have individual traits which are a product of their individual consciousness. Reading a group of poems by an author usually clarifies every individual poem, for the reader can develop a sense of the poet's distinctive style, strategies, and ideas. The total work of an author is called a **canon;** one may speak of the Milton canon or the Eliot canon. But even a sampling of a poet's work often leads a reader to expect certain procedures and attitudes, enabling a more exact and intense response. In its broadest sense, the **authorial context** may include biographical detail, psychological analysis, and specific facts about the conditions under which a poem was created, as well as dominant characteristics or tendencies in poems by a certain author.

What kind of contextual knowledge and how much of it a poem requires varies, of course, from poem to poem; many poems are readily accessible without deliberate pursuit of historical, intellectual, or authorial background, but the range and intensity of experience available through a poem is almost always enhanced by more knowledge.

12.   TRADITION AND CONVENTION

In its most inclusive sense, **tradition** is the influence—deliberate or not—of any previous event, technique, or consciousness upon subsequent ways of thought and action. Poetic tradition may involve an influence in ideas, or style, or both. Poets may deliberately seek to follow, refine, or respond to previous thinkers and poets, or they may find themselves conditioned by the past in ways over which they have no control.

Poetry, perhaps more than drama or fiction, is subject to the characteristic habits and limitations of a particular language, and it is common practice to speak of the **English tradition** (or the **English poetic tradition,** or simply the **tradition**) meaning all of the recurrent tendencies over the years, including many which oppose, modify, or contradict other tendencies. The poetry of Pound or cummings, for example, is as surely a part of the tradition as that of Milton or Tennyson, for the tradition is not something which once and for all defines itself but rather consists of continuity marked by continual modification. Participation in the tradition is not always easy to recognize or predict, for some of the English tradition's brightest lights (Shakespeare, Swift, Shelley, and Eliot are examples) at first seemed to their contemporaries most untraditional—in the sense of the tradition then understood. Tradition continually redefines itself to comprehend rebellious sons and daughters born into its line and intent on the old rituals of father-killing and mansion-burning. Sometimes the tradition is defined as if it were already complete, but it is more useful to consider it a living, changing thing which will, by definition, ultimately render any definition incomplete. Much (perhaps most) of what seems new and innovative does not, of course, last long enough in the public memory or evoke a substantial enough response in its audience to become part of the tradition. Contemporary with Shakespeare, for example, were many poets whose innovations did not "catch on" or whose distinctive appeal did not prove to be permanent; it is so in every age, and the process of developing a tradition is a perpetual matter of experimenting and sorting.

Within a language tradition are **national** and **regional traditions** as well; one may speak, for example, of a Canadian tradition, an Irish tradition, or a New England tradition. Such divisions have partly to do with local variations in linguistic usage, but they also relate to ideological concerns, cultural assumptions, and social, political, and economic movements. The same sort of division may be broadened, reaching beyond language barriers to comprehend the **European tradition** or the **Western tradition**. The latter term is often used nearly synonymously with the English tradition; such usage is not entirely precise, but many of the most characteristic features of English poetry do have origins or counterparts in ancient Greece or Rome or in more recent Continental cultures, especially those of France, Italy, and Germany.

Besides definitions based on linguistic, national, and cultural boundaries, there are other, more narrow senses of tradition in common use. Tradition may describe the history and accumulated characteristics of a literary kind or a stanza form (one might speak of the epic tradition, the sonnet tradition, the couplet tradition, or the tradition of free verse, §9 and 10), the recurrent appearances of a motif or theme (the *carpe diem* tradition, §11), the characteristics of a thought or value pattern (the Puritan tradition or the metaphysical tradition), or characteristics associated with a particular time or age (the Elizabethan tradition).

A **convention** is any characteristic which over a period of time has come to be expected in poetry or in a poem of a certain sort. There are conventions of subject matter and conventional ways of using the standard poetic devices, but conventions are especially associated with the older poetic kinds (§10). Following the standard conventions is usually less significant than not following them; when a poem ignores or contradicts a convention, a reader can be pretty sure that the convention is missing or altered for a specific reason. Conventions at their best are shortcuts in communication; they tell a reader what to look for and establish a beginning rapport between poet and reader; what happens as the expectations are satisfied or surprised is then up to the poet. Most conventions originated in the doctrine of **decorum**, which insists on appropriateness in all things: every poetic kind, for example, was assumed to require a certain level of language and persons and incidents of a specific level of dignity. Most conventions begin in necessity, flourish when they are recognizable to a large number of readers, and linger on simply as decoration, a memory of past needs. When specific conventions totally lose their use and force, they become merely ornamental, and sometimes seem amusing or absurd. This is why mechanical repetition of what is expected is often said to be "conventional" (or "merely conventional") in a negative sense. Sensible use of conventions involves taking advantage of the technical solutions and shortcuts they provide, but it involves too the personalized touch of an individual poet. No great poet leaves a convention exactly as he or she found it. In the hands of a shrewd craftsman, tradition and convention may be innovative and exciting; in the hands of a mindless ape of the past, they are nearly always dull and deadly.

ACKNOWLEDGMENTS

Franklin P. Adams: "Composed in the Composing Room" from *By and Large* by Franklin P. Adams. Copyright 1914 by Franklin P. Adams. Reprinted by permission of Doubleday & Company, Inc.

Samuel Adams: "To Satch" reprinted by permission of the author.

A. R. Ammons: "Cascadilla Falls" and "Needs" reprinted from *Collected Poems, 1951–1971,* by A. R. Ammons, by permission of W. W. Norton & Company, Inc. Copyright © 1972 by A. R. Ammons.

Maya Angelou: "Africa" from *Oh Pray My Wings Are Gonna Fit Me Well,* by Maya Angelou. Reprinted by permission of Random House, Inc.

Richard Armour: "Hiding Place" from *Light Armour* by Richard Armour. Copyright © 1954 Richard Armour. Reprinted by permission of McGraw Hill.

Margaret Atwood: "Five Poems for Dolls" from *Two Headed Poems* by Margaret Atwood. Copyright © 1978 by Margaret Atwood. Reprinted by permission of Simon & Schuster, a Division of Gulf & Western Corporation, and Oxford University Press, Canada.

W. H. Auden: "The Unknown Citizen," "Musée des Beaux Arts" and "In Memory of W. B. Yeats" copyright 1940 and renewed 1968 by W. H. Auden. Reprinted from *W. H. Auden: Collected Poems,* by W. H. Auden, edited by Edward Mendelson, by permission of Alfred A. Knopf, Inc. and Faber and Faber Ltd.

Imamu Amiri Baraka (LeRoi Jones): "In Memory of Radio" from *Preface to a Twenty Volume Suicide Note,* copyright © by LeRoi Jones. "Black Art" from *Black Magic,* copyright © 1969 by LeRoi Jones. Reprinted by permission of The Sterling Lord Agency.

John Berryman: "1 September 1939" from *Short Poems* by John Berryman. Copyright 1940, 1948 by John Berryman. Renewed Copyright © 1968 by John Berryman. Reprinted by permission of Farrar, Straus and Giroux, Inc.

John Betjeman: "In Westminster Abbey" from *Collected Poems* by John Betjeman. Reprinted by permission of John Murray (Publishers) Ltd. and Houghton Mifflin Co.

Earle Birney: "From the Hazel Bough" and "Irapuato" from *Selected Poems* by Earle Birney. Reprinted by permission of The Canadian Publishers, McClelland and Stewart Limited, Toronto.

Elizabeth Bishop: "Cootchie" from *Complete Poems* by Elizabeth Bishop. Copyright © 1941, 1969 by Elizabeth Bishop. Reprinted by permission of Farrar, Straus and Giroux, Inc.

Louise Bogan: "The Dragonfly" from *The Blue Estuaries* by Louise Bogan. Copyright © 1930, 1957, 1965, 1968 by Louise Bogan. Reprinted by permission of Farrar, Straus and Giroux, Inc.

Julian Bond: "The Bishop of Atlanta: Ray Charles" and "Rotation" reprinted by permission of the author.

Philip Booth: "One Man's Wife" from *Weather and Edges* by Philip Booth, copyright © 1966 by Philip Booth. Reprinted by permission of Viking Penguin, Inc.

Rupert Brooke: "The Soldier" reprinted by permission of Dodd, Mead & Company, Inc. from *The Collected Poems of Rupert Brooke.* Copyright 1915 by Dodd, Mead & Company. Copyright renewed 1943 by Edward Marsh.

Gwendolyn Brooks: "First Fight. Then Fiddle" from *The World of Gwendolyn Brooks.* Copyright 1949 by Gwendolyn Brooks Blakely. Reprinted by permission of Harper & Row, Publishers.

Turner Cassity: "Calvin in the Casino" and "Grace at the Atlanta Fox" from *Watchboy, What of the Night?* by Turner Cassity. Copyright © 1962, 1966 by Turner Cassity. Reprinted by permission of Wesleyan University Press. These poems first appeared in *Poetry.*

Helen Chasin: "Joy Sonnet in a Random Universe" and "The Word *Plum*" from *Coming Close and Other Poems* reprinted by permission of Yale University Press. Copyright © 1968 by Yale University.

Lucille Clifton: "at last we killed the roaches" from *An Ordinary Woman* by Lucille Clifton. Copyright © 1974 by Lucille Clifton. "Daddy" from *Good News About the Earth* by Lucille Clifton. Copyright © 1972 by Lucille Clifton. Reprinted by permission of Random House, Inc.

Leonard Cohen: "Suzanne" by Leonard Cohen © 1966 by Project Seven Music, a division of Continental Total Media Project, Inc. 41 East 42 Street, Suite 610, New York, N.Y. 10017. Reprinted by permission.

Frances Cornford: "Parting at Wartime" from *Collected Poems* by Frances Cornford. Reprinted by permission of Hutchinson Publishing Group Limited.

Countee Cullen: "For a Lady I Know" from *On These I Stand* by Countee Cullen. Copyright 1925 by Harper & Row, Publishers, Inc.; renewed 1953 by Ida M. Cullen. Reprinted by permission of Harper & Row, Publishers, Inc.

E. E. Cummings: "l(a" © 1958 by E. E. Cummings, "a salesman is an it that stinks Excuse" copyright 1944 by E. E. Cummings; renewed 1972 by Nancy T. Andrews, and "anyone lived in a pretty how town" Copyright 1940 by E. E. Cummings; renewed 1968 by Marion Morehouse Cummings are reprinted by permission of Harcourt Brace Jovanovich, Inc. from *Complete Poems 1913–1962* by E. E. Cummings. "In Just—" and "Buffalo Bill's" are reprinted from *Tulips & Chimneys* by E. E. Cummings, edited by George James Firmage, by permission of Liveright Publishing Corporation. Copyright © 1973, 1976 by Nancy T. Andrews. Copyright © 1973, 1976 by George James Firmage, "poem, or beauty hurts mr. vinal," "(ponder, darling, these busted statues," and "the season 'tis, my lovely lambs" are reprinted from *Is 5, Poems* by E. E. Cummings, by permission of Liveright Publishing Corporation. Copyright 1935 by E. E. Cummings. Copyright renewed 1963 by Marion Morehouse Cummings.

J. V. Cunningham: "Here Lies My Wife", "Epitaph for Someone or Other", "History of Ideas", and "All in Due Time" from *Collected Poems* by J. V. Cunningham, published by The Swallow Press. Reprinted by permission of Ohio University Press, Athens, Ohio.

561

C. Day Lewis: "Come Live With Me and Be My Love" from *Two Songs* in *Collected Poems*, 1954, is reprinted by permission of the Executors of the Estate of C. Day Lewis, Jonathan Cape, Ltd. and The Hogarth Press.

Walter de la Mare: "Slim Cunning Hands" from *The Complete Poems of Walter de la Mare* is reprinted by permission of the Literary Executors of Walter de la Mare and The Society of Authors as their representative.

Peter de Vries: "Bacchanal" from *The Tents of Wickedness* by Peter de Vries. Copyright 1950 by Peter de Vries. Originally appeared in *The New Yorker*. Reprinted by permission of Little, Brown and Company.

Ann Deagon: "Certified Copy", "Man and Wife Is One Flesh", and "There is no Balm in Birmingham" from *There is No Balm in Birmingham* by Ann Deagon. Copyright © 1972, 1974, 1975, 1976, 1978 by Ann Deagon. Reprinted by permission of David R. Godine, Publisher, Inc.

James Dickey: "Cherrylog Road" and "The Leap" from Poems *1957–1967*, by James Dickey. Copyright © 1963, 1964 by James Dickey. Reprinted by permission of Wesleyan University Press. "Cherrylog Road" first appeared in *The New Yorker*.

Emily Dickinson: #'s 216, 249, 341, 467, 632, 657, 712, 986, 1263, and 1277 are reprinted by permission of the Publishers and the Trustees of Amherst College from *The Poems of Emily Dickinson*, edited by Thomas H. Johnson, Cambridge, Mass.: The Belknap Press of Harvard University Press, Copyright © 1951, 1955 by the President and Fellows of Harvard College. #'s 341 and 657 are also reprinted by permission of Little, Brown and Company from *The Complete Poems of Emily Dickinson* edited by Thomas H. Johnson. Copyright 1929 by Martha Dickinson Bianchi. Copyright © 1957 by Mary L. Hampson.

Bob Dylan: "Mister Tambourine Man" © 1964 Warner Bros., Inc. All Rights Reserved. Used by Permission.

Richard Eberhart: "The Fury of Aerial Bombardment" from *Collected Poems 1930–1960*, Copyright © 1960 by Richard Eberhart. Reprinted by permission of Oxford University Press, Inc. and Chatto and Windus Ltd.

T. S. Eliot: "The Journey of the Magi" and "The Love Song of J. Alfred Prufrock" from *Collected Poems 1909–1962* by T. S. Eliot, copyright, 1936 by Harcourt Brace Jovanovich, Inc., copyright © 1963, 1964 by T. S. Eliot. Reprinted by permission of Harcourt Brace Jovanovich, Inc. and Faber and Faber Ltd.

James A. Emanuel: "Emmett Till" from *The Treehouse and Other Poems* © 1968 by James A. Emanuel. Reprinted by permission of Broadside/Crummel Press, Detroit, Michigan.

Kenneth Fearing: "Dirge" from *New and Selected Poems* by Kenneth Fearing. Reprinted by permission of the publisher, Indiana University Press.

Julia Fields: "Madness One Monday Evening" is reprinted by permission of the author.

Richard Harter Fogle: "A Hawthorne Garland: The Scarlet Letter" is reprinted by permission of the author.

Robert Frost: "Range-Finding," "The Rose Family," "Stopping By Woods on a Snowy Evening", "Birches", "Departmental", "Design", "Provide Provide", "Never Again Would Birdsong Be the Same" and "U.S. 1946 Kings X" from *The Poetry of Robert Frost* edited by Edward Connery Lathem. Copyright © 1969 by Holt, Rinehart and Winston. Copyright © 1964 by Leslie Frost Ballentine. Reprinted by permission of Holt, Rinehart and Winston, Publishers.

Allen Ginsberg: "Howl" from *Howl and Other Poems*, copyright © 1956, 1959 by Allen Ginsberg. Reprinted by permission of City Lights Books.

Nikki Giovanni: "Poetry" from *The Woman and the Men* by Nikki Giovanni, Copyright © 1970, 1974, 1975 by Nikki Giovanni. Reprinted by permission of William Morrow & Company.

Robert Graves: "The Cool Web" from *Collected Poems*. Copyright © 1955 by Robert Graves. Reprinted by permission of Curtis Brown, Ltd.

Edgar A. Guest: "The Things That Make A Soldier Great" from *Collected Verse* by Edgar Guest. Contemporary Books, Inc., Chicago, 1934. "Home" from *A Heap o' Livin'* by Edgar A. Guest. Copyright © 1916 with the permission of Contemporary Books, Inc., Chicago.

Arthur Guiterman: "On the Vanity of Earthly Greatness" by Arthur Guiterman from *Gaily the Troubadour*. Reprinted by permission of Louise H. Sclove.

Thom Gunn: "On the Move" from *The Sense of Movement*. Reprinted by permission of Faber and Faber Ltd.

Michael Hamburger: "Lines on Brueghel's Icarus" from Poems *1950–1951*, published by The Hand and Flower Press, Oldington, Kent, England, 1952. Reprinted by permission of the author.

Michael Harper: "Dear John, Dear Coltrane" from *Dear John, Dear Coltrane* published by the University of Pittsburgh Press. First published in the *Carolina Quarterly*, 1970. Reprinted by permission.

Anthony Hecht: "The Dover Bitch" and "It Out-Herods Herod. Pray You, Avoid It" from *The Hard Hours* by Anthony Hecht. Copyright © 1960, 1967 by Anthony Hecht. "A Lot of Night Music" from *Millions of Strange Shadows* by Anthony Hecht. Copyright © 1977 by Anthony Hecht. Reprinted by permission of Atheneum Publishers.

Robert G. Holland: "Eve in Old Age" is reprinted by permission of the author, Robert Holland.

John Hollander: "Adam's Task" from *The Night Mirror*, copyright © 1970, 1971 by John Hollander. "Historical Reflections by Benjamin Harrison" by John Hollander. From *Jiggery-Pokery*, edited by John Hollander and Anthony Hecht. Copyright © 1966 by Anthony Hecht and John Hollander, and "A State of Nature" from *Types of Shape*, copyright © 1967, 1969 by John Hollander are reprinted by permission of Atheneum Publishers.

Robert Hollander: "You too? Me too—Why not? Soda Pop" is reprinted from *The Massachusetts Review* © 1968 by The Massachusetts Review, Inc. by permission of the publisher.

M. Carl Holman: "Three Brown Girls Singing" is reprinted by permission of the author.

A. E. Housman: "Terence, This Is Stupid Stuff", "1887", and "To an Athlete Dying Young" from "A Shropshire Lad"—Authorized Edition—from *The Collected Poems of A. E. Housman.* Copyright 1939 1940, © 1965 by Holt, Rinehart and Winston. Copyright © 1967, 1968 by Robert E. Symons. "Epitaph on an Army of Mercenaries" from *The Collected Poems of A. E. Housman.* Copyright 1922 by Holt, Rinehart and Winston. Copyright 1950 by Barclays Bank Ltd. Reprinted by permission of Holt, Rinehart and Winston Publishers, The Society of Authors as the Literary representative of the Estate of A. E. Housman, and Jonathan Cape Ltd.

Langston Hughes: "The Negro Speaks of Rivers" copyright 1926 by Alfred A. Knopf, Inc. and renewed 1954 by Langston Hughes. Reprinted from *Selected Poems of Langston Hughes,* by permission of Alfred A. Knopf, Inc. "Dream Deferred" copyright 1959 by Langston Hughes. Reprinted from *The Panther and the Lash,* by Langston Hughes, by permission of Alfred A. Knopf, Inc. "Jazzonia" from *The Weary Blues* by Langston Hughes. Copyright 1926 by Alfred A. Knopf and renewed 1954 by Langston Hughes. Reprinted by permission of Alfred A. Knopf, Inc.

Richard Hugo: "To Women" from *White Center,* published by W. W. Norton & Co., Inc., is reprinted by permission of the author, Richard Hugo. "What Thou Lovest Well Remains American" is reprinted from *What Thou Lovest Well Remains American, Poems* by Richard Hugo, by permission of W. W. Norton & Co., Inc. Copyright © 1975 by W. W. Norton & Co., Inc.

Randall Jarrell: "The Death of the Ball Turret Gunner" is reprinted by permission of Farrar, Straus & Giroux, Inc. from *The Complete Poems* by Randall Jarrell. Copyright © 1945, 1947, 1969 by Mrs. Randall Jarrell.

Robinson Jeffers: "To the Stonecutters" copyright 1924 and renewed 1952 by Robinson Jeffers. Reprinted from *Selected Poetry of Robinson Jeffers,* by Robinson Jeffers, by permission of Random House, Inc.

Helene Johnson: "Sonnet to a Negro in Harlem." Reprinted by permission of the author.

Donald Justice: "Here in Katmandu," "Counting the Mad" and "Southern Gothic" from *The Summer Anniversaries,* copyright © 1956, 1957, 1958 by Donald Justice. Reprinted by permission of Wesleyan University Press. "Here in Katmandu" and "Southern Gothic" first appeared in *Poetry.*

Bob Kaufman: "Blues Note" reprinted by permission of the Broadside Press.

X. J. Kennedy: "Epitaph for a Postal Clerk," copyright © 1956 by X. J. Kennedy, "Ars Poetica" copyright © 1951 by X. J. Kennedy, "First Confession" copyright © 1961 by X. J. Kennedy, "Nude Descending a Staircase" copyright © 1960 by X. J. Kennedy, and "In a Prominent Bar in Secaucus One Day" are reprinted from the book *Nude Descending a Staircase* by X. J. Kennedy by permission of Doubleday & Company, Inc.

Galway Kinnell: "To Christ, Our Lord" from *What A Kingdom It Was* by Galway Kinnell, copyright © 1960 by Galway Kinnell. Reprinted by permission of Houghton Mifflin Company.

A. M. Klein: "Heirloom" from *Half Not A Jew,* by A. M. Klein, copyright by Behrman House Inc. Used with permission.

Etheridge Knight: "Hard Rock Returns to Prison From the Hospital for the Criminal Insane" and "The Idea of Ancestry" from *Poems from Prison* by Etheridge Knight, © 1968 by Etheridge Knight. Reprinted by permission of Broadside/Crummel Press, Detroit, Michigan.

Kenneth Koch: "Variations on a Theme by William Carlos Williams" and "You Were Wearing" from *Thank You and Other Poems,* Copyright © 1962 by Kenneth Koch. Reprinted by permission of Grove Press, Inc.

Maxine Kumin: "Woodchucks" from *Our Ground Time Here Will Be Brief* by Maxine Kumin. Copyright © 1971 by Maxine Kumin. Reprinted by permission of Viking Penguin, Inc.

Philip Larkin: "Church Going" is reprinted from *The Less Deceived* by permission of The Marvell Press, England. "Annus Mirabilis" from *High Windows* by Philip Larkin. Copyright © 1974 by Philip Larkin. Reprinted by permission of Farrar, Straus and Giroux, Inc.

D. H. Lawrence: "Piano" from *The Complete Poems of D. H. Lawrence.* Copyright © 1964, 1971 by Angelo Ravagli and C. M. Weekley, Executors of the Estate of Frieda Lawrence Ravagli. Reprinted by permission of Viking Penguin, Inc.

Denise Levertov: "What Were They Like?" from *The Sorrow Dance,* Copyright © 1966 by Denise Levertov Goodman. Reprinted by permission of New Directions.

Dorothy Livesay: "Green Rain" from *Collected Poems: The Two Seasons* by Dorothy Livesay. Copyright © 1972. Reprinted by permission of McGraw Hill-Ryerson, Toronto.

Donald Lloyd: "Bridal Couch" first appeared in *Prairie Schooner* and is reprinted here by permission of the author.

Audre Lorde: "Outside," "Recreation" and "Hanging Fire" are reprinted from *The Black Unicorn, Poems* by Audre Lorde by permission of W. W. Norton & Company, Inc. Copyright © 1978 by Audre Lorde.

Robert Lowell: "Skunk Hour" from *Life Studies* by Robert Lowell. Copyright © 1956, 1959 by Robert Lowell. Reprinted by permission of Farrar, Straus & Giroux, Inc.

Eugene J. McCarthy: "Kilroy" from *Other Things and the Aardvark,* copyright © 1970 by Eugene J. McCarthy. Reprinted by permission of Doubleday & Company, Inc.

David McCord: "Waiter" from *Bay Window Ballads* by David McCord. Copyright 1935 by Charles Scribner's Sons; renewal copyright © 1963 by David McCord. Reprinted by permission of Charles Scribner's Sons. "History of Education" from *What Cheer* reprinted by permission of the author.

Claude McKay: "America" and "The White House" from *Selected Poems of Claude McKay,* copyright 1953 by Twayne Publishers, Inc. and reprinted with the permission of Twayne Publishers, A Division of G. K. Hall & Co.

Archibald MacLeish: "Ars Poetica" and "Not Marble, Nor the Gilded Monuments" from *New and Collected Poems 1917–1976* by Archibald MacLeish, Copyright © 1976 by Archibald MacLeish. Reprinted by permission of Houghton Mifflin Company.

Louis MacNeice: "Aubade" and "Sunday Morning" from *The Collected Poems of Louis MacNeice* are reprinted by permission of Faber and Faber Ltd.

Eli Mandel: "On the Death of Ho Chi Minh" from *Stony Plain* and "Houdini" from **An** *Idiot's Journey* by Eli Mandel is reprinted by permission of the author.

John Masefield: "The Lemmings" is reprinted with the permission of Macmillan Publishing Co., Inc. from *Poems* by John Masefield. Copyright 1920 by John Masefield renewed 1948 by John Masefield.

James Merrill: "Watching the Dance" from *Nights and Days* by James Merrill is used by permission of Atheneum Publishers. Copyright © 1966 by James Merrill.

W. S. Merwin: "Burning the Cat" by W. S. Merwin from *The First Four Books* of *Poems* is reprinted by permission of Atheneum Publishers. Copyright © 1955, 1956 by W. S. Merwin.

Edna St. Vincent Millay: "What Lips My Lips Have Kissed" from *Collected Poems*, Harper & Row. Copyright 1923, 1951 by Edna St. Vincent Millay and Norma Millay Ellis. Reprinted by permission of Norma Millay Ellis, Literary Executor.

Vassar Miller: "Adam's Footprint" from *Wage War on Silence*, copyright © 1960 by Vassar Miller. Reprinted by permission of Wesleyan University Press.

Czeslaw Milosz: "A Poor Christian Looks at the Ghetto," from *Postwar Polish Poetry*, translated by Czeslaw Milosz. Copyright © 1965 by Czeslaw Milosz. Reprinted by permission of Doubleday & Company, Inc.

Joni Mitchell: "Woodstock" © 1969 by Siquomb Publishing Corp. All Rights Reserved. Used by permission of Warner Bros. Music.

Susan Mitchell: "From the Journals of the Frog Prince" reprinted by permission; © 1978 The New Yorker Magazine, Inc.

Marianne Moore: "Poetry" from *Collected Poems*, copyright 1935 by Marianne Moore, renewed 1963 by Marianne Moore and T. S. Eliot. Reprinted with permission of Macmillan Publishing Co., Inc. Two early versions of "Poetry" by Marianne Moore are reprinted with the permission of Lawrence E. Brinn and Louise Crane, Executors of the Estate of Marianne Moore.

Edwin Morgan: "Message Clear" and "The Computer's First Christmas Card" from *The Second Life*. Reprinted by permission of Edinburgh University Press.

Ogden Nash: "The Turtle"; copyright 1940 by Ogden Nash. Reprinted from *Verses 1929 On* by Ogden Nash by permission of Little, Brown and Co.

Howard Nemerov: "Boom," "The Goose Fish," "Epigram: Political Reflexion," "Life Cycle of Common Man," "The Vacuum," "Pockets", "The Town Dump" and "A Way of Life" from *The Collected Poems of Howard Nemerov*. University of Chicago Press 1977. Reprinted by permission of the author.

Gabriel Okara: "Piano and Drums" which originally appeared in *Black Orpheus* is reprinted by permission of the author.

Sharon Olds: "Leningrad Cemetery: Winter of 1941" reprinted by permission; © 1979 The New Yorker Magazine, Inc.

Wilfred Owen: "Disabled" and "Dulce et Decorum Est" from *The Collected Poems* by Wilfred Owen. Copyright © Chatto & Windus, Ltd., 1946, 1963. Reprinted by permission of New Directions.

Dorothy Parker: "A Certain Lady," "Comment", "Tombstones in the Starlight: The Very Rich Man", "Tombstones in the Starlight: The Fisherman" and "One Perfect Rose" from *The Portable Dorothy Parker*. Reprinted by permission of Viking Penguin, Inc.

Linda Pastan: "Marks" from *The Five Stages of Grief, Poems* by Linda Pastan is reprinted by permission of W. W. Norton & Company, Inc. Copyright © 1978 by Linda Pastan. "A Symposium: Apples" from *Aspects of Eve, Poems* by Linda Pastan is reprinted by permission of Liveright Publishing Corporation. Copyright Linda Pastan.

Raymond Patterson: "You Are the Brave" from *26 Ways of Looking at a Black Man*, an *Award* book published by Universal-Award House Inc. Copyright 1969 by Raymond Patterson. Reprinted by permission of Universal Publishing and Distributing Corporation.

Marge Piercy: "Barbie Doll" from *To Be of Use* by Marge Piercy. Copyright © 1969, 1971, 1973 by Marge Piercy. Reprinted by permission of Doubleday & Company, Inc. "Beauty I Would Suffer For" from *The Twelve-Spoked Wheel Flashing* by Marge Piercy. Copyright © 1974, 1975, 1976, and 1978 by Marge Piercy. Reprinted by permission of Alfred A. Knopf, Inc.

Sylvia Plath: "Lady Lazarus" and "Daddy" from *Ariel* by Sylvia Plath, copyright © 1963 by Ted Hughes and "Black Rook in Rainy Weather" (first published in somewhat different form by William Heinemann Ltd.) from *Crossing the Water* by Sylvia Plath, copyright © 1971 by Ted Hughes, are reprinted by permission of Harper & Row, Publishers, Inc. and Faber and Faber Ltd. "Point Shirley" copyright © 1959 by Sylvia Plath. Reprinted from *The Colossus and Other Stories*, by Sylvia Plath, by permission of Alfred A. Knopf, Inc. and Faber and Faber Ltd.

Ezra Pound: "In a Station of the Metro," "The River Merchant's Wife: A Letter," "Hugh Selwyn Mauberly, V (There died a Myriad)," "The Bathtub," "Commission," "The Garden," and "A Virginal" from *Personae* by Ezra Pound. Copyright 1926 by Ezra Pound. Reprinted by permission of New Directions.

John Press: "Womanizers" from *Guy Fawkes Night* by John Press is reprinted by permission of A. M. Heath & Company Ltd as representative of the author.

Jarold Ramsey: "Lupine Dew" is reprinted by permission of the author. "The Tally Stick" is reprinted by permission of *Northwest Review*. "Ontogeny," copyright 1978 by Washington and Lee University, Reprinted from *Shenandoah*: The Washington and Lee University Review with the permission of the Editor.

John Crowe Ransom: "Bells for John Whiteside's Daughter" Copyright 1924 by Alfred A. Knopf, Inc. and renewed 1952 by John Crowe Ransom. "The Equilibrists" Copyright 1927 by Alfred A. Knopf, Inc. and renewed 1955 by John Crowe Ransom. Reprinted from *Selected Poems* Third Edition, Revised and Enlarged, by John Crowe Ransom, by permission of Alfred A. Knopf, Inc.

Dudley Randall: "Ballad of Birmingham" from *Poem Counter Poem*, © 1969 by Margaret Danner and Dudley Randall, and "Roses and Revolutions" from *Cities Burning*, © 1968 by Dudley Randall are reprinted by permission of Broadside/Crummel Press, Detroit, Michigan.

David Ray: "A Piece of Shrapnel" from *Gathering Firewood*, copyright © 1969 by David Ray. Reprinted by permission of Wesleyan University Press.

Henry Reed: "Lessons of the War: Judging Distances" from *A Map of Verona* is reprinted by permission of the author and Jonathan Cape Ltd.

Ishmael Reed: "beware; do not read this poem" and "Sermonette," Copyright 1972 by Ishmael Reed, are reprinted by permission of the author.

Adrienne Rich: "A Clock in the Square" is reprinted by permission of the author. "Origins and History of Consciousness" is reprinted from *Dream of a Common Language, Poems 1974–1977*, by Adrienne Rich, by permission of W. W. Norton & Co., Inc. Copyright 1978 by W. W. Norton & Co., Inc. "At a Bach Concert," "Snapshots of a Daughter-in-Law," "Necessities of Life," "Orion," "Planetarium," "Trying to Talk with a Man," "Diving into the Wreck," "Storm Warnings," "Two Songs," and "Aunt Jennifer's Tigers" are reprinted from *Poems, Selected and New 1950–1974* by Adrienne Rich, by permission of W. W. Norton & Co., Inc. Copyright © 1975, 1973, 1971, 1969, 1966 by W. W. Norton & Co., Inc. Copyright 1967, 1963, 1962, 1961, 1960, 1959, 1958, 1957, 1956, 1955, 1954, 1953, 1952, 1951 by Adrienne Rich. "Coast to Coast" from *A Wild Patience Has Taken Me This Far* Copyright © 1981 by Adrienne Rich. Reprinted by permission of W. W. Norton and Co. Inc. "An Interview With Adrienne Rich" by David Kalstone, copyright © 1972 by Saturday Review, Inc. Reprinted by permission of Saturday Review, Inc. "Talking With Adrienne Rich" from *The Ohio Review*, Vol. XIII, No. 1, copyright 1971. Selections reprinted by permission of *The Ohio Review*. "When We Dead Awaken: Writing as Re-Vision" from *College English*, reprinted by permission of National Council of Teachers of English and Adrienne Rich. The chronology of the poetry of Adrienne Rich is reprinted from *Adrienne Rich's Poetry*, A Norton Critical Edition, Selected and Edited by Barbara Charlesworth Gelpi and Albert Gelpi, with the permission of W. W. Norton & Company, Inc. Copyright © 1975 by W. W. Norton & Company, Inc.

Edward Arlington Robinson: "Mr. Flood's Party" is reprinted from *Collected Poems* by Edward Arlington Robinson copyright 1921 by Edward Arlington Robinson, renewed by Ruth Nivison, with permission of Macmillan Publishing Co., Inc. "Richard Cory" from *The Children of the Night* by Edward Arlington Robinson is reprinted by permission of Charles Scribner's Sons and is fully protected by copyright. "Uncle Ananias" and "Miniver Cheevey" from *The Town Down the River* by Edward Arlington Robinson is reprinted by permission of Charles Scribner's sons. Copyright 1910 by Charles Scribner's Sons; renewal copyright 1938 by Ruth Nivison.

Theodore Roethke: "My Papa's Waltz" copyright 1942 by Hearst Magazines Inc., "I Knew a Woman" copyright 1954 by Theodore Roethke, "The Waking" copyright 1953 by Theodore Roethke, "The Mistake" copyright © 1957 by Beatrice Roethke, Administratrix of the Estate of Theodore Roethke, "She" copyright © 1956 by Theodore Roethke, and "The Dream" copyright 1955 by Theodore Roethke are reprinted from the book *The Collected Poems of Theodore Roethke* by permission of Doubleday & Company, Inc.

Siegfried Sassoon: "Repression of War Experience" from *Collected Poems* by Siegfried Sassoon. Copyright 1918 by E. P. Dutton Co., renewed 1946 by Siegfried Sassoon. Reprinted by permission of Viking-Penguin, Inc. and G. T. Sassoon.

Delmore Schwartz: "The Heavy Bear Who Goes With Me" from *Selected Poems: Summer Knowledge*. Copyright 1938 by New Directions. Copyright © 1966 by Delmore Schwartz. "A Passionate Shepherd to His Love" from *Vaudeville for a Princess*, Copyright 1950 by New Directions. Reprinted by permission of New Directions.

Anne Sexton: "The Kiss" from *Love Poems* by Anne Sexton. Copyright © 1967, 1968, 1969 by Anne Sexton. "The Truth the Dead Know" from *All My Pretty Ones* by Anne Sexton. Copyright © 1961, 1962 by Anne Sexton. Reprinted by permission of Houghton Mifflin Company.

Karl Shapiro: "Auto Wreck" and "The Fly" from *Selected Poems*, Copyright 1942 renewed 1970 by Karl Shapiro. Reprinted by permission of Random House, Inc.

Louis Simpson: "The Green Shepherd" from *At the End of the Open Road*, Copyright © 1961 by Louis Simpson. Reprinted by permission of Wesleyan University Press.

Desmond Skirrow: "Ode On A Grecian Urn Summarized" is reprinted from *The New Statesman*, London, by permission.

W. D. Snodgrass: "Leaving the Motel" from *After Experience* by W. D. Snodgrass. Copyright © 1966 by W. D. Snodgrass. Reprinted by permission of Harper & Row, Publishers, Inc. Section #7 from Heart's Needle © 1959, "The Campus on the Hill," copyright © 1958 by W. D. Snodgrass, and "These Trees Stand", copyright © 1956 by W. D. Snodgrass from *Heart's Needle* by W. D. Snodgrass. Reprinted by permission of Alfred A. Knopf, Inc.

Stephen Spender: "Judas Iscariot" from *The Edge of Being*, © 1949 by Stephen Spender. Reprinted by permission of Literistic, Ltd. and Faber and Faber Ltd. "The Express," copyright 1934 and renewed 1962 by Stephen Spender, and "An Elementary School Classroom in a Slum," copyright 1942 and renewed 1970 by Stephen Spender, from *Selected Poems* reprinted by permission of Random House, Inc. and Faber and Faber Ltd.

William Stafford: "The Epitaph Ending in And" from *The Rescued Year*, copyright © 1965 by William E. Stafford. Reprinted by permission of Harper & Row, Publishers, Inc.

George Starbuck: "On First Looking in on Blodgett's Keats's 'Chapman's Homer'" from *Bone Thoughts* by George Starbuck. Reprinted by permission of Yale University Press.

Wallace Stevens: "Of Modern Poetry", copyright 1942 by Wallace Stevens, renewed 1970 by Holly Stevens Stephenson; "Martial Cadenza," copyright 1942 by Wallace Stevens; "The World As Meditation" copyright 1952 by Wallace Stevens; "Emperor of Ice-Cream" copyright 1923 and renewed 1951 by Wallace Stevens; "The Idea of Order at Key West" copyright 1936 and renewed 1964 by Holly Stevens; "Anecdote of the Jar", "Disillusionment of Ten O'Clock", copyright 1923 and renewed 1951 by Wallace Stevens; and "Sunday Morning" copyright 1923 and renewed 1951 by Wallace Stevens. Reprinted from *The Collected Poems of Wallace Stevens*, by permission of Alfred A. Knopf, Inc.

John Stone: "Coming Home" and "Explaining About the Dachshund" from *The Smell of Matches,* Rutgers University Press, 1972, copyright John Stone, 1979. Reprinted by permission of the author.

Nancy Sullivan: "The Death of the First Man" and "Burial in the Sand" from *Telling It* by Nancy Sullivan. Copyright © 1965, 1966, 1969, 1971, 1972, 1973, 1974 1975 by Nancy Sullivan. Reprinted by permission of David R. Godine, Publishers, Inc.

Dylan Thomas: "Do Not Go Gentle Into That Good Night," "Fern Hill," "The Force That Through the Green Fuse Drives the Flower," and "In My Craft or Sullen Art," copyright 1939, 1946, reprinted by permission of New Directions Publishing Corporation from *The Poems* by Dylan Thomas, and by permission of the Trustees for the copyrights of the late Dylan Thomas and J. M. Dent & Sons Ltd. from *Collected Poems* by Dylan Thomas.

Jean Toomer: "Song of the Son" from *Cane,* copyright © 1951 by Jean Toomer. Reprinted by permission of Liveright Publishing Corporation.

Louis Untermeyer: "Edgar A. Guest Considers the Good 'Old Woman Who Lived in a Shoe' and the Good Old Truths Simultaneously" from *Selected Poems and Parodies of Louis Untermeyer.* Copyright 1935 by Harcourt Brace Jovanovich, Inc.; copyright 1963 by Louis Untermeyer. Reprinted by permission of the publisher.

Mona Van Duyn: "What the Motorcycle Said," copyright © 1973 by Mona Van Duyn from *Merciful Disguises* by Mona Van Duyn, is used by permission of Atheneum Publishers.

Peter Viereck: "Kilroy," copyright owned by author, is reprinted with his permission from his Pulitzer-prize-winning book *Terror & Decorum,* published 1948 and reprinted 1972 by Greenwood Press, Westport, Conn.; the same poem appears in Peter Viereck's *New and Selected Poems,* published 1965 and reprinted 1979 by University of Michigan Microfilms, 300 N. Zeeb Road, Ann Arbor, Michigan.

Diane Wakoski: "The Photos" from *The Man Who Shook Hands* by Diane Wakoski. Copyright © 1978 by Diane Wakoski. Reprinted by permission of Doubleday & Company, Inc. "Uneasy Rider" from *The Motorcycle Betrayal Poems,* copyright © 1971 by Diane Wakoski. Reprinted by permission of Simon & Schuster, a Division of Gulf & Western. "Belly Dancer," from *Discrepancies and Apparitions,* reprinted by permission of the author. "A Poet Recognizing the Echo of the Voice" from *The Magellanic Clouds,* reprinted by permission of Black Sparrow Press.

Tom Wayman: "Wayman in Love" and "Picketing Supermarkets," from *Waiting for Wayman* by Tom Wayman, are reprinted by permission of the Canadian publishers, McClelland and Stewart Limited, Toronto.

Alexander Whitaker: "Leaving the Dance," copyright © 1972 by Alexander Whitaker. Reprinted by permission of the author.

Richard Wilbur: "The Beautiful Changes" from *The Beautiful Changes and Other Poems,* copyright 1947, 1975 by Richard Wilbur. "Love Calls us to the Things of this World" from *The Things of This World,* © 1956 by Richard Wilbur. "Museum Piece" and "The Pardon" from *Ceremony And Other Poems,* copyright 1950, 1978 by Richard Wilbur. "She" from *Advice to A Prophet and Other Poems* © 1959 by Richard Wilbur. Reprinted by permission of Harcourt Brace Jovanovich Inc.

William Carlos Williams: "Poem" (The rose fades) and "Landscape with the Fall of Icarus" from *Pictures from Brueghel,* copyright © 1962 by William Carlos Williams. "The Red Wheelbarrow" and "This is Just to Say" from *The Collected Earlier Poems* of William Carlos Williams, copyright 1938 by New Directions Publishing Corporation. "The Dance" from *The Collected Later Poems* of William Carlos Williams, copyright 1944 by William Carlos Williams. Reprinted by permission of New Directions Publishing Corporation.

Yvor Winters: "At the San Francisco Airport" from *Collected Poems* by Yvor Winters published by the Swallow Press. Reprinted by permission of Ohio University Press.

Bruce McM. Wright: "The African Affair" reprinted by permission of the author.

James Wright: "Arrangements with the Earth for Three Dead Friends," copyright © 1957 by James Wright, from *Collected Poems* by James Wright. Reprinted by permission of Wesleyan University Press.

William Butler Yeats: "Among School Children," "Leda and the Swan" and "Sailing to Byzantium" copyright 1928 by Macmillan Publishing Co., Inc., renewed 1956 by Georgie Yeats; "Byzantium" copyright 1933 by Macmillan Publishing Co., Inc., renewed 1961 by Bertha Georgie Yeats; "The Circus Animals' Desertion" copyright 1940 by Georgie Yeats, renewed 1968 by Bertha Georgie Yeats, Michael Butler Yeats and Anne Yeats; "Easter 1916" and "The Second Coming" copyright 1924 by Macmillan Publishing Co., Inc., renewed 1952 by Bertha Georgie Yeats; "On Being Asked for a War Poem" copyright 1919 by Macmillan Publishing Co., Inc. renewed 1947 by Bertha Georgie Yeats. Reprinted by permission of Macmillan Publishing Co., Inc., Michael and Anne Yeats and Macmillan London Limited.

INDEX OF AUTHORS

INDEX OF TITLES AND FIRST LINES